"EIGHT MAJOR STEPS" HERALDS PROMISING NEW DECADE OF BELT AND ROAD COOPERATION

（ENGLISH VERSION）

共建"一带一路"
新十年良好开局

XINHUA INSTITUTE
新华社国家高端智库课题组　编著

XINHUA PUBLISHING HOUSE
新 华 出 版 社

图书在版编目（CIP）数据

共建"一带一路"新十年良好开局：英文 / 新华社国家高端智库课题组编著 .
北京：新华出版社 , 2025. 6.
ISBN 978-7-5166-8111-4

Ⅰ . F125

中国国家版本馆 CIP 数据核字第 20250YF657 号

共建"一带一路"新十年良好开局（英文版）
编著： 新华社国家高端智库课题组
出版发行： 新华出版社有限责任公司
　　　　　　（北京市石景山区京原路 8 号　邮编：100040）
印刷： 捷鹰印刷（天津）有限公司

成品尺寸： 170mm×240mm 1/16	**印张：** 18.25	**字数：** 240 千字
版次： 2025 年 7 月第 1 版	**印次：** 2025 年 7 月第 1 次印刷	
书号： ISBN 978-7-5166-8111-4	**定价：** 98.00 元（中英文版）	

微店

视频号小店

抖店

京东旗舰店

微信公众号

喜马拉雅

小红书

淘宝旗舰店

扫码添加专属客服

Contents

Report section

Thesis article

REPORT SECTION

"Eight Major Steps" Heralds Promising New Decade of Belt and Road Cooperation[①]

Xinhua Institute

Preface

In 2013, Chinese President Xi Jinping proposed the magnificent Belt and Road Initiative (BRI), marking a milestone in the history of human development. Over the past decade, with joint efforts from all sides, the BRI—centered on connectivity—has transcended geographical boundaries, bridged cultural differences, and aligned development needs. It has pioneered a new framework for international cooperation, built on the principles of consultation, collaboration, and shared benefits. Today, the BRI stands as the world's most popular international public good and the largest platform for global cooperation. It has become a path of partnership, opportunity, and prosperity for the countries involved.

During the keynote speech at the opening ceremony of the Third Belt and Road Forum for International Cooperation convened in October 2023, President Xi Jinping announced China's support for eight initiatives aimed at advancing the high-quality development of the Belt and Road. Over the past year, with the concerted efforts of BRI

---

① Released on October 15, 2024, at the Belt and Road Forum for International Think Tank Cooperation & the Second Silk Road (Xi'an) International Communication Forum in Xi'an

partner countries, these initiatives have steadily progressed and achieved remarkable results, laying a solid foundation for the second decade of the BRI. The experience has demonstrated that in today's global context, the pursuit of development, growth, and shared prosperity is a common aspiration for all nations. The BRI continues to gain worldwide consensus and has entered a phase of significant opportunity. It is well-positioned to become a ballast for building an open world economy, a driving force for collective growth, and a catalyst for global modernization.

Looking ahead, countries involved in the BRI must further implement the eight initiatives, advance practical cooperation, and jointly promote innovative development. Together, they can address risks and challenges while ensuring the steady progress of high-quality Belt and Road construction on this new journey. The goal is to create a world where peace, mutual benefit, and shared prosperity are the hallmarks of modernization and to contribute to building a community with a shared future for humanity.

Chapter One The Eight Major Steps Propel High-Quality Belt and Road Cooperation to a New Starting Point

1.1 Continued and Steady Progress in Connectivity Development

Since the introduction of the Eight Major Steps, connectivity has become a key focus. The construction of the China-Europe corridor, represented by the China-Europe Railway Express and the Trans-Caspian International Transport Corridor, continues to improve in quality. The "Maritime Silk Road" initiative advances the integrated development of port, shipping, and trade, while the Air Silk Road has steadily progressed. Under the principles of consultation, cooperation, and shared benefits, the economic and social impacts of several landmark projects have become increasingly evident, significantly contributing to the modernization of BRI partner countries.

—Official Establishment of a Diverse and Comprehensive Connectivity Framework of the Trans-Caspian International Transport Corridor Enhances the Quality of the China-Europe Corridor

In terms of connectivity across the Eurasian continent, the construction of the Trans-Caspian International Transport Corridor has progressed significantly in 2024. On July 3, Chinese President Xi Jinping and Kazakh President Kassym-Jomart Tokayev jointly attended, via video link, the launch ceremony for the China-Europe direct express line through the Caspian Sea, held at the Presidential Palace in Astana. This event marks the first time Chinese vehicles reached a Caspian port through direct highway transport, symbolizing the formal establishment of a diverse and comprehensive connectivity framework that integrates road, rail, air, and pipeline transportation. [1]

Gaidar Abdykerimov, Secretary General of the Trans-Caspian International Transport Corridor International Association, explained that this corridor was a multimodal transport route stretching over 11,000 kilometers from China across Kazakhstan, the Caspian Sea, Azerbaijan, Georgia and extending to Turkey and European countries. It has become a crucial artery for transporting goods from Southeast Asia and China to Europe, with an annual cargo throughput of approximately 6 million tons. Kazakhstan, Azerbaijan, Georgia, and Turkey have already planned to more than double the corridor's annual throughput by 2027. He noted that one of China's Eight Major Steps for the high-quality BRI involves participating in the development of the Trans-Caspian International Transport Corridor, stating, "China's support has translated into concrete actions, bringing positive news for this project."[2]

Since 2024, new China-Europe Railway Express routes have been launched via this corridor from Chinese cities such as Xi'an, Nanjing, Qingdao, and Jinan, connecting to countries like Azerbaijan, Turkey, and Italy. Currently, it takes only 29 days to travel from Xi'an, China, to Mannheim, Germany, through this corridor, with the potential to reduce the time further to around 25 days in the future. With 6-7 trains running weekly, this route has been optimized with dedicated container ships for the Caspian and Black Sea segments, significantly cutting transportation time by more than half compared to all-sea routes. This development has greatly shortened transit times, low-ered logistics costs, and led to a substantial increase in trade volume.

Driven by significant progress in the Trans-Caspian International Transport Corridor, the China-Europe Railway Express has continued to upgrade in quality. Over the past year, new records have been set for the number of trains, transport capacity, and area coverage. From January to August 2024, a total of 13,056 trains were dispatched, carrying 1.399 million TEUs (twenty-foot equivalent units) of goods, representing year-

---

[1] http://www.news.cn/20240703/d9b59485ad8d43df9a0e694ceed6f4fc/c.html
[2] http://www.news.cn/world/20240707/c6e1a7f81a4e4fc4b7aa715ba4c70c47/c.html

on-year increases of 12% and 11%, respectively. In August alone, 1,653 trains were dispatched, transporting 173,000 TEUs. Since the start of 2024, the number of trains running per month has exceeded 1,600 for six consecutive months. [1] By July 2024, the China-Europe Railway Express had reached 224 cities in 25 European countries and connected over 100 cities in 11 Asian countries, with its service network covering almost all of Eurasia. Within China, 91 scheduled lines have been established for the China-Europe Railway Express, with speeds of up to 120 kilometers per hour, linking 61 cities across the country. The range of goods transported by the trains has expanded to 53 major categories and over 50, 000 kinds of products, with a 100% container utilization rate. [2] In June 2024, the governments of China, Kyrgyzstan, and Uzbekistan signed an intergovernmental agreement for the China-Kyrgyzstan-Uzbekistan railway project. The railway will start from Kashgar in Xinjiang, pass through Kyrgyzstan, and enter Uzbekistan. In the future, it can extend to West Asia and South Asia.

Once completed, it will not only greatly enhance connectivity between the three coun-tries but also effectively promote the development of rail links between Central Asia and Europe.

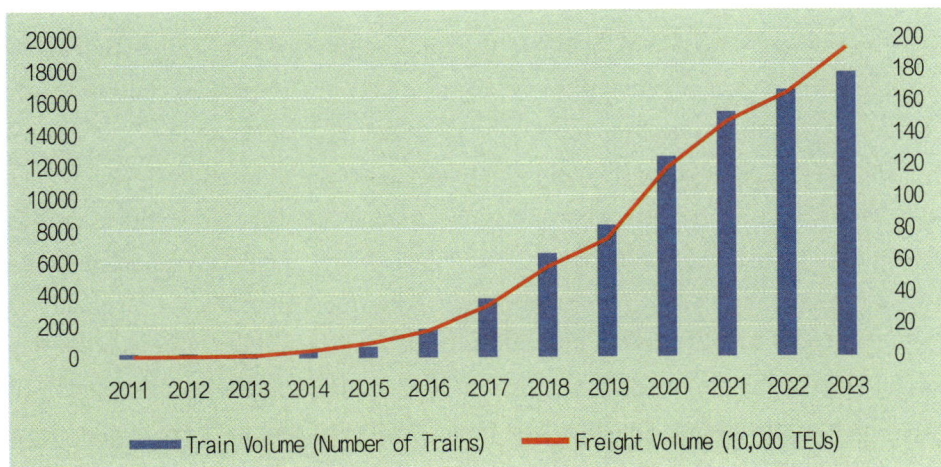

Figure 1: China-Europe Railway Express Train and Freight Volume from 2011 to 2023
Source: China-Europe Railway Express Portal

---

[1] http://paper.people.com.cn/rmrb/html/2024-09/ 19/nw.D110000renmrb_ 20240919_4-10.html
[2] http://www.news.cn/20240727/f37d543f86b3477cb3bebc7699aae955/c.html

Figure 2: China-Europe Railway Express Train and Freight Volume Since October 2023
Source: China-Europe Railway Express Portal

—Integrated Development of Ports, Shipping, and Trade of the Maritime Silk Road and Steady Progress in the Air Silk Road Construction

The integrated development of ports, shipping, and trade plays a crucial role in connectivity efforts. On September 7, during the 6th Maritime Silk Road International Cooperation Forum held in Xiamen, China, it was announced that ten new Silk Road Maritime routes were added, bringing the total number to 132. These routes now connect 145 ports across 46 countries and regions. Notably, Piraeus Port and Abu Dhabi Port have, for the first time, been included as recommended named routes. [1]

The integration of ports, shipping, and trade has proven to be mutually reinforcing, with Piraeus Port in Greece serving as a prime example. On February 6, the expansion project of the Herakleous Ro-Ro terminal at Piraeus Port was officially completed, with a total investment exceeding 20 million euros. After the expansion, the terminal can accommodate 5,100 vehicles, significantly enhancing Piraeus Port's role as a key hub for automobile shipping trade. [2] By the first half of 2024, Piraeus Port had solidified its position as the leading container port in the Mediterranean, the third-largest cruise homeport and the largest ferry port in Europe, the ship repair center of the Eastern Mediterranean, and a transshipment hub for car carriers. During the same period,

---

[1] https://www.thepaper.cn/detail/28683356

[2] http://www.news.cn/world/20240207/090804c012104af0954d5de38e31b8b3/c.html

COSCO Shipping at Piraeus Port had paid over 100 million euros in concession fees and taxes to the Greek government, with dividends for its publicly listed company increasing twelvefold. These activities directly created 4,300 jobs and indirectly generated 12,000 jobs in Greece, boosting the country's GDP by 1.56 percentage points. [1]

Where Air Silk Road development is concerned, China signed memorandums of understanding with several countries, including Kyrgyzstan, [2] Kazakhstan, and Tajikistan, [3] to jointly build the Air Silk Road during the year following the introduction of the Eight Major Steps. Regular flight routes were launched, including China's first scheduled route to Armenia, [4] the first direct passenger flight from China to Luxembourg, [5] the first direct regular passenger flight from the Chinese mainland to Saudi Arabia, [6] and the first regular commercial flight from the Chinese mainland to a South Pacific island nation. [7] Additionally, the Siem Reap Angkor International Airport in Cambodia, constructed by a Chinese company, became operational. The coverage of the Air Silk Road continues to expand, with its capacity steadily increasing.

On June 20, during the Second Zhengzhou-Luxembourg Air Silk Road International Cooperation Forum, Luxembourg's Deputy Prime Minister, Xavier Bettel, stated that the Air Silk Road between Luxembourg and Zhengzhou had become an important link strengthening the relationship between Luxembourg and China. Luxembourg is willing to use this forum as an opportunity to deepen cooperation with China in various fields within the Belt and Road framework. [8]

Fact Box: New Western Land-Sea Corridor

The New Western Land-Sea Corridor is an international trade route developed in cooperation between China's western provinces and ASEAN countries. Centered around Chongqing as the operations hub, the corridor uses rail, sea, and road transport to

---

① http://gr.china-embassy.gov.cn/zxhd/202403/t20240318_ 11262127.htm

② https://www.caac.gov.cn/XWZX/MHYW/202406/t20240617_224472.html

③ https://www.caac.gov.cn/XWZX/MHYW/202310/t20231020_221785.html

④ http://www.news.cn/2023-12/21/c_ 1130040312.htm

⑤ http://www.news.cn/photo/20240903/e99581df613e4be49551e02230296378/c.html

⑥ https://h.xinhuaxmt.com/vh512/share/ 11973574

⑦ https://h.xinhuaxmt.com/vh512/share/ 11822520

⑧ http://www.news.cn/politics/leaders/20240621/d0ee75fb546c49e6a8d4d26d329a425f/c.html

connect key nodes in China's western provinces with the world via coastal and border ports in Guangxi and Yunnan.

President Xi Jinping emphasized that building the New Western Land-Sea Corridor is of great significance in making new ground in opening China further through links running eastward and westward across land and over sea. Since the issuance of the Overall Plan for the New Western Land-Sea Corridor five years ago, the number of destinations served by the corridor has expanded from 166 ports in 71 countries and regions to 523 ports in 124 countries and regions. Over 30,000 trains have been dispatched, and the range of goods transported has increased from more than 80 types to over 1,150.

As of September 14, 2024, the rail-sea intermodal trains of the New Western Land-Sea Corridor have shipped over 600,000 TEUs. Evolving from a "single line" into a "network," the New Western Land-Sea Corridor has become a vivid representation of China's high-level opening-up to the world.

—The Principle of "Teaching to Fish" Highlights the Idea of Consultation, Cooperation, and Shared Benefits, Consolidating Long-term Mutual Gains

On May 10, 2024, a ceremony marking the achievements and future outlook of the Addis Ababa-Djibouti Railway over the past six years, as well as the official handover, was held in Addis Ababa, the capital of Ethiopia. This event symbolized the formal transfer of leading operational management for the railway to the Ethio-Djibouti Standard Gauge Railway Share Company.

The Addis Ababa-Djibouti Railway, Africa's first cross-border electrified railway, spans 752 kilometers from Addis Ababa in the west to the port city of Djibouti in the east. Built by a subsidiary of China Railway Construction Corporation (CRCC), the railway has been in commercial operation since 2018. Under the contract, the Chinese companies provided six years of operational and maintenance services. Over this period, Chinese experts certified and trained 2,840 local employees, laying a solid foundation for a successful handover. Following the handover ceremony, the Chinese team is now focusing on inspection, supervision, and guidance and plans to exit within two years fully.

Where connectivity projects are concerned, the Addis Ababa-Djibouti Railway serves as a prime example of "teaching to fish"—a hallmark of many Belt and Road initiatives.

Through such projects, BRI countries not only upgrade their infrastructure but also acquire the skills to operate and maintain it, further advancing their modernization.

On January 17, 2024, Chinese President Xi Jinping responded to a letter from Kenyan students and alumni representatives at Beijing Jiaotong University, encouraging them to continue contributing to the friendship between China, Kenya, and Africa. The Mombasa-Nairobi Railway, a flagship project and a successful model of China-Kenya cooperation under the Belt and Road Initiative, was designed to empower the Kenyan side to manage its operations. China has sponsored 100 Kenyan students to study railway operations and management at Beijing Jiaotong University. These students have since returned to Kenya, joining the Kenya Railways Corporation and becoming a new driving force for local development and enhanced bilateral cooperation. As of May 31, 2024, the Mombasa-Nairobi Railway had been in safe operation for seven years, transporting 12.86 million passengers and 32.87 million tons of cargo. It has directly and indirectly created 74,000 jobs in Kenya and trained over 2,800 highly qualified railway professionals and management personnel.

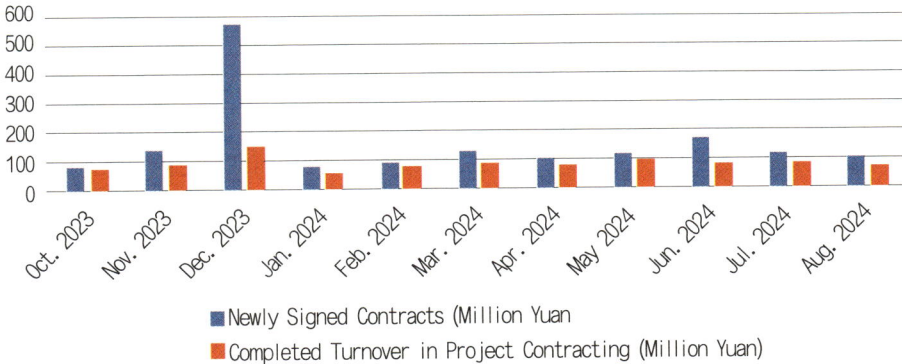

Figure 3: Contracting Projects by Chinese Enterprises in Belt and Road Partner Countries (October 2023 – August 2024)
Source: Ministry of Commerce

Under the principles of consultation, cooperation, and shared benefits, the economic and social effects of several landmark projects have increasingly become apparent, fully demonstrating the success of win-win cooperation. According to Chinese statistics, from January to August 2024, the China-Laos Railway handled 3.584 million tons of import and export goods, an increase of 22.8% year-on-year. Notably, imports of Thai durians via the China-Laos Railway reached 73,000 tons, a year-on-year increase of 74.2%. As of March 2024, the customs clearance time for international freight trains on the China-Laos Railway had been reduced from over 40 hours at the time of the railway's opening to less than 5 hours, with up to 18 international freight trains being exchanged per day at peak times. The freight service network has expanded to 12 BRI partner countries, including Laos, Thailand, Vietnam, and Myanmar, as well as major cities in 31 provinces, regions, and municipalities across China. This expansion has effectively promoted the development of economic zones such as the Vientiane Saysettha Development Zone and the Boten Economic Special Zone. [1]

Fact Box: China-Laos Railway

The China-Laos Railway starts in Kunming, Yunnan Province, China, and extends south to Vientiane, the capital of Laos. It is the first transnational railway built and operated in cooperation between China and Laos, using Chinese standards and directly connecting to China's railway network. The railway spans a total of 1,035 kilometers. In terms of freight transport, since its opening on December 3, 2021, until September 16, 2024, the China-Laos Railway has transported a cumulative 10.002 million tons of international cargo, with a total cargo value of 40.77 billion yuan. For passenger transport, since the launch of international passenger trains on April 13, 2023, the Mohan Border Inspection Station has inspected over 1,260 international passenger trains, facilitating the smooth entry and exit of more than 282,000 passengers from 101 countries and regions by September 25, 2024. The China-Laos Railway is a flagship project for promoting high-quality Belt and Road cooperation and enhancing connectivity between China and Southeast Asian countries, serving as an important link.

In Indonesia, as of July 2024, the Jakarta-Bandung High-Speed Railway had been in operation for nine months, transporting more than 4 million passengers, [2] with a strong growth in passenger numbers. The number of daily high-speed trains increased from 14 at the start of operations to 52 during peak periods, with a single-day record of 21,

---

[1] http://yn.news.cn/20240320/3981fbef4b834656800d6743844cf361/c.html

[2] http://www.news.cn/photo/20240717/0e7fa6752ad04196b516ad 1bb09815e5/c.html

537 passengers. The highest occupancy rate reached 99.6%. [1] On April 1, 2024, during talks in Beijing with Indonesia's President-elect Prabowo, Chinese President Xi Jinping noted, "The Jakarta-Bandung High-Speed Railway has become a flagship of high-quality cooperation between the two countries, marking a new phase in China-Indonesia relations as they build a community with a shared future." [2]

Fact Box: Jakarta-Bandung High-Speed Railway

The Jakarta-Bandung High-Speed Railway connects Indonesia's capital, Jakarta, with the tourist city of Bandung. Spanning 142 kilometers, it is designed for a maximum speed of 350 kilometers per hour. This railway is the first high-speed railway in Indonesia and Southeast Asia, and it serves as a "flagship project" of China-Indonesia Belt and Road cooperation. Officially opened on October 17, 2023, the railway has reduced travel time between Jakarta and Bandung from over three hours to just 46 minutes, providing a safe, green, efficient, and comfortable mode of transportation for the public.

1.2 "Green" and "Digital" Energy as Essential Themes of Innovative Development

With the implementation of the Eight Major Steps, "green" and "digital" have emerged as key themes in the new phase of BRI development. Behind these concepts is China's active cultivation of new productive forces, fostering a positive synergy with the joint construction of the BRI. This dynamic interaction has significantly contributed to the modernization processes of BRI countries, illustrating how China's path to modernization supports the development of the partner countries.

—Sustainable Development Driven by Green Silk Road

Sixty-five kilometers south of downtown Dubai in the UAE lies a futuristic megapark covering 44 square kilometers. Towering within it is a 262-meter-high solar power tower, surrounded by approximately 70,000 heliostats reflecting sunlight to the top of the tower. That is the Dubai Maktoum Solar Park Phase IV, a flagship project of the China-UAE Green Silk Road collaboration. In February 2024, all the power units of the

---

[1] http://www.news.cn/20240417/8fa72b5a1db94818b4407ec4cace0fb 1/c.html

[2] http://www.news.cn/20240401/ 1d 19b27faca748feb0e2084770924add/c.html

project were successfully connected to the grid. They began commercial operation with a total installed capacity of 950 megawatts, comprising 700 megawatts of solar thermal power and 250 megawatts of photovoltaic power. Despite the UAE's vast oil resources, the country remains committed to optimizing its energy structure. At the project's inauguration, UAE Vice President and Prime Minister Mohammed stated that the UAE aimed to become one of the world's most sustainable nations, and the commercial operation of the Dubai solar thermal and photovoltaic power project marks a significant milestone on its path to sustainable development.

As demonstrated by this project, ongoing cooperation in green infrastructure, green energy, and green transportation has become a key focus of the Eight Initiatives. In Côte d'Ivoire, two of the three units at the Gribo-Popoli hydropower station—currently the country's largest under construction—built by a Chinese enterprise were delivered in 2024, with the remaining unit set to be operational by the end of the year. The plant's total installed capacity of 112. 9 megawatts will add 554 million kilo-watt-hours of clean energy annually, helping Côte d'Ivoire meet its goal of increasing the share of renewable energy to 45% by 2030. In Uganda, the Karuma Hydro-power Station, a flagship China-Uganda Belt and Road cooperation project, began full operation at the start of 2024, generating an average of 4 billion kilowatt-hours annually, saving around 1.31 million tons of raw coal each year and reducing CO_2 emissions by 3.48 million tons. This project is also expected to lower Uganda's electricity prices by 17. 5%. In South Africa, on September 14, the 100-megawatt Redstone solar thermal power plant, built by a Chinese company, was successfully connected to the grid for the first time and will eventually provide electricity to approximately 200,000 South African households, significantly reducing reliance on traditional fossil fuels.

According to the White Paper on China's Energy Transition released in August 2024, China's BRI energy cooperation partnership now includes 33 member countries spanning six continents, including Asia and Africa. To strengthen cooperation on the Green Silk Road and incorporate sustainability principles into every aspect of the Belt and Road Initiative, China has launched the Belt and Road International Green Development Coalition. This initiative aims to help BRI partner countries meet the environmental and development-related targets of the UN 2030 Sustainable Development Goals. As of mid-2024, the coalition includes over 150 partners from more than 40 countries, including environmental authorities from over 20 Belt and Road partner nations.

Fact Box: The Green Investment Principles for the Belt and Road

The Green Investment Principles for the Belt and Road is a set of voluntary guidelines for investment enterprises, aimed at promoting green and sustainable development in Belt and Road investments. Officially launched on November 30, 2018, the principles offerseven key initiatives across strategic, operational, and innovation levels. These include corporate governance, strategy development, project management, external communication, and the use of green financial tools. The guidelines are designed for global financial institutions and companies involved in Belt and Road investments to voluntarily adopt and implement. Forty-nine signatory institutions, 20 supporting institutions, and two observer institutions from 17 countries and regions have joined the initiative as of September 2024.

—Rapid Expansion of Digital Silk Road into New Spaces

The Digital Silk Road is experiencing rapid growth in digital service trade and e-commerce. In the first half of 2024, China's digitally deliverable services imports and exports reached 1.42 trillion yuan, and cross-border e-commerce imports and exports totaled 1.22 trillion yuan—both hitting historic highs. This expansion has created vast new opportunities for participating Belt and Road countries.

At the third Global Digital Trade Expo held in Hangzhou in late September, over 30,000 professional buyers registered, including more than 6,000 international participants. The expo featured a dedicated Silk Road e-commerce section, with a "Silk Road E-Commerce Day" connecting resources for e-commerce cooperation. A special "Silk Road Cloud Products" section was set up to showcase products from Kazakhstan, Thailand, and other guest countries. That same month, the Jiangsu Central Asia Center officially launched in Nanjing, positioning Silk Road e-commerce as a core component of its operations. The center will manage production bases, warehouse resources, and logistics between Jiangsu and Central Asia through digital tools. Earlier, Shanghai's Pudong New Area released an Action Plan for Advancing the Silk Road E-Commerce Cooperation Pilot Zone, introducing a series of measures to accelerate cross-border data flows, trade facilitation, and digital trade initiatives. The plan aims to establish a comprehensive Silk Road e-commerce service system by 2025, fostering deeper trade cooperation among Belt and Road countries through e-commerce. [①]

Fact Box: "Silk Road E-Commerce"

"Silk Road E-Commerce" is an important initiative by China that leverages its strengths in e-commerce technology application, model innovation, and market scale to expand trade cooperation with BRI countries, sharing digital development opportunities. Since October 2023, China has signed new e-commerce cooperation memorandums of understanding with Serbia, Bahrain, and Tajikistan, bringing the number of "Silk Road E-Commerce" partner countries to 33.

The creation of "Silk Road E-Commerce" cooperation pilot zones is a key measure for promoting high-quality BRI development, as well as expanding institutional openness in the e-commerce sector. Since the approval from the State Council in October 2023 to establish a "Silk Road E-Commerce" cooperation pilot zone in Shanghai, 36 out of 38 construction tasks have been fully rolled out. These efforts have produced institutional breakthroughs such as cross-border e-invoice interoperability and electronic bills of lading, and have established public service platforms for talent training, think tank alliances, and national pavilions for BRI partner countries.

The practices of China's wealthiest eastern provinces and cities demonstrate that both digital service trade and the development of "cross-border e-commerce + industrial zones" have become new economic growth hotspots along the Digital Silk Road. As China continues to expand its high-level opening up, the digital economy is bound to become a key driver of growth and a major source of momentum for the Belt and Road Initiative.

In order to support the development of the digital economy, digital infrastructure has become a crucial area of cooperation. With the assistance of Chinese enterprises, Tanzania's National Fiber Optic Backbone Network project has reduced national communication costs by 57%, earning the title "Information TAZARA" (Tanzania-Zambia Railway). The Smart Senegal project has accelerated the country's digital economy, injecting new momentum into the implementation of the "Plan for an

---

① http://www.news.cn/local/2023-12/ 14/c_ 1130027225.htm

Emerging Senegal." Ahead of the 2024 Forum on China-Africa Cooperation Summit in Beijing, China announced that it would strengthen digital infrastructure development in Africa, promote high-speed Internet access, support the creation of "smart cities" in Africa, and advance China-Africa cooperation in information and network technologies, including 5G, big data, cloud computing, fintech, and artificial intelligence. The construction of the Digital Silk Road will not only promote comprehensive cooperation and exchanges between countries and regions but also effectively narrow the "digital divide," helping BRI partner countries build a community with a shared future in cyberspace and enabling them to share in the benefits of digital technology for a brighter future.

Fact Box: Action Plan for Science and Technology Innovation in BRI Cooperation

At the opening ceremony of the first Belt and Road Forum for International Cooperation convened in May 2017, President Xi Jinping proposed building the Belt and Road into one of innovation, launching Action Plan for Science and Technology Innovation in BRI Cooperation. This plan involves cooperation between China and Belt and Road partner countries in four key areas: scientific and cultural exchanges, joint laboratory construction, cooperation on science parks, and technology transfer. The goal is to jointly embrace the new wave of technological revolution and industrial transformation, advancing the path of innovation.

As of November 2023, China has signed intergovernmental science and technology cooperation agreements with over 80 BRI partner countries. More than 50 BRI joint laboratories have been established, along with over 20 agricultural technology demonstration centers and more than 70 overseas industrial parks. Nine transnational technology transfer centers have been established, and over 300 technical exchange and matchmaking events have been held, facilitating the implementation of more than 1,000 cooperative projects.

1.3 "Small Yet Smart" Projects Achieve Effective Results and Benefit Livelihood

At its core, the Belt and Road Initiative aims to improve the quality of life for people in participating countries. While large-scale landmark projects continue to advance, numerous "small yet smart" projects are also being implemented. These initiatives, ranging from education and training programs to health clinics and from mushroom cultivation workshops to clean water wells, have made tangible contributions to poverty alleviation and improving people's livelihoods.

Fact Box: BRI Chinese Government Scholarship Program

In 2017, the Ministry of Education officially established and launched the BRI Chinese Government Scholarship Program, aimed at cultivating talent from Belt and Road partner countries. The program operates through three models of cooperation: between ministries, between provinces and ministries, and between universities.

—The Luban Workshop Becomes a Shining Example of the BRI Vocational Education Cooperation

During the opening ceremony of the Forum on China-Africa Cooperation convened on September 5 in Beijing, President Xi Jinping stated, "China will implement with Africa more solidly the Future of Africa—Vocational Education Cooperation Plan, establish together an engineering technology academy, and build ten Luban Workshops." In recent years, driven by high-level diplomatic efforts, 17 Luban Workshops have already been established in 15 African countries, blossoming into a flagship model of China's international vocational education cooperation. [1]

In Central Asia, the Luban Workshop in Tajikistan has been operating successfully for over a year, while projects in Uzbekistan and Turkmenistan are progressing actively. Kyrgyzstan recently inaugurated a smart classroom for its Luban Workshop. [2] The first Luban Workshop in Kazakhstan began trial operations at the end of 2023. During talks in July 2024 between President Xi Jinping and Kazakh President Kassym-Jomart Tokayev in Astana, it was announced that China would establish a second Luban Workshop in Kazakhstan. [3]

Since the first overseas Luban Workshop was established in Thailand in 2016, it has been launched in several African countries under the Forum on China-Africa

---

[1] http://www.news.cn/politics/leaders/20240907/35e1ed2f4ec045838f5f56d491e60714/c.html

[2] http://www.news.cn/politics/leaders/20240704/ 130b35c1192e41979ad417cc34159037/c.html

[3] http://www.news.cn/20240703/d796ba 1a83b6450aa55a6620fc390d4c/c.html

Cooperation, and more have been set up across Central Asia. As of July 2024, this Chinese vocational education brand has taken root in 29 countries, offering 57 programs in 14 major fields, including artificial intelligence, electric vehicle maintenance, civil engineering, and traditional Chinese medicine. The workshops have enrolled over 10,000 students in degree programs and provided vocational training to more than 22,000 participants. [1]

—Promoting Access to Basic Health Care for People in BRI Partner Countries

For many years, "small yet smart" medical outreach programs like "Operation Brightness," "Operation Love," and "Operation Smile," which focus on treating cataracts, heart disease, and cleft lip and palate, have been widely welcomed in BRI partner countries. According to incomplete statistics, since 2024, Chinese medical teams have successfully performed nearly a thousand cataract surgeries in countries such as Mongolia, [2] Tajikistan, [3] Uzbekistan, [4] and Sri Lanka. [5] In Mongolia alone, the "Belt and Road Brightness Action" has screened 3,178 patients with eye diseases and performed 539 free cataract surgeries. In Cambodia, a 68-year-old named Duk Sarun underwent surgery at the end of January, becoming the 10,000th patient cured under China's cataract blindness elimination project in the country.

In order to further advance the Health Silk Road, China has also established various partnership mechanisms with BRI countries, assisting in building medical facilities. According to the China-Africa Belt and Road Cooperation Development Report released on August 29, 2024, as of the end of June 2024, China had helped build over 130 hospitals and clinics in Africa, dispatched medical teams to 45 African countries, and established paired cooperation mechanisms with 46 African hospitals. In Laos, the China-aided upgrade project for Luang Prabang Hospital was completed and handed over in mid-August. China constructed new surgical and cardiovascular wards and will provide three years of technical assistance to improve local healthcare and medical rescue capabilities,

---

① http://paper.ce.cn/pc/content/202408/27/content_300065.html

② http://www.news.cn/photo/20240910/e5f0072735134587993753eec3b6e624/c.html

③ http://www.news.cn/world/20240706/5cf1d23975994c96ba7fb93a76470bda/c.html

④ http://www.news.cn/20240531/a537fa86064042a1a23837b82dfb02cd/c.html

⑤ http://www.news.cn/world/20240425/ 125c589a38c34358847f12d952d74554/c.html aiming to make the hospital a central medical hub in northern Laos.

—Wells of Happiness Quench the Thirst of BRI Partner Countries' People

In order to promote access to clean water in BRI partner countries, China has initiated projects to provide drinking water facilities in various regions. On July 22, the first well of the 300-well project aided by China in Zimbabwe successfully produced water, bringing safe drinking water to local villagers. In 2024, Zimbabwe faced severe drought and food security challenges. To address this, China committed to drilling 300 wells in several provinces. Zimbabwe's Minister of National Housing and Social Amenities, Daniel Garwe, stated, "These wells will greatly alleviate the water crisis in four of the hardest-hit provinces, not only saving livestock and irrigating farmland but also laying a solid foundation for post-disaster recovery." Over the past decade, China has constructed 1,000 wells in Zimbabwe, providing water for domestic use and agricultural irrigation to approximately 400,000 people while also creating thousands of jobs.

China has been making further contributions to water supply for daily use and agricultural irrigation in 2024. In Kyrgyzstan, the first phase of China-aided irrigation system upgrades, covering three irrigation districts, was officially handed over. In Myanmar, the second phase of a rural water supply project in Naypyidaw was completed, significantly improving access to clean water for rural communities. In Sri Lanka, the China-constructed central canal project was completed in May, providing irrigation for nearly 400 hectares of farmland. Each well and every canal benefits millions of people, symbolizing the tangible cooperation and shared development between Belt and Road countries.

—The "Grass of Happiness" Continues to Drive Poverty Alleviation

In March 2024, China and the Fijian government co-hosted a "Pacific Island Countries Juncao Technology Training Workshop," attracting dozens of participants from 11 Pacific nations, including Papua New Guinea, Tonga, the Cook Islands, Samoa, and Nauru. Professor Lin Zhanxi, the inventor of Juncao technology, personally trained the participants. Juncao technology, which was first introduced as an official aid project to Papua New Guinea in 2001, has since grown in global significance. By August 2024, approximately 350 international Juncao training sessions had been held, training more than 14,000 people. [1] In Papua New Guinea, giant Juncao grass set a world record by yielding 854 tons of fresh grass per hectare annually. Prime Minister James Marape, during his meeting with Professor Lin in May, emphasized the critical role Juncao and upland rice projects have played in Papua New Guinea's agriculture and poverty reduction efforts. The government plans to expand these projects further to more provinces. In Rwanda, the Juncao industry chain has supported over 50 businesses and cooperatives, benefiting more than 4,000 households and creating employment for more than 30,000 people. In Fiji, over 2,700 technicians have been trained in Juncao technology, directly benefiting over 3,000 households. To date, the Juncao project has taken root in more than 100 countries, showing great potential in poverty reduction, job creation, desertification control, and power generation, earning its reputation as the "Grass of Happiness" that benefits the world. [2]

Fact Box: "Small Yet Smart" Projects

At the third symposium on the BRI, President Xi Jinping emphasized that "small yet smart" projects should be prioritized in international cooperation.

For many years, the BRI has focused on tangible and impactful projects that enhance the sense of satisfaction and happiness among the people of BRI partner countries. These projects cover key areas such as infrastructure, healthcare, green ecology, agricultural cooperation, water conservation, forestry, poverty alleviation and humanitarian efforts, and education and training. Guided by the principles of practicality, public engagement, low cost, and sustainability, the BRI has deeply advanced the development of "small yet smart" projects. Notable examples, such as Juncao technology and Luban Workshops, have become flagship models, with strong demonstrating effects and broad applicability.

1.4 Deepening Mechanism Building and Prominent People-to-people Exchanges

—The International Cooperation Mechanism is Improving, and Multilateral Platform Development is Progressing Steadily

---

[1] http://www.news.cn/politics/leaders/20240825/fa904ff239dc4846902b3814f06b24a2/c.html
[2] http://www.news.cn/world/20240802/6d09d74f660a470884459749086cb7e5/c.html

In line with the requirements of the Eight Major Steps, the Secretariat of the Belt and Road Forum for International Cooperation was officially inaugurated on May 11, marking the commencement of its operations. The Secretariat, located within China's Ministry of Foreign Affairs, is responsible for supporting the forum and coordinating related international cooperation efforts. Over the past year, solid progress has been made in developing multilateral cooperation platforms among BRI partner countries in various fields, such as energy, taxation, law, disaster reduction, anti-corruption, think tanks, and media, with continual new achievements.

Fact Box: Secretariat of the Belt and Road Forum for International Cooperation

In October 2023, President Xi Jinping announced the establishment of the Secretariat of the Belt and Road Forum for International Cooperation during the 3rd Belt and Road Forum for International Cooperation. Vice Minister of Foreign Affairs Ma Zhaoxu serves as the Secretary-General.

Take taxation, for example. Over 500 representatives from nearly 50 countries and regions gathered in Hong Kong in September to attend the 5th Belt and Road Tax Administration Cooperation Forum. To facilitate trade and investment for the BRI partner countries, China initiated the Belt and Road Tax Administration Cooperation Mechanism in 2019, aiming to remove tax barriers and create a tax environment that fosters development. Under this mechanism, five Belt and Road Tax Academies have been established in Yangzhou, Beijing, Astana, Macau, and Riyadh, with a new campus added in Macau (Hengqin Campus) in 2024. At the forum, it was announced that the Belt and Road Tax Academy in Algiers had officially opened, becoming the sixth such institution. As of August 2024, the mechanism has trained around 6,000 tax and finance officials from over 120 countries and regions, building a bridge for improving tax governance and facilitating trade and economic exchanges.

Over the past year, various multilateral cooperation platforms, such as the Belt and Road Energy Partnership, the Belt and Road High-level Conference on Intellectual Property, the Belt and Road International Think Tank Cooperation Committee, the Belt and Road Media Cooperation Alliance, and the Belt and Road International Cooperation Mechanism for Natural Disaster Prevention and Emergency Management, have been advancing the outcomes of the 3rd Belt and Road Forum for International Cooperation and the Eight Major Steps. These platforms have fostered international cooperation in specific fields, enhanced functional dialogues, and promoted "soft connectivity" between Belt and Road partner countries.

—Building a Clean Silk Road for Sustainable BRI Cooperation

At the Clean Silk Road Forum, held during the 3rd Belt and Road Forum for International Cooperation, Tsinghua University's Academy for Clean Governance unveiled the Belt and Road Enterprise Integrity and Compliance Evaluation System. In June 2024, the Belt and Road Corporate Integrity and Compliance Evaluation Forum was held in Yiwu, Zhejiang Province. More than 400 representatives from the Chinese government, including the Central Commission for Discipline Inspection and the National Supervisory Commission, along with international organizations, businesses, and scholars, participated. The forum focused on building consensus around the integrity and compliance system to promote high-quality corporate development. Guo Yong, Director of Tsinghua University's Academy for Clean Governance, highlighted that enterprises play a key role as a bridge in BRI cooperation, acting as key drivers in implementing various projects. He stressed that integrity was fundamental to the steady and sustainable development of the BRI, while corporate compliance was central to enhancing global competitiveness. Jaroslaw Pietrusiewicz, Secretary General of the International Anti-Corruption Academy, expressed strong support for China's Clean Silk Road initiative and pledged the academy's continued commitment to contributing to its implementation.

In August, the Belt and Road Integrity Construction Local Seminar between Yunnan, China, and Southeast Asian Countries was held in Kunming, exploring practical pathways for local exchanges and regional collaboration in anti-corruption efforts. In September, the Hong Kong Independent Commission Against Corruption (ICAC) hosted a nine-day "Anti-corruption Governance Course for Large Infrastructure Projects," attended by over 20 participants from anti-corruption agencies in more than ten BRI partner countries. The course focused on using technology to mitigate corruption risks and strengthen anti-corruption capabilities in large-scale infrastructure projects. To further enhance governmental cooperation, China has been actively promoting capacity building for the Clean Silk Road through various programs, including anti-corruption training sessions for BRI countries, international workshops on discipline inspection and supervision, and foreign aid training programs in the field of Clean Silk Road construction.

Fact Box: Beijing Initiative for the Clean Silk Road

The Beijing Initiative for the Clean Silk Road was jointly launched in April 2019 at the Clean Silk Road Sub-forum during the Second Belt and Road Forum for International Cooperation. Representatives from China, BRI partner countries, international organizations, and business and academic sectors participated in the initiative's creation. The initiative calls for greater transparency in government information, proactive prevention and resolution of disputes in trade and investment, and enhanced cooperation in finance, taxation, intellectual property, and environmental protection. It aims to establish a stable, fair, and transparent framework for rules and governance within the Belt and Road Initiative. The Beijing Initiative also urges all parties to strengthen oversight of Belt and Road cooperation projects, regulate public resource transactions, and strictly adhere to relevant laws and regulations in project bidding, construction, and management to eliminate rent-seeking opportunities and foster a standardized and law-based business environment.

—Promoting Understanding through People-to-people Exchanges, Fostering Mutual Learning between Civilizations

The countries involved in the BRI have diverse historical and cultural backgrounds, with hundreds of languages and scripts in use. This diversity underscores the need for strengthening people-to-people exchanges and cultural interactions to promote mutual understanding and foster mutual learning between civilizations.

On December 3, 2023, the inaugural Liangzhu Forum was held in Hangzhou, China. President Xi Jinping sent a congratulatory letter to the forum, in which he emphasized that mutual respect, solidarity, and harmonious coexistence are the right path for the development of human civilization. He expressed hope that all parties would fully utilize the Liangzhu Forum as a platform to deepen civilizational dialogue with BRI partner countries, implement the Global Civilization Initiative, enhance cultural exchanges, and promote the values of equality, mutual learning, dialogue, and inclusiveness. Doing so will encourage different civilizations to coexist harmoniously and achieve mutual success while fostering friendship and understanding among the peoples of various nations.

Fact Box: Liangzhu Forum

On October 18, 2023, during his keynote speech at the 3rd Belt and Road Forum for International Cooperation, President Xi Jinping announced that China would host the Liangzhu Forum to deepen civilizational dialogue with Belt and Road partner countries.

"The Liangzhu Site is a sacred place that proves the 5,000-year history of Chinese civilization," stated significantly President Xi Jinping, then Secretary of the Zhejiang Provincial Party Committee, in July 2003.

In 2016, President Xi also gave important instructions regarding the application for the Liangzhu Ancient City to be recognized as a World Heritage Site. On July 6, 2019, the Liangzhu Ancient City was successfully inscribed on the World Heritage List.

The inaugural Liangzhu Forum, co-hosted by the Ministry of Culture and Tourism and the Zhejiang Provincial Government, took place in Hangzhou, Zhejiang Province, on December 3, 2023. Themed "Implementing the Global Civilization Initiative, Promoting Civilizational Exchanges and Mutual Learning," the forum brought together more than 300 guests from China and abroad.

Over the past year, in the spirit of promoting "coexistence in harmony and facilitate progress in one another" and "forging friendship and closer bonds with other peoples," a series of cultural exchange events were held as outcomes of the 3rd Belt and Road Forum for International Cooperation. These events included the Belt and Road Media Cooperation Forum, the Belt and Road Publishing Cooperation Forum for BRI Partner Countries, the 11th Silk Road International Film Festival, the 9th China-Mongolia-Russia Tea Road City Cooperation Conference, and the 2024 Belt and Road Youth Creativity and Heritage Forum. In June, the Silk Road Tourism City Alliance held the "Silk Road Dialogue" in Istanbul, Turkey, marking the first time the alliance hosted an event outside of China. By the end of June, 63 renowned tourist cities from 28 countries had joined the coalition.

The convenience brought by connectivity and the enthusiasm generated through cultural exchanges have made two-way tourism along the Belt and Road increasingly popular. In May, China's southwestern Guizhou Province launched its first cross-border tourism train, allowing over 200 tourists to travel directly from Guiyang to Vientiane, Laos, via the China-Laos Railway. Meanwhile, in neighboring Yunnan Province, a large number of Vietnamese tourists have been entering China by high-speed trains. By mid-

August, more than 700 Vietnamese tour groups, with over 12,000 visitors, had entered China through the Hekou border, setting a new record. At the Horgos port of entry, due to it being the "Kazakhstan Tourism Year" in China and the signing of a mutual visa exemption agreement between China and Kazakhstan, the enthusiasm for tourism in the public surged. As of late August 2024, the number of people crossing the Horgos border had reached 810,000, an increase of 118% year-on-year.

Fact Box: International Tourism Alliance of Silk Road Cities

The International Tourism Alliance of Silk Road Cities was established in September 2023, jointly initiated by the China Cultural and Tourism Exchange Center of the Ministry of Culture and Tourism, along with well-known domestic and international tourist cities. Guided by the spirit of the Silk Road and based on the principles of consultation, collaboration, and shared benefits, the alliance aims to establish along-term cooperation mechanism for tourism exchange and collaboration among cities, including those along the Silk Road. The alliance plans to promote the sustainable development of tourism in its member cities through a series of thematic activities, such as international forums, joint promotional efforts, and industry matchmaking. As of June 2024, sixty-three renowned tourist cities from 28 countries, including China and others across Asia, Europe, Africa, and the Americas, have joined the alliance.

To further facilitate foreign nationals'travel to China, in 2024, the Chinese government introduced a 72-hour or 144-hour visa-free transit policy for citizens of certain countries, including over 20 BRI partner countries. This policy has significantly increased the number of tourists visiting China. On the other hand, BRI countries are also working to attract more Chinese tourists. In September, Sherif Fathy, Egypt's Minister of Tourism and Antiquities, stated that Egypt currently attracts about 200,000 Chinese tourists annually and will take further steps to increase this number, promoting bilateral tourism cooperation. According to the China-Africa Belt and Road Cooperation Development Report, China has signed bilateral tourism cooperation agreements with 31 African countries and designated 34 African nations as approved destinations for Chinese tour groups. With these reciprocal efforts, tourism cooperation between China and Belt and Road partner countries is reaching new heights.

Chapter Two The Eight Major Steps Create New Opportunities for High-Quality BRI Cooperation

As the world undergoes profound changes unseen in a century, with global political, economic, and social environments evolving rapidly and global economic governance being restructured, the introduction and implementation of the Eight Initiatives align with the common pursuit of development, growth, and shared prosperity among Belt and Road partner countries. These initiatives bring new historical opportunities for the high-quality development of the Belt and Road Initiative (BRI). In its second decade, the BRI is expected to achieve higher levels of cooperation, greater investment returns, improved quality of supply, and enhanced development resilience. The BRI has the potential to become a cornerstone for building an open world economy, a driving force for collective development, and an accelerator for global modernization.

2.1 Promoting Development on a Broader Scale: A Ballast for Building an Open World Economy

In today's world, the trend of "anti-globalization" is rising, with unilateralism, trade protectionism, and hegemonism gaining ground. Certain countries have taken unilateral, aggressive actions, using the banner of "economic security" to promote "decoupling" and "de-risking," erecting unreasonable barriers and standards, attempting to disrupt international production and supply chains, and creating exclusive trade blocs and cooperation frameworks. These actions have intensified instability within the global financial and monetary systems, undermined the multilateral trading system, and increased financial risks. As a result, international trade and investment cooperation have become more difficult, and the global trade landscape is showing signs of fragmentation.

In the face of these challenges, the international community urgently needs a ballast to support an open world economy.

—BRI Cooperation Embodies an Inherent Spirit of Openness, Aligned with the Global Trend of Inclusive Economic Globalization

As the saying goes, "Those who share the same vision will not be divided by mountains or seas." The BRI started with the goal of improving connectivity, and over the past decade, it has grown from nothing to a comprehensive network, achieving historic development. Today, more than three-quarters of the world's countries and major international organizations have joined the circle of friends of the BRI cooperation. Both in theory and practice, the BRI carries an inherent spirit of openness. The BRI cooperation has consistently upheld the Silk Road spirit of peace and cooperation, openness and inclusiveness, mutual learning, and mutual benefit. It follows the principles of consultation, collaboration, and shared benefits, promoting cooperation through openness and ensuring mutual success through joint efforts. The BRI has actively pursued a path of cooperation that avoids protectionism, exclusive arrangements, or high barriers. Despite the rising tide of anti-globalization in today'sworld, the broader trend of inclusive economic globalization remains unchanged. Most countries continue to prioritize development, work to boost their economies, and safeguard global supply chains. Peace, development, cooperation, and win-win outcomes remain the shared aspirations of the international community. As both a participant and beneficiary of economic globalization, China is committed to promoting high-level openness and maintaining the direction of economic globalization. China stands firmly in favor of free trade and genuine multilateralism, working to build an open world economy.

Within the framework of the BRI, the prospects for countries to expand openness and strengthen cooperation are broad and promising.

—The BRI Cooperation Effectively Connects with the Global Economy Across Multiple Levels and Sectors

Driven by the Eight Major Steps, the BRI enhances "soft connectivity" in terms of regulatory standards, aligning with international high-standard trade and economic rules, and actively promoting high-level openness in cross-border services, trade, and investment. It encourages deeper participation from more countries and regions, forming a collective force for development through bilateral, multilateral, and third-party market cooperation.

At regional and multilateral levels, the BRI cooperation aligns effectively with global frameworks such as the United Nations 2030 Agenda for Sustainable Development, the ASEAN Connectivity Master Plan 2025, the ASEAN Outlook on the Indo-Pacific, the African Union's Agenda 2063, and the European Union's Eurasian Connectivity Strategy, supporting regional integration and contributing to global development.

At the bilateral level, the BRI aligns with numerous national strategies, such as Russia's Eurasian Economic Union, Kazakhstan's "Bright Road" new economic policy, Turkmenistan's "Revival of the Great Silk Road" strategy, Mongolia's "Development

Road" initiative, Indonesia's "Global Maritime Fulcrum" concept, the Philippines' "Build, Build, Build" program, Vietnam's "Two Corridors and One Belt" initiative, South Africa's "Economic Reconstruction and Recovery Plan," Egypt's Suez Canal Corridor Development Project, and Saudi Arabia's "Vision 2030." These alignments strongly support the economic and social development processes of the BRI partner countries.

2.2 Expanding Growth in Broader Sectors as an Engine for Joint Development

The global economic recovery remains weak, with external economic challenges persisting. The delayed effects of the COVID-19 pandemic and the spillover impacts of geopolitical conflicts have placed some countries in economic hardship. In contrast, others face crises of poverty and potential regression in poverty alleviation. Many nations now urgently require new, sustainable drivers of growth.

—Cultivating New Growth Points through New-quality Productivity

The BRI aligns with the general trends of global economic, technological, industrial, and social development, actively engaging in cooperation in emerging fields such as health, green development, innovation, and the digital economy to foster new growth points for collaboration. In the face of the ongoing technological revolution, China is developing new types of productivity that suit local conditions. This approach aims to support partner countries in jointly pursuing innovation-driven growth. The initiative enhances innovation in areas such as the digital economy, artificial intelligence, new energy, and new materials. It promotes the full-scale, all-encompassing, and entire valuechain transformation of traditional manufacturing through modern digital technologies, the internet, and artificial intelligence. By nurturing the development of emerging and future industries, the BRI drives the deep transformation and upgrading of traditional industries. It accelerates the integration of digital technology with the real economy. It also fosters the deep coupling of digital technology and data elements, accelerates the creation of new business models and industries in the digital space, shares technological innovation achievements, deepens cooperation in digital governance, and establishes new hubs for science and technology innovation cooperation along the Belt and Road.

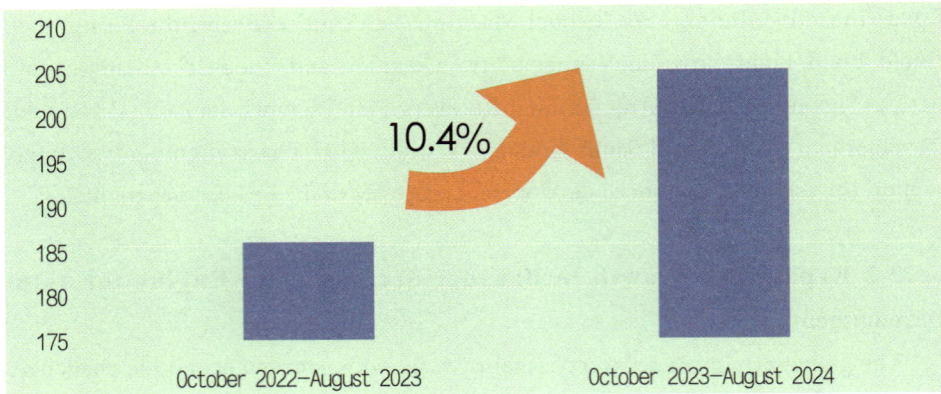

Figure 4: Growth in Non-financial Direct Investment by Chinese Enterprises in Belt and Road Partner Countries Since the Introduction of the Eight Initiatives
Source: Ministry of Commerce

—BRI Unleashes Potential in Partner Countries, Supporting Long-term Stable Growth

The BRI plays a key role in unlocking the existing potential of partner countries by effectively mobilizing various productive resources and turning natural advantages into tangible economic gains. The World Bank predicts that the BRI could reduce transportation time along economic corridors and international routes by nearly one-eighth, potentially boosting global trade by more than 6%. Data from Thailand's Ministry of Rail Transport indicates that once the China-Laos-Thailand Railway is fully operational, freight transportation costs are expected to decrease by 30% to 50% within three to five years. Such cost reductions will lead to more effective natural resource development, more efficient use of human resources, faster economic activity, and improved exchange of production outcomes.

Driven by domestic and international market demand, the BRI is transitioning from its initial "pillar and beam" phase to one of steady development. Currently, internal trade among BRI partner countries accounts for over 30% of total trade, with in termediate goods comprising more than 60%, indicating the formation of closer industrial and supply chain relationships. On this foundation, the initiative will provide strong support for the long-term, stable growth of partner countries as long as the various BRI initiatives continue to be steadily implemented and economic stability within the BRI framework is maintained.

2.3 Deepen Shared Prosperity to Accelerate Global Modernization

Due to the current global political and economic landscape, some countries lack the internal momentum needed for economic development and transformation, leading to issues such as political polarization, growing income inequality, social divisions, and a rise in populism. Developing countries face the pressing challenge of achieving modernization, while developed countries are confronted with maintaining their modernization achievements and sustaining their level of economic and social modernization.

China is now advancing its goal of national rejuvenation through the Chinese path to modernization. It is not a modernization that China seeks to achieve in isolation, but rather one that aims for joint modernization with other developing countries and the world at large. The ultimate goal of China's modernization is to improve the lives of its 1.4 billion people. For BRI partner countries, this represents access to avast market and unprecedented cooperation opportunities, injecting powerful momentum into global modernization efforts.

—Promoting Peaceful Modernization through High-quality BRI Cooperation

President Xi Jinping has emphasized that the BRI adheres to the principles of consultation, collaboration, and shared benefits. It is not a unilateral endeavor but a shared responsibility where all parties benefit equally. Consultation promotes multilateralism, encouraging collective decision-making that takes into account the interests and concerns of all involved parties, incorporating wisdom and creativity from all sides. Over the past decade, the BRI countries have embraced dialogue over confrontation and cooperation over conflict, resolving issues through diplomacy rather than violence and rejecting hegemonic and coercive thinking. Rather than a solo performance, the BRI countries have collectively played a symphony of cooperation. In the future, the BRI will continue to strengthen cooperation platforms and mechanisms, deepen dialogue and consultation across various sectors, and make "people-to-people connectivity" a fundamental pillar of high-quality Belt and Road development. The peaceful approach to achieving global modernization will continue to be widely supported and welcomed by countries around the world.

—Promoting Modernization for Shared Prosperity through High-quality BRI Cooperation

The BRI's original aspirations are to achieve joint development for partner countries, improving the lives of their people. Without shared growth and prosperity, true global peace and stability cannot be achieved, and the results of global modernization will be difficult to sustain. In the face of widening global gaps between the Global North and South, increasing challenges for developing countries to catch up, and worsening income inequality within nations, the BRI offers a realistic path to modernization for developing nations. The BRI reflects China's deep understanding and unique perspective on modernization, encompassing not only material improvements but also comprehensive social progress. It adheres to a people-centered approach to development, focusing on poverty alleviation, job creation, and improving livelihoods, ensuring that the benefits of the BRI reach all people and contribute to the local economy and society. Projects that are "small yet smart"—those that directly improve the well-being of local populations— help reduce income inequality, bridge the North-South divide, and align with the sincere aspirations of people worldwide for a better life. These projects form a key foundation of support and opportunity for the high-quality development of the BRI cooperation.

Chapter Three Advancing the Eight Major Steps and Embarking on a New Journey for High-quality BRI Cooperation

The Eight Major Steps encompass various areas, such as infrastructure connectivity, development model transformation, innovation in cooperation mechanisms, and international exchanges and training. They are a concentrated reflection of the high-quality practices and achievements of the BRI cooperation over the years and serve as a roadmap and timetable for the next phase of higher-quality and more advanced development. In order to push forward the high-quality implementation of the Eight Major Steps, we must continue to follow the guiding principles of consultation, collaboration, and shared benefits; openness, green development, and integrity; and a focus on high standards, improving livelihoods, and sustainability. Doing so will require consolidating practical cooperation, fostering innovation-driven growth, strengthening risk management, and improving systems and mechanisms to promote "hard connectivity," "soft connectivity," and "people-to-people connectivity" between nations. Together, we can create a more open, inclusive, peaceful, and mutually beneficial future.

3.1 Strengthening the Foundations of Cooperation to Build a More Resilient Connectivity Network

Looking ahead to the Eight Major Steps, BRI partner countries, regions, and international organizations must continue to enhance strategic alignment, deepen practical cooperation, and refine the integrated land-sea-air-space connectivity network to build a more resilient and multidimensional connectivity system. At the same time, it is essential to translate policy consensus into tangible outcomes that benefit people's livelihoods. Such an endeavor requires identifying priority areas for cooperation, detailing specific action plans, and drafting a list of key cooperation projects to establish a virtuous cycle of interaction.

—Coordinating the Development of Flagship Projects for Smoother and More Efficient Connectivity

Infrastructure connectivity remains central to the Eight Major Steps. Advancing it requires not only optimizing existing resources but also expanding new development opportunities. A coordinated effort is needed to develop flagship projects that will establish an integrated, intelligent, and modern multidimensional connectivity network. Data from Pakistan[1] indicates that by 2030, the China-Pakistan Economic Corridor (CPEC) is expected to boost Pakistan's economic growth by 2.5 percentage points and create 2.3 million jobs. According to estimates from Uzbekistan,[2] the China-Kyrgyzstan-Uzbekistan (CKU) Railway, once completed, will handle 15 million tons of freight annually and reduce transportation times by seven days. Peru's Ministry of Agricultural Development and Irrigation predicts that once the Chancay Port is operational, the time for Peruvian agricultural products to reach Asia will decrease from 28 days to 16 days, with shipping costs expected to drop by 30%, significantly expanding agricultural trade.[3] Additionally, the Tanzania-Zambia Railway

---

[1] https://www.radio.gov.pk/25-11-2020/cpec-is-win-win-project-of-china-pakistan-economic-cooperation-shibli

[2] Congratulatory Message by Uzbekistan President Shavkat Mirziyoyev at the Signing of the China-Kyrgyzstan-Uzbekistan Railway Project Trilateral Government Agreement on June 6, 2024 https://uza. uz/en/posts/presidents-message-to-the-participants-in-the-signing-ceremony-of-the-agreement-on-the-construction-of-the-china-kyrgyzstan-uzbekistan-railway_605632

[3] https://agraria.pe/noticias/peru-se-prepara-a-exportar-fruta-congelada-a-china-36385

Authority estimates that following the full implementation of the Memorandum of Understanding on Revitalizing the Tanzania-Zambia Railway signed by China, Tanzania, and Zambia, the railway's capacity will increase significantly, with annual freight volume rising from the current 500,000 tons to approximately 2 million tons. [1] The advancement of these flag-ship projects will not only generate growth but also drive development and yield long-term economic and social benefits.

—Enhancing the Quality of "Small Yet Smart" Projects to Deepen Strategic Alignment and Win-win Cooperation

The BRI is centered on improving people's well-being. Projects that are "small yet smart" and directly impact regional livelihoods and overall welfare are key priorities under the Eight Major Steps. According to World Bank estimates, [2] by 2030, the BRI could lift 7.6 million people out of extreme poverty and 32 million people out of moderate poverty in BRI participant countries.

As the BRI increasingly focuses on areas such as healthcare, agricultural production, food security, water resource cooperation, clean energy, ecological protection, and education and training, a series of "small yet smart" demonstration projects—characterized by low investment, quick returns, and strong economic, social, and environmental benefits—is expected to accelerate in formation. These projects will generate more grassroots-level, people-centered cooperation outcomes. Take vocational education, for example. During the launch ceremony of the track construction for Malaysia's East Coast Rail Link at the end of 2023, a flagship project of high-quality BRI cooperation between China and Malaysia, the China-Malaysia Railway Modern Craftsman Academy, jointly established by Chinese and Malaysian universities, was inaugurated. By the end of 2026, the academy is expected to enroll 50 students in degree programs, offer vocational skills training to 100 participants, and cultivate a core teaching staff of 60. [3] In the future, vocational education projects linked to major

---

[1] https://www.tazarasite.com/successful-signing-mou-concession-tazara

[2] The World Bank's June 2019 report, Belt and Road Economics: Opportunities and Risks of Transport Corridors.

[3] China-Malaysia Universities Jointly Establish Railway Craftsman Academy to Support Talent Development for the East Coast Rail Link https://www.gx.chinanews.com.cn/kjwt/2023-12-12/detail-ihcvvqfu6721482.shtml

flagship projects like this will have significant room for expansion. The individuals trained through such programs will not only meet the needs of specific projects but will also contribute to the long-term development of the local workforce in partner countries.

3.2 Expanding Innovation and Unlocking Potential in New Areas of Cooperation

Looking ahead, the Eight Major Steps aim to foster the development of new productivity by focusing on green and digital growth while further expanding cooperation in emerging fields. In addition, they will continue to promote institutional openness, leveraging the advantages of new cooperation models and exploring the potential for trilateral and multilateral market cooperation.

—Creating New Hubs for Innovation Cooperation and Advancing New-quality Productivity

Innovation serves as the core driving force behind the Eight Major Steps. Since the launch of the Belt and Road Science, Technology, and Innovation Action Plan in 2017, joint laboratories have become a crucial means of promoting technological innovation and cooperation. To date, China has established 53 Belt and Road joint laboratories with BRI partner countries, spanning key sectors such as agriculture, healthcare, information technology, new energy, and basic research. Over the next five years, China aims to expand this network to 100 joint laboratories, [1] further empowering industrial and technological advancements in partner countries and enhancing their capacity for innovative development.

Building the Digital Silk Road is a key pathway to advancing innovation cooperation under the Eight Major Steps. As the systematic and multidimensional framework of the "six corridors, six routes, multiple countries, multiple ports" becomes more refined, upgrading traditional infrastructure—such as ports, railways, highways, airports, energy, and water resources—through digital transformation will enhance the operational efficiency of economic corridors and international routes. This digital upgrade involves utilizing technologies like big data, cloud computing, the Internet of Things, and artificial intelligence for intelligent management and operation. For example, in the case of digital

---

[1] https://www.ceweekly.cn/cewsel/2024/0913/455206.html

logistics cooperation between Vietnam and China, Nguyen Xuan Hung, Vice President of the Hanoi Logistics Association, pointed out that in recent years, Vietnamese and Chinese companies have mainly cooperated in the warehousing and distribution stages of digital logistics. However, in the cross-border logistics sector, Vietnamese and Chinese companies are unable to fully track the stages of cargo in real time after it enters the destination country. There remains significant potential for further development in cross-border logistics digital cooperation.

—Unlocking Practical Cooperation Potential and Building Open Platforms Together

Openness is a key pillar of the Eight Major Steps. In order to advance these initiatives, efforts must focus on enhancing cooperation efficiency by deepening alignment in regulations, standards, and oversight among countries. Various forms of collaboration— such as public-private partnerships (PPP), bilateral cooperation, third-party market cooperation, and multilateral cooperation—should be encouraged, allowing more countries, businesses, andinstitutions to participate deeply and jointly in promoting the development of an open world economy.

Cross-border e-commerce, as a frontier of open cooperation, is strongly driving innovation in global trade. From the broader perspective of Belt and Road cooperation, this sector can effectively leverage the advantages of connectivity, industrial development, and an open economy. Promoting international cooperation in green finance will also be a key focus for achieving high-level openness within the Eight Initiatives. According to the latest United Nations estimates, [1] the annual financing gap for developing countries to achieve the Sustainable Development Goals (SDGs) by 2030 ranges between $2. 5 trillion and $4 trillion. Establishing green financial systems in developing countries and emerging economies is crucial. The Capacity-building Alliance of Sustainable Investment (CASI), co-founded by China and multiple institutions, was officially launched at the end of 2023. It is expected to provide sustainable finance capacity-building services to 100,000 participants from developing countries by 2030. [2]

---

[1] 2024 Financing for Sustainable Development Report, P16 https://sdg.iisd.org/news/annual-sdg-financing-gaps-measured-in-trillions-fsdr-2024/

[2] https://www.financialnews.com.cn/cj/sc/202312/t20231207_283686.html

3.3 Mitigating Risks and Laying a Solid Foundation for Long-term Stability

Looking ahead, the successful implementation of the Eight Major Steps will require deepening solidarity and cooperation to jointly address external risks and build stronger internal consensus among BRI partner countries. At the same time, it is crucial to enhance the risk awareness of enterprises, guided by the principles of "enterprise-led, market-driven, government-guided, and internationally rules-based." Efforts must continue to optimize the business environment along the Clean Silk Road and improve security measures for both projects and personnel.

—Cooperating to Address External Risks and Challenges

The essence of the Eight Major Steps lies in win-win cooperation. In the context of major changes unseen in a century, strengthening unity and resilience, along with collaborative development efforts, is fundamental to advancing the implementation of the steps. In addition to the political and economic risks mentioned in Chapter Two, the BRI must also remain vigilant against systemic negative propaganda promoted by certain countries. The propaganda includes false narratives that label the BRI as a "debt trap," "neo-colonialism," or a form of "systemic export," which aims to undermine and tarnish the initiative's image. Such negative campaigns can erode existing achievements, hinder project progress, and create a toxic political and social atmosphere in partner countries. A report published in April 2023 by Bruegel, a European think tank, indicated that, while the BRI's international image is largely positive, it is not immune to negative noise, much of which is driven by specific interest groups. In response to these challenges, BRI partner countries should collaborate in addressing external risks, particularly in countering smear campaigns against the BRI. Strengthening internal consensus and delivering timely, effective responses to these attacks is essential. As Mladen Ivanić, former President of Bosnia and Herzegovina, pointed out, there are many misconceptions in Western countries about the true nature of the BRI, and it is necessary to correct and eliminate these biases. [1]

---

[1] Speech by Mladen Ivanić, Former President of Bosnia and Herzegovina and Member of the Board of Directors of the Nizami Ganjavi International Center, at the Think Tank Exchange Forum of the Third Belt and Road Forum for International Cooperation, October 18, 2023. https://www.brsn.net/spjj/gjfr/detail/20231214/ 19435555_% E5% A7% 86% E6% 8B% 89% E7% 99% BB%C2%B7%E4%BC%8A%E4%B8%87%E5%B0%BC%E5%A5%87.html

—Strengthening Risk Management for Key Stakeholders

Key stakeholders play a crucial role in implementing the Eight Major Steps. As part of advancing the initiatives, it is essential to encourage these stakeholders to enhance their awareness of safety and incorporate political, economic, and cultural risks into their project planning. Analysis shows that international Belt and Road infrastructure projects are increasingly moving up the value chain, with the "investment, construction, and operation integration" model being explored. This shift places new demands on corporate management and risk control capabilities, requiring that projects meet legal and compliance standards, demonstrate financial reliability, ensure environmental sustainability, and provide social benefits. In practice, large enterprises, particularly in the energy sector, have already recognized that adhering to international market rules and local laws in project decision-making and operations is critical to ensuring the long-term sustainability of Belt and Road cooperation projects. [①]

3.4 Improving Cooperation Mechanisms to Ensure the Effective Implementation of the Eight Major Steps

Improving cooperation mechanisms is essential to ensuring the successful implementation of the Eight Major Steps. Advancing these initiatives requires continued efforts to strengthen multidimensional connectivity mechanisms, deepen trade and investment cooperation mechanisms, solidify people-to-people connectivity mechanisms, refine green development mechanisms, and improve consultation and coordination mecha-nisms.

Strengthening multidimensional connectivity mechanisms involves further integrating transportation, energy, and information networks with industrial development. Economic corridors, built on existing foundations, should lead the way, supported by major transportation routes and digital highways, with railways, highways, airports, ports, and pipelines serving as the backbone. The aim is to enhance the quality and efficiency of these systems.

---

① Speech by Yu Guo, Executive Director of the Economics and Technology Research Institute of China National Petroleum Corporation, at the Plenary Session of the Belt and Road International Think Tank Cooperation Committee, October 17, 2023. https://www.brsn.net/spjj/gjfr/detail/20231221/19435622_%E4%BD%99%E5%9B%BD.html

Deepening trade and investment cooperation mechanisms means exploring ways to deepen free trade zone development and optimize investment environments, fostering closer ties within industrial and supply chains.

Solidifying people-to-people connectivity mechanisms focuses on giving more attention to the "soft power" of the Belt and Road Initiative by promoting cultural, tourism, education, and grassroots interactions, creating a comprehensive framework for people-to-people exchanges along the BRI.

Refining green development mechanisms entails reinforcing the foundations of green mechanisms, supporting green investment and financing projects, and enhancing international cooperation on natural disaster prevention and emergency management to ensure that the BRI maintains its focus on sustainability.

Improving consultation and coordination mechanisms requires accelerating the establishment and enhancement of cooperation coordination systems for the BRI, which involves strengthening the functionality of existing BRI platforms, continuously assessing cooperation results, and promptly addressing challenges that arise during collaboration.

Conclusion

In his speech at the opening ceremony of the 3rd Belt and Road Forum for International Cooperation, Chinese President Xi Jinping emphasized that the original aspiration of the BRI is to draw inspiration from the ancient Silk Road, with connectivity at its core. The aim is to strengthen policy coordination, infrastructure connectivity, unimpeded trade, financial integration, and closer people-to-people ties with all countries. BRI will inject new momentum into global economic growth, create new opportunities for global development, and establish a new platform for international economic cooperation. The Eight Major Steps are a concrete manifestation of China's commitment to supporting high-quality Belt and Road cooperation in this new phase, reflecting the world's aspirations for peace, development, and cultural exchange.

The BRI cooperation originated in China, but its fruits and opportunities belong to the world. Over the past year, the significant achievements of the Eight Major Steps have laid a solid foundation for the second decade of the BRI. As they look ahead, partner countries are expected to continue working together to uphold the Silk Road spirit of "peace and cooperation, openness and inclusiveness, mutual learning, and mutual benefit." By deepening international cooperation under the BRI and further advancing the Eight Major Steps, we can foster higher-quality and more advanced development, promote the modernization of countries worldwide, and jointly contribute to building a community with a shared future for humanity!

Writing Explanation and Acknowledgments

The think tank report " 'Eight Major Steps'Heralds Promising New Decade of Belt and Road Cooperation" is led by Fu Hua, President of Xinhua News Agency and Chairman of the Academic Committee of Xinhua Institute, with Lyu Yansong, Editor-in-Chief of Xinhua News Agency, as the deputy head and Ren Weidong, Deputy Edi-tor-in-Chief of Xinhua News Agency, as the executive deputy head. Other members of the project team include Liu Gang, Pan Haiping, Chen Fang, Zou Wei, Cui Feng, Cao Wenzhong, Li Yue, Chen Yu, Liu Hua, Cheng Zheng, Li Tao, Zheng Mingda, Chen Weiwei, Shi Chunjiao, Ding Lei, Cao Jianing, Zhao Yixuan, Liang Qiawen, etc.

Since the initiation in the first half of 2024, the research team has taken more than 6 months for concentrated study sessions, in-depth investigations, writing, revision and proofreading.

During the process of writing and releasing the report, experts and scholars have provided valuable assistance and guidance. These include Bai Chunli, Chairman of the Belt and Road Academic Forum for Quality Development, Chen Wenling, Chief Economist of the China Center for International Economic Exchanges, Liu Weidong, Director of the Bureau of International Cooperation of the Chinese Academy of Sciences, Zhai Kun, Vice Dean of the Institute of Regional and Country Studies at Peking University, Wang Wen, Executive Dean of Chongyang Institute for Financial Studies at Renmin University of China, Wang Yiwei, Vice President of Academy of Xi Jinping Thought on Socialism with Chinese Characteristics for a New Era at Renmin University of China, Xu Peiyuan, Director of the Maritime Silk Road Research Institute of Huaqiao University, and Zong Shuren, Professor at the Hong Kong Institute for the Humanities and Social Sciences. We extend our heartfelt gratitude to all of them.

Writing Explanation and Acknowledgments

The think tank report " 'Eight Major Steps' Heralds Promising New Decade of Belt and Road Cooperation" is led by Fu Hua, President of Xinhua News Agency and Chairman of the Academic Committee of Xinhua Institute, with Lyu Yansong, Editorin-Chief of Xinhua News Agency, as the deputy head and Ren Weidong, Deputy Editor-in-Chief of Xinhua News Agency, as the executive deputy head. Other members of the project team include Liu Gang, Pan Haiping, Chen Fang, Zou Wei, Cui Feng, Cao Wenzhong, Li Yue, Chen Yu, Liu Hua, Cheng Zheng, Li Tao, Zheng Mingda, Chen Weiwei, Shi Chunjiao, Ding Lei, Cao Jianing, Zhao Yixuan, Liang Qiawen, etc.

Since the initiation in the first half of 2024, the research team has taken more than 6 months for concentrated study sessions, in-depth investigations, writing, revision and proofreading.

During the process of writing and releasing the report, experts and scholars have provided valuable assistance and guidance. These include Bai Chunli, Chairman of the Belt and Road Academic Forum for Quality Development, Chen Wenling, Chief Economist of the China Center for International Economic Exchanges, Liu Weidong, Director of the Bureau of International Cooperation of the Chinese Academy of Sciences, Zhai Kun, Vice Dean of the Institute of Regional and Country Studies at Peking University, Wang Wen, Executive Dean of Chongyang Institute for Financial Studies at Renmin University of China, Wang Yiwei, Vice President of Academy of Xi Jinping Thought on Socialism with Chinese Characteristics for a New Era at Renmin University of China, Xu Peiyuan, Director of the Maritime Silk Road Research Institute of Huaqiao University, and Zong Shuren, Professor at the Hong Kong Institute for the Humanities and Social Sciences. We extend our heartfelt gratitude to all of them.

Innovation in Local Currency Cooperation Among Global South Nations Research Report[1]

Xinhua Institute

Message from Pan Haiping
Chairman,China Economic Information Service

As unprecedented global changes continue to accelerate, the concept of the "Global South" has moved to the forefront of the world's political and economic landscape. As a collective of emerging markets and developing nations, the Global South now represents over 40% of the global economy and is reshaping the economic order, positioning itself as a pivotal force in transforming the international system.

As South-South trade expands, the closer economic ties among Global South nations

---

[1] Released on November 12, 2024, at the "Global South" Local Currency Financing Innovation Cooperation Seminar held in São Paulo, Brazil.

have spurred a growing demand for local currency settlements. This has made currency cooperation a prominent and timely topic on the agenda of Global South nations.

At the forefront of the Global South, BRICS nations are working to advance pragmatic local currency cooperation. The Johannesburg Declaration, issued at the 15th BRICS Summit in August 2023, underscores the importance of encouraging BRICS countries and their trading partners to use local currencies in trade and financial transactions, while expanding correspondent banking networks and enhancing local currency settlement mechanisms.

The Kazan Declaration of October 2024 reiterated this need, calling on BRICS finance ministers and central bank governors to continue research into local currency cooperation and payment systems.

The benefits of local currency cooperation are clear. Financing and trade conducted in local currencies can mobilize domestic savings, lower exchange rate risks and financing costs, and contribute to financial stability. Local currency bond markets, for instance, are essential for long-term financing and can mitigate currency and maturity mismatch risks, bolstering resilience against sudden capital outflows and strengthening financial stability

The report, Bridging Distances, Fostering Prosperity: Innovation in Local Currency Cooperation Among Global South Nations provides a comprehensive analysis of local currency cooperation practices in selected Global South nations, in particular highlighting the innovative approaches led by BRICS countries. Produced by Shanghai Headquarters of China Economic Information Service (CEIS) in collaboration with the Xinhua Institute, the report explores the latest achievements, challenges, and actionable strategies for advancing local currency cooperation among Global South nations. Our hope is that this report will serve as a valuable reference for Global South countries in exploring local currency cooperation pathways, helping to foster reform in the global monetary system and contribute to a fairer, more inclusive, and sustainable international economic order.

Shared purpose can transcend the most distant and tallest barriers. As a founding BRICS member and a committed part of the Global South, China has always remained closely aligned with the development goals of other Global South nations, fostering common growth and prosperity.

As a leading economic information provider in China, CEIS is one of the country's most authoritative sources of comprehensive economic data and analysis, covering sectors across the economic landscape. With its long-standing focus on monitoring international economic and financial developments, CEIS delivers comprehensive services including news, data, research reports, credit information, indices, and public opinion analysis, along with information dissemination, integrated communication, and think tank consulting services.

As the Global South's collective rise reshapes the world order, CEIS will leverage its expertise to deepen China's economic information exchanges with these nations, contributing to global prosperity and building a community with a shared future for mankind.

Message from Liu Gang
President of the Xinhua Institute

For over 2,000 years, the Silk Road has symbolized the fusion of Chinese and Western cultures.

Created by the joint efforts of China and nations along its path, this route flourished not through force or domination but through caravans and friendship, founded on principles of fairness and shared prosperity. It stands as a testament to openness and cooperation, embodying values that have shaped Chinese civilization. Today, the Silk Road's spirit endures as a powerful symbol of unity, bridging diverse cultures and fostering resilient, cooperative ties.

Since opening its doors over 40 years ago, China has embraced this spirit of openness and cooperation, positioning itself as a partner in global development. Today, as the world's second-largest economy, China is committed to offering public goods that support growth across the developing world. The Belt and Road Initiative, which has now spanned more than a decade, serves as a new pathway for connecting nations, breaking down cultural, institutional, and developmental barriers. It reflects a vision of human progress that transcends national interests.

In an era marked by crises, unpredictability, unilateralism and financial hegemony, as well as a resurgence of Cold War mentalities, the principles of inclusiveness and cooperation matter more than ever. We stand against all forms of hegemony and exclusionary practices, such as the "small yard and high fence" policies, that divide rather than unite. This is why we have launched the think tank report, Bridging Distances, Fostering Prosperity: Innovation in Local Currency Cooperation Among Global South Nations. We recognize the challenges in advancing local currency collaboration, understanding full well that progress in building robust financial systems across the Global South will not happen overnight. We are confident that as the idea of a shared future for humanity gains momentum and multipolarity shapes the global landscape, nations will seek greater collaboration in creating a more open, cooperative global economy.

The Xinhua Institute, dedicated to fuliling Xinhua's mission as a think tank, established the Belt and Road International Think Tank Cooperation Committee, which now includes over 130 global think tanks. We remain committed to conducting research that informs cooperation among Global South nations.

Introduction

In recent years, the Global South has emerged as a significant force reshaping the international economic landscape. Growing South-South trade over the past decade has fostered greater financial cooperation among Global South nations, with the BRICS framework playing a key role in this trend.

In the context of unprecedented global changes, intensifying great power competition, and increased economic nationalism, Global South nations are increasingly seeking alternatives to mitigate Western financial sanctions and USD exchange rate volatility risks. There has been growing interest in conducting trade settlements and investments in local currencies among these nations. The rise of Global South economies, their enhanced political influence, and active participation in global governance have accelerated the diversification of the international monetary system.

In the Kazan Declaration[①] issued at the 16th BRICS Summit on October 24, 2024, BRICS leaders reaffirmed their commitment to deepening financial cooperation, with a focus on innovative practices that encourage the use of local currencies in financial transactions. Moving forward, advancing local currency cooperation will not only enhance the representation of Global South countries within the international financial system but also align with the broader goals of social and economic development in the Global South.

Chapter One The Tipping Point: A New Chapter for South-South Cooperation

The development of economic globalization, the collective rise of countries in the Global South, and the advancement of South-South cooperation have significantly enhanced the Global South's international influence. This has led to a globalization of the concept of "the South," transforming it from a geographic designation to "Global South." The continued development of the Global South is reshaping the traditional international order. As the scale of South-South trade expands and areas of cooperation

---

① Source: "XVI BRICS Summit Kazan Declaration" (Full Text), Xinhua News Agency, October 24, 2024

diversify, Global South countries have come to recognize the vulnerabilities of relying heavily on a single currency, particularly the U.S. dollar. Consequently, diversifying the monetary system has become a new goal of national economic policy, with local currency cooperation emerging as a critical area of interest.

After World War II, the U.S. dollar-dominated international monetary system emerged, granting U.S. monetary policy outsized influence on the global economy. The risks associated with the U.S. dollar's dominance, particularly in terms of currency fluctuation and policy spillover effects, have increasingly prompted Global South nations to seek a multipolar currency framework. This trend has accelerated in the wake of the Ukraine crisis. Financial sanctions by the West on Russia have underscored the risks of "weaponized" financial tools and raised global concerns over the need for a diversified currency system to reduce exposure to unilateral risks.

1.1 Growing Calls for a Diversified International Monetary System

In the summer of 1944, the Bretton Woods Conference in New Hampshire, USA, established a U.S. dollar-centered monetary system, effectively replacing the British pound as a major international reserve currency. Bretton Woods emerged as a defining moment in the development of the international monetary system.

This system, which pegged the U.S. dollar to gold and other currencies to the dollar, cemented the dollar's global primacy. However, the system faced inherent challenges, notably the "Triffin Dilemma." Due to deteriorating balance of payments and shocks such as the oil crisis in the 1970s, the Bretton Woods system collapsed, and the U.S. dollar was decoupled from gold.

In January 1976, the Interim Committee of the International Monetary Fund (IMF), comprising more than 30 countries, met in Jamaica and agreed to amend the Articles of Agreement of the IMF, abandoning the fixed gold parity and officially endorsing floating exchange rates. This marked the beginning of the "post-Bretton Woods system" or "Jamaica system," in which countries could independently manage exchange rates under IMF oversight.

While the Bretton Woods system was shaken in the early 1970s, the dollar retained its dominance, pivoting from gold to oil as its anchor through the "petrodollar" arrangement. By linking oil trade with dollar transactions, the U.S. further solidified its currency's position, reinforcing the dollar's role at the core of the global energy and financial systems.

The Euro's debut and growing prominence in the 21st century initially posed a challenge to dollar dominance, causing concern in the U.S.. Released in non-physical form on January 1, 1999, by 11 European countries[1], the euro entered circulation in 2002 and quickly became an important global currency. Its emergence as a widely adopted settlement currency and a prominent reserve currency marked a significant shift in international finance. In its 25 years of existence, the Euro has established itself as one of the most significant currencies in the international economic sphere.

The international influence of a currency is closely linked to the economic and trade power of the issuing country. For instance, in trade with the Eurozone, many countries prefer to settle transactions in euros, which has bolstered the euro's international standing. Today, in terms of international trade settlements, the euro is the second most significant currency after the U.S. dollar. Additionally, the euro remains a key reserve currency choice for many countries, reflecting its strength in the global reserve currency landscape. In 2000, Iraq switched its oil export settlements from the dollar to the euro, challenging the petrodollar system.

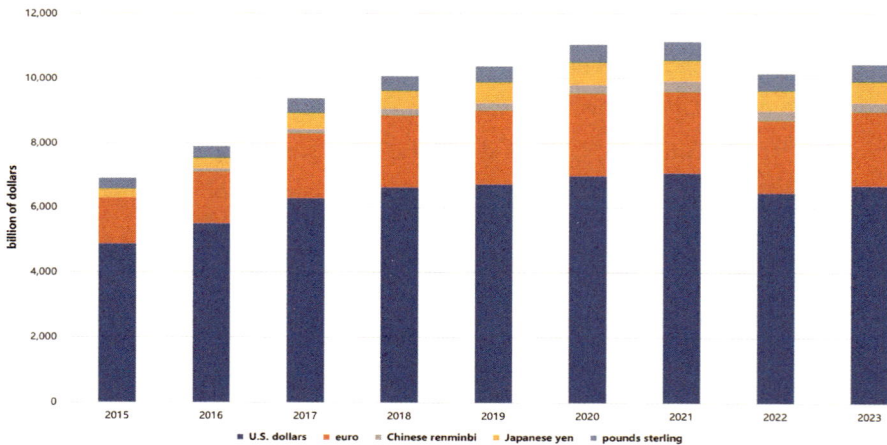

Figure 1.1 Global foreign exchange reserves by selected currencies 2015-2023
Source: IMF, Xinhua

---

[1] France, Germany, Italy, Netherlands, Belgium, Luxembourg, Ireland, Spain, Portugal, Austria and Finland

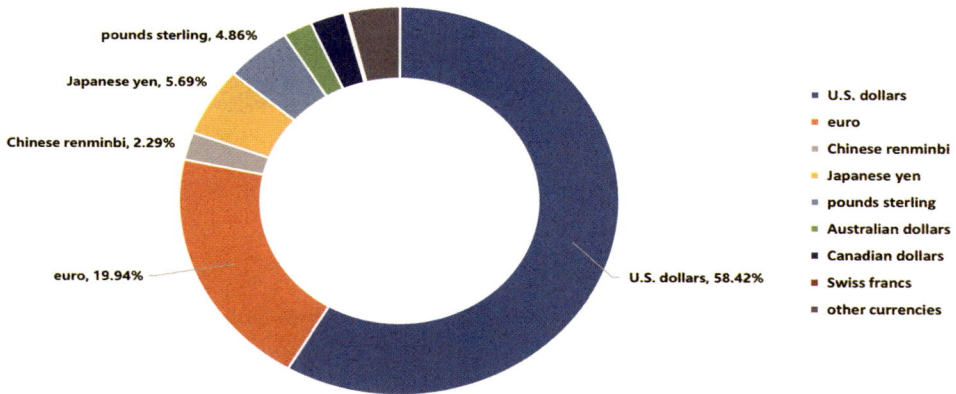

Figure 1.2 Total global foreign exchange reserves by major currencies at end-2023
Source: IMF, Xinhua Finance

In 2008, the collapse of the U. S. housing bubble triggered a global financial crisis, which sent shock waves across banking systems, stock markets, and real economies. This crisis exposed vulnerabilities and interdependencies within the global financial system, prompting many nations to reconsider the U.S. dollar's dominance and seek alternatives to mitigate risks through diversified reserves. The Ukraine crisis intensified these concerns: sweeping sanctions by Western economies led by the United States raised awareness around the world about the need for a more resilient, multipolar currency framework.

During geopolitical conflicts, the U.S. dollar has frequently been wielded as a "weapon" against sanctioned nations. This has not only driven up global food and energy prices but also exacerbated global and egional supply chain disruptions. By contributing to fragmented supply chains, this practice has posed an unprecedented challenge to globalization. Furthermore, the actions of certain developed economies in freezing the foreign exchange reserves and gold reserves of sovereign nations, coupled with unilateral actions based on unacceptable extraterritorial jurisdiction concepts, have eroded trust in Western financial institutions.

Since the onset of the Ukraine crisis, the "weaponization" of the dollar and associated financial systems has raised alarm and concerns and spurred nations to call for a more balanced international monetary system.

Quotation

"De-dollarization may not be imminent, but it is inevitable. Like the erosion of U.S.

economic dominance, the dollar's role in global reserves is likely to decline gradually for several reasons: floating exchange rates diminish the need for reserves, central banks are diversifying reserves by acquiring gold, and increasing currency swap arrangements have reduced the need for substantial dollar holdings."[1]

——Spanish media Rebelión

Case Study The Rise of Gold-A Return to the Gold Standard?

From USD 2,000 to USD 3,000 per ounce, gold prices once considered unimaginable are now becoming reality. Since the start of 2024, international gold prices have consistently broken through major price thresholds, from USD 2,100 to USD 2,800 per ounce, with a 10-month increase of over 30%, making gold one of the strongest-performing assets globally.

A range of factors are driving this surge: escalating geopolitical tensions from the Ukraine crisis to the Israel-Palestine conflict, increased risk aversion, global economic and political uncertainty, and central bank purchases. Yet, analysts and researchers increasingly believe that these factors alone fall short of fully explaining the upward trend.

There is growing recognition that the U.S. dollar, long considered the "Windows operating system" of the international monetary system, is facing limitations. For some economies, access to and functionality within this "system" have become restricted or entirely blocked, prompting them to seek alternatives. Gold, once the foundational asset underpinning the pre-dollar global monetary system, is seen as a potential fallback.

However, a full return to the gold standard is unlikely in today's economic landscape. The very flaws that led paper currency to replace the gold standard remain relevant, and the scale of the current global economy far exceeds the capacity of the gold market. The market size simply could not support a full-scale return to gold-backed currencies.

Just as open-source systems exist outside Windows, countries are exploring diverse financial alternatives to avoid "placing all eggs in one basket." This mindset is gaining traction among economies worldwide as they seek greater resilience and independence in the evolving financial landscape.

---

[1] Source: "Is De-Dollarization Only a Matter of Time?", Rebelión, September 23, 2024

1.2 The Rise of the Global South: A Stronger Foundation for Local Currency Cooperation

Since its inception in the 1960s, the term "Global South" has taken on broader significance as a collective identity for emerging markets and developing nations, reflecting their shared history, common development goals, and political aspirations. Traditionally, the Global North has dominated international affairs, but the rise of countries like China, India, and Brazil is shifting this balance, giving Global South nations a growing influence on the global stage.

Over the past two decades, emerging market economies and developing countries have contributed approximately 80% to global economic growth and nearly 85% to global consumption growth. Over the past four decades, these nations' share of global GDP has increased from 24% to over 40%.

The BRICS nations, as representatives of the Global South, have emerged as a significant force in global economics. After recent expansions, the enlarged BRICS now represents nearly half of the global population and one-fifth of global trade, with its GDP by purchasing power parity (PPP) exceeding that of the G7. The BRICS's hare in global GDP, calculated by PPP, has increased from 31.6%to 35.6%. Their share in global oil exports has risen dramatically from 15% to 36%[1].

BRICS nations demonstrate relatively rapid scale and growth rates, with their contribution to world economic growth set to surpass the G7. Currently, BRICS countries maintain an average GDP growth rate of 4%, significantly exceeding both the G7's 1.7% and the global average. In the foreseeable future, BRICS nations will become the primary driver of global GDP growth. According to IMF projections, BRICS countries' share in the world economy will reach 37.6% by 2027[2].

The sustained rapid growth of developing economies has catalyzed a fundamental shift in both North-South and South-South trade patterns. Notably, Trade among Global South countries has now surpassed their combined trade with Global North nations.

The rise of the Global South has not only transformed global power dynamics but

---

[1] Source: "From the BRIC Four to the BRIC Ten:Why Is BRICS Gaining Popularity?" CCTV, October 20, 2024

[2] Source: "Opportunities and Challenges for BRICS Economic Cooperation in the New Context", Institute of Finance, Chinese Academy of Social Sciences, October 15, 2024

also strengthened the case for local currency cooperation.

Accelerating this shift is a proactive choice in pursuit of economic independence. Local currency use can mitigate exchange rate risks, bolster domestic capital markets, and reduce financing costs. Global South economies have been particularly vulnerable to exchange rate fluctuations in recent years. The practice of using the USD as a medium of exchange in bilateraltrade has created a dual exposure: both trading partners face exchange rate risks between their domestic currencies and the U. S. dollar. Furthermore, in contexts where currency pairs demonstrate high volatility against the dollar, access to dollar liquidity becomes a constraining factor. Consequently, Global South nations have begun considering non-traditional international currencies from politically and economically more stable and reliable countries as alternatives.

Quotation

"In South America, the trend toward using the RMB for trade with China is growing, and Bolivia cannot stand on the sidelines."[1]

——President Luis Arce, Bolivia

Chapter Two Coordinated Reform: BRICS Leading Local Currency Cooperation in the Global South

Since the 2008 global financial crisis, central banks across the Global South have established a series of bilateral currency swap agreements, and the scale of these swaps has continued to grow. This trend has been particularly pronounced among BRICS nations.

These bilateral local currency swaps allow one central bank to exchange its currency with that of another, facilitating trade and investment and helping to minimize exchange costs and financial risks associated with exchange rate volatility.

---

[1] Source: "Arce: Tight Dollar Liquidity Prompts Use of the Renminbi for Trade with China", ABINews Agency (Bolivia), May 10, 2023

Statistics on the Providers of Central Bank Swap Agreements, 2007-2022

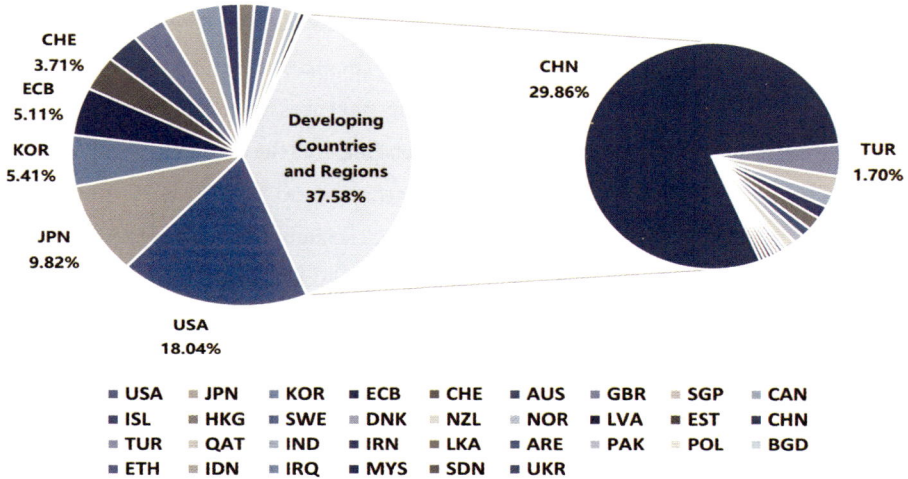

CHE
3.71%
ECB
5.11%
KOR
5.41%

Developing
Countries
and Regions
37.58%

CHN
29.86%

TUR
1.70%

JPN
9.82%

USA
18.04%

- USA   - JPN   - KOR   - ECB   - CHE   - AUS   - GBR   - SGP   - CAN
- ISL   - HKG   - SWE   - DNK   - NZL   - NOR   - LVA   - EST   - CHN
- TUR   - QAT   - IND   - IRN   - LKA   - ARE   - PAK   - POL   - BGD
- ETH   - IDN   - IRQ   - MYS   - SDN   - UKR

Statistics on the Receivers of Central Bank Swap Agreements, 2007-2022

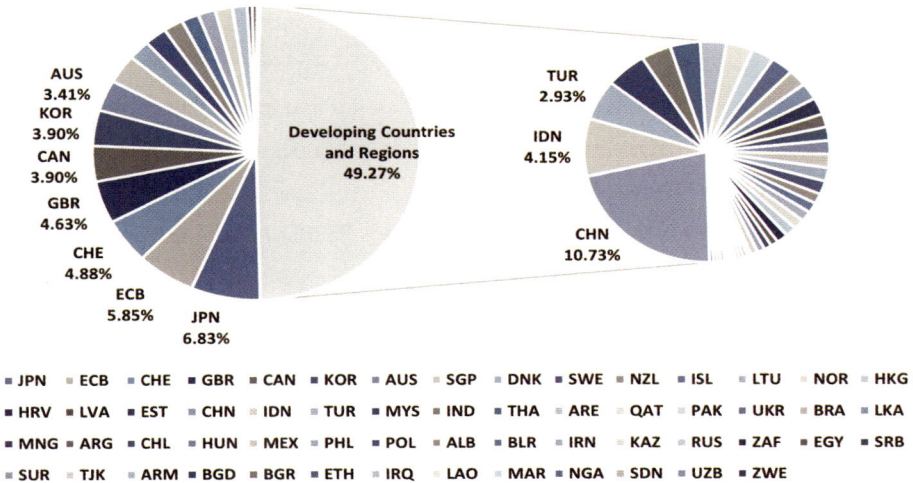

AUS
3.41%
KOR
3.90%
CAN
3.90%
GBR
4.63%

Developing Countries
and Regions
49.27%

TUR
2.93%

IDN
4.15%

CHE
4.88%
ECB
5.85%

JPN
6.83%

CHN
10.73%

- JPN   - ECB   - CHE   - GBR   - CAN   - KOR   - AUS   - SGP   - DNK   - SWE   - NZL   - ISL   - LTU   - NOR   - HKG
- HRV   - LVA   - EST   - CHN   - IDN   - TUR   - MYS   - IND   - THA   - ARE   - QAT   - PAK   - UKR   - BRA   - LKA
- MNG   - ARG   - CHL   - HUN   - MEX   - PHL   - POL   - ALB   - BLR   - IRN   - KAZ   - RUS   - ZAF   - EGY   - SRB
- SUR   - TJK   - ARM   - BGD   - BGR   - ETH   - IRQ   - LAO   - MAR   - NGA   - SDN   - UZB   - ZWE

Figure 2.1 Global currency swap agreements statistics 2007-2022
Source: Boston University Global Development Policy Center

Amidst systemic disruptions to the international order, the BRICS framework, composed of emerging and developing economies, has expanded considerably, attracting participation from other Global South nations. As BRICS countries deepen cooperation in trade, investment, and finance, discussions about establishing a BRICS cross-border payment system have become a focal point on the global stage.

The Johannesburg/l Declaration, issued at the 15th BRICS Summit in 2023, encourages BRICS countries and their trading partners to use local currencies n international trade and financial transactions. It emphasizes the importance of advancing local currency cooperation, developing payment tools and platforms, and expanding correspondent banking networks within BRICS to facilitate local currency settlements.

On October 16, 2024, the Shanghai Cooperation Organization (SCO) Heads of Government Council issued a joint communiqué opposing protectionism and unilateral sanctions and reiterated the commitment to implementing the "Roadmap for Gradually Increasing the Share of Local Currency Settlements in SCO Member States." The Kazan Declaration, issued at the 16th BRICS Summit on October 24, 2024, reaffirmed the commitment to strengthening financial cooperation among BRICS nations. The Declaration welcomed innovative financial practices and methodologies within the BRICS banking cooperation mechanism for projects and programs, particularly emphasizing the use of local currencies in financial transactions between BRICS countries and their trading partners.

Currently, nearly 90% of trade within the Eurasian Economic Union (EAEU), which comprises Russia, Belarus, Armenia, Kazakhstan, and Kyrgyzstan, is now settled in local currencies. Recently, Russia has required that natural gas and grain imports be paid for in rubles. Beyond bilateral agreements, multilateral currency negotiation mechanisms are in place, and barter trade is even being considered.

ASEAN countries, as a major force in the Asia-Pacific region, are also advancing local currency settlements in bilateral trade. With the recent sharp fluctuations in the U.S. dollar, some ASEAN member states have faced exchange rate pressures that have negatively impacted their economies to varying degrees. Currently, ASEAN countries are exploring increased use of local currencies in cross-border trade and investment to mitigate the risks associated with U.S. dollar fluctuations, ensure currency stability, and drive economic growth.

At the 2023 ASEAN Finance Ministers and Central Bank Governors' Meeting, member states unanimously agreed to strengthen local currency usage within the region to reduce reliance on major international currencies for cross-border trade and investment.

In May 2023, during the 42nd ASEAN Summit, the ten ASEAN nations jointly declared their commitment to regional payment connectivity and the promotion of local currency transactions. In August, the ASEAN Finance Ministers and Central Bank Governors' Meeting approved the establishment of a local currency trading framework across ASEAN. Meanwhile, Indonesia announced the creation of a "National Task Force on Local Currency Trading," while Malaysia proposed an initiative to "increase local currency settlement."

Moreover, all ten ASEAN countries have joined the RMB Cross-Border Payment System (CIPS), and countries such as Cambodia, Indonesia, Malaysia, the Philippines, Singapore, and Thailand have included the RMB in their official foreign exchange reserves. Data shows that from 2013 to 2022, cross-border RMB settlements between China and ASEAN grew nearly 20-fold.

Latin America has also been pursuing increased local currency settlements. Bolivia's accession to MERCOSUR (Southern Common Market) and its planned participation in the "Local Currency Payment System", which enables bilateral trade among member countries in local currencies, exemplifies this regional trend. At a business forum in Bolivia in July 2024, Brazilian President Lula stated that this move would help lower transaction costs and reduce Bolivia's dependence on the U.S. dollar.

2.1 BRICS: Leading Local Currency Cooperation in the Global South

2.1.1 NDB: Initial Success in Local Currency Financing

The New Development Bank (NDB), headquartered in Shanghai, is a hallmark achievement in deepening BRICS cooperation. As the first multilateral development bank independently established by developing countries, the NDB dedicated to supporting infrastructure and sustainable development projects in BRICS countries and other emerging economies. It aims to supplement existing international and regional financial institutions and promote global economic growth.

In July 2014, at the 6th BRICS Summit, leaders of the five countries—Brazil, Russia, India, China, and South Africa—signed the agreement to establish the NDB. In July 2015, the NDB officially commenced operations in Shanghai. In 2021, Bangladesh, Egypt, the United Arab Emirates, and Uruguay were admitted as new members. In August 2024, Algeria was approved to join the NDB, becoming the largest natural gas exporter in Africa among the bank's members.

While most multilateral development bank financing is dollar-denominated, borrowers' revenues from infrastructure projects are largely in local currencies. This poses a risk of currency mismatch between assets and liabilities. By issuing bonds denominated in local currencies in the domestic capital markets of member countries, multilateral development banks can help borrowers effectively avoid currency mismatch risks, which has significant commercial implications.

The NDB has registered local currency bond issuance programs in China, Russia, and South Africa to help mitigate these risks. The NDB issued its inaugural green financial bond on China's interbank market in July 2016, raising RMB 3 billion. On January 9, 2019, the NDB registered a RMB 10 billion bond program in China, allowing it to raise up to RMB 10 billion in the China interbank bond market within two years from the date of program registration. Since then, the NDB has successfully registered RMB bond programs in China every year, with gradually increasing scale. By 2023, the approved fundraising scale had reached nearly RMB 40 billion.

The NDB also successfully registered a Russian ruble bond issuance program in 2019, with a maximum financing scale of RUB 100 billion and no term limit. In 2023, it launched an updated South African rand bond issuance program, capped at ZAR 10 billion and with no expiration date.

Case Study NDB to Expand Local Currency Financing for Member Countries

Providing local currency financing is a key priority for the NDB. On August 30, in Cape Town, South Africa, NDB President Dilma Rousseff announced plans to expand local currency financing for its member countries to support sustainable development in emerging markets and developing countries.

Rousseff pointed out that emerging markets and developing countries face challenges in achieving sustainable development, requiring substantial resources and long-term financing. Rousseff emphasized the need for international liquidity to be channeled into developing countries, and for alternative solutions such as local currency financing to be formulated to expand fiscal space for investment.

She believes that "Using local currency is a strategic choice," highlighting that the NDB aims to raise the proportion of financing in member country currencies to 30% for the period 2022-2026. The NDB is establishing sustainable development-oriented local currency financing platforms, aiming to increase the proportion of financing in member countries' local currencies to 30%.

2.1.2 Brazil: Championing Local Currency Market Development and a Diversified Monetary System

As the largest economy in South America, Brazil is a major exporter of agricultural products and meats and a key founding member of BRICS. Brazil is also a vocal advocate for the Global South concept in various international diplomatic fora.

In recent years, the Global South has become a core concept frequently highlighted by the Brazilian government across various international diplomatic platforms. Reforming the global economic governance system has been one of Brazil's key objectives in fostering cooperation among Global South nations, especially as financial policies by the U.S. Federal Reserve have posed significant challenges for South American economies. Since his return to office, Brazilian President Luiz Inácio Lula da Silva has publicly advocated for a "multi-currency system," "local currency settlements," a "common currency," and "new payment systems," emphasizing the importance of financial independence from the U.S. dollar.

In this context, China, Brazil's largest trade partner, accounting for over one-fifth of Brazil's imports, has been a vital ally. As the largest developing countries in the Eastern and Western hemispheres and as major emerging markets, China and Brazil have continued to deepen their bilateral cooperation. Early in 2023, both countries signed a memorandum of understanding (MOU) to establish a RMB clearing arrangement in Brazil. That same year, they formalized a trade agreement to eliminate the U. S. dollar as an intermediary currency in their transactions, opting instead to conduct direct settlements in their respective currencies.

A transmission line project in Rondônia,Brazil,executed by Shandong Electric Power Construction Company under an EPC contract,traverses the Amazon rainforest.

This arrangement saw a significant milestone in August 2023, when Eldorado Brasil, a leading Brazilian pulp company exporting approximately 40% of its products to China, engaged in its first direct RMB transaction. Eldorado Brasil entered into an agreement with a Chinese importing company to use the RMB for pricing, designating Bank of China (Brazil) as the recipient bank. On September 28, Bank of China (Brazil) further advanced this goal by converting the received RMB directly into Brazilian reais, seamlessly depositing it into Eldorado Brazil's local account. This marked the first fully integrated RMB settlement solution for Brazilian exporters.

This cooperation has allowed full implementation of RMB-denominated transactions, from goods pricing to funds transfer and financing, while reducing time and cost and mitigating exchange rate risk.

Braziian coffee is presented to visitors at the 2024 China International Fair for Trade in Services, reflecting the expanding scope and scale of China-Brazil trade relations.

Beyond cross-border trade, a robust domestic currency market is another crucial foundation for currency internationalization. Despite Brazil's foreign exchange controls, foreign participation in its financial markets is significant. The Brazilian stock exchange (B3) dominates the country's securities market. As of 2023, B3's total market capitalization neared USD 1 trillion, representing approximately 45% of Brazil's GDP, with over 400 listed companies. Given Brazil's historically high interest rate environment, institutional investors maintain a dominant position in the market. International investor participation is notably high, with foreign investors accounting for over 40% of both custodial positions and trading volume as of August 2024.

Case Study Towards a Common Currency: "Sur" for South America?

In January 2023, Brazilian President Lula and Argentine President Alberto Fernández announced their intention to create a common South American currency, the "Sur." This initiative is aimed at promoting bilateral trade between Braziland Argentina and facilitating trade across South America, while mitigating the drawbacks associated with dollar-based settlements. If implemented, it could become the world's second-largest currency bloc after the eurozone.

With Brazil and Argentina accounting for over half of South America's GDP, this proposal sends a positive economic signal to the market. For Brazil, a common currency could boost exports and stimulate economic growth, while for Argentina, it could help alleviate foreign exchange shortages, reduce trade-related financial risks, and enhance bilateral economic efficiency. Regionally, the "Sur" could serve as a strategic instrument for fostering Latin American integration, representing a potential game-changer that has sparked widespread debate and interest.

Historically, regional monetary integration efforts have been proposed in South America and other regions. Although the Sur initiative reflects both actual needs on the ground and strategic rationale, and despite the strong political will expressed by the leaders of Brazil and Argentina, the project remains in its infancy, facing considerable challenges and likely to involve a lengthy and complex implementation process.

2.1.3 China: Accelerated Internationalization of the RMB

In 2009, China launched a pilot program for cross-border RMB trade settlement, marking the beginning of the RMB's journey towards internationalization. Since then, the process has shown steady, cyclical progress, with the currency gaining a larger role in global transactions. As of 2024, the RMB has become the fourth-most active currency in global payments, according to SWIFT. Its low interest rates have enhanced its appeal as a financing currency.

The growth of emerging economies is increasing demand for the RMB in trade settlements, local currency swaps, and investment activities. This shift is accelerating the maturation of the cross-border RMB ecosystem and advancing its internationalization.

2.1.3.1 Rising Share of RMB in Global Cross-Border Transactions

The steady progress of RMB internationalization has seen a rising share of regional trade settled in the RMB. As of August 2024, the RMB accounted for 4.69% of global payments, ranking fourth globally for ten consecutive months, according to SWIFT data.

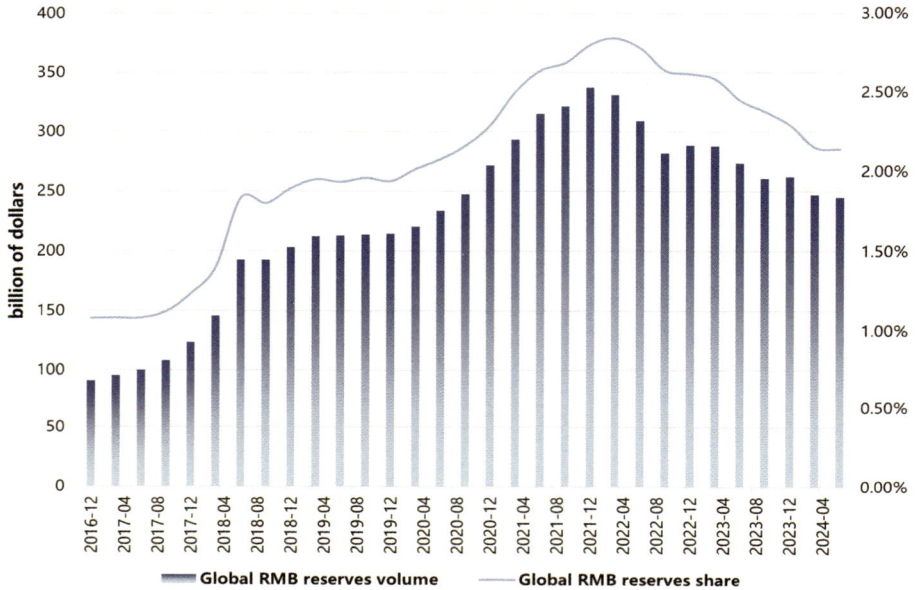

Figure 2.2 Global RMB reserves:quarterly volume and share
Source: IMF,Xinhua Finance

According to SWIFT data, in 2023, cross-border RMB transactions were recorded in 161 countries and regions, reflecting the growing network effect of RMB usage in global cross-border payments. This trend has significantly boosted the RMB's activity in international transactions. Regionally, the use of the RMB has shown particularly rapid growth within the Regional Comprehensive.

Economic Partnership (RCEP) area and along the Belt and Road Initiative (BRI) countries. Specifically, in 2023, RCEP countries (excluding China) saw a 20.4% increase in RMB remittances, while BRI countries saw a 21.1% rise.

With China's share of foreign trade growing in these regions, alongside Chinese companies expanding their global presence, the RMB is expected to see continued growth in cross-border trade settlements in the near term.

Case Study Enhanced Cross-border RMB Services Supporting the Real Economy

In the first eight months of 2024, RMB-denominated cross-border receipts and payments for corporate clients reached RMB 41.6 trillion, representing a 21.1% year-on-year increase. The RMB now accounts for 26.5% of cross-border trade settlements, up 1.7% from 2023.

China has indicated its ongoing commitment to high-level trade openness. As China maintains its status as the world's largest trading nation, with extensive ties to over 140 countries and regions, a solid foundation has been laid to support the expanded use of the RMB in international trade settlements.

Since 2023, RMB cross-border usage has grown steadily, showing balanced inflows and outflows, with an increase in its share in global payments.

The capacity of cross-border RMB transactions to support the real economy has continued to strengthen. In 2023, cross-border RMB receipts and payments in the current account totaled RMB 14 trilion, marking a 33.4% year-on-year increase. Of this, income reached RMB 6.9 trillion, up 24.5%, while expenditures amounted to RMB 7.1 trillion, a growth of 43.3%. RMB transactions accounted for 27.7% of all current account cross-border receipts and payments in both domestic and foreign currencies. From January to August 2024, cross-border RMB transactions in the current account reached RMB 10.4 trillion, a 17.3% year-on-year increase, representing 9.3% of total current account cross-border transactions in all currencies during this period.

"The 2024 RMB Internationalization Report"[1] highlights several factors contributing to the preference for the RMB in trade in recent years:

First, increased exchange rate flexibility. Ongoing reforms to the RMB exchange rate mechanism have enhanced its flexibility, resulting in more frequent two-way fluctuations. This has encouraged businesses to utilize the RMB for cross-border trade settlements to mitigate currency mismatch risks.

Second, an evolving trade landscape. The structural transformation of Chinese industries and adjustments in global supply chains have created more opportunities for RMB cross-border use, further driving demand for RMB settlements. For instance, deepening industrial and supply chain cooperation between China and ASEAN has led to

---

[1] Source: "2024 RMB Internationalization Report", People's Bank of China, September 30, 2024

a 47% year-on-year increase in RMB settlements for goods trade, reaching RMB 2 trillion in 2023.

Third, cost advantages in financing. The competitive cost of RMB financing has boosted RMB-denominated trade finance, prompting businesses to opt for the RMB in trade settlements. Fourth, emergence of new trade models. New foreign trade models, such as cross-bordere-commerce, are increasingly inclined towards RMB settlements. In 2023, third-party payment institutions processed nearly RMB 1 trillion in RMB settlements for cross-border e-commerce goods trade, marking a 24% year-on-year growth.

Fifth, progress in RMB pricing and settlement for commodities, the strengthening of the RMB's role as an investment and financing currency, and the stable share of RMB in global foreign exchange reserves all indicate the steady and prudent advancement of RMB internationalization.

2.1.3.2 Enhanced Capabilities of the RMB Cross-Border Payment System

Cross-border payment and clearing systems form the backbone of global trade and investment activities. China's Cross-Border Interbank Payment System (CIPS), a critical financial market infrastructure specifically designed for cross-border RMB payment and clearing, has continuously enhanced its functionalities since its launch in October 2015. By progressively incorporating qualified domestic and foreign banks and financial market infrastructures (FMls), CIPS plays a pivotal role as the primary channel for cross-border RMB payment and clearing, bolstering the global use of the RMB.

Over the years, CIPS has built a global RMB payment and clearing service network, connecting domestic and international banks through direct participants. As of the end of August 2024, CIPS had 152 direct participants and 1412 indirect participants across 117 countries and regions. Among the indirect participants, 1,050 are in Asia (including 563 in Mainland China), 243 in Europe, 52 in Africa, 26 in North America, 21 in Oceania, and 20 in South America. Specifically, CIPS transactions cover over 4,700 banking institutions in 184 countries and regions. Thanks to the continuous enhancement of CIPS's service capabilities, China has positioned itself as the world's third-largest cross-border payment market, trailing only the United States and the Eurozone.

2.1.3.3 Expansion of RMB Bilateral Currency Swap Agreements

Bilateral currency swaps between central banks are essential for stabilizing international financial systems. These agreements enable a central bank to exchange its currency for that of another, allowing swap funds to support bilateral trade and investment activities, thereby reducing exchange costs and mitigating currency risks.

The People's Bank of China (PBOC) has actively expanded currency swaps with foreign central banks, making them a critical component of the global financial safety net.

Since 2023, the PBOC has signed or renewed agreements with Saudi Arabia, Mauritius, Egypt, Argentina, Laos, Mongolia, and the UAE, among others. According to statistics from the Chinese Academy of International Trade and Economic Cooperation, under China's Ministry of Commerce, in July 2023 alone, China signed bilateral currency swap agreements with South Africa, Morocco, Egypt, and Nigeria, totaling RMB 73 billion.

As of August 2024, China had signed bilateral currency swap agreements with 42 countries and regions, of which 29 are currently active, with a total value exceeding RMB 4.1 trillion. Foreign central banks have used RMB swap balances totaling RMB 91. 6 billion, while the PBOC has utilized equivalent foreign currency swap balances worth RMB 680 million.

In parallel, the PBOC has expanded the overseas RMB clearing network. As of August 2024, China has designated 33 overseas RMB clearing banks (31 Chinese and 2 foreign-invested) in 31 countries and regions, effectively covering key trading partners.

Quotation

"Bilateral currency swaps are a valuable component of the financial safety net, facilitating bilateral trade and investment while providing supplementary stability to the global financial system. During periods of market turbulence or banking crises, central bank swaps have provided essential liquidity support, effectively stabilizing the financial markets."[1]

——Pan Gongsheng, Governor of the People's Bank of China

2.1.3.4 Strengthening RMB as an Investment and Financing Currency

In recent years, China's PBOC, in collaboration with relevant authorities, has optimized cross-border wealth management services, launching programs like "Wealth Management Connect" in China's Greater Bay Area and "Swap Connect" between the Chinese Mainland and Hong Kong. These initiatives have enhanced the RMB's investment and financing functions, making RMB-denominated assets increasingly attractive to international investors.

For instance, in March, State Grid Brazil Holding completed its first cross-border RMB financing transaction through the RMB payment and settlement system, reducing financial costs and exchange rate risks while promoting RMB's recognition and acceptance in Brazil.

Opening Up of the Bond Market

SWIFT data shows that, as of August 2024, the RMB's share in global trade financing reached 5.95%, making it the second-largest trade finance currency worldwide. Foreign investors continue to increase their holdings of Chinese bonds, with total holdings reaching RMB 4.6 trilion as of August 2024, representing 2.7% of total onshore bond custody, up 0.3 percentage points from the end of 2023.

Case Study CCDC Facilitating Global South's Access to China's Bond Market

In recent years, China Central Depository & Clearing Co. (CCDC) has actively supportedfinancial cooperation with the Global South, meeting the RMB financing

---

[1] Source:Pan Gongsheng:The Central Bank Has Signed Bilateral Currency Swap Agreements with 29 Countries and Regions, People's Daily Online, March 27, 2024

needs of these nations and facilitating their participation in China's bond market. CCDC has adopted a two-pronged approach, combining outward promotion with targeted engagement of key clients in the Global South.

In terms of outward promotion, CCDC has organized numerous investor roadshows both online and offine, and conducted one-on-one exchanges with central banks in Tanzania, Uganda, Angola, Mexico, Thailand, Indonesia, Mozambique, and Malaysia, among others, addressing their queries regarding market entry. As for engaging with sovereign institutions from the Global South, CCDC hosted webinars for central bank-like institutions, inviting participation from China's Ministry of Finance, the People's Bank of China, the Bank for International Settlements, and central bank-like institutions from Global South countries, including the Central Bank of Brazil.

CCDC aims to expand cooperation across cross-border issuance, settlement, collateral management, and valuation services with Global South countries, ultimately forming a complete offshore RMB financial service ecosystem.

Expanding the Panda Bond Market

Panda Bonds, named after China's iconic national animal, refer to RMB-denominated bonds issued by foreign or multilateral entities in China. Panda Bonds have grown significantly, becoming an important channel for foreign issuers seeking RMB financing to support cross-border projects and investments. In 2005, the International Finance Corporation (IFC) and the Asian Development Bank (ADB) issued RMB-denominated bonds of RMB 1.13 billion and RMB 1 billion respectively in the interbank bond market, marking the launch of Panda Bonds. The People's Bank of China (PBOC) and the State Administration of Foreign Exchange (SAFE) jointly issued regulations in 2022 to further streamline the issuance of Panda Bonds, leading to a period of rapid growth. Issuance volume reached RMB 850 billion in 2022 and over RMB 1,500 billion in 2023. By September 2024, the total issuance of Panda Bonds was RMB 941.59 billion.

Panda Bonds have attracted a diverse group of high-quality international issuers and investors, bolstering the openness of China's bond market. The New Development Bank (NDB), which entered the Chinese interbank market in 2016, has issued a cumulative RMB 55.5 billion in Panda Bonds, making it the largest issuer in the Panda Bond market. NDB Panda Bonds are widely regarded as premium assets, supporting investors' portfolio diversification goals.

Case Study Panda Bonds Maintaining High Popularity

Following record issuance levels in 2023, Panda Bonds continue to generate strong demand in 2024, surpassing previous issuance levels in the global bond market. As of today, more than 90 Panda Bonds have been issued in 2024, totaling approximately RMB 1,610 billion, a 31.71% increase compared to the same period in the previous year (For the whole of 2023, total issuance stood at RMB 154.45 billion).

While red-chip companies remain the dominant issuers, an increasing number of foreign entities have entered the market, demonstrating the growing appeal of Panda Bonds. New issuers in 2024 include global corporations like Kangshifu, Bayer, BASF, and CapitaLand, which issued Panda Bonds for the first time. The Panda bonds issued by multinational giants like Bayer and BASF have received widespread attention, underscoring the expanding attractiveness of Panda Bonds among international issuers.

In terms of maturity, Panda bonds issued this year continue to be concentrated in the short to medium term, although the scale of issuance with maturities of 5 years or more has increased significantly. Specifically, 64 Panda bonds have maturities of 3 years or less, accounting for about 70% of total issuance, representing a decrease compared to the same period last year. Among these, 3-year bonds remain the most popular maturity.

Against the backdrop of a low interest rate environment, newly issued Panda bonds with maturities of 5 years or more have notably increased compared to the same period last year. Data reveals that 20 Panda bonds with a 5-year maturity have been issued this year, compared to 11 in the same period last year. Moreover, 8 Panda bonds with a 10-year maturity have been issued this year, a maturity that was absent during the same period last year.

Developing an Offshore Financial Service Ecosystem.

China's domestic financial institutions are increasingly enhancing their international service capacity in offshore markets. This includes strengthening connections between onshore and offshore bond markets, promoting two-way connectivity of the Bond Connect program, and collaborating with the Luxembourg Stock Exchange on the Green Bond Information Channel. For instance, Chinese financial infrastructure providers like the Shanghai Clearing House are partnering with financial institutions in Shanghai to meet the cross-border RMB investment and financing needs of Global South countries, actively promoting innovative solutions such as Yulan Bonds.

In 2018, Bank of China pioneers the issuance of Panda Bond-linked investment products in Hungary

Case Study Yulan Bonds as a Financing Innovation for Domestic Issuers

In December 2020, the Shanghai Clearing House collaborated with Euroclear, an international central securities depository, to launch the "Yulan Bond" platform, providing onshore issuers access to global investors for financing in RMB and other currencies.

Yulan Bonds, as part of China's offshore bond market, align seamlessly with global issuance standards, allowing for efficient approval, listing, and investment channels that resonate with international practices. Notably, Yulan Bonds use a unique "look-through" mechanism, which enhances transparency by providing insights into the ultimate investors. This transparency enables the integration of market resources between domestic and global financial markets, empowering issuers in bond management, supporting active investor engagement, and facilitating regulatory oversight—key elements that strengthen the role of RMB assets internationally.

Today, Yulan Bonds have been successfully launched in sectors like banking and securities, with issuances in USD, EUR, and RMB. They accommodate a range of issuers, from domestic entities to offshore branches and SPVs, offering competitive financing options and access to diverse global investors. As this market gains traction, Yulan Bonds have set the stage for similar innovations, such as Japan's Origami Bonds and Singapore's Orchid Bonds. New value-added services—like payment agency support and corporate action management—are also being thoughtfully developed to enhance the Yulan platform's attractiveness in the Asian financial landscape.

2.1.4 India: Advancing Local Currency Settlement for Trade Reciprocity

Although India has sometimes taken a cautious approach to promoting a diversified currency system, as one of the few rapidly growing economies with a significant need for foreign exchange, it has actively sought to reduce the constraints imposed by its dependency on the U.S. dollar. India is working to establish or expand local currency settlement mechanisms with various countries and regions to lessen reliance on dollar-based transactions.

According to the United Nations refined Commodity Trade Statistics Database, India ranks as the UAE's second-largest trading partner, while the UAE is India's third largest. In 2023, total bilateral trade between the two nations exceeded $80 billion, with the UAE primarily exporting crude oil to India and India exporting efined chemical products and electrical goods in return. Additionally, according to The Times of India, India has a substantial workforce in the UAE, including both laborers and skilled professionals, resulting in significant annual remittances from the UAE to India. These dynamics create a strong incentive for direct currency settlements between the two nations.

In July 2023, India and the UAE reached an agreement to establish a framework for cross-border trade in their local currencies, with the added goal of developing a local currency settlement system as an alternative to SWIFT. Starting in January 2024, the two countries began direct trade transactions using their respective currencies. In August, the Reserve Bank of India (RBl) authorized selected UAE banks to open special rupee accounts in Indian banks to facilitate trade settlements, and businesses are now encouraged to use rupees and dirhams directly in trade transactions.

This local currency arrangement is expected to foster the rupee-dirham foreign exchange market, reducing dollar dependency in the short term and alleviating pressures on India's foreign exchange reserves. This shift also offers India's financial sector new opportunities by mitigating losses from exchange rate fluctuations. Over the long term, if fully developed, this rupee-dirham settlement mechanism could serve as a model for India's bilateral local currency settlements with other countries, furthering the internationalization of the rupee and reducing dollar reliance.

India's exchange rate volatility has historically been a challenge. Over the past 22 years, the rupee has depreciated by 84% against the U.S. dollar, hitting an all-time low in October 2022. To counteract the rupee's depreciation trend and streamline trade settlements with various countries, the RBl introduced a rupee settlement mechanism for international trade. Under this system, Indian traders can open special Vostro accounts in partner-country banks to conduct trade invoiced and settled exclusively in rupees, with the exchange rate determined by offshore market rates.

Case Study India-Russia Reopening Negotiations to Expand Local Currency Settlement Mechanism

In recent years, India-Russia trade has performed well. According to the Russian Presidential Press Office, bilateral trade reached a record high of USD 56.8 billion last year, marking a 60% year-on-year increase. In the first eight months of this year alone, bilateral trade grew by 9%, reaching USD 37.4 billion, primarily driven by oil supplies.

In August 2024, India and the Central Bank of Russia reopened negotiations to expand their local currency settlement mechanism to resolve the payment challenges arising from rapidly increasing trade. A key focus of this cooperation between the central banks is establishing a reference exchange rate for trade between the rupee and the ruble, bypassing the U.S. dollar as an intermediary currency. However, this approach requires larger-scale, long-term rupee-ruble transactions on a unified exchange platform, and a consensus has not yet been reached.

Beyond cross-border settlements, India is also establishing currency swap mechanisms with the South Asian Association for Regional Cooperation (SAARC). The SAARC currency swap framework, which was launched in 2012, includes Afghanistan, Bangladesh, Bhutan, India, the Maldives, Nepal, Pakistan, and Sri Lanka. This arrangement aims to provide short-term foreign exchange liquidity or temporary funds to SAARC members for balance-of-payments support until more permanent mechanisms are established.

The RBI has recently released an updated framework for its currency swap arrangements with SAARC countries for the period 2024-2027. This revised framework includes a dedicated rupee swap window and preferential support totaling INR 250 billion to enhance the rupee's use within the region.

2.1.5 Russia: Establishing Alternative International Payment Systems

Due to financial sanctions, Russia is restricted from using major international currencies-such as the U.S. dollar, euro, or British pound-in its trade settlements. Over the past two years, Russia has increasingly relied on local currency settlements for international trade. By the end of 2023, Russia's share of local currency settlements with BRICS countries surged from 26% in 2021 to 85%, with its local currency transactions with China exceeding 95%. Additionally, Russia is collaborating with other BRICS members to develop a clearing system similar to SWIFT, while refining its own local currency settlement mechanisms to improve payment efficiency and reduce risks from currency fluctuations.

Beyond enhancing its domestic payment systems and linking them with friendly nations, Russia has taken several steps toward advanced international payment solutions, exploring alternatives such as blockchain and digital currencies. Ivan Chebeskov, Russia's Deputy Minister of Finance, emphasized that Russia's top priority as the 2024 BRICS chair is to foster a fairer financial system, particularly by helping integrate new BRICS members into the multilateral cooperation framework. Establishing alternative payment systems is now a priority in Russia's external financial cooperation, with the Foreign Ministry noting that a key objective is to bolster BRICS'role in the global monetary and financial system, focusing on interbank partnerships to expand local currency settlements.

Case Study Russia-Iran Local Currency Settlements: A New Path to Bypass SWIFT

In recent years, the SWIFT system has been used as a tool for financial sanctions by Western countries, prompting several nations to seek alternatives. Iran was removed from SWIFT twice, in 2012 and 2018, and Russia was excluded in 2022. This exclusion heavily impacted Russia's oil exports to the EU, as both Russia and Iran—major energy exporters under Western sanctions have had to explore diversified settlement systems. In December 2023, Russian President Vladimir Putin noted that the U.S. dollar-centric and SWIFT-based Western financial system had lost credibility and is increasingly outdated, as countries move toward local currency settlement systems. By January 2024, Deputy Governor of Iran's Central Bank, Mohsen Karimi, reported that Moscow and Tehran had linked their interbank communication and transfer systems, enabling direct transactions between the two countries without relying on SWIFT. For instance, Iranian exporters can now invoice Russian partners in Iranian rials and receive payments directly from Russian banks in Iran.

2.1.6 South Africa: Launching Local Currency Swap Operations

South Africa formally joined BRICS in December 2010. Over the years, as economic cooperation between China and South Africa has deepened, financial activities such as cross-border payments and international financing have also flourished. To facilitate bilateral trade and investment while enhancing regional financial stability, China and South Africa have signed annual bilateral local currency swap agreements.

On April 10, 2015, the People's Bank of China and the South African Reserve Bank signed a bilateral currency swap agreement with a value of RMB 30 billion (ZAR54 billion). The agreement was subsequently renewed in 2018 and 2021, strengthening the cooperation between the two nations.

Quotation

"For many years, the dollar has been weaponized by the United States against developing nations, including Africa, China, and all other developing countries. Therefore, this weaponization is what Africa must resist, with an alternative to trade in local currencies."[1]

——Tshilidzi Munyai, Member of South African National Assembly

---

[1] Source: "Dollar Hegemony Exacerbates Global Economic Instability. Calls for Currency Diversification Intensify Worldwide", CCTV News, September 19, 2024

Case Study The African Continental Free Trade Agreement: Unlocking Africa's Economic Potential

As globalization accelerates, African countries have increasingly recognized that the economic scale of individual nations often limits their ability to compete with arger regional economies on the global stage. On May 30, 2019, African nations formally established the African Continental Free Trade Area (AFCFTA), aiming to reduce or eliminate tariffs and non-tariff barriers among member states. This initiative seeks to increase intra-African trade and strengthen Africa's competitiveness in global markets. Currently, intra-African trade represents only about 15% of the continent's total trade, but the AFCFTA is expected to significantly raise this percentage, particularly in sectors such as manufacturing, agriculture, and services.

AFCFTA has presented favorable conditions for the use of African currencies within the region. For example, Kenya's mobile payment platform M-Pesa is widely used in cross-border payments in East Africa, highlighting the growing role of African currencies in regional economic activities.

2.2 ASEAN: Building a Local Currency Settlement Ecosystem

In recent years, Southeast Asian countries have increasingly reduced their reliance on the U.S. dollar for cross-border transactions to mitigate the spillover effects of U. S. monetary policy and safeguard against potential dollar-based sanctions. By establishing local currency settlement agreements, ASEAN nations aim to create a more efficient and dynamic local currency market. As one of the world's fastest-growing economic regions, ASEAN countries have actively promoted local currency settlements and achieved several government-level agreements, steadily expanding and refining the ASEAN local currency settlement ecosystem.

2.2.1 Intra-ASEAN: Expanding Channels for Local Currency Settlements

ASEAN's primary economies have advanced bilateral local currency settlement agreements to support trade and investment while retaining foreign exchange controls. In 2016, the central banks of Indonesia, Thailand, and Malaysia signed bilateral agreements allowing designated banks (ACCD banks) to conduct local currency payments for businesses engaged in foreign trade and direct investment. Each of these countries established foreign exchange markets for each other's currency, with designated banks acting as market makers to set real-time exchange rates through a market-based approach. As the trade volume settled through these agreements grew steadily, the Philippines joined the network in 2019, further expanding the system.

In parallel, ASEAN countries have implemented local currency settlement mechanisms for border trade. Unlike bilateral local currency settlement agreements, border trade agreements allow businesses to open accounts in both their own and their trading partner's currency at designated banks, facilitating cross-border trade exclusively within border areas. These agreements primarily benefit economically developing ASEAN countries that rely heavily on border trade. Thailand, for instance, established cooperation agreements in the 1990s with Myanmar, Laos, and Cambodia, which helped form a "baht economic zone" where the Thai baht is widely used for border trade. In 2020, Thailand expanded these efforts by signing an agreement with Myanmar to enable designated banks to offer baht-kyat settlement services for border trade. Similarly, Vietnam's economic growth has attracted neighboring countries to explore local currency settlement options, with Laos signing a border trade agreement in 2023 to facilitate such settlements with Vietnam.

ASEAN has also leveraged the rise of mobile payment technology, adopting a unified QR code standard to enable direct connections between national mobile payment systems. Thailand established ts first such link with Cambodia in 2020 and later expanded to Vietnam, Singapore, Malaysia, and Indonesia, allowing Thai residents to scan local QR codes in these countries and make payments in baht. To further enhance mobile payment connectivity, ASEAN set up a dedicated task force at the 42nd ASEAN Summit in 2023 to promote seamless mobile payment integration across the region. Central banks from Indonesia, Malaysia, Thailand, Singapore, Brunei, Vietnam, and the Philippines have joined this initiative and are actively working to advance the system.

2.2.2 Beyond ASEAN: Expanding Local Currency Settlement with Non-ASEAN Partners

Building on the success of intra-ASEAN local currency agreements, Indonesia has expanded bilateral currency settlements to include non-ASEAN partners within the "ASEAN Plus Three" framework. In August 2020 and September 2021, Indonesia signed bilateral settlement agreements with Japan and China, respectively, and in May 2023, it signed a similar memorandum of understanding with South Korea to promote

Table 2.3 Overview of Bilateral Local Currency Settlement Arrangements in ASEAN Countries

No.	Category	Description	Start time	ASEAN Participants	Non-ASEAN Participants	Progress
1	Bilateral local currency settlement agreements	Designated commercial banks by currency authorities in both countries act as Authorized Cross-Currency Dealers (ACCDs). ACCDs open non-resident accounts for each other, allowing businesses to open foreign currency sub-accounts.	2016	Indonesia, Thailand, Malaysia, Philippines	China, Japan, South Korea	Agreements signed; agreements with the Philippines and South Korea not yet operational
2	Bilateral local currency settlement agreements	Limited to banks in border areas, facilitating local currency settlements for border trade transactions.	1995	Thailand-Myanmar; Thailand-Cambodia; Thailand-Laos	China-Laos; China-Cambodia; China-Myanmar; China-Vietnam	All agreements fully operational
3	Cross-border mobile payments	Using QR codes or fast-payment digital systems to enable payments in local currency across partner countries.	2018	Indonesia-Thailand; Malaysia-Singapore; Thailand-Vietnam; Singapore-Thailand; Malaysia-Thailand; Indonesia-Malaysia; Vietnam-Cambodia; Laos-Cambodia	Thailand-Japan; Thailand-Hong Kong	A dedicated ASEAN working group coordinates internal ASEAN integration; central banks manage connections with Japan and other neighboring regions, while Chinese providers like UnionPay, Alipay, and Tenpay expand services independently
4	Financial infrastructure connectivity	Direct linkage of payment and messaging systems for financial transactions.	2022	-	Russia	Currently under negotiation
5	RMB clearing banks	Local commercial banks conduct RMB settlements through designated RMB clearing banks in cooperation with Chinese commercial banks.	2013	-	China with Singapore, Philippines, Thailand, Malaysia, and Laos	Fully implemented with one-way RMB settlements
6	Cross-Border Interbank Payment System (CIPS)	Local banks access RMB settlement through direct or indirect participation in China's CIPS.	2015	-	China with all ASEAN countries	Fully implemented with one-way RMB settlements

the use of local currencies in current account and direct investment transactions. In 2023, Indonesia began discussions with India and Saudi Arabia to implement comparable local currency settlement mechanisms for trade and investment. Indonesian Central Bank Governor Perry Warjiyo said, "We are committed to expanding the use of our national currency. With a local currency settlement system, the rupiah can remain stable, independent of dollar supply, ensuring Indonesia's macroeconomic stability. This initiative willalso support trade and exchange rate stability in Southeast Asia."

ASEAN countries, including Myanmar, Cambodia, Laos, and Vietnam, have established border trade settlement agreements with China, enabling designated banks to facilitate local currency settlements for cross-border trade between these countres and China.

ASEAN nations are also working to connect mobile payment systems with neighboring regions to simplify cross-border transactions. In December 2023, the Bank of Thailand and the Hong Kong Monetary Authority announced the integration of Thailand's PromptPay and Hong Kong's Faster Payment System (FPS). This connection enables residents to make local-currency payments at merchants across both regions simply by scanning QR codes. Additionally, ASEAN countries such as Thailand, Indonesia, and Vietnam are in discussions with Japan to create similar connectivity, allowing their citizens to use local currency payments for business and tourism activities in Japan. Furthermore, some ASEAN countries are exploring direct payment linkages with Russia to stabilize bilateral trade and strengthen currency exchange mechanisms amid geopolitical uncertainties.

2.3 Diversification in Resource Trade Currency Combinations

2.3.1 Oil Trade: Local Currency Settlements Moving from Pilot to Model

In the energy sector, several BRICS members—namely Russia, Saudi Arabia, the UAE, and Iran—are among the world's most significant oil exporters, collectively accounting for approximately 40% of global oil production. Since 2000, as the "petrodollar" dominated the landscape, countries like Iraq, Iran, and Venezuela have sought ways to settle oil transactions in non-dollar currencies. Now, this trend is gaining traction as geopolitical conflicts and shifts in the global order accelerate interest in alternative currency arrangements.

Iran was an early adopter of multi-currency oil trade settlements. In response to U.S. sanctions, Iran established an international oil exchange in 2006, initially using the euro as its settlement currency. By 2007, Japanese companies were settling oil purchases from Iran in yen. In 2018, Iran and India reached an agreement for India to import Iranian crude oil with a rupee-based payment mechanism, where 50% of the payments were made in rupees and the remaining 50% was offset by Iranian imports of equivalent-value Indian goods.

In recent years, Saudi Arabia has been proactively seeking alternatives to dollar-denominated oil trade. In January 2023, Saudi Arabia made a public statement affirming its openness to settling oil transactions in currencies other than the dollar. Saudi Finance Minister Mohammed Al-Jadaan remarked, "We will not rule out any possibility that enhances the efficiency of trade settlements, whether in dollars, euros, or riyals." Analysts at the Atlantic Council note that Saudi Arabia's growing collaboration with the BRICS framework and its participation in cross-border digital currency initiatives such as the mBridge project with China, Thailand, and the UAE, indicate its gradual shift away from dollar reliance. This trend further highlights the growing focus on local currency cooperation among countries in the Global South.

2.3.2 Natural Gas Trade: Expanding Local Currency Settlements

In the natural gas sector, Russia issued the "Ruble Settlement Order" in April 2022, mandating that "unfriendly countries" pay for natural gas imports in rubles. Additionally, Russia expressed willingness to trade oil and gas with "friendly countries" in a flexible range of currencies to support diversified payment options.

In July 2023, Iraq and Iran implemented an "oil-for-gas" agreement, under which Iraq supplies crude oil to Iran in exchange for natural gas, bypassing the dollar as an intermediary currency.

China has also made notable progress in multi-currency gas trading. On March 28, 2023, China National Offshore Oil Corporation (CNOOC) and TotalEnergies completed China's first LNG import transaction settled in RMB, purchasing 65,000 tons of liquefied natural gas from the United Arab Emirates through the Shanghai Petroleum and Natural Gas Exchange. This RMB-denominated LNG transaction represents a significant step for China in using its currency for cross-border oil and gas trade, offering new channels for international resource suppliers in the Chinese market and supporting China's dual-cycle development strategy.

2.3.3 Mineral Resources Trade: Promising Outlook for Local Currency Settlements

Iron ore offers a compelling example of potential for local currency transactions in mineral resources. As a leading steel producer, China accounts for 65% of global iron ore demand. Although China has extensive iron ore reserves, most are low-grade ores with high refining costs, necessitating large-scale imports from countries like Brazil and Australia.

On November 18, 2019, Vale, the world's largest iron ore producer, signed two basis trading contracts with Chinese companies using the iron ore futures prices on the Dalian Commodity Exchange. Around the same time, Australian mining companies Rio Tinto and Fortescue Metals Group (FMG) launched trade offices in Chinese ports to conduct spot iron ore sales priced in the RMB, using port spot prices and futures prices as benchmarks.

In 2020, China Baowu Steel Group and Vale completed their first RMB cross-border iron ore settlement, valued at approximately RMB 330 million. This milestone established RMB settlement as a viable option for iron ore trade between China and Brazilian mining companies, underscoring the RMB's growing influence in international commodities transactions and advancing its internationalization.

Following this initial transaction, China Baowu expanded RMB-based cross-border settlements with the world's three major iron ore suppliers-Vale, BHP, and Rio Tinto-for iron ore from Australia and other countries. With these transactions becoming more standardized, China Baowu transitioned from trial to routine RMB settlements, becoming the first Chinese company to establish regular RMB cross-border settlements for iron ore imports. In August 2020, Ansteel Group also conducted its first RMB cross-border iron ore settlement with Rio Tinto, amounting to RMB 100 million.

Local currency settlements in China-Brazil and China-Australia trade have increased convenience, stabilized iron ore supply chains for China, and enhanced China's position in the global minerals market.

The GlobalSouth possesses abundant mineral resources, including energy commodities like oil and gas, and critical "green metals" like lithium, nickel, and copper. With the vast scale of resource and manufactured goods trade in South-South cooperation, mineral resources represent one of the most promising areas for future local currency trade and cooperation.

Chapter Three Evolving Cooperation: Advancing from Breadth to Depth across Borders

Currently, local currency cooperation among Global South countries takes many forms, including bilateral currency swaps, local currency settlement agreements, currency listings for direct exchange, and local currency financing. Notable progress has been made across primary and secondary market transactions, money markets, and financial infrastructure, with cooperation volumes steadily increasing. However, challenges remain in deepening this cooperation from broad participation to more profound integration.

In terms of scale, the volume of local currency cooperation remains limited compared to the total trade and investment flows within the Global South. In terms of pricing, bilateral currency quotes still face difficulty in fully detaching from dollar influence.

In the short term, the U.S. dollar's position and influence are unlikely to be fundamentally challenged. Political trust, economic disparities, and varying levels of financial market maturity among Global South countries continue to impact the evolution of local currency cooperation. Compared to the U.S. dollar, other currencies still exert relatively limited influence on international financial markets. Political instability and currency volatiity in some countries have added further complications to local currency initiatives. With the rise of "de-globalization," the internationalization of emerging currencies faces new constraints. Establishing a diversified currency system is a long-term endeavor that requires sustained commitment and incremental progress across multiple areas.

3.1 U.S. Dollar's Dominance Unchallenged in Short Term

Historically, a currency's international status is shaped by both enduring strength and strategic opportunities for breakthroughs. Today, the U.S. dollar continues to be the world's dominant currency for valuation, payments, investment, financing, and reserves—a position that remains secure in the short term.

For example, while ASEAN countries have actively worked to increase the share of local currency settlements in bilateral trade and investment, over 80% of ASEAN's exports were still priced in dollars as of the end of 2023. Although China is ASEAN's largest trade partner, RMB-ASEAN currency exchanges still heavily depend on U.S. dollar-based quotations. The daily exchange rates for the RMB against currencies like the Singapore dollar, Malaysian ringgit, Thai baht, and Indonesian rupiah are derived by averaging quotations from designated market makers under China's Foreign Exchange Trade System (CFETS) each morning. However, in practice, the dollar remains an essential intermediary. While direct counter transactions in the RMB and ASEAN currencies are available to businesses and individuals, the exchange rates generally hinge on dollar cross-rates due to limited market liquidity and activity. This is evidenced by the high correlation (over 0. 99) between RMB-ASEAN currency direct rates and dollar-mediated calculations for the Singapore dollar, baht, and ringgit.

Limited trading activity in these currencies also results in wider bid-ask spreads in customer exchange rates. Customer-driven demand is vital to liquidity in interbank markets, and interbank activity, in turn, influences the rates banks offer at the retail level, affecting currency exchange costs for businesses and individuals. Compared to G7 currencies like the dollar, Southeast Asian currencies lack comparable trading activity in interbank markets, limiting their market vibrancy.

To maintain the dollar's dominance, the U.S. has implemented strategic measures that complicate global currency diversification efforts. "You leave the dollar and you're not doing business with the United States because we are going to put a 100% tariff on your goods," warned U.S. Republican presidential candidate Donald Trump in a September 2024 speech[1].

As the Global South continues to explore strategies for a diversified international currency system, it is likely that the scale and depth of local currency cooperation will encounter persistent limitations.

Quotation

"In aworld increasingly shaped by great-power geopolitical competition, any shift away from the dollar—such as Latin America's potential move to adopt the 'Sur'—is likely to face opposition from the United States, with potentially severe repercussions."[2]

——Spanish economist lglesias

3.2 Infrastructure Connectivity Yet to be Enhanced

Since the 2008 global financial crisis, world economic recovery has been slow, and many developing countries face considerable challenges in financing and building infrastructure. Limited infrastructure connectivity and investment among Global South economies now stand as significant obstacles to economic transformation and growth.

Improving infrastructure connectivity, particularly financial infrastructure, is critical to enhancing the free movement of resources among Global South countries. For instance, BRICS countries must identify and address weak links in infrastructure networks to develop strategic projects that enhance connectivity. Expanding cooperation in emerging infrastructure areas such as 5G, satellite technology, and big data centers could significantly strengthen BRICS' overall connectivity.

---

[1] Source:https://www.bloomberg.com/news/articles/2024-09-07/trump-pledges-100-tarif-for-countries-that-shun-the-dollar

[2] Source: "A Currency Union for South America?A Challenging deal",Elcano Royal Institute(Spain), January 26, 2023

Beyond physical infrastructure, Global South countries must maximize existing financial infrastructure networks to support cross-market institutional activity, and facilitate greater depth in local currency cooperation. Enhanced cooperation in payment and clearing systems, for example, can improve stability and security across clearing channels.

However, many Southern economies still lack adequate physical and financial infrastructure, with underdeveloped financial markets and limited risk resilience. These factors restrict effective market operations and limit the expansion of local currency initiatives.

3.3 Disparities in Economic Development Affecting Stability of Local Currency Cooperation

The evolution of bilateral local currency cooperation is complex, shaped by the interplay of policies, market conditions, and socio-economic factors. The Global South encompasses a diverse range of countries, each with different political, economic, and financial market maturity levels, leading to varied interests or widely different capacities in currency cooperation.

Economically, Global South countries vary widely in structure and development stages. Some economies are struggling with persistent downturns, and debt issues loom large for certain nations.

Issues like social inequality, insufficient employment, and underdeveloped infrastructure further complicate international financial collaboration, often leading to divergent priorities within the Global South.

For example, Brazil's financial market has seen remarkable growth from 2000 to 2023, with the lbovespa Index-comprising Brazil's most liquid stocks-rising from 17,091.6 points to 134,185 points, a seven-fold increase with an annualized return of 9%. However, the Brazilian real experienced substantial depreciation over this period, reducing the return to just 4% when adjusted to RMB terms.

Chapter Four Steady Progress towards Joint Prosperity in the Global South

While the U.S. dollar's dominance within the international monetary system remains unchallenged in the short term, a gradual "diversification" of this system has begun. For the Global South, removing barriers to the cross-border use of local currencies and lowering transaction costs in local currency trading are vital steps. To achieve this, Global South countries must strengthen cooperation, collectively address challenges, and work towards building a more equitable and stable international financial system.

4.1 Strengthening Policy Coordination and Collaboration

To enhance local currency cooperation, particularly among Global South countries, a strategy emphasizing high-level exchanges and policy alignment is essential. Regular high-level meetings could place local currency settlement as a central agenda item in bilateral and multilateral discussions, offering a platform for exploring mutual benefits, challenges, and cooperation models. China could also proactively present detailed cooperation plans, including currency swap agreements, bilateral trade and investment accords, and initiatives for local currency settlements in infrastructure and energy projects. Such measures would reduce reliance on third-party currencies while enhancing the international standing of both currencies. Effective policy coordination mechanisms and regulatory frameworks are needed to oversee and facilitate the implementation of local currency settlements, including common standards and dispute resolution mechanisms to ensure any issues are addressed promptly and effectively.

4.2 Establishing Central Bank and Financial Institution Cooperation Mechanisms

Creating regular dialogue channels between central banks and financial institutions could enhance policy alignment and promote successful cooperation models across other countries, for instance, improving the ease of using the RMB, real, ruble and other currencies. Streamlining cross-border local currency settlement processes and improving investment and financing management would lower transaction costs, enhance settlement efficiency, and provide more convenient financial services for individuals and businesses, further supporting local currency use in international trade and investment. Such measures would also contribute to the local currency's internationalization and, in turn, global economic stability and development.

4.3 Expanding Local Currency Use Areas

First of all, Businesses should actively adopt local currencies, such as the RMB and real, for cross-border transactions, with multinationals and large corporations playing a leading role. By setting a positive example, they could encourage suppliers and partners along the value chain to accept settlements in local currencies, expanding the international use of the currencies of Global South countries. Moreover, businesses should maintain close communication with government and financial institutions to provide timely feedback on settlement challenges, helping inform policy refinement. Businesses can also leverage available government support, innovate in financing models, and ensure compliance and corporate social responsibility to build a strong international reputation. Besides, exploring digital currency applications in international trade can further reduce transaction costs and currency risk, fostering greater economic integration with Global South countries and revitalizing local currency cooperation. Such initiatives would enhance corporate competitiveness and support the internationalization of the currencies of Global South countries, contributing to a more diversified and stable global economy.

4.4 Leveraging Technology to Advance Digital Currency Adoption

A critical pathway for strengthening local currency cooperation between China and Global South countries is exploring the application of digital currency. China's leadership in mobile payments and digital currency technology has provided a solid foundation for promoting digital currency worldwide. Integrating central bank digital currency in international trade would boost a local currency's role and use in cross-border transactions and investment activities. China could collaborate with Global South countries on digital currency payment systems, by offering technical training and support to help build their digital currency infrastructure. Multilateral or bilateral agreements could also encourage digital currency use in international trade, and facilitate global trade and investment.

4.5 Building Financial Infrastructure to Attract Broader Participation

Establishing and developing local currency markets in the Global South is a long and complex process that requires multiple interdependent actions, with infrastructure as a critical foundation. Key infrastructure components include the currency market, the primary market, a solid investor base, the secondary market and cross-market clearinghouses. Cross-Border Interbank Payment System (CIPS) serves as a cornerstone for RMB cross-border payments and settlements, covering major global time zones and supporting diverse financial market transactions.

Looking ahead, efforts should focus on two main areas. Firstly, innovating cross-border payment applications and broadening product offerings are vital steps toward meeting the diverse needs of countries and regions, which in turn will strengthen the appeal of payment systems for Global South currencies. Secondly, equally important is refining business procedures, standards, and regulatory frameworks for cross-border payments to create a unified, standardized set of practices that align with international norms, thus enhancing transparency and reliability. Exploring ways to integrate cross-border payment systems for local currencies with digital currency settlement pilots also promises to deepen financial cooperation and ultimately support bilateral trade and investment among these nations.

Conclusion

The path towards local currency cooperation for Global South nations is not without its challenges. However, the steady steps led by the BRICS framework have set this journey in motion. The Global South's pursuit of local currency collaboration is underpinned by robust economic fundamentals and a strategic aim to reduce the risks associated with dependence on a single currency. This report has reviewed the evolution of the international monetary system, the current initiatives among Global South countries, and areas where local currency cooperation can be further strengthened—ranging from policy and financial infrastructure to corporate involvement and applied scenarios.

It is important to recognize that advancing local currency cooperation is not about displacing the U.S. dollar's role as a global settlement or reserve currency; rather, it is about promoting a more diversified monetary system. History shows that currency diversification is a long journey built on sustained progress and resilience. For the Global South, strengthening cooperation is essential—not just a strategic priority, but the only viable path forward. Only through collaboration can these nations forge a path that is resilient, mutually beneficial, and conducive to lasting success.

Editorial Team

Co-Directors: Liu Gang, Pan Haiping

Deputy Directors: Ji Lei

Coordinating editors: Gao Pan, He Xinrong

Researching editors: Chen Yunfu, Wang Shujuan

Research assistants: Li Yifan, Wei Yutian, Ge Jiaming, Tong Weiyuan, Liu Li, Wang Chun, Deng Kan

Special Thanks

China Central Depository & Clearing Co. , Ltd. (CCDC)

Shanghai Clearing House (SHCH)

THESIS ARTICLE

China as a Factor of Civilization Development Contribution

Zahari Zahariev

President of Bulgarian National Association for the Belt and Road

Each boundary period of development of the civilization is connected with a turbulent transposition of the geopolitical layers. There are strong social, political, economic, military and "tectonic" processes dynamically changing the aspect of all spheres of life of the public organism and international community. In their totality they trace new state frontiers, rearrange the "puzzle" of military and political unions, regroup ethno-cultural and religious communities. All this civilizing "tectonics" preceding the phase of the new civilizing balance affects deeply no only the visible sides of the international relations but also the "deep" socio-psychological layers of the personality and the human relations. It puts under "fire", consciously or not, not only the self-evaluation of the individual, personality's and social expression, but also the connected with them forms of social co-existence-family, non-formal forms and groups of communication, ideological and political and economic communities, playing the role of transmission of the individual will to the existing structures of governing the state and the society. As a result, come changes, both in the "political market" on a national and international level and in the total mechanism of international communication.

A logical consequence of these "tectonic" processes in the boundary phase of the civilizing processes is the total destabilization of the existing until now system of international security. It shows itself both on a regional and a world level. As a result of this, the list of the strong players, keeping the threads of the international policy rearranges itself. Some of them defend the prize places in the international relations, other advance to the top by force, while third ones disappear totally as subjects in the international relations. This, from its side, leads to chances in the existing mechanisms of communication in the world, too. As a result of the dynamic rearranging the forces and the formation of centers of interests, they gradually erase and turn from an instrument of regional and world balance of very often varied interests into a field of force pressure of selfish will. From mechanisms called upon to guarantee the world peace and security in the interest of prosperity and civilizing progress, they turn into a "Procrustean bed" of the social progress. All this not only destabilizes the regional and world security but activities pressure on all levels of the international relations. Considered for buried by history, national and international conflicts revive. Fireplaces of war tension, which are difficult to foresee at first sight, emerge. New and new war conflicts burst. The risks facing the world peace, threaten to go out from the life-saving control of the mechanisms and internationally approved legal norms functioning in the past.

Today, however, we are witnessing a global, not only ideological confrontation, but also a psychological war, which is taking on the proportions of a Cold War between East and West. Something more. There is a conscious effort, especially by those who aim to remove China as a factor in world affairs, to erect a new Iron Curtain as well. And it is quite natural that China, with its economic power, with its prosperity, with the example it gives of successful development and of finding successful answers to the challenges of the new civilizational phase, should be the main object of these efforts.

After the end of the Cold War, in the 1990s, it was officially declared that it was finally over. Today, however, we are witnessing not only the repetition of some of the scenarios that were used then, but also the injection of new content into efforts to isolate China and all those who tend to assume that we are all in one boat and that much depends on whether there will be peace on this planet on our ability to have constructive discussions that will enable us to lift our common boat called Earth out of the stormy sea of civilizational challenges and changes. What we observe today, unfortunately, does not have a short historical horizon. It is a long-term strategy of the USA and NATO, which carries enormous risks that the world will not only witness a geopolitical, ideological, geo-economic confrontation unknown in the past, but will also come dangerously close to its own self-destruction. Throwing enormous resources and forces into this new Cold

War, accompanied by military confrontation and psychological aggression, carries the constant danger of approaching a global thermonuclear conflict.

When we talk about China, we must keep in mind that we are talking about a third of the world economy and more than 40 percent of the budget resources of the modern world, we are talking about the scientific and technical potential of a country that is the most prosperous in terms of the discovery of a new page in the digital age of humanity. That is, we cannot try to remove China in any of these areas and not affect the stability of the world as a whole. The destructive policy towards China, read in another way, is destructive towards the overall preservation of civilizational development and the security and peaceful progress of our planet. It is quite logical that the intellectual, political and economic aggression against China by the leading imperialist powers is in effect an aggression against the tomorrow of mankind.

It is a pity that we today have the deep sympathy of the European Union for this global policy of the USA and NATO. It shows for the umpteenth time that the emancipation of Europe from American dependence is more a matter of desire than a practical possibility for the construction as a new and harmonizing the international relations factor in world politics. .

From the very beginning, when the Belt and Road initiative was launched, in an interview with China Television, I said that it would be a deep mistake to regard the Belt and Road project as a purely economic project or a project that it has above all a geopolitical focus. Of course it is both. But what distinguishes it from all the other initiatives that have been undertaken in the 20th century and now, since the beginning of the 21st century, is that it is fundamentally a civilizational project. That is, it is an attempt, practically, not only to unite the efforts and the potential (by potential I mean, apart from the economic, the intellectual potential of all the countries of the world), but also to give an answer to the question: "How far do changes in the civilizational plan around us go; how these changes reflect on the economic, geopolitical, ideological architecture of civilizational development, on the civilizational state of the world."

And I think that these 10 years confirmed this position of mine in an indisputable way. Moreover, I am glad when I see that, in one aspect or another, many of my colleagues who work in the field of geopolitical relations, first of all, step on this moment of the essence of the "One Belt, One Road" project. As for what has been achieved in these 10 years, we can definitely say that "One Belt One Road" has gained full citizenship, let me use this term, both in relation to those countries that originally joined and supported the initiative, and already globally, on a global scale.

It became, on the one hand, popular, but on the second, it left the relatively narrow framework of the Chinese Silk Road. And today, in fact, more than 140 countries from all the continents of our planet participate in this initiative. We cannot give a full assessment of this project and what has been achieved in these years, if we do not also resort to the language of numbers. During these 10 years, along the lines of "One Belt, One Road", China has provided almost as much credit and financial assistance to all other countries in the world as the World Bank has done.

In parallel, during this period, over 1 trillion dollars have been invested in a variety of projects that are related to this Chinese initiative. Of course, not only the funds involved have come officially through the government and official institutions of the People's Republic of China, but also those allocated to projects that are included in the "One Belt One Road" by those more than 140 countries that have signed treaties on participation in the project.

This picture will not be comprehensive if we do not pay attention to another direction—namely, the spiritual direction. What do I mean? Based on the initiatives and programs that are embedded in "One Belt, One Road", the academic exchange between China and other countries has greatly expanded. Something more. Joint research centers were also established in many places. I leave aside what is done along the lines of the various academies of sciences. But it is enough to also pay attention to the relationship between universities—from all over the world, and those from China. And finally yet importantly, it is related to the active presence of Chinese students in the leading universities of the world, and the presence of over 500,000 people from all over the world who to date in one form or another receive their training in the territory of the People's Republic of China.

The other thing that we should not leave out in this regard is cooperation in the field of culture. The extremely active cultural exchange that China carries out precisely along the lines of "One Belt, One Road" with all those countries that have joined this initiative, and even those that are not officially part of this initiative, but which benefit of the possibilities that this program provides.

And all this already fills with a completely concrete content, in my opinion, the defining formula in the ideological and political concept of "One Belt, One Road", expressed perhaps most precisely by the President of China, Mr. Xi Jinping, namely that the main is to come to the understanding that we are all passengers in the same boat, and from our ability to have a normal dialogue, to solve the problems that arise in this boat between us, as representatives of different ethno-cultural communities, of different countries often with different interests, depends on how steadily it will sail in the sea of civilizational changes that continue to occur; which continue, by the way, not only to advance, but to threaten us like the sword of Damocles, as representatives of the human race. This is the conceptual essence—an initial and defining idea in the overall development of the "One Belt, One Road" project during these 10 years.

Over the past 10 years, the "One Belt, One Road" initiative achieved and embodied its meaningful image, many mechanisms were successfully triggered, particularly in the area of trade, transport infrastructure, and large, promising investment projects in different countries. We can assess as success, for the Chinese side as well as for the different think-tanks, the widespread popularization of both the philosophy and the individual aspects of this civilizational initiative. At the same time, we should be sincere in noting that the capabilities of the non-governmental sector and of the civil society in Europe and other regions are not used to their full capabilities. In our view, the need to create a broad international public forum (movement) to support the civilizational aspects of the project has objectively ripened. Particular attention is paid to the problems of peace, equality, security in the regional and global context of the "One Belt, One Road" project philosophy. There are hundreds of civic initiatives in this direction, especially in Europe and America, who could find their rightful place here. Overcoming these "white spots" will not only increase our authority as a factor of peace, progress and development, but will also contribute to the mobilization of the world's potential in this direction.

At this stage, a clearer differentiation of the different aspects of the "One Belt, One Road" initiative is needed. In this regard, we propose that particular attention be paid to differing in format international forums in the following three directions:

— lawyers and international law specialists working on the legal aspects of the "One Belt, One Road" initiative

— trade unions - for social and economic aspects

— youths

It can definitely be said that, despite the changing conjuncture of international relations, the Bulgarian-Chinese relations during the past 75 years, after the establishment of diplomatic relations between the two countries, have remained largely constructive and well-intentioned, with certain peaks and troughs most already in the economic sphere of these connections. In political terms, we can boldly claim that in Bulgaria there is a consensus of goodwill and a positive attitude towards our relations with the PRC, which is not inherent in many other aspects of our foreign policy. However, the extent to which this goodwill finds its material expression in the growth of economic activity in the relations between the two countries is another question. Unfortunately, both in terms of trade and investment, Bulgaria cannot boast that it is among the leaders in Europe in this regard. I would even say that we have to state with sorrow that Bulgaria lags extremely behind compared to other countries, especially on the territory of the Balkans. I mean primarily the Western Balkans and Turkey as a Balkan country. There is also a lag in the development of economic and trade relations with China for a number of countries from the European Union. It is enough to mention only the countries of Eastern and Central Europe, which participate in the form of trade-economic and political relations with the People's Republic of China and the former socialist countries of Central and Eastern Europe and the People's Republic of China. Bulgaria lags very far behind Hungary, Poland and Slovakia. There is much to catch up on if we want our country not to miss this "train" that would allow it to join the dynamics of economic development in the context of civilizational changes in Europe and the world.

We can state with dissatisfaction that the main reason for this backwardness of our country is primarily related to the lack of an overall strategic vision of the competent state structures for the prospects in our relations with China. We do not have at all a clear conceptual strategic view of the role and place of the PRC in the efforts for higher adaptability of Bulgaria in every respect to the new requirements and criteria both in the sphere of science and technology and the sphere of economic development. This is extremely important in the context of the objective necessity, which directly concerns not only Bulgaria, but also the EU and the whole world in general, for a new paradigm of economic development. In Bulgaria, we are very far from a discussion of this topic, which is in progress extremely constructively in China itself. In many respects, China is able to be not only a locomotive of the world's economic development, but also to be a main factor of innovations in strategic visions for the economy of the 21st century.

Our National Association for the Belt and Road is trying, against the background of Bulgaria's backwardness in the field of interstate relations with China, to stimulate a secondary "breathing" of the mechanisms in the system of our interstate relations with China. Regardless of whether it is private business initiatives or projects involving the Bulgarian state in the need to develop a strategic vision for the future of Bulgarian-Chinese relations. Here I would also like to point out that many of the initiatives starting from our Bulgarian association are in harmonious unity with the high goals set in the Chinese civilizational mega project "One Belt, One Road". Therefore, I think that the association has its place and special importance in the efforts to include, and in real terms, Bulgaria in this initiative, which Bulgaria has officially recognized and in which we are an official participant.

On the occasion of the 75th anniversary of the creation of the People's Republic of China and 75 years since the establishment of diplomatic relations between Bulgaria and the People's Republic of China, the Bulgarian National Association for the Belt and Road, together with the Embassy of China in the Republic of Bulgaria, organized in Sofia from September 11 to 14 at the National Palace of Culture a Bulgarian-Chinese Business Forum "Dialogue in the Name of Mutually Beneficial Cooperation". It was attended by managers and representatives of 20 powerful world-famous Chinese companies, including 4 leading banks. Representatives of the central management of the companies presented their production list and their investment intentions. This created opportunities for establishing prospective business contacts between Chinese companies and interested representatives of the Bulgarian economic administration and Bulgarian business.

In addition, in Varna, October 28-31 there will be a meeting of twinned cities and regions of Bulgaria and China. With this meeting, again organized jointly with the Chinese Embassy, regular similar forums will be initiated with the idea of co-creating a "Club of twinned cities and regions of Bulgaria and China". It is planned that the Club members will meet annually. This year's meeting in Varna will be organized with the assistance of the Chinese People's Association for Friendship with Foreign Countries, which is one of the most authoritative and influential public structures in China.

The big problem that still hinders the commercial and economic development of relations between Bulgaria and China is mainly related to the passive position taken by the Bulgarian state institutions on the various aspects of this topic. The passive attitude to a certain extent can be explained by the general erosion processes in the statehood of Bulgaria, but also by the susceptibility of the state institutions to the existing external pressure to counteract the so-called "Chinese expansion" in the West, and in particular in relation to the EU countries. However, this is more than strange, because this politically motivated position largely does not overlap with commercial economic activity and the rapid development of investment projects by the leading countries in the EU, as well as in the USA, Great Britain and Australia in the Far East.

When we talk about the Bulgarian-Chinese relations, we should not miss the opportunity for the Bulgarian state and public structures in the country to benefit from China's innovative research and policies in the field of the country's economy and social development. In this regard, it is extremely important that the official institutions and centers that deal with the problems of sustainable construction and our economic development take advantage of some extremely promising productions that have come from China and which are largely related to the recently held Third plenum of the 20th Central Committee of the CCP. The plenum is historic because it was based not only on some specific projects for the upcoming socio-economic development of China in a closer perspective until 2027, but in a more distant plan towards the 100th anniversary of the founding of the PRC, which is coming in 2049

At the plenum, the need to develop and confirm a new paradigm of economic development in harmony with the civilizational changes in the world and the achievements of the scientific and technical development of mankind was clearly and categorically stated. This is also related to the finding that is being made in China that the previous economic model, which brought China to the position of a leading economic and scientific and technical power, is practically more or less already exhausted and the country needs comprehensive modernization, comprehensive adaptation to a completely new historical environment and to serious changes in the thinking of society and people for a future development not only of China, but also of the world as a whole.

From this point of view, the Third Plenum was also a logical extension of the three major Chinese global initiatives that were also launched within the United Nations in the last two years. It is the Global Security Initiative, the Global Governance Initiative and the Global Civilization Initiative. The objective of the Third Plenum was how the lofty goals set by these initiatives can lead to world peace, security and prosperity using the tools of economic development. The decisions of the Third Plenum are of extremely important importance for each country to consider in a new way its own future, both nationally and on a broad international level.

So, Bulgaria has many things that it could learn from and act as a wake-up call for creative searches, especially among expert circles in our country. Unfortunately, among our society, and even at the professional level, there is a lack of awareness, partly consciously imposed by ideological considerations and geopolitical interests, both about the practical goals and about the innovative efforts of the PRC in the direction of civilizational development.

We, as Bulgarian National Association for the Belt and Road, set ourselves the goal of assisting in overcoming this information deficit, which unfortunately exists in Bulgaria. This state of affairs does not allow both the interested academic structures and the Bulgarian socio-political factors to take advantage of what is being "forged" in the name of the future in the field of international relations and inter-civilizational dialogue.

The holding of international forums of different scope and target orientation on the various aspects of the "One Belt, One Road" initiative is a good opportunity to concretize the propositions that were launched by China and were accepted by the vast majority of countries in the world last November year during the Third "One Belt, One Road" meeting in Beijing dedicated to the 10th anniversary of the initiative. A good example in this regard is the recent conference in Hong Kong dedicated to building an interconnected, innovative and green world. It was attended by heads of state and government, business representatives from the "One Belt, One Road" countries. This theme is also one of the elements for concretizing the strategic issues and positions that prevailed in Chinese leader Xi Jinping's speech to the Third Forum of the 20th Central Committee of the CCP. This speech outlined how the world's successful transition to a global civilization should be ensured. In this sense, I believe that the forum in Hong Kong, as well as a number of new initiatives to come, can play a very positive role in strengthening the sense of civilizational empathy of all peoples in overcoming the increasingly alarming global challenges of our time.

China's leaders monitor the "constantly occurring changes and adapt the development model to them. The sentiment of this movement forward is remarkable, like crossing a river, along which you carefully move, feeling the bottom with your foot at each subsequent one. step, lest you sink and be swept away by the water.

In the last ten years, since President Xi Jinping has been at the head of the CCP and the People's Republic of China, China's economic power has continued its rise and today it is already the engine of the world economy, not only as a producer of 30 percent of the world's necessary goods, but also as a leader in the field of new technologies and innovations.

China has played a central role in world development over the past four decades, demonstrating that a more successful model of economic and social development than the one offered as a model by the West is possible.

The Chinese development model is successful not only economically, but also politically, because we see that liberal democracy in the West is in a severe crisis. it leads to gigantic divisions, fragmentation of societies, growing hatred, high instability. In China, as I said, it is a model that is constantly being improved and developed according to changing conditions.

It not only accelerated China's economic development, but had gigantic consequences in many fields, making it a leading country in them. Pay attention to such a moment—China not only lifted about 1 billion people out of absolute poverty in a few decades and created the largest middle class in the world, but came out on top, overtaking the United States in many other areas.

Socialism with Chinese characteristics provides a longer life for its people than crisis neoliberal capitalism. At a time when the ideas of socialism and traditional social democratic parties in Europe are collapsing, declining, losing influence, China demonstrates a model in which the improvement of the lives of such a large number of people has grown at a rate unprecedented in history.

GDP per capita has increased from $1,774 in 1978, when the reforms began, to $18,677 in 2022, calculated on international days since 2011. The strategy to eliminate the final poverty among the population in general. At the same time, China does not give up its basic principles of reforms—opening up to the world, building a socialist market economy and democratic politics, balancing reforms with stability of development, putting people at the center of development.

In recent years, China's development strategy has strengthened control over private capital and redistributive policy, emphasizing those large companies and wealthy Chinese must follow the principle of justice and redistribution of wealth. And this is possible in China because it is a system in which the party consists of three main groups, including that of private owners who support the strategy of the CCP. The improvement in the living standards of all people demonstrated by China is becoming a model for all countries that want to accelerate their development. At the same time, China's strategy is related to the continuation of peaceful development, based on the latest achievements of science and technology, which contribute to the much faster growth of productive forces. In the management of various processes today, China is much more actively using the latest technologies of the fourth industrial revolution—big data, the Internet of Things, artificial intelligence, 3D printers and synthetic biology.

It is no coincidence that the forecasts of the International Monetary Fund for the development of the world economy for the period 2023 - 2028 are that during this period 22. 6% of the world's economic growth will be carried out in China.

The vast majority of the modern world largely lives by the laws of civilizational development and sees its prosperity precisely in the direction of peaceful construction and the objective processes of internationalization—starting from the economy, passing through the spiritual sphere and reaching the field of political dialogue. Of normal, sensible political dialogue that builds, does not destroy, that which can unite all humanity.

The other thing that should also not be forgotten is that to a large extent China's policy, despite all the psychological warfare efforts being waged against it by the West, the vast majority of the public in these countries is in favor of reasonable, constructive dialogue and all-round development relations with China. An interesting paradox occurs here. Despite the efforts of imperial circles, above all in Washington, and the largely subservient to their policy by the political elites of many Western European countries, we also have a countervailing line of behavior and confrontation with this policy on the part of business, of those who move the wheel of economic development of their countries. And a concrete example of this is the deep division that occurs in these societies - between political elites and economic interests.

Despite the calls and the pressure that were made to the Western companies to leave the field of investment and economic cooperation on the territory of China, practically no serious economic structure followed these "advices" and did not succumb to this political pressure. The fact that we have a growth in foreign trade exchange between the EU and China and U.S. and China over the last 10 years by about 40 percent is also sufficient. Here I would like to draw attention to the fact that this confrontation between economic interests and the strategy of military-political opposition on the part of the

West towards China leads to deep cracks in the socio-political stability of these countries. The "China" factor, without being officially present, actively works for these rifts in Western societies and objectively contributes to the overall process of building new social relations, which the world increasingly needs.

Towards High-quality Belt and Road Cooperation: The Reconfiguration of China's Connectivity Project across Europe

Nicola Casarini

Senior Associate Fellow, Instituto Affari Internazionali and Senior Research Fellow, Bologna University

Abstract

China's Belt and Road Initiative (BRI) is being reconfigured across the old continent. In Western Europe, the BRI is moving away from physical infrastructure projects—such as ports and railways—to smaller high-quality cooperation, while most of Eastern European countries continue to promote BRI infrastructural projects. Concurrently, the whole of Europe is supportive of financial and monetary connectivity with China—a shift which is welcomed by various European actors, including some policymakers at the national level, eurozone institutions and major banks. More recently, a growing number of EU member states has opened doors to industrial cooperation in green technologies with China, suggesting that although Brussels-Beijing political relations have somehow worsened in recent times, the Belt and Road Initiative continues to make inroads into the old continent, having succeed in moving towards high-quality cooperation projects in the financial, monetary and industrial sectors.

Introduction

Since its official launch in September 2013, China's 'Belt and Road' vision has had a global scope. [1] Today, 80 percent of the United Nations' 193 member states are part of the project, including a number of European countries. [2] When the One Belt One Road (OBOR) or new Silk Roads—later renamed Belt and Road Initiative (BRI)—was announced, there was considerable enthusiasm in Europe for what was seen as an initiative that would foster Sino-European connectivity and, more generally, closer EU-China ties. [3] That was in stark contrast to the United States, where the BRI was perceived as a challenge to American primacy.

Europe was chosen as the endpoint of both the land-based and maritime routes. The Mediterranean Sea, previously neglected by Chinese strategic thinkers, would emerge as an increasingly important area connecting the Indian Ocean and Europe via the Red Sea. [4] It came as no surprise then that the early implementation of the BRI in Europe focused on financing infrastructure projects, in particular railways in Southeast Europe and ports in the Mediterranean. [5] This was accompanied by a surge of Chinese green-field investments, complemented by monetary linkages between the People's Bank of China and European central banks through the establishment of currency swap agreements and yuan or renminbi (RMB) bank clearing whose aim was to lower transaction costs of Chinese investments. [6]

---

[1] The State Council Information Office of the People's Republic of China, *A Global Community of Shared Future: China's Proposals and Actions*, September 2023 - http://www.beltandroadforum.org/english/n101/2023/1010/c127-916.html

[2] Shannon Tiezzi, 'How China's Belt and Road Took Over the World', *The Diplomat*, 12 September 2023 - https://thediplomat.com/2023/09/how-chinas-belt-and-road-took-over-the-world/

[3] As quoted in: 'China-EU Special Report: Chinese Premier Li Keqiang endorses China's big investment on Juncker's plan at 10th China-EU Business Summit', *The European Sting*, 1 July 2015 - https://europeansting.com/2015/07/01/china-eu-special-report-chinese-premier-li-keqiang-endorses-chinas-big-investment-in-junckers-plan-at-10th-china-eu-business-summit/#

[4] Xi Jinping 'East Meets West', *CGTN*, 20 March 2019.

[5] Nicola Casarini, 'When All Roads Lead to Beijing. Assessing China's New Silk Road and its Implications for Europe', *The International Spectator,* Vol. 51, Issue 4, 2016, pp. 95-108.

[6] Alessia Amighini and Alicia Garcia Herrero, *Third time lucky? China's push to internationalise the renminbi*, China Horizons, October 2023.

In 2015 a massive flood of Chinese BRI investments in the old continent came, with Italy as the main recipient in both absolute value and growth rate, with a 36 percent rise in investment compared with the previous year[1], also thanks to the acquisition by ChemChina, a state-owned Chinese company, of a 16.89 percent stake in Pirelli, the world's fifth-largest tire maker.[2] The €7.1 billion deal was completed with the participation of the Silk Road Fund, a newly established state-owned investment vehicle created to promote investment in countries along the BRI. In March 2019, the Italian government led by Giuseppe Conte signed a Memorandum of Understanding (MOU) on the Belt and Road Initiative with China's President Xi Jinping during the latter's state visit to Rome, thus making Italy the only G7 nation and the only founding member of the EU to officially endorse Xi's signature foreign policy project.

While Italy and other countries in Southern and Eastern Europe were embracing the BRI, the core nations in Western and Northern Europe adopted a more critical attitude. Beginning in 2016-2017, Germany and France had become increasingly wary of the BRI and of China's investments. This trend would reach Europe's other countries some years later. In Italy, with the appointment as Prime Minister of Mario Draghi as Conte's successor, in February 2021, BRI projects came to a halt, and eventually Italy left the BRI altogether under the conservative government that took power in 2022.

However, in Western and Northern Europe the BRI continues to be implemented at the local level. For instance, Italian and foreign media have reported that around 10 municipalities and the province of Brescia—the largest province in the northern region of Lombardy, Italy's industrial heart—are cooperating directly with China through the local government equivalent of the BRI, the Belt and Road Local Cooperation (BRLC) Committee.[3] This is only the tip of the iceberg as the number of Italian municipalities, provinces and regions that have established links with the BRLC is probably much more

---

① Joseph Percy 'Chinese FDI in the EU's Top 4 Economies', *China Briefing*, 8 May 2019, https://www.china-briefing.com/news/chinese-fdi-eu-top-4-economies/

② 'Silk Road Fund joins ChemChina in industrial investment in Pirelli & C. SpA', *China Daily*, 5 June 2015 - http://www.chinadaily.com.cn/business/2015-06/05/content_20923643.htm

③ Thomas O'Reilly, 'Italy's Local Governments Pave New Silk Road', *The European Conservative*, 11 September 2023 - https://europeanconservative.com/articles/news/italys-local-governments-pave-new-silk-road/

significant—possibly in the hundreds. Notwithstanding the decision by the central government to officially leave the BRI, various local authorities as well as important companies and political forces want to continue, or even boost, relations with China in the framework of the BRI.

While the Belt and Road Initiative continues to make inroads in Europe, it is possible to identify three trends:

— Infrastructure projects and investments under the Belt and Road have been downsized in Western and Northern Europe, while they continue in Central and Eastern Europe.

— All Europeans have kept open the doors to the financial and monetary aspects of China's connectivity project, mainly in the form of currency swap agreements and renminbi clearing hubs.

— A growing number of EU Member States is welcoming industrial cooperation with China in green technologies, suggesting that Sino-European connectivity is increasingly moving towards high-quality projects.

1. When the BRI reaches Southern Europe: the years of "enthusiasm"

Early reception of Beijing's connectivity project in Europe was pretty enthusiastic, focusing on the endless opportunities of Chinese investments flowing to the old continent and the prospect of jobs creation, at a time of sluggish economic growth in Europe and attempts at changing China's economic model. Beijing's connectivity project would serve the purpose of sustaining the Chinese economy, which was at the historical juncture of transitioning from export-oriented growth to a new model based on consumption and outward investment. Loans for infrastructure projects abroad were expected to contribute to upgrading the Chinese economy at a time of domestic production overcapacity and to the restructuring of various sectors, including heavy industries involved in the building and maintenance of transportation and energy infrastructure. Trade financing would serve to maintain existing—as well as find new—markets for Chinese products[1].

---

[1] For an examination of the BRI's economic and strategic drivers see Peter Cai, *Understanding China's Belt and Road Initiative*, Lowy Institute, March 2017 - https://www.lowyinstitute.org/publications/understanding-china-s-belt-road-initiative

Sitting at the endpoint of the Silk Roads, Europe hoped to benefit greatly from Beijing's outward economic strategy and connectivity projects. At the EU-China Summit on 29 June 2015, Jean-Claude Juncker, at the time European Commission President, called for the creation of synergies between his European Fund for Strategic Investments (EFSI) and China's Belt and Road. [1] Premier Li Keqiang replied to Juncker by making a multibillion-dollar investment commitment to the EFSI, though the precise amount was never disclosed. [2]

Southeast Europe and the Mediterranean—particularly the Greek ports—would initially be the main beneficiaries of Silk Road funds. The flagship infrastructural project in the area has been the land-sea express route which directly links the port of Piraeus —one of the largest container ports in Europe—with Central and Eastern European countries, thus turning the Piraeus into a Chinese hub for trade with Europe. The project has been financed by soft loans from China's Export-Import Bank and built by state-owned China Railway and Construction Corporation and Chinese workers. [3]

Piraeus has been central in Beijing's strategy of linking China with Europe through the Mediterranean. The Greek port is, in fact, the gateway between the Middle East and the Balkans and European markets; from a Chinese perspective, it is a unique entry point into the EU. Huawei, the Chinese electronics conglomerate, opened a logistics centre in the Pireus in 2013, followed by the June 2014 signing of a 2 billion euro deal between Greece and China to build new container ships and bulk carriers, financed by the China Development Bank, to serve the Greek port.

The most important Chinese company involved in the Piraeus port is COSCO—a state-owned, Hong Kong-listed company that is China's biggest dry bulk carrier and liner carrier—which obtained a 35-year concession from the Greek government to operate two container terminals. The deal, which carried a nominal value of 4.3 billion euros for the whole period, required COSCO to make substantial investments in Terminal II

---

[1] *EU-China summit joint statement*, 29 June 2015 - https://www.consilium.europa.eu/en/press/press-releases/2015/06/29/eu-china-statement/

[2] Robin Emmott and Paul Taylor 'Exclusive: China to extend economic diplomacy to EU infrastructure fund', *Reuters*, 15 June 2015 - http://reut.rs/1IX7LPK

[3] Dragan Pavlićević, 'China's Railway Diplomacy in the Balkans', *China Brief*, Vol. 14, No. 20 (October 2014), http://www.jamestown.org/single/?tx_ttnews[tt_news]=42992

and to build a new section of Terminal III. In September 2013, COSCO agreed to invest an extra 230 million euros to increase capacity, prompting then Greek Prime Minister Antonis Samaras to call the Piraeus Container Terminal project the most important investment in Greece. [1]

Chinese shipping companies also had a well-established presence in the Italian ports of Naples and Genoa, where both COSCO and the China Shipping Company had invested heavily. Beginning in 2015, the attention of Chinese leaders would turn to the Italian ports in the northern Adriatic Sea—ports that became the focus of the March 2019 Memorandum of Understanding on the BRI between China and Italy. By focusing on infrastructure projects on land and sea, China was seeking to build better connectivity as well as acquire political influence in the areas interested by the Belt and Road. Chinese investments would represent a great opportunity for the old continent—particularly some cash-strapped governments of the periphery—to obtain financial capital.

The BRI has certainly brought about a surge of Chinese investments in the old continent. According to the China Global Investment Tracker, a joint project of the American Enterprise Institute and the Heritage Foundation, China invested nearly $164 billion in Europe between 2005 and 2016. During that same period, it invested $103 billion in the United States. According to the Rhodium Group, a New York based consultancy, Chinese FDI in the EU increased by almost 50 times in only eight years, from less than $840 million in 2008 to a record high of $42 billion (€35 billion) in 2016. Although Chinese investments in the EU were still comparatively low, they would evolve rapidly and increasing at unprecedented growth rates in Southern Europe. [2]

2. Focus on Italy

In 2014, Italy became the recipient of a sudden flow of calibrated investments by the People's Bank of China which acquired 2 percent of several strategically important companies, including energy giant Eni, electricity producer Enel, carmaker Fiat-Chrysler (now part of the Stellantis group), telecommunication company Telecom Italia, insurer

---

① COSCO, 'The Inauguration of the Expansion of Pier III of PCT Successfully Convened', 23 January 2015 - http://en.cosco.com/art/2015/1/23/art_773_68531.html

② Thilo Hanemann, Mikko Huotari and Agatha Kratz *Chinese FDI in Europe: 2018 Trends and Impact of New Screening Policies*, Berlin: MERICS Papers on China, 6 March 2019.

Generali, and investment bank Mediobanca. [1] These purchases were a strong message from Beijing that seemed to have a positive impact on Italian public perceptions of China. Between spring 2014 and spring 2015, the Pew Research Center registered a 14 percent increase in favourable Italian public views of China, much higher than in Germany (at +6 percent) and France (+3 percent). [2] In April 2015, Italy joined the Asian Infrastructure Investment Bank (AIIB) as a founding member, along with the United Kingdom, Germany and France. That year, a massive flood of Chinese BRI investments in Europe followed, with Italy as the main recipient, with a 36 percent rise compared with the previous year.

Together with a surge of investments, there came an increased interest by EU policymakers to foster ties with Chinese leaders. For instance, Italy's former Prime Minister Paolo Gentiloni, who led a centre-left coalition government between December 2016 and June 2018, attended the first BRI Forum for International Cooperation in Beijing in May 2017. Gentiloni was the only leader of a G7 country and of a big EU member state to participate. Italy's participation in China's infrastructure projects was also endorsed by Italy's President of the Republic Sergio Mattarella. During his state visit to China in February 2017, he declared that "Italy will actively respond to China's initiative and be part of this plan." [3]

The positive image of the BRI put forward by some influential political and corporate leaders would create the conditions for the signing by then Prime Minister Conte of the MOU on the Belt and Road Initiative during Xi's state visit to Rome on 22 March 2019. While in Italy and in Southeast Europe the BRI was enjoying positive reception, in other parts of the old continent the perception of China's infrastructure project was becoming rather negative.

---

[1] Liam Moloney, 'China Central Bank Buys Stakes in Eni, Enel', *The Wall Street Journal*, 27 March 2014, https://www.wsj.com/articles/SB10001424052702304688104579465482022981014;

[2] Richard Wike, Jacob Poushter, Laura Silver and Bishop Caldwell, 'Globally, More Name U.S. Than China as World's Leading Economic Power', *Pew Research Center*, July 2017, https://www.pewresearch.org/global/wp-content/*uploads*/sites/2/2017/07/PG_2017.07.13_Views-on-China_Full-Report.pdf

[3] He Wei, 'Italian president backs Belt and Road Initiative', *China Daily*, 24 February 2017, http://www.chinadaily.com.cn/world/2017-02/24/content_28342684.htm

3. Critical views of the BRI

Beginning in 2016-2017, a growing number of scholars and policy makers begun to criticise the BRI and China's allegedly predatory investments in Europe, and argued in favour of more conditionality in EU-China relations. [1] In the same vein, the European Parliament, a number of national legislatures and some political forces within EU member states stepped up criticism of the Chinese regime and its trade practices, in particular China's lack of reciprocity. The main complaint was that Beijing limited foreign investment in its domestic market for almost all sectors. European businesses consequently faced difficulties in entering the market, while Chinese companies often received help from the government through subsidies or simpler procedures. Foreign companies—particularly those with recognised brands and technologically advanced products—were increasingly required to share their expertise before they were allowed into the market at all. European investors routinely pointed out the regulatory and administrative burden that foreign companies would have to face in China.

The acquisition of Kuka, a listed German robotics manufacturer, by the Midea Group, a Chinese-listed home appliances company, at the end of 2016—part of a larger trend characterised by the rapid increase in Chinese takeovers of European companies —fuelled concerns among experts and policymakers over a wide range of issues, including concerns that the growing 'military-civil fusion' strategy under Xi Jinping would seamlessly channel European technology to the Chinese army. [2] This led France, Germany and Italy to ask the European Commission in February 2017 to rethink the rules on foreign investment in the EU. The result was the adoption of a screening mechanism that intended to help the European Commission and the member states to evaluate whether a foreign investor was controlled by a third country government. [3] This was clearly aimed at Chinese state-backed enterprises.

---

[1] Janka Oertel, *The new China consensus: How Europe is growing wary of Beijing*, European Council on Foreign Relations, Policy Brief, 7 September 2020.

[2] Papiya Basu, 'Midea completes acquisition of German robot maker Kuka', *S&P Global Market Intelligence*, 8 January 2017 - https://www.spglobal.com/marketintelligence/en/news-insights/trending/gjozjwvrkhepx0jql2sshw2

[3] European Commission, *Proposal for a Regulation establishing a framework for screening of foreign direct investments into the European Union* (COM/2017/487), Brussels, September 2017.

Another setback in Europe-China relations came with the publication of a policy paper by the EU in March 2019—a document that would cool down the enthusiasm vis-à-vis China's BRI experienced in previous years. In it, Brussels made a shift towards a more assertive—and defensive—approach, calling China an "economic competitor" and a "systemic rival promoting alternative models of governance". [1] In the same vein, the European Council of 21-22 March 2019 voiced harsh criticism on issues ranging from the BRI and Chinese investments into the bloc, to the challenge posed by Beijing state-backed companies to Europe's competitiveness and prosperity. [2]

The election of U.S. president Joe Biden in November 2020 certainly contributed to reinforcing the EU's toughening position on China, as the new U.S. administration would seek to involve the European allies into a Washington-led containment policy towards Beijing. The pushback towards China's Silk Roads was nowhere more evident than in Italy, which had just signed the MOU on the BRI. The government of Draghi (February 2021-October 2022) would put clear limits to BRI's projects. In more than one occasion, Draghi made use of a specially created legal mechanism—the so-called "golden power"—to halt or delay acquisition of Italian companies active in strategically critical sectors (technology, cyber, energy etc.) by Chinese firms. [3] In addition China would fail to acquire stakes in the port authorities of Genoa and the various ports in the northern Adriatic Sea (Trieste, Venice, and Ravenna) that formed the backbone of the MOU. [4] Unlike the case of the port of Piraeus in Athens, where the Chinese state-owned COSCO secured the right to operate parts of the port in 2008, then acquired 51 percent of the Greek state-owned operator in 2016, and finally increased its stake to 67 percent in October 2021, Beijing has been unable to extend its reach over the ports in northern Italy, in particular those of Genoa and Trieste most coveted by COSCO.

The arrival of a nationalist-conservative coalition led by Giorgia Meloni in

---

① European Commission, *EU-China–A strategic outlook* (JOIN/2019/5 final), Brussels, 12 March 2019.

② Jing Men, *The Chinese Perspectives on the EU's Policy towards China*, IAI Papers 23/22, October 2023 - https://www.iai.it/en/pubblicazioni/chinese-perspectives-eus-policy-towards-china

③ Beatrice Gallelli, Francesca Ghiretti and Lorenzo Mariani, 'Introduction', in Beatrice Gallelli and Francesca Ghiretti (eds.), *The Belt and Road Initiative in Italy. Five Case Studies*, Bern: Peter Lang, 2023, pp. 13-25 - https://www.peterlang.com/document/1321488

④ Francesca Ghiretti, *The Belt and Road Initiative in Italy: The Ports of Genoa and Trieste*, IAI Papers, 21/17, April 2021, p. 17 - https://www.iai.it/sites/default/files/iaip2117.pdf

September 2022 accelerated the process of blocking BRI's infrastructural projects and Chinese acquisitions of industrial assets considered of strategic significance. In June 2023 the Italian government used specific legislation to block ChemChina, Pirelli's largest stakeholder, from taking control of the tire making giant. [①] The acquisition of Pirelli in 2015 had become a powerful symbol of China's investment inroads into Europe and of the opportunities that the BRI would entail for cash strapped governments and companies. In addition to blocking ChemChina's aspirations, in December 2023, the Meloni government officially exited the BRI. [②]

Italy is not the only European country to have officially turned its back on the BRI. Since 2021, anti-China sentiment has also been growing in some CEE countries with which China had tightened ties. In particular the Baltic countries have changed tack dramatically finding that the economic benefits coming from China are not as great as they had expected. In August 2022, Latvia and Estonia followed Lithuania in abandoning the so-called 16+1 grouping, a format between Beijing and CEE countries established in 2012 as a platform for cooperation on infrastructure and development projects. [③] The forum delivered little to nothing in terms of infrastructure development; besides, they were furthermore concerned about Xi's ever closer relationship with Russian President Vladimir Putin, exemplified by the declaration on the "partnership with no limits" released during the Beijing Winter Olympics in early February 2022. Russia's invasion of Ukraine in February 2022 and the decision by China to side with Moscow has exacerbated tensions between China and Baltic countries.

4. The BRI in South-East Europe: a success story

Support for Chinese-funded infrastructure projects is, however, still alive in parts

---

① Amy Kazmin and Silvia Sciorilli Borrelli, 'Italy strips China's Sinochem of its influence as Pirelli's largest investor', *Financial Times*, 18 June 2023 - https://www.ft.com/content/d69554c0-0252-4ef1-81a4-c3699ead4a54

② Aurelio Insisa, *Timing Is Everything: Italy Withdraws from the Belt and Road Initiative*, IAI Commentaries 23/67, December 2023 - https://www.iai.it/it/pubblicazioni/timing-everything-italy-withdraws-belt-and-road-initiative

③ Milda Seputyte and Ott Tammik, 'Baltic States Abandon East European Cooperation With China', *Bloomberg*, 12 August 2022 - https://www.bloomberg.com/news/articles/2022-08-11/baltic-states-abandon-eastern-european-cooperation-with-china

of Eastern and Southeast Europe, including the Western Balkan states that seek to join the EU. Serbia and Montenegro have received large amounts of BRI investments in recent years. In January 2023, a new $1 billion Chinese-funded highway outside the Montenegrin capital was officially opened. The most notable case is, however, Croatia which is a full member of the EU. Zagreb is host to the Chinese Southeast European Business Association and has actively courted Chinese investments in critical infrastructure, including ports and the EU-funded and China-built Peljesac bridge, the first example of subsidised Chinese firms beating out European firms for EU-funded projects in Europe. [1]

Other CEE countries that continue to look favourably to China's BRI include Bulgaria, Romania and Hungary. These states sent high-level delegations to the third Belt and Road Forum (BRF) held in Beijing on 17-18 October 2023. The Bulgarian National Association for the Belt and Road—an organisation which includes both active and former politicians —came to the Forum with a detailed list of projects that was given to Chinese authorities for approval. The previous month, Bulgaria had hosted a two-day conference on the 10th anniversary of the BRI with the aim to boost closer cooperation between Bulgaria/EU and China. Deputy Economy and Industry Minister Nikolay Pavlov declared that "China is a strategic partner for Bulgaria and the EU, as well as within the Belt and Road Initiative for cooperation between China and the countries in Central and East Europe". [2]

The Hungarian delegation at the BRF in October 2023 included the governor of the central bank, an avowed enthusiast of the BRI[3], who signed an agreement with the People's Bank of China to increase the level of currency-swaps. Although the overall amount of the currency swap was not revealed, it is possibly Europe's largest, suggesting that Hungary

---

[1] Nina Pejič, *Many a Mickle Makes a Muckle: Chinese Corrosive Capital in Croatia*, Central European Institute of Asian Studies, Working Paper, August 2021 - https://ceias.eu/wp-content/uploads/2021/08/Many-a-Mickle.pdf

[2] Dimitrina Solakova, 'Sofia Hosts Conference on 10th Anniversary of Belt and Road Initiative', *Bulgarian News Agency*, 13 September 2023 - https://www.bta.bg/en/news/economy/521937-sofia-hosts-conference-on-10th-anniversary-of-belt-and-road-initiative

[3] 'Hungary central bank governor: China-proposed BRI 'clear success', Xinhua, 27 September 2023 - http://english.scio.gov.cn/beltandroad/2023-09/27/content_116715074.htm

wants to become a top destination of Chinese investments in the old continent. [1] On 22 December 2023, Chinese automaker BYD announced plans to establish an electric-vehicle manufacturing plant (the biggest in Europe with a production capacity of 200, 000 vehicles per year) in the Hungarian city of Szeged, near the border with Romania and Serbia, along the Budapest-Belgrade-Skopje-Athens railway, which is the BRI's flagship project in Eastern Europe. [2]

5. Towards high-quality industrial cooperation

Hungary is by no means the only country seeking to boost industrial ties with China on key technologies. Other important European car manufacturers, such as Germany[3] and the Czech Republic[4], have signed MOUs on industrial cooperation with Beijing. In Catalonia, local authorities collaborated with the central government in Madrid to attract a significant investment by Chinese automaker Chery which in April 2024 signed a joint venture with Ebro-EV Motors to produce 150,000 cars by 2029—an investment of 500 million euros. To attract Chery, the Spanish government offered tax breaks and provided 1.7 billion-euro incentives from EU funds. [5] Chinese

---

① Márton Losonczi, 'Hungary Committed to Becoming Region's Top Destination for Chinese Investors, Minister States in Shanghai', *Hungarian Conservative*, 6 November 2023 - https://www.hungarianconservative.com/articles/current/hungary_regions_top_destination_for_chinese_investors_minister_nagy_shanghai_expo/

② 'Chinese Tesla rival BYD to open its first European EV manufacturing plant in Hungary', *Associated Press*, 22 December 2023 - https://www.euronews.com/next/2023/12/22/chinese-tesla-rival-byd-to-open-ev-manufacturing-plant-in-hungary

③ Federal Ministry for Economic Affairs and Climate Action, *Germany and China sign Memorandum of Understanding on dialogue and cooperation in the field of automated and connected driving*, Joint Press Release, 16 April 2024 - https://www.bmwk.de/Redaktion/EN/Pressemitteilung en/2024/04/20240416-germany-and-china-sign-memorandum-of-understanding-on-dialogue-and-cooperation-in-the-field-of-automated-and-connected-driving.html

④ Government of the Czech Republic, *Signing of a memorandum of understanding between the Confederation of Industry of the Czech Republic and CCPIT during the visit of a delegation from the Czech Republic to China*, 22 April 2024 - https://mzv.gov.cz/beijing/en/trade_and_economy/news/signing_of_a_memorandum_of_understanding.html

⑤ 'China's Chery to open its first European manufacturing site in Spain', *Reuters*, 16 April 2024 - https://www.reuters.com/business/autos-transportation/chinas-chery-will-open-spain-its-first-european-manufacturing-site-2024-04-16/

car manufacturer Dongfeng is currently discussing with the Meloni cabinet the plan to set up a factory in Italy capable of producing more than 100,000 hybrid and electric vehicles annually, leveraging Italy's automotive legacy and geographic position to serve the European market.

Several EU governments seem thus keen on attracting Chinese investment and technology to produce inside their territories. The goal is to manufacture electric cars and buses—but also solar panels and wind farms—that could be defined as "Made in China and Europe"—that is, made with Chinese technology and know-how together with European components and skilled labour—and thus compliant with European rules. In the automotive sector, the model is that of Stellantis, the Italian/French car producer that is partnering with Chinese battery manufacturer CATL and other Chinese players to produce electric vehicles and batteries in Europe. From this perspective, Chinese investments are expected to receive tax incentives and a favourable regulatory environment from Brussels, including monetary incentives to support research and development in green technologies—a way to effectively neutralize the recently announced EU tariffs on Chinese electric vehicles and boost the EU's Green Deal. [1]

On the heels of growing Chinese investments in the old continent, the Europeans have opened doors to financial and monetary connectivity with Beijing, a dynamic in full display at the third Belt and Road Forum in October 2023 during which China's policy banks signed a series of yuan-denominated loan contracts with foreign lenders, many of which from EU countries. [2]

6. Sino-European monetary connectivity

Since the launch of the BRI in 2013 a major goal of the Chinese leadership has been to increase the renminbi's share in trade, monetary transactions and foreign exchange

---

[1] European Commission, *Commission imposes provisional countervailing duties on imports of battery electric vehicles from China while discussions with China continue*, Press Release, 4 July 2024 - https://ec.europa.eu/commission/presscorner/detail/en/ip_24_3630.

[2] 'China ramps up yuan internationalisation under Belt and Road Initiative', *Reuters*, 19 October 2023 - https://www.reuters.com/markets/currencies/china-ramps-up-yuan-internationalisation-under-belt-road-initiative-2023-10-19/

reserves to facilitate Chinese outbound investment and lower transaction costs. [1] In the last decade, the Belt and Road and renminbi internationalisation have proceeded in lockstep, as each reinforces the other. [2] On the heels of infrastructure projects and investments, the European continent has been the main target for promoting the financial and monetary elements of the BRI.

China's monetary ambitions have been met with interest across the old continent, including by eurozone member states. Beijing has traditionally backed Europe's own monetary ambitions and supported the eurozone during the euro-crisis of 2010-2012. [3] The first BRI projects landed in Europe at the end of 2013, when peripheral countries of the eurozone, including Greece and Italy, were reeling from the effect of the sovereign debt crisis.

Furthermore, many Europeans share China's concern about the increasing tendency by the United States to weaponise the dollar. Several European companies, including French bank BNP Paribas—the largest banking group in Europe (by assets)—were fined for not submitting to Washington's extraterritorial legislation, leading Governor of the Bank of France François Villeroy de Galhau to openly call for the euro "to challenge the dollar". [4]

Europe is the world's largest trading power and has well-developed individual capital markets (even accounting for the lack of a capital market union). Since the entry into

---

① Lorenzo Bencivelli and Michele Savini Zangrandi, *The Internationalisation of the Chinese Renminbi and China's Digital Currency Plans*, IAI Papers 23/08, April 2023 - https://www.iai.it/sites/default/files/iaip2308.pdf. On the internationalization of the RMB see also:. The People's Bank of China, *2022 RMB Internationalization Report*, September 2022 - http://www.pbc.gov.cn/goutongjiaoliu/113456/113469/4666144/2022112809590450941.pdf. Bank of China, *White Paper on RMB Internationalization – RMB along the 'Belt and Road,* 2015 - https://pic.bankofchina.com/bocappd/rareport/201511/P020151109382840816047.pdf

② Bora Ly, 'The nexus of BRI and internationalization of renminbi (RMB)', *Cogent Business & Management*, Vol. 7, No. 1, August 2020 - https://www.tandfonline.com/doi/full/10.1080/23311975.2020.1808399

③ Nicola Casarini and Miguel Otero-Iglesias 'Europe's Renminbi Romance', *Project Syndicate*, 4 April 2016 - https://www.project-syndicate.org/commentary/europe-supporting-renminbi-by-nicola-casarini-and-miguel-otero-iglesias-2016-04?barrier=accesspaylog

④ Martin Arnold and Claire Jones, 'France's central banker calls for euro to challenge US dollar', *Financial Times*, 4 June 2019 - https://www.ft.com/content/12beb4e6-86c7-11e9-97ea-05ac2431f453ù

circulation of the euro in 1999, the EU has stepped up efforts to develop the global role of its currency. [1]

Chinese leaders have traditionally viewed the euro as an important element for the creation of a multipolar currency system and declared their support for the European common currency on many occasions. Moreover, China's central bank has diversified its foreign exchange reserves—the world's largest—so that it now holds over one-third in euros and slightly more than half in dollars. In turn, the Europeans have been supportive of an increased role of the Chinese currency in the world economy.

Following a surge of Chinese investments under the banner of the BRI, several European countries have established renminbi bank clearings (also called offshore hubs) where the Chinese currency can be traded. The fact that offshore renminbi hubs have emerged in Budapest, Frankfurt, Luxembourg, Madrid, Milan, Paris and Prague indicates Europe's willingness to promote the use of the Chinese currency.

In the same vein, most of Europe's central banks have accepted China's currency as a viable reserve and signed swap agreements with the People's Bank of China—a trend that benefits both sides. Through these currency swaps, Chinese companies can settle their payments using euro or renminbi to avoid exchange risks, while European businesses can make renminbi payments using clearing banks located in almost all EU member states.

Some of Europe's large companies have begun using the renminbi for their transactions with China. For instance, in April 2023 France's TotalEnergies and China National Offshore Oil Corporation completed Beijing's first purchase of imported liquefied natural gas, a transaction that was settled in renminbi through BNP Paribas and the Shanghai Petroleum and Natural Gas Exchange. [2] The deal came a few days before the state visit of French President Emmanuel Macron—a strong advocate of "EU strategic autonomy"—to China, where he declared that, when it comes to EU-China trade, "Europe

---

[1] European Commission, *Towards a stronger international role of the euro*, (COM/2018/796 final), Brussels, 4 December 2018 - https://commission.europa.eu/publications/towards-stronger-international-role-euro-commission-contribution-european-council-and-euro-summit-13_en

[2] Xu Yihe 'TotalEnergies and CNOOC complete first LNG transaction in Chinese currency', *Upstream Online*, 29 March 2023 - https://www.upstreamonline.com/lng/totalenergies-and-cnooc-complete-first-lng-transaction-in-chinese-currency/2-1-1427282

must reduce dependence on the U.S. dollar". [1]

Alongside monetary connectivity, financial centres, stock exchanges trading Chinese securities and market-connect mechanisms linking to Chinese exchanges have emerged in various European countries. Germany is at the forefront of Europe-China financial links. Based in Frankfurt, the CEINEX is a joint venture established by Shanghai Stock Exchange, Deutsche Börse Group and China's Financial Futures Exchange. It is the first dedicated trading venue for China-and RMB-related investment products outside of mainland China. Its mission is to establish a centralised marketplace for trading, risk management and asset allocation for China-related or RMB-denominated financial products in Europe.

France has developed a similar connection between Euronext Paris and the Shanghai Stock Exchange. In 2021, the two sides launched the France-China Cooperation Fund with the involvement of China Investment Corporation, BNP Paribas and Eurazeo (a leading investment group) to boost the Fund's role as a cross-border investment platform and promote the use of the renminbi among French businesses. [2]

According to the Swift-produced RMB Tracker, Europe is second only to Hong Kong when it comes to global cross-border renminbi transactions. To be sure, the gap between the two is still massive: by the end of 2023 Hong Kong had cleared 75 percent of renminbi-denominated payments and Europe just over 10 percent. However, there is every reason to think that Europe's market share will continue to rise on the back of their persistently strong bilateral trade relationship.

In this context, the use by European actors of China's Cross-Border Interbank Payment System (CIPS), an alternative to the Western-dominated SWIFT, is expected to grow. Of the 1,300+ financial institutions connected to the CIPS, more than two hundreds are based in Europe, including some large banks such as BNP Paribas, Deutsche Bank, HSBC and Intesa Sanpaolo. The European banks connected to the CIPS

---

[1] Jack Phillips, 'Macron Says Europe Should Reduce Dependence on US Dollar After Meeting With China's Xi', *The Epoch Times*, 23 April 2023 - https://www.theepochtimes.com/world/macron-says-europe-should-reduce-dependence-on-us-dollar-after-meeting-with-chinas-xi-5182353

[2] *China-France Joint Fact Sheet on the 8th High Level Economic and Financial Dialogue*, 13 December 2021 - https://www.tresor.economie.gouv.fr/Articles/7f2ddc82-fe15-4062-bcac-caf9a40ea8ec/files/22cf72c3-7b2e-4b0f-9e6d-9fbffee4dfa1

tend to clear renminbi funds used to finance infrastructure projects under Beijing's BRI, but the scope of their renminbi-denominated services keep expanding. For instance, Intesa Sanpaolo—the only Italian bank that has so far received the Silk Road Award[①]—is expanding its renminbi-clearing operations as part of its connection with China's CIPS, in line with a broader trend among European banks that are betting that the Belt and Road's next chapter will be all about the yuan. [②]

Conclusion

China's Belt and Road Initiative is being reconfigured across the old continent. In Western Europe, the BRI is moving away from physical infrastructure projects—such as ports and railways—to smaller high-quality cooperation, while most of Eastern European countries continue to promote BRI infrastructural projects. Concurrently, the whole of Europe is supportive of financial and monetary connectivity with China—a shift which is welcomed by various European actors, including some policymakers at the national level, eurozone institutions and major banks. More recently, a growing number of EU member states has opened doors to industrial cooperation in green technologies with China, suggesting that although Brussels-Beijing political relations have somehow worsened in recent times, the Belt and Road continues to make inroads into the old continent, having succeed in moving towards high-quality cooperation projects in the financial, monetary and industrial sectors.

References

Amighini, Alessia and Alicia Garcia Herrero, *Third time lucky? China's push to*

---

① Intesa Sanpaolo, 'Intesa Sanpaolo becomes first foreign bank to offer wealth management services in China through a wholly-owned subsidiary', *Press release*, 11 December 2019 - https://group.intesasanpaolo.com/en/newsroom/press-releases/2019/12/intesa-sanpaolo-becomes-firts-foreign-bank-to-offer-wealth-manag

② Diana Choyleva and Dinny McMahon. 'Belt and Road's next chapter will be all about the yuan', *Nikkei Asia*, 25 October 2022 - https://asia.nikkei.com/Opinion/Belt-and-Road-s-next-chapter-will-be-all-about-the-yuan

internationalise the renminbi, China Horizons, October 2023.

Arnold, Martin and Claire Jones, 'France's central banker calls for euro to challenge U.S. dollar', *Financial Times*, 4 June 2019.

Bank of China, *White Paper on RMB Internationalization – RMB along the 'Belt and Road*, 2015.

Basu, Papiya 'Midea completes acquisition of German robot maker Kuka', *S&P Global Market Intelligence*, 8 January 2017.

Bencivelli, Lorenzo and Michele Savini Zangrandi, *The Internationalisation of the Chinese Renminbi and China's Digital Currency Plans*, IAI Papers 23/08, April 2023.

Cai Peter, *Understanding China's Belt and Road Initiative*, Lowy Institute, March 2017.

Casarini, Nicola 'When All Roads Lead to Beijing. Assessing China's New Silk Road and its Implications for Europe', *The International Spectator*, Vol. 51, Issue 4, 2016, pp. 95-108.

Casarini, Nicola and Miguel Otero-Iglesias 'Europe's Renminbi Romance', *Project Syndicate*, 4 April 2016.

China Daily, 'Silk Road Fund joins ChemChina in industrial investment in Pirelli & C. SpA', 5 June 2015.

COSCO, 'The Inauguration of the Expansion of Pier III of PCT Successfully Convened', 23 January 2015.

Emmott, Robin and Paul Taylor 'Exclusive: China to extend economic diplomacy to EU infrastructure fund', *Reuters*, 15 June 2015.

European Commission, *Towards a stronger international role of the euro*, (COM/2018/796 final), Brussels, 4 December 2018.

European Commission, *EU-China – A strategic outlook* (JOIN/2019/5 final), Brussels, 12 March 2019.

Gallelli Beatrice and Francesca Ghiretti, *The Belt and Road Initiative in Italy. Five Case Studies*, Bern: Peter Lang, 2023.

Hanemann, Thilo, Mikko Huotari and Agatha Krat*Chinese FDI in Europe: 2018 Trends and Impact of New Screening Policies*, Berlin: MERICS Papers on China, 6 March 2019.

He, Wei 'Italian president backs Belt and Road Initiative', *China Daily*, 24 February 2017.

Hellström, Jerker *China's Acquisitions in Europe: European Perceptions of Chinese Investments and their Strategic Implications*, Stockholm: Swedish Center for China Studies, December 2016.

Men Jing, *The Chinese Perspectives on the EU's Policy towards China*, IAI Papers 23/22,

October 2023.

Oertel, Janka *The new China consensus: How Europe is growing wary of Beijing*, European Council on Foreign Relations, Policy Brief, 7 September 2020.

Pavlićević, Dragan 'China's Railway Diplomacy in the Balkans', *China Brief*, 14/20, October 2014.

Percy, Joseph 'Chinese FDI in the EU's Top 4 Economies', *China Briefing*, 8 May 2019.

Pugliese Giulio, Francesca Ghiretti, Aurelio Insisa, 'Italy's embrace of the Belt and Road Initiative: populist foreign policy and political marketing', *International Affairs*, 98/3, May 2022, pp 1033–1051.

Xu, Yihe 'TotalEnergies and CNOOC complete first LNG transaction in Chinese currency', *Upstream Online*, 29 March 2023.

The Belt and Road Initiative in Cambodia

Kun Vee Lee

Economics, Social and Cultural Council of Cambodia

Introduction to the Belt and Road Initiative (BRI)

The Belt and Road Initiative (BRI) is a global infrastructure development strategy aimed at enhancing trade and investment between China and partner nations. Introduced by Chinese President Xi Jinping in 2013, it draws inspiration from the historical Silk Road, stimulating cultural, economic, and technological exchanges (Rolland, 2017). The initiative composes of the Silk Road Economic Belt and the 21st Century Maritime Silk Road, with the former focusing on overland commerce routes in Central Asia, Eastern Europe, and South Asia, while the latter aiming to develop sea routes connecting Southeast Asia, South Asia, Africa, the Middle East, and Europe (NDRC, 2015).

Scope and Reach

The Belt and Road Initiative (BRI) represents China's all-encompassing endeavor to bolster global economic integration through enhanced infrastructure, heightened trade, cultural exchange, and policy coordination among participating nations (Maçães, 2018). China's primary objectives for launching the initiative encompass securing access to pivotal markets, mitigating transportation costs, addressing overcapacity in domestic industries, and positioning itself as a leader in global infrastructure development (Djankov & Miner, 2016). Moreover, the Belt and Road Initiative (BRI) is perceived as a strategic tool for China to expand its geopolitical influence on a global scale, particularly in regions traditionally dominated by Western powers. As of June 2023, China had entered into numerous cooperative agreements with over 150 nations and 30 international organizations, encompassing 117 ports across five continents (Xinhuanet, 2023).

Economic Impact

The Belt and Road Initiative (BRI) spans across more than 150 countries and encompasses investments exceeding $1 trillion. It is founded on China's enduring perspective of economic globalization, regional cooperation, and the cultivation of soft power influence. Between 2013 and 2022, the cumulative value of imports and exports between China and BRI partner countries reached 19.1 trillion U.S. dollars, with an average annual growth rate of 6.4 percent. The total two-way investment between China and partner countries during this period amounted to 380 billion U.S. dollars, with China contributing approximately 240 billion U.S. dollars (Xinhuanet, 2023).

Cambodia's Engagement with the BRI

Cambodia's participation in the Belt and Road Initiative (BRI) epitomizes its broader geopolitical strategy of aligning closely with China. Given its strategic location in Southeast Asia and proximity to vital maritime routes, Cambodia plays a pivotal role in China's regional ambitions. The Kingdom of Cambodia formally joined the BRI in 2016, entering into agreements to participate in infrastructure projects aimed at fostering its economic development. For Cambodia, the BRI presents an opportunity to address its infrastructure deficit, which has long posed significant barriers to economic growth and poverty alleviation (World Bank, 2022). The nation's infrastructure, particularly in transportation, logistics, and energy sectors, has fallen behind its regional counterparts, resulting in a heavy reliance on foreign investment and assistance.

Notably, the Sihanoukville Special Economic Zone (SSEZ) stands as a prominent endeavor under the Belt and Road Initiative (BRI) in Cambodia. Positioned near the Sihanoukville Autonomous Port, a pivotal transshipment center in the region, the

SSEZ represents a collaborative venture between Chinese and Cambodian investors. Functioning as a vital industrial hub for textile and electronics manufacturing and processing industries, the SSEZ is anticipated to yield tens of thousands of employment opportunities, bolster Cambodia's industrial framework, and attract further investments from global corporations. This underscores its potential to significantly influence the country's economic advancement (Cambodia Development Resource Institute [CDRI], 2020). The expansion of the port has significantly strengthened Cambodia's position as a pivotal trade gateway linking Southeast Asia with the global market. This development is particularly instrumental in fostering connectivity with China's vibrant economic hub, the Guangdong-Hong Kong-Macau Greater Bay Area (RFA, 2021).

Several significant projects in Cambodia associated with the Belt and Road Initiative (BRI) are worth highlighting. These projects encompass the development of crucial road infrastructure, including the construction of National Road No.11, facilitating connectivity between Phnom Penh and vital border areas. Additionally, the Phnom Penh-Sihanoukville Expressway has been instrumental in substantially decreasing travel duration between the capital and Cambodia's principal seaport (Thul, 2021). The aforementioned initiatives are of paramount importance in enhancing domestic connectivity and promoting regional trade. Furthermore, China has made significant investments in the enhancement of Cambodia's aviation infrastructure, particularly with regards to the expansion and modernization of Phnom Penh International Airport. These efforts are indicative of a broader commitment to bolstering regional connectivity and fostering economic development. (Cheang, 2022).

BRI projects in Cambodia

Sihanoukville Special Economic Zone (SSEZ)

The Sihanoukville Special Economic Zone (SSEZ) stands as a pivotal component of the Belt and Road Initiative (BRI) in Cambodia. Formed through a partnership between the Cambodian and Chinese governments, SSEZ accommodates over 160 enterprises spanning textile, electronics, and light manufacturing sectors. Predominantly under Chinese ownership, these entities have collectively drawn in excess of $1 billion in investments by the year 2020 (ASEAN Briefing, 2021).

Sihanoukville Autonomous Port (PAS) Expansion

The expansion of the Phnom Penh Autonomous Port (PAS) stands as a vital pillar in Cambodia's assimilation into the Belt and Road Initiative's (BRI) maritime network. Financed by Chinese loans and overseen by Chinese entities, the expansion project encompasses a deepening of the harbor, enlargement of dockyards, and the installation of state-of-the-art cargo handling infrastructure (RFA, 2021). These enhancements are meticulously crafted to amplify the port's capacity, positioning it as a pivotal transshipment center in Southeast Asia. The upgraded port is poised to catalyze amplified trade volumes, entice heightened foreign investments, and invigorate the local economy through the generation of employment opportunities and the optimization of trade logistics (Thul, 2021).

Phnom Penh-Sihanoukville Expressway

The Phnom Penh-Sihanoukville Expressway, inaugurated in October 2022, stands as a prominent example of Cambodia's participation in the Belt and Road Initiative (BRI). Spanning 187 kilometers, this vital infrastructure links the bustling capital of Phnom Penh to the strategic coastal city of Sihanoukville, a pivotal economic hub and a crucial nexus for international trade. This monumental feat, spearheaded by the China Road and Bridge Corporation (CRBC) at an estimated cost of $2 billion (Xinhuanet, 2022), has significantly slashed the travel time between these two pivotal locations from five hours to a mere two hours. This dramatic improvement in connectivity has not only expedited logistics but also fostered a more conducive environment for trade facilitation, and most important of all, an enabling environment to boost the tourism sector.

Lower Sesan 2 Dam

The Lower Sesan 2 Dam represents a substantial hydropower initiative financed by Chinese enterprises, with the primary objective of bolstering Cambodia's energy capacity. While the dam effectively enhances energy security by furnishing a consistent power source to propel industrial expansion, it has also ignited notable environmental and social apprehensions.

In addition to the Lower Sesan 2 Dam, China has invested in several other hydropower projects in Cambodia in order to bolster the country's energy capacity. These initiatives are integral to supporting industrial expansion and lessening Cambodia's dependence on energy imports (Kumar, 2022). Effectively balancing energy development with environmental sustainability remains a paramount challenge for Cambodia under the Belt and Road Initiative (BRI). The construction of the dam has resulted in the displacement of numerous indigenous communities, disruption of fisheries, and modification of the natural flow of the Mekong River, consequently impacting aquatic ecosystems and local livelihoods (International Rivers, 2020). These repercussions underscore the inherent trade-offs between economic development and environmental sustainability within the Belt and Road Initiative (BRI) framework (Kumar, 2022).

Road and Highway Development

Chinese-funded road and highway projects have played a crucial role in enhancing Cambodia's domestic connectivity. Notable examples include the development of National Road No. 11 and the Phnom Penh-Sihanoukville Expressway, both of which demonstrate the significant impact of Chinese investments on Cambodia's transportation infrastructure. These initiatives have effectively reduced transportation costs, streamlined trade logistics, and promoted regional economic integration by establishing vital links between major cities and economic zones (Tan, 2021). The enhancement of road infrastructure has also facilitated the seamless movement of goods and people, thereby contributing to the overall economic growth and development of the region.

Airport Development

The involvement of Chinese companies has been instrumental in the advancement and expansion of the Phnom Penh International Airport (PPIA). This comprehensive project encompasses the modernization of terminal facilities, expansion of runway capacity, and augmentation of cargo handling capabilities (Cheang, 2022). As a result, PPIA has emerged as Cambodia's largest airport, having achieved full operational status in October 2023. These enhancements are designed to cater to the escalating influx of passengers and bolster Cambodia's position as a pivotal regional logistics center.

In addition to the developments at PPIA, the ongoing construction of the Techo Takhmao International Airport near Phnom Penh illustrates another substantial investment under the Belt and Road Initiative (BRI). With an estimated cost of $1.5 billion, this airport, a collaborative endeavor between the Overseas Cambodia Investment Corporation (OCIC) and Chinese investors, is poised to become the largest in Cambodia upon completion. It is anticipated that the airport will be capable of accommodating 13 million passengers annually, thus alleviating congestion at the existing airport in Phnom Penh (Phnom Penh Post, 2021).

Furthermore, the Siem Reap-Angkor International Airport, another critical infrastructure project under the BRI, has been constructed by the China State Construction Engineering Corporation at an approximate cost of $880 million. The financing for this project involved a partnership between the Cambodian government and Chinese investors. The bolstered airport infrastructure not only supports the growth of tourism, a pivotal sector of Cambodia's economy, but also facilitates the movement of goods, thereby contributing to the overall expansion of the country's trade and commerce (ADB, 2020).

Hydropower Projects

In addition to the Lower Sesan 2 Dam, China has invested in several other hydropower projects in Cambodia in order to bolster the country's energy capacity. These initiatives are integral to supporting industrial expansion and lessening Cambodia's dependence on energy imports (Kumar, 2022). Nonetheless, they also give rise to environmental apprehensions such as habitat destruction, water contamination, and the displacement of local communities (International Rivers, 2020). Effectively balancing energy development with environmental sustainability remains a paramount challenge for Cambodia under the Belt and Road Initiative (BRI).

Telecommunications Infrastructure

Chinese telecommunications firms, including Huawei, have played a pivotal role in the advancement of Cambodia's digital infrastructure. Substantial investments in state-of-the-art fiber-optic networks and cutting-edge 5G technology have been made to bolster internet connectivity, foster the expansion of the digital economy, and position Cambodia as an integral part of the global digital ecosystem (Chen, 2021). The enhancement of the telecommunications infrastructure not only facilitates the growth of e-commerce, digital services, and innovation but also contributes significantly to economic diversification and modernization (ADB, 2021).

Economic Impacts of the BRI in Cambodia

The economic advantages of Cambodia's involvement in the Belt and Road Initiative (BRI) are primarily focused on infrastructure development, foreign direct investment (FDI), and industrial expansion. Cambodia has witnessed consistent economic progress in recent years, partly attributed to increased investments from China. As stated by the Ministry of Economy and Finance, Cambodia's GDP grew by an average of 7% annually from 2013 to 2019, with Chinese investment playing a significant role in this growth (MEF, 2022). BRI initiatives have resulted in enhancements to crucial infrastructure, including roads, bridges, airports, and energy facilities, leading to reduced transportation costs, improved trade logistics, and a more appealing environment for potential investors (ADB, 2020). For instance, the inauguration of the Phnom Penh-Sihanoukville Expressway in 2022 not only reduced travel time from over five hours to less than two, but also enhanced trade efficiency by facilitating the movement of goods from Cambodia's industrial zones to its primary port (Thul, 2021). This apparently has reduced transportation costs, and enhanced connectivity within Cambodia and with neighboring countries. Moreover, BRI-related projects, particularly in the SSEZ, have played a pivotal role in stimulating job creation in the manufacturing and construction sectors. With over 160 enterprises, predominantly Chinese-owned, specializing in textiles, garments, and electronics production, the SSEZ has created approximately 30, 000 jobs for local workers as of 2020, contributing to a noteworthy diversification of the Cambodian economy from agriculture to light manufacturing (ASEAN Briefing, 2021). This expansion has been instrumental in shaping Cambodia's industrial sector, previously reliant on agriculture and garment production, by diversifying into electronics, automotive parts, and other industries. This also means upgrading local skilled labor market. Consequently, Cambodia has been able to reduce its dependence on low-value-added sectors and move towards higher-value-added production. Additionally, the SSEZ has significantly contributed to Cambodia's export economy, with the zone reporting an export value of around $1. 3 billion in 2020, representing a substantial portion of the country's overall trade (ASEAN Briefing, 2021).

China has emerged as Cambodia's largest trading partner, with bilateral trade between the two countries surpassing $10 billion in 2021 (Council for the Development of Cambodia, 2022). Moreover, Chinese investments in Cambodia, particularly in the construction, energy, and manufacturing sectors, reached a record $3. 5 billion in 2020 alone (Khmer Times, 2020). The Belt and Road Initiative (BRI) has played a pivotal role in expanding Cambodia's export markets, particularly in textiles, agricultural products, and electronics. The trade relationships have been further bolstered by the 2021 Cambodia-China Free Trade Agreement (CCFTA), which has led to a reduction in tariffs on key exports and opened up new opportunities for Cambodian goods in Chinese markets (Phnom Penh Post, 2021).

The increasing reliance on Chinese investments in Cambodia has raised concerns about the country's growing debt burden. As of March 2024, Cambodia's public external debt totaled $11 billion, with China accounting for nearly 37% of it (MEF, 2024). This mounting debt has sparked debates about the sustainability of Cambodia's financial situation, with critics expressing apprehensions about the country becoming overly dependent on China for future financial support (Hurley et al. , 2018).

Social Impacts of the BRI in Cambodia

The Belt and Road Initiative (BRI) has significantly impacted Cambodia's labor market by fueling infrastructure projects and industrial zones, leading to the creation of thousands of new jobs in construction, manufacturing, and logistics (Smith, 2021). Notably, the BRI has played a pivotal role in creating employment opportunities in Cambodia. Projects like the Sihanoukville Special Economic Zone (SSEZ), which has attracted over 160 companies, have been instrumental in providing employment to thousands of Cambodian workers. According to a report from ASEAN Briefing, the SSEZ alone has generated approximately 30,000 jobs for local Cambodians by 2020, particularly in sectors such as textiles, electronics, and light manufacturing (ASEAN Briefing, 2021). The underlying benefits are reflected in the creation of a vibrant skilled labor market.

The positive impact of these employment opportunities is evident in the upliftment of families from poverty, especially in regions where agricultural work was previously the primary source of income. This transformation has been particularly significant in areas such as Sihanoukville, historically plagued by high unemployment rates. The development of the SSEZ and associated infrastructure projects has not only provided economic opportunities for local workers but has also contributed to poverty reduction and improved living standards.

Furthermore, the influx of Chinese investment has spurred rapid urbanization in cities like Phnom Penh and Sihanoukville. Improved infrastructure has facilitated the expansion of urban areas, leading to enhanced access to housing, healthcare, and education (Asian Development Bank, 2020). Urban transformation has also bolstered the local hospitality industry, attracting more foreign tourists and creating additional employment opportunities.

In addition to job creation, BRI projects have also facilitated the development of skills among Cambodian workers through training programs and capacity-building initiatives. For example, China's Belt and Road Scholarship Program has provided opportunities for Cambodian students to pursue higher education in China, focusing on fields such as engineering, infrastructure development, and technology. By 2019, more than 1, 000 Cambodian students had received scholarships to study in China, as reported by Khmer Times (2019). These educational opportunities not only benefit individuals but also have the potential to enhance Cambodia's workforce, making it more competitive in the regional labor market.

The Belt and Road Initiative (BRI) has undeniably brought about significant positive impacts on employment and urban development in Cambodia. However, it has also been associated with some negative social consequences. The rapid transformation of Sihanoukville into a "Chinese style city" has led to rising property prices, displacing local residents and small businesses (Radio Free Asia, 2021). Younger Cambodians feel left behind in the economic transformation driven by the BRI.

Environmental Impact of the BRI in Cambodia

The discourse surrounding the Belt and Road Initiative (BRI) in Cambodia has predominantly centered on the adverse environmental impacts, including deforestation and pollution. However, it is essential to acknowledge the positive efforts within the BRI framework that contribute to environmental sustainability. One notable example is the development of hydropower projects, such as the Lower Sesan 2 Dam and the Kamchay Hydropower Dam, with Chinese investment. These projects have significantly bolstered Cambodia's green energy capacity by producing around 200 MW of electricity and represent a crucial step towards sustainable energy development in the country (China Dialogue, 2021). Furthermore, the construction of the Phnom Penh-Sihanoukville Expressway has substantially reduced travel time between the capital and Cambodia's major seaport from over five hours to less than two. This achievement not only enhances transportation efficiency but also mitigates fuel consumption and vehicle emissions, thus positively impacting the environment.

The implementation of Belt and Road Initiative (BRI) projects in Cambodia has brought to the forefront environmental challenges. The expansion of infrastructure, including roads and industrial zones, under the BRI has unfortunately and unintentionally led to forest degradation Water Security and Air Pollution.

Perceived Concerns

Lack of Transparency

The management of Belt and Road Initiative (BRI) projects in Cambodia has faced substantial scrutiny due to perceived deficiencies in transparency and public engagement, particularly in the context of major infrastructure undertakings. There is a need to continue strengthening public consultation and transparency standards specifically for foreign investments such as the Belt and Road Initiative (BRI).

Border and National Security

The Belt and Road Initiative has introduced infrastructure projects near Cambodia's borders with Thailand and Vietnam, prompting purported concerns about border security and the prevention of illegal activities.

Conclusion

The Belt and Road Initiative (BRI) represents a strategic endeavor launched by China to foster global economic integration through substantial investments in infrastructure, trade, and policy coordination. Its overarching objectives encompass the augmentation of China's global influence and win-win collaboration, both economically and politically, while inducing transformative effects in partner countries such as Cambodia, particularly within the spheres of infrastructure development, energy, and telecommunications.

In Cambodia, the BRI has precipitated noteworthy economic progressions, notably evidenced through the inception of large-scale infrastructure projects such as the Sihanoukville Special Economic Zone (SSEZ), the Phnom Penh-Sihanoukville

Expressway, and various airport and hydropower developments. These initiatives have had a demonstrable and positive impact, contributing to enhanced connectivity, reduced transportation costs, and heightened industrial capabilities, thereby facilitating the creation of employment opportunities and the diversification of Cambodia's economy along with its strengthened skilled labor market.

In conclusion, the BRI has without a doubt yielded vital economic opportunities and infrastructural enhancements for Cambodia. What is required is for Cambodia to step up its readiness both from the strategic policy/regulatory framework level and the enforcement/implementation level on the ground. Ultimately, the efficacy of the BRI in Cambodia and other participating nations will hinge upon their adept management of associated economic risks, while adeptly capitalizing on the opportunities that the initiative presents.

References

Zhang, B. (2020). Cambodia and China: BRI Influence on ASEAN and South China Sea Diplomacy. The Diplomat.

U.S. Department of State. (2021). Human Rights and Cambodia's Political Landscape.

Schmitz, R. (2020). China's Naval Presence in Cambodia: A Growing Concern for the U.S. NPR.

WWF. (2019). China's Belt and Road Initiative: A Catalyst for Wildlife Destruction?

Global Forest Watch. (2022). Cambodia Deforestation Data.

International Rivers. (2020). Impact of Hydropower Dams in Cambodia: The Case of the Lower Sesan 2 Dam.

Mekong River Commission (MRC). (2021). Sesan River Fisheries and Dam Impacts.

Middleton, C., et al. (2019). Dams, Fish, and Livelihoods in the Mekong River Basin. Water International.

Rolland, N. (2017). China's Eurasian Century? Political and Strategic Implications of the Belt and Road Initiative. National Bureau of Asian Research.

National Development and Reform Commission (NDRC). (2015). Vision and Actions on Jointly Building Silk Road Economic Belt and 21st-Century Maritime Silk Road.

Maçães, B. (2018). Belt and Road: A Chinese World Order. Hurst Publishers.

Djankov, S., & Miner, S. (2016). China's Belt and Road Initiative: Motives, Scope, and

Challenges. Peterson Institute for International Economics.

Hurley, J., Morris, S., & Portelance, G. (2018). Examining the Debt Implications of the Belt and Road Initiative from a Policy Perspective. Center for Global Development.

Cambodia Development Resource Institute (CDRI). (2020). Sihanoukville Special Economic Zone: Cambodia's Growth Engine?

Thul, P. C. (2021). Cambodia Opens First Expressway in Major Belt and Road Project. Reuters.

Human Rights Watch. (2022). Cambodia: Land Disputes in BRI Projects.

International Rivers. (2020). Impact of Hydropower Dams in Cambodia: The Case of the Lower Sesan 2 Dam.

WWF. (2019). China's Belt and Road Initiative: A Catalyst for Wildlife Destruction?

Ministry of Economy and Finance (2024). Cambodia Public Debt Statistical Bulletin Volume 22 – Data as of End-Q1 2024.

Council for the Development of Cambodia (CDC). (2022). Cambodia-China Trade Relations: A Growing Partnership.

Asian Development Bank (ADB). (2021). Renewable Energy Prospects in Cambodia.

Kumar, S. (2022). Hydropower Development in Cambodia: Balancing Energy Needs and Environmental Concerns. International Journal of Sustainable Energy.

Xinhuanet (2023). Key takeaways from BRI white paper. XINHUANET.

Xinhuanet. (2021). BRI Projects Emphasizing Environmental Sustainability in Cambodia. XINHUANET.

Asian Development Bank (ADB). (2020). Impact of Road Infrastructure on Carbon Emissions in Southeast Asia. ADB.

China Dialogue. (2021). Hydropower in Southeast Asia: Balancing Development and Sustainability. China Dialogue.

The Diplomat. (2021). China's Green Belt and Road: Fact or Fiction?. The Diplomat.

Global Witness. (2019). Deforestation and Land Grabbing in Cambodia: The Role of Infrastructure Projects. Global Witness.

Human Rights Watch. (2020). Sihanoukville Industrial Zone and Environmental Health Risks. HRW.

International Rivers. (2020). The Environmental Impact of Hydropower in Cambodia: The Case of Lower Sesan 2 Dam. International Rivers.

NGO Forum on Cambodia. (2019). The Impact of the Lower Sesan 2 Dam on Local Communities and Ecosystems. NGO Forum.

The Guardian. (2018). Sand Mining in Cambodia and Its Impact on Local Ecosystems. The Guardian.

ASEAN Briefing. (2021). Sihanoukville Special Economic Zone and Cambodia's Economic Growth. ASEAN Briefing.

Human Rights Watch. (2019). Cambodian Workers Face Discrimination in Chinese-Led Projects. HRW.

Reuters. (2019). China's Online Gambling Ban Hits Cambodia's Economy Hard. Reuters.

The Diplomat. (2019). Sihanoukville's Casino Boom: Economic Growth or Bust?. The Diplomat.

Xinhuanet. (2022). Cambodia's First Expressway Opens, Cutting Travel Times and Boosting Trade. XiINHUANET.

Khmer Times. (2019). Belt and Road Scholarships Benefitting Cambodian Students. Khmer Times.

The Diplomat. (2019). Sihanoukville's Casino Boom: Economic Growth or Bust?. The Diplomat.

Phnom Penh Post. (2021). Techo Takhmao International Airport: A New Gateway for Cambodia. Phnom Penh Post.

International Rivers. (2018). Lower Sesan 2 Dam and Its Environmental and Social Impacts. International Rivers.

NGO Forum on Cambodia. (2019). Lower Sesan 2 Hydropower Dam: Impacts on Livelihoods and Environment. NGO Forum on Cambodia.

Transparency International. (2022). Corruption Perceptions Index 2022: Cambodia. Transparency International.

Global Witness. (2020). Deforestation and Corruption in Cambodia's BRI Projects. Global Witness.

ASEAN Today. (2022). The Phnom Penh-Sihanoukville Expressway: Economic Boom or Security Risk?. ASEAN Today.

Wildlife Justice Commission. (2021). Cambodia's Wildlife Trade and Security Concerns in the Mekong Region. Wildlife Justice Commission.

The Diplomat. (2021). Chinese Influence in the Sihanoukville Special Economic Zone: Opportunities and Threats. The Diplomat.

Belt and Road: the Authenticity of the Past and the Initiative of Renewal and Creativity

Hayder Qasim M. Al-Tameemi Ph.D.

Head of the Department of Historical Studies / Chief Researcher, House of Wisdom – Iraq / Baghdad

I. Introduction

This study deals with the historical roots of the Silk Road, which in ancient history linked China to the rest of the world, especially the Arab world in West Asia and North Africa. This trade route was considered a pioneering gateway to the cross-fertilization of civilizations and cultures between nations and peoples that were geographically, religiously and culturally different. We see the idea of the Silk Road, both land and sea, beginning to gain popularity over the long centuries of the history of these peoples, as is the case with the Buddhist and Islamic roads. The study then turns to the projects and discourses of cooperation shaping China's twenty-first-century "revival" of the Silk Road under the Belt and Road Initiative.

In the same context, this study aims to investigate the consequences of cultural interactions among different civilizations from ancient times through the Silk Road. The Silk Road is also known as ancient Trade Route connecting China with the West, that carried goods and ideas between the two great civilizations of Rome and China.

Originating at Xian, China this caravan tract, followed the Great Wall of China to the Northwest, bypassed the Takla Makan Desert, climbed the Pamirs, crossed Afghanistan, and went on to the Levant; from there the merchandise was shipped across the Mediterranean.

This study also finds that China received Christianity from Europe and Buddhism means of the Silk Trade Route. In the 13th and 14th centuries the route was revived under the Mongols, and at that time Marco Polo used it to travel to Cathay (China). The ancient part of the Silk Road still exists, in the form of a paved highway known as "Karakorum Highway" linking Pakistan and Xinjiang. The ancient Silk Trade Route extends to more than 7, 000 kilometers, linking most territories of Asia and Europe. To trace the ancient Silk Trade Road on the map is not an easy task, because there are several offshoots which also have many further branches while connecting East and West.

"The Silk Road" is now virtually a household word. Thousands of people all over the world wish to view and personally experience it. In fact, it was only in 1877 that the German scholar and explorer Ferdinand von Richthofen coined the term "Seidenstrasse" (Silk Road) to designate this venerable network of ancient commercial passages from East to West Asia. The Europeans and Japanese were keenly intrigued by China's Xinjiang region, and many a scholar had gone there to research the Silk Road pioneered by Zhang Qian, the Western Han Dynasty (206 BCE–25 CE) imperial envoy and explorer.

This study—Within the first section of it—principally describes the exchanges between various civilizations and societies along the length of the Silk Road. While including commerce of a host of goods such as large mammals, crops, medicines, utensils, textiles, musical instruments, jewelry, minerals, and gunpowder, it nonetheless focuses on the exchange of less tangible culture. The origins and dissemination of Zoroastrianism, Buddhism, Christianity, Manichaeism, Nestorian-Christianity, and Islam are portrayed, as well as the long-distance exchanges of scripts and spoken language, music, architecture, painting, and sculpture via the Silk Road. It outlines the historically significant migrations of various peoples from east to west, such as the Xiongnu, Yuezhi (i. e. , Yue-chi), Han, Qiang, Hephthalites, Turkic groups, Uyghurs, Mongols, and Xibe.

As for the second section of this study, I tried to trace the civilizational and cultural impact of the Belt and Road Initiative, which was launched more than ten years ago in most countries of the world. This is done by highlighting the main points on which this initiative had an impact on the cultural rapprochement between the countries of the world participating in it. In addition, there was a focus on the role of the Belt and Road Initiative in restoring the flourishing of cultural, and even social, ties between the Chinese and Arab civilizations in general, and specifically with the city of Baghdad, which during the Middle Ages was the center and capital of this civilization.

If I were to sum up in one sentence the historical significance of 2,000 years of cultural commingling along the Silk Road and throughout Eurasia, without hesitation I would say: A society evolves and thrives when it is open and inclusive, willing and accustomed to interacting with and learning from different peoples.

II. The Silk Road...historical rooting

At around 140 BC during China's Han Dynasty, Zhang Qian, a royal emissary, made a journey to the West from Chang'an (present-day Xi'an in Shaanxi Province), opening an overland route linking East and West. Centuries later, in the years of the Tang, Song and Yuan dynasties, silk routes boomed over both land and at sea. In the early 15th century, Zheng He, the famous Chinese navigator of the Ming Dynasty, made seven voyages to the Western Seas, which boosted trade along the maritime silk routes (Chang, 2023, p. 19).

For thousands of years, the ancient silk routes served as major arteries of interaction, spanning the valleys of the Nile, the Tigris and Euphrates, the Indus and Ganges, and the Yellow and Yangtze rivers. They connected the birthplaces of the Egyptian, Babylonian, Indian and Chinese civilizations, the lands of the believers of Buddhism, Christianity and Islam, and the homes of peoples of different nationalities and races (Wells, 2005, p. 101).

These routes increased connectivity among countries on the Eurasian continent, facilitated exchanges and mutual learning between Eastern and Western civilizations, boosted regional development and prosperity, and shaped the Silk Road spirit characterized by peace and cooperation, openness and inclusiveness, mutual learning and mutual benefit.

The world science's interest in the study of the Silk Road is, in its way, countdown, a glance deep into centuries; an attempt to retrace landmarks of history and "change of generations". The Silk Road is a system of caravan roads that in the ancient times and the Middle Ages traversed Eurasia from the Mediterranean to China and did much to foster the establishment and development of trade and cultural relations between peoples and states involved (Thubron, 2007, p. 27). Besides, the study aims to back the collaboration, both scientific and cultural, between scholars that had once been involved in the ancient route sphere of influence. The Silk Road that traversed steppes, seas and deserts provided every to establish contacts and dialogue, conduce to the mutual enrichment of outstanding civilizations. The objective of the complex research of the Silk Road is to make peoples realize the necessity of resuming the dialogue, seize the historical opportunity of develop mutual understanding, expand contacts and mutually enrich civilizations within the Silk Road framework (Clements, 2017, p. 9).

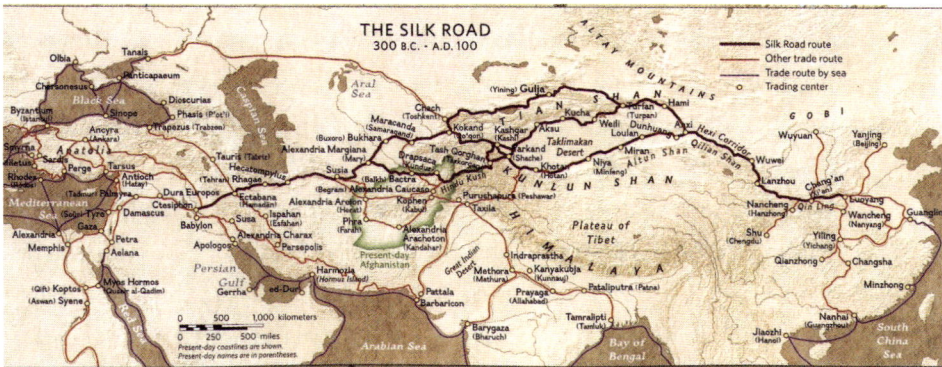

The Silk Road, other trade routes and hubs through Asia 300BC-100AD

Historically, geographically and culturologically, the Silk Road is known to have become a subject of study as far back as in the second half of the 19 century. Greatly contributing to the subject were West European, Russian and Japanese scholars. In 1877, a classical scientific work *"China"* by German scholar von Richthofen presented the Silk Road as a system of routes that connected various parts of the vast Eurasian mainland. Later on, a term "Silk Road" became firmly established. Bibliography of scientific and popular-science works about the Silk Road numbers thousands of titles, including monographs; collected works; albums; booklets and articles. They provide the history of the Silk Road; description of main and subsidiary routes; ethnic composition of population; description of towns; enumeration of goods; architecture and art; music and epos; religion. Over the past two decades, scientific and public interest in the history of transcontinental road has visibly increased (Zhang, 2005, p. 7).

It should be noted that international scientific conferences and seminars were held within the framework of the Project. These include. "Formation and Development of Silk Road Routes in the Central Asia: the Ancient and Medieval Perlods" (Samarkand, October 1990); "Interaction of Nomadic and Settled Cultures on the Silk Road" (Alma-Ata, 15-16 June, 1992); "Epos of the States along the Silk Road" (Turku, Finland, 3-7 June, 1993); "Languages and Written Languages along the Silk Road" (Cyprus, 30 September - 1 October, 1994); "Revitalization of the Silk Road: Development of Cultural Tourism and Protection of Cultural Heritage in Uzbekistan" (Bukhara, 21-22 February, 1996); "The Silk Road...between historical depth and reality" (Baghdad, House of Wisdom, September 18-19, 2019).

Of interest is the fact that special research institutions were set up in some countries of the East (India, China, Sri Lanka) to study the Silk Road: Institute of Hirayama in Kamakura (Japan) issuing a yearbook "Archaeology and Art of the Silk Road"; International Institute for Central Asian Studies in Samarkand (IICAS); International Institute for Study of Nomadic Civilizations in Ulan-Bator (Whitfield, 2004, p269).

Nevertheless, reliable sources on the life and culture of the reviewed period remain to be very scanty. The Sources proved to be the quintessence of long-term explorations archaeologists, orientalists, philosophers and culturologists of and thus gave weight to the region' potential, its ability to preserve centuries-long identity and take part in adopting geopolitical decisions (Boulnois, 2005, p. 54).

Through the instrumentality of its branching network caravan roads, the Silk Road connected the West and the East of Eurasia. Caravan routes crossed China, Kazakhstan, Kyrgyzstan, Tajikistan, Turkmenistan, and Uzbekistan. The roads led to Korea and Japan in the east; Eastern and Western Europe, Russia in the west; India in the south; Near and Middle East in the south-west. These were roads with two-way traffic to comply with achievements of scientific thought, cultural values and religions of the reviewed period. These were effective lines of information through the mediation of merchants, travelers and diplomats dissemination (Whitfield, 1999, p. 77).

No definite answer has ever existed regarding the date of the Silk Road putting into service. One can indicate separate sections of the road only that go back to the III-II millenniums BC Ancient ties had been established thanks to the development of lazurite in the mountains of Badakhshan. The mineral was exported to Iran, Mesopotamia, middle of the I millennium Anatolia, Egypt and Syria. In the BC the Badakhshan lazurite came to China. Along with "the Lazurite route", there existed "The Nephrite route" that connected Eastern Turkestan with China (Boulnois, 2005, p. 61). In the middle of the I millennium BC the so-called "Steppe route" started working; it set in a large bend of Hwang Ho, traversed the eastern and northern spurs of Altai, steppes of Kazakhstan and Black Sea region reached lands of Greeks and Etruscans (Zhang, 2005, p. 31).

The Silk Road is believed to start operating as single diplomatic and trade artery. It was Zhang Qian who initiated the idea. In 138 BC, an ambassadorial caravan came out of the Han capital to accompany prince ZhangQian sent on a mission to the unknown countries of the West by Emperor Wudi. Thirteen years later, Zhang Qian came back. He reached provinces of modern Afghanistan and was the first to have arrived in the Central Asia directly from internal regions of China. He was followed by caravans with silk to the West; and caravans with goods from the Mediterranean, Near and Middle East and the Central Asia for China (Boulnois, 1966, p. 68). However, archaeological explorations in the Central Asia, Kazakhstan, Altai, Siberia and China provided incontestable evidence of spreading the Chinese silk, Iranian carpets on the territory of Eurasia long before the Tsan's mission. A silk horse cloth with Phoenix embroidered on it, and an Iranian carpet discovered in the course of excavations of "royal" burial mounds Pazyryk on Altai are dated to the 5 century BC Contributing to the spreading of precious silk were nomadic and semi-nomadic tribes of Saks and Scythians that helped silk into the Central Asia and Mediterranean, to Europe and India (Elverskog, 2010, p. 103).

Thus, the Silk Road started in Changan, capital of China, to make for a crossing over Hwang Ho, region of Lanchjou and further along the northern spur of Nan Shan to the western outskiris of the Great Wall of China and "Outpost of Jasper Gates". In this place, the road forked to fringe the desert Taklimakan from the north and the south. The northern route crossed oases Hami, Turfan, Shiho and Beshbalyk to a valley of the river Ili; the middle route—from Goachan to Karasharu, Aksu and via a pass Bedel to the shore of Issyk Kul; the southern route—via Dunhuan, Hotan, Garkend and Kashgar to the Central Asia, Bactria, India and the Mediterranean, the so-called "southern road"; the northern route—from Hami and Turfan to Semirechye, south of Kazakhstan, Priaralye, Eastern Europe (Bonavia, 1993, p. 59).

The northern route became particularly brisk in the 6-7 centuries which is explained as being due to the following. First, Turkic kagans were headquartered in Zhetysu -

Semirechye to thus control trade routes; second, rich Turkic kagans and their entourage became large consumers of overseas commodities. This route was arterial, so a greater portion of ambassadorial and trade caravans traversed it in the 7-14 centuries (Chang, 2023, p. 36).

Two stages are singled out in the Silk Road operation period. Initial period, or "Proto-Silk Road" is chronologically related to the formation of the first states in the Central Asia and Kazakhstan (Bactria, Khorezm, states of Saks - Zhetysu and Priaralye). The Chinese silk and lranian carpets are known from excavation materials of the famous "royal" burial mounds of Altai: Pazaryk, Bashadar, Tuekty, Shibe, Katanda, Ulandryk, Uzuktala, Ak-Alah and Berel; sepulchers of Xinjiang: Subashi, Kyzyluyuk, Zathunluk; Semirechye: lssyk; Tuva: Arzhan. Thus, first, or initial stage of the Silk Road is dated to the 6 - first half of the 2 centuries BC Attached to this stage are towns-headquarters and "royal" sepulchers of Saks, Usuns, Hunnu, Savromat and Sarmats, ancient towns of the Central Asia (Che, 1989, p. 201).

The second stage of the Silk Road starts with Zhang Qian's travel in 138 BC and ends with the advent to power of the Ming dynasty in 1405 when a land segment of the Silk Road dilapidated due to China's self-isolation and rapid development of the sea route. Disputable is a date of cessation of the Silk Road. However, unreliability of land routes and the progress retained by the Chinese fleet since the 16 century mean that in the end of the said century the Silk Road as trade and cultural intermedium between the East and the West ceased to exist (Hansen, 2017, p. 136).

As has been noted above, the Silk Road initially served for export of Chinese silk to the European countries. It is also known that goods manufactured in Rome, Byzantine, India, Iran, Arab caliphate and later Russia and European countries were imported to China. A list of unusual, exotic goods is large: myrrh and labdanum; jasmine water and ambergris, cardamom and nutmeg, ginseng and bile of python, carpets and clothes, dyestuff and minerals, diamond and jasper, amber and corals, ivory and "fish tusks", gold and silver bars, furs and coins, bows and arrows, swords and spears. Transported over the Silk Road for sale were horses of Fergana Arab and Nisiya racers, camels and elephants, rhinoceros and tions, cheetahs and gazelles, hawks and falcons, peacocks, parrots and ostriches (Che, 1989, p. 217). Traders were engaged in selling cultural crops, including grape, peach, melon, vegetables and greens, as well as spice and sugar.

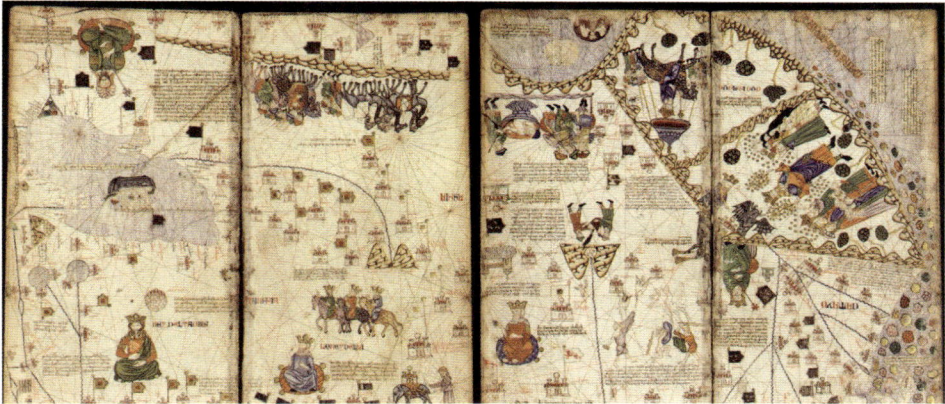

Catalan Atlas depiction of the Silk Road
Source: National Palace Museum Taipei

Still, the Chinese silk remained to be major and permanent item that, together with gold, turned into an international currency. Silk as a gift was highly appreciated; kings and ambassadors were lavishly gifted with this product; free lances were rewarded with the silk as salary; state debts were cleared off. Sources cite numerous evidences of this sort. Thus, Shahinshah of Iran Khosrov I Anushirvan received a silk Chinese garment Ushari (together with other gifts) from a Chinese Emperor that depicted a king in crown and adornments. Silk was held in reverence, as was apparent on palace frescoes of the rulers of China, Central Asia and Eastern Turkestan. Silk clothes of nobility were beautified with all the attributes, details and even stitches (Ceceri, 2011, p. 13).

Not only goods were transported through the Silk Road but also fashion for socially predetermined artistic styles within a certain ethno-cultural environment was spread along the route. An opinion is that it was the Silk Road that contributed to the wide spreading of Timurid style in ceramics notable for blue gamut against the white background. It sprang up at the imperiaf workshops of China during the dynasty of Yuan (1279-1368), then widely spread in Iran, Turkey, the Central Asia. Excellent specimens of ceramic bowls, vases in cobalt are exhibited in many museums (Fisher, 1988, p. 198).

A concept of four "world kingdoms" that symbolized vast regions and countries were spread in the early Middle Ages. Each "kingdom" had its own distinctive advantages in the eyes of contemporaries. It was the establishment of mighty states, such as China under the power of Suy (589. 618) and Tan (618-907), kingdoms of Indian rulers with a center in the town Kanaudja on Ganges, as well as a union of Turks from the Pacific to the Black sea, Persia and Byzantine - that formed a basis of the concept of "four world monarchies". Under the concept, these monarchies were located along four cardinal points: empire of "king of elephants" (India) in the south; "king of jewelry" (Iran, Byzantine) in the west "King of horses" (Turkic kaganates) in the north; "King of people" (China) in the east. Moslem adherents of this concept termed "King of elephants" as "King of wisdom" paying tribute to the importance of Indian philosophy and science; "King of people" as "King of state administration and industry" (bearing in mind famous Chinese inventions); "King of horses" as "King of predatory animals" (Elverskog, 2010, p. 109).

They distinguished two kings in the West: one of them ("King of kings") was king of Persia and then Arabs; another ("King of men" owing to population's beauty) of Byzantine. This concept is manifest in wall paintings near Samarkand where one of them depicted Chinese emperors, others—Turkish khans and Indian Brahmans: third—Persian kings and Roman emperors. It was the model nature of the Baghdad painting that explained carving on thick layer of plaster (carved stucco). Panels depicted grapevines with bunch of ripe grapes, tulips, rosettes, palmettos, belts of rhombs, borders of meanders, bunch of plants. Motifs of fretwork, separate elements of ornament, style - all these find the closest parallels in fretwork that decorates walls of palaces in Afrasiab and Varakhsha, Samarra and Fustat (Forte, 2020, p. 44). In other words, artistic tastes of Baghdad masters and fashion for capital style of the caliphate spread all over the Silk Road to embrace outlying regions of the Moslem urban expanse.

Authors from different countries, contemporaries of the remote past, glorified not only achievements of a state but also eulogized adoption of values of other cultures by native people. The development of the world culture is based on interaction of cultures as evidenced by creative work of the famous Sufi poet-Jalaleddin Rumi (1207-1273) who had his say about mutual tolerance: "It is frequent that a Turk and an Indian get along with each other. And it is frequent that two Turks are like foreigners. Hence, the language of unanimity is quite another story: unanimity is dearer than unified language" (Fisher, 1988, p. 207).

Along with merchandise, cultural samples and specimens of applied arts, architecture and wall painting, the Silk Road acted as a spreader of music and dance art, performances, a sort of medieval "variety". Performances of musicians and dancers, animal tamers, acrobats and mimes, magicians—all these called for no interpretation;

travelling troupes had no language barriers. "Those expressing themselves by bodily movements are all understood equally", wrote Erasmus from Rotterdam [1969, p. aa7]. Similar numbers were shown to Greek basileus, Kiev prince, Turkic kagan, and Chinese emperor.

It has to be kept in mind that foreign orchestras made a part of court personnel. They did performances both in case of "official court ceremonies" and "unofficial court celebrations". Of interest is a description of reception ceremony for ambassadors arranged by a Turkic kagan in his headquarters near Suyab. "Kagan,—noted witness of this ceremony, Buddhist pilgrim Xuan Zhuang,—ordered to bring wines and start music...Foreign music sounded to the accompaniment of metallic ringing. The music being of barbarians notwithstanding, it, nevertheless, fell soothingly on the ear, gladdened heart and thoughts" (Forte, 2020, p. 51). The music of the West, towns of Eastern Turkestan and the Central Asia, enjoyed particular popularity in Tan China. Musical traditions of Kucha and Kashgar, Bukhara and Samarkand blended with the Chinese musical traditions (Fisher, 1988, p. 219).

Carnivals were a great success in all times; these traditions were durable in Moslem countries in later periods as well. It is known that during Novruz masquerades were arranged in Baghdad in the presence of the caliph.

Archaeological finds along the Silk Road routes testify to the development and mutual enrichment of cultures. Thus, significant is a collection of terracotta of the Tan period depicting dancers, actors in mask, and musical ensembles on camels identifiable with representatives of the Central Asian peoples.

The Silk Road played a great role in disseminating religious ideas. Missionaries traversed it to disseminate faith across overseas countries. Buddhism came from India via the Central Asia and Eastern Turkestan; Christianity and later Islam came from Syria, Iran and Arabia (Natang, 1974, p. 77).

As viewed by researchers, Buddhism penetrated from India to China via the Central Asia since the middle of the 1 century BC Greatly contributing to the spreading of this religion in Eastern Turkestan and China were Central Asian theologians and missionaries, particularly, Sogdians, Parthians and Kangyuys. Buddhist monuments were discovered on the route of the Silk Road that traversed the Central Asia. These include a Buddhist monastery of the 1-3 centuries that has for many years been excavated in Termez on Karatobe; a cult erection in the valley of Sanzar (Sogd); Buddhist monuments discovered on the site Gyaur-kala in Merv; a Buddhist monastery of the 7-8 centuries in Adjinatepe, valley of Vakhsh in the south of Tajikistan. Testifying to the strong impact of Buddhism on Turks since the 6 century is Suang Tsan. He writes about goodwill attitude of a kagan of the western Turks to this religion. Other researchers point out that in the first half of the 7 century some rulers of the western Turks adopted Buddhism or patronized this faith (Natang, 1974, p. 81).

Note that the Silk Road also contributed to the spreading of Christianity from the West to the East. The impetus was given in the first half of the 5 century in the Eastern Roman Empire (Syria) where "a heretic sect" of adherents of priest Nestorius sprang up. A teaching of Nestorius was denounced at Ephesus Council in 431, following which Nestorians were mercilessly persecuted, and had to escape to Iran. While at Iran, they established a school at bordering Nisibin and thus close ranks of the political opposition of Byzantine. Rich Syrian merchants and artisans have lost markets in constantinople moved eastwards (Elverskog, 2010, p. 132).

Followers of Manichaeism, a religious trend in Iran, 3 century, with a great number of worshippers from Italy to China, also used the ancient route. Manichaeism as a synthesis of Zoroastrianism Christianity; Christianity; and it adopted an idea of messianism from and an idea of the struggle between good and evil, light and darkness from Zoroastrianism. It was Sodgians that played a crucial role in the spreading of this religion. In the beginning of the 8 century, a supreme leader of Manicheans had a residence in Samarkand. Note that Manichaeism had for a long time co-existed in the Central Asia equally with other religions; Buddhism had a strong influence on pantheon, terminology and even concept of Manichaeism (Forte, 2020, p. 91).

However, Islam that paved its way through the use of not only "fire and sword" but also due to "smooth-spoken speech" of Moslem merchants, gradually superseded Christianity, Buddhism, Zoroastrianism and local cults of the East. The new religion established itself in scores of Silk Road towns and in steppes. Testifying to the spreading of Islam are excavated burials. Note that in the second half of the 9-10 centuries funeral rituals changed to comply with canons typical for Moslems—in pits, crypts of raw brick. The deceased was put with a head north-westwards; face—southwards. No accessories were placed in burials. A large quantity of glazed crockery gives weight to the spreading Islam. Ceramics was based on the use of decorative elements of Arab script. A part of inscriptions is of decorative nature (cannot be read); however, some of them quote wishes, edifications, advises of religious nature. As for metal fabric, fashion for products of copper and bronze, also decorated with inscriptions of religious nature, was widely spread. The point is, in the first turn, about a large group of lamps and couplings for basic posts of yurts in the form of high cylinders on feet (Natang, 1974, p. 111).

An 18th-century map from China purporting to be a copy of one drawn there in 1418, based on the explorer Zheng He's travels around the globe. While some have claimed that it proves Zheng He arrived in the Americas before Christopher Columbus, scholars have questioned the map's authenticity.
Source: Universal Images Group / Getty Images

Archaeological excavations found that trade routes from Europe to Asia and back traversed medieval Central Asia in different places, including steppes, mountains, and fertile valleys. As main trade artery, the Silk Road concurrently contributed to the development of cooperation between many peoples. Routes of the Silk Road united ancient states from China to the Mediterranean and Eastern Europe, played a crucial role in integrating economies and cultures of the peoples of the East and the West. For thousands of years, trade and diplomatic caravans moved along the Silk Road to strictly comply with main routes East-West and North-South. Each country involved in the system of international trade and cultural contacts made its own contribution to the development and transfer of material and spiritual cultures. An eloquent testimony to this is outstanding archaeological monuments located on various sections of this ancient international route (Zhang, 2005, p. 42).

On the other side of Asia—the western side of it—Baghdad represented an important trade communication hub linking east and west in the middle ages. Along the platforms of Baghdad post, hundreds of ships from all areas of the eastern parts of the empire from China to Africa were carrying various kinds of goods and products from Baghdad (Natang, 1974, p. 156). In return, the Arab merchants carried to the Middle East and Europe various goods produced in Baghdad and then they carried these northwards to Russia, Bulgaria, Bukhara, Samarkand and South-east Asia.

In addition to the sea lane from Baghdad to Basrah and Ubulla and across the Arab gulf to the ports of India and China, there were the land routes that linked Baghdad with the east to China and Japan, with the north across Asia minor, Russia, Bulgaria and with the west to Syria, the Mediterranean and Europe (Fisher, 1988, p. 76).

From the above, it can be said that the Silk Road has affected not only the relations between the East and the West but also is considered to be a sample of bringing the cultural dialogue to life in general. Not only the traditions and customs of various medieval cultures were involved into that communication process but modern culture hasn't been left behind too. In human society there emerged a variety of methods and means of communication, storage and dissemination of information; we witness how the history of humankind is undergoing great changes. All that is provoked and closely connected with the above mentioned factors and technological progress. Since ancient times, keeping its individualism the humankind now is experiencing globalization. This means that this process requires a human communication skills and ability. For that we need to get rid of the American-Europeanism, Afro-centrism, which only recognize their values and their culture absolutism, compassionating on others (Zhang, 2005, p. 12).

The concept of "dialogism" is navigator to the better future, because the word "dialogue" has become commonly used in recent years. It is mentioned more often in political programs, research papers, discussions on the topic of educational system etc. In today's culture the concept of dialogism (the phenomenon) has attracted much attention in the social and civil sphere, the main reason for this is the fact that the dialogue has become a tool in solving problems arising in these areas. Especially now in this ever changing world the dialogue helps to solve political, religious and cultural confrontations peacefully.

The *Tabula Rogeriana*, drawn by al-Idrisi for Roger II of Sicily in 1154, one of the most advanced medieval world maps. Modern consolidation, created from al-Idrisi`s 70 double-page spreads, shown upside-down as the original had South at the top

III. Belt and Road Initiative… Closer ties

Civilization emerges from the advancement of human social practices and serves as the collective memory of a nation and its people. Rooted in the unique context of their existence, civilizations embody the wisdom and spiritual pursuits of a nation or ethnic group, manifesting their inherent value. As the future of all countries is closely connected, how can different civilizations get along with each other? The Global Civilization Initiative promotes mutual respect between civilizations, advocates equality, tolerance, coexistence, exchanges and mutual learning among different civilizations, and provides a new paradigm for fostering the harmonious coexistence of diverse civilizations.

With a population of over 8 billion today, there are more than 200 countries and regions, over 2500 ethnic groups, and more than 5000 languages. This diversity has given rise to different civilizations, each deeply rooted in its own cultural context. China's General Secretary Xi Jinping emphasized at the Conference on Dialogue of Asian Civilizations, "Civilizations only vary from each other, just as human beings are different only in terms of skin color and language. No civilization is superior to others. The thought that one's own race and civilization are superior and the inclination to re-mould or replace other civilizations are just stupid" (Xinhua, 2023). Admittedly, if human civilizations are reduced to only one single color or one single model, the world would become a stereotype and too dull a place to live in. We must cultivate mutual respect and reject both arrogance and prejudice. We need to enhance comprehension of the difference between one's own civilization and those of others, endeavoring to facilitate interactions, foster dialogue, and promote harmony among diverse civilizations.

Respecting the diversity of humans inherently requires exchanges and mutual understanding among civilizations. Also, insisting on the equality of civilizations is a way to go beyond the "civilization-centrism" and "civilization-supremacy" theories. The arguments of "Western civilization centrism" and "Western civilization superiority" have long prevailed in the international discourse. Historically, the international community has been dominated by "Western civilization centrism" and "Western civilization superiority," believing the West to be the creator of an advanced modern civilization and the central force in global civilization. This perspective implies that non-Western nations are relegated to dependency on the West, following a Western developmental model for modernization. Nevertheless, as highlighted by Marxist theory, modern Western civilization is fundamentally capitalist, grounded in private ownership, and characterized by inherent inequality and alienation. Unquestioningly adopting the Western modernization model has presented numerous challenges for some nations instead of leading to successful modernization (Bo, 2014).

The first "advocate" in the Global Civilization Initiative convincingly demonstrates that global civilizations flourish on principles of equality and tolerance, developing through exchanges and mutual understanding. This initiative introduces a novel paradigm for fostering harmonious coexistence among diverse civilizations.

From the perspective of human civilization's evolution, the shared values of all humanity represent the collective goals and aspirations pursued by societies during their developmental processes.

Historically, Global Development Initiatives have prioritized the exchange and mutual understanding of civilizations, aspiring to construct an open and inclusive world. The Global Civilization Initiative has further deepened this commitment by advocating for promoting the shared values of all humanity, focusing on understanding the varied connotations of values within different civilizations (Kissinger, 2014, p. 21).

There are different perceptions of value across civilizations, but a shared global vision for a better life persists, summarized by the pursuit of "peace, development, fairness, justice, democracy, and freedom." In the contemporary era, peace and development remain thematic priorities despite the ongoing challenges of local conflicts, hegemony, power politics, widening global disparities, and persistent issues of poverty and disease in developing nations. Fairness, justice, and democratic freedom, on the other hand, are deemed essential guarantees for individual self-development.

Contrary to self-serving interests or the specific pursuits of certain nations, regions, or ethnic groups, the Global Civilization Initiative centers on the shared value pursuits of diverse civilizations in the twenty-first century.

The shared values of all humanity surpass Western universal values. The essence of Western universal values lies in pursuing global civilization homogenization to achieve Western dominance worldwide. The United States, believing that "its own path will shape the destiny of humanity" and "its domestic principles are universally applicable," employs various means to vigorously promote its own values globally. However, the outcome, as sighed by American diplomat Henry Kissinger, is that "universality has proved elusive for any conqueror."

The second aspect of the Global Civilization Initiative highlights the pursuit of shared values in civilizational interactions, which aim to address global risks and challenges, discourage ideological confrontation, and strive to build a multi-coexisting global civilization.

Civilization development serves as a crucial indicator of human society's advancement. Achieving sustainable civilization development requires a delicate balance between inheritance and innovation. "The sustainable development of civilization requires not only passing on the flame and guarding it from one generation to the next, but also responding to the times and introducing new ideas." (Chiozza, 2002, p. 712)

Neglecting development while solely focusing on inheritance results in a civilization unable to adapt to changing times and ultimately hindering its own progress. On the contrary, an exclusive emphasis on development without the necessary attention to inheritance leaves a civilization rootless and without historical and cultural heritage, risking historical nihilism and fostering instability.

Historically, the enduring legacy of Chinese civilization, lasting thousands of years, stands as a model for the successful integration of inheritance and innovation. Overall, the desire for the development of civilization is consistent, while each country's pace and approach vary. Countries should leverage their rich cultural heritage as a driving force for modernization and, in turn, promote the innovative development of traditional culture. Besides balancing tradition and modernity, collaboration and non-interference are also crucial (Xu, 2015, p. 11).

The Global Civilization Initiative's third aspect encourages humankind's modernization with inheritance and innovation. Developing inheritance includes safeguarding historical heritage, fostering identity, and learning from history. On the other hand, promoting innovation involves pushing scientific and technological development and encouraging cultural exchanges for societal progress.

In the political context, Middle Eastern countries can actively engage in diplomatic initiatives facilitated by the GCI and utilize the platform for peaceful dialogue and conflict resolution among Middle Eastern nations and on a global scale. Moreover, they can leverage cultural exchanges and showcase their rich cultural heritage to enhance soft power and improve international perceptions (Norris, 2009, p. 239). For example, following the official listing of the Chinese New Year (also known as the Spring Festival) as a UN holiday starting from 2024, Middle Eastern countries can strive to promote traditional culture and customs, expanding the international influence of their own country's festivals and culture. To resolve conflicts through a cooperative approach, Middle Eastern countries should promote dialogue on shared challenges and collaboration on regional security issues. Additionally, by using the initiative as a platform to promote tolerance, understanding, and religious diversity, Middle Eastern countries can facilitate engagement in interfaith dialogue to address religious tensions.

From an economic perspective, Middle Eastern countries should explore opportunities for increased trade and economic integration with other nations, organize and participate in forums focused on economic development and investment, foster collaboration on innovation and technology transfer, and embrace knowledge exchange programs to enhance technological capabilities. Following the launch of the Belt and Road Initiative (BRI), bilateral connections between China and Middle Eastern countries have undergone further development. This includes signing comprehensive strategic partnerships, China's highest level in diplomatic relations, with Algeria, Egypt, Iran, Saudi Arabia, and the UAE. Additionally, strategic partnerships have been formed with another eight states in the region (Sidło et al. , 2020, p. 91). With the expansion of its geographical scope, the objectives of the BRI have also evolved. Currently, these goals encompass advancing trade, connectivity, financial integration, political coordination, and people-to-people relations

(Xu, 2015, p. 105). Still, infrastructure projects remain at the heart of the BRI; hence, Middle Eastern countries can seek support from China for infrastructure development projects to boost economic growth. In addition, environmental sustainability should be taken into consideration. Middle Eastern countries should implement policies and climate action that contribute to sustainable development, addressing environmental challenges in the region through collaborative efforts.

People-to-people ties are the social foundations of BRI cooperation. The participating countries have passed on and carried forward the spirit of friendly cooperation of the ancient Silk Road, cooperated on exchanges in culture, tourism, education, think tanks and the media, and promoted mutual learning among civilizations and cultural integration and innovation.

A model of people-to-people exchanges characterized by dynamic interactions and diversity has underpinned public support for furthering the initiative.

The Silk Road spirit is consistent with the ideal of "all states joining together in harmony and peace" long upheld by the Chinese nation, with the Chinese people's principles of amity, good neighborliness and "helping others to succeed while seeking our own success", and with the call of the times for peace, development and win-win cooperation.

For young people around the world, the initiative that originates from China's traditional culture contains universal wisdom and foresight shared by different civilizations.

"We Arabs like to use the proverbial expression 'From each orchard, pick a rose' to refer to the diversity and richness of an object", Yara Ismail, a lecturer at Cairo University, told the Global Times (Liuliu, 2023).

The BRI champions equality, mutual learning, dialogue and inclusiveness among civilizations. It upholds the shared values of peace, development, equity, justice, democracy and freedom. It transcends barriers between cultures through exchanges, resolves conflicts through mutual understanding and rejects superiority while promoting coexistence. It encourages civilizations to appreciate their differences, seek common ground and learn from one another.

The Belt and Road Initiative (BRI) is connecting countries across the globe, where people with different skin colors and speaking different languages proudly nurture their cultures. Living in a world of different civilizations, beliefs and customs, should we progress alone or together? And should we stay behind close doors or embrace one another? China's answer is clear: Build a bridge of interaction and mutual learning, and make the BRI a road connecting different civilizations.

The BRI was put forward by China in 2013. Recognizing diversity as a basic feature of the world, BRI's concept of "mutual learning among civilizations" calls for treating all civilizations in an equal and inclusive manner, respecting the systems and beliefs of all countries, and promoting understanding and trust among different civilizations. Rejecting the outdated Cold War mentality, it represents a big step forward in humanity's approach to civilization, and is garnering growing support globally (Ferdinand, 2016, p. 950).

Over the past decade, Belt and Road partner countries have carried out diverse people-to-people exchanges and cooperation, which have become bridges for mutual cultural appreciation. Chinese and foreign archaeologists are working together to explore the cultural relics of the ancient Silk Road and renew the exchanges along the Silk Road with modern-day cultural interactions. The BRI has built a platform for dialogue among civilizations, where the flowers of different civilizations bloom and shine together.

Our world is going through profound changes of a magnitude unseen in a century. China, while actively advocating dialogue among civilizations, is committed to contributing the energy of the Chinese civilization to the world, in an effort to put the concept of "mutual learning among civilizations" into practice, and add new content to the BRI. China's endeavor to further the country's development along the Chinese path to modernization and create a new form of human advancement sends a strong message—modernization does not mean Westernization, and each civilization is valuable for being uniquely its own. This strengthens the confidence of different civilizations to shine together and complement each other. China has put forward the Global Civilization Initiative that calls for respecting the diversity of world civilizations, championing the common values of humanity, promoting the inheritance and innovation of civilizations, and enhancing international people-to-people exchanges and cooperation. The aim is to open up new prospects in cultural interaction and people-to-people bonds among all countries, and contribute more to the progress of human civilization (Bo, 2014).

As once-in-a-century changes continue to unfold globally, humanity is confronted with multiple challenges and crises. The resurgence of anachronistic mentalities trumpeting the superiority of certain civilizations and clash of civilizations is posing a serious threat to world peace, stability, development and progress. At a time when all countries are interconnected with a shared future, inclusiveness, coexistence, interaction and mutual learning among civilizations play an irreplaceable role in advancing the modernization of human society and diverse human civilizations. By working together to build the Belt and Road into a road connecting different civilizations, we people of countries around the world will be able to join force and tackle all kinds of risks and challenges together (Bottici, 2006, p. 319).

This civilizational mentality and dialogue provides not only opportunities for the various parties involved, but, through the exploration of these new development strategies, the creation of a better future.

on the other hand, A sound ecosystem is essential for the prosperity of civilization. For thousands of years, the Chinese civilization has set great store by the idea that humanity must seek harmony with Nature. Into the new era, China is committed to the principle that lucid waters and lush mountains are invaluable assets, and pursuing modernization that features harmony between humanity and Nature. Thanks to persistent efforts, incredible progress has been accomplished in its eco-environmental protection and green development endeavors (Chiozza, 2002, p. 722).

While steadily advancing green development at home, China has explored to contribute its ideas and experience on green development to the Belt and Road cooperation. In 2019, at the opening ceremony of the second Belt and Road Forum for International Cooperation, China made clear that green will be a defining color of the BRI, and green infrastructure, green investment and green financing will be promoted to protect the planet we all call home. This appeal to build a green Silk Road together demonstrates China's leadership as a major country in global eco-environmental governance, and contributes Chinese wisdom to the joint endeavor for a clean and beautiful world (Bottici, 2006, p. 332).

As the world's largest market and equipment manufacturer in the field of clean energy, China has conducted green energy cooperation with more than 100 countries and regions. In Belt and Road partner countries, Chinese investment in green and low-carbon energy has surpassed that in traditional energy. This has promoted greater balance between socioeconomic development and eco-environmental protection, brought more opportunities for green development to participating countries and regions, and delivered green benefits to local communities.

With this strong emphasis on infrastructure and green development, as well as international cooperation, the BRI provides a powerful model towards increasing global prosperity between friendly nations.

Therefore, it can be said that the Belt and Road cooperation is not a solo performance, but a symphony played by all. The BRI has effectively synergized development strategies and practical demands among partners, and has helped partner countries transform their own advantages into tangible fruits of development.

Cooperation for a better world starts with thinking about ourselves and our own beliefs. We are witnessing a paradigm change from a dialogue of cultures to a dialogically born culture. These attitudes are supported by consistent dialogue with one's values. This results in a general intention to align actions with words and link ethical principles (e. g. , peace, fairness, respect, democracy) with social and civic choices. Among the questions we will address are (Jacques, 2009, pp. 66-67):

— Evaluate contemporary China's social, cultural, political, and economic characteristics; assess the impact of its global policy; and understand its compliance with international obligations/laws/norms.

— Examine new global narratives and their interactions with the SDGs to identify potential areas for global cooperation.

— Develop and network independent knowledge and expertise on contemporary China to enhance fact-based policy-making, increase knowledge sharing, create synergies between knowledge nodes, and complement existing knowledge-enhancing strategies.

Passing on the tradition of the Silk Road, today's Belt and Road Initiative (BRI) is also committed to promoting mutual understanding, respect, and admiration among different civilizations. China proposes building the BRI into a road connecting different civilizations, replacing estrangement with exchanges, replacing clashes with mutual learning, and replacing a sense of superiority with coexistence, thus boosting mutual understanding, mutual respect, and mutual trust among different countries. Over the past decade since the BRI was put forward, diverse cultural exchanges among BRI countries have been flourishing. While visioning for joint pursuit of BRI, China also put forward building a community of a shared future for humanity and introduced the Global Civilization Initiative, one of a series of far-sighted conceptions, for the benefit of the world's civilization development.

IV. Huntington's Thesis of the Clash of Civilizations in the BRI Context

In recent years, a civilizational perspective as a part of geopolitical analysis is deployed to fuel geopolitical concern. China's Belt and Road Initiative (BRI) has been viewed as a case of the clash of civilizations between the West and China. This chapter scrutinizes the civilization-based geopolitical approach and analysis. It tests the "civilizational-clash" thesis beyond the Sinic–West relations through the cases of the Sinic–Islamic. An examination and comparison of different civilizational responses to the BRI helps us to develop a critical perspective to investigate the problems in the BRI, in particular the potential civilizational fault-lines along the BRI route. The paper rejects the simplistic version of civilization-based geopolitical analysis as insufficient, problematic, and even misleading. It has sought to refine and nurture a more sophisticated and rigorous approach to the complex connection between the BRI and civilization.

The contemporary Sino-Islamic civilizational intercourse regarding BRI projects can be treated as a litmus test for Huntington's thesis of the clash of civilizations. Huntington predicted in 1996 that the clashes of the future would "arise from the interaction of Western arrogance, Islamic intolerance, and Sinic assertiveness". The "challenger civilizations" of Islam and China would, Huntington proclaimed, develop a "Confucian-Islamic connection" to challenge Western political, economic, and military superiority (Huntington, 1993, p. 33; Huntington, 1996, pp. 183–186). In hindsight, such a union has failed to materialize in the political and strategic sense. Islamic civilization is spread across countries, diluted within them, and divided across Sunni and Shia sectarian lines — rendering the emergence of a Huntingtonesque Confucian–Islamic coalition unlikely.

The scenario in which Confucian and Islamic civilizations themselves could clash, is clearly put to rest by the fact that 27 of the 65 countries that have signed up to the BRI are majority-Muslim (White Paper Media, 2018). On the contrary, the development of China's BRI in Muslim countries can also be interpreted as filling the large gap created by Washington's policies. Following the collapse of the Soviet Union, Washington's approach to development conditionally tied aid and assistance to liberal and democratic political reform. Taken to its most extreme — as in the democracy promotion agenda of the neoconservative George W. Bush administration — this included regime change and military intervention. In the Islamic world in particular, this approach has little merit

(Norris, 2009, p. 244). In contrast, China has cultivated an image of impartiality when it comes to its interaction with governing regimes. It effectively projects its respect for state sovereignty of other countries. While much has been written about the pitfalls of the BRI, the developing world's uptake of it and the adoption abroad of elements of China's development model demonstrate that Beijing's approach has genuine appeal.

The absence of the clash between Islam and Confucianism regarding the BRI can be easily understood by the comparative absence of Chinese civilizational influence in Muslim countries. Confucian penetration into Islamic areas has traditionally been negligible — indeed, the contrariwise process has been much more significant historically.

Certainly, there is no sign of China planning to "export" its religion there through the BRI. unlike the efforts to convert people from Islam to Christianity during the British colonial period which had largely failed.

Officially, Beijing depicts BRI as open and inclusive, and as a manifestation of China's benevolent civilizational force. Beijing has conceptualized the BRI as a Chinese platform for civilizational dialog and intercultural exchange. Drawing upon romantic strands of Silk Road history, China promotes the notion that the BRI will connect and facilitate dialogue and integration between different civilizations (Permanent Mission of the PRC to the UN, 2014).

In his opening speech at the inaugural Belt and Road Forum for International Cooperation in 2017, Chinese President Xi Jinping declared: "In pursuing the Belt and Road Initiative, we should ensure that when it comes to different civilizations, exchange will replace estrangement, mutual learning will replace clashes, and coexistence will replace a sense of superiority." (Xinhua, 2017) Xi reinforced the above view in his keynote speech on May 15, 2019 in the Conference on Dialogue of Asian Civilizations by declaring: "Today, the Belt and Road Initiative, together with the Two Corridors and One Belt, the Eurasian Economic Union and other initiatives, have greatly expanded inter-civilizational exchanges and mutual learning (Xinhua, 2017)". Clearly, China cognizes, and wishes others to comprehend, the BRI through a "win–win" civilizational lens. Xi Jinping also said it is advisable to discard the concept of a clash of civilizations and uphold openness, inclusiveness, and mutual learning in the June 2019 Shanghai Cooperation Organisation (SCO) meeting. SCO needs cultural common grounds just as the U.S.-led alliance system requires democracy as a common bond and norm. Xi had set up the principle of civilizational equality to deal with real-life tension between different civilizational traditions when the BRI projects have been implemented (Xinhua, 2019).

It is commonplace for academics and policymakers alike to couch their analyses of Sino-U.S. competition in geopolitical and civilizational terms. Huntington and his followers, like Kiron Skinner, provide a foundation upon which to build a framework of analysis for the extant U.S.–China rivalry, which plays out in the geopolitical arena, but is also indicative of a clash of two distinct, and possibly incompatible, civilizations. While there is undeniable value in the politics of mobilization against China, they do not capture fully the complex dynamics at play. Two key facets are overlooked, namely civilizational coexistence and the formation of new hybrid civilizations facilitated by China's BRI.

V. Conclusion

From the above, it can be said In modern cultural processes in the humanitarian sphere the concept of "border" is redefined, as it does not divide, but acts as a meeting place for one's own and another's.

In this context, the Great Silk Road, connecting countries, peoples, civilizations, contributed to the development of the alien, the synthesis of different cultural traditions and artistic systems, the inclusion of the achievements of national cultures in the world. The Central Asian region has been a cultural source of the Renaissance since ancient times. Freedom of thought prevailed in the teachings and works of Khayyam, Al-Farabi, Balasaguni and many outstanding figures of science and culture. In the mentality of the peoples, there is a trace of the great caravan routes and nomads.

The aesthetic orientation towards the synthesis of cultural influences and the dialogue of cultural traditions led them to artistic discoveries and the conviction that «starting from antiquity and the early Middle Ages, Roman and steppe, Turkic and Iranian, Arab and Chinese civilizations clashed in conflict on the territory of Central Asia. At the same time, from a geopolitical point of view, this region has always been the subject of conquest as an "intermediate belt", "buffer", "middle" zone that would protect against direct contact".

Land is neither a simple concept nor a mere physical entity despite how it naively appears. It not only generates notions of terrain, borders, territories, and regions; land has historically been thought of as a universal good, a space where crops can be grown and factories built. Land becomes a central preoccupation of human affairs inasmuch as it allows people to relate to their environments in new ways, a backdrop for human progression through time.

Trading routes have always generated vivid images of ancient connectivity due to their geopolitical and geo-cultural significance, especially for those wishing to prove that transcontinental land trade is a panacea for all ills. In Asia and the West, the so-called Silk Road became a vivid expression of this phenomenon. Operating as a pro-globalization rhetoric, the routes that became known as the Silk Road emerged during the Han Dynasty (206 BC–220 AD) and stretched throughout much of Asia, the Middle East, and Europe. Yet, to this day, the notion itself evokes a sense of universal familiarity. No matter one's culture, location, or religion, the Silk Road brings to mind the images of Oriental riches, prosperous oases, and burgeoning trade.

We should remind ourselves that the Silk Road extends far beyond the Oriental tales we are all familiar with of travelers crossing the Central Asian steppes on camels. As a concept, as an imaginary, the Silk Road has been an intrinsic product of Western imperial ambitions. Ever since the Prussian geologist Ferdinand von Richthofen (1833-1905) embarked on a mission to catalogue Chinese natural resources and coined the term "Silk Road" (Die Seidenstraße) in 1877—epitomizing what we now refer to as ancient globalization - he replicated the worldly fantasies of wealth, prosperity, and power of generations before him.

Once it received this name, the Silk Road became "revivable", allowing later engineers and technocrats to plot onto it their visions of ambitious futures to come. The Silk Road became a land in-between in the sense that it refers both to a period of antiquity that is considered a historical fact and to a form of discourse which carries real socio-political consequences.

Suspended in time and caught between often clashing, yet similar, ways of imagining the "Other", the Silk Road not only facilitated commercial and cultural exchange but also symbolized the appetite for foreign cultures, lands, and commodities, bridged distant geographies, and thus opened out unimaginable possibilities.

The Belt and Road Initiative is Beijing's most comprehensive and ambitious foreign policy enterprise to date and is emblematic of China's growing geopolitical aspirations. Studies abound on the topic, and justifiably so—yet conclusions drawn along predominantly civilizational lines are insufficient, problematic, and even misleading. This research thus rejects the simplistic version of civilization-based geopolitical analysis through an investigation of a variety of civilizational responses to the BRI and analyses of Sino-Western, and Sino-Islamic cultural interactions. It has sought to refine and nurture a more sophisticated and rigorous approach to the complex connection between the BRI and civilization.

The fourth Belt and Road Forum for International Cooperation will soon be held in Beijing. It will be the grandest event to commemorate the 10th anniversary of the BRI, and an important platform for all parties to discuss high-quality Belt and Road cooperation. We hope that all parties, standing on the new starting point, will make the pie of development increasingly bigger, so as to provide solid support for people's well-being and create more opportunities for economic growth. In doing so, we will usher in another wonderful decade on this road of global prosperity.

VI. Bibliography

Bo, Peng, "'*The Belt and the Road' and the Integration of Civilizations*", China. org.cn, November 20, 2014.

http://www.china.org.cn/opinion/2014-11/20/content_34105971.htm

Bonavia, Judy, *The Silk Road: from Xi'an to Kashgar*, Lincolnwood, Ill.: Passport Books, in conjunction with the Guidebook Co., 1993.

Bottici, Chiara and Challand, Benoît, "*Rethinking Political Myth: The Clash of Civilizations as a Self-Fulfilling Prophecy*", European Journal of Social Theory, Vol. 9, No. 3 (August 2006), pp.315–336.

Boulnois, Luce, *The Silk Road*, New York: Dutton, 1966.

Boulnois, Luce, *Silk Road: monks, warriors & merchants on the Silk Road*, trans. by: Helen Loveday, Odyssey Publications, 2005.

Ceceri, Kathy, *The Silk Road: explore the world's most famous trade route*, White River Junction, VT: Nomad Press, 2011.

Chang, H. K., *Civilizations of the Silk Road*, New York: Routledge, 2023.

Che, Muqi, *The Silk Road.. past and present*, Beijing [China]: Foreign Languages Press: Distributed by China International Book Trading Corp., 1989.

Chiozza, Giacomo, "*Is There a Clash of Civilizations? Evidence from Patterns of*

International Conflict Involvement, 1946–97", Journal of Peace Research, Vol. 39, No. 6 (2002), pp.711–734.

Clements, Jonathan, *A history of the Silk Road*, London: Armchair Traveller, 2017.

Elverskog, Johan, *Buddhism and Islam on the Silk Road*, Philadelphia: University of Pennsylvania Press, 2010.

Ferdinand, Peter, "*Westward Ho - The China Dream and 'One Belt, One Road': Chinese Foreign Policy under Xi Jinping*", International Affairs, Vol. 92, No. 4 (2016), pp.941–957.

Fisher, Richard B., *The Marco Polo expedition: a journey along the Silk Road*, London: Hodder and Stoughton, 1988.

Forte, Philippe & Andreas Kaplony (edits.), *The Journey Of Maps And Images On The Silk Road*, Brill, 2020.

Hansen, Valerie, *The Silk Road: a new history with documents*, New York: Oxford University Press, 2017.

Huntington, Samuel P., "*The Clash of Civilizations?*", Foreign Affairs, Vol. 72, No. 3 (Summer 1993), pp.22-49.

Huntington, Samuel P., *The Clash of Civilizations and the Remaking of World Order*, (New York: Simon & Shuster, 1996).

Jacques, Martin, *When China Rules the World: The Rise of the Middle Kingdom and the End of the Western World*, (London: Penguin, 2009).

Kissinger, Henry (2014)., *WORLD ORDER Reflections on the Character of Nations and the Course of History*.

Liuliu, Xu, "*BRI champions equality, mutual learning, dialogue and inclusiveness among civilizations.. Shared culture*", In: Global Times, Published: Oct 16, 2023.

https://www.globaltimes.cn/page/202310/1299952.shtml

Natang, Antony, *The Arabs: their victories and Islam glories*, Translated by: Rashed Al-Barawi, The Anglo-Egyptian library, 1974.

Norris, Pippa and Inglehart, Ronald, "*Islamic Culture and Democracy: Testing the 'Clash of Civilizations' Thesis*", in Masamichi Sasaki, ed., New Frontiers in Comparative Sociology (Leiden: Koninklijke Brill NV, 2009), pp.221–250.

Permanent Mission of the PRC to the UN, "*The Silk Road — From Past to the Future*", Chinese Ministry of Foreign Affairs, April 3, 2014.

http://www.china-un.org/eng/gyzg/t1134206.htm

Sidło, K., Andersen, L. E., Lons, C., Peragovics, T., & Rózsa, E. (2020)., The Role of China in the Middle East and North Africa (MENA) Region. Beyond Economic Interests? EuroMeSCo Joint Policy Study.

Thubron, Colin, *Shadow of the Silk Road*, London: Vintage, 2007.

Wells, Donald, *The Silk Road*, New York: Weigl Publishers, 2005.

Whitfield, Susan, *Life along the Silk Road*, Berkeley: University of California Press, 1999.

White Paper Media, *"Belt and Road Initiative puts Islamic Economy at the Forefront"*, Global Islamic Economic Gateway, November 6, 2018.

https://www.salaamgateway.com/en/story/belt_and_road_initiative_puts_islamic_economy_at_the_forefront-SALAAM06112018075409/

Whitfield, Susan (edit.), *The Silk Road: trade, travel, war and faith*, London: British Library, 2004.

Xinhua, "Full Text of President Xi's Speech at Opening of Belt and Road Forum," Xinhuanet, May 14, 2017.

http://www.xinhuanet.com/english/2017-05/14/c_136282982.htm

Xinhua, "Chinese President Calls for Closer SCO Community with Shared Future," Xinhuanet, June 14, 2019.

http://www.xinhuanet.com/english/2019-06/14/c_138144266.htm

Xinhua (2023), Full text of Xi Jinping's keynote address at the CPC in Dialogue with World Political Parties High-level Meeting, The State Council Information Office, the People's Republic of China.

Xu, S. (2015)., Visions and Actions on Jointly Building the Silk Road Economic Belt and the 21st Century Maritime Silk Road. Ministry of Foreign Affairs, China.

Zhang, Yiping, *Story of the Silk Road*, China: China Intercontinental Press, 2005.

China and Serbia: Forging a Shared Future under the BRI

Dragan Trailovic

Research Fellow, Institute of International Politics and Economics, Belgrade, Serbia

Abstract

In May 2024, the President of the People's Republic of China, Xi Jinping, visited Serbia. By then, Serbia and China had already established very strong and well-developed partnership relations, based on a comprehensive strategic partnership and conducted both bilaterally and within the China-CEEC platform and the Belt and Road Initiative (BRI). During this visit, the foundation of their partnership was elevated to the highest level, making Serbia the first country in Europe to enter into a partnership with China in building a community of China and Serbia with a shared future in the new era. This paper examines the relationship between China and Serbia, focusing on their political, economic, military, and cultural cooperation. It traces the historical development of their bilateral relations, highlights their strategic partnership, and analyses their cooperation in various areas such as diplomacy, economy, infrastructure, military, public security, and cultural exchanges. The paper aims to show how China and Serbia are building a shared future under the BRI, demonstrating the extent of their joint efforts.

Keywords: China-Serbia relations; Belt and Road Initiative (BRI), community of shared future, strategic cooperation

Introduction

In recent decades, international relations have been transformed in a way that, over time, in addition to one dominant player in the international arena, new influential regional and global actors have emerged, leading to a gradual change in the very nature of the international system from unipolar to multipolar. New forms of multilateral political, economic, and security integration have developed alongside existing international structures and institutions. Emerging economies, such as the BRICS nations, have become significant drivers of global economic flows while simultaneously challenging certain aspects of the so-called "Liberal International Order", which some of these countries perceive as a U.S.-led and U.S.-centric.

The People's Republic of China stands out as a prime example of a nation initiating new forms of regional and global political, economic, cultural, and security cooperation and connectivity among states. The rapid and substantial growth of the Chinese economy has had a profound impact on global economic currents, and consequently on global political developments, causing shifts in the balance of power at the international level. China has become a major driving force of the world economy and has achieved the capacity to actively participate in and implement policies in numerous areas of regional and global international relations, from politics, trade and finance to cultural exchange and security. The Shanghai Cooperation Organization (SCO), the Belt and Road Initiative (BRI), the Asian Infrastructure Investment Bank (AIIB), the International Organization for Mediation (IOMed) and other such initiatives are the most prominent examples of this (Stekić, 2024, p. 214-215).

China has been increasingly active on the regional and global stage in recent years, introducing new concepts and initiatives. President Xi Jinping has brought innovative ideas to the discourse on models of cooperation and partnerships among states, such as the internationally notable "community with a shared future for mankind". China has also introduced a series of new global initiatives, including the Global Development Initiative, the Global Security Initiative, and the Global Civilization Initiative. These initiatives are a clear manifestation of China's desire to play a more active and prominent role in global affairs. This reflects not only its commitment to strengthening its influence in international relations but also its response to current challenges at the global level by adapting and gaining the experience necessary to be a respected member of the international community. Beyond these specific initiatives, China has also been actively promoting its own values and narratives on the global stage. This includes advocating for a multipolar international system and inclusive multilateralism, emphasizing the importance of cooperation and mutual respect among nations, and especially respect for the principles of sovereignty and non-interference in the internal affairs of states. China is actively promoting the principle of sovereignty globally, emphasizing its importance in diplomatic discourse. Framing this within the UN Charter, China maintains a strict interpretation that prohibits any external interference in a nation's internal affairs and considers territorial integrity inviolable.

In that sense, we have also witnessed the increasing engagement of China in the region of Central and Eastern Europe, including the Balkans and the Republic of Serbia itself. Since the end of the Cold War, relations between China and Central and Eastern European Countries (CEEC) have undergone significant changes. After an initial period of cautious rapprochement, these countries increasingly opened their doors to both trade with China and Chinese investments. Although their political priorities differed from China's, common economic interests increasingly linked them. China, for its part, saw in this region an opportunity to expand its economic engagement and build new trade routes (Trailović, 2020, pp. 128-131; Trailovic & Kiculovic 2014).

During and after the global financial crisis, relations between China and these countries entered a new phase of cooperation. China showed great interest in the region, resulting in the first business forum being held in Budapest in 2011, followed by the first Summit in Warsaw in 2012. Since then, summits have been held regularly, with the last one taking place in China in 2021. The countries involved in the format adopted comprehensive annual guidelines covering various areas of cooperation, such as trade, investment, infrastructure, energy, agriculture, culture, education, and tourism (Trailović, 2020, p. 129; Mitrovic 2018). This framework for cooperation has evolved from the initial "16+1" phase to its expansion with the accession of Greece ("17+1"), and then to a phase where some countries withdrew from the format, and it became known as "14+1". At that time, cooperation within this format faced challenges due to changing geopolitical circumstances (the conflict in Ukraine), internal political tensions and different interests of participating countries, as well as external pressures from major geopolitical actors (U.S. and EU) on member states, as this growing Chinese engagement required them to choose between the West and China. Another reason for its weakening is that it was absorbed by the larger Chinese global Belt and Road Initiative, so now we most often talk about cooperation between China and CEEC within the framework of BRI. The Belt and Road Initiative (BRI) has become the overarching initiative and guiding concept for China's global strategy of economic and infrastructure development, aimed at promoting connectivity and cooperation among countries across Eurasia, Africa, and other parts of the world.

The relations between the People's Republic of China and the Republic of Serbia are based on a comprehensive strategic partnership, while Serbia is simultaneously involved in the broader Belt and Road Initiative. Serbia has been a consistent participant in the BRI, sending high-level delegations to all three Belt and Road International Cooperation Forums (Qingyun, 2024). In line with this, the Republic of Serbia has achieved a high degree of formalization, primarily of bilateral relations with China, which are in a clearly visible and stable upward trend. China is deepening its already existing interactions with Serbia by establishing institutionalized long-term cooperation, developing numerous relations with various parts of the Serbian state and society institutions. Such development of bilateral relations between the two countries was crowned by the visit of President Xi Jinping to Serbia in May 2024. On this occasion, a new chapter in relations between China and Serbia and their "ironclad friendship" was opened, marked by the transformation of the existing comprehensive strategic partnership into a "China-Serbia community with a shared future in the new era."

Compared to other countries in the Central and Eastern Europe, the Republic of Serbia is one of China's largest partners in the region, in areas such as economy, politics, culture, and security. Serbia is also the largest trading partner of China and has become one of the main centres for Chinese investments in this part of Europe. The People's Republic of China is present in Serbia in the field of infrastructure projects (construction of bridges, highways, and railways) and significant Chinese investments in Serbia have also been realized in the sectors of metallurgy, energy, mining and automotive industry. The recently signed China-Serbia Free Trade Agreement is likely to further enhance trade by easing the exchange of goods across multiple sectors (Ladjevac, 2024).

Military and security cooperation between China and Serbia has significantly increased in recent years, encompassing key areas of Serbia's national security, including the military and public security sectors. This cooperation includes equipment donations, technology transfers and significant deliveries such as UAVs and missile systems highlighted by high-profile visits. Cultural ties between China and Serbia have also strengthened, evidenced by the signing of numerous agreements for cooperation in cultural festivals, literature, art, and media.

The paper examines the complex relationship between China and Serbia, focusing on their political, economic, military and cultural cooperation. It traces the historical development of their bilateral relations, highlights their strategic partnership, and analyses their cooperation in various areas such as diplomacy, economy, trade, investment, infrastructure, military, public security, and culture.

Ironclad Friendship: The Evolution and Current State of China-Serbia Diplomatic and Political Relations

Political relations, and generally speaking, relations in various fields between China and Serbia can be traced far back in history. Thus, they can be chronologically divided into those from the distant past, referring to the Yugoslav period, and those referring to the more recent historical period which can be divided into two phases: the period during the 1990s and the period from the beginning of the 2000s until today.

Relations between Socialist Federal Republic of Yugoslavia (SFRY) and China have evolved over history, experiencing periods of both improvement and deterioration. These fluctuations were often influenced by broader structural factors at the level of the international system, particularly during the Cold War, due to the nature of the relationship between the two blocs. Yugoslavia immediately recognized the People's Republic of China after its establishment, but due to strained relations between Yugoslavia and the Soviet Union, this recognition did not provoke a reaction in China. Formal diplomatic relations were only established in January 1955, following a thaw in relations between Yugoslavia and the Soviet Union (Ladjevac, 2020, p. 273-275; Arežina, 2020; Mitrović, 2005).

In the years that followed, as already mentioned, relations between the two countries continued in the same manner, with both positive developments and crises. These ups and downs were initiated by the political dynamics within the socialist bloc (ideological issues), relations between Yugoslavia and the Soviet Union, and between China and the Soviet Union, as well as internal political developments in these countries (Arežina, 2020). Relations experienced a significant positive shift from 1978 onward, with the emergence of Deng Xiaoping and his policies of "reform and opening up" (Mitrović, 2005).

China and Serbia's current relations, while influenced by their shared communist history and China's support for the Non-Aligned Movement, is primarily shaped by more recent events. The breakup of Yugoslavia and Serbia's subsequent political rapprochement with China during the 1990s, culminating in the NATO bombing of Serbia in 1999, significantly deepened their bilateral partnership. [1] During the 1990s, the ruling political elite in Serbia (Federal Republic of Yugoslavia) sought to build strong relations with China amid the severe isolation and economic sanctions imposed on Serbia by the West. During this period, various political and economic contacts were established between the two countries, resulting in visits by high-ranking Serbian officials to China. Key agreements on trade, economic, and scientific cooperation were signed during this period (Mitrović, 2005). The shared experience of the 1999 NATO bombing of the Chinese embassy in Belgrade during the aggression on FR Yugoslavia has been a defining factor in the relationship between China and Serbia. China remains unconvinced by NATO's explanation of the incident as an "erroneous attack," fostering a strong partnership with Serbia based on mutual opposition to Western interventionism and commitment to principles of sovereignty and territorial integrity (Belt and Road Portal, 2024; Jureković 2021, p. 141).

Political relations between Serbia and China remained stable and friendly throughout the 2000s[2], despite numerous changes within the countries themselves, particularly the reorganization of the relations between the two republics of the Federal Republic of Yugoslavia, the formation of the State Union of Serbia and Montenegro, and ultimately the separation of Serbia and Montenegro and their independence in 2006. After the breakup of the SFRY, China continued to treat the FR Yugoslavia as its legal successor, followed by the State Union of Serbia and Montenegro, and then Serbia after

---

① During the NATO bombing of the Federal Republic of Yugoslavia, the Chinese embassy in Belgrade was struck, resulting in the deaths of three Chinese journalists, including a Xinhua correspondent.

② In February 2005, then-President of Serbia, Boris Tadić, made an official visit to China.

Montenegro's separation from the State Union (Dimitrijević, 2018, p. 52). Intensive relations between China and Serbia began to develop especially from 2009. During Serbian President Boris Tadić's state visit to China, both nations agreed to elevate their relationship to a strategic partnership (BBC, 2009). This new level of cooperation aimed to boost economic ties and deepen the longstanding friendship between Serbia and China. Serbia and China then agreed to expand their existing cultural, educational, scientific, and technological ties, as well as military and police cooperation, in addition to political and economic cooperation (Ladjevac, 2020, pp. 275-278; RTS, 2009).

The relationship between Serbia and China has been characterized by frequent high-level visits and significant diplomatic interactions. In 2013, Chinese President Xi Jinping and Serbian President Tomislav Nikolić signed a joint declaration on deepening the strategic partnership between China and Serbia, thereby further strengthening the already good bilateral relations between the two countries. Serbia and China agreed to strengthen their bilateral relationship by expanding cooperation in various areas, including trade, investment, infrastructure, agriculture, energy, information technology, the automobile industry, and science and technology. Both countries committed to promoting cultural exchange by establishing cultural centres in each other's states as well (Cooperation between China and Central and Eastern European Countries, 2013). A significant milestone in bilateral relations occurred in June 2016 with President Xi's visit to Serbia, the first by a Chinese president in 30 years. This visit resulted in the signing of a Joint Declaration on the Comprehensive Strategic Partnership (Ministry of Foreign Affairs, n. d.). Delegations of Serbia and China signed a total of 22 cooperation agreements. The agreements covered areas such as construction, infrastructure, telecommunications, trade, defence, media, and others (Obradović, 2016).

While cooperation between the two countries was already at a high level before the COVID-19 pandemic, it has gained further momentum both during and after the pandemic. This is particularly evident in the various forms of assistance, from medical supplies to vaccines, that China has provided to Serbia during this period. During the COVID-19 pandemic, Serbia's officials praised China for its prompt aid and vaccine donations, contrasting it with what they perceived as the EU's slow response.

As Stekić (2024, p. 2018) noted, from January 2020 to December 2022, there were 22 diplomatic activities at the bilateral level, including 13 high-level visits. In April 2020, President Xi and President Vučić had a phone call, followed by a meeting between

President Vučić and Yang Jiechi (Member of the Political Bureau of the CPC Central Committee and Director of the Office of the Foreign Affairs Commission of the CPC Central Committee) in Belgrade. Diplomatic interactions continued in 2021 with a telephone discussion between Chinese Foreign Minister Wang Yi and former Serbian Foreign Minister Nikola Selaković, as well as between president Xi and president Vučić. In October 2021, Wang Yi visited Serbia, affirming the strong relationship between the two countries, when the Protocol on Cooperation was signed, enabling regular bilateral political consultations and consular cooperation. During the Beijing Winter Olympics in February 2022, Vučić met with Xi in the margins of the event. In September 2022, Vučić and Wang Yi met again during the 77th UN General Assembly session (Stekić, 2024, p. 2018).

Serbian President Aleksandar Vučić most recently visited China in October 2023 for the Third Belt and Road Forum, where he met with Chinese President Xi Jinping. During the event, Serbia and China signed several agreements, including the action plan for implementing the Belt and Road Initiative until 2025, a memorandum on economic development cooperation, and an agreement designating the Bank of China as a clearing bank for yuan exchange. Furthermore, three commercial contracts were signed with Chinese companies for transport infrastructure, and a contract was signed for the third phase of modernization of Serbia's fixed network (Baletić, 2024; The Third Belt and Road Forum for International Cooperation, 2023). In June 2024, a Serbian parliamentary delegation visited China, where they met with Zhao Leji, the Chairman of the National People's Congress Standing Committee.

Chinese President Xi Jinping visited Serbia in May 2024, marking a significant milestone in the relations between the two countries. During this visit, a new chapter in relations was opened as the existing comprehensive strategic partnership evolved into a community of shared future between Serbia and China in the new era. Serbia became the first country in Europe to establish such a partnership with China at this level. The visit reinforced strong bilateral cooperation in multiple sectors, including economy and trade, infrastructure, healthcare and biotechnology, science and technology, innovations, digital sector, as well as information and communications, with both sides agreeing to continue high-level political dialogue.

During President Xi Jinping's visit to Serbia, discussions centred on the joint development of the Belt and Road Initiative, highlighting a commitment to enhance cooperation between the two countries. Both sides agreed to leverage the new phase of high-quality development of the BRI and implement the agreements established at the Third Belt and Road Forum for International Cooperation. They pledged to actively pursue the implementation of the Free Trade Agreement and the Mid-term Action Plan for Belt and Road Cooperation for the years 2023-2025, which were signed in October 2023 in Beijing (Ministry of Foreign Affairs, 2024).

China and Serbia have cultivated intense political relations and they share a strong alignment on several key international and domestic issues, emphasizing their support for the principles of sovereignty and territorial integrity, supporting each other in matters of vital state interest. Both nations advocate for international order grounded in international law, which highlights the importance of genuine multilateralism and equality among nations while opposing unilateralism, hegemonism and protectionism (Ministry of Foreign Affairs, 2024).

Central to their relations is Serbia's firm endorsement of the one-China principle, recognizing Taiwan as an inalienable part of China and rejecting any form of Taiwan independence. Both countries oppose the imposition of any solutions regarding the final status of Kosovo that neglect Serbia's sovereignty and United Nations Security Council Resolution 1244 (1999) (Ministry of Foreign Affairs, 2024). China's position as a permanent member of the United Nations Security Council, including its non-recognition of Kosovo's unilateral declaration of independence, is of particular importance to Serbia. In addition, China, along with several other countries, voted against a UN resolution on Srebrenica in 2024. All of this was once again confirmed at the meeting between the President of the Republic of Serbia, Aleksandar Vučić, and the Minister of Foreign Affairs of the People's Republic of China, Wang Yi, during the 79th session of the UN General Assembly in September 2024 (Tanjug, 2024). Serbia also endorses China's approaches to Hong Kong and Xinjiang. In 2019, Serbia joined a statement presented by Belarus on behalf of 54 countries at the UN General Assembly's Human Rights Committee, praising China's policies in the Xinjiang Uyghur Autonomous Region (Xiao, 2019). Serbia backs China's initiatives introduced by President Xi Jinping, including the Global Development Initiative, Global Security Initiative, Global Civilization Initiative, and actively supported China's other global efforts throughout 2022 and 2023, culminating in February 2023 with Serbia signing the Joint Statement on the Establishment of an International Organization for Mediation (IOmed) (Stekić, 2024,

p. 217; Jin, 2024; The Third Belt and Road Forum for International Cooperation, 2023).

Based on all that has been said, it can be concluded that the main characteristics of the political relations between China and Serbia are frequent high-level visits, intensive political dialogue, mutual political trust, and high degree of political coordination in multilateral settings.

Sino-Serbian Economic Partnership in the Context of Bilateral Cooperation, China–CEEC, and BRI

China and Serbia have developed a strong partnership, with their most significant cooperation occurring in the areas of economics, trade, investment, and infrastructure. This cooperation is rooted in bilateral agreements but has been further strengthened through platforms like China-CEEC and the Belt and Road Initiative. Serbia has become a major economic partner for China in the Western Balkans. It's the region's largest trading partner with China and a prime destination for Chinese investments. Chinese companies and banks have a strong presence in Serbia, particularly financing infrastructure projects and investing in sectors like metallurgy, energy, atomotive indistry, and mining. In addition to the Economic and Technical Cooperation Agreement from 2009 and the Comprehensive Strategic Partnership Agreement from 2016 (Ladjevac 2020, p. 276, 279), China and Serbia have signed several additional agreements since the launch of the Belt and Road Initiative, elevating their economic cooperation to an even higher level under the BRI framework. These agreements include: Memorandum of Understanding between the People's Republic of China and the Government of Serbia on Jointly Promoting the Construction of the Silk Road Economic Belt and the 21st Century Maritime Silk Road from 2015 and Bilateral Cooperation Plan between the Government of the People's Republic of China and the Government of the Republic of Serbia under the framework of the joint construction of the Belt and Road Initiative from 2019 (Stekić, 2024, p. 220). The newly implemented China-Serbia Free Trade Agreement (FTA) in 2024 is expected to promote trade expansion through the liberalization of trade flows in various sectors.

Serbia is China's top trading partner in Central and Eastern Europe, and China is Serbia's main trading partner in Asia. In just a few years, Serbian exports to China surged from around $20 million in 2018 to $1.2 billion in 2022. While Chinese exports to Serbia also grew to $2.2 billion in 2022, the overall bilateral trade between the two countries reached $3.55 billion (Stekić, 2024, p. 221). In 2023, trade between China and Serbia continued to grow, reaching a total value of about $6.46 billion. China was a major supplier to Serbia, with imports from China totalling $4.80 billion. At the same time, Serbian exports to China increased, reaching $1.66 billion, showing growing interest in Serbian products in the Chinese market (International Trade Centre, 2024).

China has played a pivotal role in Serbia's infrastructure development. Key projects, funded by Chinese loans, include bridges, high-speed railways, highways, power plants, and metro systems. These investments have totalled billions of dollars. China has participated in several infrastructure projects, including the construction of the Pupin Bridge in Belgrade and the modernisation of the Kostolac thermal power plant, high-speed railways (Belgrade-Stara Pazova and Novi Sad-Subotica), highways (Miloš Veliki and Corridor Fruška Gora), energy plants (Kostolac Thermal Power Plant), and metro systems (Belgrade Metro) (Ivanović & Zakić, 2023, p. 78-79; Mitrović, 2023, pp. 156-158).

Beyond infrastructure, China has made significant investments in Serbian industries. China's investment in Serbia is extensive, particularly in mining and the automotive sectors. Initiated in 2016 with the acquisition of the Železara Smederevo steel factory by the Chinese state-owned Hesteel Group, investments have grown to exceed $3 billion by June 2022 (Ivanović & Zakić, 2023, p. 80). China has made significant acquisitions, such as the mentioned Smederevo Steel Mill and Bor mines, alongside new greenfield investments like the Čukaru Peki project (Ladjevac, 2024, p. 5). In the automotive industry, Chinese companies have invested in several key projects (Shandong Linglong, Mei Ta, Yanfeng, Xingyu, and Minth) (Mileski et. al. , 2023, pp. 104-106)

Table 1. Chinese investments in Serbia

Company	Investment amount (in millions of €)
Zijin Mining	1,260
Linglong Tire	800
HBIS Group	466
Minth Group	370.9

Mei Ta	**124.4**
Hisense Group	**101.2**
Johnson Electric	**65**
Xingyu Automotive	**60**
Yanfeng	**47.1**
BMTS	**22.5**

Source: (Vojnović, 2024)

China's first tire factory in Europe began production in Serbia in 2024. The Linglong Tire factory in Zrenjanin, a $990 million investment, is expected to create over 1, 200 jobs and boost the local economy. The factory is equipped with advanced technology and has plans for further expansion (Cooperation between China and Central and Eastern European Countries, 2024a).

Economic cooperation between Serbia and China has made significant strides in connectivity. In July 2022, direct flights were established between Belgrade and Beijing, operated by Hainan Airlines. By the end of the same year, Air Serbia launched regular flights on the Belgrade-Tianjin route. This growth trend continued in 2024, when Air Serbia announced the launch of direct flights between Belgrade and Guangzhou, starting on September 30th (Cooperation between China and Central and Eastern European Countries, 2024b). This significant expansion of direct air routes between the two countries indicates increasing connectivity and facilitates travel for business people, tourists, and other passengers, which will undoubtedly contribute to further strengthening of economic relations.

China agreed to invest a record-breaking €2 billion in Serbia in 2024 to build wind and solar power plants alongside a hydrogen production facility. This project, expected to be completed by 2028, aims to provide sustainable energy for a nearby copper mine. The investment aligns with Serbia's goals of energy independence and carbon neutrality by 2050, and continues China's trend of substantial investments in Serbia as part of its Belt and Road Initiative (Reuters, 2024).

A new joint centre for China-Europe high-speed railway has been opened in Inđija, Serbia. The opening was marked by the arrival of the first Chinese train carrying raw materials for the Linglong tire factory. This new railway connection offers significant benefits such as enhanced efficiency, stability in supply, and environmental friendliness. By increasing and improving the capacity of the Inđija intermodal terminal, Serbia is becoming an important logistics centre in this part of Europe (Blečić, 2024).

Military and Public Security Cooperation between China and Serbia

Because of its strategic commitment to being a militarily neutral country, Serbia maintains a diversified approach to military cooperation and partnerships, balancing relations with Western countries and traditional allies such as Russia. However, in the past decade, Serbia has increasingly turned to China when it comes to military-technical cooperation and cooperation in the field of the military industry. This is partly driven by the growing sophistication of Chinese military technology, which has seen significant advancements in recent years, as well as new geopolitical circumstances in the world, such as the ongoing tensions between major powers and the increasing frequency of regional conflicts. Moreover, one of the most significant factors driving the accelerated development of military-to-military cooperation between China and Serbia is Serbia's strong need to modernize its defence system, particularly to upgrade its military technologically.

Serbian-Chinese military cooperation has intensified particularly since 2016/2017. It includes several directions that should be realized in the future: holding joint military exercises (was planned for 2020); development of defence technology (technology transfer); donations of military equipment and supplies; exchange of officers for training; procurement of weapons and military equipment.

A significant sign of deepening military cooperation between China and Serbia was the delivery of Chinese drones and surface-to-air missile systems. Since 2020, Serbia has started contracting for the purchase of the CH-92A and later CH-95 reconnaissance and attack unmanned aerial vehicle (drones) from China. Chinese combat drones CH-92A, were presented to the Serbian public in July 2020. Since 2023, the first public display of CH-95 combat drones from China has begun. Also, Chinese expertise was crucial for the success of the project with technology transfer that helped Serbia develop its own drone, "Pegasus" (Knezevic, 2022). Serbia has greatly improved its air defence by acquiring Chinese-made missile systems. In 2022, Serbia received the medium-range FK-3 (HQ-22) system, and in 2024, it introduced the short-range HQ-17AE system. As the first

European country to use Chinese-made missiles, Serbia has strengthened its strategic partnership with China.

Under the newly signed free trade agreement, China will gradually reduce tariffs on Serbian tanks and armoured vehicles over the next ten years, starting with a 15% tariff that will decrease by 1. 5% each year. For artillery and similar equipment, the current 13% tariff will be reduced by 2. 6% annually over the next five years. Serbia will also eliminate tariffs on Chinese weapons imports over the next ten to fifteen years, starting from the current import tax rate of 25% (Baletić, 2023).

So far, the People's Republic of China has allocated over 12 million euros through various donations for Serbian military. Representatives of the Serbian Army had the opportunity to be trained in handling with the help of Chinese instructors. These are means such as self-propelled engineering machines, transport vehicles, integral transport means as well as sanitary and fire vehicles (Vojska Srbije, 2019).

Serbia's military cooperation with China is crucial for several reasons. Firstly, it has significantly contributed to the modernization of the Serbian army, enhancing the country's security, particularly in terms of air defence. Secondly, and no less importantly, it has served as a deterrent to potential adversaries. This military cooperation aligns with Serbia's broader foreign policy objectives and contributes to its overall security posture. For China, this partnership offers several advantages. It provides China with a foothold in the European arms market, expanding its geographic reach. Also, it showcases China's technological advancements and capabilities in the military sector on the global stage.

Sino-Serbian cooperation in the field of public security represents a relatively new area of partnership between the two countries. Although cooperation in this area began as early as 2014 and 2017, it gained significant momentum in 2019. Initially, it primarily involved agreements with China regarding the Serbian procurement and use of surveillance cameras with advanced software capabilities, such as facial recognition software and license plate recognition software for perpetrators of serious traffic violations, aimed at improving public safety. For these purposes, a cooperation agreement was signed with Huawei in 2017, followed by another agreement with the same company in 2018 for the procurement of equipment, works, and services for the implementation of a traffic surveillance project in Belgrade (Mitrović, 2023, p. 153-154).

Cooperation in the field of public security saw substantial progress in 2019, when representatives of the two states signed a Memorandum of Understanding in the field of security, which related to joint police patrols and the installation of cameras with facial recognition technology in Serbia, thus initiating cooperation between the Serbian Ministry of Internal Affairs and the Chinese Ministry of Public Security. On that occasion, a document was also signed that provided for the establishment of a working group that would consider security challenges and solutions related to joint projects implemented on the territory of Serbia within the framework of the Belt and Road Initiative (Ministry of Internal Affairs, n. d.). Based on the aforementioned Memorandum, in 2019, six police officers from the People's Republic of China, together with Serbian police officers, carried out patrol activities in the areas of Belgrade, Novi Sad, and Smederevo, with the main goal of providing assistance to Chinese tourists in Serbia. In addition to joint patrols, a joint demonstration exercise of members of the Ministry of Internal Affairs of the Republic of Serbia and special police units of the Ministry of Public Security of the People's Republic of China was held in the Smederevo steel mill in November 2019 (Predsednik Republike, 2019).

In 2023, the second joint police patrols of Serbia and China were organized. Nine police officers from China and 20 police officers from China carried out patrol activities in the inner-city centres of Belgrade, Novi Sad, and Smederevo with the aim of assisting Serbian police officers in communicating with Chinese citizens, primarily Chinese tourists in Serbia (Radio Slobodna Evropa, 2023). On the other hand, in 2024, six Serbian police officers participated in joint police patrols with their Chinese colleagues in the city of Guangzhou in China (RTS, 2024a; RTS, 2024b).

In September 2024, exercises of special units of the Serbian Ministry of Internal Affairs and the Ministry of Public Security of China were held in China, in which 13 Serbian and 47 Chinese police officers participated. The exercises were attended by the Serbian Minister of the Interior, Ivica Dačić, who was in China to participate in the 2024 Conference of Global Public Security Cooperation Forum in Lianyungang (RTS, 2024a; RTS, 2024b).

Sino-Serbian Cultural Cooperation

Chinese-Serbian cultural cooperation is rich and diverse, encompassing various aspects of cultural exchange and educational activities. This cooperation includes the work of Confucius Institutes and classrooms in Serbia, the Chinese cultural centre in

Belgrade, the activities of the cultural departments of the Chinese embassy in Serbia, and initiatives of Chinese-Serbian associations for cultural exchange. The cooperation between China and Serbia in the field of culture is not one-sided, as Serbia has also established its cultural centre in Beijing. This centre, named after the renowned Serbian writer Ivo Andrić, serves as a bridge between the two cultures. Opened on November 29, 2018, the Centre promotes Serbian art, films, and language in China. The opening of the Centre was preceded by a bilateral agreement between Serbia and China on the mutual establishment of cultural centres (Ambasada Republike Srbije u Narodnoj Republici Kini, n. d.).

Although cultural cooperation between the two countries predominantly occurs at the bilateral level, it also takes various forms within the China-CEEC format and the Belt and Road Initiative, in which Serbia actively participates. For instance, Serbia hosted the 3rd China-Central and Eastern European Countries Art Cooperation Forum on November 2022. The online forum provided a platform for artists and experts to discuss ways to enhance cultural cooperation, particularly in the fields of visual art, film, and animation. The event was co-organized by Serbia's Ministry of Culture and Information and the Ministry of Culture and Tourism of China. In January 2024, Serbia and China have established an Association for the Promotion of the Economy, Trade, Culture, and Tourism, in alignment with China's Belt and Road Initiative. At the opening ceremony, Serbian Culture Minister Maja Gojković emphasized Serbia's commitment to the global development initiatives initiated by China. Over the past decade, more than 50 activities have been realized under the Belt and Road Initiative, primarily through festivals, fairs, and forums (Baletić, 2024). As an additional step in strengthening cultural cooperation between the two nations, The First China-Serbia Culture Communication Forum took place in Belgrade in April 2024 (Han, 2024).

During the official visit of the Chinese president to Serbia in May 2024, the Serbian Minister of Culture signed three documents in the field of culture, as reported by the Serbian Ministry of Culture. Also, a Cultural Cooperation Programme for the period 2025–2028, was signed by the Serbian Minister of Culture and the Chinese Ambassador to Serbia (Vreme, 2024).

Confucius Institutes play a key role in promoting Chinese culture and language in Serbia. The Confucius Institute in Belgrade, founded in 2006, promotes Chinese language and culture through courses and cultural events. Another Confucius Institute in Novi Sad, founded in 2014, offers Chinese language and culture courses, as well as programs that include Chinese calligraphy, tea ceremony, traditional medicine, and cuisine. The institute actively cooperates with local schools and businesses, and is also the official centre for taking Chinese language tests. In 2024, the third Confucius Institute in Serbia was established at the Faculty of Philosophy in Niš. Its primary goals are to offer free Chinese language courses, provide scholarships for studying in China, and foster cultural exchange by introducing Serbian students and the general public to Chinese culture, traditions, and business practices (Vojnović, 2024).

The Chinese Cultural Centre in Belgrade, the first of its kind in the Balkans, was built with the aim of deepening cultural and economic cooperation between China and Serbia. This centre includes a restaurant, hotel, business space, library, and various educational facilities, making it a central hub for promoting Chinese culture.

Educational cooperation between Serbia and China is realized through a series of cooperation agreements between universities, such as the University of Belgrade, the University of Novi Sad, and the University of Niš. These agreements enable the exchange of students and professors, contributing to cultural understanding and academic connections. The University of Kragujevac has established cooperation with Chinese companies through joint laboratories and projects in the field of information technology. The Chinese company Linglong offers scholarships to students of technical sciences, further stimulating academic exchange and cooperation (Trailovic, 2021).

Chinese media, such as China Global Television Network (CGTN) and China Radio International, have a presence in Serbia, providing content in Serbian (CRIonline Srpski). During Chinese President Xi Jinping's visit to Belgrade in May 2024, three major Serbian media outlets and the press service of President Aleksandar Vučić signed agreements with Chinese media companies. Representatives from Radio Television of Serbia and Politika newspaper exchanged agreements with the China Media Group to deepen cooperation. The Serbian President's media advisor and the news agency Tanjug signed agreements with the China Media Group and Xinhua news agency to facilitate news exchange (Stojanović, 2024).

Conclusion

In recent years, China has significantly increased its global presence, primarily through economic initiatives like the Belt and Road Initiative (BRI), but recently China also expanded its strategy to include comprehensive, not just economic, proposals (initiatives) for global transformation – GDI, GSI, GCI. These initiatives serve as vital components of China's foreign policy, offering a platform for the country to advocate its vision for the global order, but more important, Chinese understanding of the key concepts and principles. The basic principles on which the Belt and Road Initiative rests are mutual cooperation and consultation based on mutual benefit among the participating countries. An important principle underlying the Initiative is openness and inclusiveness, meaning that it is open to all countries and is designed to promote regional and global economic cooperation and development and strengthen cultural and social ties between the participating countries.

The partnership between China and Serbia under the Belt and Road Initiative (BRI) shows how two countries can work together closely in many areas. This partnership, now known as the "China-Serbia community with a shared future in the new era," highlights their strong and strategic relationship. A key part of their cooperation is the significant investments China has made in Serbia's infrastructure, including building bridges, highways, and railways. These projects have made Serbia an important part of the BRI. The new China-Serbia Free Trade Agreement signed in 2024 further strengthens their economic ties, making it easier for both countries to trade and invest in each other.

Military and security cooperation has also grown, with Serbia receiving Chinese drones and missile systems, and benefiting from technology transfers. This has helped Serbia improve its defence capabilities. Cultural and educational exchanges have become more common, with three Confucius Institutes and the Chinese Cultural Centre in Belgrade promoting mutual understanding and closer cultural ties. Politically, China and Serbia support each other's main interests, such as China's stance on Taiwan and Serbia's stance on Kosovo. Both countries value the principles of sovereignty, territorial integrity, and non-interference in each other's affairs.

Despite the new circumstances in international relations that have caused upheavals in the global geopolitical architecture, in the form of increasingly frequent regional hotspots with the potential to fundamentally shake the existing global order, the cooperation between China and Serbia not only remains stable but is intensifying. The ironclad friendship between Serbia and China has withstood the test of tectonic shifts in the international system.

In recent years, the relations between Serbia and China have seen significant growth across all areas. This progress was highlighted by President Xi Jinping's visit to Serbia in May 2024, marking a new chapter in their so-called ironclad friendship. The transformation of their comprehensive strategic partnership into a China-Serbia community with a shared future symbolizes their deepening ties and shared vision for prosperity. As the first European country to establish such a partnership with China, Serbia sets a precedent for others, emphasizing the importance of cooperation, mutual respect, and shared interests in fostering global development, and stability.

References

Ambasada Republike Srbije u Narodnoj Republici Kini. (n.d.). *U Pekingu otvoren srpski Kulturni Centar – Ivo Andrić*. Retrieved October 4, 2024, from http://www.beijing.mfa. gov.rs/lat/newstext.php?subaction=showfull&id=1543895832&ucat=118&template=He adlinesLat&

Arežina, S. Z. (2020). Sino-Yugoslav relations in the 1949-1977 period: The significance of Josip Broz Tito's 1977 visit to the People's Republic of China. *Zbornik radova Filozofskog fakulteta u Prištini*, *50*(2), 145-163. https://doi.org/10.5937/ ZRFFP50-27003

Baletić, K. (2023, October 23). *Ugovor o slobodnoj trgovini: Carina na kinesko naoružanje pada na nulu*, Retrieved September 28, 2024, from https://novaekonomija.rs/vesti-iz- zemlje/ugovor-o-slobodnoj-trgovini-carina-na-kinesko-naoruzanje-pada-na-nulu

Baletić, K. (2024, January 17). Serbia Cements China Ties with New Trade and Tourism Association. *BalkanInsight*. retrieved September 15, 2024 from https://balkaninsight. com/2024/01/17/serbia-cements-china-ties-with-new-trade-and-tourism-association/

BBC. (2009, August 9). *Strateško partnerstvo s Kinom*. Retrieved October 1, 2024, from https://www.bbc.com/serbian/news/2009/08/090820_srbchinastrategic

Belt and Road Portal. (2024, May 8). *Full text of Xi's signed article in Serbian media*. Retrieved September 4, 2024, from https://eng.yidaiyilu.gov.cn/p/05HHMCRJ.html

Blečić, M. (2024, September 8*). Zajednički centar kinesko-evropske brze železnice u Inđiji*. *IN Medija*. https://inmedija.rs/zajednicki-centar-kinesko-evropske-brze-zeleznice-u- indjiji/

Cooperation between China and Central and Eastern European Countries. (2013, Novembre

2). *China, Serbia vow to deepen strategic partnership*. Retrieved October 4, 2024, from https://www.china-ceec.org/eng/fwpt_1/qt/201610/t20161028_6832066.htm

Cooperation between China and Central and Eastern European Countries. (2024a, September 15). *China's tire factory begins mass production in Serbia*. Retrieved October 5, 2024, from https://www.china-ceec.org/eng/jmhz/202409/t20240924_11495813.htm

Cooperation between China and Central and Eastern European Countries. (2024b, July 7). *Air Serbia announces direct flights to Guangzhou*. Retrieved October 4, 2024, from https://www.china-ceec.org/eng/rwjl/202408/t20240817_11475169.htm

Dimitrijević, M. (2018). Odnosi Srbije i Kine na početku 21. veka. *Medjunarodni problem*, LXX(1), 49–67. https://doi.org/10.2298/MEDJP1801049D

Han, Z. (2024, April 30). First China-Serbia culture communication forum highlights cooperation potential under BRI. *Gobal Times*. https://www.globaltimes.cn/page/202404/1311535.shtml

International Trade Centre. (2024). *Trade Map: Bilateral trade between China and Serbia Product*, Retrieved August 28, 2024 from https://www.trademap.org/Bilateral_TS.aspx?nvpm=1%7c156%7c%7c688%7c%7cTOTAL%7c%7c%7c2%7c1%7c1%7c1%7c2%7c1%7c1%7c1%7c1%7c1

Ivanović, V. & Zakić. K. (2023). Belt and Road investments in Serbia: Is China a new saviour or a new threat?, *International Problems*, 75(1), pp. 65–92.

Jin S. (2024, April 17). Initiating the establishment of international mediation courts Background, foundation and progress. *International Cooperation Center*. Retrieved August 19, 2024, from https://en.icc.org.cn/specialties/public_diplomacy/318.html

Jureković, P. (2021). Serbia – China's Preferred Partner in the Western Balkans New, In J. Frank & D. Vogl (Eds.), *China's Footprint in Strategic Spaces of the European Union: New Challenges for a Multi-dimensional EU-China Strategy* (pp. 131-146). Vienna, Schriftenreihe der Landesverteidigungsakademie

Knezevic, J. (2022, December 15). *The growing Sino-Serbian military partnership and its implications on Western Balkans' peace and security*. Retrieved August 8, 2024, from https://mondointernazionale.org/en/focus-allegati/the-growing-sino-serbian-military-partnership-and-its-implications-on-western-balkans-peace-and-security.

Lađevac, I. (2020). The Republic of Serbia and the Belt and Road initiative. In A. Jović-Lazić, A. Troude (Eds), *Security Challenges and the Place of the Balkans and Serbia* (pp. 273–283). Belgrade: Institute of International Politics and Economics, Faculty of Security Studies, University of Belgrade. https://doi.org/10.18485/iipe_

balkans_rssc.2020.ch17

Ladjevac, I. (2024). Serbia external relations briefing: Current Bilateral Relations between Serbia and China – China-CEE Institute. *Weekly Briefing*, 69(4), 1–8. https://china-cee.eu/wp-content/uploads/2024/03/2024er01_Serbia.pdf

Mileski, T., Arnaudov, M., Nedic, P., & Klimoska, K. (2023). *The Relation Between China, North Macedonia and Serbia in the Changing Geopolitical Context*, Budapest: China-CEE Institute.

Ministarstvo unutrašnjih poslova. (n.d.). *Čelično prijateljstvo Srbije i Kine*. Retrieved September 24, 2024, from http://www.mup.gov.rs/wps/portal/sr/aktuelno/tema/!ut/p/z0/fY1BDoIwFAWvYmjYNr9gKWXJRhKRaGShdkM-pTUVLKDFeHyJB3D5JpN5IOEC0uHb3tDbw%20WG_7Kvk9SEteZjTqBAs29KspDE9VhsqCgbV6lmfqnq9R-%209gB_K_veTsfZpkBlINzuuPh8s4N71Vdb9cuoCOg-%209LeYUCx87Pu3RBQrx-4avEHE8PbUCTEcMEJUzomKMKUsDQyhnM0jWIwdvn5C3uyEXc!/

Ministry of Foreign Affairs. (2024, May 8). *Joint Statement of the President of the Republic of Serbia and the President of the People's Republic of China*, retrieved September 23, 2024 from https://www.mfa.gov.rs/en/press-service/statements/joint-statement-president-republic-serbia-and-president-people-s-republic-china

Ministry of Foreign Affairs. (n.d.). *China*, Retrieved July 13, 2024, from https://www.mfa.gov.rs/en/foreign-policy/bilateral-cooperation/china

Mitrović, D. (2005). Bilateralni odnosi SCG i NR Kine: geneza, razvoj i perspective. *Međunarodna politika*, 56(1118-1119), 15-23.

Mitrovic, D. (2018). *From Socialist Modernization to Chinese Dream*. Belgrade: Institute for Asian Studies.

Mitrović, D. (2023). The dynamics of the Republic of Serbia's cooperation with China via the Belt and Road Initiative and the "Sixteen plus One" platform, *Journal of Contemporary East Asia Studies*, 12(1), 148–178. https://doi.org/10.1080/24761028.2023.2240999

Obradović, M. (2016, June 18). Šta je sve potpisano danas: Kina i Srbija pišu novu istoriju! *Srbija Danas*. Retrieved September 18, 2024, from https://www.sd.rs/clanak/sta-je-sve-potpisano-danas-kina-i-srbija-pisu-novu-istoriju-foto-18-06-2016

Qingyun, W. (2024, May 8). *BRI projects bring benefits to Serbia*. Chinadailyhk. Retrieved October 6, 2024, from https://www.chinadailyhk.com/hk/article/582653

Radio Slobodna Evropa (2023, September 28). *MUP Srbije najavio nove zajedničke policijske patrole Srbije i Kine*. Retrieved October 7, 2024, from https://www. slobodnaevropa.org/a/zajednicke-policijske-patrole-srbija-kina/32614072.html

Redsednik Republike. (2019, November 28). *Pokazna vežba pripadnika MUP Republike Srbije i specijalnih jedinica policije Ministarstva javne bezbednosti NR Kine*. Retrieved October 6, 2024, from https://www.predsednik.rs/pres-centar/vesti/pokazna-vezba-pripadnika-mup-republike-srbije-i-specijalnih-jedinica-policije-ministarstva-javne-bezbednosti-nr-kine

Reuters. (2024, January 26). *Serbia secures $2.2 bln investment from China for renewable energy facilities*. Retrieved October 2, 2024, from https://www.reuters. com/business/energy/serbia-secures-22-bln-investment-china-renewable-energy-facilities-2024-01-26/

RTS. (2009, August 20). *Tadić u Pekingu*. Retrieved August 11, 2024, from https://www.rts. rs/lat/vesti/politika/103981/tadic-u-pekingu.html

RTS. (2024a, September 10). *Dačić u Kini: Zajedničkim patrolama jačamo prijateljstvo dva Naroda*. Retrieved October 6, 2024, from https://www.rts.rs/lat/vesti/politika/5528929/ dacic-u-kini-zajednickim-patrolama-jacamo-prijateljstvo-dva-naroda.html

RTS. (2024b, September 11). *Saradnja srpskih i kineskih specijalnih jedinica MUP-a – Dačić posmatrao zajedničke vežbe*. Retrieved October 6, 2024, from https://www.rts.rs/lat/ vesti/drustvo/5529484/vezbe-ivica-dacic-policija-.html

Stekić, N. (2024). Analysing Comprehensive Strategic Partnership between China and Serbia. In Sahakyan, M. (Ed) *Routledge Handbook of Chinese and Eurasian International Relations* (pp. 214–227). Routledge: London, New York. https://doi. org/10.4324/9781003439110-18

Stojanović, M. (2024, May 8). Serbia's Pro-Govt Media, President's Press Service, Sign Deals with Chinese Media, *BalkanInsight*. https://balkaninsight.com/2024/05/08/ serbias-pro-govt-media-presidents-press-service-sign-deals-with-chinese-media/

Tanjug. (2024, September 25). *Vučić: Još snažnija podrška Kine za KiM, Lajčaku sam preneo nezadovoljstvo*. Retrieved October 6, 2024, from https://www.tanjug.rs/ srbija/politika/112184/vucic-jos-snaznija-podrska-kine-za-kim-lajcaku-sam-preneo-nezadovoljstvo/vest

The Third Belt and Road Forum for International Cooperation. (2023, October 18). *Xi Jinping Meets with Serbian President Aleksandar Vučić—The Third Belt and Road Forum for International Cooperation*. Retrieved October 6, 2024, from http:// www.beltandroadforum.org/english/n101/2023/1018/c130-1166.html

Trailovic, D. & Kiculovic. B. (2014). Economic and Political Implications of Chinese Engagement in Central and Eastern European Countries In Stelan Scaunas, Eugen Străuţiu, Vasilie Tabara (Eds.) *Political Science, International Relations and Security Studies*, (pp. 196-203), Sibiu: Department of International Relations, Political Science and Security Studies, Faculty of Social Sciences, Lucian Blaga University of Sibiu, Research Center for Political Science, International Relations and European Studies.

Trailović, D. (2020). Vojna i bezbednosna saradnja Kine i Srbije: pokazatelj nove uloge Kine u Evropi, *Politika nacionalne bezbednosti*, 18(1), 125–145. https://doi.org/10.22182/pnb.1812020.6

Trailović, D. (2021). Kulturna diplomatija NR Kine na Zapadnom Balkanu: Srbija u uporednoj perspektivi, *Kultura*, 173, 35-67. 10.5937/kultura2173035T

Vidojković, S. (2024, September 29). Otvaranjem Instituta Konfucije kineska kultura bliža Nišlijama. *Južne Vesti*. https://www.juznevesti.com/Drushtvo/Otvaranjem-Instituta-Konfucije-kineska-kultura-bliza-Nislijama.sr.html

Vojnović, N. (2024, May 6). Trgovina i investicije se broje u milijardama: Evo kako je do sada izgledala saradnja Kine i Srbije i šta možemo da očekujemo od posete Đinpinga. *Blic*. https://www.blic.rs/biznis/privreda/evo-kako-je-do-sada-izgledala-saradnja-kine-i-srbije-i-sta-mozemo-da-ocekujemo-od/8g9pwbh

Vojska Srbije. (2019). *Prikaz sredstava iz donacije NR Kine*. Retrieved September 13, 2024, from https://www.vs.rs/sr_lat/vesti/1A9EA496DDEE11E9AC980050568F5424/prikaz-sredstava-iz-donacije-nr-kine

Vreme. (2024, May 8). *Tri dokumenta o osnaživanju kulture Srbije i Kine*. Retrieved Septenber 15. 2024, from https://vreme.com/kultura/tri-dokumenta-o-osnazivanju-kulture-srbije-i-kine/.

Xiao, H. (2019, October 30). *Joint Statement on Xinjiang at Third Committee Made by Belarus on Behalf of 54 Countries*, Retrieved August 13, 2024, from https://www.chinadaily.com.cn/a/201910/30/WS5db8f3cfa310cf3e355746e3.html.

The Silk Road Initiative (BRI) Contributes to the Promotion of "a Community of Destiny"

Jean-Pierre Page

Editor-in-chief of French Magazine Pensée Libree

The Chinese anthropologist Fei Xiaotong once stressed that *"a society is not simply a collection of individuals; it is a complex network of relationships and cultural practices that bind people together".* This seems to me to be a very good definition of what corresponds and must correspond to the purpose of the Silk Road Initiative (BRI).

It is no longer a project but a reality that is progressing through achievements that contribute to modifying day after day the modernization not only of China and Central Asia but of many countries for which development and cooperation are no longer empty words but concrete infrastructures allowing shared the right of development with other nations.

This vision promotes the response to needs through social justice, mutual understanding, democracy and peace. Therefore, international relations can be profoundly modified, because they contribute to another state of mind, another logic and vision of the future of humanity. We have the responsibility to grow this *"win-win"* approach with a view to build a *"community of destiny"* and multipolarity based on respect for the sovereignty and equality of each state. This is why, we need another architecture of international relations than the one that still prevails and which remains based on hegemony, unilateralism and violence.

From this point of view, the BRI promote a new dynamic, they are a factor of confidence and contribute to demonstrating in practice that there is no inevitability or fatality but that we can together build credible alternatives for all of humanity based on non-interference, solidarity, respect for independence and sovereignty. We can therefore reduce these obstacles that are recolonization, conflict, subordination, wars and above all the exploitation and pillage by a small oligarchy of the workforce as well as the natural resources that are the wealth that people have but of which they have been dispossessed by five centuries of western imperial domination.

Because in the face of the challenges of development and modernization, unprecedented demands for cooperation and solidarity are imposed on each and everyone as necessities. This is why we must support the demand for another logic of development like the one we are witnessing with the dynamic approach of the BRICS, the Shanghai Forum, and the New Development Bank whose existence and innovative choices contribute to give meaning and practical content to the Silk Roads (BRI). This practical and political articulation between these new and relevant institutions can promote profound changes. The upcoming BRICS Summit meeting in Kazan, Russia, will be a new step forward and an appropriate response to the arrogance of globalised financial capitalism, whose hysterical headlong rush into its deadly logic is being paid for dearly by all nations.

The time has come to completely revise the out-dated system of *Bretton Woods Institutions* and their conditionality's associated with *the Washington Consensus*? The dictatorship of an international financial system built with exclusive reference to the dollar has become anachronism. This is what it has contributes to maintain this gigantic debt on which the United States is living to the detriment of the rest of the world. There is therefore a weaponization of the dollar that must be challenged.

We have entered a new period of civilization. The world is changing quickly and like never before, which allows us to consider other outcomes, other solutions. The Silk Roads (BRI) strategy, initiated by China and involving 150 countries, is in itself a success that cannot be underestimated or trivialized. It contributes to a change in the balance of power in favour of indisputable qualitative changes for all and without exclusion. Every people, every country with no exclusion can benefit from the BRI and that include the western world, especially Europe.

Therefore, we must welcome a meeting like this one in Xi'an. In my view, it encourages new bilateral or multilateral initiatives that seek to free from the despotism of those who give orders, who themselves remain attached to an old vision that has became a growing rejection among the people. In fact, the time has come to completely revise the out-dated and anachronism legacy of economic, social and political conditionality's, coercive mechanisms, illegal sanctions and interferences imposed brutally in the name of interference that is hidden under the definition of "good governance", this concept developed in its time by the World Bank, the IMF and the U.S. Treasury in the 1980s.

Moreover, the convenience of this concept is that it is made to say one thing and its opposite. In fact, the goal remains the same: to reengineer the state by questioning its democratic functioning, to allow the transfer of popular sovereignty, the power of control of citizens over their institutions and to transfer it to the business world, if necessary by force, and in order to dispossess people of their responsibilities. "*Good governance*" is always associated with other such nebulous concepts that promote the narrative of competitive individualism and American exceptionalism for instance "*the rule of law*", "*transitional justice*", "*universal jurisdiction*", "*responsibility to protect*" (R2P), "*international community*" which in fact are reduced to the community of Western countries alone. These are concepts that constitute real dangers and obstacles to the need of understanding a new world economic order.

The changes that characterize the international situation are obviously not indifferent to this profound transformation of the world. Consequently they are not without reactions from those who see their power continue to erode. We are witnessing on the part of Western countries, mainly the United States and the European Union, a real paranoia which leads them to multiply manipulations, destabilizations, unilateral interventions, conflicts and proxy wars, interferences to the progress of the BRICS as well as universal realisations such as the Silk Roads (BRI).

This is particularly the case when seeking to destabilize China in its region, by contesting the belonging of the province of Taiwan to its territory, or in the China Seas by directly involving itself in border disputes and by instrumental international regulations on the laws of the sea, by provoking "regime change" as we have seen in Pakistan, Bangladesh, Sri Lanka, by multiplying military provocations such as the installation of long-range missiles in the Philippines with the support of the political and military authorities of this country or finally by seeking to poison the positive development of relations between China and India.

In fact, when westerners and the United States talk about applying the rules, it is nothing else than their rules that are totally opposed to the principles of multilateralism and respect of *the Charter of the United Nations*. The more they talk about respecting human rights, the more they practice this policy of double standards. The more they destroy the dignity and even the existence of peoples as illustrated at present by the conflict in the Middle East, in Lebanon, in Palestine, where a genocide is being applied with cynicism in Gaza, through the policy of extermination that Israel practices with total impunity.

Consequently, one cannot underestimate how much the international context and the influence on it of the wars and chaos wanted and deliberately organized by the United States to hinder the progress of this new movement of emancipation that we are witnessing.

Belt and Road Initiative (BRI) is precisely a concrete response in favour of another logic of development, a new international economic order. This is why the BRI has also become a target of Western media, which strives to sometimes minimize its achievements, sometimes to caricature them because they are precisely the opposite of this U.S. obsession of full *spectrum domination* over all human activities. For example, in Europe we are witnessing campaigns aimed at discrediting the BRI by designating them as responsible for the indebtedness of developing countries in Africa or even in Asia, as in the case of Sri Lanka with the achievements of the deep-water port of Hambantota. Thus, so-called experts explain in the media mainstream that indebtedness to China is a strategy to subjugate certain states. In fact, the BRIs make it possible to avoid the debt traps and therefore the hard-core neoliberal dictates of the IMF and the World Bank, as well as those of the financial oligarchy that are ruining so many countries.

The scale of the systemic crisis in Europe, of the recession, without mentioning here the consequences of the war in Ukraine, in particular for countries like France and Germany, which are supposed to be the driving forces behind European construction, bear witness to the sectarianism, arrogance and dogmatic alignment of European leaders with Washington's aggressive policy. Although this is to the detriment of our industrialization, trade, full employment, modernization, investment and peace. Europe has chosen a submission to the United States. In fact, the collective West is facing its own decline and this reality has become an inescapable fact. This is illustrated by economic paralysis, democratic crises, rising inequalities, mass poverty, corruption, the enrichment of a small oligarchy, insecurity, the abandonment of sovereignty, a collapse of moral values, the escalation of intolerance and the decline of critical thinking, the search for chaos and conflict.

However, Europe in its economic and commercial investment policy could play a positive role in favour of the unsatisfied social needs of the nations and peoples of the old continent through, the choice of mutually advantageous cooperation with the BRIs, but ideological and political preconceptions are holding back and thwarting these demands. And this is even to the detriment of Europe itself. It is therefore a fact that the BRIs must face a battle of ideas that should not be underestimated in any way but which implies an harmonization of our agendas to face them collectively.

There is therefore a need to clarify such issues and not consider them as mishaps. For my part, I continue to believe that between risks and opportunities we are engaged in a period of clarification. Consequently, we need to lead this battle of ideas together by multiplying initiatives and exchanges and this in all forms:

That is why!

We cannot conceive the promotion of the BRIs without taking into account the necessary access to modernization. We must strengthen the voice and participation of developing countries in economic decision-making at all levels regionally and internationally and for this we need new instruments. The BRICS and China contribute to this in total coherence!

Thus:

1-It is urgent to ensure the promotion of transfers as well as exchanges of technologies and the strengthening of productive capacities, as well as technological and scientific cooperation with developing countries. These are possible urgent actions and therefore indispensable to any desire for modernization.

2-There is also a need for in-depth reforms of the trading system in order to invest in sustainable projects, combat climate change and its negative effects, moderate food prices by increasing food production in order to build a global system in which no country will be left behind.

The global strategic orientation of the BRI on the development of infrastructure, not only in Eurasia but also in Africa, constitutes a major qualitative change in the geopolitical context. For many nations, it is a matter of national interest. Western powers are desperate because their "*alliance diplomacy system*" is in decline. The overwhelming majority of the countries of the South are dynamically reconfiguring themselves into a new Non-Aligned Movement (NAM). In this sense, the BRI is also a credible way to ward off all attempts to re-establish post-colonial mechanisms.

Chinese academics like to quote a 13th century imperial manual, according to which policy changes must be *"beneficial to the people".* If they only benefit corrupts officials, say this manual, the result is *loan ("chaos").* Because let us remember that it is in fact the Yuan dynasty that offers a fascinating introduction to the workings of the BRI. What was decisive and totally innovative is that at that time, that is to say in the 13th/14th century, all land and sea routes were connected to each other. The planners of the BRI of the 21st century benefit from this long historical memory.

It is therefore not difficult to predict and as we see today that China's industrial production will continue to grow while in the United States, it will continue to decline. There will be new innovations from Chinese scientists, such as artificial intelligence (AI). And so, the spirit of the 13th century Yuan Dynasty will continue to inspire the Silk Roads (BRI).

History is accelerating like never before. Fundamental changes are emerging. They concern societal choices, the requirement for another state of mind based on dialogue, multilateralism and the need for modernization of international relations.

In fact, as never before, humanity is facing challenges that call for another approach to cooperation to overcome the obstacles that hinder any project of modernization and cooperation. Consequently, we cannot conceive of the content of this cooperation independently of *"a positive common vision"* to arrive at collective and useful responses. Whether it is for example industrialization, training to create the conditions for technology transfers without which it is useless to talk about modernization. This requires above all getting out of this neo-colonial vision based on the continuation of the plundering and overexploitation of the peoples of developing countries as well as that of the workers of capitalist countries whose social alienation is widespread.

A real break requires understanding the response to the needs of modernization in a dialectical approach. This is also the case in the field of democracy in companies and the involvement of the worker in decision-making, which would make it possible to break with the lack of responsibility, demotivation, and delegations of power. A workers' democracy choosing self-management or a true self-revolution requires closer cooperation between producers from their workplace to the level of a professional group on a national or international scale. The BRI can contribute to this end. This is why; it is necessary to design common tools and practices that will allow people, workers, and future generations to exchange and share. The goal is to feel connected beyond physical and cultural borders and to implement strong and lasting relationships. It is only by getting rid of our prejudices that we will be able to appreciate and learn from other cultures.

The 3rd Plenum of the Central Committee of the Chinese Communist Party, the relevant reflections and decisions of the latter are contributions that will nourish reflection and action on the purpose of modernization and this is inseparable from our exchanges. This is true on the scale of a huge multicultural country like China, but it can also be a contribution for other nations far beyond their histories, particularities and differences.

Modernization must have as its goal social justice and the improvement of the well being of the population. If this is its goal, do we all have to learn from each other? This is why the concept of modernization is not neutral, because it directly impacts our way of life and our way of thinking. Obviously, the nature of the responses that we provide depends largely on the choice of society that we make! Thus, placing the needs of the people as the goal at the heart of modernization is to confirm the choice of socialism. This is an approach that requires us to articulate national and international, relations of production and productive forces, interaction between infrastructure and superstructure in the sense that Marx understood it. The mode of production of material life conditions the process of social, political and intellectual life. "*It is not the consciousness of men that determines their being; it is conversely their social being that determines their consciousness*".

This is the challenge that must be faced. It requires us to anticipate, to see far! As Chairman Mao Zedong said and as President Xi Jinping opportunely recalled, we must verify the correctness of the approaches by "*the primacy of practice*". The implementation and progress of the Silk Roads (BRI) is an illustration of this.

Economic progress must meet the growing needs of the population, whether in terms of their living and working conditions or the environment, or their conscious participation in the social and political life of the city. For this, innovation and the spirit of initiative must become the driving forces of change.

Wanting to make China a great modern socialist country in all areas by the middle of this century is an ambition that has the value of an example and not a model. This is what is underlined by the important resolution of the 3rd Plenum of the CPC, which does not constitute a catalogue but combat objectives that are articulated and dependent on each other in favour of modernization in the service of the people, by the people and for the people. Thus, the concept of *"new productive forces of quality,"* which emphasizes the development of advanced technologies such as biotechnology, green energy, artificial intelligence and aerospace, represents a significant change, a qualitative step compared to the previous growth model. This approach contributes to reflection and concrete action well beyond China.

I personally had the chance a month ago to visit the impressive installations of the Belt and Road Initiative (BRI) from their starting points in Kashgar and Urumqi in Xinjiang. It was a revelation for me on the relevance and coherence of what from my point of view constitutes the largest program of cooperation between nations in the history of humanity. This success is an indisputable victory of socialism because as I have seen and understood, only a progressive development of the productive forces under the leadership of the CCP has allowed such a transformation. This demonstrates the superiority of the concept of the socialist market. Unlike capitalist economies where deregulation and privatization dominate, China has been able to combine economic reforms with rigorous control by the state and positive redistribution by maintaining a socialist mode of production. In this sense, China's exploits are not only national victories but also advances for the international socialist movement that demonstrates its credibility in the service of humanity and should make us all think when we talk about alternatives. These concrete achievements, whose modernity, usefulness and efficiency are obvious, demonstrate that another path is possible than that of deregulation and privatization; it is therefore possible to make other choices in favour of the future of humanity.

This observation made me think of what Prime Minister Zhou Enlai declared in a premonitory manner in Bandung almost seventy years ago: *"Colonial powers can no longer use the methods of the past to continue their plunder and oppression. The Asia and Africa of today are no longer the Asia and Africa of yesterday. Many countries in this region have taken their destiny into their own hands after long years of endeavours".*

Belt and Road Initiative (BRI) is in fact of a simplicity that Sun Tzu would have appreciated when applied to geo-economics. *"Never interrupt the enemy when he makes a mistake".* In the years to come, what will be decisive are the political responses to be made to the choice of development as well as the preservation of our environment, those that address the social needs of the greatest number, the fight against mass poverty and especially action against the explosion of inequalities, waste and corruption as much as the reflection on the ethical purpose of Artificial Intelligence. It is all a matter of choice and political will!

We must build on the dynamics of the Silk Roads (BRI) and encourage it. There is a requirement that no one is exempt from thinking about: it is to be able to anticipate the contours as well as the content of a *"community of destiny"*, contributing to giving confidence in a credible alternative and an ambition for all peoples without exclusion. Wasn't it Sun Tzu who said, *"He who has no objectives does not risk achieving them"*? This is why it is essential to take into account the five principles of peaceful coexistence that President XI Jinping recalled in June of this year: such as *mutual trust, friendship and cooperation*. In fact, these 5 principles make it possible to open another path towards the *peaceful resolution of historical issues, triumphing over narrow-minded antagonistic and confrontational mind-sets such as bloc politics and sphere of influence.*

By demonstrating that the exploitive relations of production are neither natural nor inevitable, but the result of an explicit political decision, China's example is giving rise to alternative ideas. The growing demands to join the BRICS, the acceleration of the movement toward *dedollarization*, the new wave of decolonization in Africa and the establishment of the *Anti-imperialist Alliance of Sahel states* and the *Confederation of the Alliance of Sahel States*, the intensification of the decolonization struggle of the Palestinian people are all but manifestations of the turmoil of a world in transition, from the old to the new.

It is significant that the essence of *China's Global Civilization Initiative*, which provides a solid response to the values, and concepts that perpetuate a brutal and unjust order, has now received universal acceptance in the recently adopted resolution of the UN General Assembly. In sharp contrast to America's unilateralist vision of the world, China's vision of an *"open and inclusive world"* perceives the diversity of civilizations not as a source of global conflict, but as an engine driving the advance of human civilizations".

This rapidly changing ground reality gives us a historic opportunity to challenge the hegemonic order that has generated inequalities, injustices, exploitation, domination, conflict, wars, and plunder.

Are we ready to seize the opportunity and rise to the challenges of our time?

The Belt and Road Initiative: Catalysing Global Development and Cambodia's Strategic Growth

Kin Phea

Director General of the International Relations Institute of Cambodia

INTRODUCTION

At present, the world economy is undergoing profound changes and faces many challenges, especially under the impact of trade protectionism and anti-globalization trends. BRI, the Chinese-proposed and globally accepted common goods, has provided very important opportunities and platforms for countries to deepen their cooperation. The BRI adopts the principles of open regionalism that welcome the participation of countries around the world. Partners can take part in the cooperation at any level and in whatever area best suits their needs and priorities, domestic conditions and readiness for international cooperation. BRI is a powerful shaper of a new global order and a new global force of peace, stability, prosperity, and harmony. In short, BRI is a global non-discriminatory and inclusive platform of cooperation regardless of region, politics, level and stage of development, culture and religion.

BRI belongs to everyone, particularly the countries that are engaged in concretizing the initiative. We are all the stakeholders and owners of BRI. Intra-regional and interregional connectivity is to be improved under BRI. Political trust, mutual learning, mutual respect, and mutual interests are the foundations of cooperation under the framework of BRI. No country is willing to impose ideas or policies on other countries. Every country shares an equal say in collectively designing and implementing BRI's projects. Collective leadership for a shared opportunity is the philosophy of BRI. Sustainable and inclusive development is the vision of BRI. BRI is a potential accelerator and an effective vehicle to achieve Agenda 2030 and help in advancing several SDGs in participating countries.

Cambodia is one of the most supportive of BRI because the economic opportunities generated from the initiative are tremendous, and infrastructure development and connectivity are the Kingdom's core national interest in joining BRI. Under BRI, many tangible significant achievements have been made, including the construction of Siem Reap International Airport and the Phnom Penh-Sihanoukville Expressway, the Kingdom's first expressway project was fully completed after more than three years of construction and officially launched in October 2022. In a wider context, the importance of the Belt and Road Initiative (BRI) extends beyond the Cambodia-China partnership, serving as a key driver in strengthening China's diplomatic ties worldwide and promoting global modernization.

This paper examines the BRI's impact on development, prosperity, growth, and modernization, emphasizing the Cambodia-China partnership and exploring China's broader international relations. It also highlights the importance of promoting high-quality Belt and Road cooperation to achieve sustainable development and global modernization goals.

THE BELT AND ROAD INITIATIVE (BRI)

The Belt and Road Initiative (BRI), proposed by Chinese President Xi Jinping in 2013, is a significant global endeavor focused on infrastructure development and economic cooperation. Often referred to as a "new Silk Road," the BRI aims to strengthen economic ties and connectivity between China and various countries. Its primary goal is to enhance trade, economic growth, and infrastructure development across Asia, Europe, and Africa.

By 2023, the initiative had expanded its reach to over 150 countries and more than

30 international organizations have signed documents under the BRI framework. Since its inception in 2013 by Chinese President Xi Jinping, BRI has achieved remarkable success in transforming the world. BRI is a global non-discriminatory and inclusive platform of cooperation regardless of region, politics, level and stage of development, culture, and religion.

The initiative is composed of three main parts: (1) the Silk Road Economic Belt, which is a land-based route connecting China with Southeast Asia, South Asia, Central Asia, Russia, and Europe; (2) the 21st-Century Maritime Silk Road, a maritime route that links China's coastal areas with Southeast and South Asia, the South Pacific, West Asia, and Eastern Africa; and (3) the Digital Silk Road (DSR), which focuses on information and communications technology (ICT) partnerships and digital collaboration with developing economies and emerging markets (Sameer Patil & Gupta, 2024).

The BRI sets forth five main goals for participating countries to achieve collaborative development (Xinhua, 2017b):

1. Policy Coordination: Countries should align their economic strategies and policies, engage in intergovernmental cooperation, and build mechanisms for macro policy exchanges to strengthen mutual political trust and expand shared interests.

2. Facilities Connectivity: Improving infrastructure connectivity is a top priority, focusing on constructing international transport networks, enhancing road, port, aviation, and energy infrastructure, and creating a unified system for transport and customs operations across borders.

3. Unimpeded Trade: Efforts should be made to reduce trade and investment barriers, promote customs cooperation, and develop free trade areas to enhance trade facilitation. Countries should expand mutual investment opportunities and deepen cooperation in key sectors like agriculture, energy, and technology.

4. Financial Integration: Deepening financial cooperation is critical to the success of the BRI. This involves building stable currency and financing systems, expanding currency swaps, and promoting financial market development to support large-scale investments.

5. People-to-people Bonds: Strengthening cultural, academic, and social exchanges is essential for building public support for the BRI. Countries should promote educational exchanges, tourism, healthcare cooperation, and joint

cultural initiatives to foster strong ties between their populations.

BRI Bring Prosperity

Zhao Tingyang (2006) argued that conventional European and Anglo-American theories are insufficient for understanding China's unique challenges. According to Zhao, these theories often produce narratives and concepts like the "China threat," "debt trap diplomacy," and discussions around the "rise of China," which may not accurately reflect China's realities (Zhao, 2006).

The realist and liberal theories, which overlook traditional Chinese philosophy and its distinct worldview, values, and methods, are effective at explaining conflict but fall short in understanding harmony. In contrast, Chinese thought, with its emphasis on balance and collective well-being, provides a more complete explanation of how harmony can be achieved, which aligns with China's approach to fostering prosperity through cooperation and stability (Wren, 2023, p. 70).

The BRI has brought about positive changes in the lives of many people. It has focused on improving people's well-being, recognizing that a strong foundation is essential for a stable nation. Over the past decade, the BRI has helped lift 40 million people out of poverty and created opportunities for local communities. Numerous projects, such as schools, hospitals, and stadiums, have been implemented to enhance people's quality of life and happiness.

Particularly, the Belt and Road Initiative has mobilized nearly 1 trillion U. S. dollars in global investments, resulting in the development of over 3,000 projects and the creation of 420,000 jobs in participating nations. The initiative has supported the construction of various national landmarks, essential infrastructure projects, and significant milestones in international cooperation (Xinhua, 2023). The BRI is projected to lift over 3.7 million people out of extreme poverty in BRI regions by 2030, primarily through reductions in border delays and trade costs. This would represent about 0.7 percent of the total population. Additionally, more than 7.6 million individuals are expected to escape moderate poverty under the same conditions (Maliszewska & Van Der Mensbrugghe, 2019, p. 10).

Global Growth and Modernization: BRI's Wider Impact

The BRI has significantly reshaped international commerce and infrastructure.

Regions like Central Asia, Africa, and Eastern Europe have seen substantial benefits from BRI-funded projects, such as roads, railways, ports, and energy infrastructure. This has enhanced connectivity and economic cooperation across large geographic areas. For instance, the China-Europe Railway Express has dramatically reduced shipping times between China and Europe, revitalizing trade along the historic Silk Road.

In 2023, China's financial investments and contractual cooperation in 150 BRI countries amounted to approximately 212 deals valued at USD 92.4 billion. This marks an 18% rise compared to the USD 74.5 billion recorded in 2022. Of the 2023 total, roughly USD 44.6 billion came from investments, while USD 43.7 billion stemmed from construction contracts, some of which were partially supported by Chinese loans. Since the onset of the COVID-19 pandemic in 2020, China's overall engagement has exhibited steady growth (Nedopil, 2024, p. 8).

Chinese BRI engagement in 2023 varied significantly by region. Africa experienced a 47% rise in construction contracts and a 114% surge in investments, making it the largest recipient of Chinese involvement at USD 21.7 billion, surpassing the Middle East, which received USD 15.8 billion. Despite this, Middle Eastern countries remained a key destination for Chinese construction projects, accounting for 36.7% of total BRI construction activity, a 31% increase from 2022.

East Asian BRI countries also saw substantial growth, with Chinese investments increasing by 94% to USD 6.8 billion. In contrast, Latin American BRI countries had minimal construction engagement, receiving only USD 180 million, just ahead of Pacific BRI nations with USD 170 million. However, Latin America saw a 92% rise in investments, totaling USD 5.5 billion and capturing 20. 5% of all Chinese BRI investments abroad (Ezell, 2024, p. 6).

On top of that, A key area of expansion is technology, which has generated over USD14.3 billion in investment within BRI countries (Nedopil, 2024, p. 13). This investment is concentrated in sectors such as battery production, automotive components, electric vehicle manufacturing, and telecommunications. China has emerged as the leading market for electric vehicle (EV) manufacturing and sales. Industry experts predict that China will sell 11.5 million new EVs in 2024, surpassing sales in Europe (3.3 million) and the rest of the world (2.7 million) combined. This represents about 44% of all new vehicles sold in China this year. In 2023, EV sales in China grew by 37% compared to the previous year. In December 2023, China accounted for a significant portion of global EV sales, reaching 69% for that month and 60% for the entire year. By 2030, analysts anticipate that over 70% of annual vehicle sales in China will be electric (Ezell, 2024, p. 6).

China's Digital Silk Road and AI Ambitions

The Digital Silk Road (DSR) was formally introduced in 2015, originally referring to the integration of advanced technologies within the BRI countries. The name draws inspiration from the historic trade routes that linked Europe to East Asia through Central Asia until the 16th century. The DSR had evolved into a major aspect of China's foreign policy, with President Xi continuing to advocate for digital connectivity partnerships, particularly with ASEAN countries (Gordon & Nouwens, 2022).

Chinese companies, through the Digital Silk Road (DSR), fund and develop these digital infrastructures in Indo-Pacific countries. China's participation has involved supplying 5G technology, installing undersea cables and fibre optics, providing satellite dishes, and offering advanced technologies like cloud computing, artificial intelligence (AI), and facial recognition systems. Key initiatives under the DSR include undersea cable installation and the deployment of CCTV cameras (Sameer Patil & Gupta, 2024, p. 10).

In 2023, China launched the Global Artificial Intelligence (AI) Governance Initiative. The initiative is part of China's ambition to become a world leader in AI development. Such initiative emphasizes a people-centred approach, promoting AI technologies that benefit all nations through international cooperation, equality, and mutual benefit (China Daily, 2023). The initiative aligns with the country's broader strategic vision outlined in China's 2017 AI development plan, which sets ambitious goals for AI-driven industrial and economic transformation by 2025 and 2030.

According to the State Council of PRC (2017), China aims to achieve breakthroughs in AI theories and technologies, making China the world leader in AI innovation. By 2025, AI is expected to drive industrial upgrading and economic transformation, with its core industry surpassing 400 billion RMB and related industries reaching over 5 trillion RMB.

By 2030, China aimed to become the world's primary AI innovation hub, achieving breakthroughs in brain-inspired and swarm intelligence, while expanding AI's application across various fields such as manufacturing, defence, and social governance. The country planned to strengthen its AI-related legal and ethical systems, with the AI industry projected to exceed 1 trillion RMB in core value, and related industries topping 10 trillion RMB (State Council PRC, 2017).

The 2023 initiative's emphasis on international cooperation, ethical AI governance, and equitable technological benefits reflects China's desire not only to advance its own AI capabilities but also to influence global standards. This dual focus on domestic AI leadership and international collaboration underscores China's ambition to shape the future of AI on both a national and global scale.

BRI'S IMPACT ON CAMBODIA

Cambodia-China: A Deep-Rooted Friendship and Strategic Partnership

China-Cambodia relation is described as "ironclad" and "rock-solid,"with a shared interest in regional stability. Notably, during the COVID-19 crisis, Cambodia stood with the Chinese people, which shows Cambodia's solidarity and trust. Likewise, China responded by providing vaccines, medical equipment, and medical experts.

The friendship between Cambodia and China is rooted in the five principles of peaceful coexistence: mutual respect's territorial integrity and sovereignty, mutual non-aggression, mutual non-interference in each other's internal affairs, equality and mutual benefit, and peaceful co-existence. The two countries are jointly addressing common and global challenges, strengthening contacts at all levels and across all platforms, and deepening mutual understanding to ensure they continue great achievements at national, regional and global levels.

In April 2019, Cambodia and China signed the Action Plan 2019-2023 for Building a China-Cambodia Community with Shared Future, under which the two countries would take 31 measures in the fields of politics, security, economics, people-to-people relations, and multilateral cooperation (Phea, 2020, p. 21).

In 2022, the Cambodia-China Free Trade Agreement (CCFTA) came into effect, and there has been significant growth in trade between the two countries, along with an increase in Chinese investment in Cambodia. Under the CCFTA, 98 percent of Cambodia's exports to China and 90 percent of China's exports to Cambodia are exempt from tariffs (Kunmakara, 2023).

In 2024, during a bilateral meeting in Vientiane, Laos, at the 44th and 45th ASEAN

Summits from October 9-11, the Chinese government announced over $42 million (300 million yuan) in aid to support infrastructure development in Cambodia (Chheng, 2024).

For Cambodia, infrastructure development and connectivity are our core national interests in joining BRI. BRI has played a crucial role in helping develop its infrastructure and connectivity, such as roads, rails, airports, seaports, hydropower plants, and special economic or industrial zones. Doing so would reduce logistics costs in the kingdom, enhance economic completeness, diversify sources of growth, and become the key components to support trade and attract investment.

BRI's Transformative Impact on Cambodia's Infrastructure and Economy

Cambodia is among the most supportive of BRI because the economic opportunities generated from the initiative are tremendous. Infrastructure development and connectivity are the Kingdom's core national interests in joining BRI. By the end of 2017, more than 2, 000 km of roads, seven large bridges, and a new container terminal at Phnom Penh Autonomous Port were constructed with support from China (Xinhua, 2017a).

On top of that, Sihanoukville, which had benefited from massive Chinese commercial and corporate construction investment in the period 2017-2020, has become a city of "ghost buildings", however, those buildings are simply "underperforming and non-performing assets". The onset of COVID-19 saw many Chinese investors depart the city, leaving a large number of near and incomplete high-rise constructions. Those "grey ghosts" provide a negative view of development. The recent negative campaigns by U.S. media outlets about online casinos, digital scamming, forced labour and human trafficking have also hurt perceptions about China's engagement with Sihanoukville's development.

Under BRI, many tangible significant achievements have been made, including the construction of Siem Reap International Airport and the Phnom Penh-Sihanoukville Expressway. The Kingdom's first expressway project was fully completed after over three years of construction and officially launched in October 2022. Moreover, Cambodia's second expressway, the 135-kilometre road to Bavet City, is being built by China Bridge and Road Corp. under a 50-year build-operate-transfer contract, costing $1.35 billion and taking 48 months to construct (Panha, 2023).

Significantly, the Sihanoukville Special Economic Zone (SSEZ), a key project under China's Belt and Road Initiative (BRI), saw $628 million in trade in the first two months of 2024, a 38.3% increase from the previous year. Jointly developed by Chinese and Cambodian investors in 2008, the SSEZ is designed to accommodate up to 300 businesses and create 100,000 jobs for locals. By early 2024, it had attracted 188 enterprises, generating over 30,000 jobs, underscoring its significant contribution to Cambodia's economic growth (CGTV, 2024).

Cambodia is set to start the Funan Techo Canal project, a $1.7 billion Tonle Bassac Navigation Road and Logistics System, to connect the country's major rivers and waterways. A canal from the Mekong to the sea on the Thailand border further opens the internal riverine transport lines, which now connect 7 provinces to both land and sea routes.

Promoting Bilateral Relations

The BRI has provided Cambodia with opportunities to alleviate poverty and foster the development of its national economy. Cambodia's primary national interests in joining the BRI are focused on infrastructure development and enhancing connectivity. The project has been instrumental in promoting the development of infrastructure and enhancing connectivity, including the construction of roads, railways, airports, seaports, hydropower plants, and special economic or industrial zones.

To accelerate Cambodia's industrialization and agricultural modernization, Cambodia focuses on the "Economic Diversification and Competitiveness Enhancement (Pentagon 1)" and the "Development of Digital Economy and Society (Pentagon 5)" which emphasise agriculture, improving connectivity in transport, logistics, energy, water supply, and digital sectors, enhancing business environment, and promoting investment. The policy also improves the promotion of micro, small, and medium enterprises, strengthening public-private partnerships, and enhancing the banking system.

Therefore, BRI is an excellent opportunity for Cambodia and China to raise their bilateral relationship to a new level. Both countries are at different stages of development and have complement for each other; their political relationship at the highest level is excellent, and both countries are politically stable and peaceful. These conditions make investments and trade profitable and safe, and the BRI is the right development train for Cambodia to board.

Since the cooperation projects under the BRI were launched a decade ago, trade and investment relations between Cambodia and China have reached new heights. The BRI, combined with the Regional Comprehensive Economic Partnership (RCEP) and the CCFTA, is expected to play a crucial role in helping Cambodia reach its economic goals of becoming an upper-middle-income country by 2030 and a high-income country by 2050 (Phea, 2023).

Politically, China is a major country that has always supported the Cambodian people's independent choice of development path, the path best suited to their national conditions, and backed them in defending Cambodia's sovereignty and national security. It also supports the Cambodian people in advancing their major domestic political agenda and socioeconomic development and opposing external interference in Cambodia's internal affairs. In a wider context, the importance of the BRI extends beyond the Cambodia-China partnership, serving as a key driver in strengthening China's diplomatic ties worldwide and promoting global modernization.

CONCLUSION

The Belt and Road Initiative (BRI) has undeniably shaped global economic cooperation and infrastructure development, becoming a critical vehicle for advancing connectivity, trade, and modernization across continents. For Cambodia, BRI has served as a transformative force, fostering significant achievements in infrastructure, economic diversification, and bilateral ties with China. By enhancing road, rail, port, and digital infrastructures, Cambodia is poised to bolster its national development while promoting deeper regional integration.

Cambodia's active participation in the BRI demonstrates how smaller nations can benefit from global initiatives tailored to their specific needs, ultimately contributing to the Kingdom's long-term growth and prosperity. As BRI continues to evolve, it remains a vital platform for fostering sustainable development, supporting the UN's Agenda 2030, and strengthening international partnerships that are rooted in mutual respect, shared prosperity, and collective advancement. The enduring Cambodia-China relationship stands as a testament to BRI's potential to bridge nations and create new opportunities for development on a global scale.

BIBLIOGRAPHY

CGTV. (2024). BRI-backed economic zone in Cambodia reports 38.3% trade growth during January-February period. *CGTV*. https://news.cgtn.com/news/2024-03-27/BRI-backed-economic-zone-in-Cambodia-reports-38-3-trade-growth-1sjqFvzxrJC/p.html

Chheng, N. (2024). Despite slow growth of own economy, China provides grants to Cambodia. *The Phnom Penh Post*. https://www.phnompenhpost.com/national/despite-slow-growth-of-own-economy-china-provides-grants-to-cambodia

Daily, C. (2023). AI for good: China's proposal for global AI governance. *China Daily*. https://regional.chinadaily.com.cn/wic/2023-11/15/c_939197.htm

Ezell, S. (2024). *How Innovative Is China in the Electric Vehicle and Battery Industries?* I. T. I. Foundation.

Gordon, D., & Nouwens, M. (2022). *The Digital Silk Road: China's Technological Rise and the Geopolitics of Cyberspace*. Taylor & Francis.

Kunmakara, M. (2023). Cambodia-China FTA brings growth. *The Phnom Penh Post*. https://www.phnompenhpost.com/business/cambodia-china-fta-brings-growth#:~:text=The%20CCFTA%20was%20signed%20by, Chinese%20Foreign%20Minister%20Wang%20Yi.

Maliszewska, M., & Van Der Mensbrugghe, D. (2019). The Belt and Road Initiative: Economic, poverty and environmental impacts. *World Bank Policy Research Working Paper*(8814).

Nedopil, C. (2024). *China Belt and Road Initiative (BRI) Investment Report 2023*. Griffith Asia Institute.

Panha, H. (2023). Cambodia Breaks Ground for Construction of Second Expressway. *Ministry of Information*. https://www.information.gov.kh/articles/106628

Phea, K. (2020). Cambodia-China relations in the new decade. *New Decade, Old Challenges*, 21-26.

Phea, K. (2023). Scholar: China's BRI boosts infrastructure development, trade, investment in Cambodia. *Xinhua*. http://english.scio.gov.cn/beltandroad/2023-09/01/content_110731276.htm

PRC, S. C. (2017). *Next Generation Artificial Intelligence Development Plan* China State Council

Sameer Patil, & Gupta, P. (2024). The Digital Silk Road in the Indo-Pacific: Mapping China's Vision for Global Tech Expansion. *Observer Research Foundation*. https://

www.orfonline.org/research/the-digital-silk-road-in-the-indo-pacific-mapping-china-s-vision-for-global-tech-expansion#_edn1

Wren, D. J. (2023). An Unconventional Reading of China's Foreign Economic Policy: A Phase of Fluidity and Transformation. *BRIQ Belt & Road Initiative Quarterly*, *4*(3), 68-81.

Xinhua. (2017a). 70 pct of roads, bridges in Cambodia built under Chinese support: transport minister. *Xinhuanet*. http://www.xinhuanet.com/english/2017-07/21/c_136461623.htm

Xinhua. (2017b). Vision and actions on jointly building Belt and Road. *Belt and Road Forum for International Cooperation*, 2. http://2017.beltandroadforum.org/english/n100/2017/0410/c22-45-2.html

Xinhua. (2023). (BRF2023) Reinvestigation: Belt & Road Initiative not a tool for expanding geopolitical influence. *Xinhua*. https://english.news.cn/20231019/ec2113c725ae4 8299ecce91da402415e/c.html#:~:text=Over%20the%20past%20decade%2C%20 the,projects%20and%20milestones%20of%20cooperation.

Zhao, T. (2006). Rethinking empire from a Chinese concept 'All-under-Heaven'(Tian-xia,). *Social Identities*, *12*(1), 29-41.

Thai-Chinese Relations: Achieving Win-win Outcomes through the One Belt, One Buckle (OBOB) Strategy

Kriengsak Chareonwongsak

Senior Fellow at Harvard University

Abstract

This article examines the current state of Thai-Chinese relations and introduces the "One Belt, One Buckle" (OBOB) strategy as a framework to enhance bilateral cooperation, ensuring mutual benefits. Tracing the evolution of Thai-Chinese relations from historical trade to modern economic and diplomatic partnerships, the article identifies key challenges, such as trade concentration, limited infrastructure connectivity, underutilized cultural exchanges, and insufficient grassroots engagement. The OBOB strategy, aligned with China's Belt and Road Initiative (BRI), positions Thailand as the central "buckle" due to its strategic location and developed infrastructure. The strategy emphasizes infrastructure investment, diversification of sectors, and enhancing people-to-people connectivity to promote sustainable cooperation. Thailand's role as the buckle is reinforced by its strong infrastructure, comprehensive trade networks, cultural ties with China, and commitment to regional cooperation. The article concludes with recommendations for strengthening Thai-Chinese relations, including expanding infrastructure connectivity, establishing Thailand as a Special Economic Zone (SEZ), leveraging Thailand's strengths in agriculture and wellness, fostering educational collaboration, and promoting people-to-people exchanges. By implementing these initiatives, both countries can achieve long-term, mutually beneficial outcomes, driving economic growth and regional stability.

Keywords: One Belt, One Buckle, Belt and Road Initiative, Thai-Chinese Relations, Thailand, China

Introduction

From the past to the present, international cooperation has played a pivotal role in promoting security and fostering economic, social, and political progress. The integration of nations through cooperation has not only allowed for the exchange of resources, knowledge, and technology but also strengthened mutual economic power and security. The theory of international cooperation, such as the Interdependence Theory, posits that collaboration at the international level leads to mutual benefits among the participating countries. By sharing resources and knowledge, each country can enhance its strength through collaborative development pathways (Coate, Griffin, & Elliott-Gower, 2017).

In examining the relationship between Thailand and China, it becomes clear that the two nations have enjoyed a close and cooperative relationship in various dimensions, including economic, social, and political spheres. This regional connectivity has foste red continuous development, especially in trade and investment, which has seen exponential growth over the past decades. Strengthening and deepening cooperation between these two countries presents a critical opportunity for both nations to grow and prosper in the present and future.

This article aims to explore and analyze the current state of Thai-Chinese relations and proposes an approach to enhance bilateral relations through a strategy known as the "One Belt, One Buckle" (OBOB) strategy, designed to optimize mutual benefits for both Thailand and China.

1. The Evolution of Thai-Chinese Relations from Past to Present

The relationship between Thailand and China is one that stretches back over centuries, rooted in both cultural exchanges and economic interactions, primarily driven by trade along the historic maritime silk route. These initial interactions, which centered on the exchange of goods such as spices and silk, laid the foundation for a deep and enduring connection. Over time, this relationship evolved beyond trade, becoming multifaceted, with diplomatic and cultural exchanges further solidifying the bond between the two nations.

A pivotal moment in this shared history occurred in 1975, when Thailand and China established formal diplomatic ties (Bangkok Post Group, 2024). Over the last 49 years, this relationship has not only remained stable but has progressively deepened, particularly in strategic areas such as trade, tourism, and regional connectivity. The diplomatic milestone of 1975 was followed by increasing collaboration in various sectors, reflecting the mutual interests and benefits that have emerged between the two nations.

In recent years, China has solidified its position as Thailand's largest trading partner. Bilateral trade between the two countries now exceeds $100 billion annually, with China accounting for nearly 22% of Thailand's total trade in 2023 (Lee & Upadhyaya, 2024). Chinese investments have poured into Thailand, particularly in infrastructure projects such as the Eastern Economic Corridor (EEC) and railway development, under the framework of China's ambitious Belt and Road Initiative (BRI). Furthermore, Chinese tourists have become a critical component of Thailand's tourism industry, with over 10 million Chinese visitors annually before the COVID-19 pandemic.

This growing interdependence marks a significant transformation in Thai -Chinese relations, moving from a traditional focus on trade in goods to a comprehensive partnership encompassing economic, diplomatic, and people-to-people ties. The relationship continues to thrive, offering opportunities for both nations to further enhance cooperation and mutual growth in the coming decades.

2. Strengthening Thai-Chinese Relations-The Need for New Strategic Approaches

As the global landscape continues to evolve, it is imperative for Thailand and China to reassess and strengthen their relationship through new strategic approaches. While the existing ties between the two countries are robust, several gaps hinder the full potential of their partnership. Addressing these gaps will require a concerted effort to enhance cooperation and create a more comprehensive framework for collaboration.

2.1 Concentration of Trade in Specific Sectors

While trade and investment have grown substantially, they remain heavily concentrated in specific sectors. For example, the majority of Thai exports to China are agricultural products which accounted for 41.92 percent of its total agricultural shipments (Xinhua News Agency, 2024), which exposes Thailand to vulnerabilities in fluctuating commodity prices and market demands. Expanding the trade portfolio to include high-tech goods, services, and cultural exchanges would provide a more balanced economic relationship (The Nation Thailand, 2024).

2.2 Lack of Comprehensive Infrastructure Connectivity

There is a lack of comprehensive infrastructure connectivity that can support increased trade and tourism (Xinhua, 2023). Although projects under China's Belt and Road Initiative (BRI) aim to enhance connectivity, more focus is needed on regional integration within Thailand. Addressing this gap will require the development of logistics networks and transportation systems th at connect Thai provinces with major economic hubs in China, enabling smoother trade routes and fostering tourism.

2.3 Partially Leverage the Potential for Cultural and Educational Exchanges

The existing cultural and educational exchanges between Thailand and China do not fully capitalize on the potential for mutual understanding. While there have been efforts to promote Chinese language and culture in Thailand, there is still a significant lack of awareness among Thais about Chinese culture and vice versa (Bangkok Post, 2023b). Strengthening cultural diplomacy through educational programs, exchange visits, and collaborative research initiatives will foster greater empathy and understanding between the two nations.

2.4 The Grassroots Connections Have Been Neglected

While people-to-people connectivity is critical, current initiatives often focus on business and government-level interactions, neglecting the grassroots connections that can further enhance bilateral ties (Zawacki, 2021). There is a gap in fostering collaborations among civil society organizations, students, and local communities. Encouraging grassroots initiatives and promoting mutual visits can create lasting relationships and build a foundation for cooperation that ext ends beyond political and economic realms.

Addressing these areas of opportunity is crucial for enhancing the effectiveness and sustainability of the Thai-Chinese partnership. By focusing on these aspects, both countries can work together to elevate their relationship and achieve mutual benefits in an increasingly interconnected world.

3. The One Belt, One Buckle Strategy Explained

The OBOB Strategy represents a transformative approach to enhancing Thai-Chinese relations through integrated economic and infrastructural collaboration. This strategy seeks to position Thailand as the central "buckle" within the broader framework of China's Belt and Road Initiative (BRI), leveraging Thailand's strategic geographical location and existing infrastructure to facilitate trade and connectivity between China, Southeast Asia and beyond.

3.1 The term "One Belt" refers to the Belt and Road Initiative (BRI), while "One Buckle" emphasizes Thailand's pivotal role in this framework.

Thailand's geographical advantage places it at the crossroads of major trade routes, making it an ideal hub for logistics and transportation(Padovan, 2024). By establishing Thailand as the "buckle," the strategy aims to create a seamless connection between China and its ASEAN plus partners, enabling efficient trade flows and economic integration.

3.2 The OBOB Strategy promotes extensive investment in infrastructure development across Thailand.

Projects such as the Eastern Economic Corridor (EEC) and high-speed rail networks connecting major cities and neighboring countries are crucial components of this strategy. These infrastructure projects not only enhance domestic connectivity but also facilitate cross-border trade, creating a more interconnected regional economy.

3.3 The strategy encompasses various sectors.

By diversifying cooperation beyond traditional sectors, both Thailand and China can tap into new growth areas, fostering innovation and enhancing economic resilience. Collaborative ventures in technology transfer and joint research initiatives can also bolster Thailand's capabilities in high-value industries.

3.4 The One Belt, One Buckle Strategy emphasizes people-to-people connectivity, recognizing that fostering mutual understanding is essential for sustainable cooperation.

Educational exchanges, cultural programs, and community engagement initiatives are vital for bridging gaps between the two nations. Such connections can strengthen ties at all levels of society and promote a shared vision for the future.

In conclusion, the One Belt, One Buckle Strategy offers a comprehensive framework for elevating Thai-Chinese relations. By capitalizing on Thailand's strategic position, enhancing infrastructure connectivity, diversifying cooperation, promoting cultural exchanges, and addressing shared challenges, both nations can achieve mutual benefits and create a more prosperous future together. This strategy not only strengthens bilateral ties but also contributes to regional stability and economic growth in Southeast Asia and beyond.

4. The Reasons Thailand is Suitable as the "Buckle" of BRI

The Belt and Road Initiative (BRI) is designed to enhance connectivity across Asia through a network of infrastructure projects, both overland and maritime. Within this Asian context, Thailand stands out as the most suitable "Buckle" for the BRI, thanks to its unique advantages that distinguish it from other countries in the region.

4.1 Strategic Geographical Location

Thailand's geographical position is a significant asset, making it a natural connector within Asia. Located in the heart of Southeast Asia, Thailand provides direct access to major markets in the region, including Malaysia, Vietnam, and Cambodia. This centrality allows Thailand to serve as a logistical hub for trade routes connecting East and West, facilitating efficient transport of goods and enhancing regional supply chains. Unlike other Asian nations, Thailand's location simplifies the complexities of inter-country logistics, making it the ideal buckle for BRI projects.

4.2 Robust Infrastructure Development

Thailand has invested heavily in developing its infrastructure, particularly in transportation networks. The country's ongoing projects, such as the Eastern Economic Corridor (EEC) and the high-speed rail initiatives, enhance connectivity with neighboring countries. These infrastructure improvements ensure that Thailand can effectively manage and support the flow of people, trade and resources across the region, establishing itself as the central buckle of BRI activities in Asia.

4.3 Comprehensive Trade Networks

Thailand has established extensive trade networks with various Asian countries, including China, Japan, and India. These relationships foster a cooperative environment for BRI projects, promoting collaboration in trade, investment, and development. By serving as a single buckle, Thailand can consolidate these relationships, streamlining trade processes and optimizing logistics, which is crucial for the success of the BRI in Asia.

4.4 Cultural and Economic Ties with China

Thailand has deep-rooted cultural and economic ties with China, dating back centuries. This historical connection fosters a mutual understanding and a collaborative spirit, making it easier to navigate the complexities of BRI projects. Even though other countries like Singapore and Malaysia also maintain significant relationships, these countries lack the same level of historical cultural ties as Thailand. Moreover, countries like Indonesia and the Philippines have substantial Chinese populations but may not have the same depth of integration or influence in their political and economic systems as seen in Thailand (Skaggs, Chukaew, and Stephens, 2024) . The Sino-Thai community plays a critical role in linking Chinese investments to local businesses. The existing people-to-people connections further enhance Thailand's ability to serve as a buckle, promoting seamless cooperation with China and other countries involved in the initiative.

4.5 Commitment to Regional Cooperation

As a key member of ASEAN, Thailand actively promotes regional cooperation and integration. The country's commitment to aligning its development goals with those of its neighbors strengthens its position as the buckle for BRI initiatives in Asia. By facilitating collaborative efforts among ASEAN countries, Thailand can enhance the overall impact of the BRI, ensuring that the benefits are shared across the region.

In summary, Thailand's strategic geographical position, robust infrastructure, established trade networks, political stability, cultural ties with China, and commitment to regional cooperation make it the most suitable "Buckle" for the BRI in Asia. By centralizing efforts in Thailand, the BRI can achieve greater coherence and efficiency in connecting Asia, ultimately maximizing the potential benefits for all stakeholders involved.

5. Achieving Win-Win Outcomes through the One Belt, One Buckle Strategy

The One Belt, One Buckle (OBOB) strategy presents a unique opportunity for both Thailand and China to benefit mutually. Below is a detailed analysis of how each country stands to gain from this partnership, ensuring a win-win situation.

5.1 Benefits for Thailand

Thailand stands to gain numerous benefits from its collaboration with China under the OBOB strategy, particularly in the areas of economic growth and infrastructure development. Through large-scale infrastructure projects, such as the Eastern Economic Corridor (EEC), Thailand can attract substantial Chinese investments in sectors like transportation, logistics, and technology. These investments are expected to stimulate job creation, boost productivity, and support local businesses, thereby driving overall economic growth.

Moreover, Thailand will benefit from increased access to advanced technologies and knowledge transfer. By integrating Chinese innovations into its local industries, Thailand can enhance its production capabilities, raise quality standards, and improve its competitiveness in both domestic and global markets. This technological cooperation positions Thailand for sustained industrial advancement and economic modernization.

Additionally, the partnership with China offers Thailand the opportunity to diversify its trade relations. As Chinese companies adopt the "China +1" strategy, Thailand serves as a gateway for these firms to access ASEAN markets and beyond. This diversification of trade partners strengthens Thailand's economic resilience, reducing its dependence on any single market and making it less vulnerable to global economic shifts.

Aligning closely with China also strengthens Thailand's regional influence. By enhancing its cooperation with China, Thailand reinforces its position as a key player within ASEAN, allowing it to contribute more actively to shaping regional policies and initiatives. This strateg ic partnership bolsters Thailand's diplomatic presence and influence in Southeast Asia and on the global stage.

Furthermore, as Thailand becomes a more attractive manufacturing hub, the OBOB strategy creates new export opportunities. The development of its infrastructure and enhanced access to foreign markets allow Thai businesses to expand their exports, particular ly in light of shifting global supply chains driven by geopolitical factors. This increased export capacity is critical for Thailand's economic growth in an increasingly interconnected global economy.

Lastly, while there are concerns about the influx of Chinese products and investments, Thailand can address these challenges by implementing policies that protect local businesses. By promoting quality standards and supporting local small and medium-sized enterprises (SMEs), Thailand can create an economic environment where both domestic and foreign businesses can thrive. This balanced approach ensures that

Thailand fully leverages the benefits of its collaboration with China while safeguarding the interests of its local industries.

5.2 Benefits for China

China's engagement with Thailand offers significant strategic benefits, particularly in the context of diversifying supply chains amid rising geopolitical tensions. By investing in Thailand, China can reduce its reliance on certain trade routes and create more secure and diversified pathways for its exports and imports. This shift is crucial for mitigating risks associated with geopolitical uncertainties and ensuring the stability of China's global supply chains.

Strengthening ties with Thailand also enhances China's influence in the ASEAN region. Thailand acts as a key conduit for China to deepen its engagement with other Southeast Asian nations, facilitating collaboration on a wide range of regional initiatives. This increased cooperation helps solidify China's leadership role in the region, fostering a stronger diplomatic and economic presence within ASEAN.

In addition to regional influence, investing in Thailand provides Chinese companies with valuable access to emerging markets across ASEAN. As ASEAN economies continue to grow, Thailand serves as a strategic gateway for Chinese firms to expand their operati ons and capitalize on new business opportunities. This partnership not only benefits Chinese enterprises but also reinforces China's position as a major economic player in Southeast Asia.

Moreover, China's investments in Thailand yield economic benefits by boosting the bilateral trade relationship. As Thailand enhances its infrastructure and logistics capabilities, it becomes an efficient hub for Chinese goods to reach international markets. This logistical advantage supports China's broader economic goals by streamlining trade routes and increasing the export of Chinese goods and services.

China's investment in Thailand also strengthens bilateral ties and demonstrates its commitment to fostering mutually beneficial relationships. This helps enhance China's image as a partner in development, countering narratives of dominance and promoting goodwill among ASEAN countries. By positioning itself as a collaborative partner, China can deepen its long-term influence and strengthen its economic and diplomatic relationships in the region.

Finally, China's use of Thailand as a maritime outlet offers significant advantages over other regional alternatives like Myanmar, the South China Sea, and Pakistan. First, compared to Myanmar, which faces internal political instability, Thailand offers a much more stable political environment and well-developed infrastructure. Using Thailand's maritime routes also allows China to avoid the geopolitical tensions present in the South China Sea. While Pakistan offers China access to the Arabian Sea through the Gwadar Port, the region faces security challenges, especially in Balochistan (Aamir, 2024). The difficult terrain and risks of conflict make the route less appealing compared to Thailand's well-connected and peaceful shipping routes, which provide easier access to both the Indian Ocean and global markets.

6. How China Can Support Thailand in Becoming the "Buckle"

To establish Thailand as the "Buckle" in the OBOB strategy, China can provide significant support through various initiatives.

6.1 Enhancing connectivity is essential for maximizing Thailand's role in the Belt and Road Initiative (BRI). China can play a pivotal role by linking Thailand's smaller transportation systems to major international routes, increasing trade efficiency and regional integration. For example, expanding the rail network to connect more major cities in Thailand, such as Chiang Mai and Phuket, directly to the China-Laos railway could enhance trade and tourism. While there are ongoing discussions about expanding the rail network, specific projects and timelines for these connections remain in the planning stages (Bangkok Post, 2023a) This would not only reduce logistical bottlenecks but also support Thailand's tourism and export sectors.

From the perspective of the One Belt, One Buckle (OBOB) strategy, this approach makes sense as it aligns with the core BRI goal of improving infrastructure to facilitate trade across Asia. For China, these connectivity enhancements would provide easier acc ess to Southeast Asian markets, boosting Chinese exports and investments in the region. By improving transportation networks, both Thailand and China stand to benefit economically, with increased trade flows and stronger regional ties, ultimately reinforcing the strategic partnership between the two countries.

6.2 Designating Thailand as the 7th Special Economic Zone (SEZ), akin to established hubs like Shenzhen and Zhuhai, is a strategic move for China within the One Belt, One Buckle (OBOB) framework. This designation would not only attract

Chinese businesses to invest in Thailand but also enable them to leverage the country's strategic location as a regional operational hub. With Thailand already serving as a crucial trade partner, this initiative would further enhance economic ties and facilitate smoother trade routes throughout Southeast Asia.

By establishing Thailand as an SEZ, China would gain access to a more favorable investment climate, allowing its companies to expand their regional footprint while benefiting from Thailand's established infrastructure and skilled labor force. Additionally, this initiative would foster economic diversification in Thailand, reducing dependence on traditional sectors while creating a more robust manufacturing and technology base. Ultimately, this mutually beneficial arrangement would strengthen China's economic influence in the region and promote sustainable growth in Thailand, aligning with China's broader goals of enhancing connectivity and fostering regional development through the OBOB strategy.

6.3 China could focus on investing in sectors where Thailand has inherent strengths, promoting a win-win dynamic through the One Belt, One Buckle (OBOB) strategy.

One key area is Thailand's agricultural sector, positioning the country as a *World Food Capital*. By investing in advanced agricultural technologies and food processing capabilities, China would not only enhance Thailand's export potential but also secure a stable supply chain for Chinese consumers.

Additionally, Thailand's well-established reputation as a *Wellness Capital* for global health tourism can be further developed with Chinese support, particularly by upgrading healthcare facilities and promoting medical tourism. This aligns with China's goal of fostering regional partnerships and economic collaboration.

Moreover, China can invest in Thailand's *Tourism Capital* through infrastructure upgrades, improving accessibility for Chinese tourists, who already make up a significant portion of visitors. Another sector ripe for collaboration is elderly care, where Thailand can become an *Elderly Healthcare Capital*, offering affordable yet high-quality healthcare for retirees, including a growing number of Chinese seniors. Supporting these sectors benefits China by diversifying its investment portfolio in Thailand while ensuring access to vital services such as food, healthcare, and tourism infrastructure, fostering stronger economic ties and deepening bilateral cooperation.

6.4 China's support for the development of new cities in Thailand by establishing campuses of top-tier Chinese universities, such as Tsinghua University and Peking University, is a strategic and beneficial initiative within the framework of the One Belt, One Buckle (OBOB) strategy. This approach not only enhances Thailand's education sector but also fosters innovation and technological exchange, which are crucial for both countries' economic collaboration and modernization efforts. By investing in Thailand's educational infrastructure, China can ensure the development of a skilled workforce that meets the demands of a rapidly changing global economy. This skilled labor pool will benefit Chinese companies operating in Thailand and enhance the overall competitiveness of the region.

Moreover, the establishment of these campuses would serve as a platform for cultural exchange, helping to build strong diplomatic ties between the two nations. Chinese universities would bring their research capabilities and technological expertise to Thailand, facilitating collaboration on various projects and enhancing Thailand's capacity for innovation. This aligns with China's goals of expanding its influence in Southeast Asia while promoting its own educational models. Ultimately, this initiative would create a win-win scenario, where Thailand gains access to high-quality education and technological advancements, while China strengthens its regional presence and fosters a long-term partnership that benefits both economies.

6.5 China can enhance People Connectivity through the Belt and Road Initiative (BRI) by developing comprehensive connectivity activities and platforms that foster interaction among diverse groups, including students, businesspeople, academics, civil society, and government officials. This initiative would include creating training programs focused on foreign business practices tailored to Chinese business operations, producing educational materials such as books and online content, and organizing forums for experience sharing among these groups.

By promoting such knowledge exchange, China can help Thai entrepreneurs better understand and navigate the complexities of engaging with Chinese markets, ultimately leading to more robust business collaborations. This alignment not only enhances Thailand's competitive landscape but also benefits China by creating a more favorable environment for its businesses abroad. Strengthening these interpersonal connections will contribute to a deeper mutual understanding and cooperation, paving the way for long-term partnerships that can drive economic growth for both nations.

By implementing these targeted initiatives, China can significantly contribute to Thailand's emergence as the "Buckle" in the Belt and Road Initiative, strengthening the economic ties and ensuring a mutually beneficial partnership.

Conclusion

The Thai-Chinese relationship, under the One Belt, One Buckle (OBOB) strategy, represents a promising path for achieving mutual benefits through enhanced cooperation. Thailand's strategic location in Southeast Asia positions it as a critical partner for China's expansion and connectivity goals, aligning well with China's broader Belt and Road Initiative (BRI). The OBOB framework promotes infrastructure development, fosters economic growth, and strengthens the integration of both countries within the ASEAN region. This partnership not only boosts trade and investment but also solidifies Thailand's role in facilitating smoother regional connectivity, providing significant economic opportunities. By working together, Thailand and China are building a future of shared prosperity, deeper ties, and long-term success for both nations. The OBOB strategy exemplifies how collaboration between these two nations can lead to win-win outcomes, benefiting not only their own economies but the broader Southeast Asian region.

References

Aamir, A. (2024, March 22). Attack in Pakistan's Gwadar strikes near heart of China's interests. Retrieved October 10, 2024, from Nikkei Asia website: https://asia.nikkei.com/Politics/International-relations/Attack-in-Pakistan-s-Gwadar-strikes-near-heart-of-China-s-interests

Bangkok Post. (2023a, January 28). China-Laos-Thailand rail link plans up for talks. Retrieved October 10, 2024, from https://www.bangkokpost.com website: https://www.bangkokpost.com/business/general/2493584/china-laos-thailand-rail-link-plans-up-for-talks

Bangkok Post (2023b, September 4). *Thailand Welcomes First Chinese Curriculum School.*

Retrieved October 10, 2024, from https://www.bangkokpost.com website: https://www.bangkokpost.com/thailand/pr/2641277/thailand-welcomes-first-chinese-curriculum-school

Bangkok Post Group (2024). *48th Anniversary of the China-Thailand.* Retrieved October 10, 2024, from https://www.bangkokpost.com website: https://www.bangkokpost.com/specials/china-thailand-diplomatic-relations/ Coate, M. J. , Griffin, L. A. , & Elliott-Gower, R. (2017). *Interdependence Theory: Implications for International Cooperation.* International Relations and Global Politics.

Lee, J., & Upadhyaya, A. (2024, October 7). *Economic Relations and Opportunities Between China and Thailand - Thailand Business News.* Retrieved October 10, 2024, from Thailand Business News website: https://www.thailand-business-news.com/china/165536-economic-relations-and-opportunities-between-china-and-thailand Padovan, N. (2024). *Thailand: Strategic Global Supply Chain & Logistics Hub.* Retrieved October

10, 2024, from Jacksongrant.io website: https://www.jacksongrant.io/news/thailand-logistics-hub/

Skaggs, R. D., Chukaew, N. and Stephens, J. (2024). Characterizing Chinese Influence in Thailand. Journal of Indo-Pacific Affairs, January - February 2024, pp.7-23, Retrieved October 10, 2024, from Air University (AU) website: https://www.airuniversity.af.edu/JIPA/Display/Article/3606690/characterizing -chinese-influence-in-thailand/

The Nation Thailand. (2024, February 22). *"Thailand too dependent on a few farm export items and markets."* Retrieved October 10, 2024, from nationthailand website: https://www.nationthailand.com/thailand/economy/40035804

Xinhua. (2023). *Thailand eyes further Belt and Road cooperation with China, says Thai PM | english.scio.gov.cn.* Retrieved October 10, 2024, from Scio.gov.cn website: http://english.scio.gov.cn/beltandroad/2023-10/20/content_116762402.htm

Xinhua News Agency (2024, February 6). *Thai agricultural exports to China surge 6.1 pct in 2023 - BELT AND ROAD PORTAL.* Retrieved October 10, 2024, from Yidaiyilu.gov. cn website: https://eng.yidaiyilu.gov.cn/p/0SKUSCPI.html

Zawacki, B. (2021, June 7). *Of Questionable Connectivity: China's BRI and Thai Civil Society.* Retrieved October 10, 2024, from Council on Foreign Relations website: https://www.cfr.org/blog/questionable-connectivity-chinas-bri-and-thai-civil-society

China—the Engine of Economic Integration within the Global South

Andrei Radulescu, Sarmiza Pencea

Researcher of Institute for World Economy, Romanian Academy

ABSTRACT

In 2024 the world economy continues to be confronted with the consequences of the global exogenous shocks of recent years, including the persistence of high-level geo-political tensions.

Therefore, over the past quarters, the growth pace of the economic activity has presented an annual dynamic below the level recorded during the post-crisis economic cycle, given the geo-fragmentation of the trade flows (Euro-Atlantic vs. Euro-Asian), the high level of real interest rates (i. e. the nominal rates adjusted by inflation), the structural challenges in terms of economic competitiveness in Euroland and the gap between rhetoric and deeds (as reflected, for instance, by the fact that military spending continues to outpace the financing flows meant to counter the climate change).

Furthermore, the risks of a new global economic and financial crisis outbreak are high, given the unprecedented challenges in terms of U.S. public finance, the confrontation among the largest economic blocks in the world and the overvaluation of the financial assets.

In this context, the intensification of the economic cooperation efforts among the emerging and developing countries in the Global South have gained momentum, with China (i. e. the second largest economy in the world, with a weight of around 17% of the global GDP) playing a catalyst role, including through furthering the implementation of its Belt Road Initiative [which provided cumulated global investments of over USD 1tn since its inception (Nedopil, 2024)].

This paper is focused on the economic integration within the BRICS block, by employing standard economy tools and using the database of the International Monetary Fund (IMF). The paper has the following structure: 1. the first chapter presents the role of BRICS in the world economy; 2. the second chapter briefly describes the econometric methodology implemented in order to estimate the annual dynamics of the potential output across the BRICS member countries; 3. the economic convergence/divergence among the BRICS member countries is presented in the third chapter; 4. the IMF macroeconomic forecasts for the BRICS countries are briefly described in the fourth chapter; 5. the conclusions are drawn in the last chapter of the paper.

I. BRICS IN THE WORLD ECONOMY

Formally launched in 2009 in the context of the Great Financial Crisis (the worst economic and financial crisis since the end of the Second World War) BRICS represents a multilateral grouping of economic and development cooperation among important emerging economies (Reuters, 2023). The founding members were Brazil, Russia, India and China, while South Africa joined in 2010.

Since the 1st of January, 2024, five other countries joined this international grouping of countries (European Parliament, 2024): Iran, Saudi Arabia, the United Arab Emirates, Egypt, and Ethiopia. While Argentina was also invited to become a BRICS member starting from January the 1st, 2024, it was withdrawn by its president from joining the group a few days earlier (Plummer, 2024).

The cumulated nominal GDP of the current BRICS (10 countries) stood at USD 28. 3tn in 2023, according to the estimates of the International Monetary Fund (IMF 2024 a). This amount accounted for around 27% of the world economy, very close to the weight of the USA in the global GDP (USA is the largest economy in the world, at least since the end of the Second World War).

Within the BRICS group, China is the largest economy, contributing by 62.4% to its cumulative nominal GDP in 2023, as it can be noticed in the following chart (Figure 1). There follows India, Brazil, Russia, and South Africa with weights of 12.6%, 7.7%, 7.1%, and 3.8%, respectively. The five countries that joined the group this year contribute by less than 7% to the BRICS+ cumulative nominal GDP, according to the IMF statistics (IMF, 2024 a).

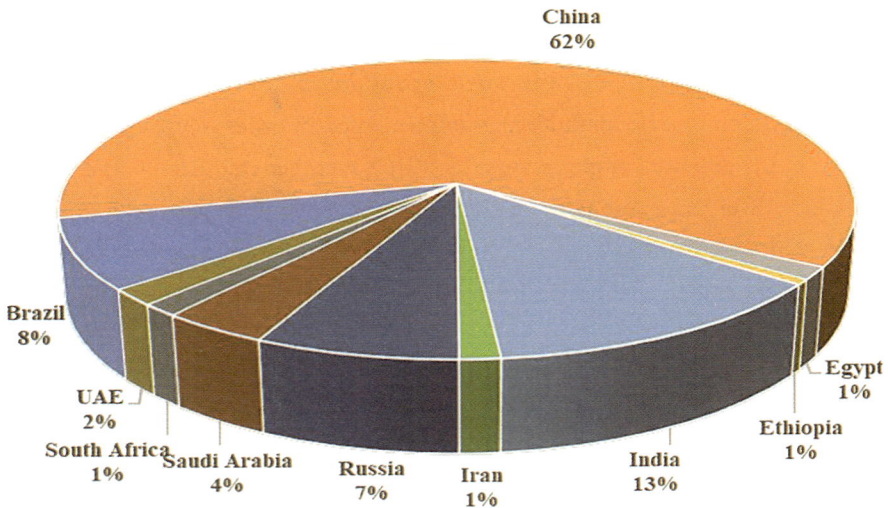

Figure 1. Member countries' contribution to the cumulative BRICS nominal GDP, 2023
Source: Representation of the author based on the statistics of International Monetary Fund (IMF, 2024, a)

However, if we take into account the GDP data in terms of purchasing power parity (PPP) in international dollars, the BRICS grouping in its current structure accounts for over 36% of the world economy (36.2% in 2023), according to the IMF statistics (International Monetary Fund, 2024 a), as shown in the following chart (Figure 2).

A convergence process of the BRICS group towards the level of the developed economies can be noticed this chart, in terms of the group's share in the global GDP (at PPP), which was more pronounced after the outbreak of the Great Financial Crisis, given the tough adjustment produced at the time, especially across the Euro Area economies. This region was confronted with two waves of the crisis, as the bankruptcies in the banking sector were immediately followed by a public debt crisis.

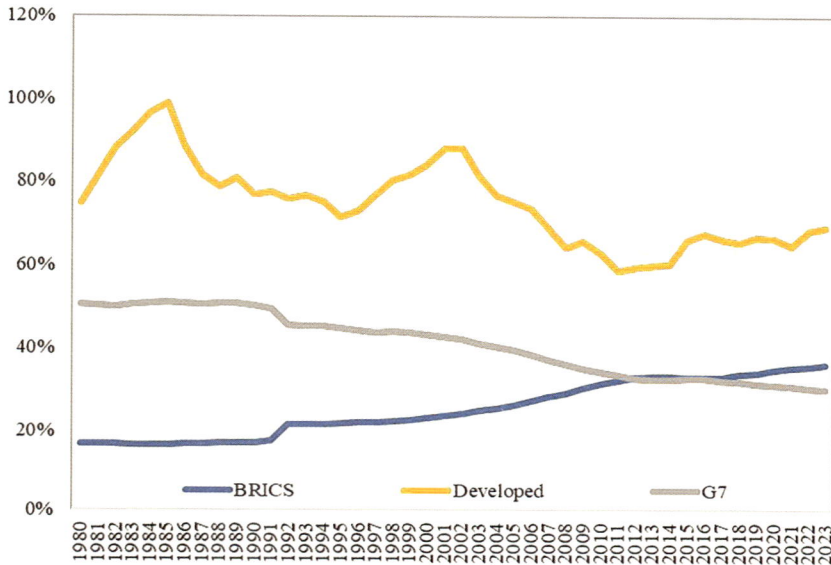

Figure 2. Share of nominal GDP in the world GDP, at PPP
Source: Representation of the author based on the statistics of International Monetary Fund (IMF, 2024, a)

Furthermore, it must be emphasized that the weight of the enlarged BRICS in the world economy is higher than that of the G7 (36.2% vs. only around 30%, in 2023), taking into account the nominal GDP at purchasing power parity, as reflected by the IMF estimates (International Monetary Fund, 2024 a).

Last, but not least, a widening gap between the BRICS and the G7 groups of states is developing after 2017, the year when BRICS surpassed G7 in terms of their cumulative share in the global GDP, setting a trend which is forecasted to intensify in the coming years and decades, given the following factors:

1. the better prospects in terms of growth and development across the emerging and developing countries, compared to the developed ones;

2. the expected progress of the economic integration process within BRICS, especially in the current context of unprecedented high level of global geo-political tensions.

However, in terms of economic development (as measured by the standard indicator GDP/capita at PPP), an important distance is still maintained between the member countries of the enlarged BRICS and the advanced economies.

On the one hand, the most developed countries in the BRICS group are the **United**

Arab Emirates and **Saudi Arabia**, where in 2023 the GDP/capita at purchasing power parity stood at 138.8% and 102.9%, respectively, of the level attained by the most advanced states of the world, as can be noticed in the next chart (Figure 3) (International Monetary Fund, 2024 a).

On the other hand, in 2023 **Russia** ranked the third in the enlarged BRICS group, with GDP/capita at PPP accounting for 53.3% of the level attained by the advanced economies.

There followed **China, Iran**, and **Brazil**, with levels of their GDP/capita at PPP above 30% of that in the advanced economies, i. e. 35.2%, 30.5%, and 30.1%, respectively.

Then, **Egypt, South Africa** and **India** had GDPs/capita at PPP representing 25.7%, 24.3%, and 14.1%, respectively, of the level cumulated by the developed countries of the world.

Finally, **Ethiopia** is the less developed country in the enlarged BRICS, with a GDP/capita accounting for less than 6% (5.7%) of the level in the advanced economies.

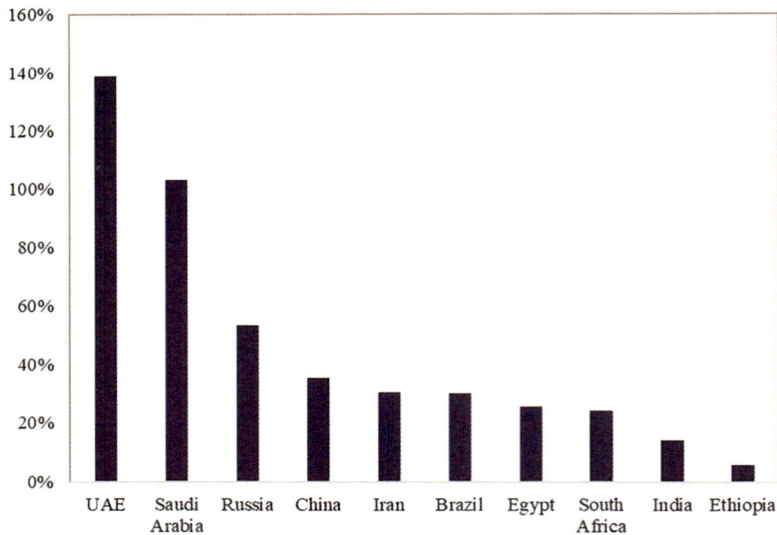

Figure 3. GDP/capita as a percentage of the level in the advanced economies
Source: Representation of the author based on the statistics of International Monetary Fund (IMF, 2024, a)

In other words, there are important differences and asymmetries among the present member countries of the BRICS in terms of their economic development. This means that the potential of economic convergence among these states is very high in the future, a theme which we will elaborate on, in the third chapter of this paper.

II. METHODOLOGY

In this paper standard econometric tools are employed and the statistics of the International Monetary Fund (IMF, 2024 a) is used in order to estimate the annual dynamics of the potential output across the member countries of the BRICS group.

The annual estimated dynamics of the potential output is important in order to assess the position of the economy on the cycle, but also the convergence/divergence among the countries, within a comparative analysis.

In this context, there must be emphasized that the economic convergence is the fundamental principle for a successful integration among several countries, especially if they are heterogenous at the beginning of the integration process.

In order to distinguish between the structural and cyclical components of the annual GDP dynamics, in this paper the filter developed by Hodrick and Prescott (1997) was implemented.

This is one of the most used econometric methods in the macroeconomic literature over the past decades for the decomposition of the macroeconomic variables, given the fact that it is transparent and simple to understand.

This econometric method is based on the following formula:

$$\mathbf{Min} \sum_{t}^{T}\left(\ln Y_t - \ln Y_t^*\right)^2 + \lambda \sum_{t}^{T-1}\left(\left(\ln Y_{t+1}^* - \ln Y_t^*\right) - \left(\ln Y_t^* - \ln Y_{t-1}^*\right)\right)^2 \qquad (2.1),$$

where Yt, Yt* și λ represent the output, the potential output, and the smoothness parameter, with the following property: the lower the value of it, the closer is the pace of GDP to its trend. In this paper a value of 100 was considered for this parameter, which is the level suggested by Hodrick-Prescott when utilising annual observations.

On the flipside, this econometric filter presents a number of shortcomings, namely the leakage effects and the compression effects, as it is impossible to perfectly distinguish between the cyclical and the structural components of the macroeconomic variables.

The IMF database (IMF, 2024 a) was used for the annual dynamics of the GDP across the BRICS member countries, during the 1995 – 2023 time-frame.

III.THE ECONOMIC CONVERGENCE/DIVERGENCE WITHIN BRICS

A high level of divergence can be also noticed among the member states of the enlarged BRICS, regarding several important macroeconomic indicators—as we have further emphasized in this chapter.

First of all, one can mention the divergence over the past decades in terms of the overall macroeconomic equilibria across the BRICS current member states, as reflected by the gap between the total investments and the national savings, both variables expressed as a percentage of the GDP.

As of 2023, the highest level of the macroeconomic disequilibria was identified in **Ethiopia**, the gap between the total investments and the national savings being at 2.8% of the GDP, according to the statistics of the International Monetary Fund (2024 a).

South Africa, Brazil, India and **Egypt** followed, with levels of their respective total investments—national savings gap of 1.6%, 1.3%, 1.2%, and 1.2% of their GDP.

On the other hand, over the past years, in **China** and in the **oil producing countries** of BRICS, the national savings presented higher levels as compared with the total investments, as reflected in the following chart (Figure 4).

In other words, these economies had a higher domestic savings rate than the total investment rate, an evolution determined by cultural aspects, including the high level of the propensity to save in China [as it was also emphasized by Zhang et al (2018)], as well as the income volatility in the oil-exporting countries [as underlined by Cherif and Hasanov (2013)].

Furthermore, according to the results of the econometric analysis implemented in this paper using the IMF annual data, there are important differences among the current member states of BRICS in terms of the dynamics of their potential output and the output gap, during the 1995-2023 time-frame (International Monetary Fund, 2024 a).

According to the results of the applied econometric methodology there are important differences in terms of the dynamics of the potential output, across the current member countries of **BRICS**.

Ethiopia and India are noticed firstly, as they are countries with the 2023 annual pace of the potential output estimated at 6.3%, and 5.7%, respectively.

They are followed by Egypt, China and Iran with levels of the 2023 annual pace of their potential GDP estimated at 4.7%, 4.4%, and 3.7%, respectively, as it can be noticed from the following chart (Figure 4).

In the United Arab Emirates, Brazil, Saudi Arabia and Russia the 2023 annual dynamics for their potential output was estimated at 3.2%, 2.2%, 1.9%, and 1.8%, respectively.

Finally, the slowest dynamics of the potential GDP was estimated for South Africa, where the annual pace was of only 0.6%, in 2023.

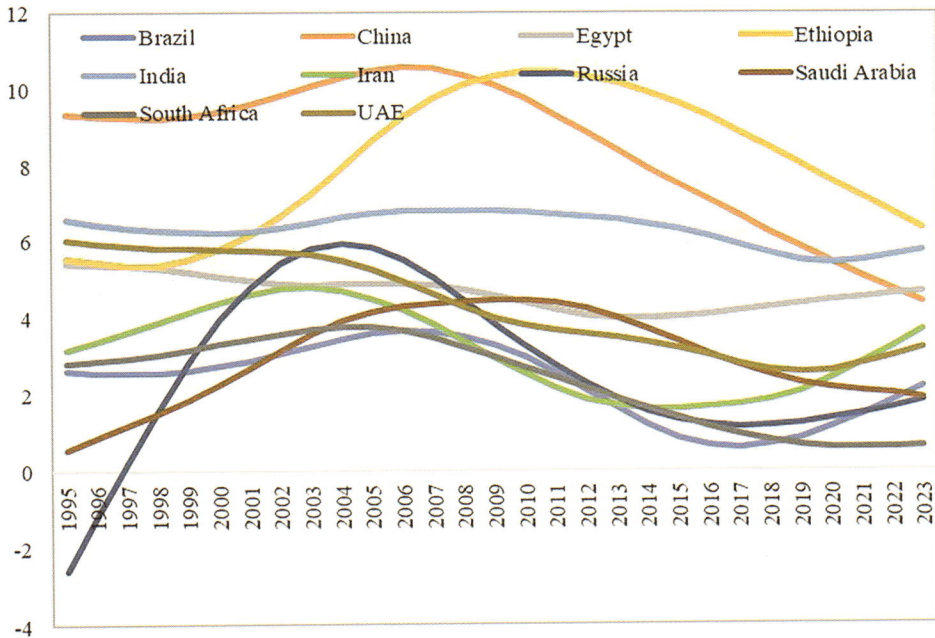

Figure 4. Annual dynamics of the potential output (%)

Source: Representation of the author based on the econometric estimates, using the above-described methodology and the annual data for GDP dynamics of the International Monetary Fund (IMF, 2024 a)

Furthermore, there are important differences among the current member countries of BRICS in terms of their position on the business cycle, as reflected by the dynamics of the output gap, according to the results of the estimates presented in the following chart (Figure 5).

As of 2023, several member economies of the enlarged BRICS presented a dynamic of their volume of the activity above the potential pace, with noticeable developments in India and Russia.

At the same time, in 2023 the output gap was also positive in Iran, China, Ethiopia and Brazil.

On the other hand, the economy of South Africa rose last year with annual pace at potential.

However, according to the results of the econometric estimates presented in Figure 5, in Egypt and Saudi Arabia the output gap stood in the negative territory in 2023.

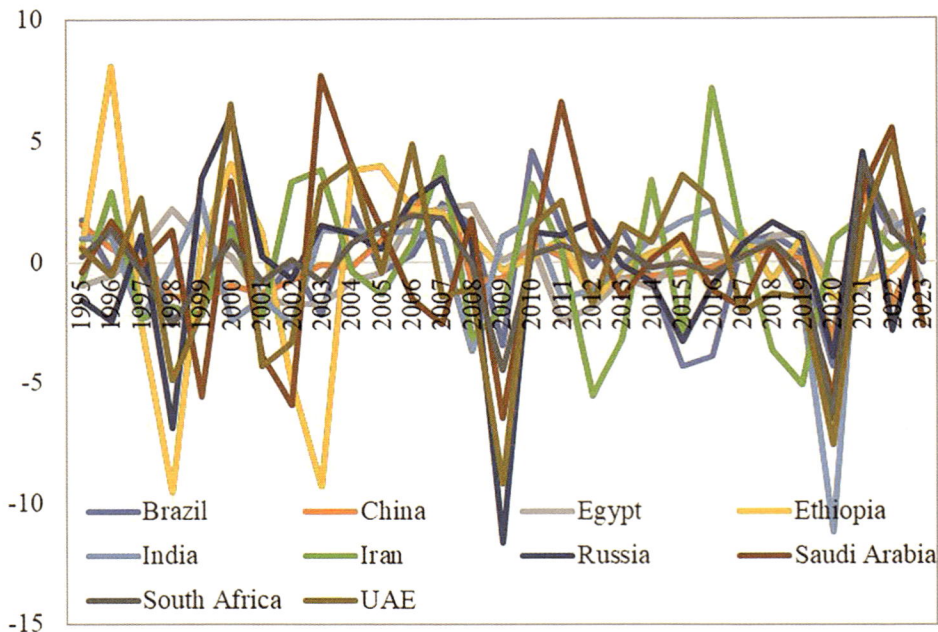

Figure 4. Annual dynamics of the potential output (%)
Source: Representation of the author based on the econometric estimates, using the above-described methodology and the annual data for GDP dynamics of the International Monetary Fund (IMF, 2024, a)

These results show that there are prospects of persistence of the structural differences and divergences across the current member countries of BRICS in terms of their future macroeconomic performance, that impact the decisions regarding the deepening of the integration process.

In this respect, we can mention one of the most debated macroeconomic topics regarding BRICS nowadays, namely the project of launching of a common currency as an alternative to the U.S. dollar and the EUR, as emphasized by many experts across the world, including Greene (2023).

IV. MACROECONOMIC OUTLOOK BRICS 2024-2025

According to the IMF's World Economic Outlook (IMF, 2024 b) published in July 2024 (updated by the incorporation of the most recent macroeconomic and financial developments) five of the current member countries of BRICS would present an average growth pace of their economic activity above the level of the world GDP pace.

The **Indian** economy can be noticed among these highly performing five BRICS countries, an economy where the GDP may advance by annual paces that are slowing down from 8.2% in 2023, to 7.0% in 2024 and 6.5% in 2025-as reflected by the following chart (Figure 6)-but still managing paces well above the world GDP average growth pace.

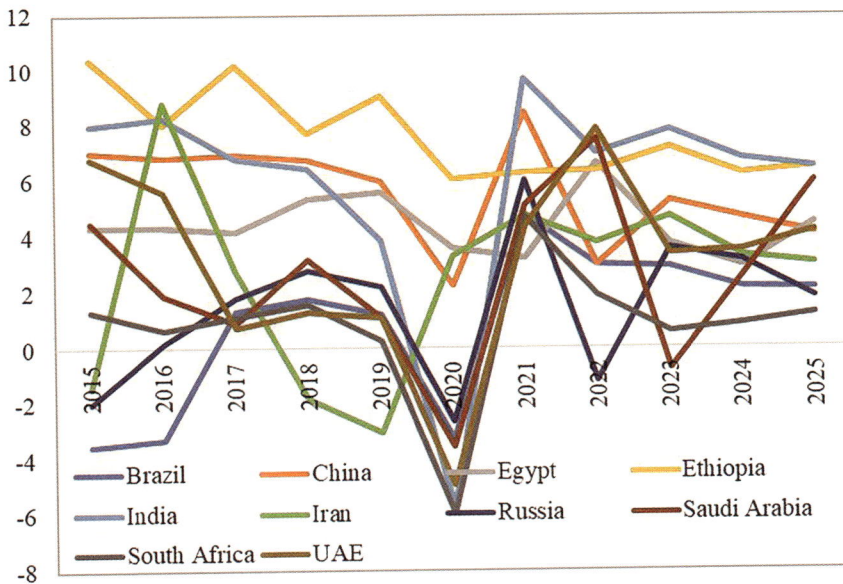

Figure 6. The GDP annual pace in BRICS countries (%)
Source: Representation of the author based on the database of the International Monetary Fund (IMF, 2024, b)

Also, in this global macroeconomic scenario of the International Monetary Fund (2024, b), the economy of **Ethiopia** may increase by annual paces of 6.2% in 2024 and 6.5% in 2025, in deceleration compared to the annual dynamics of 7.2% in 2023, but still above the average global GDP growth.

As regards **China**, the IMF's World Economic Outlook 2024 (International Monetary Fund, 2024 b) point to the increase of the GDP by annual paces slowing down from 5.2% in 2023 to 5.0% in 2024 and 4.5% in 2025, given both the weak dynamics of the global economy and the domestic challenges, including the developments in the real estate market.

The **United Arab Emirates** follow next, with prospects of increasing their economic activity by annual paces in acceleration from 3.4% in 2023, to 3.5% in 2024 and 4.2% in 2025.

For **Egypt** the Spring forecasts of IMF (2024, a) indicate annual growth pace of 2.7% in 2024 and 4.1% in 2025.

On the other hand, besides these five well performing BRICS member countries, in the resting five the GDP is forecasted to increase in 2024 and 2025 by an average annual pace below the growth of the world economy (2024, b).

For instance, the economy of **Iran** maybe slowing down from 4.6% in 2023, to 3.3% in 2024 and 3.1% in 2025.

For **Saudi Arabia** the International Monetary Fund forecasts the rebound of the economic activity in the short run, with annual growth paces of 1.7% in 2024 and 4.6% in 2025.

According to the same forecast, the GDP of **Russia** might advance by annual paces slowing down from 3.6% in 2023, to 3.2% in 2024 and 1.5% in 2025, given the war in Ukraine, the persistence of the geo-political tensions and their consequences.

In this IMF world macroeconomic scenario, the economy of **Brazil** may advance by annual paces of 2.1% in 2024 and 2.4% in 2025.

Last, but not least, according to the IMF summer forecasts of July 2024, the **South African** GDP might register a modestly accelerating annual dynamics, with growth paces improving marginally, from 0.7% in 2023, to 0.9% in 2024 and 1.2% in 2025.

As regards the climate on the labour market, the same IMF forecasts point to the general gradual decline of the average annual unemployment rate across the ten BRICS member countries during both 2024 and 2025.

In **China** the average annual rate of unemployment might register a feeble decrease from 5.2% in 2023 to 5.1% in 2024 and 2025, as reflected in the following chart (Figure 7).

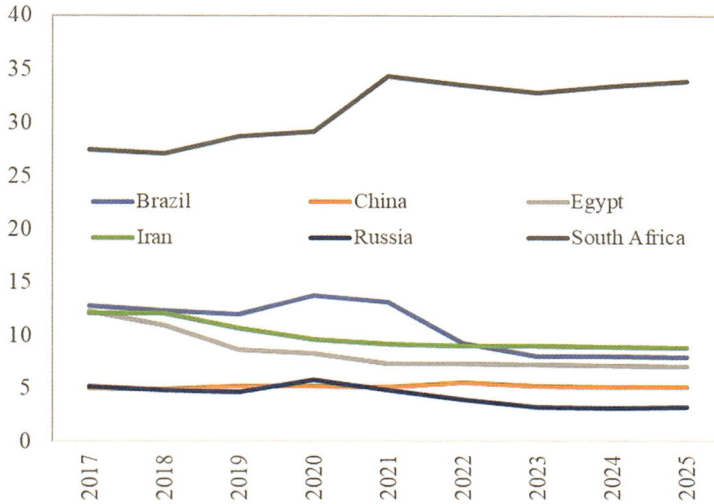

Figure 7. The average annual rate of unemployment (%)
Source: Representation of the author based on the database of the International Monetary Fund (IMF,

In **Brazil** the average annual rate of unemployment would decline from 8.0% in 2023 to 7.9% in 2025, while in **Iran** this indicator would diminish from 9.0% to 8.8% during this interval.

Furthermore, the average annual rate of unemployment would also feebly decrease in **Egypt,** from 7.2% in 2023, to 7.1% in 2024 and 7.0% in 2025.

On the other hand, the average annual rate of unemployment might consolidate in **Russia** (3.2% in 2025, the same level as in 2023) and increase in **South Africa**, from 32.8% in 2023 to 33.9% in 2025.

IMF did not release the forecasts on the dynamics of the unemployment rate in Saudi Arabia, United Arab Emirates, and India.

The IMF forecasts (IMF 2024 b) also point to the continuity of the disinflationary trend across the BRICS member countries in the coming years, an evolution in line with the developments at the global level, given the fading out of the consequences of the shocks (coronavirus and geo-political tensions) and the monetary policy under implementation.

In the case of **India**, the annual pace of consumer prices would decelerate from 5.4% in 2023, to 4.6% in 2024 and 4.2% in 2025, as shown in the following chart (Figure 8).

As regards **Russia**, consumer prices would increase by annual paces of 6.9% in 2024 and 4.5% in 2025, given the persistence of the geo-political tensions.

In **Brazil** the annual dynamics of consumer prices may decelerate from 4.6% in 2023, to 4.1% in 2024 and 3.0% in 2025, in the scenario of the international financial institution.

In **South Africa** the consumer prices may undergo an annual pace slowing down from 5.9% in 2023, to 4.9% in 2024 and 4.5% in 2025.

The persistence of high-level inflationary pressures (double digit annual pace) stands out in the IMF economic forecasts regarding **Iran, Egypt** and **Ethiopia**, but with prospects of slowing down in the coming years to levels of 32.5%, 25.7% and 18.2% respectively, by 2025.

Finally, in the coming years inflation is expected to be contained in **China, Saudi Arabia** and the **United Arab Emirates**, the international institution forecasting a convergence to an annual pace of 2% in 2025.

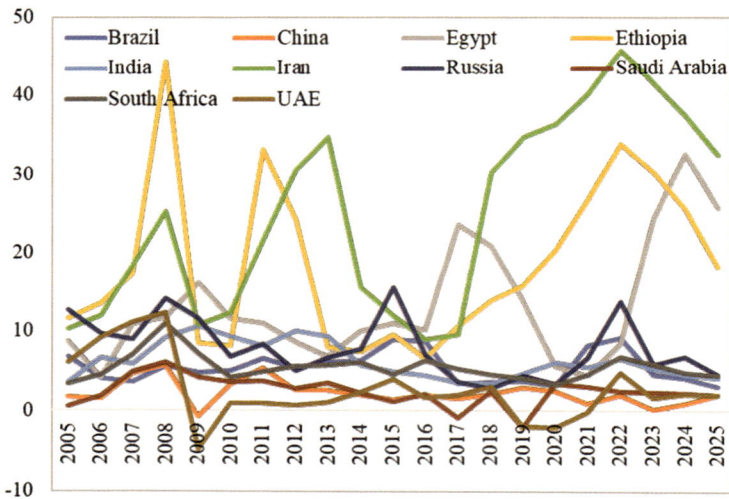

Figure 8. The annual dynamics of the consumer prices (%)
Source: Representation of the author based on the database of the International Monetary Fund
(IMF, 2024, a)

V. CONCLUSIONS

The efforts of economic integration between the emerging and developing countries within BRICS is expected to continue in the coming years, an evolution supported by the increasing role of China in the world economy and specifically in the Global South, by way of the Belt Road Initiative implementation.

In this context, the very ambitious economic component of the Shanghai Cooperation Organisation 2024 Summit should be also emphasized, with several important points, as shown by the main conclusions published in the statement of the heads of state (SCO, 2024): (i). promoting the global economic recovery by avoiding protectionism, unilateral sanctions and trade restrictions; (ii). deepening cooperation within SCO; (iii). implementing the SCO Economic Development Strategy by 2030; (iv) supporting the Belt Road Initiative (BRI); (v). accelerating the United Nations 2030 Agenda for Sustainable Development. Furthermore, the SCO Summit 2024 highlighted the priority economic sectors for the future: (a) agriculture and food security; (b) digital economy, e-commerce included; (c) technological innovation;

(d) energy; (e) entrepreneurship.

Last, but not least, the SCO Summit 2024 proposed, at the initiative of Kazakhstan, the launch of the *SCO Investment Fund* and the establishment of the *SCO Development Bank* and *SCO Development Fund.*

At the same time, the considerable challenges regarding the economic convergence among the BRICS and SCO member countries should be considered, especially in the context of the openly declared efforts aiming at de-dollarization.

In this respect, the experience of the economic integration in Europe over the past decades represents the best example of what should be done and what should be avoided by the emerging and developing countries in their endeavour of intensifying economic integration.

Bibliography

Cherif and Hasanov (2013). Oil Exporters' Dilemma: How Much to Save and How Much to Invest. *World Development*, 52, pp. 120-131, available at Oil Exporters' Dilemma: How Much to Save and How Much to Invest - ScienceDirect

European Parliament (2024). Expansion of BRICS (europa.eu)

Greene, R. (2023). The Difficult Realities of the BRICS' Dedollarization Efforts—and the Renminbi's Role, available at The Difficult Realities of the BRICS' Dedollarization Efforts—and the Renminbi's Role - Carnegie Endowment for International Peace

Hodrick, R. and Prescott, E. C. (1997). Postwar U.S. Business Cycles: An Empirical Investigation. *Journal of Money, Credit and Banking*, 29 (1), pp. 1-16.

International Monetary Fund (2024, a). World Economic Outlook, April 2024, available at World Economic Outlook, April 2024: Steady but Slow: Resilience amid Divergence (imf.org)

International Monetary Fund (2024, b). World Economic Outlook Update, July 2024, available at World Economic Outlook Update, July 2024: The Global Economy in a Sticky Spot (imf.org)

Nedopil, C. (2024). China Belt and Road Initiative (BRI) Investment Report 2023, available at China Belt and Road Initiative (BRI) Investment Report 2023 (griffith.edu.au)

Plummer, R. (2024). Argentina pulls out of plans to join BRICS bloc, https://www.bbc.com/news/world-latin-america-67842992

Reuters (2023).What is BRICS, which countries want to join and why? | Reuters

Shanghai Cooperation Organisation (SCO) (2024). ASTANA DECLARATION OF THE COUNCIL OF HEADS OF STATE OF THE SHANGHAI COOPERATION ORGANISATION | The Shanghai cooperation organisation (sectsco.org)

Zhang et al (2018). China's High Savings: Drivers, Prospects, and Policies, available at China's High Savings: Drivers, Prospects, and Policies1 in: IMF Working Papers Volume 2018 Issue 277 (2018)

Strengthening Cooperation between Analytical Centres (Think Tanks) in the Field of Scientific Exchange China-EU Countries—Key Aspects

Rybicka Magdalena

Deputy Director of the Asian Research Institute, Vistula University

The article focuses on the analysis of the research potential of Polish and Chinese think tanks. The author describes the issues in a holistic way and indicates in the conclusions how cooperation between EU and Chinese think tanks should develop.

Keywords: think tanks, quantitative research, international security, China, Poland, UE.

Introduction

Considerations regarding cooperation between analytical centers, which have been generally defined as think-thanks from English, require an attempt to define what they are and what goals they have in general and specific to their activities. This study is a consideration of understanding the idea of the activities of such units and an attempt to determine their usefulness both on a national, regional and international basis. Due to the broadness of the topic, this workshop focuses mainly on the scope related to scientific exchange, as key in relation to other trends of interest in think-thanks activities. Since it is impossible to clearly define what we understand by the concept of think-thanks, the author will initially create a general definition based on a study of available literature, which will allow for unification of what is understood by this term.

It is assumed that among other NGOs (Non Governmental Organizations), think-thanks stand out with the purpose of their activity, i. e. developing research, analyses and opinions concerning the generally understood internal and international policy of a given country or group of countries (e. g. the scope of EU activities). It is also assumed that they are independent and do not represent any interest groups, but are based on statistical data and, based on expert studies, create analyses that are intended to indicate the most universal solutions as recommendations for actions taken by governments.

In 2007, the first unofficial definition of think tanks was created. Think tanks are public policy research analysis and engagement organizations that generate policy-oriented research, analysis and advice on domestic and international issues, thereby enabling policymakers and the public to make informed decisions about public policy. Think tanks may be affiliated or independent institutions that are structured as permanent bodies, not ad-hoc commissions. These institutions often act as a bridge between the academic and policymaking communities and between states and civil society, serving in the public interest as an independent voice that translates applied and basic research into a language that is understandable, reliable and accessible for policymakers and the public (Think Tanks and Policy Advice in the U.S., Routledge 2007 and in The Fifth Estate: Think Tanks, Public Policy, and Governance, Brookings Institution Press 2016).

W historycznym ujęciu think-thank uznaje się Fabian Society. Founded in 1884, the society has been at the forefront of developing political ideas and public policy on the left for 140 years. The 1880s saw an upsurge in socialist activity in Britain and the Fabian Society was at the heart of much of it. Against the backdrop of the Match Girls' strike and the 1889 London Dock strike, the landmark Fabian Essays was published, containing essays by George Bernard Shaw, Graham Walls, Sidney Webb, Sydney Olivier and Annie Besant. All the contributors were united by their rejection of violent upheaval as a method of change, preferring to use the power of local government and trade unionism to transform society. The early Fabians' commitment to non-violent political change was underlined by the role the Fabian Society played in parliamentary politics. Having initially sought to influence the Liberal and Conservative parties, the Fabians participated in the foundation of the Labour party in 1900. The society has been affiliated to Labour throughout the party's history and is the only original founder that remains affiliated in unchanged form. None of the early figures in the society were more significant than Beatrice and Sidney Webb in developing the ideas that would come to characterise Fabian thinking and in developing the thorough research methodology that remains a feature of the Society to the present day. Both prodigious authors, Beatrice and Sidney wrote extensively on a wide range of topics, but it was Beatrice's 1909 Minority Report to the Commission of the Poor Law that was perhaps their most remembered contribution. This landmark report provided the foundation stone for much of the modern welfare state.

The members of the society were radicals for their time but their views reflected the age they lived in. Leading members of the society held racist prejudices and opinions which were not in keeping with the society's commitment to equality for all, either then or now. Fabians engaged in debates on eugenics and were racist towards people of Jewish, black and Asian origin. Views on the role of Empire varied amongst members, with some supporting rapid decolonisation and others seeing the British Empire as a potentially progressive force in the world. (fabians.org.ue)

As the historical background suggests, think tanks are often a foundation for building social groups that are transformed into parties, but their main goal is to remain impartial in the political arena as an independent advisory body. Think tanks often form partnerships with other institutions at the international level to conduct research on global challenges such as climate change, security policy, or international economics.

Think Tanks on a Global Scale

Research on international think tank cooperation is conducted mainly by institutions monitoring their activities and organizations involved in public policy analysis. Although there is no single, comprehensive database, there are some sources and reports that offer estimates and analyses. It should be noted, however, that think tanks around the world differ both in their role and methods of operation.

Tab. 1 Categories of Think Tank Affiliations

(2020 Global Go To Think Tank Index Report s.16)

Category	Definition
AUTONOMOUS AND INDEPENDENT	Significant independence from any one interest group or donor, and autonomous in its operation and funding from government.
QUASI-INDEPENDENT	Autonomous from government but controlled by an interest group, donor or contracting agency that provides most of the funding and has significant influence over operations of the think tank.
GOVERNMENT-AFFILIATED	A part of the formal structure of government.
QUASI-GOVERNMENTAL	Funded exclusively by government grants and contracts but not a part of the formal structure of government.
UNIVERSITY-AFFILIATED*	A policy research center at a university.
POLITICAL-PARTY AFFILIATED	Formally affiliated with a political party.
CORPORATE (FOR-PROFIT)	A for-profit public policy research organization, affiliated with a corporation or merely operating on a for-profit basis.

*Another typology distinguishes between three types of think tanks: "universities without students," contract researchers and advocacy tanks. Weaver (1989).

According to the 2020 Global Go To Think Tank Index Report, there are 2,397 think tanks in North America (Mexico, Canada, and the United States) of which 2,203 are in the United States. There are 2,932 think tanks in Europe. Over 47 percent of all think tanks are in North America and Europe, an increase from last year. The rate of establishment of think tanks has declined over the last 12 years in the United States and Europe. Asia, Latin America, Africa, the Middle East and North Africa continue to see an expansion in the number and type of think tanks established. Asia has experienced a dramatic growth in think tanks since the mid-2000s. Many think tanks in these regions continue to be dependent on government funding along with gifts, grants and contracts from international public and private donors. University or government-affiliated or funded think tanks remain the dominant model for think tanks in these regions. There is increasing diversity among think tanks in these regions with independent, political party affiliated and corporate or business sector think tanks that are being created with greater frequency.

In terms of geography, the distribution of think tanks in the world has remained virtually unchanged for years. The countries with the largest number of think tanks, according to the Sobieski Institute (https: //sobieski. org. pl/komentarz-is-160/), are the USA (1,828), China (426) and Great Britain (287). Further positions are occupied by India (268), Germany (194), France (177), Argentina (137), Russia (122) and Japan (108). Among the continents, North America is the leader, with 1, 984 think tanks (29. 07% of all those included in the study). Think tanks from the USA (1,828) clearly dominate there, followed by Canadian (96) and Mexican (60) think tanks. Next place is occupied by Europe with 1,818 think tanks (26.63%). In Western Europe, the largest think tank centres are the United Kingdom (287), Germany (194), France (177), Italy (89), Sweden (77), Switzerland (71), the Netherlands (57) and Belgium (52).

In Eastern and Central Europe, in terms of the number of think tanks, Poland with 41 think tanks ranked ex-aequo 4th with Hungary, behind Russia (122), Romania (54), Ukraine (47), and ahead of Bulgaria (33) and the Czech Republic (28). It is worth noting that if the number of think tanks were to be calculated per capita, Poland would rank far behind Ukraine and Russia.

Polish Perspective on Think Tanks

The presence of Polish institutions in the ranking is constantly growing. While the first reports from 2008 and 2009 listed a total of 4 Polish think tanks, in 2010 there were 5, in 2011 there were 7, in 2012 8, and this year's ranking includes as many as 9 Polish institutions. In total, since the inception of the ranking, 10 Polish think tanks and foundations have appeared in it: the Centre for Social and Economic Research, the Polish Institute of International Affairs, the Stefan Batory Foundation, the Centre for International Relations (CSM), the Adam Smith Centre, the Centre for Eastern Studies (OSW), the Institute of Public Affairs (ISP), Demos Europa, the Institute for Sustainable Development and the Jan Nowak-Jeziorański College of Eastern Europe.

Despite the aforementioned low number of think tanks per capita compared to other countries in the region, Poland ranks strongly in terms of quality. In the ranking of the 60 best think tanks in Central and Eastern Europe, CASE won, ahead of the Russian Carnegie Moscow Center, and 3rd place was taken by PISM, followed by Russian think tanks-the Institute of World Economy and International Relations of the Russian Academy of Sciences (IMEMO), the Moscow State Institute of International Relations (MGIMO) and the Center for Economic and Financial Research (CEFIR). Another Polish institution—OSW—came in 7th place. This means that there are 3 Polish think tanks in the top ten. Only Russia can boast a larger number of them (4 think tanks). In Poland, the growing role of think tanks is noticeable, as they play a key role in shaping public debate and policy. They are also a source of expert knowledge for government decision-makers and the private sector. Through reports, conferences and debates, think tanks influence the development of national strategies, while their analyses help identify threats and challenges for the Polish economy and politics. Think tanks act as a kind of "bridge" between science and politics, explaining complex issues in an accessible way. In Poland, think tanks often deal with topics related to European integration, defense, energy and systemic reforms. Some of them work on strengthening civil society and increasing citizens' participation in decision-making processes (e. g. the Civic Association "Dom Polski"). Their recommendations can influence the creation of laws and political strategies. Think tanks also cooperate with the media, organizing debates and publishing reports in the press. In the era of digitalization, the importance of analyses of new technologies and innovations is growing. The leading think tanks in Poland include the Institute of Public Affairs, the Polish Institute of International Affairs, and the Center for Eastern Studies. The Institute of Public Affairs (ISP) conducts research on public policy, European integration and civil society. The Polish Institute of International Affairs (PISM) specializes in the analysis of foreign policy, security and international relations. The Eastern Studies Center (OSW) focuses on the analysis of the countries of Eastern Europe, the Caucasus and Central Asia. The Batory Foundation is involved in research on democracy, human rights and social justice. The Jagiellonian Club Analysis Center (CAKJ) conducts research on national politics, energy, education and demography. Think tanks such as WiseEuropa analyze the economy, climate change and modern technologies. The Civic Institute Foundation also operates in Poland, dealing with research on social policy and development. The think tank Civic Association "Dom Polski" focuses on Polish-Chinese cooperation, shows the Chinese perspective in Poland and works to strengthen scientific, political and business relations between the two countries.

Think tanks in Poland have similar problems to similar institutions around the world, often struggling with major problems in financing their activities. Some of them depend on grants and external support, which can affect the independence of their research. Too many small think tanks lead to fragmentation and lack of cooperation between them. Sometimes think tanks are perceived as too closely linked to specific political parties. The influence of their recommendations on government policy is sometimes limited by the lack of openness of decision-makers to independent analyses. Competition with academic centers can lead to the marginalization of some think tanks. Maintaining a high level of expertise is also a challenge, which requires appropriate resources and staff. Some think tanks in Poland do not have sufficient tools to conduct research with a global reach. Changing political and economic priorities can affect the availability of research funds. Increasing the transparency of financing and ensuring the quality of research are challenges facing Polish think tanks, as well as all such institutions in the world. The prospects for the development of think tanks in Poland over the next 20 years are promising, although full of challenges that may affect their future role and significance. In the face of increasing globalization and dynamic technological changes, think tanks will have to adapt to new realities. A key area of development will be their role in analyzing the impact of technology on society, economy and politics. It is expected that think tanks will increasingly address topics related to digitization, artificial intelligence, armed conflicts, cybersecurity and climate change. In the coming years, Polish think tanks may increase their importance in the international arena, especially in the context of European integration and regional cooperation, due to their geographical location. However, they will have to strengthen their contacts with European institutions and international organizations to fully use the potential of global expert networks. Strengthening cooperation with international research centers can help improve the quality of analyses and better adapt to global challenges. In Poland, think tanks should and can play a key role in the debate on social problems, such as an ageing society, migration (especially currently in connection with the armed conflict in Ukraine) and the changing labor market. Demographic analyses and research on social and health policy will be key in the context of future reforms. At the same time, issues related to energy policy and green transformation will gain in importance, which will require in-depth analyses and strategic recommendations for the government and the private sector. In a broader global perspective, the role of think tanks is also important to highlight the problems of the global economy, geopolitical and business connections and mutual cooperation on many levels between, for example, Poland and China. This is a good time for Polish think tanks to take the lead in creating and explaining the right economic, business and political relations between the EU-China-Poland. A key factor for the development of think tanks is and will be financial independence and the ability to obtain funds for research activities. Private sector funding and cooperation with large corporations and non-profit organizations will become increasingly important, which can lead to potential conflicts of interest. For this reason, think tanks will have to ensure the transparency of their activities in order to maintain credibility and public trust. In terms of methodology, the development of analytical tools based on big data and artificial intelligence can revolutionize the way think tanks conduct research. Automation of analyses and increasingly advanced forecasting methods will allow for better prediction of political and economic trends, which will increase the importance of think tanks in the decision-making process. These technologies will allow for the creation of more precise models of future scenarios, which will be extremely valuable in a dynamically changing world. In the coming years, think tanks in Poland can and should also play an important role in public education.

Through cooperation with the media, schools and non-governmental organisations, think tanks will be able to educate society on the key challenges facing Poland and the world. They can also become an important source of knowledge and reliable information for citizens, especially in the face of increasing disinformation in the media and the Internet. In addition, think tanks can contribute to the shaping of modern urban and regional policies. In the face of urbanisation and the need for sustainable development of cities, they will provide recommendations on public transport, sustainable construction and the management of water and energy resources. This will be particularly important in the context of climate change and the growing demands for sustainable development. Polish think tanks can also support the government and the public sector in creating long-term political strategies. Analyses on national security, international relations and new threats such as cyberterrorism can become a key element of the activities of these institutions. Given Poland's growing importance in Central and Eastern Europe, think tanks will have the opportunity to influence the country's foreign and defence policy. It will also be important for think tanks to build stronger ties with the younger generation of researchers. Developing human capital, investing in young experts and building a network of academic contacts will be crucial for their future. Cooperation with universities, internship programs and research initiatives can help develop a new generation of experts who will be able to meet future challenges. To sum up, the development of think tanks in Poland in the coming years will be based on adaptation to global and local changes. The challenge will be to obtain funds, maintain independence, and the ability to adapt to dynamically changing technological and political realities. In response to these challenges, think tanks can gain importance as key advisors in the process of creating public policy, as well as expert centers shaping the social debate.

Think Tanks in China from a Polish Perspective.

Currently, think tanks in China play an important role in the policy-making process, although their functioning differs significantly from how similar institutions operate in countries such as the EU. Chinese think tanks are largely linked to the government, which means that their activities often fit into the official political lines of the Chinese Communist Party (CPC). Most Chinese think tanks operate under the auspices of state institutions, universities or other government organizations, and their analyses and research are intended to support government decisions and strategies. Chinese think tanks are an important tool of the CPC for formulating long-term strategies and monitoring the international political and economic situation, which is their key role. They play a key role in analyzing international trends and providing the government with data necessary for decision-making. In particular, think tanks in China are engaged in research on global politics, national security, economy and technological development, as well as relations with developing countries and great powers over the long term.

One of China's most important think tanks is the Chinese Academy of Social Sciences (CASS), which conducts research on domestic and foreign policy and analyzes social and economic trends. CASS has a huge impact on China's decision-making process, providing reports and analyses that directly reach the government and policymakers. Many other think tanks, such as the Institute of International Studies and the Chinese Academy of Military Sciences, focus on defense, international relations, and security. In recent years, China has been promoting the development of global think tanks to help improve the country's international image. The "think tanks with Chinese characteristics" initiative aims to create institutions that promote China's perspective on the international stage and increase China's influence in the global debate. In this way,

Chinese think tanks are becoming a tool of soft power, helping to build China's position as a leader in international politics and economics. On the one hand, think tanks in China are tasked with providing the government with reliable data and analysis, while on the other hand, they are also tasked with justifying the policies of the government and the CPC to society and the world. This is particularly evident in their analyses of economic development and foreign policy, which often aim to demonstrate the validity and effectiveness of the Chinese government's actions. The CPC government sees think tanks as an important tool for legitimizing its policies and strengthening China's position in the international arena. However, compared to think tanks in democratic countries, Chinese think tanks seem to have significantly limited independence. Most of them operate in close cooperation with the government, which means that they are not able to criticize official policies or make recommendations that would be contrary to the interests of the CPC, which generally distorts, for example, the actual assessment of the actions taken. A critical perspective can be a good inspiration for changes that result from the global economy or new events in the world. This limits their ability to objectively analyze social and political problems and also affects their credibility in the eyes of the international research community.

Think tanks in China are increasingly involved in research related to technological innovations, including artificial intelligence, big data, and green energy. The Chinese government recognizes that these technologies will be crucial to the country's future, and think tanks are conducting intensive research in these areas. They are also working with the private sector, including large technology companies, to develop strategies and recommendations to support China's digital economy. One challenge for Chinese think tanks in the future will be to gain greater research autonomy. Currently, they are tightly controlled by the government, which limits their ability to conduct independent research and critical analysis to a large extent. Issues of dependency and funding for think tank ingenuity are a common problem for think tanks, not only in China but also globally. Increasing global competition and the need to respond quickly to international challenges may require Chinese think tanks to be more flexible and innovative. In the context of foreign policy, think tanks in China will play an important role in the future as well, for example in analyzing and supporting initiatives such as the "One Belt, One Road" (BRI). China sees the initiative as a key element of its global strategy, and the think tanks are tasked with analysing its effects and recommending further actions that can strengthen

China's position in international markets.

In summary, Chinese think tanks have prospects for dynamic development, especially in the areas of technology, international policy and economy. However, their activities will largely depend on the policies of the CPC and on how the Chinese government decides to shape the future role of these institutions. Although their independence is limited, they have the potential to significantly influence the global debate, especially in the context of China's growing economic development, economic growth and key global roles.

Summary

Strengthening cooperation between think tanks from China and EU countries in terms of scientific exchange can contribute to a better understanding of each other's political, economic and technological priorities. Through joint research on global challenges such as climate change, technological innovation and security policy, think tanks can support dialogue between governments and societies in the two regions. Such cooperation could also accelerate the exchange of best practices, fostering knowledge transfer and innovation. However, a key challenge will be to reconcile political and systemic differences, especially in the context of the Chinese governance model and European democratic standards. This cooperation, if conducted on the basis of mutual respect and transparency, has the potential to deepen scientific and economic relations between China and the EU.

Further intensification of cooperation between Chinese and European think tanks could help build bridges between the East and the West on difficult international issues such as geopolitical changes, trade and technology. Think tanks from both sides can play a key role in developing joint research projects that focus on global issues such as sustainable development, public health and digitalization. Through exchanges of academic staff, internships and joint conferences, experts from the EU and China can learn from each other, allowing for the development of more comprehensive public policies. There is also the potential for joint initiatives related to new technologies such as artificial intelligence, 5G or renewable energy sources, which can be mutually beneficial.

However, such a partnership will require the development of a solid institutional framework that ensures a balance of interests and safeguards against undue political influence. To avoid tensions, it will be important that cooperation is based on open dialogue, respect for cultural and political differences, and transparency in the exchange of data and research results. In the context of growing concerns about data protection and security, especially in sectors such as digitalization, detailed regulations on privacy and intellectual property protection will be necessary. EU-China cooperation on think tanks could also help to mitigate trade and economic differences, if based on mutual benefits. In the longer term, a well-functioning network of think tanks can help build more stable and predictable relations between the EU and China. Increased scientific and analytical exchange will also help to prepare both sides for new challenges, such as climate change and energy transitions. Moreover, joint research projects can serve as a platform for developing better global standards that take into account the interests of both East and West.

Bibliography

Abelson, D. (2009). Do Think Tanks Matter? Assessing the Impact of Public Policy Institutes. Montreal: McGill—Queen's University Press.

Aron, R. (1995). Pokój i wojna między narodami. Warszawa: Centrum im. Adama Smitha. Bąkowski, T., Szlachetko, J. (2012). Zagadnienie think tanków w ujęciu interdyscyplinarnym. Gdańsk: Ośrodek Analiz Polityczno-Prawnych. Baylis, J., Smith, S. (2009). Globalizacja polityki światowej. Kraków: Wydawnictwo Uniwersytetu Jagiellońskiego. Bour, O. (2006). Deutsch-Polnische Stiftungstraditionen. Berlin: Maecenata Verlag. Brodie, B. (1978). The Development of Nuclear Strategy, International Security, 2, s. 65-83. Brown, Ch., Ainley, K. (2009). Understanding International Relations. New York: Palgrave Macmillan. Buzan, B. (1993). People, States and Fear. The National Security Problem in International Relations. Brighton: Wheatsheaf. Centrum Stosunków Międzynarodowych, Warszawa: http://www.csm.org. pl. [6.10.2024] Instytut Badań nad Stosunkami Międzynarodowymi, Warszawa: http:// www.ibnsm.stosunki.pl.[7.10.2024]

Fabians, https://fabians.org.ue [8.10.2024]

Global Go To Think Tank Index Report, https://repository.upenn.edu/exhibits/orgunit/think_ tanks [7.10.2024]

Instytut Studiów Strategicznych, Kraków: http://www.iss.krakow.pl. [6.10.2024]

Międzynarodowy Przegląd Polityczny: http://www.mpp.org.pl.[6.10.2024] Fundacja im. Kazimierza Pułaskiego, Warszawa: http://www.pulaski.pl.[8.10.2024] Instytut Sobieskiego, Warszawa: http://www.sobieski.org.pl. [7.10.2024]

Instytut Batorego

Infos, Biuro analiz sejmowych, Warszawa https://orka.sejm.gov.pl/WydBAS.nsf/0/AE E487CF31D5A165C12578B00047620D/$file/Infos_104.pdf Magazyn Stosunki Międzynarodowe: http://www.stosunki.pl. [8.10.2024]

Klotz, A., Prakash, D. (red.). (2009). Qualitative Methods in International Relations. A Pluralist Guide. New York: Palgrave. MacMillan, Krauz-Mozer B., Borowiec P., Ścigaj P. (t.1 i t.2, 2011-2012), Kim jesteś, politologu? Historia i stan dyscypliny w Polsce. Kraków: Wydawnictwo Uniwersytetu Jagiellońskiego.

Rich, A. (2004). Think Tanks, Public Policy, and the Politics of Expertise. Cambridge: Cambridge University Press.

Think Tanks and Policy Advice in the U.S., Routledge 2007 and in The Fifth Estate: Think Tanks, Public Policy, and Governance, Brookings Institution Press 2016)

Trachtenberg, M. (1989). Strategic Thought in America, 1952-1966. Political Science Quarterly, 104(2), s. 301-334.

Wallerstein, I. (2007). Analiza systemów-światów. Wprowadzenie. Warszawa: Wydawnictwo Dialog. Waltz, K. (2010). Struktura teorii stosunków międzynarodowych. Warszawa: Wydawnictwo Naukowe Scholar. Williams, P. (2012). Studia bezpieczeństwa. Kraków: Wydawnictwo Uniwersytetu Jagiellońskiego.

Central Asia and China from Silk Road to Belt and Road

Mirzohid Rakhimov

Head of Department at Contemporary History Center of Uzbekistan Academy of Sciences

Introduction

Central Asia and China for centuries have been an important hub for trade, economic cultural and intellectual exchange between Asia and Europe, the main link on the Silk Road routes. China and Central Asia possess the richest, unique historical heritage, which is part of the treasury of world civilization, supporting our thesis on the unity and interconnection of historical processes in various regions of the world. Modern China and the Central Asian countries, being part of the contemporary history of civilization, are closely intertwined with global processes. The Belt and Road Initiative is a good case of unity in the diversity of trans-regional and global partnerships.

From the History of Political and Diplomatic Relations

Central Asia and China historically were located at the crossroads of interaction between various civilizations and cultures. Ancient state formations of the Central Asian region had close ties with China. For example, the relations between Sogdiana and

China, and Sogdian trade missions along the Great Silk Road, including the territory of China, are well known[1]. By the end of the 2nd century BC, the state formations of the region-Davan (Fergana), Anxi (Bukhara), the confederation of tribal unions Kangju-initiated intensive diplomatic relations with China. In Chinese historiography, the ambassador of the Chinese emperor to the "Western lands" (as Xinjiang was called at that time) Zhang Qian is characterized as their discoverer. According to the "History of the Former Han Dynasty," during the reign of Emperor Wu Di (140–87 BC), not less than 10 embassies were sent annually to various states of Central Asia[2]. Also known as the war over the "heavenly horses" - the campaign of the emperor's troops to Davan[3].

In the 5th and 6th centuries, a new stage of development of trade and cultural relations between China and Central Asia began, which contributed to the establishment of diplomatic relations[4]. During the reign of Amir Timur and the Timurids, active political, diplomatic, and trade relations were established with many Asian countries, including China, India, Egypt, Turkey, and several European countries. During the existence of the Bukhara, Khiva, and Kokand Khanates, diplomatic relations were actively maintained with neighboring states. In particular, during the reign of Abdullah Khan II (1534–1598), external trade of the Bukhara Khanate experienced significant development, and economic ties were strengthened with Yarkand, the Baburid Empire, the Ottoman Empire, and the Moscow State[5]. For the Bukhara Khanate, the territory

[1] См.: Кляшторный С. Г. История Центральной Азии и памятники рунического письма. – СПб., 2003. 560 с.; Масанов Н. и др. История Казахстана. Народы и культура. – Алматы, 2001; На среднеазиатских трассах Великого шёлкового пути. Сборник статей. – Т., 1990; Ходжаев А. Китайский фактор в Центральной Азии. – Т., 2004; Его же. Буюк йўли: муносабатлар ва такдидлар. – Т., 2007; Каримова Н. Э. Взаимоотношения народов Центральной Азии и Китая в XIV-XVII вв. (по материалам китайских источников) // Автореф. дисс... докт. ист. наук. – Т., 2006. С. 42.

[2] Бичурин Н. А. Собрание сведений о народах, обитающих в Средней Азии. Т. II. – М.–Л., 1950. С. 173.

[3] Кляшторный С. Г. История Центральной Азии и памятники рунического письма. – СПб., 2003. С. 142.

[4] Смирнова О. И. Очерки из истории Согда. – М., 1971. С. 21.

[5] Мукминова Р. Г. Город – степь: Торгово-хозяйственные и этнокультурные контакты (XVI–XVII вв.) // Урбанизация и номадизм в Центральной Азии: история и проблемы. Материалы международной конференции. – Алматы, 2004. С. 84; Bregel Yu. An historical atlas of Central Asia... – Brill – Leiden – Boston, 2003. P. 68.

of the Yarkand state served as a transit route leading to China's inland areas, and the trade caravans departing from Yarkand, through the territory of Maverannahr, reached other states. The Kokand Khanate, another state in the region, also maintained intensive political and diplomatic relations with China[1].

As we know world history is full of different scales of wars and there were approximately 14, 500 armed struggles over time[2], and it is noteworthy that the history of relations between Central Asia and China belongs to the category with the least number of military conflicts. China and Central Asia experienced complex historical processes in the 19th and 20th centuries, including the Second World War—the largest conflict in human history, where the total human losses amounted to 70 million, with a large part of these losses falling on the people of the Soviet Union and China.

Trade and Civilizational Interconnectedness

Like China, Central Asia has been one of the important centres of trade, economic, and cultural exchange between Asia and Europe throughout its history, serving as a major link on the routes of the Great Silk Road[3]. Thus, in Central Asia, many items of Roman origin have been found, including coins and art objects[4]. During the reign of Kanishka, the Kushan Empire controlled the trade routes from Central Asia to Northern

---

[1] Ходжаев А. Из истории международных отношений Центральной Азии в XVIII веке. – Т.: Фан, 2003; Кулдашев Ш. Т. Политические, экономические и культурные связи между Кокандским ханством и восточным Туркестаном (XVIII – середина XIX в.) // Автореф дисс... канд. ист. наук. – Т., 2009. С. 15-18; Қўлдашев Ш. Қўқон хонлиги ва Хитой (Чинг империяси) ўртасидаги дипломатик муносабатлар. ТошДШИ. 2019. – 240 б.

[2] Jackson R., Sorensen G. Introduction to International relations: theories and approaches. Oxford University Press. 2016. Pp. 277-293.

[3] Richthofen F. F. China. Ergebnisse eigener Reisen und darauf gegrünter Studien. Berlin: Ver. D. Reimer, 1877–1883. Bd. 1–4; History of civilizations of Central Asia. Vol. I: The dawn of civilizations: earliest times to 700 B. C. Paris: UNESCO publication, 1992, Ртвеладзе Э. В. Великий шёлковый путь. Энциклопедический справочник. – Т., 2000; Waugh D. "Richtofen's «Silk Roads»: Toward the Archaeology of a Concept," The Silk Road, UW Seattle, 2007, vol. 5. № 1; Кобзева Т. История изучения Великого шёлкового пути во второй половине XIX – начале XX в. – Т., 2006; Мирзаев Р. Великий шёлковый путь: реалии XXI века. – М., 2006; and others.

[4] Ртвеладзе Э. В. Великий шёлковый путь. Энциклопедический справочник. – Т., 2000. С. 60–65.

India, along which international economic and political relations were established between Parthia, the Roman Empire, India, and China[1].

The Great Silk Road served as a transmitter of religious and cultural beliefs as well as scientific and technological achievements (Figure 1). Trade flourished, and cultural interactions occurred, including the exchange of art, ideas, and technologies. Such cities as Samarkand, Turfan, Kashgar, Xi'an and others played important roles in the Silk Road. The Ming and Qing Dynasties saw continued trade along the Silk Road, with goods like tea, porcelain, and textiles flowing between China and Central Asia. Cultural exchanges included the spread of Buddhism and Islamic influences[2].

The Sogdians played a significant role in the development of cultural interactions with China[3]. Some documents from the Mug archive (7th century) contain information about embassies sent from Sogdiana far beyond Central Asia and about the arrival of embassies from various states to Sogdiana[4]. A vivid illustration of the diplomatic relations of ancient Sogdiana with other Eastern countries can be seen in the murals of the palace of Varkhuman at Afrasiab, which depict scenes of receiving foreign embassies[5].

Almost a century before Columbus, Zheng He a eunuch admiral in the court sailed from China with three hundred ships and twenty-eight thousand men. His fleet stopped at ports in the Indian Ocean and journeyed as far as the east coast of Africa[6]. In particular, the Chinese excelled in shipbuilding technology. In the fifteenth century, they possessed the world's greatest seagoing fleet—large enough, had they willed it, to have blocked European expansion into Asian waters. The Chinese passed to traders on

---

[1] Пидаев Ш. Р. Кўхна Термиз ва «Буюк ипак йўли» // Буюк ипак йўлидаги Марказий Осиё шахарлари. – Самарқанд, 1994. Б. 52–53; Мавлянов У. М. Комммуникации и торговые пути в Средней Ази: формирование и этапы развития // Автореф. дисс... докт. ист. наук. – Т., 2009. С. 22.

[2] See: Rowe W. China's Last Empire: The Great Qing. Harvard University Press, 2009.

[3] Кляшторный С. Г. История Центральной Азии и памятники рунического письма... С. 30.

[4] Гафуров Б. Г. Таджики. Древнейшая, древняя и средневековая история. Кн. 1. – Душанбе, 1989. С. 319; Лившиц В. А. Согдийская эпиграфика Средней Азии и Семиречья. Письмо Деваштичу. – СПб., 2008. С. 84–97.

[5] Альбаум Л. И. Живопись Афрасиаба. – Т., 1975. С. 112.

[6] Kevin Reilly (ed). Worlds of History. A Comparative Reader, vol 2., since 1400. 6th. ed, Boston and New York: Bedford/St. Martin's, 2017, p.560-609; Source: Nicholas D. Kristof, "1492: The Prequel," New York Times Magazine, June 6, 1999, 5,80:1.

the Silk Road who subsequently brought the ideas to Europe the techniques of watertight bulkheads, stern-post rudders and navigational aids such as the compass. Unlike the European single-masted vessels, which could sail only downwind, their multiple-masted vessels—which influenced changes in the West—could sail into the wind. Long voyages were now feasible[①].

Looking back on this history, spanning more than a thousand years, one can make a general conclusion that in the Middle Empire and Central Asia, huge states were created in various periods, and the peoples of the region were part of various multi-ethnic formations. For instance, originating from Bukhara, General Ann Pu, Commander in Chief of Dingyuan during the Tang Dynasty, played an important role in Central Asia-China relations as well as China's history[②]. As a result, the population of Central Asia and China for a long time was characterized by inclusiveness and changed towards an increasing number of representatives of different ethnic groups, religions, and cultural-civilizational diversity.

Cultural Enrichment and Inclusiveness

Central Asia and China possess a rich, unique heritage that is part of the treasure trove of world civilization, which continues to amaze researchers today with its characteristics of sought-after universality, towards which humanity aspires. During the period of the Eastern Renaissance, great thinkers emerged in various parts of Asia, and, as noted by the famous American scholar F. Starr, for several centuries, Central Asia "was the intellectual hub of the world"[③]. Among the shared intellectual heritage, it is worth mentioning Mahmud al-Kashgari and Yusuf Balasaguni of Karakhanid Dynasty.

Mahmud al-Kashgari – an outstanding scientist, a philosopher of the XI century, the author of the first encyclopedic edition of the dictionary of Turkic dialects "The Divan Lugat at Turk" in 1071 based on a comparative analysis of the materials used among the

---

① Woodruff W. A Concise History of the Modern World 1500 to the Present A Guide to World Affairs, Fourth edition, 2002. P. 8-22.

② https://russian.news.cn/2019-06/21/c_138161529.htm (Accessed January 22, 2024).

③ Starr F. Lost Enlightenment. Central Asia's golden age. From the Arab conquest to Tamerlane. Princeton University Press, 2013. P. 5.

Turkic-speaking tribes that inhabited the territory of Central Asia. M. Kashgari received education in Bukhara, Samarkand, Baghdad and Merv, Nishapur, in the intellectual centres of the Arab world. The book provides linguistic insights into the cultural tapestry of the Turkic ethnic groups. It showcases the places inhabited by the ethnic groups using Turkic language and features approximately 800 words, idioms, proverbs and samples of poetry, accompanied by Arabic translations.

Yusuf Hajib Balasaghuni was an eleventh-century poet from the city of Balasaghun, the capital of the Karakhanid Empire in modern-day Kyrgyzstan. He wrote the *Kutadgu Bilig* ("Beneficial Knowledge") and most of what is known about him comes from his writings in this work.

The thinkers of Central Asia and China played a significant role in the development of the exchange of material and spiritual cultural achievements among the peoples of the East and Europe. According to the famous Swiss orientalist Adam Metz, the humanism of the classical European Renaissance would not have been possible without the preceding philosophical Renaissance in Central Asia[1].

The assertions of these specialists undoubtedly oppose one-sidedly oriented concepts of the development of the East and the West, supporting our thesis of the unity and interconnectedness of historical processes in various regions of the world, i. e. , the absence of a predetermined element in them.

Contemporary Relations of Central Asia and China

After the USSR's disintegration, China and Central Asian republics – Kazakhstan, Kyrgyz Republic, Tajikistan, Turkmenistan, and Uzbekistan as neighbours considerably increased bilateral and multilateral relations in all major areas, particularly in the political and economic spheres. Due to its geographical proximity and historical connections, Xinjiang Uygur Autonomous Region plays a significant role in China's relations with Central Asia. Xinjiang is a vital hub and key transit route for trade, investment, and infrastructure development between China and Central Asian countries.

China and the Central Asian countries have established a mutually beneficial

---

[1] Mez A. Die Renaissance des Islams. Heidelberg.1922. P. 504.

relationship and achieved strong cooperation.

Firstly, the continuous deepening of bilateral and multilateral policy communication and interactions between the sides;

Secondly China's trade with Kazakhstan, Kyrgyzstan, Tajikistan, Turkmenistan and Uzbekistan—increased by more than 150 times to US$70.2 billion in 2022 from US$0. 46 billion in 1992, when China established diplomatic ties with the five Central Asian countries[1];

Thirdly, China and Central Asian countries have actively promoted infrastructure connectivity, establishing a network of interconnection. Projects such as the China-Kyrgyzstan-Uzbekistan highway and at present under-construction railway line One, China-Tajikistan expressway, China-Central Asia gas pipeline, and China-Kazakhstan crude oil pipeline operate safely and steadily. China actively developed new communications links in Eurasia, in particular, communication with Europe. Its branches go in a to north-west and south-west direction, first passing through Russia, Ukraine, Belarus, Poland, and other countries and the second passing through Kazakhstan, Uzbekistan, Turkmenistan, Iran, Turkey, and Europe;

Fourthly, China and Central Asian countries have jointly implemented projects in oil and gas, mining, agriculture, textiles, manufacturing, and other sectors, contributing to industrial upgrading, and connectivity;

Fifthly, China and Central Asia have also invested in educational, cultural, and human resource development projects in Central Asia to promote people-to-people exchanges and cooperation between the two regions. Modern cultural exchanges between China and Central Asia have been multifaceted and dynamic, encompassing various aspects such as art, literature, music, cinema, language, education, and tourism. Exchange programs and academic collaborations, enhance communication between scholars, students, and professionals. Xinjiang shares cultural and ethnic ties with Central Asia and this tradition and heritage facilitates people-to-people exchanges and cultural cooperation between Xinjiang and Central Asia. Currently, there are 13 Confucius Institutes and 24 Confucius Classrooms in Central Asia[2], which help promote the popularization of China and the

---

① https://www.silkroadbriefing.com/news/2023/05/18/chinas-economic-trade-cooperation-with-central-asia/ (Accessed September 20, 2023).

② China-Central Asia cooperation in numbers. Xinhua. May 17, 2023 http://english.scio.gov.cn/interna tionalexchanges/2023-05-17/content_85354144.htm (Accessed October 5, 2023).

Chinese language in the countries of Central Asia. Major Chinese language universities also offer majors and courses in the languages of Central Asia. For sure, cultural, educational and academic exchanges contribute to a vibrant tapestry of diversity, mutual respect, and cooperation between China and Central Asia.

SCO and "PRC+ CA" Multilateral Formats

China and Central Asia were cofounders in 2001 of the Shanghai Cooperation Organisation (SCO) as an intergovernmental international organization and at present, the SCO comprises nine member states—India, Iran, Kazakhstan, China, the Kyrgyz Republic, Pakistan, Russia, Tajikistan, and Uzbekistan as well as the number of partners and observed countries. Over the years the SCO passed through several interesting phases in its institutional and political evolution and represented an international instrument to coordinate areas of multilateral cooperation. However, the existence of differences between the SCO member states and new stability challenges and problems should be noted.

Another factor contributing to the intensification of interaction is the development of China and Central Asia's "PRC+ CA" format. On May 18-19, 2023 the first and historic China-Central Asia Summit in the city of Xi'an convened the leaders of Kazakhstan, Uzbekistan, Kyrgyzstan, Tajikistan and Turkmenistan to the first China-Central Asia meeting. In his keynote speech, Xi Jinping mentioned "Over 2,100 years ago, Zhang Qian, a Han Dynasty envoy, made his journey to the West from Chang'an, opening the door to the friendship and exchanges between China and Central Asia. With their joint endeavour of hundreds of years, Chinese and Central Asian peoples made the Silk Road expand and prosper, a historic contribution to the interaction, integration, enrichment and development of world civilizations"[1]. During this summit, it was discussed a wider range of bilateral and multilateral issues and number package of documents worth 25 billion U.S. dollar was signed.

---

[1] Working Together for a China-Central Asia Community with a Shared Future - Featuring Mutual Assistance, Common Development, Universal Security, and Everlasting Friendship. Keynote Speech by Xi Jinping at the China-Central Asia Summit. 2023. https://www.chinadaily.com.cn/a/202305/20/WS6467ff4ea310b6054fad414a.html (Accessed December 10, 2023).

Belt and Road toward Global Partnership

In 2013, Chinese President Xi Jinping announced the creation of "The Silk Road Economic Belt" in Astana, Kazakhstan and "the 21st Century Maritime Silk Road" in Jakarta, Indonesia. In 2014 Silk Road Fund was established. In 2016 the Asian Infrastructure Investment Bank (AIIB) was founded, which aimed at providing investment and financial support toward cooperation in infrastructure, resources, industry, and the finance sector, as well as other transport communication projects. This involved various countries in the economic framework of the "Belt and Road" initiative. The Central Asian countries among hundreds of AIIB's member states support China's mega grant initiative.

It should be noted that the Presidents of Kazakhstan, Kyrgyzstan, Tajikistan, and Uzbekistan together with more than a dozen state and government leaders took part in "Belt and Road" international forums in Beijing in 2017, 2019, and 2023 respectively.

Today, the Belt and Road Initiative is a global initiative that requires comprehensive bilateral and multilateral cooperation on economic, political, and security matters. In Central Asia, the realization of regional and international projects is necessary. Increased connectivity and technological developments, as well as the active implementation of a diverse range of cooperation between Belt and Road participating countries, including high-tech innovations, education, public diplomacy, and tourism, are required. Moreover, China's relations with the Central Asian States began to focus more and more on long-term and comprehensive goals.

Conclusion

Historically, Central Asia and China have been one of important centres of trade, economic, and cultural exchange between Asia and Europe. The ancient Silk Road contributed a lot to civilizational development and exchanges. A deep study of the historical past provides a solid foundation for studying contemporary social transformations, and comparative analysis of the parallels and patterns of societal and state development. Today, the Belt and Road initiative is a continuation of the Silk Road traditions, but we also witness complex global processes. The wisdom coming from the depths of centuries is highly relevant. For example, there is a Chinese proverb: "Do not quarrel with your close neighbour, do not neglect your distant friend", and there is an Uzbek proverb: "A neighbour is closer than a distant relative", which is a good example of unity in diversity.

In the context of intersecting globalization and regional processes, the study of historical heritage and international humanitarian cooperation play important, complementary roles as key aspects of national and regional sustainable development. Current and future transformations will depend on the interlinks between regional and global issues and challenges.

In the context of the prospective development of relations between China and Central Asia, it seems appropriate to:

First, expand interdisciplinary approaches in studying the history and international relations of countries, regions, and the world as interconnectedness, inclusiveness and with a key point of unity in the diversity of civilizations;

Second, it is necessary to improve the functioning of the educational and scientific system in Central Asia, which will undoubtedly require a broad mobilization of resources, knowledge, and the active application of advanced international experience, including positive dynamics of the universities and research center of China;

Third, to achieve sustainability in bilateral and multilateral relations between Central Asia and China, it is advisable to intensify efforts in implementing joint integration projects, including scientific and educational ones, within the framework of the Belt and Road Initiative and others.

Undoubtedly, further deepening of political, economic, cultural, and humanitarian development and expanding international cooperation between China and Central Asia will be crucial in ensuring sustainable development and strengthening stability in Eurasia.

Sri Lanka's Strategic Role in Belt and Road Cooperation with China: A Gramscian Analysis

Asanga Abeyagoonasekera

Senior Fellow and the Executive Director of the South Asia Foresight Network

Introduction

In the aftermath of Sri Lanka's 2024 presidential election, which saw Anura Kumara Dissanayake(AKD) rise to power, the nation faces pivotal questions regarding its geopolitical future—particularly its relationship with China's Belt and Road Initiative(BRI). As the world transitions into the *"Fourth Industrial Revolution"*, marked by the convergence of technological advancements and global modernisation, high-quality Belt and Road cooperation presents an opportunity for developing nations like Sri Lanka to align with China, a global leader in economic transformation.

This paper examines Sri Lanka's evolving role within the BRI framework through the theoretical lens of Antonio Gramsci, the renowned Marxist political thinker. Gramsci's concepts of *hegemony*, *transformismo*, and *passive revolution* provide an essential framework for understanding Sri Lanka's strategic positioning under AKD's pragmatic leadership. In the backdrop of Sri Lanka's *"People's Uprising"* in 2022, a political party, National Peoples Power (NPP), with a Marxist ideological leaning with its foundational structure at Janatha Vimukthi

Peramuna (JVP), has come to power, defeating the traditional two political parties or their coalitions. The paper explores the ideological evolution of the NPP by comparing the strength of Marxist ideology in Sri Lanka's new political party and its reformist tendencies in political movements across a sample of countries, including China.

The new president AKD's approach balances Sri Lanka's national interests and the broader geopolitical dynamics influencing its development trajectory. There are many lessons that Sri Lanka could learn from China's economic miracle from 1978 to the present leadership of President Xi Jinping, who "inherited and carried forward Deng's legacy through comprehensively deepening reform". Sri Lanka's pivotal role as a strong BRI partner and a historic China-centric "Peking wing" oriented political party, the JVP in the background, will open a window of opportunity for the new administration to position with the BRI. This analysis will explore how, under AKD's stewardship, Sri Lanka might leverage its partnership with China to enhance national growth while navigating multiple geopolitical pressures.

Theoretical Framework: Gramsci's *Hegemony* and *Transformismo*

Antonio Gramsci's notion of *hegemony* asserts that power is maintained not primarily through force but through cultural and ideological dominance. China's BRI exemplifies this type of leadership. It seeks to establish global economic influence through investments in infrastructure, trade, and modernisation initiatives across partner nations. However, Gramsci's theory of *transformismo*—the absorption of local ideologies into a larger hegemonic framework—suggests that success depends on integrating the needs and aspirations of regional actors.

In Sri Lanka, AKD's leadership epitomises *transformismo*. Once rooted in Marxist ideology, the NPP has adapted to the complexities of electoral politics and economic pragmatism. Similarly, Sri Lanka's alignment with the BRI must not result in passive dependence on foreign investment but rather the strategic integration of national development goals into China's broader modernisation agenda. Gramsci's emphasis on cultural and ideological leadership offers a lens through which to view AKD's efforts to assert Sri Lanka's agency within this partnership, enabling mutually beneficial outcomes while maintaining national sovereignty.

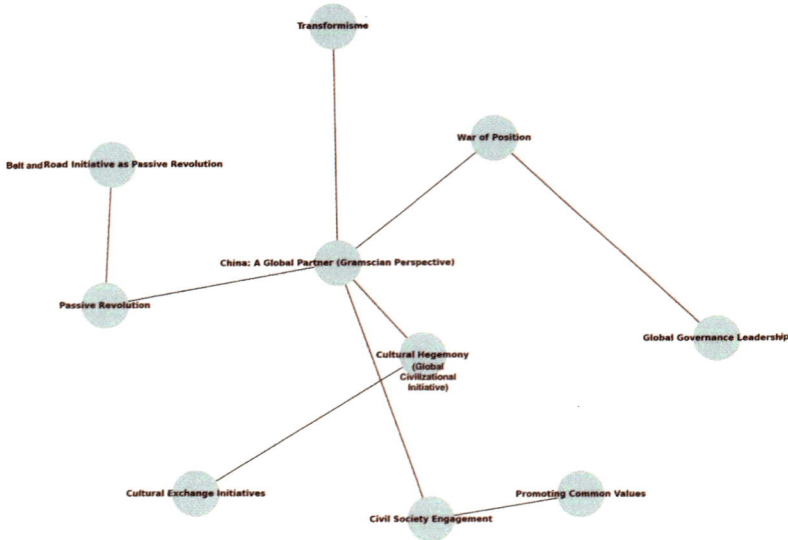

Diagram 1: Exploring China's Role as a Global Partner: A Gramscian Analysis of the BRI

The Ideological Evolution of the NPP: Marxist ideology and reformist tendencies

The People's Liberation Front, known as Janatha Vimukthi Peramuna(JVP), with its founding leader Rohana Wijeweera, was earlier in N. Shanmugathasan's Communist Party (Peking Wing), a more China-centric political party. There were two Communist Parties, the CPSL (Moscow) and the CPSL (Peking). Comrade Rohana Wijeweera was the son of a vital member of the CPSL, which influenced his thinking on the ideology of Marxism-Leninism. He was educated in the party school at the Communist Party of the Soviet Union (CPSU) while reading at Patrice Lumumba Friendship University in Soviet Russia. Comrade Wijeweera was critical of Khrushchev's revisionist line. The revisionists' thinking over Nikita Khruschev's distance from the legacy of Josef Stalin was a concern to Wijeweera, resulting in a refusal to re-enter the Soviet Union in 1964.

The shift from the Soviet camp to the Peking group was at this turning point when he saw China as the way forward for his political struggle in Sri Lanka. However, due to his internal activism, the political party the CPSL(Peking), he was expelled by the leadership. Later Wijeweera formed the JVP in 1965.

According to *Rajan Hoole,* "Wijeweera took the anti-Indianism that was a part of his political environment and represented the voiceless Plantation Tamils of recent Indian origin as an arm of Indian expansionism. The JVP avoided an explicit position on the Tamil issue by contending that once there is socialism, the issue would go away". The JVP launched the two insurrections in 1971 and 1988, and the Sri Lankan state successfully crushed them. The anti-Indian-centric position was a clear political stance from JVP's inception in 1971, and the Indo-Lanka accord on devolution of power was a clear stand against India's hegemonic behaviour over Sri Lanka's sovereignty.

Sri Lanka received Indian assistance to crush the rebellion, argues *Padmaja Murthi,* in April 1971, through five Indian 'frigates to seal off approaches to Colombo along with military equipment, six helicopters with pilots for non-combat duties and about 150 Indian troops to guard the Bandaranaike airport'. While India's action was prompted by the desire to protect the democratic system and instil domestic stability 'some in Sri Lanka opine that the speed with which Indian assistance had arrived to support the Bandaranaike's left-of-centre government in 1971 was as significant as the eagerness with which it was done'. The second insurrection was more brutal in 1988-89 that killed almost 60,000, and AKD apologised for the first time in 2014 "over the killings for which his party was responsible and also apologised to the public over such unfortunate incidents".

AKD's presidency marks a significant transformation in the NPP's political ideology, signalling a departure from the party's historical Marxist roots towards a more reformist, pragmatic stance. This evolution places the NPP within a broader context of global leftist movements that have adapted to contemporary economic and political realities.

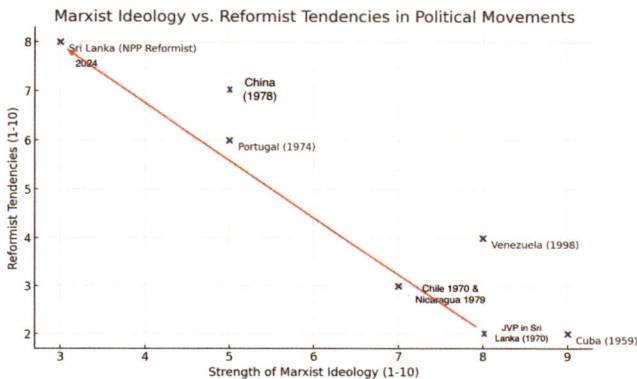

Figure 1: Marxist Ideology vs. Reformist Tendencies in Political Movements.

The NPP's ideological trajectory can be illustrated by comparing its Marxist ideological strength versus reformist tendencies, drawing parallels with other historical movements. In the 1970s, the JVP—the NPP's precursor—was a bastion of revolutionary Marxism, scoring high ideological rigidity but low reformist adaptability. By 2024, under AKD's leadership, the NPP had embraced a more flexible, reform-oriented approach, prioritising pragmatic governance over ideological purity.

Table 1: Evaluation of Marxist Ideology Strength and Reformist Tendencies

Country	Marxist Ideology Strength	Reformist Tendencies
Cuba (1959)	9	2
Chile (1970)	7	3
Venezuela (1998)	8	4
Nicaragua (1979)	7	3
Portugal (1974)	5	6
China (Post-1978 Reforms)	5	7
Sri Lanka (JVP, 1970s)	8	2
Sri Lanka (NPP, 2024)	3	8

As Table 1 reflects, the NPP's shift mirrors the pragmatic reformism seen in other leftist movements, such as Portugal's Carnation Revolution and China's post-1978 economic miracle. AKD's challenge will be to navigate the tensions between these reformist tendencies and residual ideological commitments within his party, particularly as Sri Lanka grapples with the competing influences of prominent geopolitical actors like India, U.S. and China.

Sri Lanka's pivotal role as a strong BRI partner and a historic China-centric "Peking wing"-oriented political party, with the JVP as a shadow, and its present high reformist and low Marxist-oriented values move Sri Lanka closer to the Chinese development model prescribed in 1978. This new policy prescription will open a window of opportunity for the new AKD administration to position itself better with China and its BRI than the past Sri Lankan regimes.

Gramsci in China: Application to BRI

After the Chinese Civil War ended in 1949, with the triumph of the Communist-party-led revolution led by Mao Zedong, the People's Republic of China was established on October 1, 1949. According to *Xin Liu,* the first book about Antonio Gramsci was introduced to China by the World Knowledge Press in Beijing in 1957. In this book, *Life of Antonio Gramsci* was depicted as a loyal Marxist who led the Italian Communist movement at the beginning of the twentieth century. Although Gramsci was introduced in the early days, there was resistance to accommodating his thinking in China in the 1960s and 1970s due to the critical view of foreign Western Marxist thought in China. This was due to the CPC's significant ideological break with the Communist Party of the Soviet Union led by Nikita Khrushchev. The same reason was valid in Sri Lanka, where the Peking group was formulated to retain a purer Stalinist position.

However, after the end of the Cultural Revolution in China, the new Chinese leader, Deng Xiaoping, permitted contact with the outside world and gradually loosened the strict censorship, allowing cultural communication between China and Western countries and broadening the perspective of Chinese Marxist scholars. It was Perry Anderson's *Considerations on Western Marxism,* which was made available in 1981, that became a turning point. Anderson's reintroduction of Gramsci to Chinese intellectuals was widely appreciated. Eventually, Chinese scholars saw Gramsci as a leading figure of the Western Communist movement, which had been forgotten for almost two decades.

In the present day, social and cultural organisations in China are increasingly influenced by Gramscian thinking, where *cultural hegemony* is a key concept, is used to function and disseminate a China-centric, harmonious socialist culture intellectually. BRI's *Shared Future,* where the Global Development Initiative (GDI), Global Civilizational Initiative (GCI), and Global Security Initiative (GSI), the three pillars introduced by President Xi, function to develop a harmonious world, is a Gramscian fabric wrapped together with a prime focus on creating a unique culture.

Global Civilizational Initiative (GCI), Counter-hegemonic Force

The GCI positively aligns with Antonio Gramsci's theory of *cultural hegemony*, particularly in fostering positive engagement between different civilisations. Gramsci argued that cultural hegemony operates by disseminating a dominant ideology that shapes societal values, norms, and institutions. In this context, China's initiative—focusing on harmonious coexistence and mutual respect for diverse civilisations—can be seen as a move to reshape global narratives and norms through cooperation rather than coercion.

Gramsci viewed cultural hegemony as a dynamic force evolving through consensus and intellectual leadership rather than direct political or military dominance. In this sense, China's GCI can be interpreted as an attempt to create a new global order where cultural, intellectual, and moral leadership plays a central role. By promoting intercultural dialogue, respect for sovereignty, and shared prosperity, China seeks to build a multipolar world, counteracting the historically Western-dominated narrative of global governance.

President Xi Jinping's GCI reinforces Gramsci's notion of cultural hegemony in a positive way by advocating for the respect of diverse civilisations and the shared values of humanity. In his speech, Xi emphasised the importance of respecting the diversity of civilisations, valuing both inheritance and innovation within cultures, and promoting robust international people-to-people exchanges and cooperation. This contrasts with Western notions of the "superiority of certain civilisations" and the theory of a "clash of civilisations." Instead, China promotes the principles of equality, mutual learning, dialogue, and inclusiveness among civilisations, which aligns with Gramsci's idea of creating consent and cooperation through cultural leadership.

The BRI is instrumental to this approach. While primarily economic, BRI's role in fostering connections between nations enables more profound intellectual and cultural exchanges, serving as a framework for mutual learning. Through projects that respect local traditions and promote shared development, BRI offers an alternative to Western-led development narratives, reshaping how power and leadership are understood globally. Thus, it embodies China's global civilisational ambitions and Gramsci's theories of consensual leadership, offering a path where diverse civilisations can co-exist and collaborate harmoniously, enhancing global stability.

This initiative, viewed positively, represents an opportunity for nations like Sri Lanka, under the leadership of figures like AKD, to engage in international cooperation that emphasises sovereignty and national development while participating in a global discourse on equality. It reflects Gramsci's belief that the consent of the governed (through intellectual and moral leadership) is more enduring and influential than dominance through coercion. Thus, the GCI could be seen as a *"counter-hegemony,"* offering an alternative to the hegemonic structures historically shaped by Western powers.

BRI is a practical extension of China's GCI, bringing Gramsci's cultural hegemony into economic and infrastructural realms. While Gramsci's theory emphasises the creation of consent through intellectual and artistic leadership, the BRI seeks to shape global trade and development that aligns with China's vision of international cooperation. By extending financial and technological support to developing countries through infrastructure projects, China builds physical connections and creates an intellectual and cultural influence across Asia and beyond.

For nations like Sri Lanka, BRI investments present a path towards economic growth and modernisation while providing an alternative to the development models historically shaped by Western institutions. Under the leadership of AKD, BRI participation can be framed as a partnership that respects national sovereignty while contributing to the transformation of local economies and the global system. In this view, BRI can be seen as a tool for building a new culture—where China's state-led development becomes influential globally, resonating with Gramsci's idea of creating a new "common sense" through economic, intellectual, and cultural exchange.

By integrating the GCI and the BRI, China is a leader of a new, multipolar world, embodying Gramsci's ideas of moral and intellectual leadership globally. This approach presents a *counter-hegemonic* force, potentially reshaping global norms through peaceful cooperation rather than coercion, which may appeal to Sri Lanka under a leadership aligned with socialist principles.

Gramsci's Tansformismo & Application to BRI

Gramsci introduced the concept of *transformismo* in his *"Prison Notebooks,"* written between 1929 and 1935. Gramsci used transformismo to describe how ruling classes in Italy co-opted and neutralised revolutionary movements by absorbing their leaders into the existing political framework, thus preventing radical social change. Gramsci viewed transformism as a process. The ruling class maintains its dominance by integrating opposing elements of society into its system, creating a semblance of reform while avoiding more profound systemic changes.

The *'System Change'* expressed by Sri Lankan protestors in 2022 was the change to break away from the elite ruling political class that successfully used transformismo to divide the opposition forces and further break the Marxist elements. Sri Lankan two mainstream political parties, the UNP and SLFP, with their coalition groups, managed to absorb the leftist leaders and neutralise the revolutionary movements by integrating them into the coalitions. In the present day in Sri Lanka, you witness a historical political movement in which people understood transformismo and changed the system through a democratic election.

There is an opportunity for AKD to apply *transformismo* in a positive trajectory within the context of the Belt and Road Initiative (BRI). Transformismo can be framed as a constructive strategy allowing developing countries to develop economically while maintaining their political and cultural identity. Here's how this can be interpreted positively:

1. Economic Growth and Modernization: Transformismo under the BRI allows smaller nations to embrace infrastructure and modernisation projects without being forced into ideological alignment or submission to any external hegemonic forces. By absorbing economic benefits, these countries can enhance their infrastructure and reduce poverty while maintaining their political sovereignty and cultural uniqueness. For example, many BRI nations have benefited from infrastructure projects that boost connectivity and trade.

2. Sovereignty Preservation: Rather than being dominated by external powers, nations participating in the BRI could engage in strategic partnerships that align with their national interests. Economic and political cooperation with China enhances its sovereignty by reducing economic dependency on Western financial institutions (IMF) or regional powers. For instance, developing African and Asian countries have used BRI investments to increase their bargaining power in international forums.

3. Cultural and Diplomatic Exchange: Transformismo under the BRI isn't limited to economic absorption. Cultural exchange programs, Buddhist BRI, diplomatic ties, and people-to-people connections fostered by the initiative can be seen as a positive transformation, where countries retain their cultural identities while benefiting from closer international cooperation. This can lead to more balanced global relationships based on mutual respect. Example: There is

tremendous potential for Buddhist BRI nations to align for cultural exchange and partnerships in Southeast Asia and Sri Lanka.

4. Collaborative Governance: By integrating different political and economic models through the BRI, China demonstrates a pragmatic approach to governance that can include diverse systems. Developing nations might adopt a flexible approach that blends Chinese practices with their own, creating hybrid models of governance that are responsive to local needs but benefit from China's expertise and support. With its Marxist roots, the NPP government in Sri Lanka will be open to such hybrid model experimentation.

In this context, *transformismo,* as applied to the BRI, becomes a tool for smaller nations to modernise and preserve autonomy. Through pragmatic leadership, like that potentially envisioned by AKD, countries can selectively adopt beneficial aspects of China's model. This transforms China's influence into a partnership of equals.

Gramsci's theories also provide insight into how Sri Lanka can maintain agency within the BRI framework. Rather than being a passive participant, AKD's administration can negotiate terms that align with Sri Lanka's long-term vision for sustainable development, ensuring that high-quality cooperation brings tangible benefits to its citizens. China's emphasis on win-win cooperation under the BRI and its provision of technological expertise and capacity-building offers a foundation for such a partnership.

Sri Lanka's engagement with China under the BRI offers a pivotal economic growth and modernisation opportunity. Contrary to Western concerns that Chinese investments might lead to debt dependency, AKD's administration can leverage this partnership to advance Sri Lanka's infrastructure development, job creation, and global economic standing. Projects such as the Hambantota Port and the Colombo Port City have already demonstrated the transformative potential of BRI investments. Under AKD's leadership, these projects can serve as cornerstones for a broader sustainable economic development strategy. AKD's pragmatic approach could align with Gramsci's *transformismo*, envisioning a partnership that integrates Chinese investment into Sri Lanka's national development goals rather than passively participating.

Gramsci's Application to Sri Lanka

Gramsci explains how the ruling class maintains dominance through force or coercion, ideological control, and cultural leadership. Gramsci argued that to understand political power, we must consider not just the state's coercive apparatus but also how the ruling class shapes the cultural and intellectual life of society to secure the consent of the ruled. There are several critical aspects of Gramsci's Theory of Hegemony:

1. Cultural Leadership: Gramsci emphasised that power is exercised through the ruling class's ability to influence societal norms, values, beliefs, and ideas. This process of gaining cultural and ideological leadership is what he called "hegemony." The ruling class creates a consensus that aligns the interests of subordinate groups with their own, making domination seem natural or beneficial for all.

   AKD's presidency, as the leader of the National People's Power (NPP), can exercise cultural leadership by challenging the long-established political narratives dominated by the Rajapaksa dynasty and other mainstream parties. His leadership could align with the NPP's anti-corruption platform and focus on the needs of the working class, positioning his presidency as a champion of the people. He could reshape political discourse by promoting socialist and egalitarian values, offering an alternative to neoliberal policies.

   Application: To achieve cultural hegemony, AKD must articulate a vision of a fairer, more just Sri Lanka, where public welfare is prioritised over elite interests. His leadership must also appeal to intellectuals and activists to legitimise this cultural shift.

2. Consent and Coercion: According to Gramsci, hegemony functions through consent and coercion. Consent is gained through institutions like the media, schools, and religion, which propagate the ruling class's worldview, making it seem common sense. Coercion, on the other hand, is applied through the state's legal and military institutions to manage dissent and enforce control where consent is insufficient.

   Gramsci argued that dominance is not sustained by force alone but by creating a sense of consent among the governed. In AKD's case, winning the consent of various social classes—especially the urban and rural working classes—would be crucial. The NPP's emphasis on reducing corruption, improving public services, and addressing economic inequality could secure this consent.

   Application: His presidency must carefully balance using state power and coercion with maintaining popular support. AKD could utilise the tools of media, education, and civil society to propagate a narrative that his government's policies are in the best interest of all citizens, avoiding the mistakes of purely authoritarian governance.

3. War of Position vs. War of Movement: Gramsci described the struggle for hegemony in terms of a "war of position" (gradual cultural and ideological change) and a "war of movement" (direct, often violent, revolutionary action). In modern capitalist societies, where the state and civil society are deeply intertwined, Gramsci believed that a war of position—gaining ideological and cultural influence—was essential before a war of movement could succeed.

The "war of position" refers to the gradual cultural and ideological shift necessary to challenge the existing order, while the "war of movement" is direct revolutionary action. AKD's strategy in the run-up to his election could be seen as a "war of position," in which the NPP worked to gain influence within civil society, mainly through grassroots activism and anti-establishment rhetoric.

Application: As president, he may continue this war of position by gradually introducing policies that challenge the status quo, such as land reform or state-led economic initiatives, while ensuring not to alienate the middle classes or provoke a counter-reaction from entrenched elites. The idea is to create systemic change slowly, making his policies appear as natural progress rather than radical shifts.

4. Intellectuals and Counter-hegemony: Gramsci distinguished between traditional intellectuals (aligned with the ruling class) and organic intellectuals (emerging from the working class or other subordinate groups). Organic intellectuals play a crucial role in developing counter-hegemony, creating alternative ideologies and cultural values to challenge the dominant system.

Gramsci emphasised the role of intellectuals in shaping hegemonic or counter-hegemonic forces. Organic intellectuals from the working class play a key role in constructing counter-hegemonies. Under AKD's presidency, organic intellectuals—activists, progressive academics, and left-leaning media personalities—could bolster the NPP's efforts to challenge the neoliberal narrative and promote socialist alternatives.

Application: By empowering these intellectuals to take leadership in education, media, and policymaking, AKD can strengthen his government's ideological influence. The presidency could foster an intellectual movement that redefines Sri Lanka's social and economic policies, potentially crafting a narrative where Sri Lanka's sovereignty is seen as inseparable from its socialist values.

5. Transformismo: As mentioned earlier, Gramsci introduced the concept of transformismo to explain how dominant classes prevent revolutionary change by absorbing opposition leaders and movements, co-opting their ideas and making superficial reforms to maintain the status quo.

One of the challenges AKD's administration will face is avoiding being absorbed by the very elite and capitalist structures that the NPP campaigned against. Maintaining ideological purity while also governing pragmatically could be difficult.

Application: In a positive sense, AKD could use transformismo to incorporate moderate opposition figures or reformist policies into his government without diluting his party's core principles. This might allow him to neutralise potential threats from conservative factions while advancing his socialist agenda. If successful, it would enable the NPP to maintain its anti-establishment image while effectively managing state institutions.

Challenging Indian Hegemony: Insurrections to Foreign Policy

In the context of Sri Lanka's strategic role within the BRI, Gramsci's theory of hegemony offers a compelling framework to analyse the nation's historical resistance to regional domination, mainly from India. Through its insurrections in 1971 and 1988-1989, the JVP epitomised this struggle, asserting national sovereignty against the perceived Indian hegemony exemplified in the 1987 Indo-Lanka Accord. The JVP's actions can be viewed as a positive trend toward reclaiming Sri Lankan identity, mobilising public sentiment against foreign influence and advocating for self-determination.

In this context, AKD's pragmatic leadership emerges as a contemporary response to these historical dynamics, seeking to navigate Sri Lanka's strategic interests within the BRI while resisting external pressures. AKD aims to redefine Sri Lanka's geopolitical standing, reclaim sovereignty, and establish a counter-hegemonic narrative prioritising national interests over regional domination by fostering a more equitable partnership with China and other stakeholders. AKD's balance will require calculating Indian pressure on security as explained by former Indian diplomat Ajay Bisaria: "So far, at least,

India is the preferred security partner. On its part, India is learning to build long-term equities in the neighbourhood that transcend regimes." AKD's new approach reflects an evolution of resistance from the JVP's historical insurrections to strategic manoeuvring that seeks development opportunities without sacrificing agency, highlighting a significant shift in the nation's diplomatic landscape.

Applying Gramsci's theory of hegemony, AKD's presidency could be seen as an ongoing project to reshape Sri Lanka's political culture. His ability to generate consent, engage intellectuals, and manage ideological conflict through subtle forms of leadership would be crucial in determining whether his government becomes a truly transformative force or is absorbed into the existing hegemonic order.

BRI as a Passive Revolution

Gramsci's concept of passive revolution—the notion that social and economic change can be achieved incrementally within an existing political order—provides a valuable framework for understanding Sri Lanka's role in the BRI. The BRI can be viewed as a mechanism for facilitating incremental change in global trade and infrastructure networks, aligning with the broader modernisation efforts of developing nations like Sri Lanka. AKD's presidency can be seen as a Gramscian passive revolution, where the pragmatic embrace of the BRI enables Sri Lanka to participate in global modernization while preserving sovereignty. This approach underscores Gramsci's assertion that leadership must be adaptive, responsive to local conditions, and grounded in a long-term vision for sustainable growth.

Gramsci's concept of *passive revolution* refers to gradual, reformist transformations within the system rather than through direct revolutionary means. Rather than completely overthrowing the current capitalist system or Sri Lanka's traditional reliance on foreign capital, AKD's government could approach BRI as a *passive revolution*—seeking incremental but transformative benefits from China's investments while protecting national sovereignty. By doing so, the NPP can align with China's socialist roots, mirroring the narrative that China used the BRI to assert its global presence without directly challenging Western hegemony.

Navigating Geopolitical Pressures

One of AKD's foremost challenges will be balancing the competing geopolitical pressures exerted by external powers with strategic interests in Sri Lanka's position within the Indian Ocean. China's substantial investments through the BRI must be managed carefully to avoid excessive dependency, while India seeks to counterbalance China's growing influence in the region.

Gramsci's strategy of *transformismo* offers a pathway for Sri Lanka to navigate these pressures by incorporating elements of both Chinese and Indian development models into its national strategy. This balancing act will ensure that Sri Lanka's modernisation efforts reflect its aspirations rather than being dictated by external powers.

The NPP has historically exhibited an apparent inclination towards fostering closer ties with China rather than India, reflecting its broader geopolitical strategy. This preference is deeply rooted in the NPP's ideological framework, emphasising sovereignty and autonomy in international relations. The party's founders, particularly the JVP, have historically resisted Indian hegemony, perceiving it as a threat to Sri Lanka's independence. This stance was particularly evident during the 1988 Indo-Lanka Accord, where a rejection of perceived Indian interference in Sri Lankan affairs drove the JVP's insurrection. In contrast, the NPP's engagement with China is framed as a strategic move to diversify Sri Lanka's foreign relations, enhancing economic partnerships that bolster national interests.

By aligning more closely with China, the NPP aims to counterbalance India's historical influence in the region, creating a diplomatic landscape where Sri Lanka can assert its agency. This strategic choice is significant in the context of China's BRI, which offers infrastructure development and investment opportunities that align with the NPP's vision for economic revitalisation and independence from external pressures. The NPP's pro-China sentiment thus serves as a cornerstone of its political narrative, positioning the party as a champion of Sri Lankan sovereignty while navigating the complexities of regional geopolitics.

Seven areas: Promoting High-quality Belt & Road Cooperation

The BRI, as seen through a Gramscian lens, represents China's nuanced and strategic effort to reshape the existing global hegemonic structures. By engaging in high-quality cooperation with Sri Lanka and other BRI nations, China promotes an alternative model of modernisation that integrates cultural diplomacy, technological innovation, and sustainable infrastructure development. The following are seven areas to which China can contribute:

1. Focus on Sustainable Infrastructure Development (Cultural Hegemony and Passive Revolution): From a Gramscian standpoint, the expansion of sustainable infrastructure under the BRI can be viewed as a form of *cultural hegemony*, where China promotes an alternative development model that contrasts with traditional Western-led globalisation. This passive revolution shifts the global discourse on modernisation, where sustainability and green development become dominant norms. By acting as strategic nodes in this infrastructure network, Sri Lanka and other BRI nations help legitimise China's leadership in the global sustainability agenda, subtly transforming global power relations without overtly coercive measures.

2. Modernisation of Trade and Supply Chains (Transformismo and Hegemony of Consent): The modernisation of trade routes through projects like the Colombo Port City and Hambantota Port reflects Gramsci's concept of *transformismo*, where elites from diverse sectors are co-opted to align with a broader hegemonic project—in this case, the economic integration of the Global South under the BRI. The process co-opts local elites and integrates them into a transnational capitalist framework, fostering a *hegemonic consent* where countries like Sri Lanka voluntarily align with China's vision for trade and economic connectivity. This cooperative framework subtly challenges the neoliberal global order, positioning China as a leader in global modernisation.

3. Enhancing Technological Exchange and Innovation (War of Position and Cultural Diplomacy): Gramsci's concept of the *war of position* applies to technological collaboration within the BRI. China's focus on exporting advanced technologies such as 5G, AI, and digital infrastructure is part of a long-term strategy to challenge Western technological dominance. Through *cultural diplomacy*, China subtly repositions itself as a technological leader. Sri Lanka's participation in this exchange allows it to access cutting-edge technologies while contributing to a shift in global hegemony where technological leadership is diversified. This reflects the slow yet significant cultural and ideological shifts in global leadership as non-Western countries lead innovation.

4. Strengthening Educational and Cultural Exchanges (Cultural Hegemony

and Civil Society Engagement): Educational and cultural exchanges between Sri Lanka and China expand China's GCI, offering an alternative vision of modernity, emphasising South-South cooperation and mutual development. This cooperation fosters a broader sense of solidarity among civil societies, reducing dependence on Western education and development models. Gramsci's idea of *civil society* as a space for the diffusion of hegemony becomes apparent, where values like inclusivity, cooperation, and shared prosperity are promoted. These exchanges strengthened China's leadership role while creating a new intellectual and cultural bloc that supported high-quality global modernisation efforts. Buddhist-BRI is on this path developed through the GCI focused as a Cultural development program.

5. Supporting Global Governance and Multilateralism (Transformismo and Passive Revolution): Through its Belt and Road partnerships, China promotes a shift in *global governance* that aligns with Gramsci's notion of *passive revolution*, whereby the existing international order is transformed from within. Sri Lanka's alignment with China's multilateral initiatives—such as the Asian Infrastructure Investment Bank (AIIB)—demonstrates how global governance frameworks are reconfiguring to accommodate non-Western powers. This process co-opts local elites and national governments of BRI nations into a new multilateral order where China's influence grows organically through consent rather than coercion.

6. Promoting Inclusive and People-centric Modernization (Hegemony of Consent vs. Coercion): High-quality BRI cooperation emphasises inclusive, people-centric development, aligning with Gramsci's theory of *hegemony of consent*. Rather than imposing top-down modernisation, China seeks to build consent through the participation of local communities in infrastructure projects. In Sri Lanka, initiatives focused on employment, poverty reduction, and improving living standards foster local buy-in and contribute to a broader sense of legitimacy for the BRI. This strategy represents a nuanced form of hegemony, where consent is cultivated through material benefits and cultural alignment rather than coercion.

7. Strategic Alignment with Global Development Goals (War of Position and Cultural Hegemony): Sri Lanka's role in the BRI also highlights its strategic alignment with global development frameworks, such as the UN Sustainable Development Goals. China has aligned its GDI, GCI, and GSI with the UN's

global development agenda. From a Gramscian perspective, this reflects China's *war of position* in the ideological and institutional arenas of global governance. Unlike direct political confrontation, a *war of manoeuvre*, the war of position is slow and incremental. It requires building a broad support base over time, patiently working to shift public opinion and alter the cultural landscape. By offering alternative paths to modernisation that emphasise infrastructure, sustainability, and South-South cooperation, China is engaging in a cultural and ideological contest against Western-led models. By aligning with these initiatives, Sri Lanka and other BRI nations help advance a *counter-hegemonic* project that seeks to redefine the terms of global development.

Conclusion

As Sri Lanka embarks on a new chapter under AKD's leadership, Gramsci's theoretical framework offers a profound understanding of how the country can engage with China's BRI to advance national development. High-quality cooperation, grounded in a pragmatic approach, can enable Sri Lanka and other BRI nations to assert China's role as a key player in global modernisation while preserving its sovereignty and cultural identity. This partnership represents a Gramscian *passive revolution*—an incremental transformation that aligns with sustainable and inclusive development goals. Sustainable infrastructure, modernised trade, and technological innovation reflect Gramsci's *transformismo* and *war of position*, allowing China to introduce an alternative to Western dominance through cultural diplomacy and long-term strategy. Meanwhile, people-centric modernisation and cultural exchanges help build *hegemonic consent* positively by winning the hearts and minds of the population, embedding China's influence in a subtle, cooperative manner. Through its engagement with the BRI, many developing nations could contribute to the global shift towards a new world order, positioning itself as a strategic player in this evolving landscape.

In this context, the partnership between Sri Lanka/other BRI nations and China can be considered a Gramscian passive revolution. This incremental but transformative process aligns with the broader sustainable and inclusive development goals. As Gramsci aptly observed, *"The old world is dying, and the new world struggles to be born".* Through its engagement with the BRI, Sri Lanka stands poised to contribute to this new world, positioning itself as a strategic player in the evolving global order.

References

1   Klaus Schwab, 2016, The Fourth Industrial Revolution, World Economic Forum, https://www.weforum.org/about/the-fourth-industrial-revolution-by-klaus-schwab/

2   Xinhua, 2024, Xinhua Headlines-Profile: Xi Jinping the reformer, https://english.news.cn/20240312/ed21a17a92864be2aa1cd2d33aeb5625/c.html

3   People's Liberation Front (JVP), History; https://www.jvpsrilanka.com/english/about-us/brief-history/

4   Hoole Rajan, Colombo Telegraph; https://www.colombotelegraph.com/index.php/the-jvp-towards-a-second-comeback/

5   Padmaja Murthy, 2000, Indo-Sri Lankan Security Perceptions: Divergences and Convergences , Columbia University, https://ciaotest.cc.columbia.edu/olj/sa/sa_may00mup01.html

6   K.M. de Silva, 1996, Regional Powers and Small State Security (Delhi: Vikas Publishing House, 1996), pp. 25.

7   Asia Mirror, 2014, JVP Tenders Public Apology Over 6000 Killings During 88-89 Uprising, https://asianmirror.lk/news/item/1386-jvp-tenders-public-apology-over-6000-killings-during-88-89-uprising

8   Lombardo Radice, 1957, Life of Antonio Gramsci, trans.Yinxing Huang (Beijing:World Knowledge Press, 1957).

9   Perry Anderson, 1981, Considerations on Western Marxism, trans. Kuo Gao (Beijing: People's Publishing House, 1981).

10   Xinhua, 2024, 3 things to know about China's Global Civilization Initiative, http://english.scio.gov.cn/in-depth/2024-04/03/content_117103205.htm

11   Saroj Pathirana, 2024, 'Only the beginning': Sri Lankans hope for deep changes under new president', Aljazeera, https://www.aljazeera.com/news/2024/9/25/only-the-beginning-sri-lankans-hope-for-deep-changes-under-new-president

12   Murali Krishnan, 2024, 'Will a new president shift Sri Lanka's foreign policy?', https://www.dw.com/en/will-a-new-president-shift-sri-lankas-approach-to-india-and-china/a-70322311

Asanga Abeyagoonasekera is a distinguished scholar and strategic advisor specializing in international security and geopolitics. He currently serves as the Executive Director of the South Asia Foresight Network (SAFN) based in Washington, DC. He is the author of several internationally recognized books and has held the position of visiting professor in the United States. With nearly two decades of experience in Sri Lanka's government, particularly within foreign policy and defense think tanks, he was the founding Director General of the Institute of National Security Studies in Sri Lanka.

Uzbekistan-China: Dynamics of Strategic Partnership and the BRI

Farrukh Khakimov

Head of Department, Development Strategy Center, Uzbekistan

Uzbekistan's contemporary foreign policy among other fundamental principles, characterized with its commitment to a multi-vector approach and non-interference. Uzbekistan is actively working to strengthen its position on the international stage, which is particularly evident in its cooperation with neighboring countries in Central Asia and with traditional strategic partners.

Neighboring states such as Kazakhstan, Tajikistan, Kyrgyzstan, and Turkmenistan are becoming important partners within Uzbekistan's new foreign policy agenda. This collaboration is reaching a new level, reflecting the desire for integration and joint solutions to regional issues.

Moreover, Uzbekistan is actively developing relations with major global powers such as China, Russia, the USA, Turkey, European Union and other countries by diversifying the geography of its international partners. This not only strengthens the Uzbekistan's economic and political ties but also allows it to play a more active role in international processes.

Thus, Uzbekistan demonstrates a flexible approach to foreign policy, contributing to its sustainable development and strengthening its position both in the region and beyond.

As of today, China is an important foreign policy and economic partner of Uzbekistan. Over the more than 30 years of diplomatic relations between the two countries, a solid foundation has been established for the activation of multifaceted strategic cooperation. As a result, during this period, relations between Uzbekistan and China have risen to the highest level of a strategic partnership in all areas.

It is particularly important to emphasize the rapidly developing economic, trade, and investment relations between two countries. In particular, over the past years, China has taken a key position in the trade and investment sector of Uzbekistan. For example, from 2017 to 2023, total investments from China in Uzbekistan's economy exceeded 14 billion dollars. The total trade volume in 2023 also reached 14 billion dollars. As of 2023, the number of enterprises with Chinese capital in Uzbekistan has reached 2, 337, which is 16. 6 percent of the total number of foreign companies operating in the country.

Notably, major companies such as Huawei, ZTE, Eximbank of China, Wenzhou Jinsheng Trading, Peng Sheng Joint Venture, Sinotruk, HengBang Textile Central Asia, and many others are actively operating in Uzbekistan. For instance, Huawei is implementing the "Safe City" project aimed at developing e-government, the digital economy, information technology, telemedicine, and IT telephony, with a budget of 300 million dollars.

Currently, Uzbekistan and China are achieving success in traditional areas of cooperation such as energy, agriculture, and the textile industry, while also witnessing growth in new areas, including cross-border e-commerce, green development, biomedicine, and poverty reduction.

The development of the strategic partnership between the two countries has opened up broad opportunities for studying China's advanced experience in poverty reduction. Evidence of this is the agreement reached in 2022 to hold joint activities aimed at learning from and implementing Chinese experience in the fight against poverty. To practically implement this agreement, a visit by Chinese scholars to Uzbekistan was organized in February 2023, and they became advisors to the Ministry of Employment and Poverty Reduction of the Republic of Uzbekistan.

Moreover, within the framework of long-term national development "Uzbekistan-2030" strategy Uzbekistan plans to halve poverty in the country by the end of 2026, drawing on China's experience.

At the same time, it is worth noting the actively developing interregional cooperation between Uzbekistan and China. In recent years, both countries have paid special attention to the development of economic, trade, and investment ties at the regional level. For example, trade turnover between Uzbekistan and the Xinjiang Uygur Autonomous Region (XUAR) is growing, with this region currently accounting for about 10 percent of mutual trade between the countries. The portfolio of investment projects with leading companies from XUAR amounts to 3. 5 billion dollars and currently encompasses areas such as green energy, the electrical engineering sector, construction, production of new types of building materials, metallurgy, infrastructure modernization, and others. A cultural exchanges program are also actively underway.

In May 2023, during the state visit of the President of Uzbekistan Shavkat Mirziyoyev to China, agreements were signed to establish partnership relations between the city of Tashkent and Sichuan Province, between Syrdarya Region and Shaanxi Province, and between Samarkand Region and Shaanxi Province. Following the state visit, in 2024, agreements were signed to establish partnership relations between Tashkent Region and Shaanxi Province and between the cities of Samarkand and Qingdao.

It is important to note that after prolonged quarantine measures due to the pandemic, Uzbekistan was one of the first countries visited by the Chinese leader on a state visit in September 2022, and also participated in the Samarkand Shanghai Cooperation Organization Summit (September 15-16, 2022).

On May 18, 2023, during the state visit of the President of Uzbekistan to China, bilateral negotiations were held between the leaders of the two countries. During the negotiations, the leaders of Uzbekistan and China signed a Joint Statement and adopted a Program for the Development of Comprehensive Strategic Partnership in a New Era for 2023-2027.

On May 19, 2023, Shavkat Mirziyoyev participated in the first "Central Asia–China" summit in Xi'an, where he presented several important proposals and initiatives for the development of regional cooperation.

In particular, President of Uzbekistan proposed the further formation of a New Economic Dialogue and the strengthening of interconnectedness, aiming to double the trade turnover between the countries of Central Asia and China by 2030.

The summit marked the official establishment of the "Central Asia–China" mechanism. Emphasizing its "epoch-making significance," the summit opened a new stage in the development of cooperation between China and the Central Asian states.

To confirm their intention to strengthen and support cooperation, the parties agreed to institutionalize the mechanism by creating a permanent secretariat in China, which began functioning this year.

The cooperation mechanism in the "Central Asia–China" format can serve as an effective regional diplomatic platform for promoting economic cooperation, security, and sustainable development in Central Asia. Additionally, the formation of new formats and dialogue platforms enhances the geopolitical and economic significance of Central Asia.

During the state visit of the President of Uzbekistan to China in January of this year, the leaders elevated Uzbek-Chinese relations to the level of all-weather comprehensive strategic partnership.

Uzbekistan and China are building close relations within the framework of international organizations. Uzbekistan and China coordinate closely within multilateral structures such as the United Nations, the Shanghai Cooperation Organization, and the Conference on Interaction and Confidence-Building Measures in Asia, supporting each other on pressing issues of the international and regional agenda.

Uzbekistan also actively supports the Belt and Road Initiative (BRI), proposed by China in 2013, which has significantly contributed to the interconnectedness among participating countries and facilitated regional economic development, especially in landlocked Central Asia.

The BRI projects, involving large-scale construction of roads, trade hubs, and logistics infrastructure on the way to Europe, impacts all Central Asian countries, including Uzbekistan.

It is important to note that the initiative to expand cooperation under the BRI is in harmony with specific provisions of national strategic documents, such as "Uzbekistan-2030" strategy, which will promote the progressive development of Uzbek-Chinese all-weather comprehensive strategic partnership and mutually beneficial cooperation in areas such as industry, energy, infrastructure development, transport, logistics, agriculture, tourism, education, and others.

In 2017, 2019, and 2023, President Shavkat Mirziyoyev visited China to participate in three high-level forums on international cooperation for the BRI.

It should be noted that within the framework of the BRI, Uzbekistan has several advantages – firstly, convenient geographical location of Uzbekistan and abundant natural resources. Due to its geographical position, Uzbekistan has become an integral part of the BRI. Secondly, political stability and a rapidly developing economy. Thirdly, an open, pragmatic, and peaceful foreign policy.

Several infrastructure projects are being implemented in Uzbekistan as part of the BRI. One of the first successfully completed projects is the improvement of the railway section "Andijan-Pap-Angren-Tashkent," specifically the construction of the 19-kilometer Kamchik tunnel and the electrification of the railway lines from 2013 to 2016.

Additionally, the PVC production complex launched in Navoi in 2019, as part of the BRI, changed the country's dependence on PVC and caustic soda imports, while also creating a significant number of new jobs, which has been vital for the country's economic development.

The throughput potential of the "China-Kyrgyzstan-Uzbekistan" road corridor, the "China-Kazakhstan-Uzbekistan" railway, and the multimodal transport corridor "China-Kyrgyzstan-Uzbekistan" is continuously being unlocked.

During Chinese President Xi Jinping's state visit to Uzbekistan in September 2022, China, Kyrgyzstan, and Uzbekistan signed a memorandum of understanding on cooperation concerning the Kyrgyz section of the "China-Kyrgyzstan-Uzbekistan" railway, achieving significant progress in the construction of the transport corridor on the Eurasian continent.

In June of this year, a document on cooperation to jointly promote the "China-Kyrgyzstan-Uzbekistan" railway project was signed in Beijing, establishing mechanisms for financing, construction, and other related issues. In October, an office for the construction company of this railway was opened in Bishkek. In July, the President of Uzbekistan instructed to allocate 255 million dollars to the charter fund of the project company, while Kyrgyzstan planned to allocate about 130. 5 million dollars in its budget. The construction of the railway within China will be fully implemented and financed by the Chinese side.

Given the current circumstances, the delivery of goods via the northern route makes the implementation of the "China-Kyrgyzstan-Uzbekistan" railway project extremely significant and relevant.

According to World Bank estimates, improvements in transport infrastructure under the BRI will reduce delivery times to Uzbekistan by nearly 15%, the largest reduction among BRI involved countries.

The reduction in shipping times, in turn, will increase Uzbekistan's exports by 13-23%. The higher estimated growth is a cumulative effect of completed transport projects under the BRI and reforms that have halved delays at border crossings.

As noted by President Shavkat Mirziyoyev in his speech at the "Central Asia–China" summit: a priority project for reviving the Great Silk Road is the Trans-Eurasian Highway, with significant components being the road and rail connections between China, Kyrgyzstan, and Uzbekistan. In the long term, the implementation of this project and the construction of the Trans-Afghan corridor will allow for alternative routes connecting China with the countries of South Asia under the BRI.

Indeed, the construction of the strategically important "China-Kyrgyzstan-Uzbekistan" railway will significantly reduce delivery times for cargo between Central Asian countries and China, alleviate freight traffic on existing routes, and strengthen the interconnectedness of the Eurasian region.

Overall, Uzbekistan and China are making joint efforts to implement the BRI, which gives a positive impetus to the development and prosperity of the region and the world. The countries also maintain a high level of political, trade-economic, and scientific-technical interaction, consistently elevating the level of bilateral relations.

In conclusion, it is worth noting that Uzbekistan's modern foreign policy is characterized by an active pursuit of a multi-vector approach and cooperation at both regional and global levels. Strengthening ties with neighboring Central Asian states and major world powers serves as the foundation for stable economic and political development in the country.

At the same time, cooperation with China within the framework of the "Belt and Road" initiative, as well as with other international organizations and dialogues, along with the development of bilateral relations, demonstrate the growing economic potential and mutually beneficial partnerships for both sides. The signed agreements in various areas, including energy, transport, and technology, reflect Uzbekistan's readiness to actively participate in international processes and initiatives that contribute to its development.

Key Projects under the BRI in Nepal

Chauyenlai Shrestha

Secretary General, Institute of International Relations, Nepal

The Belt and Road Initiative (BRI) is a global infrastructure development strategy adopted by the Chinese government in 2013.

. It aims to enhance regional connectivity and embrace a brighter economic future by building infrastructure and broadening trade links between China and other countries1. Nepal, as a neighboring country, has formally joined the BRI with the anticipation of mutually beneficial cooperation in various fields including infrastructure upgrading, economic development, and enhancement of capacity in the service sector, technology transfer, cultural collaboration, and above all, the growth of the tourism sector.

Pokhara International Airport: This project is one of the flagship projects under the BRI in Nepal

The airport is expected to boost tourism and economic activities in the region[1]

Panda Pack Project: This project focuses on improving the quality of education by providing educational materials and infrastructure[2]

Amity Living Water Project: This project aims to provide clean drinking water to communities in need.

Challenges and Concerns

Despite the potential benefits, there have been challenges and concerns regarding the implementation of BRI projects in Nepal4 One of the main concerns is the financial burden that these projects might impose on Nepal Additionally, there have been delays and stalling of some projects due to various reasons, including political changes and geopolitical complexities[3].

Future Prospects

The future of the BRI in Nepal looks promising, with both countries working towards enhancing cooperation and addressing the challenges[4]. The success of the BRI projects in Nepal will depend on effective collaboration, transparency, and mutual benefits for both nations.

Strategic Importance

Nepal's strategic location between China and India makes it a key player in the Belt and Road Initiative. The landlocked nation serves as a bridge between these two Asian giants, and the development of infrastructure through BRI can help Nepal harness its geographic advantages to boost trade and connectivity. By integrating Nepal into a broader network of trade routes, the BRI aims to transform the country's economic landscape and enhance its position in the region.

Infrastructure Development

Trans-Himalayan Multidimensional Connectivity Network: This ambitious project aims to build a network of roads, railways, and airways, linking Nepal with Tibet and other regions in China. The construction of the Kathmandu-Kerung railway is a key component, which will establish a direct rail link between Nepal and China, reducing travel time and cost.

Energy Projects: Nepal has significant hydropower potential, and the BRI has facilitated investments in the energy sector. Projects like the Budhi Gandaki Hydropower Plant are expected to provide clean and sustainable energy, reducing Nepal's dependence on imported fossil fuels and addressing its energy deficit.

Improvement of Border Infrastructure: Upgrading border facilities and infrastructure at key points like Rasuwagadhi and Tatopani can enhance trade efficiency and boost economic activities. The development of dry ports and customs facilities is crucial for streamlining trade processes and facilitating the movement of goods.

Economic Impact

The BRI has the potential to drive economic growth in Nepal by creating job opportunities, attracting foreign investments, and fostering industrial development. Improved infrastructure can stimulate tourism, agriculture, and manufacturing sectors, contributing to Nepal's overall economic development. Additionally, the BRI aims to promote regional cooperation and economic integration, enabling Nepal to access larger markets and benefit from increased trade.

Cultural and Educational Exchanges

The BRI is not limited to infrastructure development; it also emphasizes people-to-people connectivity. Cultural and educational exchanges between Nepal and China have increased, with initiatives such as scholarship programs, language courses, and cultural events. These exchanges foster mutual understanding, strengthen bilateral ties, and create opportunities for collaboration in various fields, including science, technology, and research.

Challenges and Criticisms

Despite the potential benefits, the BRI in Nepal faces several challenges and criticisms:

Debt Burden: Concerns about the rising debt burden have been raised, as Nepal borrows heavily to finance infrastructure projects. Ensuring sustainable financing and avoiding debt distress is crucial for the long-term success of the BRI.

Environmental Impact: Large-scale infrastructure projects can have significant environmental impacts, including deforestation, habitat destruction, and disruption of ecosystems. Implementing environmentally sustainable practices and mitigating adverse effects is essential.

Geopolitical Tensions: The BRI has geopolitical implications, and Nepal must navigate its relationships with both China and India carefully. Balancing these relationships and avoiding potential conflicts of interest is a delicate task.

Future Prospects

The future of the BRI in Nepal depends on effective implementation, addressing challenges, and ensuring that the benefits outweigh the costs. Key areas to focus on include:

Strengthening Institutions: Building strong institutions and governance frameworks is essential for managing BRI projects effectively. Transparent and accountable institutions can ensure the efficient use of resources and mitigate corruption.

Enhancing Regional Cooperation: Promoting regional cooperation and integration can amplify the benefits of the BRI. Collaboration with neighboring countries on infrastructure projects, trade facilitation, and policy harmonization can create a more connected and prosperous region.

Sustainable Development: Emphasizing sustainable development principles is crucial for balancing economic growth with environmental protection and social well-being. Integrating sustainability into project planning and implementation can ensure long-term benefits for Nepal.

The Belt and Road Initiative presents both opportunities and challenges for Nepal. While it has the potential to transform Nepal's infrastructure, economy, and regional connectivity, careful planning, effective implementation, and addressing concerns are essential for maximizing its benefits. By fostering cooperation, promoting sustainable development, and leveraging its strategic location, Nepal can harness the full potential of the BRI to achieve long-term prosperity and development.

Let's take a deeper dive into some other aspects of the BRI in Nepal:

Tourism Boost and Cultural Exchange

Nepal, renowned for its stunning landscapes and rich cultural heritage, stands to gain significantly from the tourism boost driven by BRI-related infrastructure improvements. Projects like the Pokhara International Airport and enhanced road connectivity are likely to make travel more accessible, attracting more tourists to Nepal's picturesque destinations. Furthermore, increased tourism can lead to a ripple effect, positively impacting local businesses, creating employment opportunities, and fostering cultural exchange.

Technological Advancements

The BRI also includes technology transfer and cooperation between China and Nepal. This collaboration can facilitate the modernization of Nepal's industries and enhance the country's technological capabilities. Areas such as renewable energy, telecommunications, and digital infrastructure can benefit from Chinese expertise and investments. By embracing technological advancements, Nepal can improve its productivity, innovation capacity, and overall competitiveness in the global market.

Social and Economic Upliftment

Employment Generation: The construction of infrastructure projects under the BRI requires a significant workforce, leading to job creation and economic upliftment in local communities. These employment opportunities can help alleviate poverty and improve living standards for many Nepali families.

Capacity Building: BRI projects often include capacity-building components, such as training programs and skill development initiatives. By enhancing the skills of the local workforce, Nepal can build a more capable and knowledgeable labor force, contributing to long-term economic growth.

Economic Diversification: The BRI provides an opportunity for Nepal to diversify its economy by attracting investments in various sectors, such as manufacturing, agriculture, and services. By reducing dependence on a single sector, Nepal can build a more resilient and robust economy.

Environmental Considerations

Sustainable Practices: To mitigate the environmental impact of infrastructure projects, it is crucial to adopt sustainable practices. This includes conducting thorough environmental impact assessments, implementing green construction techniques, and incorporating renewable energy solutions. By prioritizing sustainability, Nepal can ensure that economic development does not come at the cost of environmental degradation.

Conservation Efforts: Nepal's rich biodiversity and natural resources must be preserved. BRI projects should include measures to protect wildlife habitats, forests, and water bodies. Additionally, promoting eco-tourism can help raise awareness about environmental conservation and generate revenue for conservation efforts.

Healthcare Improvements

Improved infrastructure can also enhance healthcare delivery in Nepal. By developing better transportation networks and healthcare facilities, the BRI can facilitate access to medical services, especially in remote and rural areas. This can lead to improved health outcomes, reduced mortality rates, and a better quality of life for the Nepali population.

Strengthening Bilateral Relations

The BRI serves as a platform for strengthening bilateral relations between Nepal and China. Through increased collaboration and cooperation, both countries can build a strong foundation for future partnerships. Diplomatic ties, trade agreements, and cultural exchanges can further solidify the relationship, fostering mutual understanding and trust.

Lessons Learned and Best Practices

As Nepal continues to implement BRI projects, it is essential to learn from the experiences of other countries and adopt best practices. This includes:

Transparent Governance: Ensuring transparency in project planning, implementation, and financial management is crucial. Transparent governance can build public trust, attract investments, and minimize corruption.

Stakeholder Engagement: Engaging local communities, civil society organizations, and other stakeholders in the decision-making process can lead to more inclusive and sustainable development outcomes. By addressing the needs and concerns of various stakeholders, Nepal can ensure that BRI projects have a positive impact on society.

Monitoring and Evaluation: Regular monitoring and evaluation of BRI projects can help identify challenges, measure progress, and make necessary adjustments. This can improve project efficiency, effectiveness, and accountability.

Conclusion

The Belt and Road Initiative offers Nepal a unique opportunity to transform its infrastructure, economy, and regional connectivity. While challenges exist, careful planning, effective implementation, and a focus on sustainable development can maximize the benefits of the BRI. By leveraging its strategic location, enhancing regional cooperation, and fostering mutual understanding with China, Nepal can pave the way for long-term prosperity and development. The Belt and Road Initiative presents both opportunities and challenges for Nepal. While it has the potential to transform Nepal's infrastructure, economy, and regional connectivity, careful planning, effective implementation, and addressing concerns are essential for maximizing its benefits. By fostering cooperation, promoting sustainable development, and leveraging its strategic location, Nepal can harness the full potential of the BRI to achieve long-term prosperity and development.

REFERENCES

.This article discusses the challenges and delays in implementing BRI projects in Nepal.

The Hindu: "Nepal: What happened to China's 'Belt and Road' projects?" 1

.This article explores the status of BRI projects in Nepal and the concerns surrounding Chinese loans

.Academia.edu: "Belt and Road Initiative: Prospects for Nepal-China Cooperation" 2

.This paper examines the potential benefits and challenges of BRI cooperation between Nepal and China

.NIICE Nepal: "China's Belt and Road Initiative (BRI): Opportunities" 3

Asia News Network: "7 years on, Nepal and China still at odds over Belt and Road Initiative execution" 4

Postscript

On October 13 to 15, 2024, the Belt and Road Forum for International Think Tank Cooperation & the Second Silk Road (Xi'an) International Communication Forum were successfully convened in Xi'an, Shaanxi Province. The event brought together over 300 distinguished guests, including diplomats, think tank scholars, and media professionals from 50 countries, to share insights and propose strategies for advancing the high-quality development of the Belt and Road Initiative (BRI). Held at the outset of the BRI's "Second Golden Decade", this forum carried profound significance and far-reaching influence.

At the forum, Xinhua Institute released a research report entitled " 'Eight Major Steps' Heralds Promising New Decade of Belt and Road Cooperation", which comprehensively reviewed the progress and achievements of the BRI in the year following President Xi Jinping's announcement of the "Eight Actions" initiative. Focusing on the theme of "High-Quality Co-Building of the BRI to Advance Global Modernization," participants engaged in dynamic discussions, exploring the BRI's impact in their respective nations, tracing its historical roots, addressing practical challenges, and envisioning future collaboration. These vibrant exchanges of ideas yielded substantial results.

To preserve and share the conference's outcomes, the organizing committee included the full text of the report " 'Eight Major Steps' Heralds Promising New Decade of Belt and Road Cooperation". Additionally, 14 exceptional papers were selected from a wealth of submissions and compiled into this volume. The book also features a report released by Xinhua Institute at the Global South Media and Think Tank Forum in Brazil in November 2024, titled "Bridging Distances, Fostering Prosperity: Innovation in Local Currency Cooperation Among Global South Nations".

We hope this book will ignite intellectual curiosity and inspire innovative thinking in BRI research. We are confident that the BRI's transformative journey will continue to yield a wealth of think tank contributions, transcending geographical and cultural boundaries, enriching practical applications, and fostering greater global connectivity.

The editorial team for this publication, comprising Wen Jian, Chen Yi, Li Cheng, Chen Yina, and He Xiaofan from the Strategic Communication Research Center of Xinhua Institute, has diligently curated this collection. We warmly invite readers to share their critiques and suggestions. Any comments and suggestions will be appreciated warmly.

Editorial Committee

May 2025

"EIGHT MAJOR STEPS"
HERALDS PROMISING NEW DECADE
OF BELT AND ROAD COOPERATION

共建"一带一路"
新十年良好开局

新华社国家高端智库课题组　编著

新 华 出 版 社

图书在版编目（CIP）数据

共建"一带一路"新十年良好开局 / 新华社国家高端智库课题组编著 .
北京：新华出版社 , 2025. 6.
ISBN 978-7-5166-8111-4

Ⅰ . F125

中国国家版本馆 CIP 数据核字第 2025ZA6412 号

共建"一带一路"新十年良好开局（中文版）

编著：新华社国家高端智库课题组
出版发行：新华出版社有限责任公司
（北京市石景山区京原路 8 号　邮编：100040）
印刷：捷鹰印刷（天津）有限公司

成品尺寸：170mm×240mm　1/16　　　**印张：** 16　**字数：** 200 千字
版次： 2025 年 7 月第 1 版　　　　　　**印次：** 2025 年 7 月第 1 次印刷
书号： ISBN 978-7-5166-8111-4　　　　**定价：** 98.00 元（中英文版）

微店　　视频号小店　　抖店　　京东旗舰店

微信公众号　　喜马拉雅　　小红书　　淘宝旗舰店　　扫码添加专属客服

目录
Contents

报告篇

八项行动奠定共建"一带一路"新十年良好开局 ①

前　言

2013 年，中国国家主席习近平提出共建"一带一路"宏伟倡议，成为人类发展史上具有里程碑意义的事件。十多年来，在各方携手努力下，共建"一带一路"以互联互通为主线，打破地理限制，融合文化差异，统筹发展需求，开拓共商、共建、共享的国际合作新格局，成为当今世界最受欢迎的国际公共产品和最大规模的国际合作平台，也成为共建国家携手发展的合作之路、机遇之路、繁荣之路。

2023 年 10 月，在第三届"一带一路"国际合作高峰论坛开幕式主旨演讲中，习近平主席宣布中国支持高质量共建"一带一路"的八项行动。一年来，在共建国家的共同努力下，八项行动稳步推进，成果斐然，为共建"一带一路"第二个十年奠定良好开局。实践证明，在当前国际形势下，谋发展、促增长、共繁荣，是世界各国的普遍诉求。共建"一

---

① 2024 年 10 月 15 日发布于在西安举行的"一带一路"国际智库合作论坛暨第二届丝绸之路（西安）国际传播大会。

带一路"日益凝聚全球共识,迎来发展重大机遇,完全可以成为构建开放型世界经济的压舱石,成为推动各国共同发展的发动机,成为实现世界现代化的加速器。

面向未来,共建"一带一路"国家需进一步落实八项行动,推进务实合作,共同推动创新发展,携手应对风险挑战,推动高质量共建"一带一路"在新征程上稳步前行,实现和平发展、互利合作、共同繁荣的世界现代化,推动构建人类命运共同体。

第一章 八项行动推动高质量共建"一带一路"迈上新起点

1.1 互联互通持续发展稳步推进

八项行动提出一年来,互联互通建设成为其中重点推进方向。以中欧班列和跨里海国际运输走廊为代表的中欧通道建设持续提质升级,"丝路海运"继续推进港航贸一体化发展,空中丝绸之路建设稳步推进。在共商共建共享原则下,一批标志性工程的经济社会效益进一步显现,有力推动共建国家的现代化进程。

——跨里海国际运输走廊多元立体格局正式建成,推动中欧通道持续提质升级

在欧亚大陆互联互通建设方面,跨里海国际运输走廊建设在 2024 年实现重大进展。7 月 3 日,中国国家主席习近平同哈萨克斯坦总统托卡耶夫在阿斯塔纳总统府以视频方式共同出席中欧跨里海直达快运开通仪式。此次是中方车辆首次以公路直达的运输方式抵达里海沿岸港口,这标志着集公路、铁路、航空、管道运输为一体的多元立体互联互通格局正式建成。[①]

---

① http://www.news.cn/20240703/d9b59485ad8d43df9a0e694ceed6f4fc/c.html

　　跨里海国际运输走廊国际协会秘书长盖达尔·阿布季克里莫夫介绍，这一走廊属于多式联运路线，从中国横跨哈萨克斯坦、里海沿岸、阿塞拜疆、格鲁吉亚并延伸至土耳其和欧洲国家，全长 1.1 万公里，已成为从东南亚和中国向欧洲运输货物的重要动脉，目前年货物吞吐量约为 600 万吨，哈萨克斯坦、阿塞拜疆、格鲁吉亚和土耳其四国已计划在 2027 年前将该路线的年吞吐量增加一倍以上。他表示，中国提出的高质量共建"一带一路"八项行动包括参与跨里海国际运输走廊建设，"中方的支持落在实际行动中，为这一建设带来好消息"。[①]

　　正是经由这一走廊，2024 年以来，中国的西安、南京、青岛、济南等城市先后开通了新的中欧班列车次，通达阿塞拜疆、土耳其、意大利等国家。如今，从中国西安到德国曼海姆，通过这一走廊仅需 29 天，未来可进一步缩短至 25 天左右。由于每周班次已达到 6-7 列，这一路线在里海、黑海段相应优化为"专线专用"集装箱船，运输时间相比全程海运节省一半以上，大大缩短了货物在途时间，降低了物流成本，贸易量随之大幅增加。

　　在跨里海国际运输走廊实现重大进展的推动下，中欧班列持续提质升级，一年来，开列车次、运力运量、覆盖范围等指标不断创下新佳绩。2024 年 1 月至 8 月份，中欧班列累计开行 13056 列，发送货物 139.9 万标箱，同比分别增长 12%、11%，其中 8 月份开行 1653 列，发送货物 17.3 万标箱。2024 年以来，中欧班列已连续 6 个月单月开行数量突破 1600 列。[②] 截至 2024 年 7 月，中欧班列已通达欧洲 25 个国家 224 个城市，连接 11 个亚洲国家 100 多个城市，服务网络基本覆盖欧亚全境。

---

① http://www.news.cn/world/20240707/c6e1a7f81a4e4fc4b7aa715ba4c70c47/c.html

② http://paper.people.com.cn/rmrb/html/2024-09/19/nw.D110000renmrb_20240919_4-10.html

中国境内已铺画时速 120 公里的图定中欧班列运行线 91 条，联通中国境内 61 个城市。中欧班列运输的货物品类达 53 大类 5 万余种，综合重箱率稳定在 100%。[①]2024 年 6 月，中吉乌铁路项目三国政府间协定签署。这条铁路起自新疆喀什，经吉尔吉斯斯坦进入乌兹别克斯坦境内，未来可向西亚、南亚延伸，建成后不仅将极大促进三国互联互通，还将有效促进中亚、中欧铁路通道的联通发展。

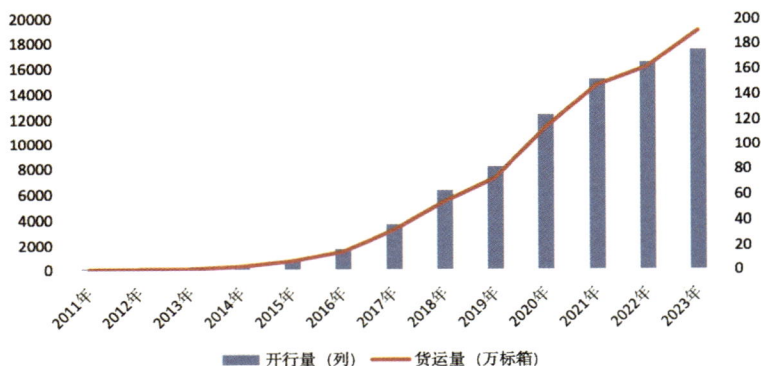

图 1 2011—2023 年中欧班列开行量及货运量

数据来源：中欧班列门户网站

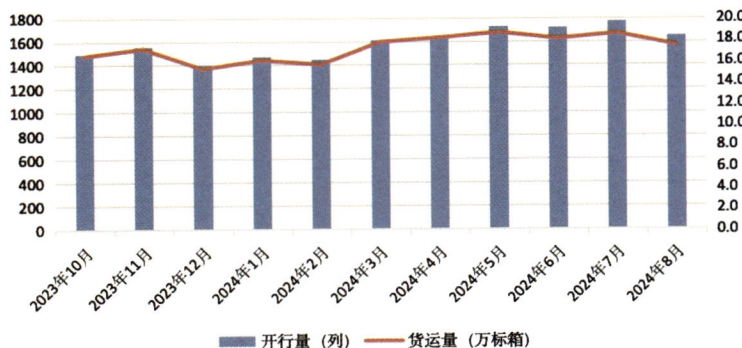

图 2 中欧班列开行量及货运量（2023 年 10 月以来）

数据来源：中欧班列门户网站

---

① http://www.news.cn/20240727/f37d543f86b3477cb3bebc7699aae955/c.html

——"丝路海运"港航贸一体化发展，空中丝绸之路建设稳步推进

港航贸一体化发展在互联互通建设中发挥重要作用。9月7日，在中国厦门举行的第六届"丝路海运"国际合作论坛宣布新增10条"丝路海运"命名航线，总数量增加到132条，通达46个国家和地区的145个港口。其中，境外港口比雷埃夫斯港、阿布扎比港系首次推荐命名航线。[①]

港口、航运与贸易一体化发展，相互促进、相得益彰，这在希腊比雷埃夫斯港得以充分体现。2月6日，比雷埃夫斯港赫拉克莱乌斯滚装码头扩建工程正式落成，项目投资总额超过2000万欧元。码头扩建后，可停放5100辆汽车，将大幅提升比港的汽车船贸易枢纽地位。[②] 截至2024上半年，比雷埃夫斯港已站稳地中海领先集装箱大港、欧洲第三大邮轮母港、欧洲第一大渡轮港口、东地中海修船中心和汽车船中转枢纽的行业地位。同期，中远海运比港已累计向希腊政府上缴特许经营权费和税金超过一亿欧元，上市公司分红水平提高12倍，为希腊直接创造4300个就业岗位，间接创造12000个就业岗位，带动希腊GDP提高1.56个百分点。[③]

在空中丝绸之路建设方面，八项行动提出后一年间，中国与吉尔吉斯斯坦[④]、哈萨克斯坦、塔吉克斯坦[⑤]等多个国家签署了关于共建"空中丝绸之路"的谅解备忘录。中国至亚美尼亚首条定期航线[⑥]、中国至卢

---

① https://www.thepaper.cn/detail/28683356

② http://www.news.cn/world/20240207/090804c012104af0954d5de38e31b8b3/c.html

③ http://gr.china-embassy.gov.cn/zxhd/202403/t20240318_11262127.htm

④ https://www.caac.gov.cn/XWZX/MHYW/202406/t20240617_224472.html

⑤ https://www.caac.gov.cn/XWZX/MHYW/202310/t20231020_221785.html

⑥ http://www.news.cn/2023-12/21/c_1130040312.htm

森堡首条直飞客运航线[①]，中国内地至沙特阿拉伯首条定期直飞客运航线[②]、中国内地至南太平洋岛国的首条定期商业航线等相继开通[③]。由中国企业建设的柬埔寨暹粒吴哥国际机场通航运营。[④] "空中丝绸之路"覆盖范围持续拓展，承载能力愈来愈强。

6月20日，在与中方领导人共同出席第二届郑州－卢森堡"空中丝绸之路"国际合作论坛期间，卢森堡副首相贝泰尔表示，从卢森堡到郑州的"空中丝绸之路"已经成为拉近卢中关系的重要纽带。卢方愿以这次论坛为契机，同中方密切"一带一路"框架下各领域合作。[⑤] 如今，郑州－卢森堡航空通道"一点连三洲、一线串欧美"，通达24个国家200多个城市。郑州机场由此成为高度信息化、数字化的航空枢纽，货运量已跻身中国第六大机场。来自欧洲的生鲜、南美的水果，在入境郑州机场以后，12小时内就能转运至中国各地。依托郑州机场位居中国中部的优势，诸多国家纷纷加强对这一枢纽的运用。2024年，仅从比利时列日到郑州的货运航线航班量已经从每周7班加密到9班，河南－柬埔寨－东盟"空中丝路"已加密至每周3班，并计划在2024年底加密至每周7班。

【知识卡片】西部陆海新通道

西部陆海新通道是由中国西部省份与东盟国家合作打造的国际陆海贸易新通道，以重庆为运营中心，各西部省区市为关键节点，利用铁路、

---

① http://www.news.cn/photo/20240903/e99581df613e4be49551e02230296378/c.html

② https://h.xinhuaxmt.com/vh512/share/11973574

③ https://h.xinhuaxmt.com/vh512/share/11822520

④ http://www.news.cn/world/2023-10-16/c_1129919776.htm

⑤ http://www.news.cn/politics/leaders/20240621/d0ee75fb546c49e6a8d4d26d329a425f/c.html

海运、公路等运输方式，向南经广西、云南等沿海沿边口岸通达世界各地。

习近平主席指出，建设西部陆海新通道，对于推动形成"陆海内外联动、东西双向互济"的对外开放格局具有重要意义。《西部陆海新通道总体规划》印发 5 年来，通道目的地已从 71 个国家和地区的 166 个港口，拓展到 124 个国家和地区的 523 个港口，班列开行总量超 3 万列，货物品类从 80 余种增加至 1150 余种。

截至 9 月 14 日，西部陆海新通道铁海联运班列 2024 年发运货物突破 60 万标箱。从"一条线"到"一张网"，西部陆海新通道已成为中国扩大高水平对外开放的生动写照。

——"授人以渔"彰显共商共建共享，标志性工程巩固互利共赢长效

2024 年 5 月 10 日，亚吉铁路六年成就和未来展望发布会暨交钥匙仪式在埃塞俄比亚首都亚的斯亚贝巴举行，这标志着埃塞俄比亚·吉布提标准轨距公司正式开始主导运营亚吉铁路。

亚吉铁路是非洲首条跨国电气化铁路，西起亚的斯亚贝巴，东至吉布提首都吉布提的港口，全长 752 公里。这条铁路由中国铁建下属企业承建，自 2018 年转入商业运营。按照合同，中方企业向业主提供六年的铁路运营维护服务。六年来，中方累计完成培训认证当地员工 2840 人，为按时顺利移交夯实基础。交钥匙仪式后，中方团队主要进行重点巡视和指导监督工作，并将在两年内完全退出。

在互联互通建设中，像亚吉铁路这样"授人以渔"的案例，成为诸多工程的鲜明特色。通过项目建设，共建"一带一路"国家不仅实现了基础设施的升级，还掌握了基础设施的运营维护，进一步推动了本国现代化的发展。

2024 年 1 月 17 日，中国国家主席习近平复信北京交通大学肯尼亚留学生及校友代表，鼓励他们继续为中肯和中非友好事业发光发热。蒙内铁路是中肯共建"一带一路"旗舰项目和成功典范。正是为了让肯方

能够掌握蒙内铁路的运营工作，中方先后资助支持 100 名肯尼亚学生，到北京交通大学学习铁路运营管理知识。如今，他们已经陆续回国进入肯尼亚铁路公司工作，成为促进当地发展、增强两国合作的重要新生力量。截至 2024 年 5 月 31 日，蒙内铁路已安全运行 7 周年，累计发送旅客 1286 万人次、货物 3287 万吨，为肯尼亚直接和间接创造 7.4 万个就业岗位，培养 2800 余名高素质铁路专业技术和管理人才。

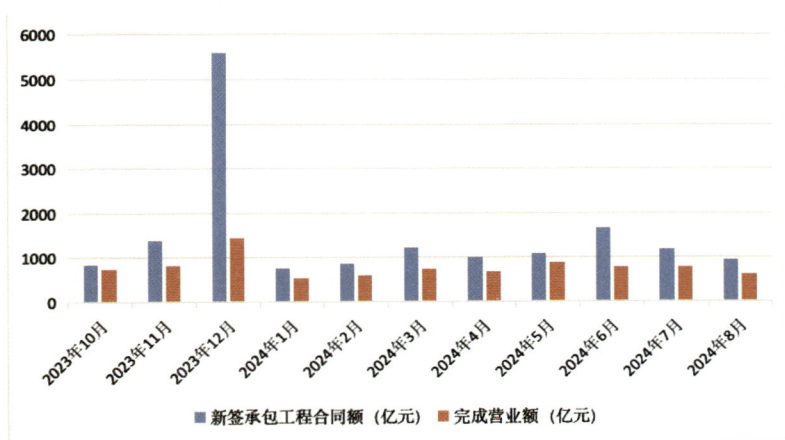

图 3　中国企业在"一带一路"共建国家承包工程情况
（2023 年 10 月—2024 年 8 月）
数据来源：商务部

在共商共建共享原则的保障下，一批标志性工程的经济社会效果日益显现，充分体现合作共赢效果。据中方统计，2024 年 1 月至 8 月，中老铁路进出口货物量 358.4 万吨，同比增长 22.8%。其中，仅经过中老铁路进口的泰国榴莲就达 7.3 万吨，同比增长 74.2%。截至 2024 年 3 月，中老铁路国际货物列车通关时间已从开通初期的 40 多个小时压缩至 5 个小时内，单日交接的国际货物列车数量最高可达 18 列。货物运输服务已经辐射至老挝、泰国、越南、缅甸等 12 个"一带一路"共建国家以及国内 31 个省（区、市）的主要城市，有效带动了万象赛色塔综合开发区、磨丁经济特区等经济园区发展。①

【知识卡片】中老铁路

中老铁路北起中国云南昆明，南至老挝首都万象，是第一条采用中国标准、中老合作建设运营，并与中国铁路网直接连通的跨国铁路，全长1035公里。货物运输方面，自2021年12月3日通车运营以来，截至2024年9月16日，中老铁路已累计运输国际货物1000.2万吨，货值407.7亿元。客运方面，自2023年4月13日国际旅客列车正式开行以来，截至2024年9月25日，磨憨边检站共计查验国际旅客列车1260余列次，保障来自101个国家和地区的28.2万余名出入境旅客顺畅通关。中老铁路是中国同中南半岛国家推进高质量共建"一带一路"、促进互联互通的龙头项目，已成为联结域内国家的重要纽带。

在印度尼西亚，截至2024年7月，雅万高铁正式开通运营9个月，累计发送旅客就超400万人次，②客流呈现强劲增长态势，特别是每日开行动车组列车由开通初期的14列增至高峰期的52列，单日最高旅客发送量21537人次，旅客上座率最高达99.6%。③2024年4月1日，中国国家主席习近平在北京同印尼当选总统普拉博沃会谈时指出，"雅万高铁成为两国高质量合作的金字招牌，中印尼关系进入共建命运共同体的新阶段"。④

---

① http://yn.news.cn/20240320/3981fbef4b834656800d6743844cf361/c.html
② http://www.news.cn/photo/20240717/0e7fa6752ad04196b516ad1bb09815e5/c.html
③ http://www.news.cn/20240417/8fa72b5a1db94818b4407ec4cace0fb1/c.html
④ http://www.news.cn/20240401/1d19b27faca748feb0e2084770924add/c.html

【知识卡片】雅万高铁

雅万高铁连接印度尼西亚首都雅加达和该国旅游名城万隆，全长142公里，设计最高时速350公里，是印尼和东南亚的第一条高速铁路，也是中国和印尼共建"一带一路"的"金字招牌"。雅万高铁于2023年10月17日正式开通运营，将雅加达和万隆两城间的交通时间由原来的3个多小时缩短至46分钟，为民众提供了安全、绿色、高效、舒适的出行方式。

1.2 "绿色""数字"成为创新发展关键词

随着八项行动实施落实，在"一带一路"发展新空间中，"绿色""数字"成为创新发展的关键热词。在其背后，是中国积极培育发展新质生产力的过程，与共建"一带一路"形成相互促进、相互赋能的良性互动作用，成为中国式现代化对于共建国家现代化进程的有效助力。

——绿色丝绸之路推动可持续发展

在阿联酋迪拜市区以南65公里，有一处占地面积44平方公里、充满科幻感的巨大园区——高达262米的集热塔位居其中，周围排布约7万面定日镜，将太阳光反射至集热塔顶端。这是中阿共建绿色丝绸之路重点合作项目——迪拜马克图姆太阳能公园四期光热光伏综合发电项目。2024年2月，这一项目所有发电机组正式并网发电并投入商业运行，总装机容量950兆瓦，其中包括700兆瓦光热发电机组和250兆瓦光伏发电机组。尽管阿联酋拥有丰富的石油资源，但一直致力于优化本国能源结构。阿联酋副总统兼总理穆罕默德在出席项目落成仪式时表示，阿联酋致力于推动本国跻身全球"最可持续国家"行列，迪拜光热光伏综合发电项目投入商业运行，是阿联酋可持续发展道路上的又一重要里程碑。

正如这一项目所示，绿色基建、绿色能源、绿色交通等领域的持续合作，成为落实八项行动进程中的重点方向。在科特迪瓦，中国企业承建的该国在建最大水电站格西波－波波里水电站 2024 年已有 2 台机组交付，剩余 1 台将于年底前投入使用。电站总装机容量 112.9 兆瓦，建成后每年将为科特迪瓦增添 5.54 亿度清洁电力，帮助科特迪瓦实现 2030 年可再生能源份额提升至 45% 的目标。在乌干达，中乌"一带一路"合作旗舰项目卡鲁玛水电站于 2024 年年初全容量投产，年平均发电量约 40 亿千瓦时，每年将节约原煤约 131 万吨，减少二氧化碳排放 348 万吨，并将使该国电价降低 17.5%。在南非，中企承建的红石 100 兆瓦光热电站于 9 月 14 日首次并网成功，未来可满足约 20 万户南非家庭用电需求，大幅减少对传统化石能源的依赖。

2024 年 8 月发布的《中国能源转型白皮书》显示，中国倡导建立的"一带一路"能源合作伙伴关系成员国已达到 33 个，覆盖亚洲、非洲等六大洲。为加强绿色丝绸之路合作，特别是将可持续发展理念融入共建"一带一路"的各个领域，中方倡议发起"一带一路"绿色发展国际联盟，助力共建国家实现联合国 2030 年可持续发展目标中环境与发展有关指标。截至 2024 年上半年，联盟已有来自 40 余个国家的 150 多家合作伙伴，其中包括 20 多个共建国家的环境主管部门。

【知识卡片】"一带一路"绿色投资原则

《"一带一路"绿色投资原则》是一套鼓励投资企业自愿参加和签署的行为准则，旨在推动"一带一路"投资绿色化和可持续发展，于 2018 年 11 月 30 日正式发布。该原则从战略、运营和创新三个层面制定了七条原则性倡议，包括公司治理、战略制定、项目管理、对外沟通，以及绿色金融工具运用等，供参与"一带一路"投资的全球金融机构和企业在自愿基础上采纳和实施。截至 2024 年 9 月，已有来自 17 个国家和地区的 49 家签署机构、20 家支持机构以及 2 家观察机构。

——数字丝绸之路快速拓展新空间

在数字丝绸之路建设中，数字服务贸易与数字电商呈现迅速发展态势。2024 年上半年，中国可数字化交付的服务进出口规模已达 1.42 万亿元人民币，同期跨境电商进出口 1.22 万亿元人民币，均创历史新高，这为共建国家带来了广阔新空间。

在 9 月下旬于中国杭州举行的第三届全球数字贸易博览会上，超过 3 万名专业采购商登记注册参会，其中国际客商超过 6 千名。博览会专门设立丝路电商区，举办"丝路电商日"，对接丝路电商合作资源，并为哈萨克斯坦、泰国等主宾国设立"丝路云品"推荐周产品专区。同月，江苏中亚中心在南京正式启幕，其将丝路电商中心作为重要业务版块，通过数字化手段管理江苏与中亚的生产基地、货仓资源和物流运输。此前，上海市浦东新区发布《浦东新区推进"丝路电商"合作先行区建设行动方案》，在推动跨境数据流动、实施贸易便利化措施、试点贸易数字化举措等方面推出一系列措施，加快建设"丝路电商"合作先行区中心功能区，计划至 2025 年基本建成"丝路电商"综合服务体系，推动共建"一带一路"国家通过电子商务进一步促进贸易合作。[1]

【知识卡片】"丝路电商"

"丝路电商"是中国充分发挥电子商务技术应用、模式创新和市场规模等优势，与"一带一路"共建国家拓展经贸合作领域、共享数字发展机遇的重要举措。2023 年 10 月以来，中国与塞尔维亚、巴林、塔吉克斯坦 3 国新签电子商务合作备忘录，"丝路电商"伙伴国扩展至 33 个。

创建"丝路电商"合作先行区是推进高质量共建"一带一路"的重

---

[1] http://www.news.cn/local/2023-12/14/c_1130027225.htm

大举措，也是扩大电子商务领域制度型开放的重要内容。2023 年 10 月国务院批复同意在上海创建"丝路电商"合作先行区以来，上海"丝路电商"合作先行区 38 项建设任务中 36 项全面推开，形成跨境电子发票互操作、电子提单等一批制度型示范引领开放成果，建成人才培训、智库联盟、伙伴国国家馆等一批公共服务平台。

中国东部最富裕省市的实践表明，无论是数字服务贸易，还是"跨境电商＋产业带"建设，均已成为数字丝绸之路的新经济风口。随着中国持续扩大高水平对外开放，数字经济必将成为共建"一带一路"的重要增长要素和动力来源。

为保障数字经济的发展，数字基建也已成为重要共建合作领域。在中国企业的支持下，坦桑尼亚国家光缆骨干网项目使全国通信成本下降了 57%，被誉为"信息坦赞铁路"；智慧塞内加尔项目推动塞内加尔加快数字经济发展，为落实"振兴塞内加尔"计划注入新动力。在 2024 年中非合作论坛北京峰会前夕，中方宣布中非将加强数字基础设施建设，促进非洲高速互联网接入，支持非洲建设"智慧城市"，推进中非以 5G、大数据、云计算、金融科技、人工智能等为代表的信息网络技术合作。数字丝绸之路的建设，不仅将推动各个国家和地区的全方位交流合作，还必将有效缩小"数字鸿沟"，推动共建国家构建网络空间命运共同体，共享数字技术带来的美好未来。

【知识卡片】共建"一带一路"科技创新行动计划

2017 年 5 月，习近平主席在首届"一带一路"国际合作高峰论坛开幕式上提出，要将"一带一路"建成创新之路，启动共建"一带一路"科技创新行动计划。共建"一带一路"科技创新行动计划是指中国与共建"一带一路"国家在科技人文交流、共建联合实验室、科技园区合作、技术转移等四方面开展合作，共同迎接新一轮科技革命和产业变革，推动创新之路建设。

截至 2023 年 11 月，中国已与 80 多个共建国家签署政府间科技合作协定，共建 50 多家"一带一路"联合实验室，在共建国家建成 20 多个农业技术示范中心和 70 多个海外产业园，建设了 9 个跨国技术转移中心，累计举办技术交流对接活动 300 余场，促进千余项合作项目落地。

1.3 "小而美"项目卓有成效普惠民生

共建"一带一路"归根结底是为了让各国人民都过上更好的生活。在各项标志性工程持续推进的同时，一批批"小而美"项目也在陆续落地发展，从教育培训到健康义诊，从菌草作坊到洁净水井，这些项目在消除贫困、改善民生领域作出了实实在在的贡献。

【知识卡片】"丝绸之路"中国政府奖学金项目

教育部于 2017 年正式设立并启动"丝绸之路"中国政府奖学金项目，通过部委合作、省部合作、高校合作 3 种模式培养共建国家人才。

——"鲁班工坊"成为"一带一路"职教合作闪亮名片

9 月 5 日，习近平主席在中非合作论坛北京峰会开幕式上表示："中方愿同非方深入推进'未来非洲职业教育'计划，共建工程技术学院，建设 10 个'鲁班工坊'。"近年来，在元首外交的关心推动下，仅在非洲大地，就已有 17 家鲁班工坊在 15 个国家落地扎根、开花结果，成为中国职业教育国际合作的一张闪亮名片。[1]

---

[1] http://www.news.cn/politics/leaders/20240907/35e1ed2f4ec045838f5f56d491e60714/c.html

在中亚地区，塔吉克斯坦鲁班工坊已顺利运营一年多，乌兹别克斯坦、土库曼斯坦积极推进项目建设，吉尔吉斯斯坦鲁班工坊智慧教室新近揭牌。① 哈萨克斯坦首家鲁班工坊 2023 年底投入试运行。2024 年 7 月，习近平主席在阿斯塔纳同哈萨克斯坦总统托卡耶夫会谈时表示，中方决定在哈萨克斯坦开设第二家鲁班工坊。②

从 2016 年首个海外鲁班工坊在泰国设立，到中非合作论坛框架下在非洲多国设立鲁班工坊，再到中亚地区鲁班工坊的陆续开设，截至 2024 年 7 月，这一中国职教品牌已在 29 个国家落地生根，开设了 14 大类 57 个专业，涵盖人工智能、电动汽车维修、土木工程、中医药等多个领域，累计参与学历教育的学生超万人，实施职业培训超过 2.2 万人次。③

——推动共建国家民众获得基本健康保障

长期以来，以治疗白内障、心脏病、唇腭裂等疾病为目标的"光明行""爱心行""微笑行"等"小而美"义诊项目在共建国家广受欢迎。据不完全统计，2024 年以来，来自中国的医疗队先后为蒙古国④、塔吉克斯坦⑤、乌兹别克斯坦⑥、斯里兰卡⑦等多个国家的白内障患者成功实施近千例白内障复明手术。仅在蒙古国，"一带一路·光明行"蒙古国行动就已累计筛查蒙古国眼疾患者 3178 人，成功实施免费复明手术 539

---

① http://www.news.cn/politics/leaders/20240704/130b35c1192e41979ad417cc34159037/c.html

② http://www.news.cn/20240703/d796ba1a83b6450aa55a6620fc390d4c/c.html

③ http://paper.ce.cn/pc/content/202408/27/content_300065.html

④ http://www.news.cn/photo/20240910/e5f0072735134587993753eec3b6e624/c.html

⑤ http://www.news.cn/world/20240706/5cf1d23975994c96ba7fb93a76470bda/c.html

⑥ http://www.news.cn/20240531/a537fa86064042a1a23837b82dfb02cd/c.html

⑦ http://www.news.cn/world/20240425/125c589a38c34358847f12d952d74554/c.html

例。[①] 在柬埔寨，68 岁的杜洛沙伦在 1 月底接受手术，成为中方在柬埔寨消除白内障致盲项目的第一万名治愈患者。

为进一步推动健康丝路建设，中国还与共建国家建立各类对口合作机制，援建共建各类医疗设施。2024 年 8 月 29 日发布的《中国－非洲国家共建"一带一路"发展报告》中显示，截至 2024 年 6 月底，中国已在非洲援建了 130 多家医院和诊所，向 45 个非洲国家派遣中国医疗队，与 46 家非洲医院建立对口合作机制。在老挝，中国援助的琅勃拉邦医院升级改造项目于 8 月中旬正式启用并移交老方，中方为医院新建外科和心血管科楼，并将开展三年技术援助，继续提升当地医疗卫生水平和医疗救助能力，将这一医院打造为老挝北部地区的中心医院。

——幸福水井滋润共建国家民众

为推动共建国家民众获得洁净用水，中国在多个国家开展了生活用水设施援助。7 月 22 日，中国援助津巴布韦 300 口水井项目的首井成功出水，让当地村民从此吃上了放心水。2024 年以来，津巴布韦遭遇严重干旱，面临严重粮食安全挑战。为应对灾情，中国决定为津巴布韦多个省份援建 300 口水井。津巴布韦地方政府和公共工程部长丹尼尔·加鲁韦表示："这些水井将显著缓解 4 个重灾省份的用水危机，不仅能够拯救牲畜、浇灌农田，还将成为当地灾后重建的坚实基础。"在津巴布韦，中国在过去十年已建设 1000 口水井，为约 40 万民众提供了生活和农业灌溉用水，并创造了数千个就业岗位。

在生产生活用水领域，2024 年以来，中国援助吉尔吉斯斯坦灌溉系统改造项目一标段的 3 个灌区正式交接；在缅甸，内比都农村生产生活用水设施二期项目交工，极大改善缅甸首都农村地区的民众用水状况；

---

① https://h.xinhuaxmt.com/vh512/share/12186310

在斯里兰卡，中国承建的斯中部水渠项目于 5 月正式完工，可灌溉农田近 400 公顷。一口口水井，一条条水渠，润泽数百万人民群众生活，成为共建"一带一路"务实合作、携手发展的生动写照。

——"幸福草"持续推动共建国家减贫事业

2024 年 3 月，中方与斐济政府联合主办"太平洋岛国菌草技术培训班"，吸引来自巴布亚新几内亚、汤加、库克群岛、萨摩亚、瑙鲁等 11 个太平洋国家的数十位学员参加。菌草技术发明人林占熺教授为学员亲自授课。2001 年，来自中国的菌草技术首次作为官方援助项目走出国门，在巴布亚新几内亚落地。截至 2024 年 8 月，菌草技术国际培训班已举办了约 350 期，培训 1.4 万余人。[1] 在巴布亚新几内亚，巨菌草已创下每公顷年产 854 吨鲜草的世界纪录。巴布亚新几内亚总理马拉佩 5 月在会见林占熺时表示，中国菌草旱稻项目在巴新农业和减贫事业中发挥重要作用，巴新政府将继续积极支持这一项目发展，在巴新更多省份推广。在卢旺达，这一产业链已经扶持 50 多家企业和合作社，涵盖农户超过 4 千户，带动 3 万多人就业。在斐济，接受菌草培训的技术人员已超过 2700 人，直接受益农户达 3 千多户。截至目前，菌草项目已在 100 多个国家落地生根，在脱贫、就业、治沙、发电等领域释放巨大潜力，成为造福世界的"幸福草"。[2]

【知识卡片】"小而美"项目

习近平主席在第三次"一带一路"建设座谈会上强调，要将"小而美"项目作为对外合作优先项目。

---

[1] http://www.news.cn/politics/leaders/20240825/fa904ff239dc4846902b3814f06b24a2/c.html

[2] http://www.news.cn/world/20240802/6d09d74f660a470884459749086cb7e5/c.html

多年来，共建"一带一路"聚焦共建国家民众"看得见、摸得着"，容易提升获得感、幸福感的基础设施建设、卫生健康、绿色生态、农业合作、水利、林草发展、减贫和人道主义、教育培训等重点领域，以接地气、聚人心、低成本、可持续为导向，深入推进共建"一带一路""小而美"项目建设，着力打造了"菌草""鲁班工坊"等一批有示范效应的代表性项目。

1.4 机制建设持续深化，民间交往亮点频现

——国际合作机制日益完善，多边平台建设扎实推进

根据八项行动要求，5月11日，"一带一路"国际合作高峰论坛秘书处揭牌，正式启动秘书处工作。秘书处设于中国外交部，负责为高峰论坛提供支持，协调推动相关国际合作。一年来，在能源、税收、法律、减灾、反腐败、智库、媒体等领域，共建"一带一路"国家多边合作平台建设扎实推进，不断取得新的进展。

【知识卡片】"一带一路"国际合作高峰论坛秘书处

2023年10月，习近平主席在第三届"一带一路"国际合作高峰论坛上宣布成立高峰论坛秘书处。外交部副部长马朝旭任秘书长。

以税收领域为例，9月，来自近50个国家和地区的500余名代表汇聚香港，出席第五届"一带一路"税收征管合作论坛。为保障共建国家贸易和投资自由便利化，中国于2019年推动成立"一带一路"税收征管合作机制，旨在移除税务障碍，建设促进发展的税务环境。在这一机制推动下，共建国家先后在扬州、北京、阿斯塔纳、澳门和利雅得先后设立了5所"一带一路"税务学院，2024年增设了"一带一路"税务学院·澳门（横琴校区）。本届合作论坛宣布，"一带一路"税务学院·阿尔及尔正式成立，成为第六所"一带一路"税务学院。截至2024年8月，

这一机制已培训了 120 多个国家和地区的约 6000 名财税官员，为各方架构了促进经贸畅通、提升税收治理能力的桥梁纽带。

一年来，"一带一路"能源合作伙伴关系、"一带一路"知识产权高级别会议、"一带一路"国际智库合作委员会、"一带一路"新闻合作联盟、"一带一路"自然灾害防治和应急管理国际合作机制等在各自领域落实第三届"一带一路"国际合作高峰论坛成果和八项行动要求，不断推进"一带一路"具体领域国际合作，强化功能性议题对话，持续促进共建国家"软联通"进程。

——建设廉洁之路，保障共建"一带一路"行稳致远

在第三届"一带一路"国际合作高峰论坛廉洁丝绸之路专题论坛上，清华大学纪检监察研究院公布了"一带一路"企业廉洁合规评价体系。2024 年 6 月，"一带一路"背景下企业廉洁合规发展论坛在中国浙江义乌举行。来自中国的中央纪委国家监委、国家发改委等政府代表，与国际组织、中外企业代表和专家学者等 400 余人出席论坛，围绕这一体系凝聚共识，推动企业廉洁合规建设高质量发展。清华大学纪检监察研究院院长过勇表示，在"一带一路"建设中，企业发挥着重要的桥梁纽带作用，是各项合作具体实施的重要推动者。廉洁是"一带一路"行稳致远的重要基础，廉洁合规是企业提升全球竞争力的核心要义。国际反腐败学院总务长雅罗斯瓦夫·彼得鲁谢维奇在论坛上表示，国际反腐败学院高度认同中国政府提出的建设廉洁之路倡议，未来将继续发挥重要的执行角色，为打造廉洁丝绸之路作出贡献。

8 月，"一带一路"廉洁建设中国云南与东南亚国家地方研讨会在昆明举行，探讨"一带一路"廉洁建设和反腐败国际合作中地方交流、区域协作的实践路径。9 月，香港廉政学院为共建"一带一路"国家举办了为期 9 天的"大型基建反腐治理专业课程"，来自 10 余个共建国家反贪机构的 20 多名学员参与课程，学习如何运用科技手段，在大型

基建项目中降低腐败风险、提升反贪能力。为加强政府层面合作力度，中国正在通过"一带一路"合作伙伴反腐败研修班，反腐败、纪检监察等领域国际研修、"一带一路"廉洁建设领域援外培训等各类项目，持续开展廉洁丝绸之路能力建设。

【知识卡片】《廉洁丝绸之路北京倡议》

《廉洁丝绸之路北京倡议》于2019年4月在第二届"一带一路"国际合作高峰论坛廉洁丝绸之路分论坛上，由中国与有关国家、国际组织以及工商学术界代表共同发起。《廉洁丝绸之路北京倡议》倡议各方增强政府信息公开透明，积极预防和妥善解决贸易、投资中的有关争端，推进金融、税收、知识产权、环境保护等领域合作，为共建"一带一路"构建稳定、公平、透明的规则和治理框架。呼吁各方加强对"一带一路"合作项目的监督管理，规范公共资源交易，在项目招投标、施工建设、运营管理等过程中严格遵守相关法律法规，努力消除权力寻租空间，打造规范化、法治化营商环境。

——以民间交往促进民心相通，以人文交流推动文明互鉴

共建"一带一路"国家拥有各自不同的历史渊源和文化背景，上百种语言文字并存。正因如此，在共建进程中，更需要加强民间交往、人文交流，实现民心相通和文明互鉴。

2023年12月3日，首届"良渚论坛"在中国杭州举办。中国国家主席习近平向论坛致贺信，他在贺信中强调，相互尊重、和衷共济、和合共生是人类文明发展的正确道路。希望各方充分利用"良渚论坛"平台，深化同共建"一带一路"国家的文明对话，践行全球文明倡议、加强文明交流借鉴，弘扬平等、互鉴、对话、包容的文明观，推动不同文明和谐共处、相互成就，促进各国人民出入相友、相知相亲。

【知识卡片】"良渚论坛"

2023 年 10 月 18 日，习近平主席在第三届"一带一路"国际合作高峰论坛开幕式上发表主旨演讲时宣布，中方将举办"良渚论坛"，深化同共建"一带一路"国家的文明对话。

"良渚遗址是实证中华五千年文明史的圣地"，2003 年 7 月，时任浙江省委书记习近平对遗址的历史地位作出重要论断。

2016 年，习近平主席又对良渚古城遗址申遗作出重要指示。2019 年 7 月 6 日，良渚古城遗址成功列入《世界遗产名录》。

2023 年 12 月 3 日，由文化和旅游部、浙江省人民政府共同主办的首届"良渚论坛"在浙江省杭州市举办，主题为"践行全球文明倡议，推动文明交流互鉴"，来自海内外的 300 余名嘉宾出席论坛。

为了"和谐共处、相互成就"，为了"出入相友、相知相亲"，一年来，作为第三届"一带一路"国际合作高峰论坛成果，"一带一路"媒体合作论坛、"一带一路"共建国家出版合作体论坛、第十一届丝绸之路国际电影节、第九届中蒙俄万里茶道城市合作大会、2024"一带一路"青年创意与遗产论坛等人文交流活动相继举行。6 月，丝绸之路旅游城市联盟"丝路对话"在土耳其伊斯坦布尔召开。这是联盟成立以来首次在中国以外举办活动。截至 6 月底，已有 28 个国家的 63 个知名旅游城市加入联盟。

互联互通带来的便利，人文交流产生的热情，促使"一带一路"双向旅游热度凸显。5 月，中国西南的贵州省开通了首个跨境旅游专列，200 多名游客能够通过中老铁路从贵阳直抵老挝万象；而在相邻的云南省，大批越南游客乘坐动车组进入中国旅游，截至 8 月中旬，仅河口口岸入境的越南旅游团队就突破 700 个，人数超过 1.2 万人次，创历史新高。在中国的霍尔果斯口岸，由于恰逢中国"哈萨克斯坦旅游年"，中哈两国又签署互免签证协定，激发了民众的旅游热情。截至 8 月下旬，2024 年霍尔果斯口岸出入境人员已达 81 万人次，同比增长 118%。

【知识卡片】丝绸之路旅游城市联盟

丝绸之路旅游城市联盟于 2023 年 9 月成立，由中国文化和旅游部中外文化交流中心联合国内外知名旅游城市共同发起，旨在以丝绸之路精神为指引，以共商共建共享为原则，为包括丝绸之路沿线在内的中外城市旅游领域交流合作建设长效合作机制。联盟拟通过国际论坛、联合推介、产业对接等一系列主题活动，助推会员城市旅游业可持续发展。截至 2024 年 6 月，已有包括中国和来自亚洲、欧洲、非洲、美洲等地区 28 个国家的 63 个海内外知名旅游城市加入联盟。

为进一步便利外籍人员来华，中国政府 2024 年对部分国家人员实施 72 小时或 144 小时过境免签政策，其中 20 余个为共建"一带一路"国家，促使来华游客大幅增加。另一方面，共建国家也正在努力吸引更多中国游客。埃及旅游和文物部长谢里夫·法特希 9 月就此表示，目前埃及每年能吸引约 20 万中国游客赴埃旅游，后续将采取措施努力增加中国游客人数，促进两国旅游业合作发展。《中国－非洲国家共建"一带一路"发展报告》显示，中国已与 31 个非洲国家签署双边旅游合作文件，将 34 个非洲国家列为中国公民组团出境旅游目的地。在双向奔赴之下，中国与共建国家的旅游合作正在向更高层次迈进。

第二章 八项行动打造高质量共建"一带一路"新机遇

当今世界百年未有之大变局加速演进，全球政治、经济和社会环境出现深刻变化，全球经济治理格局加快重构。在此背景下，八项行动的提出和落实，契合共建国家谋发展、促增长、共繁荣的普遍追求，为高质量共建"一带一路"带来新的历史机遇。共建"一带一路"在第二个十年中有望实现更高合作水平、更高投入效益、更高供给质量和更高发展韧性的高质量发展，完全可以成为构建开放型世界经济的压舱石，成为推动各国共同发展的发动机，成为实现世界现代化的加速器。

2.1 更大范围谋发展：成为构建开放型世界经济的压舱石

当前世界范围内，"逆全球化"思潮涌动，单边主义、贸易保护主义、霸凌主义等不断抬头，个别国家采取单方面激进行为，以"经济安全"名义推动"脱钩断链""去风险"，持续设置不合理规则标准壁垒，试图破坏国际产供链布局，打造排他性贸易集团与合作框架，现有国际金融货币体系的不稳定性加重，多边贸易体制受到冲击，金融风险明显增加，国际投融资与产供链合作难度提升，国际贸易格局呈现局部碎片化趋势。

面临这种形势，国际社会急需构建开放型世界经济的压舱石。

——共建"一带一路"拥有与生俱来的开放基因，顺应普惠包容的经济全球化大趋势

志合者，不以山海为远。"一带一路"建设起自互联互通，十多年来从无到有、由点及面、连线成网，实现了全方位布局和历史性发展。全球已有超过四分之三的国家和重要国际组织加入共建"一带一路"朋友圈。无论是从理论还是实践上，"一带一路"带有与生俱来的开放基因。

共建"一带一路"始终坚持和平合作、开放包容、互学互鉴、互利共赢的丝路精神，坚持共商共建共享原则，坚持在开放中合作，在合作中共赢，共同努力探索走出一条不画地为牢、不设高门槛、不搞排他性安排、反对保护主义的正确合作道路。尽管当今世界逆全球化浪潮抬头，但普惠包容的经济全球化大趋势不会变，绝大多数国家依旧把发展作为

主要任务，努力促进经济发展，维护全球产供链稳定。和平、发展、合作、共赢依旧是人心所向、大势所趋。中国是经济全球化的参与者、受益者和贡献者，中国坚持推进高水平对外开放，坚持经济全球化大方向，旗帜鲜明主张自由贸易和真正的多边主义，推动建设开放型世界经济。在"一带一路"框架内，未来各国扩大开放、加强合作的前景广阔。

——共建"一带一路"能够多层次多领域有效对接全球经济

在八项行动的具体推动下，共建"一带一路"通过加强规则软联通，对标国际高标准经贸规则，主动推进跨境服务贸易和投资高水平开放等形式，鼓励来自更多国家和地区的合作伙伴深入参与，通过双多边合作、第三方市场合作等方式形成发展合力。

在区域和多边层面，共建"一带一路"同联合国2030年可持续发展议程、《东盟互联互通总体规划2025》、东盟印太展望、非盟《2063年议程》、欧盟欧亚互联互通战略等有效对接，支持区域一体化进程和全球发展事业。

在双边层面，共建"一带一路"可与俄罗斯欧亚经济联盟建设、哈萨克斯坦"光明之路"新经济政策、土库曼斯坦"复兴丝绸之路"战略、蒙古国"草原之路"倡议、印度尼西亚"全球海洋支点"构想、菲律宾"多建好建"规划、越南"两廊一圈"、南非"经济重建和复苏计划"、埃及苏伊士运河走廊开发计划、沙特"2030愿景"等多国战略实现对接，有力支持对象国经济社会建设进程。

2.2 更宽领域促增长：成为推动各国共同发展的发动机

当前，全球经济复苏整体乏力，外部经济环境负面影响持续存在。新冠疫情影响的滞后效应以及地缘冲突的外溢影响，导致部分国家面临经济困境，一些国家面临减贫和"返贫"危机，各国普遍需要新的可持续增长动能。

——以新质生产力培育共建合作新增长点

"一带一路"顺应世界经济、技术、产业、社会发展普遍规律和时代大势，积极开展健康、绿色、创新、数字等新领域合作，致力于培育合作新增长点。面对新技术革命浪潮，中国正在因地制宜发展新质生产力。这将有效助力共建国家共同创新发展，不断加强数字经济、人工智能、新能源、新材料等领域创新力度，充分利用现代数字信息、互联网和人工智能等技术对传统制造业进行全系统、全角度、全链条的改造，培育发展新兴产业和未来产业，推进传统产业深度转型升级，促进数字技术与实体经济深度融合、数字技术和数据要素深度耦合发展，加快培育数字领域合作新业态新模式，分享科技创新成果，深化数字治理合作，打造"一带一路"科技创新合作新高地。

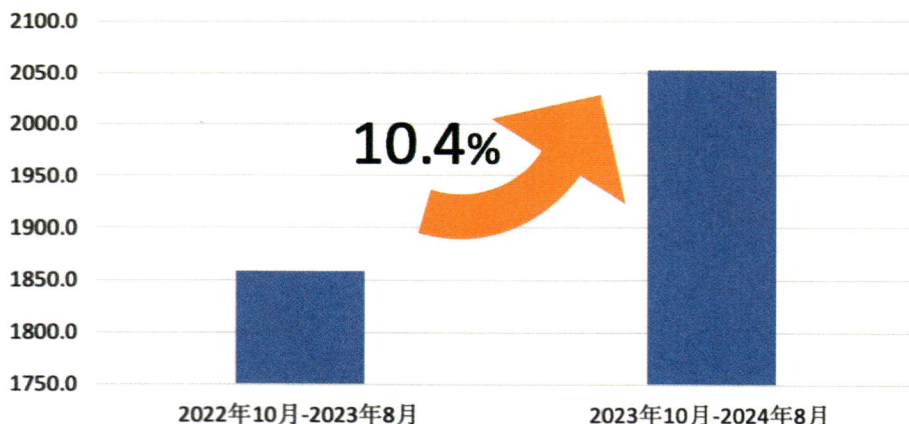

图 4 八项行动提出以来，中国企业在"一带一路"共建国家非金融类直接投资增长情况
数据来源：商务部

——"一带一路"激发共建国家既有潜能，助力长期稳定增长

"一带一路"互联互通建设的重要意义，在于有效激活共建国家既有资源禀赋，有效调动各类生产要素，将资源优势转化为实实在在的经济成果。世界银行预测，共建"一带一路"倡议有望使经济走廊和国际

通道沿线运输时间缩短近八分之一，可使全球贸易往来增加 6% 以上。泰国铁路运输部数据显示，中老泰铁路全线通车后，将在 3 至 5 年内使货物运输成本降低 30% 至 50%。这必将带来自然资源的有效开发、人力资源的高效利用、经济生活的高速运转、生产成果的高效交换。

在国内国际两个市场增长需求驱动下，"一带一路"将由过去"立柱架梁"转入稳步发展阶段。当前"一带一路"共建国家间的内部贸易占比已超 30%，其中中间品贸易占比超 60%，说明共建国家内部已形成更加紧密的产业链、供应链关系。在此基础上，只要稳步推进"一带一路"各项建设，促进"一带一路"框架下各项经济稳定发展，就能够为共建国家长期稳定增长提供有力支撑。

2.3 更深层次共繁荣：成为实现世界现代化的加速器

受前述全球政经形势影响，部分国家经济发展和转型内生动力不足，导致内部呈现政治极化、贫富分化加剧、社会对立、民粹主义盛行等问题。对于广大发展中国家而言，面临如何实现现代化目标的现实问题，对于发达国家而言，也同样面临如何维系现代化成果、保持经济社会现代化水平的深层次问题。

当前，中国正在以中国式现代化全面推进强国建设、民族复兴伟业。中国追求的不是独善其身的现代化，而是期待同广大发展中国家在内的各国一道，共同实现现代化。中国式现代化的出发点和落脚点是让 14 亿多中国人民过上更加美好的生活。对共建"一带一路"国家而言，这意味着更加广阔的市场和前所未有的合作机遇，也将为世界现代化注入强大动力。

——以高质量共建"一带一路"推动世界实现的是和平的现代化

习近平主席指出，"一带一路"倡议坚持共商共建共享，不是一家说了算，而是大家共担责任，共享成果。共商，就是倡导多边主义，大家的事大家商量着办,使"一带一路"建设兼顾各方利益和关切,体现各方智慧和创意。十多年来,共建国家秉持对话而非对抗,合作而非冲突的理念,通过外交方式而非暴力手段解决问题,坚决摒弃霸权思维、强权思维,不搞一家的独奏,而是努力唱响共建国家的大合唱。未来,共建"一带一路"仍会继续加强"一带一路"合作平台与机制建设,加强各领域对话协商,把同共建国家人民"心联通"作为重要基础,推动共建"一带一路"高质量发展,以和平方式共同实现世界现代化的做法势必仍将得到广大国家支持与欢迎。

——以高质量共建"一带一路"推动世界实现的是共同繁荣的现代化

实现共建国家共同发展,让民众过上好日子是"一带一路"倡议的初心。没有共同发展、共同繁荣,就不会实现世界真正的和平与稳定,世界的现代化成果就难以维存。在全球南北差距不断扩大、发展中国家追赶难度持续增加、各国内部贫富差距加剧的背景下,共建"一带一路"倡议为发展中国家提供了一条实现现代化的现实选择。共建"一带一路"倡议体现了中国对于现代化的深刻理解和独特视角,既有对物质生活的提升,更有社会全面的进步,始终坚持以人民为中心的发展思想,聚焦消除贫困、增加就业、改善民生,让共建"一带一路"成果更好惠及全体人民,为当地经济社会发展作出实实在在的贡献。聚焦共建国家民众"看得见、摸得着",容易提升获得感、幸福感的"小而美"项目,助力缩小贫富差距,弥合南北鸿沟,这将契合各国人民对实现更美好生活的淳朴真挚期许,是高质量共建"一带一路"重要的民心基础与时代机遇。

第三章 持续推进八项行动,开启高质量共建"一带一路"新征程

八项行动涵盖设施联通建设、发展方式转型、合作机制创新、国际交流培养等多个方面,既是对共建"一带一路"多年来高质量实践成果

的高度浓缩，也是下一步实现更高质量、更高水平新发展的路线图时间表。推进高质量共建"一带一路"八项行动，要继续以共商共建共享、开放绿色廉洁、高标准惠民生可持续为指导原则，巩固务实合作，聚焦创新发展，强化风险防控，完善体系机制，共促各国"硬联通""软联通""心联通"，创造更加开放包容、和平发展、合作共赢的美好未来。

3.1 夯实合作根基，构建更高韧性互联互通网络

展望八项行动，共建国家、区域和国际组织要持续加强战略对接，不断深化务实合作，完善陆海天网"四位一体"布局，构建更高韧性立体互联互通网络；同时，要将政策共识进一步落实至民生焦点和生活福祉，确定重点合作领域，细化具体行动方案，制定重点合作清单，形成良性互动链条。

——统筹打造标志性工程 推进互联互通更畅通高效

设施互联互通是八项行动的核心。推进设施联通，不仅要调整盘活存量，还要进一步做优做强增量，统筹打造好标志性项目，构建一体化、智能化、现代化的立体互联互通网络。

巴基斯坦方面数据显示[1]，到2030年，中巴经济走廊有望拉动巴基斯坦经济增速2.5个百分点，为当地创造230万个就业岗位。据乌兹别克斯坦方面估算[2]，中吉乌铁路建成后，铁路干线年货运量可达1500万

---

[1] https://www.radio.gov.pk/25-11-2020/cpec-is-win-win-project-of-china-pakistan-economic-cooperation-shibli

[2] 乌兹别克斯坦总统米尔济约耶夫2024年6月6日在中吉乌铁路项目三国政府间协定签字上的贺词 https://uza.uz/en/posts/presidents-message-to-the-participants-in-the-signing-ceremony-of-the-agreement-on-the-construction-of-the-china-kyrgyzstan-uzbekistan-railway_605632

吨，货物运输时间将缩短 7 天。秘鲁农业发展与灌溉部预计 ①，钱凯港启用后，秘鲁农产品到达亚洲的时间有望从当前的 28 天缩短至 16 天，海运运费预计将降低 30%，这对扩大农产品贸易意义重大。坦赞铁路管理局测算 ②，中国、坦桑尼亚、赞比亚三方共同签署的《坦赞铁路激活项目谅解备忘录》全面落实后，坦赞铁路运力将大幅提高，年运载量有望从目前的 50 万公吨提升到 200 万公吨左右。这些标志性项目的推进，将有效形成增量、带动发展，并衍生长期经济社会效益。

——擦亮"小而美"品牌成色 深化战略对接与共赢合作

"一带一路"建设以人民为中心。关系地区民生和整体福利的"小而美"项目是八项行动合作的重要优先事项。世界银行测算 ③，到 2030 年，共建"一带一路"有望使相关国家 760 万人摆脱极端贫困、3200 万人摆脱中度贫穷。

随着"一带一路"建设更加聚焦卫生健康、农业生产、粮食安全、水利合作、清洁能源、生态环保、教育培训等领域，一批投资小、见效快、经济社会环境效益好的"小而美"示范项目将加速形成，凝聚更多接地气、聚人心的合作成果。以职业教育为例，2023 年底，在中马高质量共建"一带一路"旗舰项目——马来西亚东海岸铁路项目轨道工程启动仪式上，中马高校共建的中国—马来西亚铁路现代工匠学院挂牌。预计到 2026 年底，该学院将实现学历教育学生 50 人，开展职业技能培训 100 人次，培养核心教师队伍 60 人 ④。今后一段时间，类似这样依托标志性

---

① https://agraria.pe/noticias/peru-se-prepara-a-exportar-fruta-congelada-a-china-36385

② https://www.tazarasite.com/successful-signing-mou-concession-tazara

③ 世界银行 2019 年 6 月发布的《一带一路经济学：交通走廊的机遇与风险》报告

④ 《中马高校共建铁路工匠学院 为马东铁路提供人才支撑》https://www.gx.chinanews.com.cn/kjwt/2023-12-12/detail-ihcvvqfu6721482.shtml

工程和重大项目的职业教育还有广阔拓展空间，其培训的人员不仅可满足项目需求，还可为对象国人力资源厚植长期基础。

3.2 壮大创新火种，解锁更多新领域合作潜力

展望八项行动，要着力推动发展新质生产力，进一步聚焦绿色发展、数字发展，深入拓展新领域合作空间；同时，继续扩大制度型开放，发挥新型合作模式优势，进一步挖掘三方、多方市场合作潜力。

——打造创新合作新高地 推动提升新质生产力

创新是八项行动的核心驱动力。自2017年"一带一路"科技创新行动计划启动以来，共建"一带一路"联合实验室已成为推进科技创新合作的重要方式。目前，中国与相关国家在农业、医疗、信息、新能源、基础研究等多个领域共同建设了53家"一带一路"联合实验室，并将在未来5年内把同各方共建的联合实验室扩大到100家[①]。这将有效赋能共建国家产业技术进步，进一步提升创新发展能力。

建设数字丝绸之路是推动实施八项行动创新合作的重要途径。随着"六廊六路多国多港"空间架构的系统性、立体性进一步健全，通过对传统基础设施如港口、铁路、公路、机场、能源、水利等进行数字化升级改造，同时运用大数据、云计算、物联网、人工智能等技术实现智能化运营管理，将进一步提高经济走廊和国际通道的运效。以越中数字物流合作为例，越南河内物流协会副会长阮春雄指出，近年来越南企业与中国企业在数字物流方面的合作多保持在仓储配送环节，针对跨国物流动态货运环节，越中双方企业尚无法实时掌握货物入境对象国后的各阶段信息，跨国物流数字合作还有很大发展空间。[②]

---

① https://www.ceweekly.cn/cewsel/2024/0913/455206.html
② 《云南日报》https://yndaily.yunnan.cn/content/202407/28/content_216531.html

——挖掘务实合作潜力 共同建设开放型平台

开放是八项行动的重要支撑。推进八项行动,要继续协同增效,加强各国在规制、标准、监管等方面的深度对接,通过政府和社会资本合作(PPP模式)、双边合作、第三方市场合作、多边合作等多种形式,使更多国家、企业和机构深度参与其中,共同推动建设开放型世界经济。

跨境电商作为开放合作的前沿,正有力推动全球贸易创新发展。从共建"一带一路"的整体格局来看,这一领域能够充分发挥互联互通、产业发展与开放型经济的综合优势。推进绿色金融国际合作将是落实八项行动高水平开放的重要方向。根据联合国最新测算[1],2030年前发展中国家为实现可持续发展目标每年的投融资缺口在2.5万亿美元至4万亿美元之间。在发展中国家和新兴经济体中建立绿色金融体系至关重要。由中国和多国机构共同发起成立的可持续投资能力建设联盟(The Capacity-building Alliance of Sustainable Investment,简称CASI)于2023年底正式启动,预计其所提供的可持续金融能力建设服务将在2030年前覆盖来自发展中国家10万人次参与者。[2]

3.3 遏制风险苗头,共筑行稳致远坚实基底

展望八项行动,要深化团结协作,共同应对外部风险,凝聚加强共建国家内部共识。同时,要坚持推动企业的防范风险意识,根据"企业主体、市场运作、政府引导、国际规则"的原则,持续优化廉洁丝绸之路营商环境,完善对项目和人员的安全保障措施。

——合作应对外部风险挑战

---

① 2024 Financing for Sustainable Development Report, P16 https://sdg.iisd.org/news/annual-sdg-financing-gaps-measured-in-trillions-fsdr-2024/

② https://www.financialnews.com.cn/cj/sc/202312/t20231207_283686.html

　　合作共赢是八项行动的要义。在百年未有之大变局下，增强团结韧性、共商合作发展是推进八项行动落实落地的前提。除本报告第二章所述的政治、经济等方面风险外，"一带一路"还需警惕个别国家在全球范围内的系统性负面舆论宣传。此类宣传持续炒作"一带一路"是"债务陷阱""新殖民主义""制度输出"等谬论，抹黑和唱衰共建"一带一路"，甚至通过渗透和干预共建国家内政等方式，破坏共建"一带一路"存量成果，阻碍相关建设项目进程，毒化共建"一带一路"的政治社会氛围，产生诸多负面影响。欧洲智库布鲁盖尔研究所2023年4月发布的一份报告显示，"一带一路"国际形象总体正面，但也不乏负面杂音，这与一些势力的推动密切相关。对此，共建国家应合作应对外部风险，特别是针对个别国家对"一带一路"的抹黑攻击，更要凝聚加强内部共识，予以及时有效的因应回击。正如波黑前总统姆拉登·伊万尼奇所说[1]，西方国家对于共建"一带一路"倡议的本质存在许多偏见，有必要纠正和消除这种成见。

　　——推动经营主体加强风险防控

　　经营主体是实施八项行动的重要力量。推进八项行动，应推动经营主体增强安全意识，将政治、经济、文化等方面的风险作为确立项目的参考。分析显示，当前"一带一路"国际工程建设越来越向价值链高端发展，探索"投建营一体化"模式，这对企业运营管理以及风险管控能力提出了新要求，需确保项目符合法律合规、财务可靠、环境可持续、社会有益等指标。在实践中，已有大型能源企业等主体认识到，按照市

---

[1] 波黑前总统、尼扎米·甘伽维国际中心董事会成员姆拉登·伊万尼奇2023年10月18日在第三届"一带一路"国际合作高峰论坛智库交流专题论上的发言 https://www.brsn.net/spjj/gjfr/detail/20231214/19435555_%E5%A7%86%E6%8B%89%E7%99%BB%C2%B7%E4%BC%8A%E4%B8%87%E5%B0%BC%E5%A5%87.html

场化国际规则和当地法律进行项目决策和运作，才能保证"一带一路"项目合作的可持续性。①

3.4 完善合作机制，助力八项行动见实见效

完善合作机制是推进八项行动落实的保障。推进八项行动，要继续夯实立体互联互通机制，深化贸易投资合作机制，筑牢民心相通机制，完善绿色发展机制，健全协商协同对接机制。

夯实立体互联互通合作机制，就是要在现有基础上，继续以经济走廊为引领，以大通道和信息高速公路为骨架，以铁路、公路、机场、港口、管网为依托，将交通、能源、信息网络与产业有机结合，进一步实现提质增效。

深化贸易投资合作机制，就是要通过探索深化自由贸易区建设、优化投资环境等方式，形成更加紧密的产业链、供应链关系。

筑牢民心相通机制，就是要对"一带一路"软能力建设给予更多关注，增强文化、旅游、教育、民间等方面的互动，形成"一带一路"多元互动的人文交流大格局。

完善绿色发展机制，就是要强化绿色机制基石，支持绿色投融资项目，加强自然灾害防治和应急管理国际合作，让共建"一带一路"的底色更加鲜亮。

健全协商协同对接机制，就是要加快建立和完善共建"一带一路"合作工作协调机制，强化已建成的"一带一路"平台合作功能，不断总结合作成效，及时协调解决合作中的困难和问题。

---

① 中国石油集团经济技术研究院执行董事余国 2023 年 10 月 17 日在"一带一路"国际智库合作委员会全体大会上的发言 https://www.brsn.net/spjj/gjfr/detail/20231221/19435622_%E4%BD%99%E5%9B%BD.html

结　语

中国国家主席习近平在第三届"一带一路"国际合作高峰论坛开幕式上指出，"一带一路"倡议提出的初心，是借鉴古丝绸之路，以互联互通为主线，同各国加强政策沟通、设施联通、贸易畅通、资金融通、民心相通，为世界经济增长注入新动能，为全球发展开辟新空间，为国际经济合作打造新平台。八项行动，正是中国在新阶段支持高质量共建"一带一路"的具体体现，承载着世界对和平发展的追求、对美好生活的向往、对交流互鉴的渴望。

共建"一带一路"源自中国，成果和机遇属于世界。一年来，八项行动的丰硕成果，为"一带一路"第二个十年建设奠定良好开局。期待共建国家携手前行，弘扬"和平合作、开放包容、互学互鉴、互利共赢"的丝路精神，继续深化"一带一路"国际合作，持续推进八项行动，迎接共建"一带一路"更高质量、更高水平的新发展，推动实现世界各国的现代化，共同推进构建人类命运共同体！

编写说明与致谢

《八项行动奠定"一带一路"新十年良好开局》智库报告课题组由新华通讯社社长、新华社国家高端智库学术委员会主任傅华任组长，新华通讯社总编辑吕岩松任副组长，新华通讯社副总编辑任卫东任执行副组长。课题组成员包括刘刚、潘海平、陈芳、邹伟、崔峰、曹文忠、李月、陈瑜、刘华、程征、李桃、郑明达、陈炜伟、史春姣、丁蕾、曹家宁、赵熠煊、梁洽闻等。

课题自 2024 年上半年启动以来，历时半年多采访、调研、撰写、修改、审校完成。

在报告写作和发布过程中，"一带一路"高质量发展学术论坛主席白春礼、中国国际经济交流中心总经济师陈文玲、中国科学院国际合作局局长刘卫东、北京大学区域与国别研究院副院长翟崑、中国人民大学重阳金融研究院执行院长王文、中国人民大学习近平新时代中国特色社会主义思想研究院副院长王义桅、华侨大学海上丝绸之路研究院院长许培源、香港人文社会研究所教授宗树人等专家学者给予了多方面的帮助和指导，在此一并表示诚挚谢意。

"全球南方"本币合作创新研究 ①

寄语

中国经济信息社董事长　潘海平

随着百年未有之大变局加速演进，"全球南方"正逐渐成为世界政治经济版图中新的焦点和热土。作为新兴市场国家和发展中国家的集合体，"全球南方"占世界经济比重已提升到 40% 以上，正在深刻改写世界经济版图，成为国际秩序变革的关键力量。

近年来，"南南贸易"份额持续上升，"全球南方"国家之间的贸易合作更加紧密，本币结算需求不断增长，本币合作已成为一个新议题、

---

① 2024 年 11 月 12 日发布于在巴西圣保罗举行的"全球南方"本币融资创新合作研讨会。

新热点。

作为"全球南方"的第一方阵，金砖国家致力于推进本币的务实合作。2023 年 8 月发布的《金砖国家领导人第十五次会晤约翰内斯堡宣言》强调了金砖国家及其贸易伙伴使用本币进行交易的重要性，并鼓励加强金砖国家之间的代理银行网络，以及推进本币结算。

2024 年 10 月，《金砖国家领导人第十六次会晤喀山宣言》重申了加强金砖国家金融合作，并授权金砖国家财长和央行行长适时继续研究本币合作、支付工具和平台。

本币合作有诸多好处。以本币计价投融资，可有效动员当地储蓄，降低汇率风险和融资成本，维护金融稳定。对于本币债券市场来说，可有效降低货币错配和期限错配风险，提升金融风险防控能力。

《跨越山海合作共赢——"全球南方"本币合作创新研究》报告，聚焦以金砖国家为代表的"全球南方"在本币合作方面的创新实践，由中国经济信息社上海总部、新华社研究院精心编制。报告力求展示"全球南方"本币合作的最新成果，探讨本币合作面临的挑战和障碍，并尝试提出一些针对性的政策建议。我们期待这份报告能够为"全球南方"国家探索本币合作，提供更多有价值的参考，为推动国际金融货币体系改革，为构建更加公平、包容、可持续的国际经济秩序贡献一份力量。

志合者，不以山海为远。作为金砖创始成员国、"全球南方"大家庭的重要成员，以及世界上最大的发展中国家，中国始终心系"全球南方"、扎根"全球南方"，始终与其他发展中国家同呼吸、共命运，积极促进"全球南方"发展繁荣。

作为国家级经济信息旗舰，中国经济信息社（简称"中经社"）是中国权威性最强、服务领域最广、信息种类最全的经济信息服务机构。中经社长期关注国际经济金融形势最新动向，为用户提供资讯、数据、研报、信用、指数、舆情，以及信息发布、融合传播、智库咨询等综合信息服务。

潮起南方，万象更新。在"全球南方"群体性崛起的世界大变局中，中经社将充分发挥自身优势，持续推动中国与"全球南方"国家间的经济信息合作，为促进世界经济繁荣发展、推动构建人类命运共同体贡献智慧和力量。

寄　语

新华社研究院院长　刘　刚

回首 2000 多年古代丝绸之路的历史，这条由中国人民和沿线各国人民，共同开辟的东西方文明交融之路之所以能够名垂青史，靠的不是战马和长矛，而是驼队和友谊；不是垄断和强权，而是公平和互利。丝绸之路是开放包容的象征，也是合作共赢的象征，滋养了中华文化的气度与胸襟。

改革开放 40 多年来，作为发展中的大国，中国正是秉承开放包容、合作共赢的精神，在经济全球化浪潮中得到快速发展，成为世界第二大经济体。为帮助更多发展中国家走向现代化道路，中国致力于为世界贡献更多公共产品。共建"一带一路"10 多年来，这一倡议跨越不同文明、文化、社会制度、发展阶段差异，开辟了各国交往的新路径，搭建起国际合作的新框架，汇集着人类共同发展的最大公约数。

当今世界危机四伏，充满不确定因素，单边主义、金融霸权、冷战思维魅影重重，不时卷土重来，人类社会不断面临新的重大挑战。本着开放包容、合作共赢的精神，我们反对一切霸权行径和"小院高墙"。为此，我们推出《跨越山海合作共赢——"全球南方"本币合作创新研究》智库报告，我们深知本币合作任重道远，有利于"全球南方"的金融体系建设不会蹴而就。但我们相信，随着人类命运共同体理念更加深入人心，多极化成为世界基本趋势，就会推动形成更高水平开放型经济新体制，激励人们携手合作，共同推动高质量发展，形成彼此互助的命运共同体。

新华社研究院是新华社履行智库职责的专门机构，牵头发起"一带一路"国际智库合作委员会，目前已有 130 多家中外智库参与，我们希望以更多智库研究成果为促进"全球南方"合作贡献力量。

引　言

随着全球经济的发展，南方国家逐渐成为影响国际经济格局的重要力量。尤其是近年来"南南贸易"的占比逐步扩大，全球南方国家的金融合作基础日益增多，贸易往来紧密的金砖国家，成为全球南方金融领域合作的引领性力量。

当今世界正处于百年未有之大变局，大国博弈加剧，经济全球化遭遇逆流，为规避西方金融制裁和美元汇率波动风险，全球南方国家对于使用本币进行投融资和贸易结算表现出日益浓厚的兴趣。全球南方经济的崛起、政治影响力的提升和对全球治理的积极参与，也促进了国际货币体系改革朝着多元化方向迈进。2024 年 10 月 24 日发布的《金砖国家领导人第十六次会晤喀山宣言》[①]，重申致力于加强金砖国家金融合作，欢迎金砖国家银行合作机制聚焦促进和扩大项目、计划的创新金融

---

① 来源：新华社，《金砖国家领导人第十六次会晤喀山宣言（全文）》；2024 年 10 月 24 日

实践和方法，及金砖国家同其贸易伙伴在开展金融交易时使用本币。未来，推动全球南方国家本币合作，进一步提升全球南方国家在国际金融货币体系中的代表性和发言权，势必是新时代的重要课题，也是全球南方社会经济发展的应有之义。

第一章　水到渠成：南南合作谱写新篇章

随着经济全球化的发展、南方国家的群体崛起和南南合作的推进，南方国家越发具有全球影响力。南方的概念也逐渐被全球化，南方发展成为"全球南方"。"全球南方"的持续发展，改变了传统的国际格局，尤其是随着南南贸易的规模不断扩大，南南合作的领域逐渐拓展。与此同时，"全球南方"国家日益感受到过度依赖单一货币结算所带来的弊端，开始将多元化货币体系作为一项国家经济政策目标，本币合作成为新议题、新热点。

二战后，以美元为主导的国际货币体系，使美国的货币政策对世界经济的影响过大，美国经济的风险透过美元在国际货币体系中的主导地位不断传导给世界各国。为减少对美元的依赖，降低风险，在国际贸易、投资甚至储备货币选择上，越来越多的"全球南方"国家开始寻求构建多样化的货币体系。尤其是此轮乌克兰危机加剧以来，欧美亦将金融手段"武器化"，制裁与自身政治外交立场或价值观不同的国家，这不仅抬高全球粮食和能源价格，还进一步导致全球和区域性"断链"，向各国敲响了警钟，加速了多元化货币体系的进程。

1.1 国际货币体系多元化呼声高涨

1944 年的夏天，在美国新罕布什尔州的布雷顿森林召开了次国际会议，44 个国家参加并商定建立了以美元为中心的国际货币制度。这里至此载入国际货币发展史，美元彻底取代英镑成为主要国际储备货币。

布雷顿森林体系应运而生，美元与黄金挂钩，其他国家的货币与美元挂钩，美元在全球货币中的主导地位由此而来。然而，这一体系也暴露出诸多问题，比如"特里芬悖论"，20世纪70年代，随着美国国际收支恶化和石油危机等冲击，二战后建立起来的布雷顿森林体系瓦解，美元与黄金脱钩。

1976年1月，由30多个国家组成的"临时委员会"在牙买加召开会议达成《牙买加协定》，决定修改国际货币基金组织章程，废除各国货币的金平价，承认浮动汇率的合法性，允许各国自行调整汇率并同时接受基金组织对汇率事务的监督。人们称之为"后布雷顿森林体系"或"牙买加体系"。

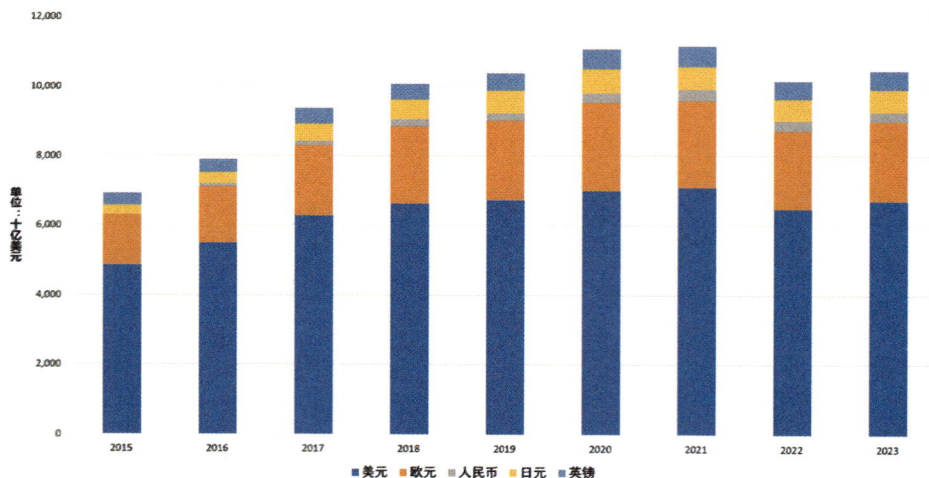

图 1.1 2015-2023 年部分货币全球外汇储量

数据来源：IMF 新华财经

不过，尽管布雷顿森林体系于1970年代初崩溃，美元不再具有法理上的特殊地位，但美元的主导地位并未随之动摇。为维系美元的主导地位，美国把美元的锚定物从黄金转向石油，开始建立"石油美元"体系。

通过石油贸易与美元结算的绑定，美元地位再次上升到又一高度，进一步巩固了其在全球能源和金融体系中的核心地位。

进入 21 世纪以来，欧元横空出世并走强，一度令美国感到忧心。1999 年 1 月 1 日，欧元以非实体形式在法国、德国、意大利、荷兰、比利时、卢森堡、爱尔兰、西班牙、葡萄牙、奥地利、芬兰共 11 个欧元区国家正式发行。2002 年 1 月 1 日起，欧元纸币和硬币正式流通，并于同年 1 月 4 日登陆国际金融市场。在数十个主权国家发行共同货币称得上是一次伟大创举，诞生 25 年以来，欧元成为了国际经济领域中备受瞩目的货币之一。

货币的国际影响力和经贸实力紧密相关。由于许多国家在与欧元区进行贸易往来时，倾向于使用欧元进行结算，这使得欧元在国际舞台上一度走强。时至今日，从国际贸易结算的角度来看，欧元是仅次于美元的重要结算货币。在国际储备货币方面，欧元也是各国重要的储备选择之一。2000 年，伊拉克政府宣布将石油出口从美元结算改为欧元结算，这对"石油美元"体系构成了威胁。

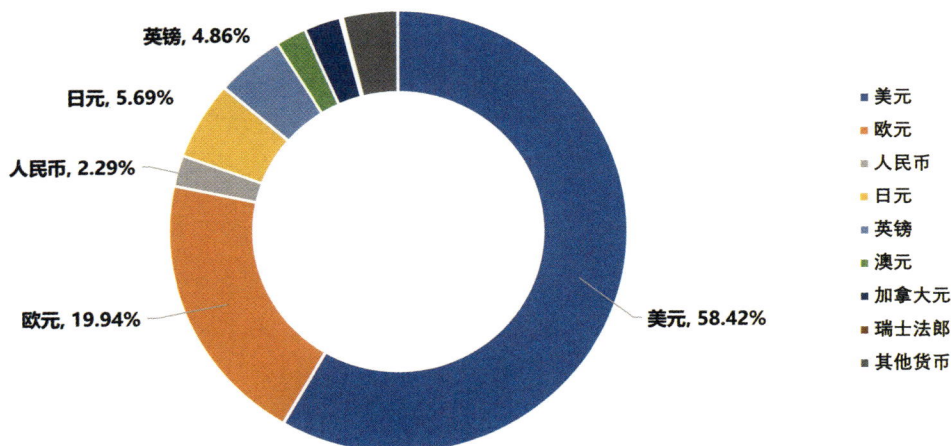

图 1.2　2023 年末全球主要货币外汇储备总量

数据来源：IMF 新华财经

2008 年，美国房地产市场泡沫破裂，引发了全球金融海啸，众多国家的银行系统、股市和实体经济遭受重创。这场金融危机揭示了全球金融体系的脆弱性和相互依赖性,许多国家开始反思美元主导的国际货币体系,并探索多元化外汇储备,减少对美元独大的依赖。此轮乌克兰危机爆发以来,以美国为首的西方经济体对俄全方位制裁再次惊醒其他国家,也把构建多元化货币体系更迫切地推向了国际金融市场的台前。

在地缘政治冲突中,美元被当作"武器"用来制裁相关国家,这不仅抬高了全球粮食和能源价格,还进一步导致全球和区域性"断链",全球化遭遇空前挑战,"碎片化"的土壤逐渐发育。部分发达经济体动辄冻结主权国家外汇储备、黄金储备,以及基于不可接受的域外管辖权概念的相关单边主义行径,导致国际社会对西方金融机构资产安全的疑虑。

此轮乌克兰危机以来,美国将美元和国际结算体系等国际公共产品"武器化",引发越来越多国家的警觉和担忧。一段时期以来,构建多元化货币体系已持续成为国际社会讨论的热点话题,国际货币体系变革的呼声高涨。

声音

"尽管未必迫在眉睫,但逐步去美元化是不可避免的,而这和美国逐步丧失在全球经济中的参与度和国际霸主地位如出一辙……即使没有发生地缘政治或经济灾难,美元在全球储备中的作用也可能继续下降,原因有几个:浮动汇率导致各国对储备的需求减少;各央行的储备多样化政策,比如购买黄金;央行越来越多地使用货币互换额度,进而减少了对大量储备的需求[1]。"

——西班牙《起义报》

---

[1] 来源:西班牙《起义报》,《去美元化只是时间问题吗?》;2024年9月23日

案例　黄金上涨，世界会回到金本位吗？

从 2000 美元到 3000 美元，两年前市场不敢想象的黄金价格正在变成现实。2024 年以来，国际金价接连突破 2100 到 2700 美元的所有整数关口，10 个月涨幅超过 30%，市场表现"牛冠"全球。

此轮乌克兰危机、巴以冲突不断升温带动避险情绪升温，经济、政治形势不确定，央行购买……在一系列上涨的解释因素中，分析师、研究员越来越觉得现有的因素解释力有限。

越来越多的研究认识到，美元作为国际货币体系的"windows 操作系统"正在受到限制，部分使用者的功能受限或者不能继续使用这一系统，让部分经济体开始寻找替代系统，而黄金曾经是当前美元主导的国际货币体系之前的"基础"。

但全球经济发展到今天，世界经济已不能回到"金本位"，方面是纸币体系之所以替代金本位体系，本身是其优势使然，而另一方面，当前全球经济的规模早已不是此前"金本位"时期的规模，全球黄金市场的规模早已不足以支撑"金本位"。

在 windows 系统之外，还有哪些开源系统可以补充，"鸡蛋不能放在一个篮子里"，是当前不少经济体国家的普遍心态，也是正在努力探索的方向。

1.2 "全球南方"崛起：南南本币合作基础更坚实

"全球南方"这一诞生于 20 世纪 60 年代的概念，并非单纯的地理或经济概念，而是新兴市场国家和发展中国家的集合体，是这些国家基于相似历史境遇、现实发展阶段、共同发展目标、相同政治诉求而形成的身份认同。传统上，国际事务主要由北方国家主导。随着中国、印度、巴西等南方国家的集体崛起，全球的力量中心正逐渐向南方转移，打破了长期以来国际事务由北方国家主导的格局。

过去 20 年，新兴市场国家和发展中国家对世界经济增长的贡献率高达 80%，占全球消费增长的近 85%；过去 40 年，这些国家国内生产总值（GDP）的全球占比从 24% 增至 40% 以上。

作为"全球南方"代表的金砖国家，已成为国际舞台上一支不可忽视的重要力量。扩员后的"大金砖"，人口占全球近一半、贸易占全球 1/5，经济总量按购买力平价计算已经超七国集团（G7）。金砖扩员后在全球 GDP 中的占比，按购买力平价计算，从 31.6% 提高到 35.6%。金砖国家在世界原油出口中的占比更是从 15% 提高到 36%[①]。

金砖国家规模和成长速度相对较快，对世界经济增长的贡献率将超越七国集团。目前，金砖国家 GDP 平均增长速度为 4%，远超七国集团的 1.7%，也超过世界的平均增长速度。在可预见的未来，金砖国家将成为全球 GDP 增长的主要动力。根据国际货币基金组织预测，2027 年金砖国家在世界经济中的占比将达到 37.6%[②]。

发展中经济体的持续快速增长，推动南北贸易、南南贸易模式发生改变。"全球南方"国家内部的贸易额逐渐超过其与全球北方国家的贸易额。

"全球南方"崛起，不仅改变全球的实力结构，也让南南本币合作基础更加牢固。

南南本币合作提速，是"全球南方"追求经济独立和自主发展的战略选择。使用本币有助于减少成员国面临的汇率风险，同时提振国内资本市场，降低融资成本。近年来，"全球南方"经济体深受汇率大幅波动的影响，对于双方的贸易而言，相互的贸易以美元作为介质，双方都

---

① 来源：央视网，《从"金砖四国"到"金砖十国"为什么"金砖"越来越受欢迎？》；2024 年 10 月 20 日

② 来源：中国社会科学院金融研究所，《新形势下"大金砖"经济合作的机遇与挑战》；2024 年 10 月 15 日

面临美元和本币的汇率风险，同时在一些经济体货币与美元的汇率大幅波动环境下，美元本身也是稀缺资源，无疑限制南南双方的自由贸易。因此，"全球南方"国家近年来开始将政治经济形势更为稳定可靠的非传统国际货币纳入考虑范围。

声音

　　"在对华贸易中使用人民币结算正成为南美地区的趋势，玻利维亚不能选择'袖手旁观'。[①]"

——玻利维亚总统路易斯·阿尔塞

第二章　协同促改：金砖国家引领"全球南方"本币合作实践

　　自 2008 年全球金融危机爆发以来，"全球南方"国家的中央银行之间签订了诸多双边货币互换协议，且这些协议下的货币互换规模持续增长，金砖国家表现尤为突出。

　　央行间的双边本币互换作为一种融资机制，允许一国中央银行用本国货币置换另一国的货币。互换资金可以用来促进双边贸易和投资活动，有助于节省汇兑成本，降低汇率波动等带来的金融风险。

　　在国际秩序经历系统性震荡的当下，由新兴国家和发展中国家组成的金砖国家合作机制近年来显著壮大，吸引了众多"全球南方"国家的加入，成为国际格局变化中的亮点。随着金砖国家在经贸、投资、金融等领域的合作不断深化，推动金砖国家跨境支付合作、建立金砖支付体系成为国际社会热议的焦点话题。

---

① 来源：玻利维亚 ABI 通讯社，《阿尔塞：美元流动性"紧张"，倾向用人民币进行中国贸易》；2023 年 5 月 10 日

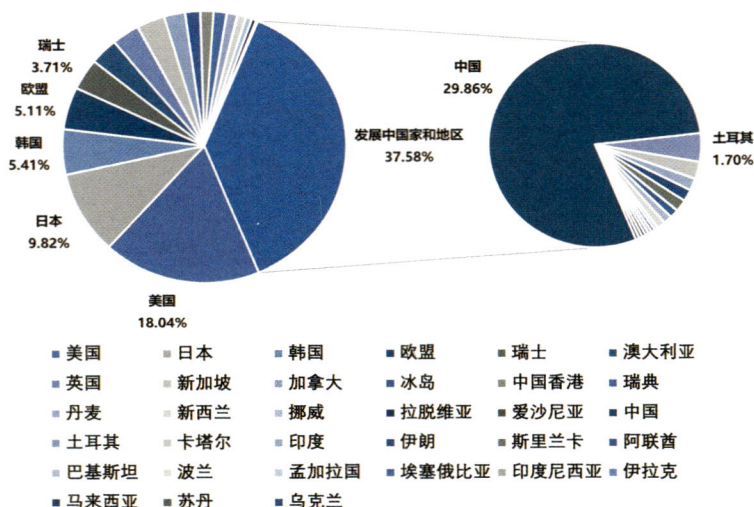

瑞士
3.71%
欧盟
5.11%
韩国
5.41%
日本
9.82%
美国
18.04%
发展中国家和地区
37.58%
中国
29.86%
土耳其
1.70%

■ 美国　　■ 日本　　■ 韩国　　■ 欧盟　　■ 瑞士　　■ 澳大利亚
■ 英国　　■ 新加坡　　■ 加拿大　　■ 冰岛　　■ 中国香港　　■ 瑞典
■ 丹麦　　■ 新西兰　　■ 挪威　　■ 拉脱维亚　　■ 爱沙尼亚　　■ 中国
■ 土耳其　　■ 卡塔尔　　■ 印度　　■ 伊朗　　■ 斯里兰卡　　■ 阿联酋
■ 巴基斯坦　　■ 波兰　　■ 孟加拉国　　■ 埃塞俄比亚　　■ 印度尼西亚　　■ 伊拉克
■ 马来西亚　　■ 苏丹　　■ 乌克兰

图 2.1　2007-2022 年全球货币互换协议供给侧统计

数据来源：波士顿大学全球发展政策研究中心（Global Development policy center）

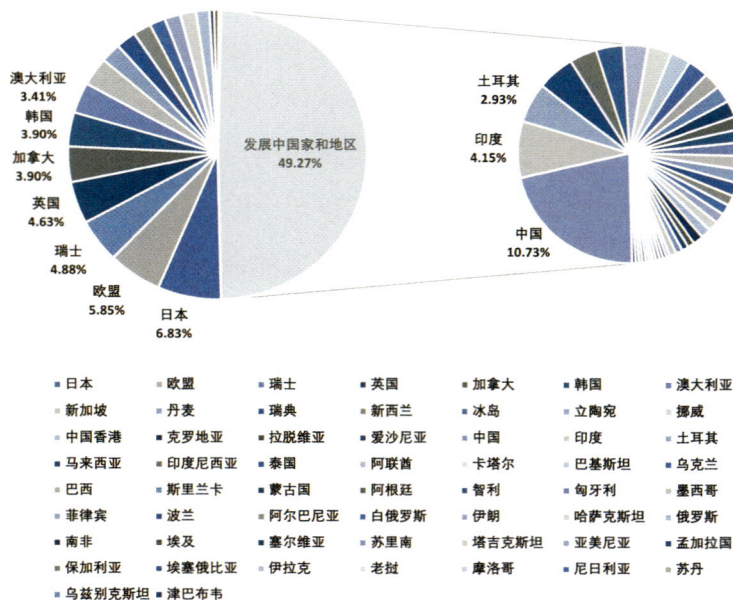

澳大利亚
3.41%
韩国
3.90%
加拿大
3.90%
英国
4.63%
瑞士
4.88%
欧盟
5.85%
日本
6.83%
发展中国家和地区
49.27%
土耳其
2.93%
印度
4.15%
中国
10.73%

■ 日本　　■ 欧盟　　■ 瑞士　　■ 英国　　■ 加拿大　　■ 韩国　　■ 澳大利亚
■ 新加坡　　■ 丹麦　　■ 瑞典　　■ 新西兰　　■ 冰岛　　■ 立陶宛　　■ 挪威
■ 中国香港　　■ 克罗地亚　　■ 拉脱维亚　　■ 爱沙尼亚　　■ 中国　　■ 印度　　■ 土耳其
■ 马来西亚　　■ 印度尼西亚　　■ 泰国　　■ 阿联酋　　■ 卡塔尔　　■ 巴基斯坦　　■ 乌克兰
■ 巴西　　■ 斯里兰卡　　■ 蒙古国　　■ 阿根廷　　■ 智利　　■ 匈牙利　　■ 墨西哥
■ 菲律宾　　■ 波兰　　■ 阿尔巴尼亚　　■ 白俄罗斯　　■ 伊朗　　■ 哈萨克斯坦　　■ 俄罗斯
■ 南非　　■ 埃及　　■ 塞尔维亚　　■ 苏里南　　■ 塔吉克斯坦　　■ 亚美尼亚　　■ 孟加拉国
■ 保加利亚　　■ 埃塞俄比亚　　■ 伊拉克　　■ 老挝　　■ 摩洛哥　　■ 尼日利亚　　■ 苏丹
■ 乌兹别克斯坦　　■ 津巴布韦

图 2.1　2007-2022 年全球货币互换协议接收侧统计

数据来源：波士顿大学全球发展政策研究中心（Global Development Policy Center）

2023 年，《金砖国家领导人第十五次会晤约翰内斯堡宣言》鼓励金砖国家同其贸易伙伴在开展国际贸易和金融交易时使用本币，强调推进金砖国家本币合作、支付工具和平台研究的重要性，并鼓励加强金砖国家间的代理银行网络，以促进本币结算。10 月 16 日，上海合作组织成员国政府首脑理事会发表联合公报，反对保护主义及单边制裁，强调应继续落实《上合组织成员国逐步扩大本币结算份额路线图》。2024 年 10 月 24 日，《金砖国家领导人第十六次会晤喀山宣言》重申，致力于加强金砖国家金融合作，欢迎金砖国家银行合作机制聚焦促进和扩大项目、计划的创新金融实践和方法，及金砖国家同其贸易伙伴在开展金融交易时使用本币。

目前，由俄罗斯、白俄罗斯、亚美尼亚、哈萨克斯坦和吉尔吉斯斯坦组成的欧亚经济联盟成员国间的贸易本币结算比例已接近 90%。近期，俄罗斯已经要求使用卢布支付天然气和粮食的进口款项。除了双边本币支付协议，还存在多边货币协商机制，甚至不排除实物交易的可能性。

东盟作为亚太地区的重要力量，同样正在积极推进双边贸易中本币结算的比重。近年来，随着美元的剧烈波动，东盟部分成员国的货币汇率遭遇压力，给东盟国家的经济直接造成了不同程度的负面影响。目前，东盟各国正寻求在跨境贸易和投资中增加本币使用的频率，以降低因美元波动导致的汇率和通胀风险，确保货币稳定，推动经济增长。

2023 年东盟财长和央行行长会议上，东盟各成员国一致同意加强本地区内本地货币的使用，减少在跨境贸易和投资中对现行国际主要货币的依赖。2023 年 5 月 11 日，东盟十国在第 42 届领导人峰会期间共同发表了关于推进区域支付互联互通和促进本币交易的集体宣言。2023 年 8 月，东盟财政部长和央行行长会议批准建立东盟范围内的本币交易框架。同时，印度尼西亚宣布成立"本币交易国家特别工作组"，而马来西亚提出了"增加本币结算"的倡议。

此外,目前东盟10国均已加入人民币跨境支付系统(CIPS),柬埔寨、印度尼西亚、马来西亚、菲律宾、新加坡、泰国等国已将人民币纳入外汇官方储备。相关数据显示,2013至2022年,中国与东盟跨境人民币结算量增长近20倍。

拉美地区也在试图增加本币结算的规模。其中玻利维亚加入南方共同市场(简称"南共市"),并计划加入南共市的"本地货币支付系统"。该系统允许南共市成员国之间使用本币结算双边贸易。2024年7月,巴西总统卢拉在玻利维亚举行的商业论坛闭幕式上表示,这一举措有助于降低交易成本,减少玻利维亚对美元的依赖。

2.1 金砖国家:引领南南本币合作潮流

2.1.1 新开发银行:本币融资初见成效

总部位于上海的新开发银行(NDB)是金砖国家合作走深走实的标志性成果之一。作为全球首个由发展中国家独立创建的多边开发银行,新开发银行致力于支持金砖国家以及其他新兴经济体和发展中国家的基础设施和可持续发展项目,旨在作为现有国际多边和区域金融机构的补充,推动全球经济增长与发展。

2014年7月,在金砖国家领导人第六次会晤期间,五国领导人(巴西、俄罗斯、印度、中国、南非)签署了《成立新开发银行的协议》。2015年7月,新开发银行在上海正式开业。2021年,孟加拉国、埃及、阿联酋和乌拉圭被吸纳成为新开发银行的新成员。2024年8月,阿尔及利亚获准加入新开发银行,成为该银行成员中非洲地区最大的天然气出口国。

多边开发银行目前的融资大多以美元形式提供,但对借款人而言,从基础设施项目获得的大部分收入都以当地货币计价,因此存在负债端和资产端的货币错配风险。多边开发银行通过在成员国的国内资本市场上发行以当地货币计价的债券进行融资，能帮助借款人有效避免货币错配风险，具有重大的商业意义。

目前，新开发银行已经成功注册人民币、俄罗斯卢布和南非兰特债券发行计划。2016 年 7 月，新开发银行在中国银行间债券市场发行第一期绿色金融债券，发行规模 30 亿元人民币。2019 年 1 月 9 日，新开发银行在中国注册 100 亿元人民币债券计划，即获准自项目注册之日起 2 年内在中国银行间债券市场募集不超过 100 亿元人民币。此后，新开发银行每年均成功在中国注册人民币债券计划，且规模逐渐扩大。到 2023 年，新开发银行获准的募集规模已达到近 400 亿元人民币。

在其他当地货币方面，2019 年，新开发银行成功注册了俄罗斯卢布债券发行计划，最大融资规模 1000 亿卢布，无有效期限限制。2023 年，新开发银行推出修订后的南非兰特债券发行计划，最大筹资规模为 100 亿南非兰特，无有效期限限制。

案例　新开发银行将扩大成员国本币融资

提供本币融资是新开发银行的重要价值体现。新开发银行行长罗塞芙 8 月 30 日在南非立法首都开普敦表示，新开发银行将扩大成员国本币融资，以支持新兴经济体和发展中国家的可持续发展。

罗塞芙指出，新兴市场和发展中国家在实现可持续发展方面面临挑战，需要大量资源和长期融资，应将国际流动性引入发展中国家，并制定本币融资等替代方案以扩大投资的财政空间。

罗塞芙认为，"使用本币是一种战略选择"，扩大本币融资是新开发银行 2022 年至 2026 年期间的主要战略目标之一。新开发银行正在建立以可持续发展为导向的本币融资平台，目标是将以成员国本币进行融资的比例提升到 30%。

2.1.2 巴西：积极发展本币市场，推进多元货币体系

作为南美最大的经济体，巴西是全球最大的农产品和肉类出口国之一，作为金砖国家合作机制的重要创始成员国，巴西也是"全球南方"概念的积极推动者。

"全球南方"已成为巴西政府在各种国际外交场合中频繁提及的核心概念，而改革全球经济治理体系则是巴西推动"全球南方"合作的重要议题。近年来，美联储的金融政策对南美造成了严重影响。自卢拉重新执政以来，其多次在公开场合讨论了"多元货币体系""本币结算""共同货币"以及"新支付体系"等议题。

在巴西朗多尼亚州，山东电建一公司承担 EPC 总承包任务的 EDP 输变电项目线路穿越热带雨林。

中国是巴西最大的贸易伙伴，占巴西进口总额度的五分之一以上。作为关系紧密的贸易伙伴，以及东西半球最大的发展中国家和重要新兴市场国家，中国和巴西持续推动双方在本币交易市场的合作。2023年初，两国签署了在巴西建立人民币清算安排的合作备忘录。2023 年，双方签署贸易协议，同意在未来的双边贸易中不再使用美元作为中间货币，

而是直接使用双方本币进行结算。首次尝试这一新结算方式的是巴西纸浆工业领域龙头企业巴西埃尔多拉多纸浆公司（Eldorado Brasil），其产品约有 40% 销往中国。2023 年 8 月，该公司与厦门某进口企业达成协议，采用人民币作为计价货币，并指定中银巴西作为收款银行，尝试人民币结算。9 月 28 日，中银巴西即时将收到的人民币直接兑换为雷亚尔入境巴西，汇入客户本地账户，为巴西出口商提供了人民币结算一站式解决方案。

目前两国之间已实现从货物交易的人民币计价，到资金交易的人民币结算、融资和本币直兑的全流程操作，将进一步降低两国交易的时间和费用成本，也将规避汇率风险，减少对第三方货币或者单一货币的依赖。

近年来中国巴西贸易规模、领域持续扩大。图为在 2024 年中国国际服务贸易交易会上，工作人员向观众介绍巴西咖啡。

发展本币市场，除了跨境贸易，本币金融市场的完备度亦是重要基础。巴西尽管实行外汇管制，但境外的参与者已占据较高的比重。巴西股票市场由巴西证券交易所（B3）主导。截至 2023 年，B3 上市证券的总市值接近 1 万亿美元，占当年巴西 GDP 的约 45%，共有 400 多家上市公司，由于巴西市场习惯高利率，机构投资者在巴西股市中占据主导地位，国际投资者占比较高。截至 2024 年 8 月，国外投资者的托管头寸和交易量占比均在 40% 以上。

案例　巴西与阿根廷筹建共同货币："南美元"要来了？

2023 年 1 月，巴西总统卢拉和阿根廷时任总统费尔南德斯宣布双方有意创建南美洲共同货币"苏尔"。该倡议旨在促进巴阿双边及南美国家间贸易，避免美元结算的弊端，并有望将南美洲建成仅次于欧元区的全球第二大货币区。

巴西与阿根廷两国的国内生产总值占南美洲国家经济总量超过 50%。两国携手提出共同货币的倡议，向市场传递了积极的经济信号：若该倡议得到妥善设计与执行，对巴西而言，有望提升其出口量并刺激经济增长；对阿根廷，则有助于缓解其美元外汇储备的紧张状况，减少贸易和长期利率风险，同时提高两国间的贸易、投资及经济效率。此外，对整个区域而言，该倡议亦可作为推动拉丁美洲一体化进程的战略举措之一。因此，这倡议具有不可忽视的潜力与重要性，自提出以来，已在社会各界引发了广泛而热烈的讨论。

历史上，区域货币一体化的概念和实践在南美洲以及其他地区频繁出现，此次提出的南美洲共同货币倡议同样具有其时代的必然性和内在的合理性。然而，尽管巴西和阿根廷两国领导人在相关计划的声明中表现出了坚定的政治决心，但该项目目前仍处于初步构想阶段，面临诸多争议和挑战，未来也将经历一个漫长且复杂的实施过程。

2.1.3 中国：人民币国际化进程持续加快

2009 年，中国启动人民币跨境贸易结算试点，标志着人民币开始走向国际。此后，人民币国际化进程呈现周期性发展、稳步上升的趋势。目前，人民币的国际地位和全球影响力正在持续提升，在全球交易中，人民币的使用比例持续稳步增长，根据 SWIFT 数据，人民币已成为全球支付中第四大活跃货币。同时，由于人民币利率较低，其作为融资货币的属性也不断增强。随着新兴经济体的发展，人民币跨境贸易结算、本币互换、投融资需求的旺盛以及外汇风险管理需求的增加，将加速推进跨境人民币生态圈的成熟，进一步推动人民币国际化进程。

2.1.3.1 人民币在全球跨境交易使用中的占比提高

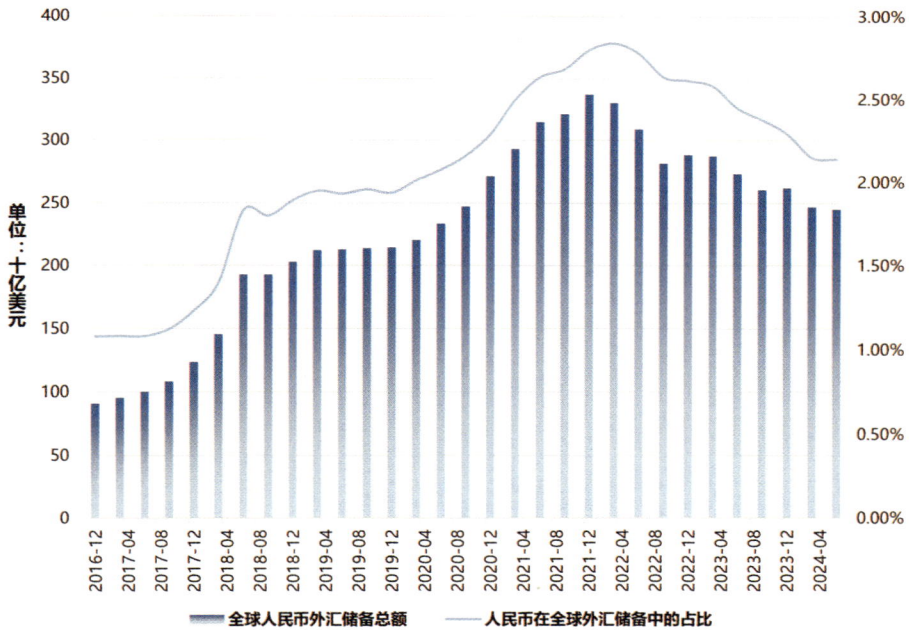

图 2.3 全球人民币储备规模及份额

数据来源：IMF 新华财经

随着人民币国际化进程的加快，越来越多的区域贸易开始采用人民币进行结算。据 SWIFT 数据，截至 2024 年 8 月，人民币结算额占全球支付总额的 4.69%，这已经是人民币在全球支付排名中连续第 10 个月位列第四。

根据 SWIFT 数据，2023 年共有 161 个国家和地区发生跨境人民币客户汇款收付，人民币跨境使用的网络效应正在逐步显现，促进了人民币跨境使用活跃度提升。从地域结构上看，人民币在 RCEP 区域及"一带一路"沿线国家的使用保持了较快增长。2023 年，RCEP 成员国（不含中国自身）人民币客户汇款规模增长了 20.4%，"一带一路"沿线国家人民币客户汇款规模增长了 21.1%。

随着共建"一带一路"以及 RCEP 等新兴市场国家在中国外贸中的占比不断上升，加上中国企业加大出海力度，未来一段时间内，人民币在跨境贸易结算中的使用预计将展现出强劲的增长前景。

案例 跨境人民币业务服务实体经济能力持续提升

2024 年 1 至 8 月，银行代客人民币跨境收付金额合计为 41.6 万亿元，同比增长 21.1%，增速保持在较高水平，其中，货物贸易人民币跨境收付金额占同期本外币跨境收付金额比例进一步提升至 26.5%，较 2023 年全年提高 1.7 个百分点。

伴随着中国持续推进高水平对外开放，连续 7 年保持货物贸易第一大国地位，是全球 140 多个国家和地区的主要贸易伙伴，企业在对外贸易中使用人民币进行结算具有扎实、良好的基础。

2023 年以来，人民币跨境使用规模稳步增长，收支总体平衡，人民币在中国本外币跨境收付中的占比进一步提高，在全球支付中占比和排名提升。

其中，跨境人民币业务服务实体经济能力持续提高。2023 年，经常项目人民币跨境收付金额合计为 14 万亿元，同比增长 33.4%，其中，收入 6.9 万亿元，同比增长 24.5%；支出 7.1 万亿元，同比增长 43.3%。2023 年，经常项目人民币跨境收付占同期经常项目本外币跨境收付金额的比例为 27.7%。2024 年 1 至 8 月，经常项目人民币跨境收付金额合计为 10.4 万亿元，同比增长 17.3%，占同期本外币跨境收付金额的比例为 9.3%。

对于近年来货物贸易人民币结算呈现出的新特点，《2024 年人民币国际化报告》[1] 显示：一是随着人民币汇率形成机制改革不断深化，人民币汇率弹性增强，人民币汇率双向波动成为常态，企业更倾向于在跨境贸易结算中使用人民币，以减轻货币错配影响。二是中国产业结构转型升级，全球产业布局调整，为人民币跨境使用创造了更多场景，进一步带动人民币使用需求上升。例如，近年来，中国持续深化与东盟国家产业链供应链合作，2023 年中国与东盟货物贸易人民币跨境结算金额为 2 万亿元，同比增长 47%。三是人民币融资成本优势推动人民币贸易融资增加，带动经营主体在贸易结算中选择人民币。四是跨境电商等外贸新业态经营主体更倾向于使用人民币结算。2023 年，第三方支付机构办理的跨境电商货物贸易人民币结算金额近 1 万亿元，同比增长 24%。此外，大宗商品人民币计价结算取得新进展、人民币投融资货币功能进一步强化、人民币国际储备占比总体稳定等特点，均显示出人民币国际化正稳慎扎实推进。

2.1.3.2 人民币跨境支付系统服务能力提升

跨境支付清算系统为跨境贸易和投融资活动提供了基础性支持，是全球经济金融运行的重要基础。人民币跨境支付系统（CIPS）作为专门服务于人民币跨境支付清算业务的关键金融市场基础设施，自 2015 年

---

[1] 来源：中国人民银行，《2024 年人民币国际化报告》；2024 年 9 月 30 日

10 月上线运行以来，持续完善系统功能，陆续接入符合条件的境内外银行和金融基础设施（FMI），发挥了跨境人民币支付清算的"主渠道"作用，为全球范围内人民币的跨境使用提供了坚实支撑。

经过几年发展，人民币跨境支付系统以直参为主要节点、联通境内外银行的全球人民币支付清算服务网络已基本形成。截至2024年8月末，人民币跨境支付系统共有直接参与者152家，间接参与者1412家。间接参与者中，亚洲1050家（境内563家），欧洲243家，非洲52家，北美洲26家，大洋洲21家，南美洲20家。具体来看，人民币跨境支付系统的参与者分布在全球117个国家和地区，其业务通过4700多家法人银行机构覆盖至全球184个国家和地区。随着人民币跨境支付系统服务能力的不断提升，目前中国已成为仅次于美国和欧元区的全球跨境支付第三大市场。

2.1.3.3 人民币双边本币互换协议规模扩大

各国央行间的双边本币互换是一种融资合作，一国央行可以用自己的货币置换另一国货币，互换资金可用于支持双边贸易投资活动，有助于节约汇兑成本、降低汇率风险。

近年来中国人民银行持续深化与境外央行间的货币合作，货币互换已成为全球金融安全网的重要组成部分。

2023 年以来，中国人民银行与沙特阿拉伯、毛里求斯、埃及、阿根廷、老挝、蒙古国、阿联酋等国家和地区的中央银行或货币当局签署或续签双边本币互换协议。据中国商务部国际贸易经济合作研究院统计，2023 年 7 月，中国已与南非、摩洛哥、埃及和尼日利亚签署了总额达 730 亿元人民币的双边本币互换协议。截至 2024 年 8 月，中国人民银行共与 42 个国家和地区的中央银行或货币当局签署过双边本币互换协议，其中有效协议 29 份，互换规模超过 4.1 万亿元人民币；境外货币当局实际动用人民币余额 916 亿元，中国人民银行实际动用外币互换资金余额折合人民币 6.8 亿元。

同时，2023 年以来，中国人民银行不断优化人民币海外清算网络，人民币清算行覆盖范围持续扩大。截至 2024 年 8 月，中国人民银行已在 31 个国家和地区授权 33 家境外人民币清算行，其中中资清算行 31 家，外资清算行 2 家，基本覆盖与中国贸易往来密切的国家和地区。

声音

"双边的货币互换是金融安全网的重要组成部分。双边货币互换既可促进双边贸易和投资，又是全球金融安全网有益的补充。如在国际金融市场动荡或一些国家发生银行业危机期间，主要经济体央行之间通过双边互换提供了紧急的流动性支持，有效缓解了全球金融市场的波动。"[①]

——中国人民银行行长潘功胜

[①] 来源：人民网，《潘功胜：央行已与 29 个国家和地区签署双边本币互换协议》；2024 年 3 月 27 日

2.1.3.4 人民币投融资货币功能深化

近年来，中国人民银行会同有关部门优化粤港澳大湾区"跨境理财通"业务，上线内地与香港"互换通"业务，支持"熊猫债"发行，人民币投融资功能深化。随着投资人民币资产的可操作性得到较大改善，国际投资者对人民币资产的投资日益活跃。

例如，2024 年 3 月，国家电网巴西控股公司所属席尔瓦尼亚输电特许权公司完成了首笔跨境人民币融资，借助人民币跨境支付清算路径，不仅降低了财务成本、减少了汇兑风险，也有助于提升巴西企业对人民币的认知度、接受度。

一是推进债券市场高水平对外开放。

SWIFT 数据显示，2024 年 8 月，人民币在全球贸易融资中的占比为 5.95%，是全球第二大贸易融资货币。境外投资者持续买入中国债券，截至 2024 年 8 月末持仓规模约 4.6 万亿元，占境内债券托管总量的 2.7%，较 2023 年末上升 0.3 个百分点。

案例 中国中央结算公司加大服务"全球南方"进入中国债券市场

近年来，中央结算公司积极支持与"全球南方"金融领域相关合作，持续对接其人民币融资需求，服务"全球南方"国家深度参与中国债券市场，助力中国债券市场高水平对外开放。中央结算公司采取"走出去"与"引进来"相结合的方式，聚焦"全球南方"国家主权类机构等重点客户开展定向营销和服务。在"走出去"方面，中央结算公司采取线上线下相结合的方式，举办多场境外投资者推介会，并先后与坦桑尼亚、乌干达、安哥拉、墨西哥、泰国、印度尼西亚、莫桑比克、马来西亚等国央行开展一对一交流，为其解答入市过程中的相关问题；在"引进来"方面，中央结算公司举办境外央行类机构线上研讨会，邀请财政部、中国人民银行、国际清算银行，以及包括巴西央行等"全球南方"国家境外央行类机构参与会议。

下一步，中央结算公司将在跨境发行、跨境结算、担保品管理、金融估值等多个领域推动与"全球南方"国家开展金融合作，服务"全球南方"国家发行人和投资人，形成体系完整、功能完善的离岸金融服务体系。

二是推动熊猫债市场持续扩容。

在支持境外发行主体的跨境融资需求方面，熊猫债发挥了重要作用。以中国国宝命名的熊猫债，是指境外和多边金融机构等在中国发行的人民币债券。2005 年，国际金融公司（IFC）和亚洲开发银行（ADB）在银行间债券市场分别发行人民币债券 11.3 亿元和 10 亿元，标志着熊猫债正式启航。2022 年，人民银行和外管局联合发布《关于境外机构境内发行债券资金管理有关事宜的通知》，加之中美利差影响，熊猫债进入高速发展阶段。2022 年发行 850 亿元；2023 年发行 1500 多亿元；2024 年 1-9 月发行规模 1610 亿元，截至 2024 年 9 月底，熊猫债总发行规模达 9415.9 亿元。熊猫债吸引了优质国际发行人和投资人的广泛参与，提升了中国债券市场开放程度。新开发银行自 2016 年进入银行间市场以来，已累计发行熊猫债 555 亿元，未偿还余额共计 315 亿元，是迄今为止熊猫债市场上最大的发行人。新开发银行的熊猫债已成为投资者的优质资产，并有助于投资者实现债券投资的多样化。

案例　熊猫债发行热度空前

继 2023 年发行量创历史新高后，2024 年以来，熊猫债发行延续火热局面，在全球债券市场中不断刷新热度。数据显示，以发行起始日计，截至目前，2024 年熊猫债已发行 90 余只，发行规模约为 1610 亿元，超过 2023 年全年发行额 1544.5 亿元，与去年同期相比，发行额增长了 31.71%。

从发行人结构来看，虽然红筹企业仍是熊猫债发行的主力，但伴随熊猫债认可度的不断提升，纯境外发行人发行熊猫债的规模也有所提升。值得一提的是，在今年熊猫债的纯境外发行人中，还出现了不少"新面孔"。康师傅、拜耳、巴斯夫、凯德等多家企业首次出现在发行人名单中。拜耳、巴斯夫等作为大型跨国企业发行的熊猫债获得了市场的广泛关注，凸显了熊猫债的吸引力。

从债券期限看，今年以来，熊猫债发行期限仍主要集中在中短期，但 5 年期及以上发行规模明显增加。具体来看，发行期限在 3 年及 3 年以下的熊猫债有 64 只，占比约为 70%，与去年同期相比有所下降，其中 3 年期仍为发行规模最大的债券品种。

在低利率环境下，5 年期及以上发行规模与去年同期相比明显增长。数据显示，今年以来，发行期限为 5 年的熊猫债有 20 只，去年同期为 11 只；发行期限为 10 年的熊猫债有 8 只，去年同期未出现 10 年期限债券。

三是健全离岸金融服务体系。

中国本土金融机构在全球离岸市场的国际服务能力也在持续提升，包括在债券业务上加强境内外市场连接，推动"债券通"南北双向通车，与卢森堡证券交易所开展"绿债信息通"合作等。例如，上海清算所等本土金融基础设施协同在沪金融机构，持续对接"全球南方"国家的跨境人民币投融资诉求，积极开展推动玉兰债等业务创新。

早在 2018 年，中国银行在匈牙利发行熊猫债挂钩票据类投资产品。

案例 创新"玉兰债"业务，服务境内发行人发债融资

2020年12月，上海清算所与国际中央证券存管机构（ICSD）欧清银行合作推出"玉兰债"业务，服务境内发行人走到国际市场进行人民币等各币种的发债融资。

"玉兰债"产品作为离岸债券市场的组成部分，在发行审批、上市挂牌及投资渠道等与传统境外发债制度安排和操作惯例顺畅对接的基础上，创新引入最终投资者信息穿透机制，便利了境内外金融市场要素资源的共享，为发行人债券存续期管理、投资者主动管理以及监管机构提供有效工具，有力支持了人民币资产国际化发展。

目前，"玉兰债"产品已先后在银行业、证券业有序落地，计价币种涵盖美元、欧元、人民币，发行机构包括境内主体直发、境外分支机构及SPV间接发行，发行成本理想、投资者分布广泛。随着业务红利稳步积累，"玉兰债"已经引领了日本、新加坡的"折纸债"、"兰花债"模式创新，支付代理、公司行为等增值服务也在稳慎探索中。

2.1.4 印度：推行本币结算增进贸易互惠

在推动多元货币体系的议题上，印度尽管一直表现出犹豫且摇摆不定，但作为美元创汇难的较大的快速发展经济体，印度也一直试图降低美元对其经济发展的制约，减少对美元结算的依赖，同多个国家和地区建立或正在建立本币结算机制。

联合国商品贸易统计数据库的数据显示，印度是阿联酋的第二大贸易伙伴，阿联酋则是印度的第三大贸易伙伴，两国2023年总贸易额超过800亿美元。阿联酋主要向印度出口原油，而印度向阿联酋出口一部分精炼化工产品和电器等。同时，据《印度时报》报道，印度有大量劳工和专业技术人员在阿联酋工作，每年有大量侨汇需要从阿联酋转回印度。因此印度和阿联酋对两国实现货币直接结算有较大需求。

2023 年 7 月，印度与阿联酋两国达成共识，同意建立本币跨境贸易框架，并开发替代 SWIFT 支付系统的本币结算系统。2024 年 1 月起，两国已经开始使用各自的本币进行直接贸易。8 月，印度中央银行授权部分阿联酋银行在印度银行开设特别卢比账户用于贸易结算，并鼓励进出口商直接使用卢比和迪拉姆进行交易。

实现两国之间的本币结算不仅有助于发展卢比－迪拉姆外汇市场，短期内减少对美元的依赖有助于缓解外汇储备的压力，并降低汇率波动带来的损失，为印度金融业带来新的机遇。长远来看，卢比和迪拉姆结算机制若发展完善，将为印度与其他国家开展双边本币结算建立示范，推动卢比的国际化进程，进一步降低对美元的依赖。

此外，长期以来，印度卢比的汇率波动性较大。过去 22 年中，印度卢比对美元汇率贬值了 84%，并在 2022 年 10 月达到了历史最低点。为了遏制卢比的贬值趋势，同时方便印度与各国进行贸易交易结算，印度储备银行（RBI）实施了国际贸易的卢比结算机制。根据该机制，印度的贸易商可以在特定贸易伙伴国银行开设特别 vostro 账户，但所有进出口贸易均以卢比进行结算和开具发票。双方采用的卢比汇率由国际离岸市场汇率决定。

案例　印俄重启扩大本币结算机制谈判

近年来，印度与俄罗斯之间的贸易额表现良好。根据俄罗斯总统新闻办公室的数据，去年双边贸易额创下了 568 亿美元的历史新高，增长超过 60%。今年 1 月至 8 月，由于石油供应的推动，俄印之间的贸易额同比增长了 9%，达到了 374 亿美元。

2024 年 8 月，印度与俄罗斯中央银行重启了扩大本币结算机制的谈判，旨在解决近年来双边贸易急剧增长后出现的支付问题。两国央行合作的关键问题在于设定两国货币之间的贸易参考汇率，而不是通过美元作为中介货币来确定印俄本币之间的汇率。但这将需要印度卢比和俄罗斯卢布在统一的货币兑换平台上进行更大规模和更长时间的交易，目前双方尚未就此达成共识。

除了跨境结算，印度也在与南亚区域合作联盟国家建立货币互换机制，这一南盟货币互换机制自2012年起开始运作，成员国包括阿富汗、孟加拉国、不丹、印度、马尔代夫、尼泊尔、巴基斯坦和斯里兰卡等，旨在为南盟国家提供短期外汇流动性支持或应对国际收支危机的临时资金，直至建立起长期机制。

印度储备银行此前还发布了2024年至2027年间与南亚区域合作联盟（SAARC）国家货币互换安排的修订框架。该框架新增了独立的卢比互换窗口，并为印度卢比的互换提供了共计2500亿卢比的优惠支持。

2.1.5 俄罗斯：搭建国际替代支付系统

由于金融制裁的影响，俄罗斯在国际贸易中无法使用美元、欧元或英镑等主要国际货币进行结算，近两年俄罗斯的国际贸易通常采用本币结算方式。截至2023年底，俄罗斯与金砖国家的本币结算份额已从2021年的26%跃升至85%，其中与中国的本币结算比例超过95%。此外，俄罗斯正与金砖国家合作，建立一个类似于SWIFT的清算系统，并不断完善本币结算机制，以提高支付效率并降低汇率波动带来的风险。

除完善本国结算系统以及与友好国家接通结算系统外，俄罗斯还推出了多种举措，尝试使用更先进的国际支付手段和解决方案，包括区块链和数字货币。

俄罗斯财政部副部长伊万·切别斯科夫表示，创建公平的金融体系是俄罗斯担任金砖国家轮值主席国的首要任务，2024年的重点就是帮助金砖国家新成员融入多边合作架构。俄罗斯将创建替代支付系统作为当前对外金融合作的优先事项之一，俄罗斯外交部称，要加强金砖国家在国际货币和金融体系中的作用，以增加本币结算为重点发展银行间合作。

案例　俄伊本币结算：绕开 SWIFT 束缚的新路径

近年来，SWIFT 系统多次被西方国家用作金融制裁的工具，迫使更多国家寻找替代方案。2012 年和 2018 年，伊朗两次被从 SWIFT 系统除名；2022 年，俄罗斯被从 SWIFT 系统除名。受西方制裁影响，俄罗斯对欧盟的原油出口份额大幅下降。作为能源出口大国，西方制裁下的俄罗斯和伊朗均需要寻找或建立多元化的替代结算系统。2023 年 12 月，俄罗斯总统普京表示，基于美元主导和 SWIFT 系统结算的西方金融体系已信誉扫地，该系统已经或至少正在过时，正在被本币结算系统取代。2024 年 1 月，据俄新社报道，伊朗央行副行长卡里米表示，莫斯科与德黑兰已经接通了两国间的银行间通信和转账系统，双方贸易无需通过 SWIFT 系统，可直接通过双方银行完成交易。例如，伊朗出口商现在能够以本币里亚尔为计价单位向俄罗斯贸易伙伴开具账单，并直接从设在伊朗的俄罗斯银行收取里亚尔货款。

2.1.6 南非：启动本币互换便利操作

2010 年 12 月，南非正式加入金砖国家。近年来，随着中非经贸合作不断走深，与经贸合作相伴而生的跨境支付、跨国融资等金融活动更加繁盛，中国与南非已连续多年签署双边本币互换协议，旨在便利双边贸易和投资，维护区域金融稳定。

2015 年 4 月 10 日，中国人民银行与南非储备银行签署了规模为 300 亿元人民币（540 亿南非兰特）的双边本币互换协议。2018 年、2021 年，中国人民银行与南非储备银行两次续签 300 亿元人民币规模的双边本币互换协议，双方合作更加紧密。

声音

多年来，美国一直利用美元作为武器，对抗包括非洲在内的所有发展中国家。因此非洲必须抵制这种将美元武器化的行为，寻找用本地货币进行贸易的替代方案①。

——南非国会议员孟亚

案例　签署非洲自由贸易协定，释放非洲经济潜力

随着全球化步伐的加快，非洲国家逐渐意识到，单个国家的经济规模在全球市场上难以与更大的区域经济体抗衡。2019 年 5 月 30 日，非洲国家正式批准成立非洲大陆自由贸易区（AFCFTA），其核心目标是通过减少或消除成员国之间的关税和非关税障碍，提高区域内的贸易流动性，加强非洲在全球市场中的竞争力。目前，非洲内部的贸易额仅占其总贸易量的大约 15%，而非洲大陆自由贸易区的成立预计将显著提高这一比例，尤其是在制造业、农业和服务业领域。随着时间的推移，非洲大陆有望成为一个更加统一的政治和经济实体，在全球事务中增强其集体影响力。

非洲大陆自由贸易区建立，为非洲货币在区域内部的使用提供了有利条件。以肯尼亚的移动支付平台 M-pesa 为例，其在东非地区的跨境支付中得到广泛应用，表明非洲货币在区域经济活动中的作用正在扩大。

2.2 东盟：建设本币结算生态圈

近年来，为减轻美联储货币政策的外溢效应并防范美元制裁风险，东南亚国家在跨境交易中逐渐减少对美元的依赖，并通过签订本币结

---

① 来源：央视新闻，《美元霸权加剧全球经济动荡多国人士呼吁货币多样化》，2024 年 9 月 19 日

算协议来促进彼此之间的合作，旨在建立一个更高效、更具活力的本币市场。作为全球经济增长的热点区域，东盟国家积极推广本币结算，并在政府层面达成了多项协议，东盟本币结算生态圈正在持续扩大和优化。

2.2.1 东盟内部：本币结算渠道逐渐增多

积极推进双边本币结算协议。双边本币结算协议是东盟主要国家在保留外汇管制情况下，实现贸易投资本币结算的特殊机制。2016 年，印度尼西亚、泰国、马来西亚三国央行签署双边本币结算协议，允许本国从事外贸和开展对外直接投资的企业，通过指定银行（ACCD 银行）完成本币支付。为支持双边本币结算协议实施，三国央行还在国内建立了对方货币外汇市场，由本国 ACCD 银行组成做市商，通过市场化方式形成实时汇率。随着三国通过双边本币结算协议结算的贸易量稳步上升，菲律宾于 2019 年加入三国间的本币结算协议网络。

同时加大边贸本币结算协议执行力度。东盟边贸本币结算协议与双边本币结算协议类似，通过指定银行互开同业往来账户实施本币结算，但与双边本币结算协议不同，边贸本币结算协议允许两国企业在指定银行同时开设本币及对方货币账户，且仅能开展边境贸易。目前，边贸本币结算协议主要在东盟内以边贸为主、发展相对落后的国家实施。早在20 世纪 90 年代，缅甸、老挝、柬埔寨已与泰国就泰铢结算达成相关合作协议，泰铢在四国外贸结算中的使用频率迅速上升并形成"泰铢经济圈"。为进一步促进泰铢跨境使用，2020 年泰国又与缅甸签订协议，允许两国指定银行为从事边贸的企业同时提供泰铢和缅元结算服务。此外，越南经济的快速发展也吸引了周边邻国与其开展本币结算合作，例如老挝于 2023 年与越南签订边贸本币结算谅解备忘录，力争尽早实现两国边贸本币结算。

而在移动支付方面。东盟利用愈发普及的移动支付技术，通过统一的二维码标准推进移动支付系统的直接连接。泰国在 2020 年与柬埔寨实现了移动支付系统的直连，随后又与越南、新加坡、马来西亚、印尼等国家相继建立了双边移动支付系统的直连，泰国居民能够使用本国的移动支付软件，在上述国家扫描当地的二维码，并以本国货币进行支付。此外，为进一步提高移动支付的互联互通效率，2023 年第 42 届东盟峰会组建了专门工作组，在东盟全域推进移动支付系统的直连。目前，印尼、马来西亚、泰国、新加坡、文莱、越南、菲律宾七国的中央银行均已加入并开展相关工作。

2.2.2 东盟与域外国家（地区）：本币结算范围不断扩大

在双边本币结算领域，继印尼、泰国、马来西亚双边本币结算协议取得一定成效后，印尼又在东盟"10+3"框架下，与日本、中国、韩国分别签订了双边本币结算协议。2020 年 8 月和 2021 年 9 月，印尼分别与日本和中国签订实施双边本币结算协议；2023 年 5 月，印尼与韩国签署了双边本币结算谅解备忘录，鼓励在经常项目和直接投资业务中使用双边本币。此外，今年以来，印尼正与印度、沙特协商，在贸易投资领域推进类似双边本币结算合作。印尼央行行长佩里·瓦吉约表示，"我们将不断扩大本国货币的使用。有了本币结算机制，印尼盾的汇率可以更加稳定，因为它将不取决于美元的供应，印尼经济的宏观稳定将继续得到有力维护，此举也将为东南亚地区的贸易和汇率稳定提供支持。"

在边贸本币结算领域，缅甸、柬埔寨、老挝、越南与中国均达成了边贸本币结算协议，允许双方指定银行为两国企业提供本币结算服务。

东盟国家还积极推进与周边地区移动支付系统互联互通，以便利双边人员往来交流。2023 年 12 月，泰国央行与中国香港金融管理局宣布，香港金融管理局推出的快速支付系统"转数快"与泰国央行推出的快速支付系统 promptpay 成功实现联通，两地居民可使用本地移动支付软件在对方城市商户扫描当地二维码并使用本币支付。此外，泰国、印尼、越南等东盟国家正在与日本进行协商，推进日本－东盟移动支付系统的互联互通，便利本国居民在境外使用本币开展商务和旅游等活动。同时，为稳定双边经贸往来，部分东盟国家与俄罗斯的支付和报文系统直连也已进入协商阶段。

类别	内容	开始时间	参与方（东盟内）	参与方（东盟以外）	进展
双边本币结算协议	协议两国货币当局指定若干商业银行作为特许做市商（ACCD），两国ACCD银行互相为对方开设非居民账户，两国企业在本国ACCD银行开立对方货币子账户	2016年	印尼、泰国、马来西亚、菲律宾	中国、日本、韩国	已签署协议，菲律宾和韩国尚未正式运行
边贸本币结算协议	仅允许边境地区银行为边贸提供本币结算服务	1995年	泰国－缅甸；泰国－柬埔寨；泰国－老挝	中国－老挝；中国－越南；中国－缅甸；中国－越南	均已实施
跨境移动支付	使用二维码/快速支付的数字支付系统在协议国境内使用本国货币进行支付	2018年	印尼－泰国；马来西亚－新加坡；泰国－越南；新加坡－泰国；马来西亚－泰国；印尼－马来西亚；越南－柬埔寨；老挝－柬埔寨	泰国－日本；泰国－中国香港	东盟内部已有东盟工作组集中推进，与日本等周边地区由双边央行推进，中国主要由银联国际、支付宝、财付通自主开拓市场
金融基础设施互联互通	支付和报文系统直连	2022年	——	俄罗斯	正在协商
人民币清算行	当地商业银行通过人民币清算行与中国商业银行完成人民币结算	2013年		中国与新加坡、菲律宾、泰国、马来西亚和老挝五国	已实施，单向使用人民币结算
人民币跨境支付系统（CIPS）	当地商业银行通过接入CIPS的直参间接代理人民币结算业务	2015年	——	中国与东盟全部国家	已实施，单向使用人民币结算

图 2.4　东盟国家双边本币结算情况统计表

2.3 资源贸易趋向采用多元化货币组合

2.3.1 石油交易本币结算从试点到示范

在能源领域，金砖国家中，俄罗斯与沙特、阿联酋、伊朗均为重要的能源出口国，石油产量达到全球40%左右的份额。2000年以来，在"石油美元"的大环境下，包括伊拉克、伊朗、委内瑞拉等在内的多个国家曾尝试构建以非美货币结算石油贸易，如今，这种趋势正因地缘政治冲突以及世界变局加速显现。

伊朗是较早尝试用多种货币进行石油贸易结算的国家之一。在美国对伊朗的制裁下，2006年，伊朗正式成立了以欧元为结算货币的国际石油交易所，2007年，日本部分企业开始以日元结算其从伊朗购买的石油。2018年，伊朗和印度达成协议，印度将采用基于卢比的支付机制从伊朗进口原油，其中50%款项将用卢比支付，另外50%款项伊朗可以通过从印度进口等值产品进行交换。

近年来，沙特不断寻求用非美元货币结算石油贸易。2023年1月，沙特就"参与非美元石油交易"做出公开说明，称对于用美元以外货币结算石油贸易持开放态度。沙特财政部部长穆罕默德·贾丹表示："我们不会放弃或排除任何有助于改善贸易结算体系的可能性，愿意对石油贸易结算安排进行讨论，不管是美元、欧元还是沙特里亚尔。"大西洋理事会（Atlantic Council）分析认为，沙特参与金砖合作机制，以及与中国、泰国、阿联酋等国家和地区合作开展mBridge跨境央行数字货币项目，也能表明沙特在逐渐减少对美元的依赖。这也让外界更加关注"全球南方"本币合作的发展方向。

2.3.2 天然气交易本币结算零星扩展

在天然气交易方面，俄罗斯于2022年4月推出"卢布结算令"，对"不友好国家"的天然气贸易实施卢布结算，同时表示愿意与"友好国家"进行币种多样化、支付灵活的石油和天然气交易。

2023年7月，伊拉克和伊朗落实了"油换气"协议，伊拉克将通过原油换取伊朗的天然气，而非通过美元中转结算。

中国同样在多币种交易天然气方面取得了一定突破。2023年3月28日，中国海油与道达尔能源通过上海石油天然气交易中心平台完成国内首单以人民币结算的进口液化天然气（LNG）采购交易，LNG资源来自海湾合作委员会国家阿联酋，成交量约为6.5万吨。这是中国开展油气贸易人民币结算的有益尝试，标志着中国在油气贸易领域的跨境人民币结算交易探索迈出实质性一步，是为国际资源商参与中国市场提供新渠道、助力构建国内国际双循环发展新格局的重要实践。

2.3.3 矿产本币交易前景广阔

以铁矿石为例，中国作为全球钢铁大国，对铁矿石的需求巨大，在全球铁矿石市场占据着 65% 的份额。虽然中国储量丰富，但大部分是贫矿，提炼成本较高，因此需要从国外大量进口铁矿石，主要进口国家集中在巴西和澳大利亚。

2019 年 11 月 18 日，全球最大的铁矿石生产商——巴西淡水河谷与山东莱钢永锋国贸等国内大型钢铁企业签订了两笔以大连商品交易所铁矿石期货价格为基准的基差贸易合同。同时，澳大利亚矿企力拓和 FMG 当年也成立了中国贸易公司，在中国港口开展人民币计价的现货贸易，其价格参考港口现货和期货价格等。

2020 年，中国宝武首次与巴西淡水河谷完成了部分铁矿石合同的人民币跨境结算，合同结算的金额高达近 3.3 亿元人民币，这标志着中国与巴西矿企在铁矿石使用人民币跨境贸易结算实现了新突破，人民币在国际大宗商品的结算影响力已开始提升，推动人民币走向国际化。

随后，中国宝武先后与全球三大铁矿石供应商（淡水河谷、必和必拓、力拓集团）就产自澳大利亚等国的铁矿石进行了人民币跨境结算的初步尝试。随着交易流程的日益完善，中国宝武进口铁矿石人民币跨境结算已开始从试单向一定数量的常态化结算过渡，中国宝武也成为国内首家常态化进行铁矿石人民币跨境结算的中国企业。

2020 年 8 月，鞍钢集团也与力拓集团实现了鞍钢集团首单、全国第二家人民币跨境结算铁矿石交易，合计金额约 1 亿元。

中巴、中澳等国之间的本币结算为双方贸易合作带来了更多便利，将有助于稳固中国的铁矿石供应，同时也为中国在全球矿产市场上增添了话语权。

事实上，"全球南方"国家拥有丰富的矿产资源，包括石油、天然气等能源类品种，以及锂矿、镍、铜等被称为绿色金属的资源品，南南贸易中的资源贸易、制成品贸易规模庞大，是未来最具潜力的本币合作交易场景之一。

第三章　合作进化论：跨越山海，从广度到深度有待深化

当前，"全球南方"本币合作的形式多样，涵盖双边本币互换、双边本币结算、货币挂牌交易、本币融资等，并在一级市场、二级市场交易、货币市场以及金融基础设施等领域取得一定成效，合作资金规模也不断提升。但要理性看到的是，南南深化本币合作仍存在不少困境，从"广度"走向"深度"还有待进一步深化。从量的维度看，与"全球南方"的贸易和投资总体规模相比，本币合作的规模仍然有限。从价的维度看，双边本币直接交易报价仍然难以完全摆脱美元的影响。

短期内美元的地位和影响力仍难以根本改变，"全球南方"各国之间的政治互信、经济发展差异、金融市场水平等都在影响着本币合作的"进化"。与美元相比，目前其它货币在国际金融市场上的影响力仍相对处于弱势，一些国家的政局、币值不稳，也给本币合作带来挑战。"逆全球化"的趋势下，新兴货币国际化发展空间受到挤压。构建多元化货币体系是一个长期过程。

3.1 美元主导地位短期内仍难以摆脱

从货币国际地位演化的历史看，国际货币不仅是一个实力长期积累的过程，也是一个抓住机遇不断取得突破的过程。美元仍是当前全球最主要的计价货币、支付货币、投融资货币和储备货币，短期内美元的主导地位仍难以扭转。

以东盟为例，东盟尽管积极推进双边贸易和投资中增加本币结算的比重，但截至 2023 年底，东盟 80% 以上的出口贸易仍以美元计价。中国是东盟第一大贸易国，但中国与东盟双边本币交易合作中，直接交易报价仍难以绕开美元。人民币对新加坡元、林吉特、泰铢、印尼盾的中间价是在每日开盘前由中国外汇交易中心向做市商（报价行）询价，将做市商（报价行）报价平均得到。但在实践中，美元仍是重要的转换中介，企业和个人在柜台实现人民币对四国货币的直接兑换，并不等同于兑换价格完全绕开美元。由于市场缺乏足够的流动性和活跃度，银行往往习惯于通过美元套算得出直接交易的汇率报价。通过计算境内银行间外汇市场人民币对新加坡元、泰铢和林吉特的即期汇率可以发现，人民币对这三种货币的直接汇率与通过美元套算得出的汇率呈现较强正相关性，相关系数高达 0.99 以上。

此外，交易不活跃造成银行对客报价点差较大。客盘需求是银行间市场流动性的重要来源，反过来，银行间市场的活跃度又会影响银行在柜台市场的报价，进而影响企业和个人的货币兑换成本。相较于美元等七国集团（G7）货币，东南亚货币在银行间市场的交易活跃度整体欠佳。

为维护美元主导地位，美国采取的"护持方略"也增加了全球货币多元化的难度。"如果不使用美元，那么与美国做生意就将面临100%的关税。"在2024年9月的一次演讲中，特朗普在当时的竞选活动中就警告威胁说[1]。

可以预计，"全球南方"围绕构建多元化国际货币体系的战略博弈将持续，"全球南方"的本币合作规模和深度仍将受到一定制约。

声音

当今世界愈发由大国间的地缘政治竞争主导，若未来随着"苏尔"的推出，拉美国家减少了美元的使用，很可能会遭到美国方面的反对与阻碍，并由此产生严重的后果[2]。

——西班牙经济学家伊格莱西亚斯

3.2 基础设施的互联互通水平待提高

2008年全球金融危机爆发以来，世界经济复苏缓慢，许多发展中国家在基础设施融资和建设上面临不小的困难。当前"全球南方"经济体的基础设施互联互通水平低、投资不足，已成为制约"全球南方"经济转型发展的突出问题。

---

① 来源：参考消息，《特朗普放话：不用美元就别和美国做生意》，2024年9月9日
② 来源：西班牙埃尔卡诺皇家学院研究所，《南美洲的货币联盟？一个难以实现的理想》，2023年1月26日

　　基础设施互联互通尤其是金融基础设施进一步健全对提升"全球南方"国家之间的要素自由流动便利度起着至关重要的作用。以金砖国家为例，要积极推进金砖国家基础设施建设，找准金砖国家基础设施薄弱环节，打造一批金砖国家基础设施项目，继续深化5G、通信卫星、大数据中心等新型基础设施领域合作，提升金砖国家全方位互联互通水平。

　　除了基础设施互联互通，"全球南方"国家还要充分利用现有金融基础设施互联互通机制，进一步支持机构跨市场开展相关业务，扩大本币合作深度。例如，深化支付清算体系合作，推动支付系统的互联互通，提升清算渠道的稳定性和安全性。

　　实际上，对于不少南方国家，不只是基础设施缺乏互联互通，一些经济体的金融基础设施也还不健全，发展本币合作的相关金融市场运行不畅，抗风险能力薄弱，市场功能发挥不全。

3.3 经济发展程度不一带来本币合作的稳定性有待提升

双边本币合作的深化与发展并非一日之功，是政策与市场、政治与经济等多方面因素共同作用的结果。"全球南方"的覆盖面庞杂多元，不同经济体的政治、经济、金融市场发展程度各不相同。经济发展水平不一，加上一些国家金融市场不够成熟，导致不同国家在本币合作中的利益诉求不同或能力差异较大。

经济层面上，"全球南方"国家在经济结构和发展阶段上存在显著差异。部分经济体的经济形势持续萎靡不振，部分国家的债务问题尤为突出。此外，社会不平等、就业不足、基础设施落后等问题也是国际金融合作中的阻碍。这些因素都可能导致"全球南方"国家在金融合作方面的分歧。

比如对于巴西金融市场而言，2000 年至 2023 年，由巴西最具流通性的 80 多支股票组成的 bovEspa 指数从 17091.6 点涨至 134185 点，涨幅接近 7 倍，年化投资回报率 9%。但因巴西雷亚尔同期经历大幅贬值，经汇率调整后以人民币计价的投资回报率就降至仅 4%。

第四章　行稳致远：携手合作共促南南繁荣

尽管美元在国际货币体系中的主导地位短期内不会被动摇，但国际货币体系"多元化"的进程已然开启。扫清本币合作的跨境使用障碍，降低本币交易成本，便成为"全球南方"国家本币合作的应有之义。在此进程中，"全球南方"国家各国应加强合作，共同应对挑战，构建更加公平、稳定的国际金融体系。

4.1 加强政策协调与配合

促进"全球南方"国家本币合作的策略应当着重于加强高层交流与

政策协调。首先，可以通过定期的高层访问和会谈，将本币结算作为双边和多边会谈的核心议题。这样的对话能够为双方提供一个平台，共同探讨本币结算的潜在利益、挑战和合作模式。其次，中国可以主动提出具体的合作方案，包括但不限于货币互换协议、双边贸易和投资协议，以及在基础设施和能源项目中使用本币结算的倡议。这些方案旨在减少对第三方货币的依赖，同时增强双方货币的国际地位。为了确保合作的顺利进行，双方应致力于建立有效的政策协调机制和监管框架，以监督和指导本币结算的实施。这包括制定共同的规则和标准，以及建立争端解决机制，确保合作过程中的任何问题都能得到及时和有效的处理。

4.2 建立央行及金融机构间互动和协调机制

可以通过建立双边央行及金融机构间的定期对话机制，促进政策互通和协调，同时复制并推广成功的合作模式至其他国家，以增强金融合作的深度和广度，比如提升人民币、雷亚尔、卢布等货币使用的便利性。同时，简化跨境本币结算流程和优化跨境投融资管理，不仅能够降低交易成本，提高结算效率，还能为个人和企业提供更加便捷的金融服务，从而促进本币在国际贸易和投资中的使用，推动本币国际化进程，为全球经济的稳定和发展贡献力量。

4.3 积极拓展本币合作应用场景

首先，企业应积极采用人民币、雷亚尔等本国货币进行跨境交易结算，特别是跨国企业和大型企业应发挥引领作用，通过自身的示范效应，鼓励供应链上的合作伙伴接受本币结算，从而扩大南方国家本币的国际使用范围。其次，企业应加强与政府及金融机构的沟通，及时反馈在结算过程中遇到的障碍，为政策的制定和优化提供实际依据。同时，企业应充分利用政府提供的政策支持，创新投融资模式，注重合规经营和履行社会责任，以树立良好的国际形象。此外，企业还应积极探索数字货币在国际贸易中的潜在应用，利用已有的本币结算合作框架，以降低交易成本和汇率风险。通过这些措施，企业可以加快与"全球南方"国家的经贸往来，共同推动本币合作的深化，为双方的经济发展注入新的活

力。这样的合作不仅能够增强企业的国际竞争力，还能促进南方国家货币的国际化，为全球经济的多元化和稳定做出贡献。

4.4 技术引领，积极推进数字货币落地

促进中国与"全球南方"国家本币合作的一个关键途径是探索数字货币的应用。中国在移动支付和数字货币领域已经处于世界领先地位，这为中国在全球范围内推广数字货币提供了坚实的基础。通过在国际贸易中应用央行数字货币（CBDC），可以显著提升人民币等南方国家货币在跨境交易和投资活动中的地位和使用频率。中国可以与"全球南方"国家合作，共同开发和推广数字货币支付系统，提供技术培训和支持，帮助这些国家建立和完善数字货币基础设施。同时，中国还可以通过多边或双边协议，推动数字货币在国际贸易中的使用，为全球贸易和投资提供更多便利。

4.5 建设金融基础设施，吸引更多参与者

建立和发展"全球南方"本币市场是一个漫长而复杂的过程，需要采取多项相互依赖的行动，基础设施是关键的一环。关键基础设施包括货币市场、一级市场、投资者基础、二级市场、跨市场清算机构。其中，中国人民币跨境支付系统（CIPS）作为人民币跨境支付和结算的关键金融基础设施，目前已经实现了对全球主要时区的全面覆盖并且可以支持多样化的金融市场业务资金结算。未来，一方面，要创新跨境支付业务的使用场景和丰富产品服务，满足不同国家和地区的多样化需求，增强南方国家货币跨境支付系统的吸引力。另一方面，要完善跨境支付相关的业务制度、标准和规则，以提供规范、统一且符合国际通行做法的行为范本，提升系统的透明度和可靠性。此外，可以探索将南方国家本币跨境支付系统与"全球南方"国家的数字货币跨境结算试点相结合，加强与这些国家的金融合作，促进双边贸易和投资。

结　语

"全球南方"国家的本币合作并非路坦途，但随着金砖机制的引领，坚定的步伐已经迈出，南方国家的本币合作既有经济发展的基础，也有降低单一货币风险的考量。本报告通过梳理国际货币体系的演变，以及当前南方国家间本币合作的实践和探索，提出在政策、金融基础设施、企业以及应用场景等多方面推进本币合作的建议。要看到，南方国家发展本币合作，并非是取代美元的结算货币、储备货币地位，而是更好地促进货币多元化体系进程。

国际货币体系演变史告诉我们，货币的多元化是数十年的进击和坚守。加强合作，是"全球南方"国家的发展要义，也是唯一正确选择，只有合作，才能团结一致、互惠互利；只有合作，才能行稳致远、进而有为。

报告课题组

组　　长：刘　刚　潘海平

副组长：季　蕾

统　　筹：高　攀　何欣荣

研究主笔：陈云富　王淑娟

参与调研：李一帆　魏雨田　葛佳明　童威远

　　　　　柳　理　王　纯　邓　侃

特别感谢

中央结算公司

上海清算所

论文篇

"一带一路"与中国文明发展

扎哈里·扎哈里耶夫（保加利亚"一带一路"全国联合会主席）

    文明发展的每一个分界时期都与地缘政治层面的动荡转换有关。强大的社会、政治、经济、军事和"构造"进程在不断改变公共组织和国际社会生活的各个领域。总的来说，它们追踪新的国家边界，重新排列军事和政治联盟的"拼图"，重组民族文化和宗教团体。在新的文明平衡阶段之前的所有这些文明"构造"不仅深刻影响了国际关系的可见方面，而且深刻影响了人格和人际关系的"深层"社会心理层面。它不仅有意无意地使个人的自我评价、个性和社会表达受到"攻击"，还使与之相关联的社会共存形式——家庭、非正式的交流形式和群体、意识形态和政治经济共同体——受到"攻击"，起到了将个人意志传递到现存国家和社会治理结构的作用。因此，无论是国家和国际层面的"政治市场"，还是国际交往的整体机制，都发生了变化。

    文明进程边界阶段的这些"构造"过程的必然结果是导致迄今为止的现有国际安全体系不稳定。它既体现在地区层面，也体现在世界层面。因此，强大参与者的名单会重新排列。他们有的捍卫着国际关系中的桂冠，有的靠武力上位，还有的将彻底从国际关系主体中消失。这也给这个世界现有的交流机制带来了机会。由于力量的不断改变和利益中心的形成，它们逐渐被抹去，并从一个经常是各种利益的地区和世界平衡工具变成了一个自我意志的武力压力场。它们从为了繁荣和文明的进步而被要求保障世界和平与安全的机制，变成了社会进步的"普洛克拉斯提之床"。所有这一切不仅破坏了区域和世界安全，还给国际关系的各个层面带来了压力。认为已被历史埋葬的国家和国际冲突死灰复燃。乍一看难以预见的战争紧张局面出现了。新的战争冲突爆发。世界和平面临的危险有可能脱离过去发挥作用的挽救生命的机制和国际认可的法律规范。

然而，今天，我们正在目睹一场全球性的不仅是意识形态的对抗，而且是一场心理战，将达到东西方冷战的程度。此外，那些旨在将中国从世界事务中剔除的人，也在有意识地努力竖起一道新的铁幕。中国拥有强大的经济实力，繁荣昌盛，在成功发展和成功应对新文明阶段的挑战方面树立了榜样，自然会成为这些行动的主要目标。

20世纪90年代，正式宣布冷战结束。然而，今天，我们不仅再次目睹了当时的一些场景，而且还为孤立中国和所有那些认为我们都在一条船上的人的行为注入了新的内容，这在很大程度上取决于这个星球上是否会有和平，取决于我们进行建设性讨论的能力，这些讨论将使我们同舟共济驶出文明挑战和变革的惊涛骇浪。不幸的是，我们今天所看到的并不是一个短暂的历史时期。它是美国和北约的一项长期战略，它带来了巨大的风险，世界不仅将目睹一场前所未有的地缘政治、意识形态和地缘经济对抗，而且还将危险地接近自我毁灭。将巨大的资源和力量投入这场新的冷战，并伴随着军事对抗和心理攻击，会不断带来接近一场全球热核冲突的危险。

当我们谈论中国时，我们必须记住，我们谈论的是世界经济体量的三分之一和现代世界40%以上的预算资源，我们谈论的是一个在开辟人类数字时代新篇章方面最为繁荣的国家的科学和技术潜力。也就是说，我们不可能在不影响整个世界稳定的情况下，试图将中国从这些领域清除。对中国的破坏性政策，从另一个角度来看，是对全面维护文明发展以及我们星球的安全与和平进步的破坏。其逻辑是，帝国主义列强在思想上、政治上、经济上对中国的侵略，实际上是对人类明天的侵略。

遗憾的是，我们今天看到，欧盟对美国和北约的全球政策深表赞同。这无数次地表明，欧洲摆脱对美国的依赖更多的是一种愿望，而不是作为世界政治中一个新的、协调的国际关系因素的实际可能性。

从"一带一路"倡议提出之初，我在接受中国电视台采访时就说过，如果仅仅把"一带一路"看作是一个经济项目，或者是地缘政治项目，那就大错特错了。当然它两者都是。但它与 20 世纪和 21 世纪初以来提出的所有其他倡议的区别在于，它从根本上来说是一项文明工程。也就是说，它实际上是一种尝试，不仅要把各种努力和潜力（我所说的潜力是指，全球所有国家除经济和智力潜力之外的潜力）结合起来，而且要回答这个问题："我们身边的文明计划的变化能走多远？这些变化如何反映文明发展的经济、地缘政治和意识形态架构，以及全球文明状态？"

我认为，这 10 年无可争辩地证实了我的这一立场。此外，我很高兴地看到，我的许多地缘政治关系领域的同事们，至少从一个方面，首先抓住了"一带一路"项目的本质。至于这 10 年来取得的成就，可以肯定地说，"一带一路"无论是在一开始加入并支持该倡议的国家，还是在全球范围内，已经获得了充分的公民权，请允许我使用这个词。

一方面，它变得流行起来，另一方面，它脱离了中国丝绸之路相对狭窄的框架。事实上，今天，来自地球各大洲的 150 多个国家参与了这一倡议。如果我们不使用数字语言，我们就不能对这一项目和这些年来所取得的成就做出充分的评价。10 年来，在"一带一路"倡议下，中国向世界各国提供的信贷和金融援助几乎与世界银行的总和相当。

与此同时，在此期间，对与这一中国倡议相关的各种项目的投资超过 1 万亿美元。当然，所涉及的资金不仅是通过中华人民共和国政府和官方机构正式提供的，而且还有 150 多个签署了参与"一带一路"项目条约的国家分配给包括在"一带一路"内的项目的资金。

如果我们不注意另一个方向，即精神方向，这幅图景就是不全面的。什么意思呢？在"一带一路"倡议和项目的推动下，中国与世界各国的学术交流得到了极大的拓展。此外，许多地方还建立了联合研究中心。我先撇开各科学院所做的工作不谈。关注一下世界各地大学和中国大学之间的关系也足够了。最后，同样重要的是，这与中国学生活跃在世界一流大学有关，也与来自世界各地的 50 多万人以这样或那样的形式在中华人民共和国境内学习有关。

在这方面，我们也不能忽视文化领域的合作。中国正沿着"一带一路"的路线，与所有已加入这一倡议的国家，甚至那些没有正式加入这一倡议但受益于这一计划提供的可能性的国家进行极其活跃的文化交流。

这一切已经充满了非常具体的内容，在我看来，"一带一路"这一意识形态和政治概念的定义公式，中国国家主席习近平先生可能表达得最为准确，即首先要认识到我们共乘一条大船，从我们是否有能力进行正常的对话，到解决我们这条船上出现的问题，由于不同国家，不同民族文化社群的代表，往往有着不同的利益，这取决于不断发生的文明变革海洋中航行的平稳程度；顺便说一下，它不仅仍在继续前行，而且像"达摩克利斯之剑"一样威胁着我们。这是"一带一路"项目 10 年来整体发展的一个最初的、决定性的概念。

10 年来，"一带一路"倡议实现并体现了其富有意义的形象，成功启动了许多机制，特别是在贸易、交通基础设施和各国有前景的大型投资项目方面。无论是对中方还是对不同的智库而言，我们都可以将这一文明倡议的理念和各个方面的普惠发展视为成功。与此同时，我们应该真诚地指出，欧洲和其他区域的非政府部门和民间团体并没有充分发挥其能力。在我们看来，建立一个广泛的国际公共论坛（运动）来支持该项目文明方面的需求客观上已经成熟。特别关注一下"一带一路"项目理念在区域和全球背景下的和平、平等和安全问题。在这方面有成百上千的公民倡议，特别是在欧洲和美国，它们可以在这里找到自己应有的位置。克服这些问题不仅将增强我们作为和平、进步和发展因素的权威，而且还将有助于在这方面调动世界的潜力。

在这个阶段，需要对"一带一路"倡议的不同方面进行更清晰的区分。在这方面，我们建议特别注意区分以下三个方面国际论坛的形式。

——从事"一带一路"法律方面工作的律师和国际法专家。

——工会—社会和经济领域。

——青年群体。

可以肯定地说，尽管国际关系风云变幻，但保中建交75年来，两国关系在很大程度上保持了建设性和善意。在这些联系的经济领域中会有一些高峰和低谷。在政治方面，我们可以大胆地宣称，保加利亚对我们与中国的关系有着善意的共识和积极的态度，这在我们外交政策的许多其他方面不是固有的。然而，这种善意在两国经济活动的增长中得到多大程度的物质表现是另一个问题。不幸的是，在贸易和投资方面，保加利亚不能夸口说它在欧洲是这方面的领导者之一。我甚至要说，我们不得不遗憾地指出，与其他国家相比，保加利亚远远落后，特别是在巴尔干领土上。我指的主要是西巴尔干和作为巴尔干国家的土耳其。对一些欧盟国家来说，与中国的经贸关系发展也比较滞后。只有东欧和中欧各国值得一提，前中东欧的社会主义国家与中华人民共和国建立了经贸和政治关系。保加利亚远远落后于匈牙利、波兰和斯洛伐克。如果希望我们的国家不会错过这趟"列车"，那么我们还有很多事情要做，这趟列车将使我们能够在欧洲和世界文明变革的背景下加入经济发展的动态。

我们很不满地指出，我国落后的主要原因与国家机构对我们与中国关系的前景缺乏全面的战略眼光有关。对于中华人民共和国在保加利亚在科学技术领域和经济发展领域的新要求和标准的各个方面提高适应能力的努力中所起到的作用及其地位，我们根本没有一个明确的概念性战略观点。这在客观必要性的背景下是极其重要的，这不仅直接关系到保加利亚，还关系到欧盟和整个世界，我们需要一种新的经济发展模式。在保加利亚，我们还远没有去讨论这个话题，而在中国，正在极具建设性地对这个话题进行讨论。在许多方面，中国不仅能够成为世界经济发展的"火车头"，而且能够成为 21 世纪经济战略愿景创新的主要因素。

保加利亚"一带一路"全国联合会正努力在保加利亚在对华国家关系领域较为落后的背景下，促进我们与中国的国家间关系。无论是私营企业倡议还是涉及保加利亚国家的项目，都需要为保中关系的未来发展制定战略愿景。在这里，我还想指出，我们保加利亚"一带一路"全国联合会提出的许多倡议，都与中国的文明大工程"一带一路"倡议的崇高目标和谐统一。因此，我认为全国联合会在努力使保加利亚真正参与这一倡议方面具有其地位和特殊重要性，保加利亚已正式承认这一倡议，我们是该倡议的正式参与者。

值此中华人民共和国成立 75 周年和保加利亚与中华人民共和国建交 75 周年之际，保加利亚"一带一路"全国联合会与中国驻保加利亚共和国大使馆一道，于 9 月 11 日至 14 日在索非亚国立文化宫举办了"以互利合作之名对话"的保中经贸论坛。20 家中国知名企业的管理人员和代表参加了会议，其中包括 4 家主要银行。这些公司的高管介绍了他们的生产清单和投资意向。这为中国企业与感兴趣的保加利亚经济管理部门和保加利亚商界代表之间建立潜在的商业联系创造了机会。

此外，10 月 28 日至 31 日在瓦尔纳举办了保加利亚和中国的友好城市和地区的交流会。这次会议也是与中国大使馆联合举办的，定期举办类似论坛，共同创建"保中友好城市和地区俱乐部"。俱乐部成员计划每年聚会一次。今年在瓦尔纳举行的交流会得到了中国人民对外友好协会的支持。中国人民对外友好协会是中国最具权威和影响力的公共机构之一。

目前阻碍保中两国经贸关系发展的主要问题主要与保加利亚国家机构在这一问题的各个方面所采取的消极立场有关。在某种程度上，这种被动的态度可以用保加利亚国家地位的普遍侵蚀过程来解释，但也可以用国家机构对抵制所谓的"中国在西方扩张"的现有外部压力的敏感性来解释。然而，这并不奇怪，因为这种出于政治动机的立场在很大程度上与商业经济活动和欧盟主要国家以及美国、英国和澳大利亚投资项目的快速发展并不重叠。

在谈论保中关系时，我们不应错过保加利亚国家和公共机构从中国在该国经济和社会发展领域的创新研究和政策中受益的机会。在这方面，应对可持续建设和经济发展问题的官方机构和中心利用来自中国的一些非常有前景的成果是非常重要的，这些成果在很大程度上与最近召开的中国共产党第二十届中央委员会第三次全体会议有关。这次全会是历史性的，因为它不仅是基于从更近的角度来看直到2027年的中国社会经济发展的一些具体项目，而且是基于2049年中华人民共和国成立100周年的一个更长远的计划。

此次全会明确和直截了当地指出，需要建立和确认一种与世界文明变革和人类科技发展成就相协调的新的经济发展模式。这也与中国正在做出的改变有关，即以前那种使中国成为领先的经济和科技强国的经济模式实际上或多或少已不再适用，国家需要全面现代化，全面适应一个全新的历史环境，适应社会和人民思想的重大变化，不仅是为了中国的未来发展，也是为了整个世界的未来发展。

从这个角度来看，中共二十届三中全会也是中国过去两年在联合国发起的三大全球倡议，即全球安全倡议、全球治理倡议和全球文明倡议的合理延伸。中共二十届三中全会的目标是，这些倡议所确立的崇高目标如何能够利用经济发展的工具带来世界和平、安全和繁荣。中共二十届三中全会的决定对于每一个国家以新的方式去考虑自己的未来，无论是在国内还是在广泛的国际层面，都具有极其重要的意义。

因此，保加利亚有很多东西可以向中国学习，尤其是在我国的专家圈子里。不幸的是，在我们的社会中，甚至在专业层面，对中华人民共和国在文明发展方向上的奋斗目标和创新努力都缺乏认识，一定程度上是有意识地受到意识形态考量和地缘政治利益的影响。

我们保加利亚"一带一路"全国联合会，为自己设定的目标是帮助克服保加利亚不幸存在的这一信息差。这种情况不允许有兴趣的学术机构和保加利亚社会政治因素利用在国际关系和文明间对话领域以未来之名义正在"打造"的东西。

就"一带一路"倡议的各个方面举办不同范围和目标导向的国际论坛，是将 2023 年 11 月在北京举行的第三次"一带一路"倡议会议期间中国提出并为世界绝大多数国家所接受的主张具体化的好机会，那次会议旨在纪念"一带一路"倡议提出 10 周年。最近在香港举行的会议就是这方面的一个很好的例子，会议的主题是建设一个相互联系、创新和绿色的世界。"一带一路"共建国家的国家元首和政府首脑、企业代表出席了会议。这一主题也是中国领导人习近平在中国共产党第二十届中央委员会第三次全体会议上的讲话中所强调的战略问题和立场具体化的要素之一。这篇演讲概述了应如何确保世界成功过渡到全球文明。从这个意义上讲，我相信在香港举行的论坛，以及一些新的倡议，可以在加强各国人民的文明共鸣方面发挥非常积极的作用，以克服我们这个时代日益令人担忧的全球挑战。

中国领导人密切关注不断发生的变化，并根据这些变化调整发展模式。这种向前推进的感觉是非凡的，就像过河一样，你小心翼翼地沿着河走，用脚感受踏在河床上的每一步，免得沉下去或被水冲走。

过去十年，自从习近平主席成为中国共产党和中华人民共和国的领导人以来，中国的经济实力持续提升，今天它已经是世界经济的引擎，不仅是全球 30% 的必需品的生产国，同时也是新技术和创新领域的领导者。

过去 40 年，中国在全球发展中发挥了核心作用，证明了一种比西方模式更成功的经济和社会发展模式是可能的。

中国的发展模式不仅在经济上是成功的，在政治上也是成功的，因为我们看到西方的自由民主正处于严重的危机之中。它导致了巨大的分裂、社会的分裂、日益增长的仇恨和严重的不稳定。在中国，正如我所说的，这是一种根据变化不断改进和发展的模式。

它不仅加速了中国的经济发展，而且在许多领域产生了巨大的影响，使中国成为这些领域的领导者。请关注这样一个时刻——中国不仅在几十年内让大约 10 亿人摆脱了绝对贫困，创造了世界上最大规模的中产，而且在许多其他领域超越了美国，处于领先地位。

中国特色社会主义比危机中的新自由资本主义为人民提供了更长的寿命。当欧洲的社会主义思想和传统的社会民主党正在崩溃、衰落、失去影响力的时候，中国展示了一个模式，在这个模式中，如此之多人民的生活水平在以历史上前所未有的速度提高。

中国的人均 GDP 从 1978 年改革开放开始时的 1774 美元，增加到了 2022 年的 18677 美元。其战略就是在一般人口中消除贫穷。与此同时，中国没有放弃改革的基本原则，即对外开放，建设社会主义市场经济和民主政治，平衡改革与稳定发展，坚持以人为本的发展理念。

近年来，中国的发展战略加强了对私有资本和再分配政策的控制，强调大公司和中国富人必须遵循正义和财富再分配的原则。这在中国是可能的，因为在这个体制中，党由三个主要群体组成，其中包括支持中国共产党战略的私人所有者。中国人民生活水平的提高，正在成为世界各国加快发展的榜样。与此同时，中国的战略涉及以最新的科学技术成果为基础的和平发展的继续，科技将促进生产力的更快发展。在当今各种流程的管理中，中国更加积极地使用第四次工业革命的最新技术——大数据、物联网、人工智能、3D 打印机和合成生物学。

国际货币基金组织对 2023 年至 2028 年世界经济发展的预测是，在此期间，全球经济增长的 22.6% 发生在中国，这并非巧合。

现代世界的绝大多数人很大程度上是按照文明发展的规律生活的，在和平建设的方向和国际化的客观进程中——从经济出发，传到精神层面，到达政治对话领域。正常的、明智的政治对话，可建立而不是摧毁能够团结全人类的东西。

另一件不应忘记的事情是，尽管西方对中国发起了各种心理战，但在很大程度上，这些国家的绝大多数公众都赞成与中国进行合理的、建设性的对话并与之全面发展关系。这里出现了一个有趣的悖论。尽管帝国主义集团做出了努力，尤其是在华盛顿，而且许多西欧国家的政治精英在很大程度上服从于他们的政策，但是，就商业和那些推动国家经济发展车轮的人而言，我们也有与这一政策相抗衡的行为和对抗力量。一个具体的例子就是这些社会中政治精英和经济利益之间的深刻分歧。

尽管西方公司被要求离开中国领土上的投资和经济合作领域，但实际上没有一个重要的经济结构听从这些"建议"，也没有屈服于这种政治压力。过去 10 年，我们看到欧盟与中国以及美国与中国的对外贸易往来增长了约 40%，这一事实也足够了。在此，我想提请注意这样一个事实，即经济利益与西方对中国的军事政治反对战略之间的对抗，导致这些国家的社会政治稳定出现了深刻的裂痕。"中国"因素虽然没有正式出现，但在西方社会的这些裂痕中发挥着积极作用，客观上有助于建立世界日益需要的新型社会关系的整体进程。

迈向高质量的共建"一带一路"倡议
——中欧互联互通项目的重新配置

尼古拉·卡萨里尼（意大利国际事务研究院高级研究员、亚洲研究中心主任）

自 2013 年 9 月正式启动以来，中国共建"一带一路"的愿景已遍及全球。如今，联合国 193 个会员国中有 80% 参与了该项目，其中包括一些欧洲国家。当"一带一路"或新丝绸之路（后称为共建"一带一路"倡议）宣布时，欧洲对这一被视为促进中欧互联互通、密切欧中国关系的倡议充满了热情。这与美国形成鲜明对比，后者认为共建"一带一路"倡议是对美国主导地位的挑战。

一、共建"一带一路"倡议在欧洲推进现状

欧洲被选为陆地和海上路线的终点。以前被中国战略思想家所忽视的地中海，将成为通过红海连接印度洋和欧洲的一个日益重要的地区。因此，共建"一带一路"倡议在欧洲早期的实施重点是为基础设施项目融资，特别是东南欧的铁路和地中海的港口。与此同时，中国绿地投资

激增，中国人民银行与欧洲央行通过建立货币互换协议和人民币银行清算建立货币联系，旨在降低中国投资的交易成本。

2015 年，中国的"一带一路"投资大量涌入欧洲大陆，无论在绝对值还是增长率上，意大利都是主要投资对象，与前一年相比，投资增长了 36%，这也得益于中国国有企业中国化工集团有限公司收购了世界第五大轮胎制造商倍耐力集团 16.89% 的股份。这笔 71 亿欧元的交易在丝路基金的参与下完成，丝路基金是新成立的国有投资工具，旨在促进对"一带一路"沿线国家的投资。2019 年 3 月，意大利总理朱塞佩·孔特领导的政府在习近平主席对罗马进行国事访问期间，与中国签署了关于共建"一带一路"倡议的谅解备忘录，从而使意大利成为唯一正式支持习近平主席标志性外交政策项目的七国集团国家和欧盟创始成员国。

在意大利和其他南欧、东欧国家接受共建"一带一路"倡议的同时，西欧和北欧的核心国家却采取了更为挑剔的态度。从 2016 年开始，德国和法国对共建"一带一路"倡议和中国投资越来越警惕。几年后，这一趋势波及欧洲其他国家。在意大利，随着马里奥·德拉吉于 2021 年 2 月被任命为总理，成为孔特的继任者，"一带一路"项目也随之停止，最终意大利在 2022 年上台的保守派政府领导下完全退出了共建"一带一路"倡议。

然而，在西欧和北欧，共建"一带一路"倡议仍在地方层面持续推进。例如，媒体报道称，意大利约有 10 个市镇及布雷西亚省（意大利工业中心伦巴第北部地区最大的省份）正通过"一带一路"地方合作委员会这一地方政府层面的"一带一路"合作机制，直接与中国开展合作。这仅仅是冰山一角，因为与"一带一路"地方合作委员会建立联系的意大利市镇、省和地区的数量可能要多得多，或许有数百个。尽管意大利中央政府决定正式退出共建"一带一路"倡议，但众多地方当局以及重要企业和政治力量仍希望继续推进，甚至加强在"一带一路"框架下与中国的合作。

共建"一带一路"倡议继续在欧洲取得进展，有三个趋势值得关注：

一是西欧和北欧的"一带一路"基础设施项目和投资规模有所缩小，而中东欧的此类项目和投资仍在继续。

二是所有欧洲国家都对中国互联互通项目的金融和货币领域敞开了大门，主要形式是货币互换协议和人民币清算中心。

三是越来越多的欧盟成员国欢迎与中国在绿色技术领域进行产业合作，这表明中欧互联互通正日益向高质量项目迈进。

二、共建"一带一路"倡议到达南欧："激情"岁月

在欧洲经济增长乏力、中国试图改变经济模式之际，人们对中国在欧洲互联互通项目的早期反响相当热烈，关注中国投资进入欧洲大陆创造的无限机会和就业前景。中国的互联互通项目将服务于保持中国经济增长的目的，中国经济正处于从出口导向型增长向以消费和对外投资为基础的新模式过渡的历史关头。在国内产能过剩之际，为海外基础设施项目提供的贷款预计将有助于中国经济升级，并有助于各个部门的重组，贸易融资将有助于维护中国产品的现有市场，并为其寻找新的市场。

欧洲位于丝绸之路的终点，希望从中国的外向经济战略和互联互通项目中受益。在 2015 年 6 月 29 日举行的欧盟－中国峰会上，时任欧盟委员会主席的让－克洛德·容克呼吁在欧洲战略投资基金与中国的"一带一路"倡议之间建立协同效应。李克强总理回应容克，承诺向欧洲战略投资基金投资数十亿美元，但具体金额从未透露。

东南欧和地中海特别是希腊港口，最初是丝路基金的主要受益者。该地区的旗舰基础设施项目是陆海快速通道，直接连接欧洲最大的集装箱港口之一——比雷埃夫斯港和中东欧国家，从而使比雷埃夫斯成为中

欧贸易中心。该项目由中国进出口银行提供软贷款，由国有企业中国铁道建筑集团有限公司和中国工人建造。

比雷埃夫斯一直是中国通过地中海连接中国与欧洲战略的核心。事实上，这个希腊港口是中东、巴尔干半岛和欧洲市场之间的门户；从中国的角度来看，这是一个进入欧盟的独特入口。2013年，中国华为集团在比雷埃夫斯港开设了一个物流中心。随后在2014年6月，希腊和中国签署了一项20亿欧元的协议，由中国国家开发银行提供资金，建造新的集装箱船和散货船，为这个希腊港口服务。

参与比雷埃夫斯港项目最重要的中国企业是中国远洋海运集团。中远海运是一家在香港上市的国有企业，是中国最大的干散货运输公司和班轮运输公司。该公司获得了希腊政府35年的特许经营权，经营两个集装箱码头。该交易整个期间的名义价值为43亿欧元，要求中远海运对二号码头进行大量投资，并建造三号码头的新建部分。

中国航运公司也在意大利那不勒斯港和热那亚港建立了良好业务，中远海运和中国海运集团对这两个港口都进行了大量投资。从2015年开始，中国领导人的注意力转向亚得里亚海北部的意大利港口，这些港口成为2019年3月中意签署共同推进"一带一路"谅解备忘录的焦点。通过专注于陆地和海上基础设施项目，中国正在寻求建立更好的互联互通并在"一带一路"倡议感兴趣的地区获得政治影响力。中国的投资将为欧洲大陆特别是一些现金短缺的外围国家政府，提供获得金融资本的绝佳机会。

共建"一带一路"倡议无疑让中国对欧洲大陆的投资激增。根据美国企业研究所和传统基金会联合公布的《中国全球投资追踪》报告，2005年至2016年间，中国在欧洲投资了近1640亿美元。同期，它在美国投资了1030亿美元。根据纽约荣鼎咨询公司数据，中国对欧盟的直接投资在短短八年内增长到近50倍，从2008年的不到8.4亿美元增加到 2016 年的 420 亿美元（350 亿欧元）的历史新高。尽管中国对欧盟的投资仍然相对较低，但它将迅速发展，并在南欧以前所未有的速度增长。

三、共建"一带一路"倡议在意大利取得积极进展

2014 年，意大利成为中国人民银行突然进行校准投资的接受国。中国人民银行收购了意大利多家具有战略重要性的公司 2% 的股份，包括能源巨头埃尼公司、国家电力公司、汽车制造商菲亚特—克莱斯勒公司（目前是斯泰兰蒂斯集团的一部分）、意大利电信公司、忠利保险有限公司和中期银行。

这些收购行动是中国发出的强烈信息，似乎对意大利公众对中国的看法产生了积极影响。皮尤研究中心的数据显示，从 2014 年春季到 2015 年春季，意大利公众对中国的好感增加了 14%，远高于德国（+6%）和法国（+3%）。2015 年 4 月，意大利与英国、德国和法国一道，作为创始成员国加入了亚洲基础设施投资银行。当年，中国对欧洲的投资随之而来，比上年增长 36%，其中意大利是主要投资对象。

随着投资激增，欧盟政策制定者对加强与中国领导人关系的兴趣也随之增加。例如，2016 年 12 月至 2018 年 6 月领导中左翼联合政府的意大利前总理保罗·真蒂洛尼于 2017 年 5 月出席了在北京举行的首届"一带一路"国际合作高峰论坛。真蒂洛尼是七国集团国家和欧盟大成员国中唯一参会的领导人。意大利参与中国基础设施项目也得到了意大利总统塞尔焦·马塔雷拉的支持。2017 年 2 月他对中国进行国事访问期间宣布，"意大利将积极响应中国的倡议并参与这一计划"。

一些有影响力的政治领导人和企业领袖为共建"一带一路"倡议塑造积极形象，为两国在 2019 年 3 月习近平主席访意期间签署共建"一

带一路"倡议谅解备忘录创造了条件。尽管在意大利和东南欧,共建"一带一路"倡议受到了积极欢迎,但在欧洲大陆其他地区,人们对中国基础设施项目的看法却在变得相当负面。

四、部分国家对共建"一带一路"倡议的批评

从 2016 年开始,越来越多的学者和政策制定者开始批评共建"一带一路"倡议和中国在欧洲所谓的掠夺性投资,并主张在欧中关系中增加条件。同样,欧洲议会、一些国家立法机构和欧盟成员国内部的一些政治力量加大了对中国政权及其贸易行为的批评,尤其是中国缺乏互惠。主要抱怨内容是,中国政府在国内市场几乎所有领域都限制外国投资。因此,欧洲企业在进入中国市场时面临困难,而中国企业往往通过补贴或简化程序得到欧洲国家政府帮助。越来越多的外国企业尤其是那些拥有知名品牌和技术先进产品的公司,在获准进入中国市场之前,必须分享自己的专业知识。欧洲投资者经常指出,外国公司在中国将不得不面临监管和行政负担。

中国家电企业美的集团在 2016 年底收购德国库卡机器人集团——这是中国收购欧洲企业数量迅速增加这一大趋势的一部分——加剧了专家和政策制定者对一系列问题的担忧,包括担心日益壮大的"军民融合"将欧洲技术无缝输送给中国军队。这导致法国、德国和意大利在 2017年 2 月要求欧盟委员会重新考虑关于欧盟外国投资的规定。其结果是采用了一种筛选机制,旨在帮助欧盟委员会和成员国评估外国投资者是否受到第三国政府的控制。这显然是针对中国国有企业的。

欧中关系的另一个挫折来自欧盟于 2019 年 3 月发布的一份政策文件,这份文件终结了前几年欧洲对共建"一带一路"倡议的热情。在文件中,布鲁塞尔转向更为强硬、防御性的态度,称中国为"经济竞争对手"

和"推动替代治理模式的系统性对手"。同样，2019 年 3 月 21 日至 22 日的欧洲理事会对一系列问题提出了严厉批评，包括共建"一带一路"倡议、中国对欧盟的投资以及中国国有企业对欧洲竞争力和繁荣构成的挑战。

2020 年 11 月美国总统乔·拜登的当选无疑有助于加强欧盟对中国的强硬立场，因为美国新政府寻求让欧洲盟友参与美国主导的遏华政策。刚刚签署了共建"一带一路"倡议谅解备忘录的意大利，态度逆转最为明显。德拉吉政府（2021 年 2 月至 2022 年 10 月）对共建"一带一路"项目作出明确限制。德拉吉多次利用特别创建的法律机制——所谓的"黄金权力"，来阻止或延迟中国企业收购活跃在关键领域（如技术、网络、能源等）的意大利公司。此外，中国将无法获得热那亚港和亚得里亚海北部各港口（的里雅斯特、威尼斯和拉韦纳）港务局的股份，而这些港口构成了谅解备忘录的支柱。中国国有企业中国远洋运输公司于 2008 年获得了雅典比雷埃夫斯港部分运营权，然后于 2016 年收购了这家希腊国有运营商 51% 的股份，并最终在 2021 年 10 月将其股份增至 67%。此后，中国一直无法将其影响力扩大到意大利北部的港口，特别是中远海运最渴望的热那亚港和的里雅斯特港。

2022 年 9 月，由焦尔吉娅·梅洛尼领导的民族主义保守派联盟上台，加速了阻止共建"一带一路"基础设施项目和中国收购被认为具有战略意义的工业资产的进程。2015 年对倍耐力的收购是中国投资进入欧洲的有力象征。2023 年 6 月，意大利政府利用特定立法，阻止了倍耐力集团最大股东中国化工集团控制这家轮胎制造巨头。除了阻止中国中化的雄心外，2023 年 12 月，梅洛尼政府正式退出了共建"一带一路"倡议。

意大利并不是唯一一个正式背弃共建"一带一路"倡议的欧洲国家。自 2021 年以来，一些原与中国加强关系的中东欧国家的反华情绪也有所上升，特别是波罗的海国家发现来自中国的经济利益并未达到预期后，也大幅改变了策略。2022 年 8 月，拉脱维亚和爱沙尼亚继立陶宛之后退出了所谓的"16+1 合作"机制。"16+1 合作"机制是中国和中东欧国家于 2012 年建立的基础设施和发展项目合作平台。此外，他们还担心中俄日益密切的关系，2022 年 2 月初北京冬奥会期间宣布的两国"友好无止境"就是这一关系的例证。在 2022 年 2 月的俄乌战争中，中国决定站在俄罗斯一边也加剧了中国与波罗的海国家之间的紧张局势。

五、共建"一带一路"倡议在东南欧：一个成功的故事

在东欧和东南欧的部分地区，包括寻求加入欧盟的西巴尔干国家，对中国资助的基础设施项目的依旧支持。塞尔维亚和黑山共和国近年来获得了大量"一带一路"投资。2023 年 1 月，中国出资 10 亿美元在黑山共和国首都郊外新建的高速公路正式通车。然而，最引人注目的例子是欧盟成员国克罗地亚。萨格勒布是中国东南欧洲商业协会的所在地，积极吸引中国在关键基础设施方面的投资，包括港口和欧盟资助、中国建造的佩列沙茨大桥，这是首个获补贴的中国公司在欧盟资助的欧洲项目上击败欧洲公司的例子。

其他继续看好中国共建"一带一路"倡议的中东欧国家包括保加利亚、罗马尼亚和匈牙利。这些国家派出高级别代表团出席 2023 年 10 月 17 日至 18 日在北京举行的第三届"一带一路"国际合作高峰论坛。保加利亚"一带一路"全国协会——一个由现任和前任政治家组成的组织带着一份详细的项目清单来到论坛，并提交给中国政府批准。上月，保加利亚举办了为期两天的"一带一路"倡议十周年会议，旨在促进保加利亚／欧盟与中国之间的更密切合作。经济和工业部副部长尼古拉·帕夫洛夫宣称，"中国是保加利亚和欧盟的战略伙伴，也是共建'一带一路'倡议范围内中国与中东欧国家合作的战略伙伴"。

2023年10月出席"一带一路"国际合作高峰论坛的匈牙利代表团中包括匈牙利央行行长,他公开支持共建"一带一路"倡议,与中国人民银行签署了一项协议,以提高货币互换水平。尽管货币互换的总金额并未公布,但有可能是欧洲最大的一笔,这表明匈牙利希望成为欧洲大陆中国投资的首选目的地。2023年12月22日,中国车企比亚迪股份有限公司宣布计划在匈牙利的塞格德市(位于匈牙利与罗马尼亚、塞尔维亚边境附近,在布达佩斯—贝尔格莱德—斯科普里—雅典铁路沿线)建立一家电动汽车制造厂,这将是欧洲最大的电动汽车制造厂,年产能达20万辆。这是共建"一带一路"倡议在东欧的旗舰项目。

六、共建"一带一路"倡议迈向高质量产业合作

匈牙利绝非唯一一个寻求在关键技术领域加强与中国产业联系的国家。其他重要的欧洲汽车制造国,如德国和捷克共和国,也已与中国签署了产业合作谅解备忘录。在加泰罗尼亚,当地政府与马德里中央政府合作,吸引了中国车企奇瑞汽车股份有限公司的重大投资。奇瑞于2024年4月与埃夫罗电动汽车公司签署了一项合资协议,计划到2029年生产15万辆汽车,投资金额达5亿欧元。为了吸引奇瑞,西班牙政府提供了税收优惠,并从欧盟基金中拿出17亿欧元作为激励。中国车企东风汽车集团有限公司目前正在与意大利梅洛尼内阁讨论在意大利建厂的计划,该厂将具备年产超过10万辆混合动力和电动汽车的能力,利用意大利的汽车工业遗产和地理位置优势,服务于欧洲市场。

许多欧盟政府似乎热衷于吸引中国投资和技术,以在其境内生产。目标是制造可以被定义为"中国制造和欧洲制造"的电动汽车和公交车,也包括太阳能板和风力发电场。也就是说,使用中国技术和专业知识,结合欧洲的零部件和熟练劳动力生产,从而符合欧洲规则。在汽车领域,

斯泰兰蒂斯集团是这一模式的代表，它与中国电池制造商宁德时代新能源科技股份有限公司以及其他中国企业合作，在欧洲生产电动汽车和电池。从这个角度来看，预计中国投资将从布鲁塞尔获得税收优惠和有利的监管环境，包括货币激励措施以支持绿色技术的研发——这是一种有效中和最近宣布的欧盟对中国电动汽车征收关税，并推动欧盟绿色协议的方式。

随着中国在欧洲大陆投资的不断增长，欧洲人已经向中国敞开了金融和货币联通的大门，这一动态在2023年10月举行的第三届"一带一路"国际合作高峰论坛上得到了充分展示，当时中国的政策性银行与外国贷款机构签署了一系列以人民币计价的贷款合同，其中许多来自欧盟国家。

七、中欧货币互联互通

自2013年共建"一带一路"倡议启动以来，中国领导层的一个主要目标是增加人民币在贸易、货币交易和外汇储备中的份额，以促进中国对外投资并降低交易成本。过去十年，共建"一带一路"倡议的推进和人民币国际化步调一致，相辅相成。继基础设施项目和投资之后，欧洲大陆一直是推广"一带一路"金融和货币政策的主要目标。

中国的货币政策在包括欧元区成员国在内的欧洲大陆引起了广泛兴趣。中国一直支持欧洲自身的货币政策，并在2010-2012年的欧元危机期间支持欧元区。首批"一带一路"项目于2013年底登陆欧洲，当时欧元区的边缘国家，包括希腊和意大利，正受到主权债务危机的冲击。

此外，许多欧洲人和中国一样，对美国将美元武器化的趋势感到担忧。数家欧洲公司，包括欧洲以资产计算最大的银行集团法国巴黎银行因违反美国的对外制裁法规而被罚款，导致法国法兰西银行行长弗朗索瓦·维勒鲁瓦·德加约公开呼吁欧元"挑战美元"。

欧洲是世界上最大的贸易体，拥有发达的个体资本市场（即使考虑到缺乏资本市场联盟）。自 1999 年欧元进入流通以来，欧盟加大了发挥欧元全球作用的努力。

中国政府一直将欧元视为创建多极货币体系的重要元素，并在许多场合表示对欧洲共同货币的支持。此外，中国人民银行已经实现其外汇储备多元化，欧元占其持有量超过三分之一。作为回报，欧洲人也支持人民币在世界经济中发挥更大作用。

随着中国在共建"一带一路"倡议下投资激增，一些欧洲国家建立了人民币银行清算中心（也称离岸中心），在那里可以进行人民币交易。布达佩斯、法兰克福、卢森堡、马德里、米兰、巴黎和布拉格都出现了离岸人民币中心。这一事实表明，欧洲愿意推动人民币的使用。

同样，大多数欧洲央行已经接受人民币作为可行的储备货币，并与中国人民银行签署了货币互换协议，这一趋势对双方都有利。通过这些货币互换，中国企业可以使用欧元或人民币结算支付，以避免汇率风险，而欧洲企业可以通过位于几乎所有欧盟成员国的清算银行进行人民币支付。

一些欧洲大型企业已开始使用人民币进行与中国的交易。例如，2023 年 4 月，法国道达尔能源公司和中国海洋石油集团有限公司完成了中国的首笔进口液化天然气采购，该交易通过法国巴黎银行和上海石油天然气交易中心以人民币结算。这笔交易发生在法国总统埃马纽埃尔·马克龙——"欧盟战略自主性"的坚定倡导者访华前几天。在访华期间，他宣称在欧盟与中国的贸易中，"欧洲必须减少对美元的依赖"。

除了货币互联互通，金融中心、交易中国证券的证券交易所，连接中国交易所的市场联通机制也在欧洲各国纷纷涌现，德国在这方面处于欧洲前沿。总部位于法兰克福的中欧国际交易所股份有限公司是由上海证券交易所、德意志交易所集团和中国金融期货交易所共同建立的合资企业。它是首个在中国大陆以外专门用于交易中国和人民币相关投资产品的交易场所。其使命是在欧洲建立一个集中化的交易、风险管理及资产配置市场，用于交易、管理风险和配置与中国相关或以人民币计价的金融产品。

法国在巴黎泛欧证券交易所和上海证券交易所之间建立了类似联系。2021 年，双方启动了由中国投资有限责任公司、法国巴黎银行和优拉吉欧公司（一家主要投资集团）参与的中法合作基金，以提升该基金作为跨境投资平台的作用，促进人民币在法国企业中的使用。

根据环球银行间金融通信协会发布的人民币追踪报告，欧洲在全球跨境人民币交易中的占比仅次于中国香港。确实，两者之间的差距仍然很大：截至 2023 年底，香港处理全球约 75% 离岸人民币结算业务，而欧洲仅略高于 10%。然而，有充分理由认为，凭借其持续强劲的双边贸易关系，欧洲的市场份额将继续上升。

在此背景下，欧洲参与者对人民币跨境支付系统的使用预计将会增加。在参与人民币跨境支付系统的 1300 多家金融机构中，有 200 多家位于欧洲，其中包括法国巴黎银行、德意志银行、汇丰银行和联合圣保罗银行等一些大型银行。参与人民币跨境支付系统的欧洲银行倾向于清算用于为共建"一带一路"倡议下的基础设施项目融资的人民币资金，但其人民币计价服务范围不断扩大。例如，意大利联合圣保罗银行——迄今为止唯一一家获得丝路奖的意大利银行，正在扩大其人民币清算业务，作为其参与人民币跨境支付系统的一部分，这符合欧洲银行的更广泛趋势，这些银行押注"一带一路"的下一章将全部与人民币有关。

八、结论

中国共建"一带一路"倡议正在整个欧洲大陆重新配置。在西欧，共建"一带一路"倡议正在从港口和铁路等实体基础设施项目转向规模较小的高质量合作，而大多数东欧国家则继续推进"一带一路"基础设施项目。同时，整个欧洲都支持与中国在金融和货币方面的互联互通——这一转变得到了包括一些国家层面的政策制定者、欧元区机构和大型银行在内的欧洲参与各方的欢迎。最近，越来越多的欧盟成员国对与中国在绿色技术领域的产业合作敞开了大门，这表明尽管欧中政治关系在近期有所恶化，但共建"一带一路"倡议仍在不断深入欧洲大陆，并成功地向金融、货币和工业领域的高质量合作项目迈进。

柬埔寨与共建"一带一路"倡议

李伟光（柬埔寨经济、社会和文化理事会技术顾问）

共建"一带一路"倡议是一项全球基础设施发展战略，旨在促进中国与伙伴国之间的贸易和投资。它是中国国家主席习近平 2013 年提出的，从历史上的丝绸之路汲取灵感，促进文化、经济和技术交流。该倡议由"丝绸之路经济带"和"21 世纪海上丝绸之路"组成，前者侧重于中亚、东欧和南亚的陆上商业路线，后者旨在发展连接东南亚、南亚、非洲、中东和欧洲的海上路线。

一、共建"一带一路"倡议的范畴及经济影响

共建"一带一路"倡议代表了中国通过加强基础设施、贸易、文化交流和参与国之间的政策协调来增进全球经济一体化的全面努力。中国发起这一倡议的主要目标包括确保进入关键市场，降低运输成本，解决国内行业产能过剩问题，并将自身定位为全球基础设施发展领域的主导。此外，共建"一带一路"倡议被视为中国在全球范围内扩大地缘政治影响力的战略工具，尤其是在传统上由西方大国主导的地区。截至 2023 年 6 月，中国已与 150 多个国家和 30 多个国际组织签署了多项合作协议，

涉及五大洲 117 个港口。

"一带一路"倡议横跨 150 多个国家,投资超过 1 万亿美元。它建立在中国对经济全球化、区域合作和培养软实力影响力的持久看法之上。2013 年至 2022 年,中国与共建"一带一路"国家累计进出口总额 19.1 万亿美元,年均增长 6.4%。在此期间,中国与共建国家的累计双向投资超过 3800 亿美元,其中中国对共建国家的直接投资超过 2400 亿美元。

二、柬埔寨参与共建"一带一路"倡议的情况

柬埔寨参与共建"一带一路"倡议体现了其与中国密切合作的地缘政治战略。鉴于其在东南亚的战略位置以及靠近重要海上航线,柬埔寨在中国的区域战略中扮演着关键角色。2016 年,柬埔寨王国正式加入"一带一路"倡议,并签署协议,参与旨在促进其经济发展的基础设施项目。对柬埔寨来说,共建"一带一路"倡议提供了一个解决其基础设施赤字的机会。长期以来,该问题一直对经济增长和减贫构成严重障碍。该国的基础设施,特别是运输、物流和能源领域的基础设施,严重依赖外国投资和援助,明显落后于地区其他国家。

值得一提的是,西哈努克港经济特区(以下简称"西港特区")是共建"一带一路"倡议在柬埔寨的一项显著努力。该特区位于西哈努克港附近,是中国和柬埔寨投资合作项目。作为纺织和电子制造加工业的重要工业中心,西港特区预计将带来数万个就业机会,加强柬埔寨的工业框架,并吸引全球企业的进一步投资。这凸显了倡议对该国经济发展产生重大影响的潜力。该港口的扩建大大加强了柬埔寨作为连接东南亚与全球市场的关键贸易门户的地位。这一发展尤其有助于促进与中国充满活力的经济中心——粤港澳大湾区的互联互通。

柬埔寨与共建"一带一路"倡议相关的几个重大项目值得强调。这

些项目中包括建设关键道路基础设施（比如 11 号国家公路的建设），以促进金边与重要边境地区之间的互联互通。此外，金边—西哈努克港高速公路（以下简称"金港高速公路"）在大大缩短首都与柬埔寨主要海港之间的旅行时长方面发挥了重要作用。可见，倡议对加强柬埔寨国内互联互通和促进区域贸易至关重要。此外，中国在加强柬埔寨航空基础设施方面进行了大量投资，特别是在金边国际机场的扩建和现代化升级方面。这些努力表明，中国致力于加强区域互联互通，促进经济发展。

共建"一带一路"倡议在柬埔寨的重点项目如下：

1. 西哈努克港经济特区（SSEZ）

"西港特区"是共建"一带一路"倡议在柬埔寨的一个重要组成部分。该特区由柬中两国政府合作成立，容纳了 160 多家企业，涵盖纺织、电子和轻工制造业。这些实体主要由中国所有，到 2020 年总共吸引了超过 10 亿美元的投资。

2. 西哈努克自治港（PAS）扩建

金边自治港的扩建是柬埔寨融入共建"一带一路"倡议的海上网络的重要支柱。该扩建项目由中国贷款提供资金，并由中国实体监督，包括增加港口水深、扩大船坞和安装最先进的货物装卸基础设施。这些改进是精心设计的，旨在扩大港口的能力，将其定位为东南亚的关键转运中心。升级后的港口有望通过创造就业机会和优化贸易物流来提升贸易量，吸引更多的外国投资，振兴当地经济。

3. 金港高速公路

金港高速公路于 2022 年 10 月通车，是柬埔寨参与共建"一带一路"倡议的突出例证。这条重要的高速公路全长 187 公里，将繁华的首都金边与具有战略意义的西哈努克港连接起来，西哈努克港是一个关键的经济中心和国际贸易的重要枢纽。这一巨大的壮举由中国路桥工程有限责任公司（CRBC）投资，耗资 20 亿美元，将这两个关键地点之间的通行时长从 5 小时大幅缩短到不到 2 小时。这一显著改善不仅加快了物流速度，也为贸易便利化创造了更有利的环境，更为旅游业的发展创造了有利的环境。

4. 桑河下游 2 号等一系列水电项目

桑河下游 2 号水电项目是中国企业资助的一项重大水电项目，其主要目的是增加柬埔寨的能源供给。虽然大坝通过提供持续的电力来源来推动产业扩张，有效地加强了能源安全，但它也引发了对于环境和民生的担忧，有舆论担心项目实施影响到湄公河水生态系统和沿河居民生计。

除了桑河下游 2 号水电项目，中国还在柬埔寨投资了其他几个水电项目，这些举措对于支持柬埔寨工业扩张和减少其对能源进口的依赖是不可或缺的。在共建"一带一路"倡议下，有效平衡能源发展与环境可持续性仍然是柬埔寨面临的最大挑战。

5. 道路及公路发展

中国投资的道路和公路项目为柬埔寨国内互联互通发挥了重要作用。值得注意的例子包括 11 号国家公路和金港高速公路的发展，这两个项目都显示了中国投资对柬埔寨交通基础设施的重大影响。这些举措有效降低了运输成本，简化了贸易物流，并通过建立主要城市和经济区之间的重要联系，促进了区域经济一体化，从而带动了该地区的全面经济增长和发展。

6. 机场建设

中国企业在金边国际机场（PPIA）的扩建中发挥了重要作用。这一综合项目包括航站楼设施的现代化、跑道容量的扩大和货物装卸能力的增强。目前，该机场已成为柬埔寨最大的机场，并于 2023 年 10 月全面投入运营。这些改进的目的是为了适应旅客数量的日益增加，并巩固柬埔寨作为关键区域物流中心的地位。

除了该机场的发展，金边附近正在建设的德崇国际机场是共建"一带一路"倡议下的另一项重大投资。该机场由海外柬华投资公司（OCIC）和中国投资者合作建设，预计耗资 15 亿美元，建成后将成为柬埔寨最大的机场。预计该机场每年将能够接待 1300 万名旅客，从而缓解金边现有机场的拥堵。

此外，共建"一带一路"倡议下的另一个重要基础设施项目暹粒—吴哥国际机场已由中国建筑工程总公司建设，耗资约 8.8 亿美元。该项目的融资涉及柬埔寨政府和中国投资者之间的伙伴关系。机场基础设施的加强不仅支持了旅游业的增长，这是柬埔寨经济的重要来源，而且还促进了货物的流动，从而促进了该国贸易和商业的全面升级。

7. 电信基础设施

包括华为公司在内的中国电信公司在柬埔寨数字基础设施的发展中发挥了关键作用。它们对最先进的光纤网络和尖端的 5G 技术进行了大量投资，以加强互联网连接，促进数字经济的发展，并将柬埔寨定位为全球数字生态系统不可分割的一部分。电信基础设施的加强不仅促进了电子商务、数字服务和创新的增长，而且柬埔寨对经济多样化和现代化作出了重大贡献。

三、"一带一路"倡议在柬埔寨的经济影响

柬埔寨参与共建"一带一路"倡议的经济优势主要集中在基础设施建设、外国直接投资（FDI）和发展工业上。近年来，柬埔寨经济持续发展，其中一个主要原因是中国投资的增加。正如柬埔寨财经部所说，从 2013 年到 2019 年，柬埔寨的 GDP 年均增长 7%，中国的投资在这一增长中发挥了重大作用。共建"一带一路"倡议改善了关键基础设施，包括道路、桥梁、机场和能源设施，从而降低了运输成本，改善了贸易物流，并为潜在投资者提供了更具吸引力的环境。例如，2022 年金港高速公路的开通不仅将旅行时间从 5 小时缩短到不到 2 小时，而且通过为货物从柬埔寨工业区向其主要港口的流动提供便利，提高了贸易效率。这显然降低了运输成本，并加强了柬埔寨国内以及与邻国的连通性。此外，与共建"一带一路"倡议相关的项目，特别是在西港特区的项目，在刺激制造业和建筑业创造就业方面发挥了关键作用。截至 2020 年，西港特区拥有 160 多家专门从事纺织品、服装和电子产品生产的企业，其中以中资企业为主，为当地工人创造了约 3 万个就业岗位，为柬埔寨经济从农业到轻工业的显著多元化作出了贡献。通过向电子、汽车零部件和其他行业进行拓展，对塑造柬埔寨的工业起到重要作用，而柬埔寨经济原本依赖于农业和服装生产，这也意味着升级本地熟练劳动力市场。因此，柬埔寨能够减少对低附加值部门的依赖，并转向高附加值的生产。此外，西港特区还为柬埔寨的出口经济作出了重大贡献，该特区 2020 年的出口额约为 13 亿美元，占该国整体贸易额的很大一部分。

中国已成为柬埔寨最大的贸易伙伴，2021 年两国双边贸易额超过 100 亿美元。此外，中国在柬埔寨的投资，特别是在建筑、能源和制造业领域，仅 2020 年就达到创纪录的 35 亿美元。共建"一带一路"倡议在扩大柬埔寨出口市场方面发挥了关键作用，特别是在纺织品、农产品

和电子产品方面。2021 年签署的柬中自由贸易协定（CCFTA）进一步加强了贸易关系，该协定降低了主要出口产品的关税，为柬埔寨商品进入中国市场开辟了新的机会。

另一方面，柬埔寨对中国投资的依赖，引发了部分人对该国偿债能力的担忧。由于柬埔寨的许多共建"一带一路"倡议项目都是由中国贷款资助的，柬埔寨的公共债务增加明显。截至 2024 年 3 月，柬埔寨的公共外债总额为 110 亿美元，其中近 37% 来自中国。不断增加的债务引发了关于柬埔寨财政状况可持续性的讨论，有人建议柬埔寨应使其收入和投资来源更加多样化。

四、"一带一路"倡议在柬埔寨的社会影响

值得注意的是，共建"一带一路"倡议在柬埔寨创造就业机会方面发挥了关键作用。共建"一带一路"倡议通过推动基础设施项目和工业区，对柬埔寨的劳动力市场产生了重大影响，从而在建筑、制造业和物流领域创造了大量新工作岗位。例如，西港特区等项目吸引了 160 多家公司，为数千名柬埔寨工人提供了就业机会。根据《东盟简报》的一份报告，到 2020 年，仅西港特区就为当地柬埔寨人创造了大约 3 万个就业机会，特别是在纺织、电子和轻工业等领域。潜在的好处体现在创造了一个充满活力的熟练劳动力市场。

这些就业机会在使家庭摆脱贫困方面是显而易见的，特别是在以前以农业为主要收入来源的地区。这种转变在西哈努克港等地区尤为显著，这些地区历来受到高失业率的困扰。特区的发展和相关的基础设施项目不仅为当地工人提供了经济机会，而且有助于减少贫困和提高生活水平。

此外，中国投资的涌入刺激了金边和西哈努克城等城市的快速城市化。基础设施的改善促进了城市地区的扩张，从而增加了获得住房、医

疗保健和教育的机会。城市转型也提振了当地的酒店业，吸引了更多的外国游客，创造了更多的就业机会。

除了创造就业机会，共建"一带一路"倡议项目还通过培训项目和能力建设倡议促进了柬埔寨工人的技能发展。例如，中国的"一带一路"奖学金项目为柬埔寨学生提供了在中国接受高等教育的机会，重点是在工程、基础设施建设和技术等领域。据《高棉时报》2019 年报道，截至2019 年，已有 1000 多名柬埔寨学生获得奖学金到中国留学。这些教育机会不仅使个人受益，而且有可能增强柬埔寨的劳动力，使其在区域劳动力市场上更具竞争力。

毋庸置疑，共建"一带一路"倡议为柬埔寨的就业和城市发展带来了重大积极影响。然而，它也带来一些误解和疑虑，如中国工人和企业的涌入是否会使柬埔寨工人被边缘化，是否会影响当地文化，是否和当地政府协商妥善处理补偿安置等问题。

五、"一带一路"倡议在柬埔寨的环境影响

我们必须承认中国在共建"一带一路"框架下为促进环境可持续性所做的积极努力。一个值得注意的例子是中国投资的水电项目的开发，比如桑河下游 2 号水电项目以及甘再水电站项目。这些项目通过生产约 200 兆瓦的电力，大大增强了柬埔寨的绿色能源能力，是该国朝着可持续能源发展迈出的关键一步。此外，金港高速公路的建设大大缩短了首都和柬埔寨主要海港之间的旅行时间，从而减少了燃料消耗和车辆排放，对环境产生了积极影响。

同时，个别项目也引发当地一些担忧，如道路和工业区等基础设施的增加是否会导致森林退化水土流失；采矿项目是否会造成空气污染；水电项目是否会改变水环境影响渔业发展，后续是否能将太阳能和风能

等可再生能源纳入柬埔寨的能源构成等。

六、在柬埔寨推进共建"一带一路"倡议需要妥善把握的问题

针对部分民众对于共建"一带一路"项目的疑虑和争论，在下一步推进中需要妥善把握两个问题。

（一）进一步增加透明度

特别是在重大基础设施建设中，前期需增加地方社区和民间社会组织在决策过程中的参与度，建议企业共享关键信息，特别是有关项目的环境和社会影响的信息。尽管《环境保护和自然资源管理法》规定了环境影响评估的必要性，但执行力度可能仍然不足。加强公众参与特别是社区参与，可以减少共建"一带一路"项目推进的阻力，提升其推进效率。

（二）注重边境安全管理

共建"一带一路"倡议在柬埔寨与泰国和越南边境附近引入了基础设施项目，虽然改善的基础设施大大促进了贸易和其他经济活动，但也可能引发对边境安全管理的担忧。建议加强监测和管理，防止有不法分子滥用这一基础设施从事非法活动或实施跨境犯罪。

七、结论

共建"一带一路"倡议是中国发起的一项战略努力，旨在通过在基础设施、贸易和政策协调方面的投资，促进全球经济一体化。其总体目标包括增强中国的全球影响力和促进共建国家的双赢合作，这一倡议在柬埔寨等伙伴国引发变革性的积极影响，特别是在基础设施发展、能源

和电信领域，有助于加强联通性，降低运输成本，提高工业能力，从而促进就业机会的创造，促进柬埔寨经济多样化，并加强熟练劳动力市场。

总之，"一带一路"倡议无疑为柬埔寨带来了重要的经济机遇。柬埔寨需要从战略政策／监管框架层面和实地执法／实施层面加强准备。此外，更有效和及时的公众沟通将缓解对所谓的经济和政治脆弱性产生的担忧。随着柬埔寨继续参与共建"一带一路"倡议，柬埔寨和其他参与国的成效将取决于它们能否充分利用倡议所带来的机遇并共同管理风险。

"一带一路"历史探源与创新实践

海德尔·卡西姆·M·塔米米（伊拉克"智慧宫"历史研究所所长）

一、简介

本文研究丝绸之路的历史根源。在古代历史上，丝绸之路把中国与世界其他地区（特别是与西亚和北非的阿拉伯世界）联系起来。这条贸易路线被认为是一个开创性门户，促进了不同地理、宗教和文化的国家和民族之间文明和文化的相互交融。我们看到，在这些民族的漫长历史中，丝绸之路的概念（无论是陆上还是海上）开始越来越受欢迎，就像佛教和伊斯兰教的传播路线一样。然后，研究转向共建"一带一路"倡议下的合作项目和对话，这些项目和对话塑造了中国丝绸之路在 21 世纪的"复兴"。

在上述背景下，本研究旨在探讨古代不同文明之间通过丝绸之路进行文化交流的影响。丝绸之路也被称为连接中国和西方的古代贸易路线，在罗马和中国这两个伟大的文明之间输送货物和传播思想。

这个商队路线起源于中国西安，沿着中国的长城向西北延伸，绕过塔克拉玛干沙漠，翻过帕米尔高原，穿越阿富汗，然后前往黎凡特；货物从那里经航运抵达地中海彼岸。

在公元13和14世纪,这条路线在蒙古人的统治下复兴,当时马可·波罗经由这条线路来到中国。丝绸之路的这部分古老的路线至今仍然存在,但已经成为一条铺设柏油的公路,连接着巴基斯坦和中国新疆地区,被称为"喀喇昆仑公路"。古代丝绸之路绵延7000多公里,连接了亚洲和欧洲的大多数领土。在地图上追踪古代丝绸之路的路线并不容易,因为它有多个分支路线,这些联通东西方的分支又会衍生出更多支线。

"丝绸之路"这个词现在几乎是家喻户晓,全世界成千上万的人都希望走访和亲身体验它。事实上,直到1877年,德国学者和探险家费迪南·冯·李希霍芬才创造了"丝绸之路"一词,用以指代这个从东亚到西亚的古老商业运输网络。欧洲人和日本人对中国的新疆地区非常感兴趣,许多学者去那里研究西汉时期,作为汉武帝特使和探险家的张骞所开创的丝绸之路。

本研究的第一部分主要描述了丝绸之路沿线各种文明和社会之间的交流。这种交流虽然包括大量商品的贸易,如大型哺乳动物、农作物、药品、餐具、纺织品、乐器、珠宝、矿物和火药,但本研究仍然侧重于物质之外的文化交流,包括拜火教、佛教、基督教、摩尼教、景教和伊斯兰教的起源和传播,以及通过丝绸之路实现的文字和语言、音乐、建筑、绘画和雕塑的远距离交流。它概述了历史上从东到西的不同民族的重要迁移,如匈奴、月氏、汉、羌、嚈哒、突厥、维吾尔、蒙古和锡伯等民族。

至于本研究的第二部分,我试图追溯十多年前获得世界大多数国家参与的共建"一带一路"倡议对文明和文化的影响。研究强调了这一倡议对世界"一带一路"共建国家之间的文化和解产生影响的主要观点。此外,研究重点关注"一带一路"在恢复中国和阿拉伯文明之间文化联系甚至社会纽带繁荣方面的作用,特别是与巴格达市的联系。在中世纪,巴格达市曾是阿拉伯文明的中心和首都。

如果要用一句话来概括丝绸之路沿线和整个欧亚大陆 2000 年文化交融的历史意义,我会毫不犹豫地说:当一个社会保持开放和包容,愿意并习惯于与不同民族互动和学习时,这个社会就会兴旺繁荣。

二、丝绸之路历史溯源

大约在公元前 140 年左右的中国汉朝时期,汉武帝的使者张骞从长安(今陕西省西安市)启程前往西域,开辟了一条连接东西方的陆路通道。在此后的几个世纪,陆上和海上丝绸之路在唐、宋、元时期都蓬勃发展。15 世纪初,明朝著名的航海家郑和七次下西洋,促进了海上丝绸之路的贸易。

几千年来,古代丝绸之路一直是互动交流的主要动脉,它跨越了尼罗河、底格里斯河和幼发拉底河、印度河和恒河,以及黄河和长江;连接了埃及、巴比伦、印度和中国文明的发源地,穿越了佛教徒、基督教徒和伊斯兰教徒生活的地区,也连通了不同民族和种族的家园。

这些路线增强了欧亚大陆国家之间的互联互通,促进了东西方文明的交流和相互学习,促进了地区发展和繁荣,塑造了和平合作、开放包容、互学互惠的丝绸之路精神。

世界学术界对丝绸之路研究的兴趣与日俱增,学者试图了解其绵延多个世纪的历史;追溯历史上的标志性事件和"世代更替"的里程碑。丝绸之路是一个商队通道体系,在古代和中世纪穿越了从地中海到中国的欧亚大陆,为促进民族和国家之间贸易和文化纽带的建立和发展作出了巨大贡献。此外,该研究旨在支持曾经参与这条古代路线影响范围研究的学者之间的科学和文化合作。穿越草原、海洋和沙漠的丝绸之路提供了建立联系和对话的机会,促进了优秀文明的交流互鉴。对丝绸之路开展广泛研究的目的是让人们认识到恢复对话的必要性,抓住历史机遇,在丝绸之路框架内发展相互理解、拓展联系、交流互鉴的文明。

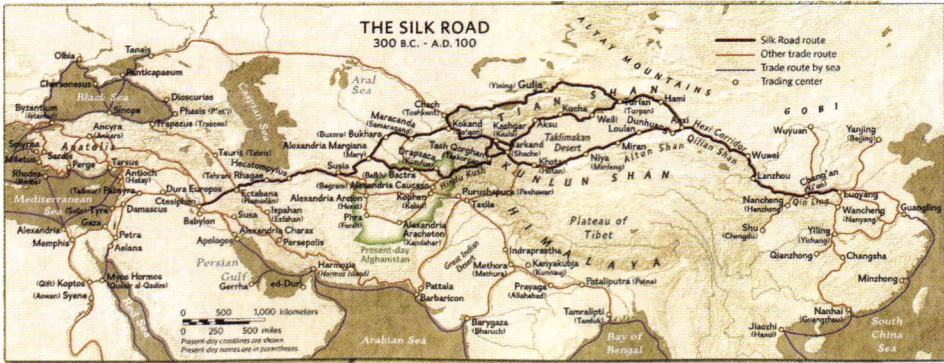

丝绸之路，亚洲其他的贸易路线和枢纽，公元前 300 年－公元 100 年

在历史、地理和文化领域，丝绸之路早在 19 世纪下半叶就已成为研究课题。西欧、俄罗斯和日本学者在这一研究课题上成果突出。1877 年，德国学者费迪南·冯·李希霍芬的经典著作《中国》提出"丝绸之路"的概念，将其描述为连接广阔欧亚大陆各个区域的道路系统。后来，"丝绸之路"一词深入人心。关于丝绸之路的学术和科普著作数以千计，包括专著、作品集、图册、手册和文章。它们的内容涵盖丝绸之路的历史、主要和次要路线介绍、人口的民族构成、沿途城市介绍、商品的列举、建筑和艺术、音乐和诗歌、宗教等等。在过去的二十年间，学界和公众对这条横贯大陆之路的历史的兴趣明显增加。

值得注意的是，在该课题的框架内举行了多场国际学术会议和研讨会。其中包括："中亚丝绸之路路线的形成和发展：古代和中世纪时期"（撒马尔罕，1990 年 10 月）；"丝绸之路上游牧文化和定居文化的相互作用"（阿拉木图，1992 年 6 月 15 日至 16 日）；"丝绸之路沿线国家的诗歌"（芬兰图尔库，1993 年 6 月 3 日至 7 日）；"丝绸之路沿线的语言和书面语言"（塞浦路斯，1994 年 9 月 30 日至 10 月 1 日）；"丝绸之路的振兴：乌兹别克斯坦文化旅游发展和文化遗产保护"（布哈拉，1996 年 2 月 21 日至 22 日）；"丝绸之路：历史深度与现实之间"（巴格达，智慧之家，2019 年 9 月 18 日至 19 日）。

值得关注的是，一些国家设立了专门的机构来研究丝绸之路，例如日本镰仓的平山丝绸之路研究所，它出版了《丝绸之路的考古学和艺术》年鉴；此外还有撒马尔罕的国际中亚研究所和乌兰巴托的国际游牧文明研究所。

然而，关于所研究时期的生活和文化的可靠来源仍然非常少。这些来源是考古学家、东方学家、哲学家和文化学家长期探索的成果，因此凸显了该地区的潜力、保持历史身份认同和参与地缘政治决策的重要性。

通过其分支丰富的商队道路网络，丝绸之路连接了欧亚大陆的西部和东部。商队路线穿过中国、哈萨克斯坦、吉尔吉斯斯坦、塔吉克斯坦、土库曼斯坦和乌兹别克斯坦。这些道路向东直抵韩国和日本；向西通往东欧和西欧、俄罗斯，向南抵达印度；向西南则延伸到近东和中东。这些路线保持双向流动，反映了所研究时期在科学思想、文化价值观和宗教方面的成就。商人、旅行者和外交官通过这些线路实现了信息的有效传播。

关于丝绸之路启用的日期，学界从来没有明确的答案。人们只能指出某些路段的历史可以追溯到公元前 2 世纪到 3 世纪，由于巴达赫尚山区青金石的开发，联系已经建立。这种矿石被出口到伊朗、美索不达米亚、安纳托利亚、埃及和叙利亚。巴达赫尚青金石早在公元前就来到了中国。除了"青金石之路"，还有连接当时新疆地区和中国中原地区的"玉石之路"。在公元前 5 世纪，所谓的"草原之路"开始形成，它始于黄河的一个大转弯区域，翻过阿尔泰山脉进入哈萨克草原和黑海地区，到达希腊人和伊特鲁里亚人的土地。

丝绸之路在形成之初被认为是一条单独的外交和贸易动脉。张骞提出了这个想法。公元前 138 年，一个使节团队从汉朝都城出发，受命于汉武帝，陪同张骞开启了出使西域未知国家的旅程。13年后，张骞得以返回长安。他的足迹最远到达了如今的阿富汗地区，成为第一个从中国中原地区直接到达中亚的人。自此之后，中国商队带着丝绸运往西方；来自地中海、近东、中东和中亚的商队把货物运向东方。不过，中亚、哈萨克斯坦、阿尔泰、西伯利亚和中国的考古探索也提供了无可争辩的证据，证明中国丝绸和波斯地毯早在张骞通西域之前就已经在欧亚大陆上传播了。绣有凤凰的绸缎，以及在阿尔泰地区巴泽雷克的"皇家"墓穴挖掘过程中发现的波斯地毯，可追溯到公元前5世纪，当时游牧和半游牧的斯基泰人部落促进了珍贵丝绸的传播，帮助丝绸进入中亚和地中海地区，到达欧洲和印度。

因此，丝绸之路始于中国都城长安，跨越黄河、兰州地区，到达长城的西端外围地区和玉门关。在这里，路线分为南北两支以绕开塔克拉玛干沙漠。北方路线穿过哈密、吐鲁番、庭州等，到达伊犁河谷；中间路线是从高昌到焉耆、阿克苏，并通过别迭里山口到达伊塞克湖岸边；南部路线通过敦煌、和田、喀什等地到达中亚、巴克特里亚王国、印度和地中海。

北方路线在6世纪到7世纪变得特别繁忙，这被认为是由于以下原因：首先，当时的突厥汗国的总部设在七河地区，从而控制了贸易路线；其次，富有的突厥汗国人及其家族成为海外商品的主要消费者。这条路线成为主干道，因此在7—14世纪，更多的使节和商队在这条路上穿行。

丝绸之路的历史分为两个阶段。初始阶段，即"原始丝绸之路"，在时间上与中亚和哈萨克斯坦的第一批政权（巴克特里亚王国、花剌子模王国、七河地区政权等）相联系。中国丝绸和波斯地毯以阿尔泰著名的"皇家"墓穴的出土文物而闻名。因此，丝绸之路的第一阶段或初始阶段可以追溯到公元前2世纪的前半叶，与此阶段相关的是斯基泰人、乌孙人、匈奴人、萨马尔泰人的城镇和王室墓葬，以及中亚的古老城市。

丝绸之路的第二阶段始于公元前138年张骞出使西域，结束于公元1405年的明朝时期，当时陆上丝绸之路的一段由于中国的闭关政策和海路的快速发展而陷入衰落。学术界对陆上丝绸之路的废止日期仍有争议，但自16世纪以来，陆路的不确定性增加和中国舰队的进步，意味着到16世纪末作为东西方贸易和文化通道的丝绸之路不复存在了。

如前文所述，丝绸之路最初用于向欧洲国家出口中国丝绸。我们也知道，古罗马、拜占庭、印度、伊朗、阿拉伯哈里发国以及后来的俄国和欧洲国家制造的商品由此被运送到中国。不寻常的异国情调的商品有很多：没药和劳丹脂、茉莉花水和龙涎香、豆蔻和肉豆蔻、人参和蛇胆、地毯和衣服、染料和矿物、钻石和碧玉、琥珀和珊瑚、象牙和"鱼牙"、金条和银条、毛皮和硬币、弓箭、剑和长矛。通过丝绸之路运输出售的有大宛汗血宝马、骆驼和大象、犀牛、猎豹和瞪羚、鹰和隼、孔雀、鹦鹉和鸵鸟。商贩们还销售不同地区的特产作物，包括葡萄、桃子、甜瓜、各种蔬菜，以及香料和糖。

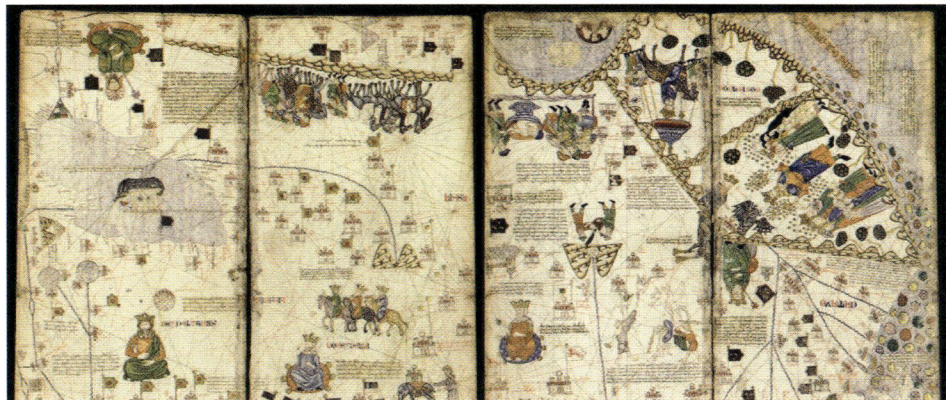

加泰罗尼亚地图集对丝绸之路的描绘
来源：台北故宫博物院

尽管如此，中国丝绸仍然是重要且持久的物品，它与黄金一起充当着国际货币的角色。丝绸作为礼物受到高度赞赏；国王和使节被慷慨地赠送这种产品；打短工的会得到绸缎作为薪水。有大量证据证明这一点。因此，伊朗的霍斯劳一世从一位中国帝王那里收到了一件丝绸中国服装（连同其他礼物），上面绣了一个戴着王冠和装饰品的国王。丝绸受到崇敬，这在中国、中亚和东突厥统治者的宫殿壁画上都有体现。贵族的丝绸服装会从方方面面的细节进行美化。

通过丝绸之路输送的不仅是货物，还有不同民族文化环境中所特有的艺术时尚。一种观点认为，正是丝绸之路促成了在陶瓷中广泛传播的帖木儿风格，以在白色背景下绘制蓝色图案而著称。这种风格的瓷器在元朝（1279—1368）期间在中国的官窑中兴起，然后在伊朗、土耳其、中亚广泛传播。许多博物馆陈列有精美的青花瓷碗和花瓶标本。

世界"四天子"的概念在中世纪早期传播开来，每个"王国"在同时代人眼中都有其独特的优势。强大政权的建立构成了"四天子"概念的基础，包括中国的隋朝和唐朝时期、印度统治者以恒河城市根瑙杰为中心建立的王国、从太平洋到黑海的突厥人联盟以及伊朗和拜占庭帝国。在这个概念下，这些王国位于四个方位：南部的"象主"之国（印度）；西部的"宝主"之国（伊朗、拜占庭）；北部的"马主"之国（突厥汗国）；东部的"人主"之国（中国）。接受这个概念的穆斯林信徒称"象主"为"智慧之王"，用以致敬印度哲学和科学的重要地位；称"人主"为"国家治理和工业之王"（考虑到著名的中国发明）；称"马主"为"狮子之王"。

他们又把西方的两个国王进行了区分：其中一个（"万王之王"）是波斯和阿拉伯国王；另一个（由于人口的美丽而被称为"人类之王"）是拜占庭国王。这个概念在撒马尔罕附近的壁画中得到了体现，其中一个描绘了中国帝王，其他人为突厥可汗和印度梵天；第三个是波斯国王和古罗马皇帝。巴格达画作的模式解释了在厚厚的石膏层（雕刻灰泥）上的这些雕刻。这些面板上描绘了葡萄藤和成串的葡萄、郁金香、玫瑰花、棕榈、菱形带、蜿蜒的边界以及一堆植物。这些花纹图案，不同的装饰元素和风格，都在古城阿弗拉西亚布和瓦拉赫沙、萨迈拉等地的官殿壁画中找到了风格最接近的作品。换句话说，巴格达艺术家的品味和这座哈里发国首都的时尚风格沿着丝绸之路传播，抵达了穆斯林城市的边远地区。

这些生活在历史上的同一时期但来自不同国家的作者们，不仅歌颂本国的成就，也展现了当地人对其他文化价值观的接纳。世界文化的发展基于不同文化的互动，正如著名苏菲派诗人贾拉鲁丁·鲁米（1207—1273）的创造性作品所证明的那样，他谈到了互相包容："一个土耳其人和一个印度人经常融洽相处。两个土耳其人经常格格不入。因此，语言相通是另一码事：心意一致比语言相通更可贵。"

随着商品、应用艺术、建筑和壁画的样本的传播，丝绸之路充当了音乐和舞蹈艺术、表演的传播渠道，形成了一种中世纪的"多样性"。音乐家和舞蹈家、驯兽师、杂技演员和哑剧演员、魔术师的表演，巡演剧团不存在语言障碍，不需要翻译。"那些通过肢体动作表达自己的人都能同样得到理解。"荷兰思想家伊拉斯谟在鹿特丹写道。同样的表演被展示给希腊国王、基辅王子、突厥可汗和中国皇帝。

别忘了，在当时，外国管弦乐团是宫廷人员的一部分。他们会在"官方宫廷仪式"和"非官方宫廷庆典"的场合进行表演。一位突厥可汗在碎叶城附近的帐篷款待使节的场景描写十分有趣。这场仪式的见证人、著名的佛教取经人玄奘写道："可汗命陈酒设乐……杰侏兜离之音，铿锵互举。虽蕃俗之曲，亦甚悦耳目、乐心意也。"来自东突厥汗国和中亚城市的西域音乐，在唐朝的中国特别受欢迎。来自库车和喀什、布哈拉和撒马尔罕的音乐风格与中式音乐传统融合在一起。

狂欢节在所有时代都是巨大的成功；这些传统在后来的穆斯林国家也有持久的生命力。众所周知，在诺鲁孜节期间，巴格达会在哈里发的见证下安排化装舞会。

丝绸之路沿线的考古发现证明了文化的发展和互惠互鉴。因此，一组唐代时期的舞蹈俑的出土具有重要意义，它们描绘了舞者、戴面具的演员和骑着骆驼的乐团，可以辨认出中亚民族的特征。

丝绸之路在传播宗教思想方面也发挥了重要作用。传教士沿着这条路线在其他国家传教。佛教来自印度，途经中亚和东突厥汗国；基督教和后来的伊斯兰教来自叙利亚、伊朗和阿拉伯。

研究人员认为，自公元前 1 世纪中叶以来，佛教通过中亚从印度传入中国。中亚僧侣对佛教在东突厥汗国和中国的传播作出了巨大贡献。在穿越中亚的丝绸之路沿途，人们发现了多处佛教遗迹。其中包括在卡拉托别发掘的公元 1 世纪到 3 世纪的佛教寺庙；撒马尔罕附近河谷的寺院遗存；梅尔夫的古代堡垒遗址上的佛教纪念碑；塔吉克斯坦南部瓦赫什河谷的一处 7 世纪到 8 世纪的佛教寺庙。玄奘证明了自 6 世纪以来佛教对土耳其人的强烈影响。他讲述了一位西域突厥人可汗对这种宗教的好感。其他研究人员指出，在 7 世纪上半叶，西突厥一些统治者接纳了佛教或支持这种信仰。

值得一提的是，丝绸之路也促进了基督教从西方到东方的传播。5 世纪上半叶，东罗马帝国（叙利亚）出现了一个由景教信徒组成的"异端教派"。431 年，在以弗所公会议上，景教的教义被谴责，随后，景教信徒受到无情迫害，不得不逃往伊朗。在伊朗，他们在与努赛宾接壤的地方建立了一所学校，从而同拜占庭的政治反对派加深了联系。富裕的叙利亚商人和工匠在君士坦丁堡东移时失去了市场。

摩尼教是伊朗在 3 世纪兴起的一种宗教，从意大利到中国都有大量的信徒。这种宗教的传播也利用了古老的丝绸之路。摩尼教是拜火教—基督教的综合体，它采用了救世主的理论和一种善与恶、光明与黑暗斗争的思想。粟特人在这种宗教的传播中发挥了至关重要的作用。8 世纪初，摩尼教的最高领袖在撒马尔罕拥有住所。需要指出的是，摩尼教长期以来与其他宗教平等地共存于中亚；佛教对摩尼教的众神构成、术语甚至概念都有很大影响。

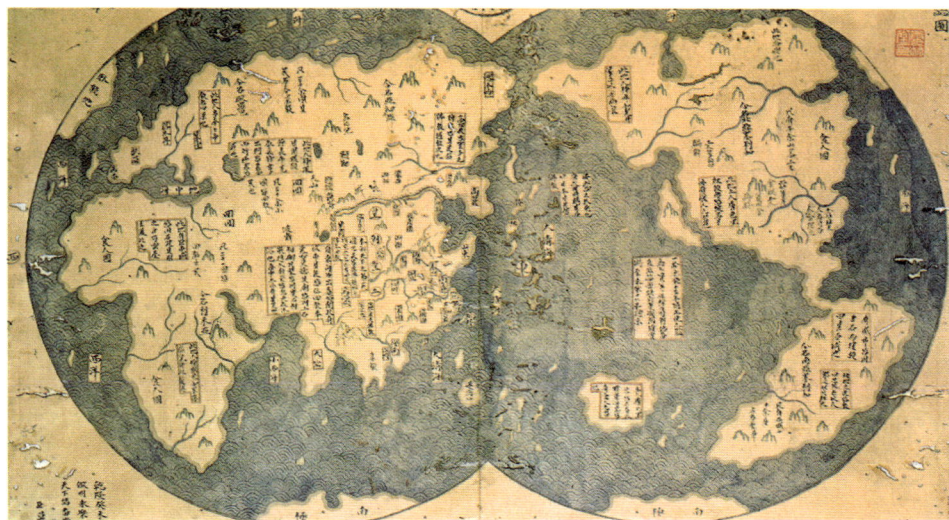

一张 18 世纪来自中国的地图，据称是 1418 年中国所绘地图的复制品，该地图基于探险家郑和的出海之行。虽然有人声称这证明郑和比哥伦布更早到达美洲，但学者们质疑该地图的真实性。

来源：环球图片集团 /345 盖蒂图像

然而，伊斯兰教不仅使用"火和剑"，还凭借穆斯林商人的"能说会道"，为自己的传播铺平了道路，逐渐超越了基督教、佛教、拜火教和东方的本地宗教。这种新宗教在丝绸之路的许多城市和草原上确立了自己的地位。一些墓葬发掘成果证明了伊斯兰教的传播。请注意，在 9 世纪到 10 世纪的后半叶，葬礼仪式发生了变化，以符合穆斯林典型的教规：葬在坑里，由生砖砌成的地窖中。死者的头向西北方。墓穴中没有放置任何随葬品。大量的釉面陶器印证了伊斯兰教传播的影响力。这些陶瓷使用了基于阿拉伯文字的装饰元素。铭文的一部分是装饰性的（无法阅读）；然而，其中一些铭文描述了宗教愿望、教义和建议。此外，金属物品,铜和青铜制品的风格,也装饰有宗教性质的铭文,被广泛传播。

考古发现,在中世纪,从欧洲到亚洲的贸易路线途经中亚不同地区,包括草原、山脉和肥沃的山谷。作为主要的贸易动脉,丝绸之路同时促进了许多民族之间的合作发展。丝绸之路的路线连通了从中国到地中海和东欧的古代政权,在整合东西方人民的经济和文化方面发挥了至关重要的作用。数千年来,贸易商队和外交团队沿着丝绸之路移动,严格遵循从东到西和从南到北的主要路线。参与这一国际贸易和文化接触体系的每个国家都为物质和精神的发展和传播做出了自己的贡献。在这条古老跨国路线各段发掘的杰出考古成果构成了极具说服力的证据。

在亚洲的另一侧,即西亚地区,巴格达代表了中世纪连接东西方的重要贸易交流中心。沿着巴格达运输平台,来自帝国东部各个地区的数百艘船只从中国到非洲,从巴格达运送各种货物和产品。随后,阿拉伯商人将巴格达生产的各种货物运往中东和欧洲,然后将这些货物运往俄罗斯、保加利亚、布哈拉、撒马尔罕和东南亚。

除了从巴格达到巴士拉和乌剌国,以及穿过阿拉伯海湾到印度和中国港口的海上通道外,还有陆上通道向东连接巴格达与中国和日本;向北穿过小亚细亚、俄罗斯、保加利亚;向西抵达叙利亚、地中海和欧洲。

综上所述,丝绸之路不仅影响了东西方之间的关系,而且被认为是让文化交流活起来的一个样本。不仅各种中世纪文化的传统和习俗参与了这个交流过程,现代文化也没有被落下。在人类社会中,出现了各种交流、存储和传播信息的方法和手段;我们见证了人类历史正在经历巨大的变化。所有这些都与上述因素和技术进步密切相关。自古以来,保持个人主义的人类现在正在经历全球化。这意味着这个过程需要人类的沟通技巧和能力。为此,我们需要摆脱美国欧洲主义、非洲中心主义,这些理论只承认自己的价值观和文化专制主义。

"对话理论"是通向更美好未来的导航器,因为"对话"一词近年来已经越来越常见。它在政治节目、研究论文、教育系统讨论等方面被更频繁地提及。在当今文化中，对话的概念在社会和公民领域引起了广泛关注，主要原因是对话已成为解决这些领域所出现问题的工具。特别是在这个不断变化的世界中，对话有助于和平解决政治、宗教和文化对抗。

1154 年，地理学家伊德里西为西西里国王罗杰二世绘制的世界地图，这是最先进的中世纪世界地图之一。本图对伊德里西 70 个双页进行了合并并上下翻转，因为原始地图为上南下北。

三、"一带一路"倡议——更密切的联系

文明源于人类社会实践的进步，是一个民族及其人民的集体记忆。文明植根于其存在的独特语境，体现了一个国家或民族的智慧和精神追求，体现了其内在价值观。由于所有国家的未来紧密相连，不同的文明如何相处？全球文明倡议促进文明之间的相互尊重，倡导不同文明之间的平等对话、交流互鉴和包容共存，为培育多元文明和谐共存提供了新范式。

如今全球有 80 亿人口，200 多个国家和地区，2500 多个民族，5000 多种语言。这种多样性催生了不同的文明，每个文明都深深植根于自己的文化语境中。中国领导人习近平在亚洲文明对话大会上强调："人类只有肤色语言之别，文明只有姹紫嫣红之别，但绝无高低优劣之分。认为自己的人种和文明高人一等，执意改造甚至取代其他文明，在认识上是愚蠢的。"诚然，如果人类文明被简化为单一的颜色或单一的模式，世界将陷入刻板印象，变得沉闷无聊。我们必须倡导相互尊重，拒绝傲慢和偏见。我们需要加强对自身文明与其他文明差异的理解，努力增进互动，提倡对话，促进不同文明之间的和谐。

尊重人类的多样性本质上需要不同文明之间的交流和相互理解。此外，坚持文明平等是超越"文明中心论"和"文明至上论"的一种方式。"西方文明中心论"和"西方文明至上论"长期以来一直在国际话语中盛行。历史上，国际社会一直被这两种论调所主导，认为西方是先进现代文明的创造者和全球文明的中心力量。这种观点意味着非西方国家被降级为西方的附庸，必须遵循西方的现代化发展模式。然而，正如马克思主义理论所强调的那样，现代西方文明基本上是资本主义的，以私有制为基础，其特征是固有的不平等和疏离感。毫无疑问，套用西方现代化模式给一些国家带来了许多挑战，而不是带来成功。

全球文明倡议中的第一部分"倡导"令人信服地证明，全球文明应该在平等和包容的原则下蓬勃发展，通过交流和相互理解来发展。该倡议提出了一种促进不同文明和谐共存的新范式。

从人类文明演进的角度来看，全人类共同价值代表了社会在发展过程中追求的集体目标和愿望。

此前，全球发展倡议已经提出重视文明的交流和相互理解，旨在构建一个开放和包容的世界。全球文明倡议进一步深化了这一承诺，倡导弘扬全人类共同价值，重点是理解不同文明对价值内涵的认识。

不同文明对价值有不同的看法，但对更美好生活的追求仍然是共同的全球愿景，这是体现于对"和平、发展、公平、正义、民主、自由"的共同追求。在当代，尽管有地区冲突、霸权、强权政治、不断扩大的全球差距以及发展中国家持续存在的贫困和疾病问题，但和平与发展仍然是优先事项。另一方面，公平、正义、民主和自由被认为是个人发展的重要保障。

与自私的利益或某些国家、地区或族裔群体的特定追求相反，全球文明倡议的核心是 21 世纪不同文明的共同价值追求。

全人类的共同价值超越了西方普世价值。西方普世价值的本质在于追求全球文明同质化，以实现西方在全球范围内的主导地位。美国认为"自己的道路将塑造人类的命运"，"其国内原则是普遍适用的"，采用各种手段在全球范围大力推行自己的价值观。然而，正如美国外交官亨利·基辛格所叹息的那样，结果是"普世性对于任何征服者来说都是镜花水月"。

全球文明倡议的第二个方面强调在文明互动中倡导弘扬全人类共同价值，旨在应对全球风险和挑战，遏制意识形态对抗，努力建设多元共存的全球文明。

文明发展是人类社会进步的关键指标。实现可持续文明发展需要在传承和创新之间保持微妙的平衡。"文明永续发展，既需要薪火相传、代代守护，更需要顺时应势、推陈出新。"

忽视发展而只关注传承，会导致文明无法适应时代的变化，最终阻碍自身的进步。相反，只强调发展而不关注传承，会使文明失去根基和历史文化遗产，有历史虚无主义和不稳定的风险。

历史上，中国文明的持久遗产延续了数千年，是传承与创新成功融合的典范。总体而言，文明发展的愿望是一致的，而每个国家的步伐和方法各不相同。各国应利用其丰富的文化遗产作为现代化的驱动力，进而促进传统文化的创新性发展。除了平衡传统和现代，合作和不干涉也至关重要。

全球文明倡议的第三个方面鼓励人类通过传承和创新实现现代化。发展传承包括保护历史遗产、培养身份认同和以史为鉴。另一方面，促进创新包括推动科技发展和鼓励文化交流以促进社会进步。

在政治层面，中东国家可以积极参与由全球文明倡议促成的外交倡议，并利用这一平台，在中东国家之间和全球范围内开展和平对话和寻找冲突解决方案。此外，它们可以利用文化交流展示其丰富的文化遗产，增强自己的软实力和改善国际形象。例如，中国春节从 2024 年开始正式被列为联合国假期，中东国家也可以努力推广自己的传统文化和习俗，扩大本国节日和文化的国际影响力。为了通过合作方式解决冲突，中东国家应促进对话，应对共同挑战和讨论区域安全合作。此外，中东国家可以将该倡议作为促进包容、理解和宗教多样性的平台，倡导跨宗教对话以解决宗教紧张局势。

从经济角度来看，中东国家应该探索与其他国家促进贸易和经济一体化的机会，组织和参与以经济发展和投资为重点的论坛，促进创新和技术转让方面的合作，并积极参与知识交流计划以增强技术能力。随着"一带一路"倡议的推进，中国和中东国家之间的双边联系得到了进一步发展。这包括与阿尔及利亚、埃及、伊朗、沙特阿拉伯和阿联酋签署全面战略伙伴关系。此外，中国还与该地区的另外八个国家建立了战略伙伴关系。随着其地理范围的扩大，"一带一路"倡议的目标也发生了变化。目前，这些目标包括促进贸易、互联互通、金融一体化、政治合作和民间交往等。然而，基础设施项目仍然是"一带一路"倡议的核心；因此，中东国家可以向中国寻求基础设施发展项目的支持，以促进经济增长。此外，应考虑环境可持续性。中东国家应实施有助于可持续发展的政策和气候行动，通过合作努力解决该地区的环境挑战。

人民之间的联系是"一带一路"合作的社会基础。参与国传承和发扬了古丝绸之路的友好合作精神，在文化、旅游、教育、智库和媒体交流方面进行了合作，促进了文明间的互学互鉴和文化融合创新。

以动态互动和多样性为特征的民间交流模式支撑了公众对推进该倡议的支持。

丝绸之路精神与中华民族长期坚持的"和平、和谐、和睦"的外交理念相一致，与中国人民的与邻为善和立己达人的原则相一致，与和平、发展、合作共赢的时代召唤相一致。

对于世界各地的年轻人来说，这一源自中国传统文化的倡议包含了不同文明共享的普遍智慧和远见。正如阿拉伯人喜欢使用谚语"从每个花园都摘一朵玫瑰"来指代物品的多样性和丰富性。

"一带一路"倡议倡导文明之间的平等、互鉴、对话和包容。它维护和平、发展、公平、正义、民主和自由的共同价值观。它通过交流超越文化之间的障碍，通过相互理解消弭冲突，拒绝优越感，促进共存。它鼓励文明之间求同存异，互学互鉴。

"一带一路"倡议正在联通全球各国，有不同肤色、说不同语言的人自豪地弘扬他们自己的文化。生活在一个不同文明、信仰和习俗的世界里，我们应该独自进步还是共同进步？我们应该闭门造车还是相互拥抱？中国的答案很明确：架起交流互动和互学互鉴的桥梁，使"一带一路"成为连接不同文明的纽带。

"一带一路"倡议由中国于 2013 年提出。该倡议认识到多样性是世界的基本特征，其"文明互鉴"的概念呼吁以平等和包容的方式对待所有文明，尊重所有国家的制度和信仰，促进不同文明之间的理解和信任。它拒绝过时的冷战思维，代表了人类文明理念的重大进步，并在全球范围内获得了越来越多的支持。

过去十年间,共建"一带一路"伙伴国家开展了多元化的民间交流与合作,构建了相互文化欣赏的桥梁。中外考古学家正在共同探索古代丝绸之路的文化遗迹,并通过现代文化互动续写丝绸之路上的交流新篇。"一带一路"搭建了文明对话的平台,不同文明的花朵在这里共同绽放和闪耀。

我们的世界正在经历百年未有之大变局。中国在积极倡导文明对话的同时,致力于为世界贡献中华文明的能量,努力将"文明互鉴"的概念付诸实践,并为"一带一路"增添新的内容。中国沿着中国式现代化的道路推进国家发展,创造人类进步的新形式,发出了一种强烈信息:现代化并不意味着西方化,每个文明都有独特的价值。这增强了不同文明共同闪耀、相得益彰的信心。中国提出了全球文明倡议,呼吁尊重世界文明的多样性,倡导人类共同价值,促进文明的传承与创新,加强国际人文交流与合作。其目的是为各国之间的文化互动和民间交往开辟新的前景,为人类文明的进步作出更多贡献。

随着百年变局在全球范围内继续演进,人类面临着多重挑战和危机。鼓吹特定文明优越论和文明冲突的不合时宜的论调正在对世界和平、稳定、发展和进步构成严重威胁。在所有国家参与构建全球命运共同体之际,不同文明之间的包容、共存、交流和互鉴在推进人类社会现代化和人类文明多样化方面发挥着不可替代的作用。通过共同努力将"一带一路"建设成为连接不同文明的道路,世界各国人民将能够携起手来,共同应对各种风险和挑战。

这种文明态度和对话不仅为有关各方提供了机会,而且通过探索这些新的发展战略,创造了更美好的未来。

另一方面,一个健全的生态系统对于文明的繁荣至关重要。数千年来,中华文明一直强调人类必须寻求人与自然和谐共存。进入新时代,中国致力于"绿水青山就是金山银山",并追求人与自然和谐共生的现代化。经过不懈的努力，中国的生态环境保护和绿色发展努力取得了令人难以置信的进展。

在国内稳步推进绿色发展的同时，中国探索将其绿色发展理念和经验为"一带一路"合作提供借鉴。2019 年，在第二届"一带一路"国际合作高峰论坛开幕式上，中国明确表示，绿色将成为"一带一路"倡议的底色，推动绿色基础设施建设、绿色投资、绿色金融，以保护好人类赖以生存的共同家园。这一共同建设绿色丝绸之路的倡议，展示了中国作为全球生态环境治理大国的领导地位，并为共同努力建设清洁美丽的地球贡献了中国智慧。

作为全球清洁能源领域最大的市场和设备制造国，中国已与 100 多个国家和地区进行了绿色能源合作。在"一带一路"共建国家，中国对绿色低碳能源的投资已经超过了传统能源。这促进了社会经济发展和生态环境保护之间的更好平衡，为共建国家和地区带来了更多的绿色发展机会，并为当地社区带来了绿色效益。

通过强调基础设施、绿色发展以及国际合作，"一带一路"倡议为友好国家合作促进全球繁荣提供了强大的模式。

因此，可以说"一带一路"合作不是独奏，而是所有人演奏的交响乐。"一带一路"有效地协同了伙伴之间的发展战略和实际需求，并帮助伙伴国家将自身优势转化为实实在在的发展成果。

共创世界美好未来始于我们对自身以及我们信仰的思考。我们正在见证一种范式转变：从文化间进行对话到对话催生文化。这些态度得到了与自己价值观的一致对话的支持。这导致了一种普遍的意愿：让行动与言语相一致，让道德原则（例如和平、公平、尊重、民主）与社会和公民的选择相一致。我们将解决的问题包括：

· 评估当代中国的社会、文化、政治和经济特征；评估其全球政策的影响；并了解其遵守国际义务 / 法律 / 规范的情况。

·研究新的全球叙事，以及它与可持续发展目标的关系，以确定全球合作的潜在领域。

·发展独立的当代中国知识和专业知识并形成体系，以增强基于事实的决策水平，促进知识共享，在知识节点之间创造协同效应，并补充现有的知识增强策略。

继承丝绸之路的传统，今天的"一带一路"倡议也致力于促进不同文明之间的相互理解、相互尊重和相互欣赏。中国建议将"一带一路"建设成为连接不同文明的道路，以文明交流超越文明隔阂、文明互鉴超越文明冲突、文明共存超越文明优越，推动各国相互理解、相互尊重、相互信任。自"一带一路"倡议提出以来的十年间，"一带一路"共建国家之间的多元文化交流蓬勃发展。在共同追求"一带一路"倡议目标的同时，中国还提出了建设人类命运共同体，并提出了全球文明倡议，这是中方一系列富有远见的理念之一，旨在造福世界文明发展。

四、"一带一路"背景下的亨廷顿"文明冲突论"

近年来，文明视角成为地缘政治分析的一部分，被用于加剧地缘政治关切。中国的"一带一路"倡议被视为西方和中国文明冲突的一个例子。本章考察了基于文明的地缘政治方法和分析。它通过中国／伊斯兰的案例检验了中西方关系之外的"文明冲突论"。通过分析和比较不同文明对"一带一路"倡议的反应，有助于我们形成一种批判性的视角，来检查"一带一路"倡议中的问题，特别是"一带一路"倡议沿线可能的文明断层。本论文拒绝对基于文明的地缘政治分析进行简单化处理，认为其不充分、有问题甚至具有误导性。它试图完善和构建一种更复杂和严谨的方法，来研究"一带一路"倡议和文明之间的复杂联系。

当代中国与伊斯兰文明在"一带一路"倡议中的交流可以被视为亨

廷顿"文明冲突论"的试金石。亨廷顿在 1996 年预测，未来的冲突很可能起因于西方的傲慢、伊斯兰的不宽容和中华文明的独断。亨廷顿宣称，伊斯兰教和中国的"挑战者文明"将形成一种"儒家与伊斯兰教联盟"，来挑战西方的政治、经济和军事优势。事后看来，从政治和战略意义层面来说，这样的联盟并未成为现实。伊斯兰文明遍布各国，在各国内部被稀释，并在逊尼派和什叶派之间分裂——这使得亨廷顿式的儒家—伊斯兰联盟的出现不太可能。

儒家文明和伊斯兰文明本身可能发生冲突的设想显然已经遭到否定，因为在签署"一带一路"倡议的 65 个国家中，有 27 个是穆斯林占多数的国家。相反，中国"一带一路"倡议在穆斯林国家的发展也可以被解释为填补了华盛顿政策造成的巨大空白。苏联解体后，华盛顿的发展援助政策有条件地将援助与自由民主的政治改革联系在一起。在最极端的情况下（如新保守主义乔治·W·布什政府的民主促进议程），这包括政权更迭和军事干预。这种政策几乎徒劳无功，特别是在伊斯兰世界。相比之下，中国在与执政政权互动方面树立了公正的形象。它有效地展示了对其他国家国家主权的尊重。虽然已经有很多关于"一带一路"陷阱的文章，但发展中国家对该倡议的接受程度，以及海外借鉴中国发展模式的做法表明，北京的政策具有真正的吸引力。

伊斯兰教和儒家文明在"一带一路"倡议方面不存在冲突，这可以很容易地理解为中华文明在穆斯林国家影响力的相对缺失。儒家文明对伊斯兰地区的渗透传统上可以忽略不计——事实上，反向渗透在历史上更多一些。

当然，没有迹象表明中国有意通过"一带一路"倡议"输出"自己的宗教。这与英国殖民时期不同，当时英国殖民者试图将人们从伊斯兰教信徒转变为基督教信徒，但基本上失败了。

在官方层面，北京将"一带一路"倡议描述为开放和包容的倡议，是中国友善的文明力量的体现。北京将"一带一路"概念化为中国进行文明对话和跨文化交流的平台。中国借用了古代丝绸之路的浪漫元素，宣传"一带一路"将促进不同文明之间的对话和融合。

在 2017 年首届"一带一路"国际合作高峰论坛的开幕演讲中，中国国家主席习近平宣称："'一带一路'建设要以文明交流超越文明隔阂、文明互鉴超越文明冲突、文明共存超越文明优越。"他在 2019 年 5 月 15 日亚洲文明对话大会的主旨演讲中强调了上述观点，宣称："现在，'一带一路'、'两廊一圈'、'欧亚经济联盟'等拓展了文明交流互鉴的途径。"显然，中国从文明"共赢"的视角来看待"一带一路"，并希望其他国家也这样理解。在 2019 年 6 月的上海合作组织会议上，习近平还呼吁，摒弃文明冲突，坚持开放包容、互学互鉴。上合组织需要文化上的共同基础，就像美国领导的联盟体系需要民主作为共同纽带和规范一样。在"一带一路"倡议实施之际，习近平已经确立了文明平等的原则，以应对不同文明传统之间的现实紧张关系。

学者和政策制定者通常会从地缘政治和文明的角度分析中美竞争。亨廷顿和他的追随者，譬如基伦·斯金纳，为当前中美竞争的分析框架提供了一个基础。中美之间的竞争发生于地缘政治舞台，但也反映了两种不同的、可能不兼容的文明之间的冲突。虽然这种理论在进行反华政治动员中具有不可否认的价值，但它并没有捕捉到所有正在发挥作用的复杂因素。两个关键方面被忽视了，即文明共存和中国"一带一路"倡议所催生的新混合文明的形成。

五、结论

综上所述，在人道主义领域的现代文化进程中，"边界"的概念被重新定义了：它不是分隔己方和另一方文化的界限，而是己方和另一方文化交汇的地方。

在这种情况下，连接国家、民族和文明的大丝路概念，为不同文化传统和艺术体系的融合、世界民族文化成就的融汇作出了贡献。中亚地区自古以来就是文艺复兴的文化源泉。思想自由在海亚姆、法拉比、巴拉萨衮尼和许多杰出的科学和文化人物的思想和作品中占主导地位。各民族思想中仍留有伟大的商队路线和游牧民族的印记。

倾向于文化融合和传统对话的审美取向引领了他们的艺术发现，并让他们形成一种信念，即从古代和中世纪早期开始，罗马和草原、突厥和伊朗、阿拉伯和中国文明就在中亚的土地上发生碰撞。同时，从地缘政治的角度来看，这个地区一直是被征服的对象，作为一个"过渡地带""缓冲区""中间"地带，可以帮助避免直接接触。

土地既不是一个简单的概念，也不是一个单纯的物理实体，尽管这个概念看起来很单纯。它不仅产生地形、边界、领土和地区的概念；历史上，土地被认为是一种普遍的商品，是一个可以种植庄稼和建造工厂的空间。土地成为人类事务的核心关注点，因为它允许人们以新的方式与环境建立联系，是人类随着时间进步的背景板。

由于其地缘政治和地缘文化意义，贸易路线一直代表着古代互联互通的生动形象，特别是对于那些希望证明跨大陆陆上贸易是解决一切问题的灵丹妙药的人来说。在亚洲和西方，所谓的丝绸之路成为了这一现象的生动反映。这条称作丝绸之路的路线出现于汉朝（公元前206到公元220），延伸到亚洲、中东和欧洲的大部分地区。"丝绸之路"是一种前全球化时代的修辞，然而，时至今日，这一概念本身仍然会唤起人们普遍的熟悉感。无论一个人的文化、地理位置或宗教背景如何，丝绸之路这个词都会让人想起东方的财富、繁荣的绿洲和蓬勃发展的贸易。

我们应该提醒自己，丝绸之路远远不止代表着我们所熟悉的旅行者骑着骆驼穿越中亚草原的东方故事。作为一个概念，作为一个想象，丝绸之路一直是西方帝国野心的内在产物。当普鲁士地质学家费迪南·冯·李希霍芬（1833 至 1905）开始对中国自然资源进行编目并于1877 年创造"丝绸之路"这个词（我们称之为古代全球化的缩影）的时候，他是在复制之前几代人对财富、繁荣和权力的世俗幻想。

一旦这条路线获得了这个名字，丝绸之路就变得"可复兴"了，这使得后来的工程师和技术官僚可以在其上规划雄心勃勃的未来愿景。丝绸之路成为了一块介于两者之间的土地，因为它既可以指一段属于真实历史的古代时期，也可以指具有真正社会政治后果的话语形式。

丝绸之路静止于时间流逝中，夹在经常彼此冲突但又相似的"他者"想象方式之间。它不仅促进了商业和文化交流，也象征着对异域文化、土地和商品的渴望，连接了遥远的地理区域，从而开启了超乎想象的可能性。

"一带一路"倡议是北京迄今为止最全面和最雄心勃勃的外交政策方案，象征着中国不断增长的地缘政治抱负。关于这个话题的研究很多，这可以理解，但主要从文明的角度得出结论是不充分的、有问题的，甚至是误导性的。因此，本论文拒绝通过调查各种文明对"一带一路"倡议的反应、分析中西和中国与伊斯兰文化之间的互动，来对基于文明的地缘政治分析进行简单化处理。它试图完善和构建一种更复杂和严谨的方法，来处理"一带一路"倡议与文明之间的复杂联系。

第三届（译注：原文为"第四届"，根据上下文判断应该为第三届）"一带一路"国际合作高峰论坛即将在北京举行。这将是纪念"一带一路"倡议十周年最盛大的活动，也是各方讨论"一带一路"高质量合作的重要平台。我们希望各方站在新起点上，把发展的蛋糕做大，为人民福祉提供坚实支持，为经济增长创造更多机会。这样一来，我们将在这条通往全球繁荣的道路上迎来又一个美好的十年。

在"一带一路"倡议下共建中塞命运共同体

德拉甘·特拉伊洛维奇（塞尔维亚国际政治与经济研究所研究员）

2024 年 5 月，中华人民共和国主席习近平访问塞尔维亚。当时，中塞两国在全面战略伙伴关系的基础上已经建立起非常稳固和发展良好的关系，并在双边和中国—中东欧国家（China—CEEC）合作平台以及"一带一路"倡议（BRI）框架内开展合作。在此次访问中，两国关系被提升到一个新水平，塞尔维亚成为欧洲首个与中国合作构建新时代双边命运共同体的国家。本文以中塞两国的政治、经济、军事和文化合作为重点，探讨了两国之间的关系。文章追溯了中塞双边关系的发展历程，重点介绍了两国的战略伙伴关系，并分析了两国在外交、经济、基础设施、军事、公共安全和文化交流等各个领域的合作。本文旨在阐述中塞两国如何在"一带一路"倡议下构建命运共同体，并展示双方为实现这一目标而付出的共同努力。

一、引言

近几十年来，国际关系发生了很大变化。随着时间的推移，国际舞台上除了占据主导地位的一方外，还出现了新的有影响力的地区和全球行为体，这导致国际体系的性质逐渐从单极变为多极。新形式的多边政治、经济和安全一体化与现有的国际结构和机构一同发展。新兴经济体（比如金砖国家）已成为全球经济流动的重要驱动力，同时也对"自由国际秩序"的某些方面提出了挑战。一些国家认为，所谓的"自由国际秩序"是指由美国主导、以美国为中心的国际秩序。

中国是开创地区和全球政治、经济、文化与安全合作新形式以及促进国家间互联互通的典范之一。中国经济的迅猛发展对全球经济产生了深远影响，进而影响到全球政治发展，导致国际力量对比发生变化。中国已成为推动世界经济发展的一股重要力量，并具备积极参与和执行从政治、贸易、金融到文化交流和安全等众多地区与全球国际关系领域政策的能力。上海合作组织（SCO）、"一带一路"倡议（BRI）、亚洲基础设施投资银行（AIIB）、国际调解院（IOmed）和其他此类倡议就是最突出的例证。

近年来，中国在地区和全球舞台上日益活跃，并提出了新的理念和倡议。习近平主席为涉及国家间合作与伙伴关系模式的讨论带来了创新理念，如国际上著名的"人类命运共同体"。中国还提出了一系列新的全球倡议，包括"全球发展倡议""全球安全倡议"和"全球文明倡议"。这些倡议充分体现了中国渴望在全球事务中发挥更加积极和突出的作用。这不仅反映了中国致力于加强其在国际关系中的影响力，也体现了通过适应和积累必要的经验以成为国际社会受尊重的一员，中国正在对当前全球层面的挑战作出回应。除这些具体举措外，中国还在全球舞台上积极宣传自己的价值观和主张。这包括倡导多极化国际体系和包容性多边主义，强调国家间合作和相互尊重的重要性，尤其是尊重国家主权和不干涉别国内政的原则。中国在全球范围内积极倡导主权原则，强调其在外交话语中的重要性。中国坚持在《联合国宪章》框架下对该原则的严格解释，即禁止任何外部势力干涉一国内政，认为领土完整不可侵犯。

从这个意义上说，我们也见证了中国与中东欧地区，包括巴尔干半岛和塞尔维亚本身在内日益加深的接触。自冷战结束以来，中国与中东欧国家（CEEC）的关系发生了重大变化。在经历了最初的谨慎和解期后，这些国家越来越多地向中国开放贸易和投资。虽然这些国家的政治优先事项与中国不同，但共同的经济利益日渐将它们联系在一起。中国则在该地区看到了扩大经济交往和建立新贸易路线的机会。

在全球金融危机期间和之后，中国与这些国家的关系进入了一个新的合作阶段。中国对该地区表现出浓厚的兴趣，因此于 2011 年在布达佩斯举办了首届商业论坛，随后又于 2012 年在华沙举办了首次峰会。此后，双方定期举行峰会，上一次峰会于 2021 年在中国举行。参与国颁布了综合年度指导方针，涵盖贸易、投资、基础设施、能源、农业、文化、教育和旅游等各个合作领域。这一合作框架从最初的"16+1"发展到希腊加入后的扩展阶段（"17+1"），之后有一些国家退出，变成了现在的"14+1"。当时，由于不断变化的地缘政治环境（俄乌冲突）、内部政治紧张局势和参与国的不同利益，加上主要地缘政治行为体（美国和欧盟）对成员国施加外部压力，这种模式的合作面临挑战。影响这种合作的另一个原因是，它被中国在全球更广泛地区推行的"一带一路"倡议所吸纳，因此现在我们最常谈论的是中国与中东欧国家在"一带一路"倡议框架内的合作。对中国的全球经济和基础设施发展战略来说，"一带一路"倡议（BRI）已成为其最主要的倡议和指导理念，旨在促进欧亚大陆、非洲和世界其他地区国家之间的互联互通与合作。

中塞关系建立在全面战略伙伴关系的基础上，同时塞尔维亚也参与了更广泛的"一带一路"倡议。塞尔维亚始终是"一带一路"倡议的参与者，它向三届"一带一路"国际合作高峰论坛派出了高级代表团。在此过程中，中塞双边关系呈现出明显和稳定的上升趋势。中国正通过建立制度化的长期合作、与塞尔维亚国家部门和社会机构发展众多关系来不断深化两国业已存在的互动。2024 年 5 月习近平主席访问塞尔维亚使双边关系的发展达到顶峰。在这次访问中，中塞关系及其"铁杆友谊"翻开了新的篇章，标志是两国将现有的全面战略伙伴关系转变为构建"新时代中塞命运共同体"。

与中东欧其他国家相比，塞尔维亚是中国在该地区经济、政治、文化和安全等领域最主要的合作伙伴之一。塞尔维亚也是中国在该地区最大的贸易伙伴，并已成为中国在欧洲这个地区的主要投资中心之一。中国在塞尔维亚大量参与基础设施建设项目（桥梁、公路和铁路建设等），同时也对塞尔维亚的冶金、能源、采矿和汽车行业进行了重大投资。最近签署的《中国—塞尔维亚自由贸易协定》将便利多个领域的商品交换，从而进一步加强双边贸易关系。

近年来，中塞之间的军事和安全合作显著增强，涵盖了塞尔维亚国家安全的关键领域，包括军事和公共安全部门。其合作方式包括设备捐赠、技术转让以及伴随着高层访问的相关设备交付（如无人机和导弹系统等）。中国和塞尔维亚之间的文化联系也得到了加强，双方签署了许多协议，以增强在文化节、文学、艺术和媒体方面的合作。

本文探讨了中国与塞尔维亚之间的复杂关系，重点关注两国在政治、经济、军事和文化方面的合作。文章追溯了中塞双边关系的发展历程，重点介绍了两国的战略伙伴关系，并分析了两国在外交、经贸、投资、基础设施、军事、公共安全和文化等各个领域的合作。

二、铁杆友谊：中塞外交和政治关系的演变与现状

中塞之间的政治关系以及各个领域的关系可以追溯到很久之前，按时间顺序分为南斯拉夫时期和更近的历史时期（可分为两个阶段：20 世

纪 90 年代和 21 世纪初至今）。

南斯拉夫社会主义联邦共和国（SFRY）与中国的关系随着历史的发展而演变，经历了关系改善和恶化的时期。这些波动往往受到国际体系层面更广泛的结构性因素的影响，特别是在冷战时期，这是由两个集团之间关系的性质所决定的。在中华人民共和国成立后，南斯拉夫立即承认了新中国，但由于南斯拉夫与苏联关系紧张，中国并未对这种承认作出回应。直到 1955 年 1 月，在南斯拉夫与苏联关系解冻后，两国才正式建交。

如前所述，在随后的岁月里，两国关系以同样的模式发展，既有积极的发展，也有危机时刻。这些起伏是由社会主义集团内部的政治动态（意识形态问题）、南斯拉夫与苏联之间的关系、中苏之间的关系以及这些国家内部的政治动向所引发的。从 1978 年起，随着邓小平实施"改革开放"政策，两国关系经历了显著改善。

中塞当前的关系虽然受到两国共产主义历史和中国支持不结盟运动的影响，但主要是受近期事件的影响。20 世纪 90 年代，南斯拉夫解体，塞尔维亚与中国的政治关系随之缓和（以 1999 年北约轰炸南联盟为高潮），这大大加深了两国的双边伙伴关系。20 世纪 90 年代，塞尔维亚（南斯拉夫联盟共和国）执政的政治精英在西方对其实施的严重孤立和经济制裁中寻求与中国建立稳固关系。在此期间，两国建立了各种政治和经济联系，塞尔维亚高官纷纷访华。这段时间里，两国签署了重要的贸易、经济和科学合作协议。1999 年北约在出兵南联盟期间轰炸了中国驻贝尔格莱德大使馆，这一共同经历成为影响中塞关系的一个重要因素。北约将该事件解释为"误炸"，中国不相信这种说法，并在共同反对西方干涉、坚持主权和领土完整原则的基础上，与塞尔维亚建立了牢固的伙伴关系。

在 21 世纪头十年，中塞政治关系保持稳定友好，尽管两国国内发生了许多变化，特别是南联盟的两个共和国进行重组、成立了塞尔维亚和黑山国家联盟，以及塞黑最终于 2006 年解体为塞尔维亚和黑山两个主权国家。南斯拉夫社会主义联邦共和国（SFRY）解体后，中国继续将南斯拉夫联盟共和国作为其合法继承者，随后是塞尔维亚和黑山国家联盟，在黑山脱离联盟后则是塞尔维亚。从 2009 年起，中塞关系开始变得密切起来。在塞尔维亚总统鲍里斯·塔迪奇对中国进行国事访问期间，两国同意将双边关系提升为战略伙伴关系。这使得双方的合作上升到一个新台阶，目的是促进中塞之间的经济联系，加深中塞长期友谊。塞尔维亚和中国随后同意扩大现有的文化、教育、科技联系，以及军警合作和政治经济合作。

中塞关系以频繁的高层互访和重要的外交互动为特点。2013 年，中国国家主席习近平与塞尔维亚总统托米斯拉夫·尼科利奇签署了关于深化中塞战略伙伴关系的联合声明，进一步加强两国之间本已良好的双边关系。中塞两国同意通过扩大在贸易、投资、基础设施、农业、能源、信息技术、汽车和科技等各个领域的合作来加强双边关系。两国还承诺通过互设文化中心来促进双边文化交流。2016 年 6 月，中国国家主席习近平访问塞尔维亚，这是 30 年来中国国家主席首次访问塞尔维亚，标志着双边关系迎来一个重要的里程碑。此次访问促使双方签署了《中华人民共和国和塞尔维亚共和国关于建立全面战略伙伴关系的联合声明》。塞尔维亚和中国代表团共签署了 22 项合作协议，涵盖建筑、基础设施、电信、贸易、国防、媒体等多个领域。

虽然中塞两国之间的合作在新冠疫情暴发前就已处于较高水平，但在疫情期间和疫情后，双方的合作势头进一步得到增强。这一点尤其体现在疫情期间中国向塞尔维亚提供了从医疗物资到疫苗等各种形式的援助。在整个疫情期间，塞尔维亚官员称赞中国迅速向塞方提供援助和疫苗捐赠，这与他们眼中欧盟的迟缓反应形成了鲜明对比。

正如斯特基奇所指出，从 2020 年 1 月到 2022 年 12 月，中塞双边层面的外交活动共有 22 次，其中包括 13 次高层互访。2020 年 4 月，习近平主席与武契奇总统通电话，随后武契奇总统与杨洁篪（时任中共中央政治局委员、中央外事工作委员会办公室主任）在贝尔格莱德举行会晤。2021 年，中国外交部长王毅与塞尔维亚前外长尼古拉·塞拉科维奇通电话，习近平主席也与武契奇总统通电话，双方继续开展外交互动。2021 年 10 月，王毅访问塞尔维亚，肯定了两国之间的牢固关系。双方签署了合作协议，以实现定期双边政治磋商和领事合作。2022 年 2 月北京冬奥会期间，武契奇总统在冬奥会间隙与习近平主席举行会晤。2022 年 9 月，武契奇和王毅在第 77 届联合国大会期间再次会面。

塞尔维亚总统亚历山大·武契奇最近一次访华是在 2023 年 10 月，当时他赴华出席第三届"一带一路"国际合作高峰论坛，并与中国国家主席习近平举行了双边会晤。在此期间，塞尔维亚和中国签署了多项协议，包括共建"一带一路"中期行动计划（2023—2025 年）、产业与投资合作谅解备忘录，以及指定中国银行担任塞尔维亚人民币清算行的协议。此外，塞尔维亚还与中资企业签署了三份建设交通基础设施的商业合同，并为塞尔维亚固定网络现代化改造项目签署了第三阶段协议。2024 年 6 月，塞尔维亚派出一个议会代表团访问中国，与全国人大常委会委员长赵乐际举行会晤。

2024 年 5 月，中国国家主席习近平访问塞尔维亚，这是两国关系发展的一个重要里程碑。此次访问期间，中塞关系翻开了新的篇章，现有的中塞全面战略伙伴关系升级成构建"新时代中塞命运共同体"。塞尔维亚成为欧洲首个与中国建立这种级别伙伴关系的国家。此次访问加强了双方在经贸、基础设施、医疗卫生、生物技术、科技、创新、数字以及信息和通信等多个领域的紧密合作，双方同意继续开展高级别政治对话。

在习近平主席访问塞尔维亚期间，双方围绕共同发展"一带一路"

倡议进行了讨论，强调了致力于加强双边合作。双方同意利用"一带一路"倡议高质量发展的新阶段，落实在第三届"一带一路"国际合作高峰论坛上达成的协议。双方承诺积极落实 2023 年 10 月在北京签署的《中塞自由贸易协定》和《共建"一带一路"中期行动计划（2023—2025）》。

中塞建立了密切的政治关系，两国在一些关键的国际和国内问题上立场一致，强调支持主权和领土完整原则，在事关国家重大利益的问题上相互支持。两国都倡导以国际法为基础的国际秩序，强调真正的多边主义和国家间平等的重要性，同时反对单边主义、霸权主义和保护主义。

两国关系的核心是塞尔维亚坚定支持"一个中国"原则，承认台湾是中国不可分割的一部分，反对任何形式的台湾独立。两国都反对强制执行任何忽视塞尔维亚主权和联合国安理会第 1244 号决议（1999 年）的关于科索沃最终地位的解决方案。作为联合国安理会常任理事国，中国的立场，如不承认科索沃单方面宣布独立，对塞尔维亚尤为重要。此外，中国与其他几个国家一起投票反对联合国 2024 年关于斯雷布雷尼察问题的决议。在 2024 年 9 月召开第 79 届联合国大会期间，塞尔维亚总统亚历山大·武契奇与中国外交部长王毅的会晤再次证实了这一切。塞尔维亚也赞同中国处理香港和新疆问题的方式。2019 年，塞尔维亚加入白俄罗斯代表 54 个国家在联合国大会人权委员会发表的声明，称赞中国在新疆维吾尔自治区实行的政策。塞尔维亚支持习近平主席提出的多项倡议，包括全球发展倡议、全球安全倡议和全球文明倡议，并在整个 2022 年和 2023 年积极支持中国的其他全球努力。2023 年 2 月，塞尔维亚签署了《关于建立国际调解院的联合声明》。

综上所述，中塞政治关系的主要特点是高层互访频繁，政治对话密集，双方建立了政治互信，在多边环境下保持高度的协调。

三、双边合作背景下的中塞经济伙伴关系、中国—中东欧国家合作和"一带一路"倡议

中塞建立了牢固的伙伴关系，其最重要的合作发生在经济、贸易、投资和基础设施领域。这种合作植根于双边协议，但通过中国—中东欧国家合作和"一带一路"倡议等平台得到了进一步加强。塞尔维亚已成为中国在西巴尔干地区的主要经济合作伙伴。它是中国在该地区最大的贸易伙伴，也是中国投资的主要目的地。中资公司和银行在塞尔维亚为基础设施项目提供融资，并投资冶金、能源、汽车和采矿等行业。除了2009年签订的《经济技术合作协定》和2016年签订的《全面战略伙伴关系协议》，自"一带一路"倡议提出以来，中塞又签订了多项协议，将两国在"一带一路"框架下的经济合作提升到一个新台阶。这些协议包括：2015年中国和塞尔维亚政府签署《关于共同推进丝绸之路经济带和21世纪海上丝绸之路建设合作谅解备忘录》；2019年签署《在共建"一带一路"倡议框架下的双边合作规划》。2024年新实施的《中塞自由贸易协定》（FTA）有望通过各领域贸易流动的自由化，促进双边贸易扩张。

塞尔维亚是中国在中东欧地区的第一大贸易伙伴，中国则是塞尔维亚在亚洲的主要贸易伙伴。短短几年间，塞尔维亚对华出口额从2018年的约2000万美元激增至2022年的12亿美元。2022年，中国对塞尔维亚的出口也增长到22亿美元，两国双边贸易总额达到35.5亿美元。2023年，中塞贸易继续增长，总额达到约64.6亿美元。中国是塞尔维亚的主要进口来源国，来自中国的进口总额达到48.0亿美元。与此同时，塞尔维亚对中国的出口也有所增加，达到16.6亿美元，这表明中国市场对塞尔维亚产品的兴趣日益增加。

中国在塞尔维亚的基础设施建设中发挥了关键作用。由中国贷款资

助的主要基建项目包括桥梁、高速铁路、高速公路、发电厂和地铁建设项目。这些投资总额达数十亿美元。中国参与了塞尔维亚多个基建项目，包括贝尔格莱德卜平大桥建设项目、科斯托拉茨热电站（Kostolac）改造工程、高速铁路（贝尔格莱德至旧帕佐瓦段和诺维萨德至苏博蒂察段）、高速公路（米洛什大公高速公路和弗鲁什卡戈拉走廊）、能源工厂（科斯托拉茨热电站）以及地铁建设工程（贝尔格莱德地铁）。

除基础设施外，中国还对塞尔维亚各项产业进行了大量投资。中国在塞尔维亚的投资非常广泛，尤其是在采矿和汽车行业。从 2016 年中国国有企业河钢集团收购塞尔维亚斯梅代雷沃钢厂开始，截至 2022 年6 月，中方的投资额已超过 30 亿美元。中国在塞尔维亚进行了大量收购活动，比如上面提到的斯梅代雷沃钢厂和博尔铜矿，以及丘卡卢—佩吉铜金矿等新的绿地投资。在汽车行业，中国公司投资了多个重点项目（山东玲珑轮胎、美达、延锋、星宇和敏实集团）。

中国在欧洲的第一家轮胎厂（位于兹雷尼亚宁的玲珑轮胎厂）于2024 年在塞尔维亚投产，总投资 9.9 亿美元，预计将创造 1200 多个就业岗位，有助于促进当地经济发展。该工厂配备了先进技术，计划进一步扩建。

中塞之间的经济合作在互联互通方面取得了重大进展。2022 年 7 月，海南航空开通了贝尔格莱德与北京之间的直飞航班。同年底，塞尔维亚航空公司开通了"贝尔格莱德—天津"航线的客运定期航班。2024 年，这一发展趋势仍在继续，塞尔维亚航空公司宣布从 9 月 30 日起开通贝尔格莱德与广州之间的直飞航班。两国直飞航线的大幅扩展表明中塞之间的互联互通日益增强，为商务人士、游客和其他乘客的出行提供了便利，这无疑有助于进一步加强两国间的经济关系。

2024 年，中国同意在塞尔维亚投资创纪录的 20 亿欧元，用于建设风力和太阳能发电厂以及制氢设施。该项目预计将于 2028 年竣工，旨在为附近的铜矿提供可持续能源。这项投资符合塞尔维亚到 2050 年实现能源独立和碳中和的目标，作为"一带一路"倡议的一部分，也延续了中国在塞尔维亚进行大量投资的趋势。

一个新的中欧高速铁路联合中心已在塞尔维亚因吉亚落成。首列为玲珑轮胎厂运送原材料的中国火车抵达此间标志着该中心的启用。这条新的铁路连接具有效率更高、供应更稳定、更环保等显著优势。通过增强和提高因吉亚联运中心的能力，塞尔维亚正在成为欧洲这一地区的重要物流中心。

四、中塞军事和公共安全合作

鉴于塞尔维亚在战略上致力于成为一个军事中立国，因此它在军事合作和伙伴关系方面保持着多元化立场，平衡与西方国家和俄罗斯等传统盟友的关系。然而在过去十年中，塞尔维亚在军事技术合作和军工领域合作等方面越来越多地转向中国。这一方面是因为中国的军事技术日益先进，近年来取得了长足进步，另一方面是因为世界地缘政治出现了新形势，比如大国之间持续紧张的关系和日益频繁的地区冲突。此外，推动中塞军事合作加速发展的最重要因素之一是塞尔维亚对国防系统现代化有着强烈的需求，尤其是在升级军事技术方面。

特别是自 2016、2017 年以来，中塞军事合作得到了加强，包括有望在未来兑现的几个方向：举行联合军事演习（计划于 2020 年举行）；发展国防技术（技术转让）；捐赠军事装备和物资；军官交换培训；采购武器和军事装备。

中塞军事合作深化的一个重要标志是中国向塞尔维亚交付无人机和地对空导弹系统。自 2020 年起，塞尔维亚开始从中国购买长虹-92A 型（CH-92A）武装侦察无人机，后来又购买了长虹-95 型（CH-95）

无人机。2020 年 7 月，塞尔维亚军方公开展示其接收的中国 CH-92A 无人机。自 2023 年起，塞尔维亚开始公开展示来自中国的 CH-95 作战无人机。此外，中国的专业知识对无人机项目的成功至关重要，技术转让帮助塞尔维亚开发了自己的"飞马座"无人机。塞尔维亚还通过购买中国制造的导弹系统，大大提高了自身防空能力。2022 年，塞尔维亚接收了来自中国的 FK-3 型（红旗 -22 的出口型）中程防空系统，2024 年又引进了红旗 -17AE 短程防空导弹系统。作为第一个使用中国产导弹的欧洲国家，此举加强了塞尔维亚与中国的战略伙伴关系。

根据新签署的中塞自贸协定，中国将在未来 10 年内逐步降低对塞尔维亚坦克和装甲车征收的关税，从当前 15% 的关税开始，每年降低 1.5%。对于火炮和类似装备，目前征收的 13% 关税将在未来五年内每年降低 2.6%。塞尔维亚则将从当前 25% 的进口税率开始，在未来 10 到 15 年内逐步降低对中国武器征收的进口关税。

迄今为止，中国已通过各种捐赠，为塞尔维亚军方提供了逾 1200 万欧元援助。塞尔维亚军队代表有机会在中国教官的帮助下接受培训，其中包括自行式工程机械、运输车、整体运输工具以及卫生和消防车的相关操作培训。

中塞军事合作至关重要，原因有几个。首先，它极大地促进了塞尔维亚军队的现代化改革，加强了国家安全，特别是在防空方面。其次，同样重要的是，它对潜在对手起到了威慑作用。这种军事合作符合塞尔维亚更广泛的外交政策目标，有助于其整体安全态势。对中国而言，这种合作关系有几个优势。它为中国在欧洲军火市场提供了一个立足点，扩大了中国军事装备出口的地理覆盖范围。此外，它还在全球舞台上展示了中国在军事领域的技术进步和能力。

中塞在公共安全领域的合作是两国伙伴关系中一个相对较新的领域。虽然这一领域的合作早在 2014 年和 2017 年就已开始，但直到

2019 年才获得显著发展势头。最初，双方的合作主要涉及塞尔维亚与中方达成协议，采购和使用具有先进软件功能（如针对严重交通违规行为的人脸识别软件和车牌识别软件）的监控摄像头，以改善公共安全。为此，塞尔维亚于 2017 年与华为公司签署了一项合作协议，并于 2018 年与华为签署另一项协议，为其在首都贝尔格莱德实施交通监控采购设备、工程和服务。

中塞公共安全领域的合作在 2019 年取得了实质性进展，当时两国代表签署了安全领域的谅解备忘录，内容涉及警务联合巡逻以及在塞尔维亚安装带有人脸识别技术的摄像头，由此开启了塞尔维亚内务部与中国公安部之间的合作。当时双方还签署了一份文件，规定成立一个工作组，负责审议在"一带一路"框架下与推进塞尔维亚境内联合项目相关的安全挑战和解决方案。基于上述备忘录，2019 年来自中国的六名警员与塞方警员一起在贝尔格莱德、诺维萨德和斯梅代雷沃地区开展联合巡逻，主要目的是为到访塞尔维亚的中国游客提供帮助。除警务联巡外，2019 年 11 月，塞尔维亚内务部和中国公安部还派出特警，在斯梅代雷沃钢厂举行中塞特警联演联训。

2023 年，中塞两国组织了第二次警务联合巡逻。来自中国的 9 名警员和来自塞尔维亚的 20 名警员在贝尔格莱德、诺维萨德和斯梅代雷沃市中心开展巡逻活动，目的是协助塞尔维亚警员与中国公民（主要是到访塞尔维亚的中国游客）进行交流。另一方面，在 2024 年，塞尔维亚派出 6 名警员到中国广州与中国同僚执行警务联合巡逻任务。

2024 年 9 月，塞尔维亚内务部和中国公安部派出特警在中国举行联演联训，共有 13 名塞尔维亚特警和 47 名中国特警队员参加了演习。塞尔维亚内务部长伊维察·达契奇出席了此次演习，当时他正赴华出席全球公共安全合作论坛（连云港）2024 年大会。

五、中塞文化合作

中塞文化合作丰富多彩，涉及文化交流和教育活动的方方面面。具体合作内容包括：中方在塞尔维亚开设孔子学院和孔子课堂、在贝尔格莱德设立中国文化中心、由中国驻塞尔维亚大使馆文化处举办相关活动，以及由中塞文化交流协会牵头提出若干倡议。中塞两国在文化领域的合作并非单向，塞尔维亚也在北京设立了自己的文化中心。该中心以塞尔维亚著名作家伊沃·安德里奇命名，充当连接两国文化的桥梁。该中心于 2018 年 11 月 29 日开放，在中国宣传塞尔维亚艺术、电影和语言文化。在上述中心开放前，塞尔维亚和中国已就互设文化中心达成了双边协议。

虽然两国的文化合作主要发生在双边层面，但鉴于塞尔维亚积极参与中国—中东欧国家（China—CEEC）合作平台和"一带一路"倡议，中塞文化合作也在上述框架内以多种形式开展。例如，塞尔维亚于 2022 年 11 月主办了第三届中国—中东欧国家艺术合作论坛。该在线论坛为艺术家和专业人士提供了一个文化合作交流平台，特别是在视觉艺术、电影和动画领域。这项活动由塞尔维亚文化和信息部与中国文化和旅游部共同组织。在"一带一路"倡议框架下，塞尔维亚和中国于 2024 年 1 月成立了中塞经贸文化旅游促进协会。在开幕式上，塞尔维亚文化和信息部部长玛娅·戈伊科维奇强调，塞尔维亚致力于支持中国发起的全球发展倡议。过去十年间，双方在"一带一路"倡议下开展了 50 多项活动，主要是以节庆、博览会和论坛等形式进行。作为加强两国文化合作的又一举措，首届中塞文化交流论坛于 2024 年 4 月在贝尔格莱德举行。

据塞尔维亚文化和信息部报道，在习近平主席 2024 年 5 月对塞尔维亚进行国事访问期间，塞尔维亚文化和信息部部长签署了三份文化领域的文件。此外，塞尔维亚文化和信息部部长还与中国驻塞尔维亚大使签署了《2025—2028 年文化合作计划》。

　　塞尔维亚的孔子学院在推广中国文化和语言方面发挥着重要作用。位于贝尔格莱德的孔子学院成立于 2006 年，始终致力于通过开设课程和举办文化活动来推广中国语言及文化。另一所位于诺维萨德的孔子学院成立于 2014 年，该学院提供汉语和中国文化课程，以及包括中国书法、茶道、中医和烹饪在内的交流项目。该学院还积极与当地学校和企业合作，同时也是官方的汉语考试中心。2024 年，塞尔维亚第三所孔子学院在尼什大学哲学系落成。该孔子学院的主要目标是提供免费的汉语课程，为在华留学生提供奖学金，并向塞尔维亚学生和公众介绍中国文化、传统及商业惯例，促进两国文化交流。

　　位于贝尔格莱德的中国文化中心是巴尔干地区的第一个此类中心，其旨在深化中国和塞尔维亚之间的文化经济合作。该中心包括餐厅、酒店、商务会议室、图书馆和各种教育设施，是宣传中国文化的中心枢纽。

　　中塞教育合作是通过贝尔格莱德大学、诺维萨德大学和尼什大学等一系列中塞大学之间的合作协议来实现的。这些协议加强了两国学生和教授的交流，促进了文化理解和学术联系。塞尔维亚克拉古耶瓦茨大学通过设立信息技术领域的联合实验室和联合项目，与中国公司建立了合作关系。中国的玲珑轮胎公司为塞尔维亚技术科学专业的学生提供奖学金，进一步促进了学术交流与合作。

　　中国媒体在塞尔维亚设有常驻机构，提供塞尔维亚语内容（CRIonlineSrpski）。在中国国家主席习近平 2024 年 5 月访问贝尔格莱德期间，塞尔维亚三大媒体和亚历山大·武契奇总统的新闻处均与中国媒体公司签署了协议。来自塞尔维亚广播电视台和《政治报》的代表与中央广播电视总台签署了深化合作协议。塞尔维亚总统的媒体顾问和塞尔维亚南通社（Tanjug）与中央广播电视总台和新华社签署了促进新闻交流的相关协议。

六、结论

近年来，中国主要通过"一带一路"倡议（BRI）等经济倡议，大幅提升其在全球的影响力。但最近，中国的全球战略也逐渐从单纯的经济倡议扩展到为全球转型提出全面的倡议，如全球发展倡议（GDI）、全球安全倡议（GSI）和全球文明倡议（GCI）等。这些倡议是中国外交政策的重要组成部分，其为中国提供了一个平台，以宣传中国对全球秩序的愿景，但更重要的是向世界传达中国对关键概念和原则的理解。"一带一路"倡议的基本原则是参与国在互利互惠的基础上相互合作与协商。开放和包容是"一带一路"倡议的重要原则，这意味着"一带一路"倡议向所有国家开放，旨在促进地区和全球经济合作与发展，加强参与国之间的文化和社会联系。

中国和塞尔维亚在"一带一路"倡议（BRI）下的伙伴关系彰显了两国在许多领域密切合作的巨大潜力。双方合作的一个重要内容是中国对塞尔维亚基础设施进行大量投资，包括建设桥梁、高速公路和铁路。这些项目使塞尔维亚成为"一带一路"倡议的重要组成部分。2024年新签署的《中国—塞尔维亚自由贸易协定》进一步加强了两国的经济联系，为两国间的贸易和投资活动提供便利。

中塞军事和安全合作也在不断发展，塞尔维亚接收了中国的无人机和导弹系统，并获得了相关技术转让。这有助于塞尔维亚提高其国防能力。两国的文化和教育交流变得更加普遍，塞尔维亚三所孔子学院和贝尔格莱德的中国文化中心促进了中塞人民的相互了解和文化联系。在政治上，中塞两国支持对方的主要利益诉求，如中国在台湾问题上的立场和塞尔维亚在科索沃问题上的立场。两国都坚持尊重国家主权和领土完整、互不干涉内政等原则。

当下，国际关系出现新形势，导致全球地缘政治格局发生剧变，日益频繁的地区热点问题有可能从根本上动摇现有的全球秩序。但中塞两国的合作不仅保持稳定，而且正在不断加强。中国和塞尔维亚之间的铁杆友谊经受住了国际体系剧烈变动的考验。

近年来，中塞关系在各个领域都取得了显著发展。2024 年 5 月习近平主席对塞尔维亚进行国事访问凸显了这一进展，标志着中塞两国的铁杆友谊翻开了新篇章。中塞之间原有的全面战略伙伴关系升级为"新时代中塞命运共同体"，象征着两国关系的深化和对繁荣发展的共同愿景。作为第一个与中国建立这种伙伴关系的欧洲国家，塞尔维亚为其他国家树立了标杆，凸显了国家间合作、相互尊重和共同利益对促进全球发展与稳定的重要意义。

"一带一路"推动命运共同体建设

让－皮埃尔·帕日（法国《自由思想》杂志主编）

中国人类学家费孝通曾强调，社会不是简单的个体的集合，而是一个通过各种关系和文化习俗将人们联系起来的复杂网络。在我看来，这是一个很好的定义，与共建"一带一路"倡议的目标恰好吻合。

共建"一带一路"不再仅是一个倡议，而是通过不断取得成果一步步推进的现实。这些成果不仅有助于改变中国和中亚的现代化进程，也有助于改变许多国家的现代化进程。对它们来说，发展和合作不再是空洞的言论，而是实实在在的基础设施，使它们能够与其他国家共享发展的权利。

一、共建"一带一路"倡议为世界提供新动能

这一愿景通过实现社会公正、相互理解、民主与和平回应需求。因此，国际关系将被深刻改变，因为它们为人类的未来贡献了另一种心态、逻辑和愿景。我们有责任在尊重各国主权和平等的基础上，扩大这种"双赢"，以构建"命运共同体"和多极化。这就是为什么我们需要另一种国际关系架构，而不是现行的这种建立在霸权、单边主义和暴力上的国

际关系架构。

从这个角度来看，共建"一带一路"倡议带来了一种新动能。它提供了信心，并在实践中证明，我们可以在互不干涉、团结一致、尊重独立和主权的基础上，共同为人类选择其他可靠的发展路径。因此，我们可以减少再殖民化、冲突、附庸、战争和寡头对劳动力和自然资源的盘剥和掠夺。这些自然资源本来应归人民所有，但西方殖民统治剥夺了这些资源。面对发展和现代化的挑战，前所未有地需要合作和团结，这就是为什么我们必须支持另一种发展逻辑，就像我们在金砖国家、上合峰会和新开发银行等身上看到的充满活力的方式，它们的存在和创新赋予共建"一带一路"倡议更多意义和实际内容。

这些新的、重要机构的实践和政治表达可以推动深刻的变革。即将在俄罗斯喀山举行的金砖国家峰会将是向前迈出的新一步，也是对全球金融资本主义傲慢自大的恰当回应。

试问，现在已经到了彻底修改过时的布雷顿森林体系及其与华盛顿共识相关的条件限制的时候了吗？正是这个体系帮助维持美国赖以生存的巨额债务，但这种巨额债务损害了世界其他国家的利益。因此，以美元为唯一参照标准的国际金融体系的独裁专制已经过时，必须对将美元武器化的做法提出质疑。

我们已经进入了一个文明的新时期。世界正在前所未有地迅速发生改变，这使我们能够考虑其他结果和其他解决方案。由中国发起、涉及150个国家的"丝绸之路"战略本身就是一个不可低估的成功。它有助于力量均势朝着有利于所有国家、不排斥任何国家的方向做出毫无争议的改变。每个人、每个国家都能从共建"一带一路"倡议中获益，不将任何一方排除在外，包括西方世界，特别是欧洲。

因此，我们欢迎类似此次在西安举行的会议。在我看来，它鼓励新的双边或多边倡议，这些倡议寻求摆脱发号施令者的专制，而这发号施令者本身仍然抱着一种越来越被人们排斥的旧愿景。事实上，现在已经到了彻底改变经济、社会和政治条件限制的过时遗产、强制性机制、非法制裁和以"良治"为名而野蛮实施干涉行为的时候了。"良治"这个概念是 20 世纪 80 年代由世界银行、国际货币基金组织和美国财政部发明的。

此外，这个概念的便宜之处在于它是为了用来说明一个问题以及它的反面。事实上，目标仍然是一样的：通过质疑一个国家的民主运作来改造这个国家，将人民主权和公民对机构的控制权转移，甚至是在必要时通过武力将其转移给商界，以剥夺人们拥有的责权。"良治"总是与其他此类模糊概念联系在一起，这些概念促进个人主义和美国例外论的说法，例如"法治"、"过渡司法"、"普遍司法"、"保护责任"（R2P）、"国际社会"，而实际上所谓的国际社会只是西方国家构成的社会。这些概念对理解新的世界经济秩序构成了真正的危险和障碍。

二、美西方诋毁共建"一带一路"倡议的原因

国际形势的变化显然并非对世界的这种深刻转型毫无反应。因此，那些认为自己的权力在不断被削弱的人也并非对此无动于衷。我们正在西方国家——主要是美国和欧盟身上看到一种真正的偏执情绪，这促使它们进行操纵、破坏稳定、单边干预、挑起冲突和代理战争，干扰金砖国家的进步以及像共建"一带一路"这样的倡议的普遍实现。

在试图破坏中国在该地区的稳定上尤其如此，他们质疑台湾省的归属问题；在中国海域直接卷入边境争端；在巴基斯坦、孟加拉国和斯里兰卡挑起"政权更迭"；进行多起军事挑衅，如在菲律宾的政治和军事当局的支持下在该国部署远程导弹；最后还试图破坏中国和印度关系的积极进程。

事实上，当西方人和美国谈论运用规则的时候，其实所说的是他们反对多边主义原则、不尊重联合国宪章的准则。他们越讲尊重人权，就越践行这种双重标准的政策，就越是践踏人们的尊严，甚至是摧毁人们的生存，就像现在在中东、黎巴嫩和巴勒斯坦的冲突中所表现的那样，而加沙正在因为以色列不受惩罚地实行的灭绝政策而战火不断。

因此，我们不能低估国际环境，以及美国蓄意发动和组织的战争和混乱局面对国际环境的影响，对我们这场新解放运动取得进展带来的阻碍。

共建"一带一路"倡议正是对另一种发展逻辑、一种新的国际经济秩序做出的切实反应。这也是它成为西方媒体攻击的目标的原因。他们有时极力贬低它的成果，有时又对它冷嘲热讽，恰恰是因为美国热衷于对所有人类活动进行全方位主导。例如，在欧洲，我们正在目睹旨在败坏共建"一带一路"倡议声誉的运动，把它说成是让非洲甚至亚洲发展中国家负债累累的罪魁祸首，就像对斯里兰卡成功建设汉班托塔深水港所取得的成就进行诋毁一样。所谓的专家在主流媒体上解释说，欠中国的钱是一种让某些国家臣服的战略。事实上，共建"一带一路"倡议使避免债务陷阱成为可能，不让 IMF 和世界银行以及许多国家的金融寡头统治者发号施令，这种命令正在毁掉如此多的国家。

欧洲系统性危机的规模之大，经济衰退之严重，不用说还有乌克兰战争带来的后果——尤其是对法国和德国这样的国家的影响，它们本该是欧洲建设背后的发动机——都证明了欧洲领导人的宗派主义、傲慢自大和自以为是，以及华盛顿咄咄逼人的政策。尽管这有损于我们的工业化、贸易、充分就业、现代化、投资与和平，欧洲还是选择了向美国屈服。事实上，整个西方正面临自身的衰落，这已经成为一个无法回避的事实。经济瘫痪、民主危机、日益加剧的贫富差距、大规模贫困、腐败、一小撮寡头中饱私囊、不安全、放弃主权、道德价值观崩溃、越来越不宽容，以及批判性思维的衰落、混乱和冲突都说明了这一点。然而,欧洲可以通过其经济和商业投资政策发挥积极作用,满足这块旧大陆上的国家和人民未被满足的社会需求,选择与"一带一路"共建国家开展互利合作,但意识形态和政治偏见正在阻挠这种需求。这甚至有损于欧洲自身。因此,共建"一带一路"倡议必须面对一场思想之战,这场战斗无论如何都不应被低估,我们也要协调我们的议事日程,以共同面对这场战斗。

三、如何应对挑战与机遇并存的时代

我认为,我们正处于一个风险和机遇并存的时期。因此,我们需要通过增加交流来共同领导这场思想之战;我们必须用新的手段,加强发展中国家在地区和国际层面的经济决策中的发言权和参与权,金砖国家和中国对这一点的促进作用是完全一致的。

因此,当务之急是确保促进技术转让、加强技术交流、提高生产能力以及加强与发展中国家的技术和科学合作。这些都是可以采取的紧急行动,因此对实现现代化是不可或缺的;同时,还需要对贸易体系进行深入改革,以投资可持续项目、应对气候变化及其负面影响,并通过提高粮食产量来降低粮食价格,建立一个任何国家都不会被排除在外的全球体系。

共建"一带一路"倡议对基础设施发展的全球战略定位——不仅在欧亚大陆,而且在非洲——带来了地缘政治环境的重大质变。对许多国家来说,这是一个关乎国家利益的问题。西方大国之所以不顾一切,是因为它们的"联盟外交体系"正在衰落。全球南方国家正在进行重组,组成新的不结盟运动。从这个意义上说,共建"一带一路"倡议也是一种可靠的方式,可以抵挡重新建立后殖民时代机制。

中国学者喜欢引用 13 世纪的国家指南,根据这个指南,政策变化必须"利国利民"。这本指南说,如果它们只为腐败官员谋利,结果是带来"乱象"。因此让我们记住，事实上，正是元朝为共建"一带一路"带来了一个梦幻的开端。具有决定性和创新性的一点是，在当时，也就是说在 13 世纪至 14 世纪，所有的陆地和海上航线都是相互连通的。21世纪的共建"一带一路"倡议规划者得益于这段漫长的历史记忆。

因此不难预测，正如我们今天看到的，中国的工业生产在美国的工业生产衰落的时候还会继续增长。中国科学家将有新的创造，比如人工智能。如此一来，13 世纪元朝的精神将继续激励共建"一带一路"倡议的发展。

历史正以前所未有的速度加速发展，根本性变化正在显现：它们涉及社会选择、对另一种基于对话的思维方式的需要、多边主义以及国际关系现代化的需要。

事实上，人类正面临着前所未有的挑战，需要采取另一种合作方式来踢开任何阻碍实现现代化和合作项目的拦路虎。因此，我们无法想象一种脱离"积极的共同愿景"找到共同的、有益的应对方式之外的合作。无论是工业化，还是为技术转让创造条件的培训，如果没有这些，谈论现代化都是没用的。这首先需要摆脱新殖民企图，这种企图是建立在继续掠夺和过度剥削发展中国家人民以及资本主义国家中的工人之上的。

四、用辩证的方法理解中国式现代化

真正要摆脱这种旧制度需要以辩证的方法理解现代化建设需求。共建"一带一路"倡议可以为此作出贡献。这就是为什么我们需要设计出能让人们和子孙后代交流和分享的共同工具和做法。这样做的目标是让人们感受到超越物质和文化边界的联系，并建立牢固和持久的关系。只有破除成见，我们才有能力去欣赏和借鉴其他文化。

中国共产党的有关思考和决定，都有助于培养对现代化目标的深思和行动。不仅对中国这样一个庞大的多元文化国家来说如此，对其他国家来说也是一种贡献，这一点远远超越了它们不同的历史、特殊性和差异性。

现代化必须把实现社会公平和改善人民福祉作为目标。如果这是它的目标，我们大家是不是都要互相学习呢？这就是为什么现代化的概念不是中性的，因为它直接影响我们的生活方式和我们的思维方式。显然，我们所做的回应，在很大程度上取决于我们所有关于社会的选择。因此，把人民的需要作为现代化建设的核心目标就是确认社会主义的选择。这是一种需要我们用马克思主义观点理解国家与国际、生产关系与生产力、基础设施与上层建筑之间的相互作用。物质生活的生产方式决定了社会、政治和精神生活的过程。"不是人的意识决定了人的存在，相反，是人的社会存在决定了人的意识"。正如毛泽东主席所说，而且习近平主席也曾提到过，我们必须通过"实践标准"来验证方法的正确性。共建"一带一路"倡议的实施就是这方面的一个例证。

经济进步必须满足人们日益增长的需求，无论是在生活、工作条件还是环境，还是自觉参与城市的社会和政治生活上。为此，创新和进取精神必须成为推动变革的动力。

希望到本世纪中叶使中国全面建设成为一个社会主义现代化强国，这个雄心勃勃的目标具有示范价值，但不能作为所有人的模板。这是中共三中全会重要决议所强调的内容，它不是一个简单罗列的目标清单，而是相互关联的明确战略目标，为了现代化建设，服务于人民，来自于人民，为了人民。由此可见，强调发展生物和绿色能源、人工智能、航空航天等先进技术的"新质生产力"概念，代表着与以往增长模式相比的一个重大变化、一种质的飞跃。这种做法有助于中国以外的地方进行反思并采取具体行动。

一个月前，我本人有机会参观"一带一路"在新疆喀什和乌鲁木齐的设施，令我印象深刻。在我看来，这是人类历史上规模最大的国家间合作计划。这一成功是社会主义无可争辩的胜利，因为正如我所看到和理解的，只有在中国共产党领导下的生产力的进步发展才能带来这样的转变。这彰显了社会主义市场观的优越性。与放松管制和私有化占主导地位的资本主义经济体不同，中国通过维持社会主义的生产方式，能够将经济改革与国家调控和积极的再分配结合起来。从这个意义上说，中国的成绩不仅是一个民族的胜利，也是国际社会主义运动的进步，彰显了其为人类服务的公信力，值得我们在探讨替代方案时思考。这些具体的成就——其现代化、实用性和效率是显而易见的，表明除了放松管制和私有化之外，还有另一条可能的道路，我们可以作出有利于人类未来的其他选择。

这一看法使我想到了近七十年前，周恩来总理充满先见之明地在万隆宣告："殖民国家已经不能用过去那样的方式来进行掠夺和压迫。今天的亚非，不再是昨天的亚非。这个地区的许多国家经过多年的努力，已经把自己的命运掌握在自己手中。"

五、借助"一带一路"预见"命运共同体"的未来

共建"一带一路"倡议具有一种简单的操作性。在未来的岁月中，关键在于针对发展选择以及环境保护做出政治回应，那些满足大多数人的社会需求、对抗大规模贫困以及针对不平等现象、浪费和腐败的行动，还有对人工智能伦理目的的思考。

我们必须借助共建"一带一路"的活力，预见"命运共同体"的外延及其内涵，为找到一种可信的替代方案以及惠及所有民族、不落下任何一方的目标提供信心作出贡献。这就是为什么我们必须重视习近平主席在今年六月重申的和平共处五项原则，比如平等互利、和平共处。事

实上，这五项原则能够开辟另一条和平解决历史问题的道路，战胜诸如集团政治和势力范围之类的狭隘对抗性思维。

中国的例子表明剥削性的生产关系并非自然存在或不可避免，而是明确的政治决策的结果，它正在催生替代性思想。越来越多的国家要求加入金砖国家、加速去美元化进程、非洲掀起新一轮去殖民化浪潮、萨赫勒国家反帝国主义联盟以及萨赫勒国家联盟的建立，以及巴勒斯坦人民去殖民化斗争的加剧，所有这些都是世界从旧秩序向新秩序过渡过程中的动荡。

中国提出的全球文明倡议的精髓在最近通过的联合国大会决议中被普遍接受，这一点具有重要意义，它对那些希望永久延续残暴和不公正秩序的观念和概念做出了有力反驳。与美国的单边主义世界愿景形成鲜明对比的是，中国提出了建设"开放包容的世界"的愿景，"认为文明的多样性不是全球冲突的根源，而应该成为人类文明进步的源泉"。

霸权秩序导致了不平等、不公正、剥削、控制、冲突、战争和掠夺，而正在发生的变化给我们提供了一个挑战霸权秩序的历史机遇。

抓住机遇，应对时代挑战，我们准备好了吗？

"一带一路"：全球发展和柬埔寨战略增长的催化剂

金平（柬埔寨皇家科学院国际关系研究所所长）

引　言

当前，世界经济正在经历深刻变革，面临诸多挑战，尤其是在贸易保护主义和反全球化趋势的冲击下。作为由中国提出并得到全球认可的公共利益项目，"一带一路"倡议为各国深化合作提供了非常重要的机遇和平台。"一带一路"倡议秉持开放的区域主义原则，欢迎世界各国参与。合作伙伴可以根据自身需求和优先事项、本国国情以及国际合作的准备程度，在任何层面、任何最契合自身的领域参与合作。"一带一路"倡议是全球新秩序的有力塑造者，是促进和平、稳定、繁荣与和谐的一股新兴全球力量。"一带一路"倡议是一个全球性的、非歧视性的包容性合作平台，各国不论地区、政治、发展水平与阶段、文化及宗教有何差异，都可参与合作。

"一带一路"倡议属于所有国家，尤其是那些致力于将这一倡议落到实处的国家。我们都是"一带一路"倡议的利益攸关方和主人翁。在

"一带一路"倡议下,区域内和区域间的互联互通将得到提升。政治互信、互学互鉴、相互尊重和互利共赢是"一带一路"倡议框架下合作的基础。没有一个国家会将自己的想法或政策强加给其他国家。各国在共同设计和实施"一带一路"项目中都拥有平等的话语权。凝聚领导力量,共享发展机遇,是"一带一路"倡议秉持的理念。实现可持续和包容性发展是"一带一路"倡议的愿景。"一带一路"倡议有望成为实现联合国 2030 年可持续发展议程和推动参与国实现若干可持续发展目标的加速器和有效载体。

柬埔寨是"一带一路"倡议最坚定的支持者之一,因为该倡议带来的经济机遇巨大,而基础设施建设和互联互通是柬埔寨加入"一带一路"倡议的核心国家利益所在。在"一带一路"倡议框架下,已取得许多显著的实质性成果,包括建设暹粒国际机场以及金边至西哈努克港高速公路(即金港高速)。金港高速是柬埔寨首个高速公路项目,历经三年多建设全面完工,并于 2022 年 10 月正式通车。从更广泛的层面来看,"一带一路"倡议的重要性不仅体现在柬中伙伴关系上,它还是加强中国与世界各国的外交关系、推动全球现代化的关键驱动力。

本文探讨"一带一路"倡议对发展、繁荣、增长和现代化的影响,着重分析柬中伙伴关系,并对中国更广泛的国际关系进行研究。同时,本文还强调推动高质量的"一带一路"合作对于实现可持续发展和全球现代化目标的重要性。

一、"一带一路"倡议

"一带一路"倡议由中国国家主席习近平于 2013 年提出,是一项重大的全球举措,重点聚焦基础设施建设和经济合作。"一带一路"常被称作"新丝绸之路"。该倡议旨在加强中国与各国之间的经济联系和互联互通，其主要目标是促进亚洲、欧洲和非洲的贸易发展、经济增长及基础设施建设。

截至 2023 年，"一带一路"倡议已覆盖 150 多个国家，30 多个国际组织在"一带一路"倡议框架下签署了相关文件。"一带一路"倡议自 2013 年中国国家主席习近平提出以来，在改变世界方面取得了显著成就。"一带一路"倡议是一个全球性的、非歧视性的包容性合作平台，各国不论地区、政治、发展水平和阶段、文化及宗教有何差异，都可参与合作。

该倡议由三个主要部分组成：（1）丝绸之路经济带，这是一条连接中国与东南亚、南亚、中亚、俄罗斯及欧洲的陆上通道；（2）21 世纪海上丝绸之路，一条将中国沿海地区与东南亚、南亚、南太平洋、西亚和东非相连的海上通道；（3）数字丝绸之路（DSR），它专注于与发展中经济体和新兴市场在信息通信技术领域的合作以及数字协作（引自 Sameer Patil 与 Gupta2024 年发表的文章）。

"一带一路"倡议为参与国提出了实现协同发展的五大主要目标（引自新华社 2017 年播发的文章）：

1. 政策协调：各国应协调经济战略和政策，开展政府间合作，建立宏观政策交流机制，以增进相互政治信任，扩大共同利益。

2. 设施联通：提升基础设施互联互通水平是重中之重，重点在于建设国际运输网络，加强公路、港口、航空和能源基础设施建设，并建立统一的跨境运输和海关作业体系。

3. 贸易畅通：应努力减少贸易和投资壁垒，促进海关合作，建设自由贸易区以提高贸易便利化水平。各国应扩大相互投资机会，深化农业、能源、科技等关键领域的合作。

4. 资金融通：深化金融合作对"一带一路"倡议的成功至关重要。这包括构建稳定的货币和融资体系、扩大货币互换，以及推动金融市场发展，以支持大规模投资。

5.人文交流：加强文化、学术和社会交流对于构建"一带一路"倡议的民意基础至关重要。各国应推动教育交流、旅游、医疗合作以及联合开展文化活动，以增进人民之间的紧密联系。

二、"一带一路"带来繁荣

赵汀阳（在 2006 年的相关论述中）强调，传统的欧洲和英美理论不足以理解中国面临的独特挑战。赵汀阳指出，这些理论常常衍生出"中国威胁论""债务陷阱外交"等叙事和概念以及围绕"中国崛起"的讨论，而这些可能并不能准确反映中国的实际情况。

现实主义和自由主义理论忽视了中国传统哲学及其独特的世界观、价值观和方法论。这些理论在解释冲突方面颇为有效，但在理解和谐方面却有所不足。相形之下，中国思想强调平衡和集体福祉，能更全面地阐释如何实现和谐，这与中国通过合作与稳定促进繁荣的方式相契合（引自 Wren2023 年发表的文章）。

"一带一路"倡议给许多人的生活带来了积极的变化。它注重改善民生，认识到稳固的根基对于国家的稳定至关重要。在过去十年里，"一带一路"倡议帮助 4000 万人摆脱了贫困，并为当地社区创造了机会。诸多项目，如建设学校、医院和体育场馆等项目得以实施，提升了人们的生活质量和幸福感。

特别是，"一带一路"倡议已在全球范围内拉动近万亿美元投资规模，形成 3000 多个合作项目，为沿线国家创造 42 万个工作岗位。该倡议支持了众多国家标志性建筑的建设、重要基础设施项目以及国际合作中的重大里程碑项目。预计到 2030 年，"一带一路"倡议将使相关国家超 370 万人摆脱极端贫困，这主要通过减少边境延误和降低贸易成本来实现。这一人口数量将占到"一带一路"沿线国家总人口的约 0.7%。此外，在相同的条件下，预计将有超过 760 万人摆脱中度贫困（数据来自 Maliszewska 与 Van Der Mensbrugghe 于 2019 年发表的文章）。

三、全球增长与现代化："一带一路"倡议的更广泛影响

"一带一路"倡议极大地重塑了国际商业和基础设施格局。中亚、非洲和东欧等地区从"一带一路"倡议资助的项目中受益匪浅，比如公路、铁路、港口和能源基础设施。这增强了广大地区之间的互联互通和经济合作。例如，中欧班列大幅缩短中国与欧洲之间的运输时间，使古老的丝绸之路沿线贸易重焕生机。

2023 年，中国在 150 个"一带一路"倡议相关国家的金融投资和合作项目约达 212 个，总价值 924 亿美元。与 2022 年的 745 亿美元相比，这一数字增长 18%。在 2023 年的资金总额中，约 446 亿美元来自投资，437 亿美元来自工程合同，其中一些工程项目部分得到了中方贷款的支持。自 2020 年新冠疫情暴发以来，中国在这方面的总体参与度呈现出稳步增长态势（数据来自 Christoph Nedopil 于 2024 年撰写的报告）。

2023 年，在"一带一路"倡议下，中国在不同地区的参与度差异显著。中国在非洲地区的工程合同增长 47%，投资增长 114%，总价值达 217 亿美元。非洲成为中国参与度最高的地区，超过获得 158 亿美元投资的中东地区。尽管如此，中东地区国家仍然是中国工程承包的主要接收国，2023 年获得 36.7% 的"一带一路"工程承包，较 2022 年增长 31%（数据来自 Christoph Nedopil 于 2024 年撰写的报告）。

东亚地区的"一带一路"沿线国家也实现了大幅增长，中国对其投资增长 94%，达到 68 亿美元。相比之下，拉美地区的"一带一路"沿线国家在工程项目方面的参与度较低，仅获得 1.8 亿美元投资，略高于太平洋

地区的"一带一路"沿线国家获得的投资（1.7亿美元）。不过，拉美地区获得的投资增长92%，总额达55亿美元，占中国对海外"一带一路"沿线国家投资总额的20.5%（数据引自Ezell于2024年发表的文章）。

除此之外，技术领域是一个重要的扩张领域，在"一带一路"沿线国家已吸引超过143亿美元的投资（数据引自Christoph Nedopil于2024年撰写的报告）。这些投资主要集中在电池生产、汽车零部件、电动汽车制造和电信等行业。中国已成为电动汽车制造和销售的领先市场。行业专家预测，2024年中国将销售1150万辆新电动汽车，超过欧洲（330万辆）和世界其他地区（270万辆）的销量总和。这约占今年中国所有新车销量的44%。2023年，中国电动汽车销量同比增长37%。2023年12月，中国在全球电动汽车销量中当月占比69%，全年占比为60%，引人瞩目。分析师预计，到2030年，中国汽车年销量的70%以上将是电动汽车（数据引自Ezell于2024年发表的文章）。

四、中国的数字丝绸之路与人工智能宏图

数字丝绸之路于2015年正式提出，最初指的是"一带一路"沿线国家的先进技术融合。这个名称的灵感来源于16世纪前通过中亚连接欧洲和东亚的历史贸易路线。数字丝绸之路已发展成为中国外交政策的一个重要方面，习近平主席继续倡导建立数字互联互通伙伴关系，特别是与东盟国家的合作（引自Gordon与Nouwens在2022年发表的文章）。

中国企业通过数字丝绸之路，在印太地区国家资助和发展数字基础设施。中国的参与包括提供5G技术、铺设海底电缆和光纤、提供卫星天线，以及提供云计算、人工智能和面部识别系统等先进技术。数字丝绸之路的关键举措包括铺设海底电缆和安装闭路电视摄像头（引自Sameer Patil与Gupta于2024年发表的文章）。

2023 年，中国提出《全球人工智能治理倡议》。该倡议是中国立志成为全球人工智能发展领军者的一部分。这一倡议强调以人为本的理念，通过国际合作、秉持平等互利原则，推动惠及所有国家的人工智能技术发展（引自《中国日报》于 2023 年发表的文章）。该倡议与中国 2017 年提出的人工智能发展规划中概述的更广泛战略愿景相一致，该规划为 2025 年和 2030 年由人工智能驱动的产业和经济转型设定了宏伟目标。

根据中华人民共和国国务院（2017 年）的规划，中国旨在实现人工智能理论和技术的突破，使中国成为全球人工智能创新的引领者。到 2025 年，人工智能有望推动产业升级和经济转型，其核心产业规模将突破 4000 亿元人民币，相关产业规模将超过 5 万亿元人民币。

到 2030 年，中国的目标是成为全球主要的人工智能创新中心，在类脑智能和群体智能方面取得突破，同时将人工智能的应用拓展到制造、国防和社会治理等各个领域。中国计划加强与人工智能相关的法律和伦理体系建设，预计人工智能核心产业规模将超过 1 万亿元人民币，相关产业规模将突破 10 万亿元人民币（引自中华人民共和国国务院 2017 年的规划）。

2023 年提出的这一倡议强调国际合作、合乎伦理的人工智能治理以及公平的技术惠益，这不仅反映出中国提升自身人工智能能力的愿望，也体现了其影响全球标准的诉求。这种既注重在国内引领人工智能发展，又强调国际合作的双重关注，凸显了中国在国家和全球层面塑造人工智能未来的雄心。

五、"一带一路"倡议对柬埔寨的影响

1. 柬埔寨—中国：深厚友谊和战略伙伴关系

中柬关系被形容为"坚如钢铁""稳如磐石"，双方在维护地区稳定方面有着共同利益。值得注意的是，在新冠疫情危机期间，柬埔寨与

中国人民站在一起，这体现了柬埔寨的团结与信任。而且中国也相应地提供了疫苗、医疗设备和医学专家。

柬中友谊植根于和平共处五项原则：互相尊重领土完整和主权、互不侵犯、互不干涉内政、平等互利及和平共处。两国正在共同应对共同的全球性挑战，加强各层级、各平台的交流与联系，加深相互理解，以确保在国家、地区和全球层面不断取得巨大成就。

2019 年 4 月，柬埔寨和中国签署了《构建中柬命运共同体行动计划（2019—2023 年）》。根据该计划，两国将在政治、安全、经济、人文交流以及多边合作等领域采取 31 项举措（引自 Phea 于 2020 年撰写的报告）。

2022 年，《柬中自由贸易协定》正式生效。两国贸易显著增长，中国对柬埔寨的投资也有所增加。根据该协定，98% 的柬埔寨对华出口商品和 90% 的中国对柬埔寨出口商品免征关税（引自 Kunmakara 于 2023 撰写的文章）。

2024 年 10 月 9 日至 11 日，在老挝万象举行的第 44 届和第 45 届东盟峰会期间的双边会谈上，中国政府宣布将向柬埔寨提供 3 亿元人民币（约合 4200 万美元）的援助，以支持其基础设施建设（引自 Chheng 于 2024 年发表的文章）。

对柬埔寨而言，基础设施建设和互联互通是我们参与"一带一路"倡议的核心国家利益所在。"一带一路"倡议为帮助柬埔寨修建公路、铁路、机场、港口、水电站、经济特区、工业特区等基础设施和实现互联互通发挥了重要作用。这将降低柬埔寨的物流成本，增强经济完整性，使增长来源多元化，并成为支撑贸易和吸引投资的关键要素。

2. "一带一路"倡议对柬埔寨基础设施和经济的变革性影响

柬埔寨是"一带一路"倡议最坚定的支持者之一，因为该倡议带来的经济机遇十分巨大。基础设施建设和互联互通是柬埔寨加入"一带一路"倡议的核心国家利益。截至 2017 年底，在中国的支持下，柬埔寨已建成超过 2000 公里的公路、七座大型桥梁以及金边自治港的一个新集装箱码头（引自新华社于 2017 年播发的文章）。

除此之外，西哈努克市在 2017 年至 2020 年间受益于中国大量的商业和企业建设投资，如今却成了一座"鬼城"。不过，那些建筑只是"表现不佳和不良的资产"。新冠疫情暴发后，许多中国投资者离开了这座城市，留下了大量未完工和接近完工的高层建筑。这些"灰色幽灵"给这座城市的开发带来了负面印象。最近，美国媒体关于网络赌场、数字诈骗、强迫劳动和人口贩卖的负面报道，也损害了人们对中国参与西哈努克市开发的看法。

在"一带一路"倡议下，柬埔寨已取得许多实实在在的重大成就，包括修建暹粒国际机场和金边至西哈努克港高速公路（即金港高速）。柬埔寨的首条高速公路项目（金港高速）历经三年多建设全面完工，于 2022 年 10 月正式通车。此外，柬埔寨的第二条高速公路——全长 135 公里通往巴韦市的公路，由中国路桥公司承建。该项目采用为期 50 年的"建设—运营—转让"的合同模式，造价 13.5 亿美元，建设工期 48 个月（引自 Panha 于 2023 年发表的文章）。

值得注意的是，作为中国"一带一路"倡议下的重点项目，西哈努克港经济特区在 2024 年前两个月的贸易额达到 6.28 亿美元，同比增长 38.3%。该经济特区由中国和柬埔寨投资者于 2008 年共同开发，旨在容纳多达 300 家企业，并为当地创造 10 万个就业岗位。截至 2024 年初，它已吸引 188 家企业入驻，创造超过 3 万个就业岗位，这凸显出其对柬埔寨经济增长的重要贡献（引自中国环球电视网 2024 年的报道）。

柬埔寨即将启动德崇富南运河项目，这是一个耗资 17 亿美元的巴塞河航道及物流系统工程，旨在连接该国的主要河流和水道。这条从湄公河延伸至泰国边境沿海地区的运河将进一步打通内河运输线路。目前这些线路已将 7 个省份与陆路和海路连接起来。

六、促进柬中双边关系

"一带一路"倡议为柬埔寨提供了减贫和推动国民经济发展的机遇。柬埔寨加入"一带一路"倡议,其主要国家利益集中在基础设施建设和提升互联互通水平方面。该倡议在推动基础设施建设和提升互联互通方面发挥了重要作用,涵盖公路、铁路、机场、海港、水电站以及经济特区或工业园区的建设。

为加快柬埔寨的工业化和农业现代化进程,柬埔寨重点关注"经济多元化与竞争力提升"("五角战略"之一)以及"数字经济与社会发展"("五角战略"之五)。这两个方面强调发展农业,改善交通、物流、能源、供水和数字领域的互联互通,优化营商环境以及促进投资。该政策还将加大对微型、小型和中型企业的扶持力度,加强公私合作,并提升银行体系。

因此,"一带一路"倡议为柬埔寨和中国将双边关系提升至新高度提供了绝佳机遇。两国处于不同的发展阶段,具有互补性;两国最高层面的政治关系十分良好,且两国政治稳定、社会安宁。这些条件使得投资和贸易能够获利且安全可靠,而"一带一路"倡议正是柬埔寨应搭乘的发展列车。

自"一带一路"倡议下的合作项目在十年前启动以来,柬埔寨与中国之间的贸易和投资关系达到了新的高度。"一带一路"倡议,加之《区域全面经济伙伴关系协定》以及《柬中自由贸易协定》,有望在帮助柬埔寨实现到 2030 年成为中等偏上收入国家、到 2050 年成为高收入国家的经济目标方面发挥关键作用(引自 Phea 于 2023 发表的文章)。

　　在政治上，中国作为一个大国，始终支持柬埔寨人民独立自主地选择最适合本国国情的发展道路，支持柬埔寨捍卫国家主权和国家安全。中国还支持柬埔寨推进国内重大政治议程和社会经济发展，反对外部力量干涉柬埔寨内政。从更广泛的层面来看，"一带一路"倡议的重要性不仅体现在柬中伙伴关系上，它还是加强中国与世界各国的外交关系、推动全球现代化的关键驱动力。

结　论

　　"一带一路"倡议无疑重塑了全球经济合作与基础设施建设格局，已然成为推动各大洲互联互通、贸易发展与现代化进程的关键载体。对柬埔寨而言，"一带一路"倡议发挥了变革性作用，在基础设施建设、经济多元化发展以及柬中双边关系等方面均取得了显著成就。通过加强公路、铁路、港口及数字基础设施建设，柬埔寨不仅有望推动本国发展，同时还能促进更深入的区域一体化。

　　柬埔寨积极参与"一带一路"倡议，表明了小国能够从契合自身特定需求的全球倡议中获益，最终推动本国的长期增长与繁荣。随着"一带一路"倡议不断发展，它仍是促进可持续发展、支持联合国 2030 年可持续发展议程，以及巩固基于相互尊重、共享繁荣和共同进步的国际伙伴关系的重要平台。柬中两国之间长久的友好关系证明了"一带一路"倡议在连接各国、为全球发展创造新机遇方面的潜力。

泰中关系：通过"一带一扣"战略实现双赢

江萨·差伦翁沙（哈佛大学高级研究员、国家建设国际研究所主席、未来发展研究院院长）

摘要：本论文研究了泰中关系的现状，并引入"一带一扣"（OBOB）战略作为加强双边合作、确保互利共赢的框架。通过追溯泰中关系从历史贸易到现代经济和外交伙伴关系的演变，本文指出了关键挑战，如贸易过度集中、基础设施互联互通有限、文化交流利用不足以及基层参与不够等问题。"一带一扣"战略与中国的"一带一路"倡议（BRI）契合，考虑到泰国的战略位置和发达的基础设施，将泰国定位为核心的"扣"。该战略强调基础设施投资、产业多元化以及加强人文交流以促进可持续合作。泰国作为"扣"的角色因其强大的基础设施、全面的贸易网络、与中国的文化联系以及对区域合作的承诺而得到强化。论文最后提出了加强泰中关系的建议，包括扩大基础设施互联互通、将泰国设立为经济特区、发挥泰国在农业和健康产业的优势、促进教育合作以及推动人文交流等。通过实施这些举措，两国能够实现长期互利的成果，推动经济增长和区域稳定。

从古至今，国际合作在促进安全以及推动经济、社会和政治进步方面发挥了关键作用。国与国通过合作实现一体化，不仅促进了资源、知识和技术的交流，还增强了相互的经济实力和安全。国际合作理论如相互依赖理论认为，国际层面的合作会给参与国带来互利。通过共享资源和知识，每个国家都能通过合作发展增强自身实力。

在研究泰国和中国的关系时，很明显，两国在经济、社会和政治等各个领域都保持着密切的合作关系。这种区域连通性促进了持续发展，特别是在贸易和投资方面，在过去几十年中实现了指数级增长。加强和深化两国之间的合作对双方在当前和未来的发展与繁荣提供了关键机遇。

本文旨在探索和分析泰中关系的现状，并提出通过"一带一扣"战略来加强双边关系的方法，以实现泰中两国的利益最大化。

一、泰中关系的历史演变

泰国和中国的关系可以追溯到几个世纪以前，植根于文化交流和经济互动，主要由历史上的海上丝绸之路贸易驱动。最初的两国交往以香料和丝绸等商品交换活动为核心，为深厚而持久的联系奠定了基础。随着时间的推移，这种关系超越了贸易，层次越来越多样化，外交和文化交流进一步巩固了两国之间的纽带。

这段共同历史中的一个关键时间节点是 1975 年，当时泰国和中国建立了正式外交关系。过去的 49 年来，这种关系不仅保持稳定，而且逐步深化，特别是在贸易、旅游和区域连通性等战略领域。1975 年这个外交里程碑之后，各个领域的合作不断增加，反映了两国之间的共同利益。

近年来，中国已巩固其作为泰国最大贸易伙伴的地位。两国双边贸易额现在每年超过 1000 亿美元，2023 年中国占泰国贸易总额的近

22%。在中国"一带一路"倡议框架下，中国投资大量涌入泰国，特别是东部经济走廊（EEC）的基础设施项目和铁路建设项目。此外，中国游客已成为泰国旅游业的重要组成部分，在新冠疫情之前，每年有超过1000万中国游客到访。

这种日益增长的相互依存关系标志着泰中关系的重大转变，从传统的货物贸易转向涵盖经济、外交和人文联系的全面伙伴关系。这种关系继续蓬勃发展，为两国未来几十年的进一步合作和共同增长提供了机会。

二、加强泰中关系——新战略方法的必要性

随着全球格局不断演变，泰国和中国迫切需要通过新的战略方法重新评估和加强彼此关系。虽然两国之间现有的联系很牢固，但仍存在一些差距阻碍了伙伴关系充分发挥潜力。解决这些差距需要共同努力加强合作，并创建一个更全面的协作框架。

一是贸易集中在特定领域。虽然贸易和投资大幅增长，但它们仍然高度集中在特定领域。例如，泰国对中国的出口大部分是农产品，占其农产品总出口的41.92%，导致泰国容易受到商品价格波动和市场需求变化的影响。扩大贸易品组合，加入高科技产品、服务和文化交流，将使经济关系更加平衡。

二是缺乏全面的基础设施连通性。缺乏全面的基础设施连通性来支持贸易和旅游的增长。虽然中国"一带一路"倡议下的项目旨在加强连通性，但需要更多地关注泰国境内的区域一体化。解决这一差距需要发展连接泰国各省与中国主要经济中心的物流网络和交通系统，以实现更顺畅的贸易路线并促进旅游业发展。

三是文化和教育交流的潜力未充分发挥。泰国和中国之间现有的文化和教育交流项目没有充分发挥潜力来增进相互理解。虽然泰国在努力

推广汉语和中国文化，但泰国人对中国文化的了解仍然严重不足，反之亦然。通过教育项目、互访和合作研究倡议来加强文化外交将促进两国之间的共情和理解。

四是基层联系一直被忽视。虽然人文方面的连通性至关重要，但当前的倡议往往侧重于商业和政府层面的互动，忽视了能够进一步加强双边关系的基层联系。在促进民间社会组织、学生和当地社区之间的合作方面仍旧存在差距。鼓励基层项目和促进互访可以建立持久的关系，并为超越政治和经济领域的合作奠定基础。

解决这些领域对于提高泰中伙伴关系的有效性和可持续性至关重要。通过关注这些方面，两国可以共同努力提升关系，并在日益互联互通的世界中实现互利。

三、"一带一扣"战略解析

"一带一扣"战略是一种通过一体化经济和基础设施合作来加强泰中关系的变革性方法。该战略旨在将泰国定位为中国"一带一路"倡议大框架内的核心之"扣"，利用泰国的战略地理位置和现有基础设施，促进中国、东南亚及其他地区之间的贸易和连通性。

"一带"指的是"一带一路"倡议，而"一扣"则强调泰国在该框架中的关键作用。泰国的地理优势使其处于主要贸易路线的交汇点，使其成为物流和运输的理想枢纽。通过将泰国确立为"扣"，该战略旨在中国与其东盟及其他伙伴之间建立无缝连接，实现高效的贸易流动和经济一体化。

"一带一扣"战略促进了对泰国基础设施建设的大量投资。东部经济走廊和连接主要城市及邻国的高速铁路网络等项目是该战略的关键组成部分。这些基础设施项目不仅增强了国内的连通性，还促进了跨境贸易，创造了一个更加互联互通的区域经济。

该战略涵盖多个领域。通过在传统行业之外更加多元地开展合作，泰中两国可以开拓新的增长领域，促进创新并增强经济的韧性。在技术转让和联合研究项目方面的合作也可以增强泰国在高价值产业中的能力。

"一带一扣"战略强调人文方面的连通性，认识到增进相互理解对于可持续合作至关重要。教育交流、文化项目和社区参与项目对于弥合两国之间的差距至关重要。这种联系可以加强社会各层面的纽带，并促进对未来的共同设想。

总之，"一带一扣"战略为提升泰中关系提供了一个全面的框架。通过利用泰国的战略地位、加强基础设施连通性、实现合作多元化、促进文化交流以及应对共同挑战，两国可以实现互利共赢，共同创造一个更加繁荣的未来。该战略不仅加强了双边关系，还有助于东南亚及其他地区的区域稳定和经济增长。

四、泰国适合成为"一带一路"倡议之"扣"的原因

"一带一路"倡议旨在通过陆上和海上的基础设施网络加强亚洲各地的连通性。在亚洲的背景下，泰国因其独特优势在该地区脱颖而出，成为"一带一路"倡议最适合的"扣"。

一是战略地理位置。泰国的地理位置是一项重要资产，使其成为亚洲的天然交汇点。位于东南亚中心地带的泰国可直接通往该地区的主要市场，包括马来西亚、越南和柬埔寨。这种中心地位使泰国能够作为连接东西方贸易路线的物流枢纽，促进货物的高效运输并增强区域供应链。与其他亚洲国家不同，泰国的地理位置降低了国家间物流运输的复杂性，使其成为"一带一路"倡议项目的理想之"扣"。

二是健全的基础设施。泰国在基础设施建设方面投入巨大，特别是在交通网络方面。该国正在进行的项目，如东部经济走廊和高速铁路项目，都增强了与邻国的连通性。这些基础设施的改善确保了泰国能够有效地管理和支持区域内人员、贸易和资源的流动，确立了其作为亚洲"一带一路"活动核心之扣的地位。

三是全面的贸易网络。泰国与包括中国、日本和印度在内的多个亚洲国家建立了广泛的贸易网络。这些关系为"一带一路"倡议项目营造了一个合作的环境，促进了贸易、投资和发展方面的合作。作为唯一的扣，泰国可以整合这些关系，简化贸易流程并优化物流，这对于"一带一路"倡议在亚洲的成功至关重要。

四是与中国的文化经济关系。泰国与中国有着深厚的文化和经济联系，这种联系可以追溯到几个世纪以前。这种历史渊源培养了一种相互理解和合作的精神，使其能更容易应对"一带一路"倡议项目的复杂性。虽然新加坡和马来西亚等其他国家也与中国保持着重要关系，但这些国家没有达到与泰国同等程度的历史文化纽带。此外，印度尼西亚和菲律宾等国拥有大量华裔人口，但在政治和经济体系中的融合程度或影响力可能不如泰国。泰国华人社区在将中国投资与当地企业联系起来方面发挥着关键作用。现有的人文联系进一步增强了泰国作为扣的能力，促进了与中国及其他一带一路倡议共建国家的无缝合作。

五是对于区域合作的承诺。作为东盟的关键成员，泰国积极推动区域合作与一体化。泰国致力于使其发展目标与邻国的目标保持一致，加强了其作为亚洲"一带一路"倡议之扣的地位。通过促进东盟国家之间的合作，泰国可以增强"一带一路"倡议的整体影响，确保整个地区可以共享利益。

总之，泰国的战略地理位置、健全的基础设施、完善的贸易网络、与中国的文化联系以及对区域合作的承诺，使其成为亚洲"一带一路"

倡议最适合的"扣"。通过将重点放在泰国,"一带一路"倡议可以在亚洲互联互通方面达到更大的连贯性和效率,最终为所有相关利益攸关方创造最大的潜在利益。

五、通过"一带一扣"战略实现双赢

"一带一扣"战略为泰国和中国提供了一个独特的互利共赢机会。以下是对泰中两国如何从这种伙伴关系中获益的详细分析,确保实现双赢局面。

对于泰国的好处。在"一带一扣"战略下,泰国与中国的合作将带来诸多好处,特别是在经济增长和基础设施发展方面。通过大规模基础设施项目如东部经济走廊,泰国可以吸引中国对于交通、物流和技术等领域的大量投资。这些投资预计将刺激创造就业机会,提高生产力,支持当地企业,从而推动整体经济增长。

此外,泰国将受益于有可能获得先进技术和知识的转让。通过将中国的创新项目融入其本地产业,泰国可以提高其生产能力,提升质量标准,并增强其在国内和全球两个市场的竞争力。这种技术合作使泰国能够实现持续的工业进步和经济现代化。

与中国的伙伴关系还为泰国提供了实现贸易关系多元化的机会。随着中国企业采用"中国 +1"战略,泰国成为这些企业进入东盟及其他市场的门户。贸易伙伴的多元化增强了泰国的经济韧性,减少了其对单一市场的依赖,使其在全球经济变化中更具抗风险能力。

与中国紧密合作也增强了泰国的区域影响力。通过加强与中国的合作,泰国巩固了其作为东盟关键参与者的地位,使其能够更积极地参与制定区域政策和倡议。这种战略伙伴关系提升了泰国在东南亚及全球舞台上的外交影响力。

此外，随着泰国成为更具吸引力的制造业中心，"一带一扣"战略创造了新的出口机会。其基础设施的发展和进入外国市场机会的增加使泰国企业能够扩大出口，特别是考虑到地缘政治因素造成全球供应链发生变化。在日益互联互通的全球经济中，这种出口能力的提升对泰国的经济增长至关重要。

最后，虽然有人担心中国产品和投资的涌入，但泰国可以通过实施保护本地企业的政策来应对这些挑战。通过推行质量标准并支持本地中小企业，泰国可以营造一个国内外企业都能蓬勃发展的经济环境。这种平衡的方法确保泰国可以充分利用与中国合作的好处，同时保护本土产业的利益。

对于中国的好处。中国与泰国的合作提供了重要的战略利益，特别是在地缘政治紧张局势加剧的情况下可以实现供应链的多元化。通过投资于泰国，中国可以减少对某些贸易路线的依赖，并为其进出口创造更安全、更多样化的途径。这一转变对于降低与地缘政治不确定性相关的风险以及确保中国全球供应链的稳定至关重要。

加强与泰国的联系也增强了中国在东盟地区的影响力。泰国是中国深化与其他东南亚国家接触的关键渠道，促进了在许多区域倡议上的合作。这种合作的增加有助于巩固中国在该地区的领导地位，在东盟内培育更大的外交和经济影响力。

除了区域影响力，投资于泰国为中国公司提供了进入东盟新兴市场的宝贵机会。随着东盟经济体的持续增长，泰国成为中国企业扩大业务和利用新商业机会的战略门户。这种伙伴关系不仅使中国企业受益，还巩固了中国作为东南亚主要经济参与者的地位。

中国对泰国的投资还通过促进双边贸易关系产生经济效益。随着泰国基础设施和物流能力的提升，它成为中国商品进入国际市场的高效枢纽。这种物流优势通过简化贸易路线和增加中国商品及服务的出口，支持中国更广泛的经济目标。

中国对泰国的投资也加强了双边关系，并展示了其对于促进互利关系的承诺。这有助于提升中国作为发展伙伴的形象，反驳主流叙事，并在东盟国家中促进友好关系。通过将自己定位为合作伙伴，中国可以深化其长期影响力，并加强其在该地区的经济和外交关系。

最后，中国利用泰国作为海上出口通道相较于其他区域选择具有显著优势。首先，与面临内部政治不稳定的缅甸相比，泰国提供了更为稳定的政治环境和发达的基础设施。使用泰国的海上航线还使中国能够避免南海已有的地缘政治紧张局势。虽然巴基斯坦通过瓜达尔港为中国提供了进入阿拉伯海的通道，但该地区面临安全挑战，特别是在俾路支省。崎岖的地形和冲突风险使该路线相较于泰国四通八达且和平的航运路线缺乏吸引力，后者更容易进入印度洋和全球市场。

六、中国如何支持泰国成为"扣"

为了确立泰国在"一带一扣"战略中的"扣"的地位，中国可以通过各种举措提供重要支持。

一是加强连通性对于最大限度地发挥泰国在"一带一路"倡议中的作用至关重要。中国可以发挥关键作用，将泰国较小范围的交通系统与主要国际航线连接起来，提高贸易效率和区域一体化。例如，扩展铁路网络，将泰国更多的主要城市（如清迈和普吉岛）直接与中老铁路相连，促进贸易和旅游业的发展。虽然关于扩展铁路网络的讨论正在进行中，但这些铁路的具体项目和时间表仍处于规划阶段。它不仅将减少物流瓶颈，还将支持泰国的旅游和出口部门。

从"一带一扣"战略的角度来看，这种方法是合理的，因为它符合"一带一路"倡议改善基础设施以促进亚洲贸易的核心目标。对中国而言，连通性的增强将使其更容易进入东南亚市场，促进中国在该地区的出口和投资。通过改善交通网络，泰国和中国都将在经济上受益，贸易往来增加，区域联系加强，最终巩固两国之间的战略伙伴关系。

二是可考虑在"一带一扣"框架内，给予泰国经济特区地位。这不仅将吸引中国企业在泰国投资，还将使它们能够利用泰国作为区域运营枢纽的战略位置。鉴于泰国已经是重要的贸易伙伴，这一举措将进一步加强经济联系，并促进整个东南亚更顺畅的贸易路线。

通过将泰国设为经济特区，中国将获得更有利的投资环境，使其公司能够扩大在区域内的业务版图，同时受益于泰国已有的基础设施和熟练劳动力。此外，这一举措将促进泰国的经济多元化，减少对传统部门的依赖，同时创建更强大的制造业和技术基础。最终，这种互利安排将加强中国在该地区的经济影响力，并促进泰国的可持续增长，符合中国通过"一带一扣"战略加强连通性和促进区域发展的更广泛目标。

三是中国可以重点投资泰国具有固有优势的领域，通过"一带一扣"战略促进双赢局面。一个关键领域是泰国的农业部门，将泰国定位为"世界粮食之都"。通过投资于先进农业技术和食品加工能力，中国不仅可以提高泰国的出口潜力，还可以为中国消费者确保稳定的供应链。

此外，泰国已经有着作为全球健康旅游养生之都的良好声誉，在中国的支持下，可以进一步发展，特别是通过升级医疗设施和促进医疗旅游。这符合中国促进区域伙伴关系和经济合作的目标。

此外，中国可以通过基础设施升级，投资于泰国的"旅游之都"，提高中国游客的可达性。中国游客已经在泰国游客中占了很大一部分。另一个适合合作的领域是养老护理，泰国可以成为"养老医疗之都"，为包括越来越多的中国老年人在内的退休人员提供负担得起但高质量的医疗保健。支持这些领域有利于中国在泰国实现投资组合多元化，同时确保可以获得食品、医疗保健和旅游基础设施等重要服务，促进更紧密的经济联系和深化双边合作。

四是通过在泰国建立中国顶尖大学的分校，支持泰国新城发展。这是"一带一扣"战略框架内一项具有战略意义和有益的举措。这种方式不仅提升了泰国的教育部门，还促进了创新和技术交流，这对两国的经济合作和现代化努力都至关重要。通过投资于泰国的教育基础设施，中国可以确保培养出满足快速变化的全球经济所需的熟练劳动力。这支熟练的劳动力队伍将使在泰国运营的中国公司受益，并提高该地区的整体竞争力。此外，这些校区的建立将成为文化交流的平台，有助于建立两国之间牢固的外交关系。中国大学把其研究能力和技术专长带到泰国，促进在各种项目上的合作，提高泰国的创新能力。这符合中国在东南亚扩大影响力同时推广自身教育模式的目标。最终，这一举措将创造一个双赢的局面，泰国在教育和技术方面获得了高质量的进步，而中国则加强了其在该地区的存在，形成对双方经济都有利的长期伙伴关系。

五是通过"一带一路"倡议促进人员的互联互通，组织全面的交流活动和平台。促进包括学生、商人、学者等和政府官员在内的不同群体之间的互动。这一倡议包括创建为中国商业活动量身打造的外国商业实操培训项目，制作书籍和在线内容等教育材料，组织这些群体之间的经验分享论坛。通过促进这种知识交流，中国可以帮助泰国企业家更好地理解和应对与中国市场合作的复杂性，最终促成更深入的商业合作。这种协同不仅增强了泰国的竞争格局，也为中国创造了更有利的海外商业环境。加强这些人际联系将有助于更深入的相互理解和合作，为两国的长期伙伴关系铺平道路，推动经济增长。

通过实施这些有针对性的举措，中国可以为泰国成为"一带一路"倡议中的"扣"做出重大贡献，加强经济联系并确保互利的伙伴关系。

结　论

　　"一带一扣"战略下的泰中关系代表了一条通过加强合作实现互利的光明道路。泰国在东南亚的战略位置使其成为中国扩大影响力和促进互联互通的关键伙伴，与中国更广泛的"一带一路"倡议高度契合。"一带一扣"框架促进基础设施发展，促进经济增长，并加强两国在东盟地区的一体化。这种伙伴关系不仅促进了贸易和投资，还巩固了泰国在促进更顺畅的区域互联互通方面的作用，提供了重要的经济机会。通过共同努力，泰国和中国正在为两国构建一个共同繁荣、关系更紧密和长期成功的未来。"一带一扣"战略体现了这两个国家之间的合作如何能够带来双赢的结果，不仅有利于它们自身的经济，还有利于更广泛的东南亚地区。

"中国－全球南方"经济融合的引擎

安德烈·勒杜列斯库、萨尔米扎·彭恰（罗马尼亚科学院世界经济研究所研究员）

2024 年，世界经济继续面对着近年来全球外生冲击带来的后果，包括持续处于高位的地缘政治紧张关系。因此，过去几个季度以来，经济活动的增长速度呈现出的年度走势低于后危机经济周期所记录的水平，原因包括贸易往来的地缘分化格局（欧美对欧亚）、处于高位的实际利率（即经通胀调整后的名义利率）、欧元区经济竞争力方面的结构性挑战等。此外，考虑到美国公共财政面临前所未有的挑战、世界最大经济集团之间爆发对抗以及金融资产估值过高等问题，爆发新的全球经济和金融危机的风险很高。在此背景下，全球南方新兴发展中国家之间加强经济合作的进程获得了越来越强的推动，中国（作为世界第二大经济体，占全球 GDP 的比重约为 17%）进一步推进"一带一路"倡议（该倡议自启动以来已累计提供超过 1 万亿美元的全球投资），发挥了催化作用。

本论文聚焦于金砖国家组织内部的经济一体化，采用标准经济工具并使用国际货币基金组织的数据库。论文的结构如下：第一章介绍金砖国家在世界经济中的作用；第二章简要描述了计量经济学方法，以估算金砖国家潜在产出的年度走势；第三章展示金砖国家成员之间的经济趋

同 / 分化；第四章简要介绍国际货币基金组织对金砖国家的宏观经济预测；最后一章得出结论。

一、世界经济中的金砖国家

金砖国家是 2009 年全球金融危机（即二战以来最严重的经济和金融危机）的背景下正式成立的，是一个重要新兴经济体之间开展经济与发展合作的多边组织。其创始成员为巴西、俄罗斯、印度和中国，南非于 2010 年加入。自 2024 年 1 月 1 日起，又有五个国家加入这一国际组织：伊朗、沙特阿拉伯、阿联酋、埃及和埃塞俄比亚。

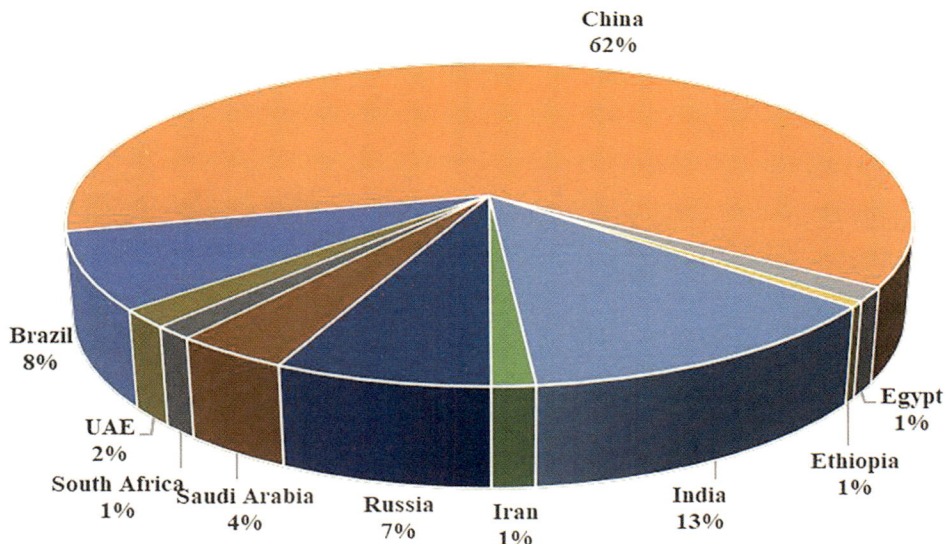

图 1 2023 年金砖国家成员对总的名义 GDP 的贡献率

资料来源：作者根据国际货币基金组织的统计数据绘制

根据国际货币基金组织的估算，当前金砖国家（包括十个国家）2023 年的名义 GDP 总计达到 28.3 万亿美元。这一数额约占世界经济总量的 27%，非常接近美国在全球 GDP 中的占比（美国自二战结束以来一直是世界最大经济体）。

在金砖国家组织内部，中国是最大的经济体，2023 年对总的名义 GDP 的贡献率为 62.4%，如下图所示（图 1）。其次是印度、巴西、俄罗斯和南非，占比分别为 12.6%、7.7%、7.1% 和 3.8%。根据国际货币基金组织的统计数据，今年加入该组织的五个国家对"金砖国家+"总的名义 GDP 的贡献率不到 7%。

然而，如果我们按照购买力平价（PPP）并按国际美元计算来考虑 GDP 数据，那么根据国际货币基金组织的统计数据，当前结构下的金砖国家组织占世界经济的比重超过36%（2023年为36.2%），如下图所示（图2）。

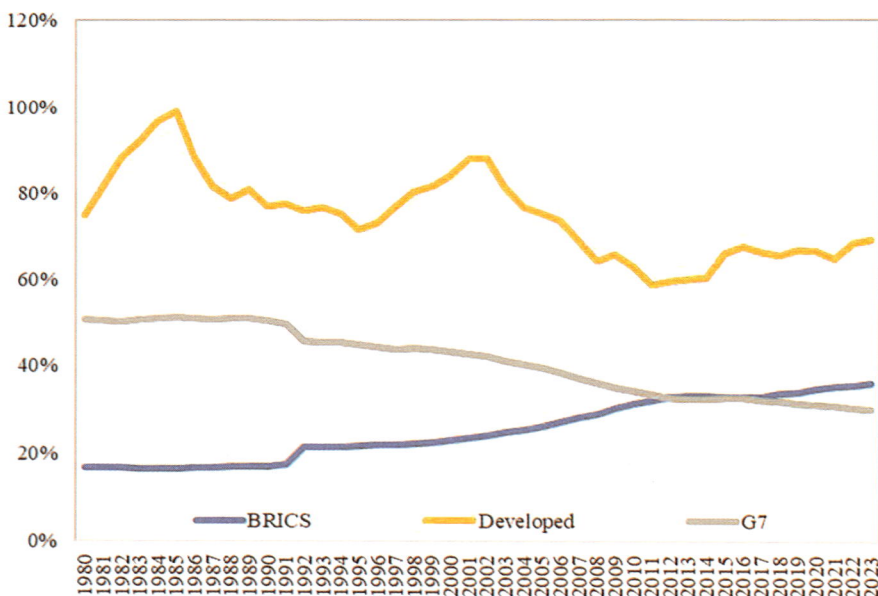

图 2　按 PPP 计算的名义 GDP 在世界 GDP 中的份额
资料来源：作者根据国际货币基金组织的统计数据绘制

从这张图中可以看出金砖国家在全球 GDP（按 PPP 计算）中所占份额向发达经济体水平的趋近过程，这一趋势在全球金融危机爆发后更为明显。这是由于当时欧元区经济体进行了艰难的调整。欧元区当时经历了两波危机，先是银行业破产，紧接着是公共债务危机。

此外，必须强调的是，考虑到按购买力平价计算的名义 GDP，扩员后的金砖国家在世界经济中的占比高于七国集团（2023 年为 36.2% 对 30% 左右），这也反映在国际货币基金组织的估算中。

最后但同样重要的是，自 2017 年金砖国家在全球 GDP 中的总占比超过七国集团以来，两者之间的差距正在不断扩大。考虑到以下因素，预计这一趋势在未来几年和几十年内还会拉大：（1）与发达国家相比，新兴和发展中国家在增长和发展方面具有更好的前景；（2）金砖国家内部经济一体化进程有望取得进展，特别是在当前全球地缘政治紧张局势处于前所未有的高水平的背景下。

然而，就经济发展（以标准指标人均 GDP 衡量）而言，扩员后的金砖国家成员与发达经济体之间仍存在较大差距。

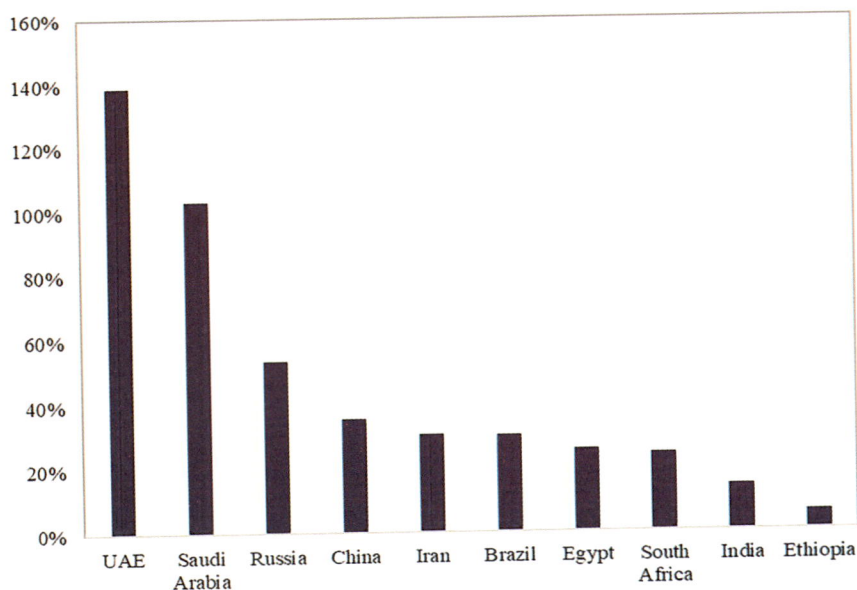

图 3 人均 GDP 相比发达经济体水平的百分比

资料来源：作者根据国际货币基金组织的统计数据绘制

一方面，金砖国家中最发达的国家是阿联酋和沙特阿拉伯，2023年其购买力平价 GDP 分别达到世界最发达国家水平的 138.8% 和 102.9%，如下图所示（图 3）。

另一方面，2023 年俄罗斯在扩员后的金砖国家中排名第三，其购买力平价 GDP 相当于发达经济体水平的 53.3%。其次是中国、伊朗和巴西，其购买力平价 GDP 水平均高于发达经济体水平的 30%，分别为 35.2%、30.5% 和 30.1%。接下来，埃及、南非和印度的购买力平价 GDP 分别相当于世界发达国家水平的 25.7%、24.3% 和 14.1%。最后，埃塞俄比亚是扩员后的金砖国家中最不发达的国家，其人均 GDP 不到发达经济体水平的 6%（5.7%）。

换句话说，当前金砖国家成员在经济发展方面存在显著差异和不对称。这意味着这些国家未来经济趋同的潜力非常高，本文第三章将详细阐述这一主题。

二、方法

本文采用标准计量经济学工具，并使用国际货币基金组织的统计数据，以估算金砖国家集团成员潜在产出的年度走势。潜在产出的年度估算走势对于评估经济在周期中的所处位置以及在比较分析中评估各国之间的趋同 / 分化情况非常重要。在这种情况下，必须强调经济趋同是不同国家成功实现一体化的基本原则，尤其是在一体化进程开始时这些国家存在差异的情况下。

为了区分年度 GDP 走势的结构性和周期性成分，本文采用了霍德里克和普雷斯科特的滤波公式。鉴于其透明且易于理解，这是过去几十年宏观经济文献中最常用的计量经济学方法之一，用于分解宏观经济变量。该计量经济学方法基于以下公式：

$$\textbf{Min} \sum_{t=1}^{T} (\ln Y_t - \ln Y_t^*)^2 + \lambda \sum_{t=2}^{T-1} ((\ln Y_{t+1}^* - \ln Y_t^*) - (\ln Y_t^* - \ln Y_{t-1}^*))^2$$

其中（Yt）、（Yt*）和 λ 分别代表产出、潜在产出和平滑参数，具有以下性质：值越低，GDP 增长速度越接近其趋势。本文中该参数取值为 100，这是霍德里克－普雷斯科特在使用年度观测值时建议的值。

另一方面，该计量经济学滤波公式存在一些缺点，即泄漏效应和压缩效应，这是因为无法完美区分宏观经济变量的周期性和结构性成分。

本文使用国际货币基金组织数据库中 1995—2023 年期间金砖国家成员的 GDP 年度动态数据。

三、金砖国家内部的经济趋同和分化

在扩员后的金砖国家成员国之间，就几个重要的宏观经济指标而言，也可以明显看出有高度的分化情况出现，本章将进一步强调这一点。

首先，我们可以看到金砖国家现有成员国过去几十年来在总体宏观经济平衡方面的差异，这反映在总投资与国民储蓄之间的差额上，这两个变量均以 GDP 的百分比表示。截至 2023 年，埃塞俄比亚的宏观经济失衡程度最高，根据国际货币基金组织的统计数据，其总投资与国民储蓄之间的差额相当于 GDP 的 2.8%。南非、巴西、印度和埃及紧随其后，其总投资与国民储蓄的差额占 GDP 的比例分别为 1.6%、1.3%、1.2% 和 1.2%。

另一方面，在过去几年中，中国和金砖国家中的石油生产国的国民储蓄水平高于总投资水平。换句话说，这些经济体的国内储蓄率高于总投资率，这一变化是由传统因素决定的，包括中国的高储蓄偏好以及石油出口国的收入波动。

此外，根据本文使用国际货币基金组织年度数据进行的计量经济学分析结果，在 1995—2023 年期间，金砖国家现有成员国在潜在产出走势和产出缺口方面存在显著差异，如下图所示（图 4）。

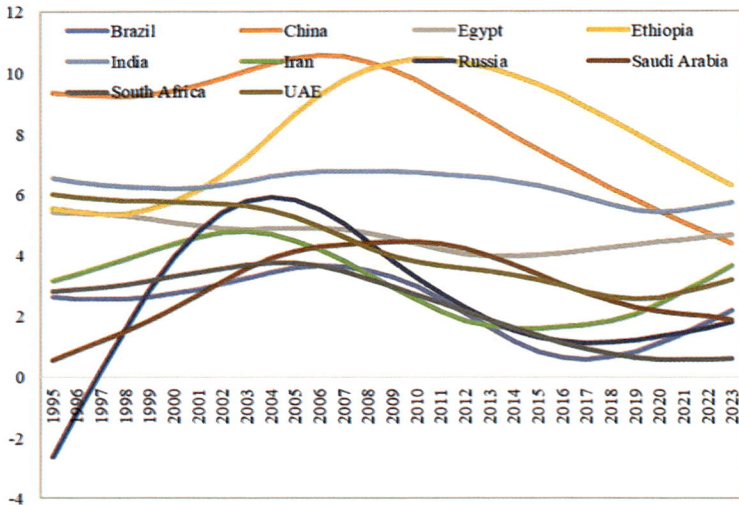

图 4 潜在产出的年度走势（%）

资料来源：作者根据计量经济学估计数字，使用上述方法和国际货币基金组织的 GDP 年度数据绘制

　　首先值得注意的是埃塞俄比亚和印度，这两个国家 2023 年潜在 GDP 的年增长率估计分别为 6.3% 和 5.7%。其次是埃及、中国和伊朗，其 2023 年潜在 GDP 的年增长率估计分别为 4.7%、4.4% 和 3.7%。在阿联酋、巴西、沙特阿拉伯和俄罗斯，2023 年潜在 GDP 的年增长率估计分别为 3.2%、2.2%、1.9% 和 1.8%。最后，南非的潜在 GDP 增速最慢，2023 年的年增长率仅为 0.6%。

　　此外，根据以下图表（图 5）中的估计结果，金砖国家现有成员国在商业周期中的位置也存在显著差异，这反映在产出缺口的走势上。截至 2023 年，在扩员后的金砖国家中，有几个成员国的经济活动高于潜在速度，印度和俄罗斯尤为显著。同时，2023 年伊朗、中国、埃塞俄比亚和巴西的产出缺口也为正。另一方面，南非经济去年的增长速度与潜在速度持平。

然而，根据计量经济学估计结果，2023 年埃及和沙特阿拉伯的产出缺口为负。

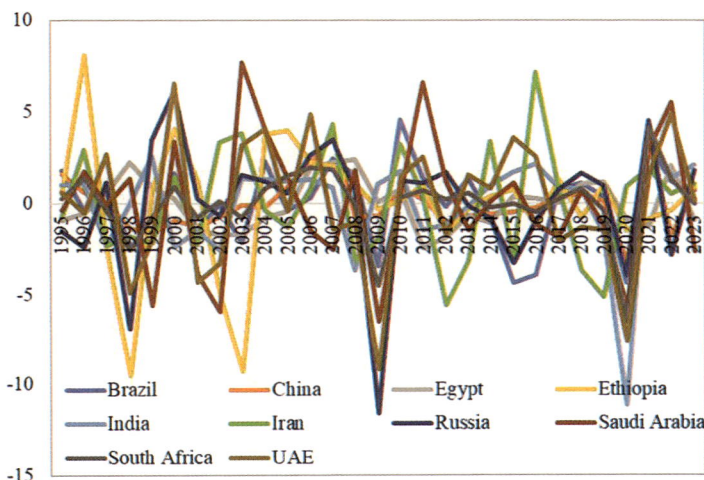

图 5　产出缺口——实际 GDP 与潜在 GDP 的偏差——占潜在 GDP 的百分比 **

资料来源：作者根据计量经济学估计数字，使用上述方法和国际货币基金组织的 GDP 年度数据绘制

这些结果表明，金砖国家现有成员国在未来宏观经济表现方面存在结构性差异和分化持续存在的可能性，这会影响深化一体化进程的决策。在这方面，我们可以提到当今关于金砖国家最具争议的宏观经济话题之一，即推出一种替代美元和欧元的共同货币的方案，正如世界各地许多专家所强调的那样。

四、2024—2025 年金砖国家宏观经济展望

根据国际货币基金组织 2024 年 7 月发布的《世界经济展望》（更新版纳入最新的宏观经济和金融发展情况），金砖国家现有成员国中有五个成员国的经济活动平均增长速度将高于世界 GDP 增长速度。

印度经济是这五个表现出色的金砖国家之一，其 GDP 年增长率可能

从 2023 年的 8.2% 放缓至 2024 年的 7.0% 和 2025 年的 6.5%，如下图所示（图 6），但仍远高于世界 GDP 平均增长速度。

在国际货币基金组织的全球宏观经济图景中，埃塞俄比亚经济在 2024 年和 2025 年可能分别以 6.2% 和 6.5% 的年增长率增长，与 2023 年 7.2% 的年增长率相比有所放缓，但仍高于全球平均 GDP 增长速度。

对于中国而言，国际货币基金组织 2024 年《世界经济展望》指出，由于全球经济疲软以及国内挑战（包括房地产市场出现的新情况），GDP 年增长率将从 2023 年的 5.2% 放缓至 2024 年的 5.0% 和 2025 年的 4.5%。阿联酋紧随其后，其经济活动的年增长率有望从 2023 年的 3.4% 加速至 2024 年的 3.5% 和 2025 年的 4.2%。国际货币基金组织春季预测显示，埃及 2024 年和 2025 年的年增长率分别为 2.7% 和 4.1%。

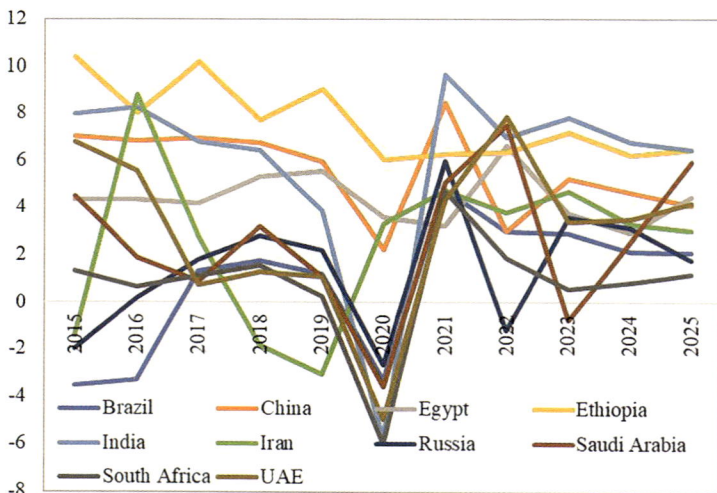

图 6 金砖国家 GDP 年增长率（%）
资料来源：作者根据国际货币基金组织的数据库绘制

另一方面，除了这五个表现良好的金砖国家成员外，其余五个国家的 GDP 增速在 2024 年和 2025 年预计将低于世界经济增长的平均年增长率。例如，伊朗经济可能从 2023 年的 4.6% 放缓至 2024 年的 3.3%

和 2025 年的 3.1%。国际货币基金组织预测，沙特阿拉伯经济短期内将反弹，2024 年和 2025 年的年增长率分别为 1.7% 和 4.6%。

根据同一预测，由于乌克兰战争、持续的地缘政治紧张局势及其后果，俄罗斯的 GDP 年增长率可能从 2023 年的 3.6% 放缓至 2024 年的 3.2% 和 2025 年的 1.5%。在国际货币基金组织的世界宏观经济图景中，巴西经济在 2024 年和 2025 年可能分别以 2.1% 和 2.4% 的年增长率增长。

最后但同样重要的是，根据国际货币基金组织 2024 年 7 月的夏季预测，南非 GDP 可能会出现适度加速的年度走势，增长率略有提高，从 2023 年的 0.7% 提高到 2024 年的 0.9% 和 2025 年的 1.2%。

关于劳动力市场状况，国际货币基金组织预测指出，2024 年和 2025 年期间，十个金砖国家成员国的平均年失业率总体上将逐渐下降。在中国，平均年失业率可能从 2023 年的 5.2% 微弱下降至 2024 年和 2025 年的 5.1%，如下图所示（图 7）。

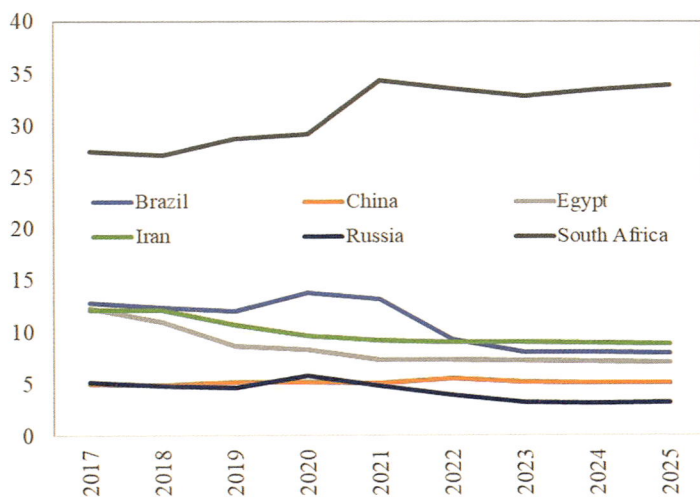

图 7 平均年失业率（%）

资料来源：作者根据国际货币基金组织的数据库绘制

在巴西，平均年失业率将从 2023 年的 8.0% 下降 2025 年的 7.9%，而在伊朗，这一指标在此期间将从 9.0% 降至 8.8%。此外，埃及的平均年失业率也将微弱下降，从 2023 年的 7.2% 降至 2024 年的 7.1% 和 2025 年的 7.0%。另一方面，俄罗斯的平均年失业率可能保持稳定（2025 年为 3.2%，与 2023 年持平），而南非的失业率将从 2023 年的 32.8% 上升到 2025 年的 33.9%。国际货币基金组织没有公布对沙特阿拉伯、阿拉伯联合酋长国和印度失业率的预测。

国际货币基金组织的预测还指出，未来几年，金砖国家成员国的反通胀趋势将持续下去，鉴于冲击（包括新冠疫情和地缘政治紧张局势）的影响逐渐消退以及正在实施的货币政策，这一变化过程与全球层面的趋势相符。就印度而言，如下图表（图 8）所示，消费者价格的年增长率将从 2023 年的 5.4% 降至 2024 年的 4.6% 和 2025 年的 4.2%。

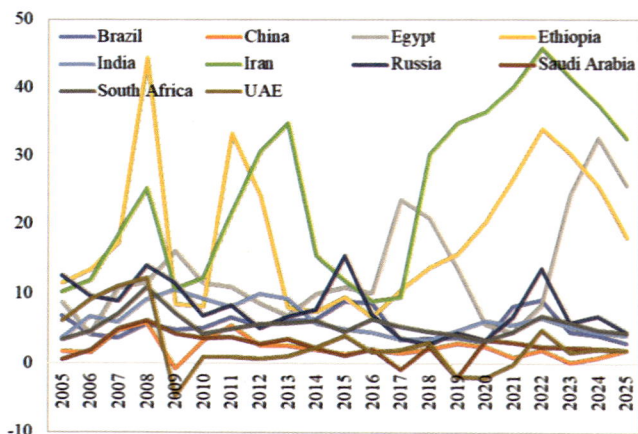

图 8　金砖国家消费者价格年增长率（%）
资料来源：作者根据国际货币基金组织的数据库绘制

就俄罗斯而言，考虑到地缘政治紧张局势的持续存在，2024 年消费者价格将以 6.9% 的年增长率上涨，2025 年为 4.5%。在国际货币基金组织的图景中，巴西消费者价格的年增长率可能从 2023 年的 4.6% 降至 2024 年的 4.1% 和 2025 年的 3.0%。在南非，消费者价格的年增长率可能从 2023 年的 5.9% 放缓至 2024 年的 4.9% 和 2025 年的 4.5%。

在国际货币基金组织对伊朗、埃及和埃塞俄比亚的经济预测中，高通胀压力（即两位数的增长速度）持续存在较为突出，但预计未来几年将放缓，到 2025 年分别降至 32.5%、25.7% 和 18.2%。最后，预计未来几年，中国、沙特阿拉伯和阿拉伯联合酋长国的通货膨胀将得到控制，该国际机构预测到 2025 年将收敛至 2% 的年增长率。

五、结论

预计未来几年，金砖国家新兴和发展中国家之间的经济一体化进程将继续下去，其背后的支持因素是中国通过实施"一带一路"倡议，在世界经济中特别是在全球南方中所发挥的作用日益重要。

在此背景下，我们还应强调上海合作组织 2024 年峰会在经济领域提出的宏伟目标。有几个重要方面，正如国家元首宣言中公布的主要结论所示：（一）反对保护主义、单边制裁和贸易限制，促进全球经济复苏；（二）深化上合组织内部合作；（三）落实《上合组织至 2030 年经济发展战略》；（四）支持"一带一路"倡议；（五）加快落实联合国 2030 年可持续发展议程。此外，2024 年上合组织峰会强调了未来的优先经济部门：农业和粮食安全领域；数字经济，包括电子商务；技术创新；能源；创业。

最后但同样重要的是，应哈萨克斯坦的倡议，2024 年上合组织峰会提议启动上合组织投资基金，并设立上合组织开发银行和上合组织发展基金。同时，应考虑到金砖国家和上合组织成员国在经济趋同方面面临的巨大挑战，特别是在公开宣布致力于去美元化的背景下。在这方面，欧洲过去几十年来的经济一体化经验是新兴和发展中国家在加强经济一体化进程中应该做什么和应该避免什么的最佳范例。

中国和欧盟智库合作交流研究

玛格达莱娜·雷比茨卡（波兰维斯瓦大学亚洲研究中心常务主任、经济学家）

摘要： 要考虑智库之间开展合作，需要尝试定义它们是什么，以及它们活动的总体目标和具体目标。这项研究是为了了解这些机构活动的理念，并尝试明确它们在国家、区域和国际层面的用处。由于这个主题十分宽泛，本文主要侧重与科学交流相关的范围，以及与智库活动其他有趣趋势相关的重点。由于无法明确定义我们对智库概念的理解，因此作者将首先基于对现有文献的研究创建一个通用定义，这将可以统一对该术语的理解。

人们认为，相对其他 NGO（非政府组织），智库会因其活动目的而脱颖而出，即针对人们普遍了解的特定国家或国家集团（例如欧盟活动范围）的内部和对外政策进行研究、分析和发表意见。人们还认为，它们地位独立，不代表任何利益集团，而是基于统计数据和专家研究进行分析，旨在提出最普适的解决办法，作为政府采取行动的建议。

2007 年出现首个对智库的非官方定义。智库是公共政策研究、分析和参与组织，对国内和国际问题开展政策导向的研究、分析并提出建议，从而使决策者和公众能就公共政策做出明智的决定。智库可以是附属机构或独立机构，其在结构上为常设机构，而不是临时委员会。这些机构通常充当学术界和决策层之间以及国家和民间社会之间的桥梁，作为独立的声音为公共利益服务，将应用和基础研究转化为容易理解的语言，供政策决策者和公众放心使用。

从历史背景来看，智库经常发展成社会团体进而转型为政党，但其主要目标是成为保持政治公正的独立咨询机构。智库经常与其他国际机构建立伙伴关系，对气候变化、安全政策或国际经济等全球性挑战展开合作研究。

一、全球范围的智库概况

国际智库合作的研究主要由监测它们活动的机构和参与公共政策分析的组织进行。虽然没有单一的、全面的数据库，但有一些来源和报告提供了评估和分析。然而，应当指出，世界各地的智库在扮演的角色和运作方式等方面各不相同。

据《2020 年全球智库指数报告》显示，北美（墨西哥、加拿大和美国）共有 2397 家智库，其中美国有 2203 家。欧洲有 2932 家智库。超过 47% 的智库位于北美和欧洲，比上一年有所增加。在过去 12 年里，美国和欧洲的新智库成立速度有所下降。亚洲、拉美、非洲、中东和北非地区的智库数量和类型继续增加。自 2000 年中期以来，亚洲的智库数量急剧增加。这些地区的许多智库继续依赖政府资助以及国际公共和私人捐助者的捐助、赠款和合同。大学或政府附属或资助的智库仍然是这些地区智库运营的主流模式。随着独立智库、政党智库、企业智库、商业智库的成立步伐越来越快，这些地区的智库也越来越多样化。

从地理位置看，智库在世界范围内的分布多年来基本没有变化。据索比斯基研究所（sobieski）的统计，智库数量最多的国家依次是美国（1828家）、中国（426家）、英国（287家）。其他分别是印度（268家）、德国（194家）、法国（177家）、阿根廷（137家）、俄罗斯（122家）和日本（108家）。在各大洲中，北美处于领先地位，拥有1984家智库（占研究中所有智库的29.07%）。来自美国的智库（1828家）明显占据主导地位，接着是加拿大（96家）和墨西哥（60家）。其次是欧洲，有1818家智库（26.63%）。在西欧，最大的智库中心依次是英国（287家）、德国（194家）、法国（177家）、意大利（89家）、瑞典（77家）、瑞士（71家）、荷兰（57家）和比利时（52家）。

在东欧和中欧，波兰有41家智库，排在俄罗斯（122家）、罗马尼亚（54家）、乌克兰（47家）之后，在保加利亚（33家）和捷克（28家）之前。值得注意的是，如果按人均计算，波兰的智库数量远远落后于乌克兰和俄罗斯。

二、波兰智库发展现状

波兰智库的排名在不断上升。2008年和2009年的报告分别有4家波兰智库入榜，2010年有5家，2011年有7家，2012年有8家，今年有多达9家波兰机构入榜。自该排名开始以来，总共有10家波兰智库和基金会上榜：社会和经济研究中心、波兰国际事务研究所、斯蒂芬·巴托里基金会、国际关系中心、亚当·斯密中心、东方研究中心、公共事务研究所、Demos Europa、可持续发展研究所和东欧扬·诺瓦克－耶焦兰斯基学院。

尽管波兰的人均智库数量与该地区其他国家相比较少，但在质量方面却排名靠前。在中欧和东欧60个最佳智库排名中，社会和经济研究中心领先于俄罗斯卡内基莫斯科中心，波兰国际事务研究所排名第三，接着是俄罗斯几家智库——俄罗斯科学院世界经济与国际关系研究所（IMEMO）、莫斯科国立国际关系研究所（MGIMO）和经济与金融研究中心（CEFIR）。另一所波兰机构东方研究中心排名第七。这意味着前十名中有 3 家波兰智库，仅次于俄罗斯（4 家）。

在波兰，智库的作用日益显著，因为它们在塑造公共辩论和政策方面发挥着重要作用。它们也是政府决策者和私营部门的专业知识来源。通过报告、会议和研讨会，智库影响国家战略的制定，而它们的分析有助于明确波兰经济和政治面临的威胁和挑战。智库充当了科学与政治之间的"桥梁"，以一种通俗易懂的方式解释复杂的问题。波兰智库经常研究与欧洲一体化、国防、能源和系统改革有关的话题。其中一些机构致力于赋能民间团体和增加公民对决策过程的参与（例如公民协会"Dom Polski"）。他们的建议可以影响法律和政治战略的制定。智库还与媒体合作，组织辩论并在媒体上发表报道。

在数字化时代，分析新技术和创新的重要性越来越大。波兰的主要智库包括公共事务研究所、波兰国际事务研究所和东方研究中心。公共事务研究所（ISP）研究公共政策、欧洲一体化和公民社会。波兰国际事务研究所（PISM）专门研究外交政策、安全和国际关系。东方研究中心（OSW）侧重于对东欧、高加索和中亚国家的分析研究。巴托里基金会致力于民主、人权和社会正义的研究。雅盖隆俱乐部分析中心（CAKJ）对国家政治、能源、教育和人口问题进行研究。智慧欧洲（Wise Europa）等智库分析经济、气候变化和现代技术。公民研究所基金会也在波兰开展活动，进行有关社会政策和发展的研究。波兰智库"Dom Polski"关注波中合作，展示波兰对中国的观点，致力于加强两国之间的科学、政治和商业关系。

波兰的智库面临着与世界各地类似机构相同的问题，经常在为活动筹措资金方面遇到重大挑战。其中一些机构依赖拨款和外部支持，可能会影响它们研究的独立性。小型智库太多，导致碎片化，相互之间缺乏合作。有时，人们认为智库与特定政党联系过于紧密。它们就政府政策的建议，有时会因决策者对独立分析态度不够开放而影响受限。与学术中心的竞争可能导致一些智库被边缘化。保持高水平的专业学识也是一项挑战，这需要适当的资源和人员。波兰的一些智库没有足够的手段进行具有全球影响力的研究。不断变化的政治和经济优先事项可能影响研究资金的供应。提高融资透明度和确保研究质量是波兰智库以及世界上所有此类机构面临的挑战。

波兰智库在未来20年的发展前景是光明的，不过也面临可能影响其未来作用和意义的挑战。面对日益加深的全球化和日新月异的技术变革，智库必须适应新的现实。一个关键的发展领域将是他们在分析技术对社会、经济和政治的影响方面的作用。预计智库将越来越多地讨论与数字化、人工智能、武装冲突、网络安全和气候变化相关的话题。由于波兰的地理位置，未来几年，波兰智库在国际舞台上的重要性可能会提升，尤其是在欧洲一体化和区域合作的背景下。但是，它们必须加强与欧洲机构和国际组织的联系，以充分利用全球专家网络的潜力。加强与国际研究中心的合作有助于提高研究分析质量，更好地适应全球挑战。

在波兰，智库应该而且能够在社会问题的讨论中发挥重要作用，如老龄化社会、移民（尤其是目前与乌克兰武装冲突有关的问题）和不断变化的劳动力市场。人口分析和关于社保政策的研究将是今后改革的关键。与此同时，与能源政策和绿色转型相关的问题将变得越来越重要，这将需要对政府和私营部门进行深入研究并提出战略建议。

在更广阔的全球舞台，智库的作用也很重要，可重点关注全球经济、地缘政治和商业联系以及波兰和中国之间多层次的相互合作等问题。这是波兰智库带头建立和阐释欧盟—中国—波兰之间正确的经济、商业和政治关系的好时机。智库成长的一个关键因素是财政独立和获得研究活动经费的能力。私营部门的资助以及与大企业和非营利组织的合作将变得越来越重要，这可能导致潜在的利益冲突。因此，为了维持公信力和民众的信任，必须确保活动的透明度。

在方法论上，基于大数据和人工智能的分析工具的发展可能彻底改变智库的研究方式。分析自动化和日益先进的预测方法将使人们能够更好地预测政治和经济趋势，这将增加智库在决策过程中的重要性。这些技术可让智库创建更精确的未来情景模型，这在一个动态变化的世界中将非常有价值。未来几年，波兰的智库可以也应该在公共教育方面发挥重要作用。

通过与媒体、学校和非政府组织的合作，智库将能够引导社会了解波兰和世界面临的主要挑战。它们还可以成为公民获取知识和可靠信息的重要来源，尤其是在媒体和互联网上虚假信息日益增多的情况下。此外，智库可以为现代城市和区域政策的形成作出贡献。面对城市化和城市可持续发展的需要，它们将在公共交通、可持续建筑以及水和能源资源管理方面提供建议。在气候变化和对可持续发展日益增长的需求的背景下，这一点尤其重要。波兰的智库也可以支持政府和公共部门制定长期的政治战略。对国家安全、国际关系和网络恐怖主义等新威胁的分析可以成为这些机构活动的重要任务。鉴于波兰在中欧和东欧日益重要的地位，智库将有机会影响波兰的外交和国防政策。与年轻一代的研究人员建立更紧密的联系也很重要。发展人力资本、投资年轻专家和建立学术联系网络对他们的未来至关重要。与大学、实习项目和研究项目的合作可以帮助培养能够应对未来挑战的新一代专家。综上所述，未来几年波兰智库的发展将以适应全球和本土变化为基础。智库面临的挑战将是获得资金、保持独立性以及适应动态变化的技术和政治现实的能力。为了应对这些挑战，智库可以在制定公共政策的过程中发挥重要的顾问作用，也可以成为引导社会讨论的专家中心。

三、从波兰视角看中国智库

目前,中国的智库在政策制定过程中发挥着重要作用,尽管它们的功能与欧盟等国的类似机构的运作方式有很大不同。中国的智库在很大程度上与政府有联系,这意味着它们的活动往往符合中国共产党的官方政治路线。大多数中国智库在国家机构、大学或其他政府组织的支持下运作,它们的分析和研究旨在支持政府的决策和战略。中国智库是中国共产党制定长期战略、监测国际政治经济形势的重要工具,发挥着重要作用。它们在分析国际趋势和向政府提供决策所需的数据方面发挥着重要作用。中国的智库尤其致力于全球政治、国家安全、经济和科技发展以及与发展中国家和大国关系的长期研究。

中国最重要的智库之一是中国社会科学院,它研究国内外政策,分析社会和经济趋势。社会科学院对中国的决策过程有着巨大影响,它提供的报告和分析直接传达给政府和决策者。许多其他智库,如中国国际问题研究院和中国军事科学院,专注于国防、国际关系和安全问题研究。近年来,中国一直在推动全球智库的发展,以帮助改善中国的国际形象。"中国特色智库"意见旨在建立在国际舞台宣扬中国立场的机构,增加中国在全球舆论中的影响力。通过这种方式,中国的智库正在成为软实力的工具,帮助建立中国在国际政治和经济领域的领导地位。中国的智库一方面承担着为政府提供可靠数据和分析研究的任务,另一方面也承担着为政府和中国共产党的政策向社会和世界说明的任务。这一点在它们对经济发展和外交政策的分析中尤为明显。中国智库的大多数与政府密切合作,这意味着它们可能难以有效批评官方政策,这也在一定程度上限制了它们客观分析社会和政治问题的能力。

中国的智库越来越多地参与与技术创新相关的研究,包括人工智能、大数据和绿色能源。中国政府认识到这些技术对国家的未来至关重要,智库正在这些领域进行深入研究。它们还与包括大型科技公司在内的私营部门合作，制定支持中国数字经济的战略和建议。中国智库未来面临的一个挑战将是获得更大的研究自主权。不仅在中国，在全球范围内，对智库创造力的依赖和资助问题都是智库面临的普遍问题。日益激烈的全球竞争和快速应对国际挑战的需要可能要求中国的智库更加灵活和创新。在外交政策方面，中国的智库在未来也将发挥重要作用，例如在分析和支持"一带一路"等倡议方面。中国将"一带一路"倡议视为其全球战略的一个关键要素，这些智库的任务是分析其影响，并就下一步行动提出建议，加强中国在国际市场上的地位。

总之，中国智库在动态发展研究方面前景良好，特别是在技术、国际政策和经济领域。然而，它们的活动将在很大程度上取决于中国共产党的政策，以及中国政府决定如何塑造这些机构未来的角色。未来，它们有可能对全球舆论产生重大影响，尤其是在中国经济不断发展、经济增长和发挥关键全球作用的背景下。

四、结语

加强中欧智库在科学交流方面的合作，有助于双方更好地了解彼此在政治、经济和科技领域的重点关切。通过在气候变化、技术创新和安全政策等全球挑战方面展开联合研究，智库可以推动中欧政府和社会之间的对话。这种合作还可以加快交流最佳合作实践，促进知识转让和创新。然而，一个重要的挑战将是调和政治和制度上的差异，尤其是在中国治理模式和欧洲民主标准方面。这种合作如果在相互尊重和透明的基础上进行，将有可能深化中国与欧盟之间的科学和经济关系。

中欧智库之间进一步加强合作，有助于在地缘政治变化、贸易和技术等棘手的国际问题上架起东西方之间的桥梁。双方智库可在制定以可持续发展、公共卫生和数字化等全球性问题为重点的联合研究项目方面发挥关键作用。通过学术人员交流、培训、联合会议等方式，中欧专家可以相互学习，制定更全面的公共政策。双方也有可能在人工智能、5G或可再生能源等新技术领域开展合作，实现互利共赢。

但是，这种伙伴关系需要建立一个稳固的体制框架，确保利益平衡和防止不恰当的政治影响。为了避免紧张局势，合作必须建立在公开对话、尊重文化和政治差异以及数据和研究成果透明交流的基础上。在对数据保护和安全日益关注的背景下，特别是在数字化等领域，有必要制定有关隐私和知识产权保护的详细规定。中欧在智库方面的合作，如果以互利为基础，也有助于弥合贸易和经济方面的分歧。从长远来看，一个运作良好的智库网络可以帮助欧盟和中国建立更加稳定和可预测的关系。加强科学和分析交流也将有助于双方为应对气候变化和能源转型等新挑战做好准备。此外，联合研究项目可以成为制定更好的全球标准的平台，考虑到东西方的利益。

从"一带一路"看中国与中亚关系

米尔佐希德·拉希莫夫（乌兹别克斯坦科学院当代历史研究中心主任）

几个世纪以来，中亚和中国一直是亚洲和欧洲之间贸易、经济、文化和知识交流的重要枢纽，是丝绸之路上的主要纽带。中国和中亚拥有最丰富、最独特的历史遗产，是世界文明宝库的一部分，这为我们关于世界各地区历史进程的统一性和相互联系的论点提供了支持。作为当代文明史的一部分，现代中国和中亚国家与世界发展进程紧密相连。"一带一路"倡议是跨区域和全球伙伴关系多样化的一个很好的案例。

一、从政治和外交关系史来看

中亚和中国历史上处于各个文明和文化的交汇之地。中亚地区古代国家的形成与中国有着密切的联系。例如，粟特人和中国的关系，粟特人沿丝绸之路（包括中国境内）的贸易活动闻名遐迩。到公元前2世纪末，该地区的一些国家形态——达万（费尔干纳）、安西（布哈拉）、康居部落联盟——与中国建立了密切的外交关系。在中国史学著作中，中国皇帝派往"西域"（今新疆地区）的使节张骞被描述为这些国家的发现者。

据《汉书》记载，汉武帝时期（公元前 140—87 年），每年向中亚各国派遣不下 10 个使节。此外还有著名的"天马之战"——汉武帝的军队攻打大宛的战役。

公元 5 世纪和 6 世纪，中国与中亚的贸易和文化关系进入了一个新的发展阶段，推动双方建立使团往来。在埃米尔·帖木儿和帖木儿帝国统治时期，中亚与许多亚洲国家建立了积极的政治、外交和贸易联系，包括中国、印度、埃及、土耳其和几个欧洲国家。在布哈拉、希瓦和浩罕汗国存在期间，它们与邻国积极保持外交关系。特别是在阿卜杜拉汗二世（1534—1598）统治期间，布哈拉汗国的对外贸易得到显著发展，与叶尔羌汗国、莫卧儿帝国、奥斯曼帝国和莫斯科公国的经济联系得到加强。对于布哈拉汗国来说，叶尔羌汗国的领地是通往中国内陆地区的中转站；从叶尔羌汗国出发的商队，通过马维兰纳赫尔的领地，可以到达其他国家。该地区的另一个国家浩罕汗国也与中国保持着密切的政治和外交关系。

我们知道，世界历史上充斥着各种不同规模的战争，大约记录了 14500 场战争，值得注意的是，在中亚与中国的关系史上，双方的军事冲突属于最少的范畴。中国和中亚在 19 世纪和 20 世纪经历了复杂的历史进程，包括第二次世界大战，这是人类历史上规模最大的冲突，人口损失达 7000 万，其中苏联和中国人民承担了很大一部分损失。

二、贸易和文明的相互联系

和中国一样，中亚在历史上一直是亚洲和欧洲之间重要的贸易、经济和文化交流枢纽之一，是丝绸之路上的重要一环。因此，在中亚发现了许多源于罗马的物品，包括硬币和艺术品。在迦腻色伽王朝期间，贵霜帝国控制着从中亚到北印度的贸易路线，沿着这条路线，帕提亚帝国、罗马帝国、印度和中国之间建立了国际经济和政治关系。

丝绸之路是宗教文化信仰和科技成果的传播者。沿线贸易繁荣发展，文化交流活动频繁，包括艺术、思想和技术方面的交流。撒马尔罕、吐鲁番、喀什、西安等城市在丝绸之路上发挥了重要作用。明清两朝，丝绸之路沿线的贸易继续进行，茶叶、瓷器和纺织品等商品在中国和中亚之间流通。文化交流包括佛教和伊斯兰教影响的传播。

粟特人在中亚与中国文化交流发展中发挥了重要作用。史料记载了距离中亚很远的粟特国派遣使节的信息，以及不同国家使节抵达粟特国的信息。古粟特国与其他东方国家的外交往来，在阿夫拉西阿卜瓦克胡曼宫的壁画中有生动写照，这些壁画描绘了接待外国使节的场景。

在哥伦布发现新大陆之前大约一个世纪，宫廷太监郑和率领三百艘船和两万八千人从中国出发。他的船队在印度洋沿岸港口停靠，并远行至非洲东海岸。中国人在造船技术方面尤为出色。他们在 15 世纪就拥有世界上最强大的远洋舰队——如果他们愿意，完全可以阻止欧洲人向亚洲海域扩张。中国人在丝绸之路沿线把水密舱壁、船尾舵和指南针等导航设备技术传给贸易商，这些贸易商随后把这些技术带到欧洲。与欧洲单桅帆船只能顺风航行不同，他们的多桅帆船——影响西方技术变革——可以逆风航行。长途航行变得可行。

回顾这一千多年的历史，我们可以得出一个大致的结论：在中央帝国和中亚，不同时期都建立了幅员辽阔的国家，地区人民由多民族组成。例如，来自布哈拉的唐朝定远将军安菩，在中亚与中国的关系乃至中国历史上都发挥了重要作用。因此，中亚和中国人民在很长一段时间内呈现出包容性的特征，并向民族、宗教和文化文明多样性转变。

三、文化丰富性和包容性

中亚和中国拥有丰富而独特的遗产，是世界文明宝库的一部分，它以其令人向往的普世性和人类所渴望的特点，不断让今天的研究人员惊叹。在东方文艺复兴时期，亚洲各地涌现出许多伟大的思想家，正如美国著名学者斯塔尔所指出的那样，几个世纪以来，中亚"是世界的知识中心"。在共同的知识遗产中，值得一提的是喀拉汗王朝的马赫穆德·喀什噶里和玉素甫·哈斯·哈吉甫。

马赫穆德·喀什噶里——11世纪的杰出科学家、哲学家，他在对居住在中亚地区的讲突厥语的部落所使用的语言进行比较分析的基础上，于1071年出版了第一本百科全书式的突厥语方言词典《Divan Lugatat Turk》。喀什噶里在布哈拉、撒马尔罕、巴格达和梅尔夫、内沙布尔接受过教育，这些都是阿拉伯世界的知识中心。这本书提供了对突厥民族文化的语言学阐释。它展示了使用突厥语的少数民族的生活场所，并列举了大约800个单词、成语、谚语和诗歌样本，并配有阿拉伯语译文。

玉素甫·哈斯·哈吉甫是一位生活在11世纪的诗人，来自喀拉汗王朝的首都八刺沙衮（位于今天的吉尔吉斯斯坦）。他写了《Kutadgubileg》（有益的知识），大部分关于他的信息都来自这部作品。

中亚和中国的思想家们在东方和欧洲各国人民之间的物质和精神文化交流发展中发挥了重要作用。瑞士著名东方学家亚当·梅茨认为，如果没有较早的中亚哲学复兴，欧洲文艺复兴时期的人文主义是不可能出现的。

这些专家的论断无疑反对片面的东西方发展概念，支持我们有关世界各地区历史进程的统一性和相互联系的论点，即在这些历史进程中没有预先确定的因素。

四、当代中亚与中国关系

苏联解体后，中国和中亚各国——哈萨克斯坦、吉尔吉斯斯坦、塔吉克斯坦、土库曼斯坦和乌兹别克斯坦作为邻国，在所有主要领域，特别是政治和经济领域，大大加强了双边和多边关系。由于地理上的邻近和历史上的联系，新疆维吾尔自治区在中国与中亚的关系中发挥着重要作用。新疆是中国与中亚国家开展贸易、投资和基础设施建设合作的重要枢纽和重要通道。

中国与中亚国家建立了互利共赢的关系，开展了强有力的合作。

一是双方双边和多边政策沟通与互动不断深化。

二是中国同哈萨克斯坦、吉尔吉斯斯坦、塔吉克斯坦、土库曼斯坦和乌兹别克斯坦的贸易额，从 1992 年与中亚五国建交时的 4.6 亿美元增长到 2022 年的 702 亿美元，增长了 150 多倍。

三是中国与中亚国家积极推进基础设施互联互通，构建互联互通网络。中吉乌高速公路及在建的铁路线、中塔高速公路、中国—中亚天然气管道、中哈原油管道等项目平稳推进。中国积极发展欧亚地区的交通新纽带，特别是同欧洲的交通。通道分支向西北和西南方向延伸，第一条经过俄罗斯、乌克兰、白俄罗斯、波兰等国家，第二条贯穿哈萨克斯坦、乌兹别克斯坦、土库曼斯坦、伊朗、土耳其和欧洲。

四是中国与中亚国家在油气、矿业、农业、纺织、制造业等领域合作实施项目，促进产业升级和互联互通。

五是中国和中亚还投资中亚地区的教育、文化、人力资源开发项目，促进双方人文交流与合作。中国与中亚地区的现代文化交流是多方面的，充满活力，涵盖了艺术、文学、音乐、电影、语言、教育和旅游等各个方面。交流项目和学术合作加强了学者、学生和专业人士之间的交流。新疆与中亚有着文化和民族联系，这一传统和遗产为新疆与中亚的人文交流和文化合作提供了便利。目前，中亚地区共有 13 所孔子学院和 24 个孔子课堂，推动了中国形象和汉语在中亚国家的普及。中国主要语言类大学也开设中亚语言的专业和课程。文化、教育和学术交流为中国和中亚之间的多元化交流、相互尊重和合作做出了贡献。

五、上海合作组织和"中国＋中亚"多边形式

2001 年，中国和中亚共同发起上海合作组织这一政府间国际组织。目前，上海合作组织由印度、伊朗、哈萨克斯坦、中国、吉尔吉斯斯坦、巴基斯坦、俄罗斯、塔吉克斯坦和乌兹别克斯坦 9 个成员国组成，此外还有一些合作伙伴和观察员国。多年来，上海合作组织在体制和政治发展方面经历了几个有趣的阶段，成为一支协调多边合作的国际力量。但也要看到，上合组织成员国之间存在分歧，影响稳定的新挑战和问题也需要关注。

促进中国与中亚互动加强的另一个因素是"中国＋中亚"模式的发展。2023 年 5 月 18 日至 19 日，历史性的中国—中亚峰会在西安举行，哈萨克斯坦、乌兹别克斯坦、吉尔吉斯斯坦、塔吉克斯坦和土库曼斯坦领导人出席了首届中国—中亚峰会。习近平在主旨讲话中指出："2100多年前，中国汉代使者张骞自长安出发，出使西域，打开了中国同中亚友好交往的大门。千百年来，中国同中亚各族人民一道推动了丝绸之路的兴起和繁荣，为世界文明交流交融、丰富发展作出了历史性贡献。"在这次峰会上，双方讨论了广泛的双边和多边问题，签署了价值 250 亿美元的一揽子合作文件。

六、共建"一带一路"，迈向全球伙伴关系

2013 年，中国国家主席习近平在哈萨克斯坦阿斯塔纳提出建设"丝绸之路经济带"，在印度尼西亚雅加达提出建设"21 世纪海上丝绸之路"。2014 年，丝路基金成立。2016 年，亚洲基础设施投资银行成立，旨在为基础设施、资源、产业、金融等领域的合作以及其他交通通信项目提供投资和金融支持。它向参与共建"一带一路"倡议的各国开放。中亚

国家在内的亚投行成员国都支持中国的倡议。

需要指出的是，哈萨克斯坦、吉尔吉斯斯坦、塔吉克斯坦、乌兹别克斯坦等国总统和十几个国家和政府领导人先后出席了 2017 年、2019 年和 2023 年在北京举行的"一带一路"国际论坛。

如今，"一带一路"倡议已成为一个全球性倡议，需要在经济、政治、安全等领域开展全面的双边和多边合作。在中亚，有必要实施区域和国际项目。需要加强互联互通和技术发展，积极开展高科技创新、教育、公共外交、旅游等各领域合作。此外，中国与中亚国家的关系开始越来越注重长期和全面的目标。

结　语

历史上，中亚和中国一直是亚洲和欧洲之间重要的贸易、经济和文化交流枢纽之一。古丝绸之路为文明发展和交流作出了巨大贡献。对过去历史的深入研究为研究当代社会转型以及对社会和国家发展的相似之处和模式的比较分析提供了坚实基础。今天，"一带一路"既是丝绸之路传统的延续，也见证了复杂的全球发展进程。各国几个世纪以来沉淀的智慧有时高度相似。例如，中国有句谚语："远亲不如近邻"，乌兹别克斯坦有句谚语："邻居比远亲更近"，这是多样性中存在一致性的一个很好例子。

在全球化和区域发展进程相互交织的背景下，历史遗产研究和国际人道主义合作形成重要互补，是国家和区域可持续发展的重要方面。当前和未来的变革将取决于区域和全球问题和挑战之间的相互联系。

在中国与中亚关系未来发展的大背景下，我们有必要：一是拓展国家、地区、世界历史与国际关系研究的跨学科研究思路，以相互联系、包容为核心，在文明多样性寻找统一性。二是有必要改善中亚地区的教育和科学体系的功能，这无疑需要广泛调动资源、掌握知识和积极应用先进的国际经验，包括中国大学和研究中心的积极助力。三是为实现中亚与中国双边和多边关系的可持续性，应在"一带一路"倡议等框架下，加强实施联合一体化项目，包括科教一体化项目。

毫无疑问，进一步深化中国与中亚的政治、经济、文化和人道主义发展合作，并扩大国际合作，对确保欧亚地区的可持续发展和巩固稳定至关重要。

斯里兰卡在"一带一路"中的战略角色研究：基于葛兰西理论的分析

阿桑加·阿贝亚古纳塞克拉（南亚前瞻网络高级研究员兼执行董事）

阿努拉·库马拉·迪萨纳亚克在赢得 2024 年斯里兰卡总统选举并上台执政后，斯里兰卡面临有关其地缘政治未来的关键问题，尤其是与中国"一带一路"倡议的关系。随着世界迈入以技术进步和全球现代化融合为标志的"第四次工业革命"时代，高质量的"一带一路"合作为像斯里兰卡这样的发展中国家提供了一个与全球经济转型领导者中国合作的契机。

本文通过著名马克思主义政治思想家安东尼奥·葛兰西的理论视角，探讨斯里兰卡在"一带一路"倡议框架内不断演变的角色。葛兰西的文化领导权（Hegemony）、变革融合（Transformismo）和消极革命（Passive Revolution）等概念提供了一个重要框架，有助于理解斯里兰卡在迪萨纳亚克务实领导下的战略定位。在 2022 年斯里兰卡"人民起义"的背景下，具有马克思主义思想倾向、以人民解放阵线为基础结构的国家人民力量党（NPP）击败了传统的两大政党及其联盟，上台执政。本文通过比较斯里兰卡新政党中马克思主义思想的力量，及其在中国等各国政治运动中的改革主义倾向，探讨国家人民力量党的意识形态演变。

新总统迪萨纳亚克的施政方针，平衡了斯里兰卡的国家利益与影响其发展轨迹的更广泛的地缘政治态势。从 1978 年至今，中国创造了经济奇迹，当前在习近平主席的领导下正"通过全面深化改革继承和发扬邓小平的改革思想"，斯里兰卡可以从中汲取许多经验。斯里兰卡作为"一带一路"倡议重要合作伙伴的关键角色，以及人民解放阵线脱胎于"亲北京派"政党的历史背景，将为新政府与"一带一路"倡议的定位打开一扇机会之窗。本文将探讨在迪萨纳亚克的领导下，斯里兰卡如何利用与中国的伙伴关系，在应对多重地缘政治压力的同时，推动国家发展。

一、理论框架：葛兰西的文化领导权与变革融合理论

安东尼奥·葛兰西的文化领导权概念认为，权力的维系并非主要依靠武力，而是文化和意识形态的主导地位。中国的"一带一路"倡议就是这种领导力的例证。该倡议旨在通过对伙伴国的基础设施、贸易和现代化建设投资，建立全球经济影响力。然而，葛兰西的变革融合理论将地方意识形态吸收到更大的领导权框架中，表明成功与否取决于能否将地区行为体的需求和愿望整合进来。

在斯里兰卡，迪萨纳亚克的领导层就是变革融合的缩影。曾植根于马克思主义思想的国家人民力量党已经适应选举政治和经济实用主义的复杂性。同样，斯里兰卡与"一带一路"倡议的合作决不能导致对外国投资的被动依赖，而是要将国家发展目标战略性地融入中国更广泛的现代化议程。葛兰西对文化领导权的强调为我们提供了一个视角，可以借此审视迪萨纳亚克在这一伙伴关系中为维护斯里兰卡自主性，从而在维护国家主权的同时实现互惠互利所做的努力。

二、人民解放阵线的意识形态演变：马克思主义意识形态和改革倾向

人民解放阵线（JVP）的创始领导人罗哈纳·维杰维拉早先加入了N·桑穆加塔桑领导的斯里兰卡共产党（亲北京派），这是一个更以中国为中心的政党。当时斯里兰卡有两个共产党，一个是亲莫斯科派，另一个是亲北京派。罗哈纳·维杰维拉同志是斯里兰卡共产党一名重要成员之子，这对他的马克思列宁主义思想产生了重要影响。他在苏联帕特里斯·卢蒙巴人民友谊大学读书时，曾在苏联共产党党校接受教育。维杰维拉对赫鲁晓夫的修正主义路线持批评态度，修正主义者对尼基塔·赫鲁晓夫远离约瑟夫·斯大林遗产的想法让维杰维拉深感担忧，因此他在1964年拒绝再次进入苏联。

正是在这个转折点上，他从苏联阵营转向亲华阵营，将中国视为斯里兰卡政治斗争的前进方向。然而，由于在斯里兰卡共产党（亲北京派）内部的积极活动，他被领导层驱逐。后来，维杰维拉于1965年创立了人民解放阵线。

根据拉詹·胡尔的说法，"维杰维拉从他所处的政治环境中吸取了反印度的思想，并将无发言权的近代印度裔种植园泰米尔人视为印度扩张主义的爪牙。人民解放阵线在泰米尔人的问题上没有表明立场，声称一旦实现社会主义，这个问题就会迎刃而解。"人民解放阵线在1971年和1988年两次发动起义，但被斯里兰卡当局成功镇压。从1971年人民解放阵线成立之初，反印度中心论就是其明确的政治立场。

帕德马贾·穆尔蒂认为，1971年4月，斯里兰卡接受了印度的援助，以镇压起义，"印度提供五艘护卫舰和军事装备，封锁通往科伦坡的道路，六架用于非战斗任务且配有飞行员的直升机，以及约150名印度士兵守卫班达拉奈克机场"。1988年至1989年的第二次起义更为惨烈，造成

近 6 万人丧生。2014 年，迪萨纳亚克首次"就其政党应为之负责的屠杀事件向公众道歉"。

迪萨纳亚克担任总统标志着，国家人民力量党政治意识形态的重大转变，标志着该党从马克思主义的历史渊源转向更加改革、务实的立场。这一演变将国家人民力量党置于已经适应当代经济和政治现实的全球左翼运动的大背景下。

通过比较国家人民力量党的马克思主义意识形态力量和改革倾向，并与其他历史运动进行比较，可以看出国家人民力量党的意识形态轨迹。20 世纪 70 年代，国家人民力量党的前身人民解放阵线是马克思主义革命的堡垒，其意识形态僵化程度高，但改革适应性低。到 2024 年，在迪萨纳亚克的领导下，国家人民力量党采取了更加灵活、以改革为导向的方法，将务实的治理置于纯粹的意识形态之上。

国家人民力量党的转变反映了与其他左翼运动相似的务实改革，如葡萄牙的康乃馨革命和中国 1978 年后的经济奇迹。迪萨纳亚克所面临的挑战将是，如何处理这些改革倾向与党内残余意识形态之间的矛盾，尤其是在斯里兰卡努力应对印度、美国和中国等主要地缘政治行为体的竞争性影响之时。

斯里兰卡是"一带一路"倡议的重要合作伙伴，人民解放阵线脱胎于以中国为中心、"亲北京派"的政党，如今，斯里兰卡推崇改革，这使其更接近于 1978 年中国开启的发展模式。这一新的政策走向，为迪萨纳亚克领导的新政府提供了契机，使其能比以往的斯里兰卡政权更好地巩固与中国的关系，更深入地参与"一带一路"倡议。

三、葛兰西思想在中国：在"一带一路"倡议中的应用

1949 年中国内战结束，毛泽东领导的中国共产党取得革命胜利，中

华人民共和国于 1949 年 10 月 1 日成立。据介绍，1957 年北京世界知识出版社将第一本关于安东尼奥·葛兰西的书籍引入中国。在这本《安东尼奥·葛兰西的一生》中，葛兰西被描绘成二十世纪初领导意大利共产主义运动的忠诚的马克思主义者。虽然葛兰西在早期就被介绍到中国，但在 20 世纪 60 年代至 70 年代，由于中国对西方马克思主义思想的批判，中国在吸收他的思想时遇到了阻力。这是由于中国共产党与尼基塔·赫鲁晓夫领导的苏联共产党在意识形态上发生重大决裂。同样的情况也发生在斯里兰卡。

然而，中国文化大革命结束后，新的中国领导人邓小平允许与外部世界接触，中国与西方国家的文化交流，拓宽了中国马克思主义学者的视野。1981 年出版的佩里·安德森的《西方马克思主义探讨》成为一个转折点。安德森将葛兰西重新介绍给中国知识分子，受到广泛赞誉。最终，中国学者将葛兰西视为被遗忘了近二十年的西方共产主义运动的领袖人物。

今天，中国的社会和文化组织日益受到葛兰西思想的影响。"一带一路"倡议下的人类命运共同体理念，以及习近平主席提出的全球发展倡议、全球文明倡议和全球安全倡议这三大支柱，都致力于构建一个和谐的世界，这是一种带有葛兰西思想特质的架构，其核心在于打造一种独特的文化。

四、全球文明倡议和反霸权力量

全球文明倡议与安东尼奥·葛兰西的文化领导权理论有着积极的契合点，尤其体现在促进不同文明之间的积极互动方面。葛兰西认为，文化领导权通过传播一种主导性意识形态来发挥作用，这种意识形态塑造着社会的价值观、规范和制度。在此背景下，中国聚焦于不同文明和谐共处、相互尊重的这一倡议，可被视为一种通过合作而非强制手段来重塑全球叙事和规范的举措。

葛兰西将文化领导权视为一种通过共识和知识领导力不断演变的动态力量，而非直接的政治或军事统治。从这个意义上说，中国的全球文明倡议可被解读为试图创建一种新的全球秩序，文化、知识和道德领导力在其中发挥核心作用。通过推动跨文化对话、尊重主权以及共享繁荣，中国力求构建一个多极世界，抗衡历史上由西方主导的全球治理叙事。

习近平主席提出的全球文明倡议以积极的方式强化了葛兰西的文化领导权理论，倡导尊重不同文明和全人类共同价值。习近平在讲话中强调了尊重文明多样性、重视文化的传承与创新，以及大力推动国际人文交流与合作的重要性。这与西方"某些文明优越论"以及"文明冲突论"形成鲜明对比。与西方相反，中国倡导文明之间平等、互鉴、对话、包容的原则，这与葛兰西通过文化领导权达成共识与合作的理念相契合。

"一带一路"倡议对这一理念的实施至关重要。尽管"一带一路"倡议主要侧重于经济领域，但其在促进国家间联系方面的作用，为更深入的知识和文化交流创造了条件，成为相互学习的一个框架。通过尊重当地传统、促进共同发展的项目，"一带一路"倡议提供了在西方主导的发展叙事之外的另一种选择，重塑了全球对权力和领导力的认知。因此，它体现了中国在全球文明层面的抱负以及葛兰西的共识性领导理论，为不同文明和谐共处与合作、增进全球稳定开辟了一条道路。

从积极的角度看，"一带一路"倡议为斯里兰卡这样的国家提供了一个契机，在迪萨纳亚克等领导人的带领下，参与强调主权和国家发展的国际合作，并参与关于平等的全球对话。它反映了葛兰西的信念，即（通过知识和道德领导）获得被统治者的认同比通过强制手段取得的统治权更持久、更有影响力。因此，全球文明倡议可被视为一种"反霸权"力量，提供了在历史上由西方列强塑造的霸权结构之外的另一种选择。

　　"一带一路"倡议是中国全球文明倡议的切实延伸，将葛兰西的文化领导权理论延伸到经济和基础设施领域。葛兰西的理论强调，通过知识和艺术领导力来达成共识，而"一带一路"倡议寻求塑造符合中国国际合作愿景的全球贸易和发展。通过基础设施项目向发展中国家提供资金和技术支持，中国建立起了有形的联系，并在整个亚洲乃至其他地区创造了知识和文化影响力。

　　对斯里兰卡这样的国家而言，"一带一路"倡议投资提供了一条通往经济增长和现代化的道路，同时也提供了不同于历史上由西方塑造的发展模式。在迪萨纳亚克的领导下，斯里兰卡参与"一带一路"倡议可被视为一种尊重国家主权的合作伙伴关系，同时有助于当地经济转型和全球体系变革。从这个角度看，"一带一路"倡议可被视为构建一种新文化的工具。在这种文化中，中国国家主导的发展将在全球范围内产生影响，这与葛兰西通过经济、知识和文化交流创造新"常识"的理念不谋而合。

　　通过将全球文明倡议与"一带一路"倡议相结合，中国成为新多极世界的领导者，在全球范围内践行葛兰西关于道德与知识领导力的理念。这种方式构成了一种反霸权力量，有可能通过和平合作而非胁迫重塑全球规范，对于秉持社会主义原则的斯里兰卡领导层而言，这可能颇具吸引力。

五、葛兰西的变革融合理论及其在"一带一路"倡议中的应用

　　葛兰西在 1929 年至 1935 年间撰写的《狱中札记》中提出了"变革融合"这一概念。葛兰西用"变革融合"来描述意大利统治阶级如何通过将革命运动的领袖吸纳进现有政治框架，从而收编并消解这些革命运动，以此来阻止激进的社会变革。葛兰西将"变革融合"视为一个过程。

统治阶级通过把社会中的对立元素整合进自身体系来维持统治地位，营造出一种改革的假象，以避免更深刻的体制变革。

2022 年斯里兰卡抗议者所表达的"体制变革"，就是要摆脱精英统治的政治阶层，这个阶层成功运用"变革融合"分化了反对派力量，进一步瓦解了马克思主义势力。斯里兰卡的两个主流政党，统一国民党和自由党及其联合团体，设法吸纳了左翼领导人，并通过将他们纳入联合阵营来消解革命运动。今天在斯里兰卡，人们见证了一场具有历史意义的政治运动，民众认清了"变革融合"，并通过民主选举改变了体制。

在"一带一路"倡议的背景下，迪萨纳亚克有机会积极应用"变革融合"。"变革融合"可被构建为一种建设性策略，使发展中国家在保持其政治和文化特性的同时实现经济发展。以下是对其积极意义的解读：

1. **经济增长与现代化**："一带一路"倡议下的变革融合允许较小的国家接受基础设施和现代化项目，而不必被迫在意识形态上保持一致或屈服于任何外部霸权势力。通过吸收经济利益，这些国家可以加强基础设施建设，减少贫困，同时保持其政治主权和文化独特性。例如，许多"一带一路"国家都受益于促进互联互通和贸易的基础设施项目。

2. **维护主权**：参与"一带一路"倡议的国家可以建立符合其国家利益的战略伙伴关系，而不受外部势力支配。与中国的经济和政治合作可以减少对西方金融机构（如国际货币基金组织）或地区大国的经济依赖，从而增强其主权。例如，非洲和亚洲发展中国家利用"一带一路"倡议投资来提高其在国际上的议价能力。

3. **文化与外交交流**："一带一路"倡议下的"变革融合"并非局限于经济层面的融合。该倡议所推动的文化交流项目、外交联系以及民间交往，可被视为一种积极的转变，各国在受益于更紧密的国际合作的同时，还能保留自身的文化特性。这能促成建立在相互尊重基础上更加平衡的全球关系。例如：在东南亚和斯里兰卡，佛教在"一带一路"相关国家间的文化交流与合作方面有着巨大的潜力。

4. 协同治理： 通过"一带一路"倡议整合不同的政治和经济模式，中国展示了一种务实的治理方式，这种方式能兼容多种体制。发展中国家可能会采取一种灵活的做法，将中国的实践经验与本国情况相结合，创造出既符合当地需求，又能从中国的专业知识和支持中受益的混合治理模式。有着马克思主义渊源的斯里兰卡国家人民力量党政府会乐于尝试此类混合模式。

在此背景下，应用于"一带一路"倡议的"变革融合"成为小国实现现代化和维护自主性的工具。通过务实的领导（就像迪萨纳亚克可能设想的那样），各国可以有选择性地采纳中国模式中有益的方面。这将中国的影响力转化为平等的伙伴关系。

葛兰西的理论也为斯里兰卡在"一带一路"框架内如何保持自主性提供了深刻见解。迪萨纳亚克领导的政府不应是被动的参与者，而是可以协商出与斯里兰卡可持续发展长期愿景相符的条款，确保高质量的合作能为其国民带来切实利益。中国在"一带一路"倡议下对合作共赢的重视以及提供的技术专长和能力建设，为这样一种伙伴关系奠定了基础。

斯里兰卡在"一带一路"倡议下与中国的合作提供了一个实现经济增长和现代化的关键机遇。与西方所担忧的中国投资可能导致债务依赖的观点相反，迪萨纳亚克领导的政府可以利用这种伙伴关系推动斯里兰卡的基础设施建设、创造就业机会，并提升其在全球经济中的地位。汉班托塔港和科伦坡港口城等项目已经展现出"一带一路"倡议投资所具有的变革潜力。在迪萨纳亚克的领导下，这些项目能成为更广泛的可持续经济发展战略的基石。迪萨纳亚克的务实做法可以与葛兰西的"变革融合"相契合，设想一种将中国投资融入斯里兰卡国家发展目标的伙伴关系，而非被动参与。

六、葛兰西理论在斯里兰卡的应用

葛兰西阐释了统治阶级如何通过武力或强制手段、意识形态以及文化领导来维持其统治地位。葛兰西认为，要理解政治权力，不能仅仅考虑国家的强制机构，还必须考虑统治阶级如何塑造社会的文化和思想生活，以获取被统治者的认同。葛兰西的理论包含以下几个关键方面：

1. 文化领导：葛兰西强调，权力的行使体现在统治阶级影响社会规范、价值观、信仰和观念的能力上。统治阶级营造出一种共识，使从属群体的利益与自身利益相一致，让统治看起来对所有人都是自然或有益的。

作为斯里兰卡国家人民力量党的领导人，迪萨纳亚克在总统任期内可以通过挑战长期以来由拉贾帕克萨王朝及其他主流政党主导的政治叙事来发挥文化领导作用。他的领导可以与国家人民力量党反贪腐的纲领相契合，并聚焦工人阶级的需求，将自己定位为民众权益的捍卫者。他可以通过倡导社会主义和平等主义价值观来重塑政治话语，为新自由主义政策提供另一种替代选择。

为实现文化领导权，迪萨纳亚克必须清晰阐述建设一个更公平、更公正的斯里兰卡的愿景，在这个愿景中，公共福利优先于精英阶层的利益。他的领导还必须吸引知识分子和活动家，使这种文化转变合法化。

2. 认同与强制：葛兰西认为，权力通过认同与强制来发挥作用。认同通过媒体、学校和宗教等机构获得，这些机构传播统治阶级的世界观，使其看起来像是常识。而强制则通过国家的法律和军事机构来实施，用于管控异见，在认同不足的情况下实施管控。

葛兰西指出，统治并非仅靠武力来维持，而是通过在被统治者中营造一种认同感。就迪萨纳亚克而言，赢得各社会阶层（尤其是城乡工人阶级）的认同至关重要。国家人民力量党强调减少腐败、改善公共服务以及解决经济不平等问题，这些举措有助于获取这种认同。

他在总统任内必须谨慎平衡运用国家权力和强制手段与维持民众支持这两方面的关系。迪萨纳亚克可以利用媒体、教育和公民社会等工具来传播一种叙事，即其政府的政策符合全体公民的最佳利益，避免重蹈纯粹威权治理的覆辙。

3. 阵地战与运动战：葛兰西从"阵地战"（渐进的文化和意识形态变革）和"运动战"（直接的、往往带有暴力性质的革命行动）的角度描述了争夺领导权的斗争。在现代资本主义社会中，鉴于国家和公民社会深度交织，葛兰西认为，在运动战能取得成功之前，通过阵地战获取意识形态和文化影响力必不可少。

"阵地战"指的是挑战现有秩序所必需的渐进式文化和意识形态转变，而"运动战"则是直接的革命行动。迪萨纳亚克在竞选前的策略可被视为一场"阵地战"，在此期间，国家人民力量党主要通过基层活动和反建制言论来努力获得在公民社会中的影响力。

担任总统后，他可以继续这场阵地战，通过逐步推行挑战现状的政策，比如土地改革或国家主导的经济举措等，同时确保不会疏远中产阶级或引发既有精英阶层的反制行动。其理念在于，缓慢推动系统性变革，使其政策看起来像是自然的进步，而非激进的转变。

4. 知识分子与反霸权：葛兰西对传统知识分子（与统治阶级结盟的知识分子）和有机知识分子（来自工人阶级或其他从属群体的知识分子）进行了区分。有机知识分子在发展反霸权方面起着至关重要的作用，他们创造替代性的意识形态和文化价值观，以挑战占主导地位的体系。

在迪萨纳亚克的总统任内，有机知识分子，即活动家、进步学者以及左倾媒体人士，能助力国家人民力量党挑战新自由主义叙事并推广社会主义替代方案。

通过赋予这些知识分子在教育、媒体和政策制定方面的领导权，迪萨纳亚克可以强化其政府的意识形态影响力。他担任总统可以推动一场知识运动，重新定义斯里兰卡的社会和经济政策，并有可能塑造一种叙事，即斯里兰卡的主权与其社会主义价值观不可分割。

5. 变革融合：如前文所述，葛兰西提出了"变革融合"概念，用以解释统治阶级如何通过吸纳反对派领导人和运动、采纳他们的部分理念并进行表面性的改革来防止革命性变革，从而维持现状。

迪萨纳亚克政府将要面临的挑战之一是，避免被国家人民力量党曾反对的精英阶层和资本主义结构所同化。在秉持意识形态纯粹性的同时做到务实治理可能颇有难度。

从积极的方面来看，迪萨纳亚克可以利用"变革融合"，将温和的反对派人物或改革派政策纳入政府，同时又不稀释本党的核心原则。这或许能让他化解来自保守派的潜在威胁，同时推进其社会主义议程。倘若成功，这将使国家人民力量党既能维持其反建制形象，又能有效管理国家机构。

七、挑战印度霸权：从起义到外交政策

在斯里兰卡于"一带一路"倡议中扮演战略角色这一背景下，葛兰西的霸权理论为分析该国长期以来抵抗地区（主要是来自印度的）统治提供了一个极具说服力的框架。通过 1971 年以及 1988 年至 1989 年的起义，斯里兰卡人民解放阵线成为这种抗争的典型代表，它针对 1987 年《印斯协议》所体现的印度霸权，坚决维护国家主权。人民解放阵线的行动可被视为一股积极的潮流，旨在重拾斯里兰卡的国家特性，调动民众对外国影响的抵触情绪，并倡导自决。

在此背景下，迪萨纳亚克务实的领导风格成为对这些历史的当代回应。他试图在"一带一路"倡议框架内协调斯里兰卡的战略利益，同时抵御外部压力。迪萨纳亚克的目的是重新定义斯里兰卡的地缘政治地位，恢复主权，并通过与中国及其他利益相关方建立更公平的伙伴关系，构建一种反霸权叙事，将国家利益置于首位，而非屈从于地区统治。正如印度前外交官阿贾伊·比萨里亚所解释的，迪萨纳亚克要实现平衡就需要考量印度在安全方面的施压："至少到目前为止，印度仍是首选的安全合作伙伴。而印度自身正在学习在周边地区建立超越政权更迭的长期权益。"迪萨纳亚克的新举措反映了从人民解放阵线历史上的起义式抵抗到战略性策略调整的演变，这种转变在不牺牲自主权的前提下寻求发展机遇，凸显了该国在外交格局上的重大转变。

　　运用葛兰西的霸权理论，迪萨纳亚克的总统任期可被视为重塑斯里兰卡政治文化的一个持续进程。他能否通过巧妙的领导方式赢得民众认同、吸引知识分子参与并处理意识形态冲突，将决定其政府是成为真正推动变革的力量，还是会被现有霸权秩序所同化的关键。

八、"一带一路"倡议：一场"消极革命"

　　葛兰西提出的"消极革命"概念，即社会和经济变革可以在现有政治秩序内逐步实现，为理解斯里兰卡在"一带一路"倡议中的角色提供了一个宝贵的框架。"一带一路"倡议可被视为一种推动全球贸易和基础设施网络逐步变革的机制，与斯里兰卡等发展中国家更广泛的现代化努力相契合。在迪萨纳亚克的总统任内，斯里兰卡将进行一场葛兰西式的"消极革命"，在这一过程中，斯里兰卡务实接受"一带一路"倡议，在维护主权的同时参与全球现代化进程。这种做法强调了葛兰西的观点，即领导力必须具有适应性，能够响应当地实际情况，并以可持续增长的长远愿景为基础。

　　葛兰西的"消极革命"概念是指，在体系内通过渐进式的改良而非直接的革命手段实现变革。迪萨纳亚克政府不会彻底推翻当前的资本主义体系，也不会摒弃斯里兰卡对外国资本的传统依赖，而是可以在捍卫国家主权的同时，从中国的投资中获取渐进但具有变革性的利益。由此，国家人民力量党可以与中国的社会主义根源相契合，这与中国利用"一带一路"倡议在不直接挑战西方霸权的情况下提升全球影响力的理念相呼应。

九、应对地缘政治压力

迪萨纳亚克面临的首要挑战之一，是在外部大国施加的相互竞争的地缘政治压力与斯里兰卡基于自身在印度洋地区地位的战略利益之间寻求平衡。必须谨慎管理中国通过"一带一路"倡议进行的大量投资，以避免过度依赖；与此同时，印度试图制衡中国在该地区日益增长的影响力。

葛兰西的"变革融合"战略为斯里兰卡应对这些压力提供了途径，即把中国和印度的发展模式要素融入其国家战略。这种平衡举措将确保斯里兰卡的现代化努力反映自身诉求，而非受外部大国摆布。

国家人民力量党历史上明显倾向于与中国而非印度建立更紧密的关系，这反映了其更广泛的地缘政治战略。这种偏好深深植根于国家人民力量党的意识形态框架，强调国际关系中的主权和自主。该党的创始人，尤其是人民解放阵线，长期以来一直抵制印度霸权，将其视为对斯里兰卡独立的威胁。这一立场在1988年《印斯协议》期间表现得尤为明显，当时对印度干涉斯里兰卡事务的抵制促使人民解放阵线发动起义。相比之下，国家人民力量党与中国的接触被视为一种战略举措，旨在使斯里兰卡的外交关系多元化，加强经济合作以促进国家利益。

通过与中国更紧密地合作，国家人民力量党旨在制衡印度在该地区的历史影响力，营造一个斯里兰卡能够彰显自身能动性的外交环境。在中国"一带一路"倡议的背景下，这一战略选择意义重大，因为"一带一路"倡议提供的基础设施建设和投资机遇与国家人民力量党实现经济复兴、摆脱外部压力的愿景相契合。因此，国家人民力量党的亲华倾向成为其政治叙事的基石，使该党在应对地区地缘政治复杂性的同时，树立起斯里兰卡主权捍卫者的形象。

十、七个领域：推动高质量"一带一路"合作

从葛兰西理论的视角来看，"一带一路"倡议体现了中国为重塑现有全球霸权结构所做的微妙且具有战略性的努力。通过与斯里兰卡及其他"一带一路"国家开展高质量合作，中国推广了一种替代性的现代化模式，该模式融合了文化外交、技术创新和可持续基础设施建设。以下是中国可以做出贡献的七个领域：

1. 聚焦可持续基础设施建设： 从葛兰西的观点出发，"一带一路"倡议下可持续基础设施的扩展可被视为一种文化领导权形式。在此过程中，中国推广了一种有别于传统上由西方主导的全球化的替代性发展模式。这场"消极革命"改变了全球关于现代化的话语体系，使可持续性和绿色发展成为主导规范。斯里兰卡和其他"一带一路"国家作为这一基础设施网络中的战略节点，有助于使中国在全球可持续发展议程中的领导地位合法化，在不公然采取强制手段的情况下，微妙地改变全球权力关系。

2. 贸易与供应链现代化： 通过科伦坡港口城和汉班托塔港等项目实现贸易路线的现代化，体现了葛兰西的变革融合概念。在"一带一路"倡议下的全球南方经济一体化过程中，当地精英融入跨国资本主义框架，促成一种共识，使斯里兰卡这样的国家与中国在贸易和经济连通性方面

的愿景保持一致。这种合作框架微妙地挑战了新自由主义的全球秩序，将中国定位为全球现代化的引领者。

3. 加强技术交流与创新： 葛兰西的阵地战概念适用于"一带一路"倡议内的技术合作。中国注重出口 5G、人工智能和数字基础设施等先进技术，这是其挑战西方技术主导地位的长期战略的一部分。通过文化外交，中国巧妙地将自身重新定位为技术领导者。斯里兰卡参与这种交流，使其能够获取前沿技术，同时也推动了全球霸权的转变，使技术领导权更加多元化。这反映了随着非西方国家引领创新，全球领导格局在文化和意识形态方面缓慢但重大的转变。

4. 加强教育与文化交流： 斯里兰卡与中国之间的教育和文化交流扩大了中国的全球文明倡议，提供了一种替代性的现代性愿景，强调南南合作和共同发展。这种合作在公民社会中培养了更广泛的团结意识，包容、合作和共享繁荣等价值观得到推广，减少了对西方教育和发展模式的依赖。这些交流加强了中国的领导作用，同时创造了一个新的知识和文化阵营，支持高质量的全球现代化努力。

5. 支持全球治理与多边主义： 通过"一带一路"伙伴关系，中国推动了全球治理的转变，这与葛兰西的"消极革命"概念相一致，即现有国际秩序从内部发生转变。斯里兰卡与中国的多边倡议（如亚洲基础设施投资银行）保持一致，这表明全球治理框架正在重新调整，以适应非西方大国的参与。这一过程将"一带一路"国家的当地精英和各国政府纳入一个新的多边秩序中，中国在其中的影响力通过共识而非强制手段自然增长。

6. 促进包容和以人为本的现代化： 高质量的"一带一路"合作强调包容、以人为本的发展，这与葛兰西基于共识的领导权理论相一致。中国并非自上而下地强加现代化模式，而是让当地社区参与基础设施项目，通过物质利益和文化契合而非强制手段来培育共识。在斯里兰卡，以就业、减贫和提高生活水平为重点的举措促进了当地的支持，为"一带一路"倡议赢得了更广泛的合法性。

7. 与全球发展目标的战略对接：斯里兰卡在"一带一路"倡议中的角色也凸显了其与全球发展框架（如联合国可持续发展目标）的战略对接。中国已将其全球发展倡议、全球文明倡议和全球安全倡议与联合国的全球发展议程相结合。从葛兰西的视角来看，这反映了中国在全球治理的意识形态和制度领域的阵地战。与直接的政治对抗（运动战）不同，阵地战是缓慢且渐进的。它需要随着时间的推移建立广泛的支持基础，耐心地努力改变公众舆论和文化格局。通过提供强调基础设施、可持续性和南南合作的替代性现代化路径，中国正在与西方主导的模式展开一场文化和意识形态的较量。通过与这些倡议对接，斯里兰卡和其他"一带一路"国家帮助推进了一项反霸权事业，其目标是重新定义全球发展的条件。

十一、结论

在迪萨纳亚克的领导下，斯里兰卡开启了新篇章。葛兰西的理论框架为我们深入理解斯里兰卡如何通过参与中国的"一带一路"倡议推动国家发展提供了深刻的视角。以务实态度为基础的高质量合作，能使斯里兰卡及其他"一带一路"国家在维护自身主权和文化身份的同时，彰显中国在全球现代化进程中的关键作用。这种伙伴关系体现了葛兰西式的"消极革命"，一种与可持续和包容性发展目标相契合的渐进式变革。可持续基础设施、现代化贸易以及技术创新，体现了葛兰西的变革融合理论和阵地战思想，这使中国能通过文化外交和长期战略，提供一种有别于西方主导模式的发展路径。与此同时，以人为本的现代化进程和文化交流，以积极的方式构建共识，赢得了民心。通过参与"一带一路"

倡议，许多发展中国家可以推动全球向新的世界秩序转变，并在这一不断演变的格局中确立自身的战略地位。

在此背景下，斯里兰卡及其他"一带一路"国家与中国的伙伴关系可被视为一场葛兰西式的"消极革命"。这一渐进却具变革性的进程与更广泛的可持续和包容性发展目标相一致。葛兰西恰如其分地指出："旧世界正在消亡，而新世界正在艰难诞生。"通过参与"一带一路"倡议，斯里兰卡已准备好为这个新世界做出贡献，在不断演变的全球秩序中确立自身的战略地位。

"一带一路"与中乌战略伙伴关系

法鲁赫·哈基莫夫（乌兹别克斯坦发展战略中心部门负责人）

乌兹别克斯坦当代外交政策的基本原则之一是坚持多方位外交方针和不干涉原则。乌兹别克斯坦正积极努力提升自身在国际舞台上的地位，这一点在其与中亚邻国以及传统战略伙伴的合作中尤为明显。

哈萨克斯坦、塔吉克斯坦、吉尔吉斯斯坦和土库曼斯坦等邻国，正成为乌兹别克斯坦新外交政策议程中的重要伙伴。这种合作正迈向新高度，反映出各方对于区域一体化以及共同解决地区问题的渴求。

此外，乌兹别克斯坦通过扩大国际合作伙伴的地域范围，积极发展与中国、俄罗斯、美国、土耳其、欧盟等全球主要经济体和其他国家的关系。这不仅加强了乌兹别克斯坦的经济和政治联系，还使其能够在国际事务中发挥更积极的作用。

因此，乌兹别克斯坦在外交政策上展现出灵活的策略。这有助于乌兹别克斯坦实现可持续发展，并巩固其在地区及更广泛范围内的地位。

当前，中国是乌兹别克斯坦重要的外交政策和经济伙伴。建交30多年来，两国为积极开展多方面战略协作奠定了坚实基础。因此，在这一时期，乌兹别克斯坦与中国的关系在各领域都提升至战略伙伴关系的最高水平。

　　尤其需要强调的是，两国之间迅速发展的经贸和投资关系。特别是过去几年，中国在乌兹别克斯坦的贸易和投资领域占据了关键地位。例如，2017 年至 2023 年，中国对乌兹别克斯坦经济的投资总额超 140 亿美元。2023 年的中乌双边贸易总额也达到 140 亿美元。截至 2023 年，在乌兹别克斯坦的中资企业数量已达 2337 家，占该国外资企业总数的16.6%。

　　值得注意的是，华为、中兴通讯、中国进出口银行、温州金盛贸易、鹏盛合资公司、中国重汽、恒邦纺织中亚等众多大型中资企业都在乌兹别克斯坦积极开展业务。例如，华为正在乌兹别克斯坦开展"智慧城市"项目，预算 3 亿美元，旨在发展电子政务、数字经济、信息技术、远程医疗和互联网电话。

　　目前，乌兹别克斯坦和中国正在能源、农业、纺织业等传统合作领域取得成效。同时，两国在跨境电子商务、绿色发展、生物医学和减贫等新领域的合作也在不断发展。

　　两国战略伙伴关系的发展为乌兹别克斯坦学习中国在减贫方面的先进经验开辟了广阔机遇。2022 年双方达成的开展联合活动以学习和借鉴中方减贫经验的协议便是明证。为切实落实该协议，2023 年 2 月中方学者受邀访问乌兹别克斯坦，这些学者成为了乌兹别克斯坦就业与减贫部的顾问。

　　此外，在"乌兹别克斯坦 2030"这一长期国家发展战略框架下，乌兹别克斯坦计划借鉴中国的经验，在 2026 年底前将本国的贫困人口减半。

　　同时，乌兹别克斯坦与中国之间积极发展的区域间合作也值得关注。近年来，两国特别重视在区域层面发展经济、贸易和投资关系。例如，乌兹别克斯坦与中国新疆维吾尔自治区之间的贸易额不断增长，目前该地区约占两国贸易总额的 10%。乌兹别克斯坦与来自中国新疆的龙头企业合作的投资项目总额达 35 亿美元，涵盖绿色能源、电气工程、建筑、新型建筑材料生产、冶金、基础设施现代化升级等领域。两国文化交流项目也在积极开展中。

2023 年 5 月，乌兹别克斯坦总统沙夫卡特·米尔济约耶夫对中国进行国事访问期间，签署了关于建立塔什干市与四川省、锡尔河州与陕西省、撒马尔罕州与陕西省友好合作关系的协议。在此次国事访问之后，2024 年双方又签署了关于建立塔什干州与陕西省、撒马尔罕市与青岛市友好合作关系的协议。

值得注意的是，在因疫情实施长时间的隔离措施之后，乌兹别克斯坦是中国领导人于 2022 年 9 月展开国事访问的首批到访国家之一。同时，乌兹别克斯坦还参加了 2022 年 9 月 15 日至 16 日在撒马尔罕举行的上海合作组织峰会。

2023 年 5 月 18 日，在乌兹别克斯坦总统对中国进行国事访问期间，两国领导人举行了双边会谈。会谈期间，两国领导人签署了联合声明，并通过了《中华人民共和国和乌兹别克斯坦共和国新时代全面战略伙伴关系发展规划（2023—2027 年）》。

2023 年 5 月 19 日，乌兹别克斯坦总统沙夫卡特·米尔济约耶夫出席了在西安举行的首届"中国—中亚"峰会。在会上，他就区域合作的发展提出了若干重要建议和倡议。

尤其是，米尔济约耶夫提议进一步构建新的经济对话机制并加强互联互通，目的是到 2030 年使中亚国家与中国之间的贸易额翻一番。

此次峰会标志着"中国—中亚"合作机制正式建立。峰会强调其具有"划时代意义"，开启了中国与中亚各国合作发展的新阶段。为表明加强和支持合作的意愿，各方商定在中国设立一个常设秘书处，以将这一机制制度化。该秘书处已于今年开始运作。

"中国—中亚"合作机制可成为促进中亚地区经济合作、安全与可持续发展的有效区域外交平台。此外，新机制和对话平台的形成提升了中亚地区的地缘政治和经济意义。

2024年1月，在乌兹别克斯坦总统对中国进行国事访问期间，两国领导人将乌中关系提升为全天候全面战略伙伴关系。

乌兹别克斯坦和中国正在国际组织框架内建立密切关系。乌兹别克斯坦和中国在联合国、上海合作组织以及亚洲相互协作与信任措施会议等多边机构中密切协调，在国际和地区议程中的紧迫问题上相互支持。

乌兹别克斯坦还积极支持中国于2013年提出的"一带一路"倡议。该倡议极大地促进了参与国之间的互联互通，推动了区域经济发展，对地处内陆的中亚地区而言尤其如此。

"一带一路"倡议项目涉及在通往欧洲的沿途大规模建设公路、贸易中心和物流基础设施，这对包括乌兹别克斯坦在内的所有中亚国家都产生了影响。

需要指出的是，"一带一路"倡议扩大合作的举措与"乌兹别克斯坦2030"等国家战略文件中的具体规定相契合。这将推动乌中全天候全面战略伙伴关系不断发展，促进双方在工业、能源、基础设施建设、交通、物流、农业、旅游、教育等领域的互利合作。

2017年、2019年和2023年，乌兹别克斯坦总统沙夫卡特·米尔济约耶夫访问了中国，并参加了三届"一带一路"国际合作高峰论坛。

应当指出的是，在"一带一路"倡议框架下，乌兹别克斯坦具有若干优势。首先，乌兹别克斯坦地理位置便利，自然资源丰富。因其地理位置，乌兹别克斯坦已成为"一带一路"倡议的重要组成部分。其次，乌兹别克斯坦政治稳定，经济发展迅速。第三，乌兹别克斯坦奉行开放、务实、和平的外交政策。

作为"一带一路"倡议的一部分，乌兹别克斯坦正在实施多个基础设施项目。首批成功完工的项目之一是对"安集延—帕普—安格连—塔什干"铁路段进行升级改造，具体包括 2013 年至 2016 年期间修建 19 公里的卡姆奇克隧道以及对铁路线路的电气化改造。

此外，作为"一带一路"倡议的一部分，2019 年在纳沃伊投产的聚氯乙烯生产综合体改变了乌兹别克斯坦对聚氯乙烯和烧碱进口的依赖，同时还创造了大量新的就业机会，这对该国的经济发展至关重要。

"中国—吉尔吉斯斯坦—乌兹别克斯坦"公路走廊、"中国—哈萨克斯坦—乌兹别克斯坦"铁路以及"中国—吉尔吉斯斯坦—乌兹别克斯坦"多式联运走廊的运输潜力正不断得到释放。

2022 年 9 月，中国国家主席习近平对乌兹别克斯坦进行国事访问期间，中国、吉尔吉斯斯坦、乌兹别克斯坦就"中吉乌"铁路吉尔吉斯斯坦段建设签署合作谅解备忘录，欧亚大陆交通走廊建设因此取得重大进展。

2024 年 6 月，一份关于共同推进"中吉乌"铁路项目的合作文件在北京签署，确立了融资、建设等相关问题的机制。同年 10 月，该铁路建设公司的办事处在比什凯克揭牌。同年 7 月，乌兹别克斯坦总统指示向相关项目公司的特许基金拨款 2.55 亿美元，同时吉尔吉斯斯坦计划在预算中拨款约 1.305 亿美元。中国境内的铁路段将由中方全面实施建设并提供资金。

鉴于当前形势，通过北线运输货物使得"中吉乌"铁路项目的实施极具重要性和现实意义。

据世界银行估计，"一带一路"倡议下交通基础设施的改善将使货物运往乌兹别克斯坦的时间缩短近 15%，这是"一带一路"倡议参与国中货运时间降幅最大的。

相应地，运输时间的缩短将使乌兹别克斯坦的出口增长 13% 至 23%。这一较高的增长估计值是"一带一路"倡议下已完工的交通项目以及将边境通关延误时间减半的改革所产生的累积效应。

正如乌兹别克斯坦总统沙夫卡特·米尔济约耶夫在"中亚—中国"峰会的演讲中所指出的：复兴伟大丝绸之路的一个优先项目是跨欧亚公路，其中重要的组成部分是中国、吉尔吉斯斯坦和乌兹别克斯坦之间的公路和铁路连接。从长远来看，在"一带一路"倡议下，该项目的实施以及阿富汗走廊的建设，将使中国与南亚国家之间有了可供选择的交通路线。

的确，具有战略重要性的"中吉乌"铁路的建设，将大幅缩短中亚国家与中国之间的货运时间，缓解现有路线的货运压力，并增强欧亚地区的互联互通。

总体而言，乌兹别克斯坦和中国正共同努力落实"一带一路"倡议，这为地区乃至世界的繁荣发展注入了积极动力。此外，两国还保持着高水平的政治、经贸和科技互动，不断推动双边关系迈上新台阶。

总之，值得注意的是，乌兹别克斯坦的现代外交政策以积极奉行多方位外交方针及在地区和全球层面开展合作为特点。加强与中亚邻国以及世界主要大国的关系，是该国经济稳定发展和政治保持稳定的基础。

与此同时，在"一带一路"倡议框架下与中国的合作，以及与其他国际组织的合作和对话，再加上双边关系的发展，都彰显出双方不断增长的经济潜力和互利共赢的伙伴关系。在能源、交通、科技等各个领域签署的协议，反映出乌兹别克斯坦积极投身有助于其自身发展的国际进程和倡议的意愿。

"一带一路"倡议在尼泊尔

召严·什雷斯塔（尼泊尔国际关系研究所秘书长）

共建"一带一路"倡议 (BRI) 是中国政府 2013 年通过的全球基础设施发展战略。它旨在通过建设基础设施和扩大中国与其他国家的贸易联系，来加强地区互联互通，迎来更加光明的经济未来。

作为邻国，尼泊尔已正式加入 BRI，并期待在基础设施升级、经济发展、服务业壮大、技术转让、文化合作等各领域开展互利合作。

一、总体情况

1.BRI 在尼泊尔建设的关键项目

博克拉国际机场项目：该项目是 BRI 在尼泊尔的旗舰项目之一。机场预计将促进地区旅游和经济活动。

"熊猫包裹"项目：该项目聚焦于通过提供教材和基础设施，提高教育质量。

阿米蒂生活用水项目：该项目旨在为有需要的社区提供清洁饮用水。

2. 挑战和担忧

尽管有诸多潜在好处，但尼泊尔的 BRI 项目的执行也面临一些挑战和担忧。一个主要的担忧是这些项目可能给尼泊尔带来经济负担，此外，由于种种原因，包括政治变动和地缘政治复杂性等，一些项目出现了拖延和搁置。

3. 未来前景

BRI 在尼泊尔的前景看上去充满光明，两国都在努力加强合作，应对挑战。BRI 项目在尼泊尔的成功将取决于两国的有效合作、透明和互惠互利。

4. 战略重要性

尼泊尔处于中国和印度之间，这一战略位置使其成为 BRI 的关键参与者。这个内陆国家是中印两个亚洲大国之间的桥梁，发展基础设施可以帮助尼泊尔利用其地理优势促进贸易和连通。通过将尼泊尔纳入更广泛的贸易通道网络，BRI 旨在改变这个国家的经济格局，提升其在该地区的地位。

5. 基础设施发展

跨喜马拉雅多维连通网络：这个雄心勃勃的项目旨在建设一个公路、铁路和航空网络，将尼泊尔与中国西藏和其他地区连接起来。加德满都 – 吉隆铁路的建设是关键的组成部分，它将建立尼泊尔与中国之间的直通铁路，减少旅行时间和成本。

能源项目：尼泊尔拥有巨大的水电潜力，BRI 促进了对能源部门的投资。像布迪甘达基水电站这样的项目有望提供清洁和可持续的能源，减少尼泊尔对进口化石燃料的依赖，并解决其能源短缺问题。

改善边境基础设施：在拉苏瓦堡和塔托帕尼等关键地点升级边境设施和基础设施，可以提高贸易效率，促进经济活动。建设陆港和海关设施，对于简化贸易流程、方便货物流动至关重要。

6. 经济影响

BRI 有望通过创造就业机会、吸引外国投资和促进工业发展来推动尼泊尔的经济增长。改善基础设施可以刺激旅游业、农业和制造业的发展，为尼泊尔整体经济发展做出贡献。此外，BRI 旨在促进地区合作和经济融合，使尼泊尔能够进入更大的市场，并从贸易增加中获益。

7. 文化和教育交流

BRI 不仅限于基础设施建设，还强调人文交流。尼泊尔与中国的文化教育交流不断增加，有奖学金项目、语言课程、文化活动等倡议。这些交流促进了相互了解，加强了双边关系，为包括科学、技术和研究在内的各领域合作创造了机会。

8. 质疑与批评

尽管有潜在的好处，但 BRI 在尼泊尔仍面临着一些挑战和批评：

债务负担：人们对不断增加的债务负担感到担忧，因为尼泊尔大量举债为基础设施项目融资。确保可持续融资和避免债务危机对 BRI 的长期成功至关重要。

环境影响：大型基础设施项目可能带来严重的环境影响，包括导致森林被砍伐、栖息地和生态系统被破坏。因此，采取环境上可持续的做法并减轻不利影响至关重要。

地缘政治紧张关系：BRI 具有地缘政治意义，尼泊尔必须谨慎处理与中国和印度的关系。平衡这些关系并避免潜在的利益冲突是一项微妙的任务。

9. 未来前景

BRI 在尼泊尔的未来取决于倡议的有效落实、应对挑战，并确保好处大于代价。需要重点关注的关键领域包括：

加强机构建设：建立强有力的机构和治理框架对于有效管理 BRI 项目至关重要。透明、可问责的机构，可以保证资源的高效利用，减少腐败。

加强区域合作：促进区域合作和一体化可以放大 BRI 的好处。与周边国家在基础设施项目、贸易便利化、政策协调等方面的合作，可以创造一个更加紧密、更加繁荣的地区。

可持续发展：强调可持续发展原则对于平衡经济增长与环境保护和社会福祉至关重要。将可持续性纳入项目规划和实施可以确保尼泊尔的长期利益。

BRI 给尼泊尔带来的既有机遇也有挑战。虽然它有潜力改变尼泊尔的基础设施、经济和地区连通性，但精心规划、有效落实和消除担忧对于实现其利益最大化至关重要。通过加强合作，促进可持续发展，并借力其战略位置，尼泊尔可以利用 BRI 的全部潜力，实现长期繁荣发展。

二、"一带一路"在尼泊尔的其他方面

1. 促进旅游业和文化交流

尼泊尔以令人叹为观止的风景和丰富的文化遗产而闻名，与 BRI 相关的基础设施改善将极大促进旅游业的发展，这将令尼泊尔大大受益。像博克拉国际机场这样的项目加强道路连通后，很可能会使旅行更加便捷，吸引更多游客前往尼泊尔风景如画的旅游目的地。此外，旅游业的发展会带来连锁反应，对当地企业产生积极影响，创造就业机会，促进文化交流。

2. 技术进步

BRI 还包括中国和尼泊尔之间的技术转让和合作。这种合作可以促进尼泊尔产业的现代化，增强这个国家的技术能力。可再生能源、电信和数字基础设施等领域可以从中国的专业知识和投资中获益。通过拥抱技术进步，尼泊尔可以提高生产力、创新能力和在全球市场上的整体竞争力。

3. 社会和经济进步

创造就业：BRI 的基础设施项目建设需要大量劳动力，在当地促进了就业和经济振兴。这些就业机会有助于减少贫困，提高许多尼泊尔家庭的生活水平。

能力建设：BRI 项目往往包括能力建设部分，比如培训项目和技能开发项目。通过提高当地劳动力的技能，尼泊尔可以建立一支更有能力和知识的劳动力大军，为长期的经济增长做出贡献。

经济多元化：通过吸引对制造业、农业和服务业等各领域的投资，BRI 为尼泊尔提供了一个实现经济多样化的机会。通过减少对单一部门的依赖，尼泊尔可以建立更有韧性和更稳健的经济。

4. 环境考虑

可持续做法：要减轻基础设施项目带来的环境影响，采取可持续的做法至关重要。这包括开展全盘的环境影响评估，采取绿色建筑技术，并纳入可再生能源解决方案。通过优先考虑可持续性，尼泊尔可以确保经济发展不会以环境恶化为代价。

环保努力：尼泊尔丰富的生物多样性和自然资源必须得到保护。BRI 项目应该包括保护野生动物栖息地、森林和水体的措施。此外，推动生态旅游有助于提高人们的环境保护意识，并为保护努力带来收入。

5.医疗水平提高

改善基础设施还能提高尼泊尔的医疗服务水平。通过改善交通网络和医疗设施，BRI 可以方便人们获取医疗服务，尤其是在偏远地区和农村地区。这会带来健康状况的改善，降低死亡率，提高尼泊尔人的生活质量提高。

6.加强双边关系

BRI 是尼泊尔和中国加强双边关系的一个平台。通过加强协作与合作，两国可以为未来的伙伴关系建立强有力的基础。外交关系、贸易协定和人文交流可以进一步夯实两国关系，促进相互理解和信任。

7.吸取经验和最佳做法

随着尼泊尔继续实施 BRI 项目，学习其他国家的经验并采取最佳做法至关重要。这包括：

保证管理透明：确保项目规划、实施和财务管理的透明度至关重要。透明的管理可以建立公众信任，吸引投资，最大限度减少腐败。

利益相关方的参与：让当地社区、民间组织和其他利益相关方参与决策过程，可以带来更多包容和可持续的发展成果。通过解决各利益相关方的需求和关切，尼泊尔可以确保 BRI 项目对社会产生积极影响。

监督和评估：对 BRI 项目进行定期监督和评估，有助于发现问题、评估进展，并作出必要调整。这样可以提高项目的效率、效益和问责。

三、结论

BRI 为尼泊尔提供了一个改善基础设施、促进经济发展和地区连通的独特机会。尽管存在挑战，但精心规划、有效落实和对可持续发展的重视可以使 BRI 的好处最大化。通过利用自己的战略位置，加强区域合作，促进与中国的相互了解，尼泊尔可以为国家的长期繁荣和发展铺平道路。BRI 给尼泊尔带来了机遇和挑战。虽然它有潜力改善尼泊尔的基础设施、促进经济发展和地区连通性，但精心规划、有效落实并解决各方关切对于实现 BRI 的收效最大化至关重要。通过加强合作，促进可持续发展，并借力其战略位置，尼泊尔可以利用 BRI 的全部潜力，实现长期的繁荣发展。

后　记

　　2024 年 10 月 13 日—15 日，"一带一路"国际智库合作论坛暨第二届丝绸之路（西安）国际传播大会在陕西西安成功举办。来自 50 个国家的驻华外交官、智库专家、媒体记者等 300 余名嘉宾济济一堂，为"一带一路"高质量发展建言献策。此次论坛在共建"一带一路"第二个"金色十年"的新起点上召开，意义重大，影响深远。

　　会上，新华社国家高端智库发布了《八项行动奠定共建"一带一路"新十年良好开局》研究报告，系统总结了习近平总书记提出"八项行动"倡议一周年以来，共建"一带一路"取得的新发展新成就。与会嘉宾围绕"高质量共建'一带一路'助力世界各国现代化"主题，立足"一带一路"在各自国家的发展，或探究历史渊源，或讨论实践难题，或展望合作前景……在观点碰撞与思想交流中，会议取得丰硕成果。

　　为了更好地纪录、展示、传播本次会议成果，组委会全文收录《八项行动奠定共建"一带一路"新十年良好开局》研究报告，同时从海量投稿中选取了 14 篇优秀论文，集结成册。此外，本书还收录了新华社国家高端智库 2024 年 11 月在巴西"全球南方"媒体智库高端论坛上发布的报告《跨越山海 合作共赢——"全球南方"本币合作创新研究》，以飨读者。

我们希望，这本书能够为"一带一路"研究传递思想火花、激发智慧力量。我们相信，在"一带一路"建设的伟大实践土壤中，将会不断结出更多穿越山海、跨越文化的智库成果，更好发挥反哺实践、加强融通的作用。

承担本书编辑工作的是新华社研究院传播战略研究室的文建、陈怡、李成、陈谊娜、何小凡等同志。欢迎各位读者批评指正。

本书编写组

2025 年 5 月